Physician of the Soul,
Healer of the Cosmos

STANFORD STUDIES IN JEWISH HISTORY AND CULTURE

EDITED BY *Aron Rodrigue and Steven J. Zipperstein*

Physician of the Soul, Healer of the Cosmos

Isaac Luria and His Kabbalistic Fellowship

Lawrence Fine

STANFORD UNIVERSITY PRESS

STANFORD, CALIFORNIA

2003

Stanford University Press
Stanford, California

©2003 by the Board of Trustees of the
Leland Stanford Junior University. All rights reserved.

Published with the assistance of the
Lucius N. Littauer Foundation.

Printed in the United States of America
on acid-free, archival-quality paper.

Library of Congress Cataloging-in-Publication Data
Fine, Lawrence.
  Physician of the soul, healer of the cosmos: Isaac Luria and his
kabbalistic fellowship / Lawrence Fine.
      p. cm.— (Stanford studies in Jewish history and culture)
   Includes bibliographical references and index.
   ISBN 0-8047-3825-4—ISBN 0-8047-4826-8
   1. Luria, Isaac ben Solomon, 1534-1572. 2. Luria, Isaac ben
Solomon,
1534-1572—Disciples. 3. Cabala—History. 4. Mysticism—Judaism. 5.
Judaism—Israel—Tsefat—History. I. Title. II. Series.
BM525.L835 F56 2003
296.8'33'092—dc21   2002154139

Original Printing 2003

Last figure below indicates year of this printing:
12   11   10   09   08   07   06   05   04

Typeset by Classic Typography in 10.5/14 Galliard

For Deb, with love beyond measure

Contents

Acknowledgments

It is my great pleasure to acknowledge individuals and institutions that have supported my work on this book. It was my considerable good fortune to have begun the study of Jewish mysticism in earnest at Brandeis University under the tutelage of the late Professor Alexander Altmann, one of the masters of the history of Judaism in the twentieth century. I am indebted to him, not only for what he taught me, but also for the rigorous standards of scholarship he exemplified, and for the personal interest he showed in his students. It was Altmann who said to me, in one of the earliest conversations I had with him after I arrived at Brandeis, that "nobody truly understands Lurianic Kabbalah, not even Scholem," referring, of course, to the preeminent historian of Jewish mysticism, Gershom Scholem. While I couldn't fathom exactly what he meant at the time, I knew enough to be impressed (but was too naive to be frightened) by such a statement, coming from a scholar's scholar. Over the course of time, I have come to realize that Altmann was right, by which I mean that the irreducible complexities of Lurianic Kabbalah cannot be grasped in some unequivocal fashion. Its ambiguities, paradoxes, and elaborate multitiered mythic edifice resist simple resolution or intellectual closure.

During the years in which I first began to be intrigued by the spiritual renaissance in Safed and its mystical communities, my wife and I were lucky enough to take part in our own experiment in community, during the earliest years of the Havurat Shalom in Somerville, Massachusetts. In addition to the many enduring friendships gained there, I had the opportunity to experience firsthand the joys and challenges of communal fellowship. As I look back, I believe that my interest in studying intentional community had something important to do with my own experience in community during the early 1970s. I am immeasurably grateful to all the people with whom I shared those wonderful, exciting years.

This work began while I was a member of the faculty of Indiana University. I am grateful for the research support I enjoyed there, as well as for the exceedingly stimulating intellectual environment provided by my colleagues in the Department of Religious Studies. I am especially indebted to James Ackerman, the late J. Samuel Preus, and David Smith for their support. Other friends and colleagues of mine at Indiana during that time, with whom I had significant conversations about the subject of this book, include Howard Eilberg-Schwartz, Todd Endelman, and George Savran. More recently, I have also benefited from the collegiality of the members of the Department of Religion and the Jewish Studies Program at Mount Holyoke College, and from the generous financial support of the college.

Friends and colleagues who read all or parts of this book in manuscript form include the following scholars: Robert Goldenberg, Arthur Green, Eric Lawee, Daniel Matt, Ivan Marcus, and Aron Rodrigue. I am indebted to each of them for their helpful suggestions and comments. Special thanks to Art Green for his encouragement and friendship over the years. My gratitude goes to Professors Aron Rodrigue and Steven J. Zipperstein of Stanford University, co-editors of the distinguished series of which this book is a part, for their enthusiastic interest in this project, as well as to Norris Pope, program director at Stanford University Press, and Mariana Raykov, production editor. I am especially grateful to Peter Dreyer for the meticulous care with which he helped edit this book.

This work would not have been possible without the support of members of my family. My deep gratitude to my father, Jack Fine; my late mother, Mildred Fine; and my mother-in-law, Jean Segal, for their love. My late father-in-law, Rabbi Jacob E. Segal, took a warm interest in my scholarly career during the all too few years I was privileged to know this remarkable man. My thanks as well to my brother and sister-in-law, Roger and Rebecca Fine, for their love and friendship. I am grateful for the blessing of my two sons, Jacob and Aaron, who have watched their father pore over kabbalistic texts for much of their lives. They inspire me by their passions and commitments, and by being such beautiful souls. My deepest gratitude and appreciation belongs to my wife, Deborah. It is hard to imagine life without her uncommonly good sense, her stimulating companionship, and most of all, her endless love and friendship.

In a remarkable coincidence, her paternal great-grandfather, Shalom of Podayetz, migrated from Poland and ended up in Safed, where he became known as a kabbalistic enthusiast. We are told that melodies he composed, preserved in family memory, are still sung in synagogues in Safed even today. He is buried in the ancient cemetery in Safed, among the mystical luminaries of the sixteenth century, including Isaac Luria. Even more remarkable, in light of the contents of this book, over the past several years his grave has become the object of veneration and pilgrimage. Thus, my gratitude to Shalom of Podayetz, through whom I enjoy some small but meaningful measure of personal connection to the orbit of Safed and its mysteries.

Note to Readers

Inconsistencies in the transliteration from Hebrew are deliberate. I have retained the common English usage of certain words in the interest of familiarity. Thus, for example, Kabbalah rather than Qabbalah, and Safed rather than Tsfat. Certain Hebrew words that are relatively well known, such as mitsvah and halakha, do not appear in italicized form. While this book is highly technical and specialized in many ways, I have sought to write in such a way as to make it as accessible as reasonably possible to a general reader. For example, I have included some background to kabbalistic ideas and symbolism in Chapter 2 and, more generally, provided certain information with which scholarly readers will be familiar. Unless otherwise noted, all translations from Hebrew to English are my own. In some instances, I have slightly modified existing English translations upon which I have drawn.

Abbreviations

BT	Babylonian Talmud	*ShG*	Hayyim Vital, *Shaʿar ha-Gilgulim*
Deut.	Deuteronomy		
Eccles.	Ecclesiastes	*ShH*	Hayyim Vital, *Shaʿar ha-Haqdamot*
EH	Hayyim Vital, *ʿEts Ḥayyim*		
EJ	*Encyclopedia Judaica*	*ShK*	Hayyim Vital, *Shaʿar ha-Kavvanot*
Exod.	Exodus		
Gen.	Genesis	*ShMR*	Hayyim Vital, *Shaʿar Maʾamarei Rashbi*
Isa.	Isaiah		
Jer.	Jeremiah	*ShM*	Hayyim Vital, *Shaʿar ha-Mitsvot*
JT	Jerusalem Talmud		
Lev.	Leviticus	*ShP*	Hayyim Vital, *Shaʿar ha-Pesuqim*
MY	*Meḥqarei Yerushalayim*		
Num.	Numbers	*SRH*	Hayyim Vital, *Shaʿar Ruaḥ ha-Qodesh*
Ps.	Psalms		
QS	*Qiryat Sefer*	*ShY*	Hayyim Vital, *Shaʿar ha-Yiḥudim*
REJ	*Revue des études juives*		
2 Sam.	2 Samuel	*WZ*	Isaiah Tishby and Fischel Lachower, eds., *The Wisdom of the Zohar: An Anthology of Texts*
SeA	*Sefer ha-Ari ve-gurav,* ed. Yaʿakov Moshe Hillel		
SeG	Hayyim Vital, *Sefer ha-Gilgulim*		
SeH	Hayyim Vital, *Sefer ha-Ḥezyonot*		
STA	*Sefer Toldot ha-Ari*, ed. Meir Benayahu		

Physician of the Soul,
Healer of the Cosmos

Introduction: Embodying the Study of Lurianic Kabbalah

Isaac Luria is one of the several most extraordinary and influential mystical personalities that the Jewish tradition has ever produced. Along with Moses de Leon, the primary author of the *Zohar*; Abraham Abulafia, the originator of prophetic Kabbalah; Sabbatai Sevi, the infamous Turkish Jew whose messianic pretensions threw the Jewish world into turmoil for much of the seventeenth century; and Israel ben Eliezer, the charismatic figure at the center of early Hasidism, Luria (b. 1534) may be credited with having helped shape the course of Jewish mysticism in decisive and profound ways. Thus, even though Luria (also called the Ari) lived in the Galilean city of Safed for less than three years—from early 1570 until his death at the age of thirty-eight in August 1572—his name is virtually synonymous with the great renaissance of mystical community that took place there between approximately 1530 and 1590.

During these six decades, Safed spawned an astounding array of impressive religious personalities—rabbinic legalists, poets, preachers, biblical exegetes, ethicists, and above all kabbalists. Moses Cordovero, Solomon Alkabets, Jacob Berab, Moses di Trani, Joseph Karo, Hayyim Vital, Joseph ibn Tabul, Abraham ben Eliezer ha-Levi Berukhim, Israel Najara, Eleazar Azikri, Elijah de Vidas, and Moses Alsheikh were just a few of those whose creativity made Safed such a remarkable place. Among the kabbalists, however, it was Isaac Luria whose powerful religious imagination and personal charisma served to arouse the most fervent enthusiasm.

Not only did Luria's presence dominate the kabbalistic community in Safed during the relatively brief time that he lived there, but following his death, the impression his personality had made lived on, providing grist for a rich legendary tradition. Two important collections of such traditions, one most commonly known as *Shivḥei ha-Ari* (In Praise of the Ari) and *Toldot ha-Ari* (The Life of the Ari), reflect the degree to which Luria's personality continued to capture the imagination of subsequent generations. *Shivḥei ha-Ari*, based upon a series of letters written from Safed by Solomon Shlomiel of Dresnitz at the beginning of the seventeenth century, is among the first works of its kind in Hebrew literature, a full-fledged set of hagiographical narratives organized around the life of a single individual. It is certainly the most influential such collection. The stories in these two books reverberated over the course of time in a broad range of adaptations and translations. Even today, stories about Isaac Luria based upon these earlier works are preserved and widely transmitted, especially in Jewish communities whose roots are in the Near East.

Along completely different lines, Isaac Luria's highly imaginative mythic teachings gave birth to a literature of unusually complex kabbalistic theosophy among certain elite thinkers. Despite the fact that his immediate disciples—particularly Hayyim Vital (1543–1620)—sought to conceal their master's teachings altogether, or at least severely to restrict dissemination of them, following his death, they eventually had a powerful impact on various circles throughout the Jewish world. This is one of the great ironies of the history of Lurianic Kabbalah. The intense concern on Luria's own part that his teachings be restricted to a small circle of initiates eventually gave way to the production of a very extensive number of manuscripts and printed publications, the so-called (and misnamed) "Lurianic Writings" (*Kitvei ha-Ari*). For, in addition to the elaborate array of editions and recensions of Luria's teachings produced by certain of his disciples, Lurianic Kabbalah inspired the composition of numerous other treatises of diverse types by people who had not personally studied with him. The questions surrounding the repercussions of Luria's speculative and theosophical teachings are exceedingly intricate, but a few brief examples should suffice to at least suggest their influence. My goal here is not to describe this phenomenon in detail, but rather to provide examples of the afterlife of Luria's teachings.

A small, but exceedingly important, constellation of northern Italian scholars were the first individuals outside Palestine to acquire knowledge of Lurianic mysticism and to subject it to their own creative, interpretive forces. Although it was once believed that the kabbalist Israel Sarug (d. 1610) was responsible for introducing Lurianic teachings to these scholars, it now appears that even before Sarug's activities in Italy in the last years of the sixteenth century, Lurianic manuscripts had reached there.[1]

The study of these manuscripts, along with the distinctive version of Lurianic thought taught by Sarug, deeply influenced such illustrious individuals as Menahem Azariah da Fano (1548–1620), Joseph Solomon Delmedigo (1591–1655, also known as YaSHar of Candia [Iraklion, Crete]), Abraham Herrera (d. 1635), and Aaron Berekhiah of Modena (d. 1639). These authors fashioned highly sophisticated, philosophically oriented Lurianic treatises, nurtured significantly by Renaissance Neoplatonism.[2] They were interested in the metaphysical rather than the practical dimensions of Lurianic teaching, and over time their works gained considerable appeal (most particularly those of Menahem Azariah da Fano) and influenced various other elite kabbalistic thinkers.[3] Other highly influential European kabbalistic scholars from the first half of the seventeenth century whose writings were based upon Lurianic teaching include Shabbetai Sheftel Horowitz of Prague (c. 1561–1619) and Naphtali Bacharach of Frankfurt, among others.[4]

Another consequential repercussion of Lurianic Kabbalah is associated with the Sabbatean movement in the middle of the seventeenth century. While there has been much debate about the precise nature of the relationship between Lurianic Kabbalah and Sabbateanism, there is no question that the writings of Nathan of Gaza (1643/4–1680), the central propagandist and religious ideologue of the Sabbatean movement, were thoroughly suffused with Lurianic teaching of a theosophical and mythological type. As Moshe Idel observed, Nathan "employed Lurianic terminology creatively, giving it a special twist that 'illuminated' the personal myth of [Sabbatai] Sevi. Moreover, the theological language of Sevi's followers was predominantly Lurianic, although . . . it was used and understood only by the very few."[5] In the

Figure 1. The title page of *Sefer Limmudei ʾAtsilut* (Lemberg [Lvov], 1850), by Israel Sarug, mistakenly attributed to Hayyim Vital.

arena of religious practice, Nathan promoted penitential exercises (*tiqqunei ʿavonot*) adapted directly from penances developed by Luria for his disciples.[6]

A similar observation may be made with respect to the popular pietistic movement known as Hasidism, which swept through eastern Europe beginning in the eighteenth century. As with Sabbateanism, the exact relationship between Lurianic Kabbalah and Hasidism continues to be the subject of considerable discussion. Moshe Idel has argued, for example, that Hasidism was forged out of a range of earlier Jewish mystical traditions, of which Lurianic mysticism was only one.[7] Nevertheless, it is unequivocally clear that Hasidic teachers creatively adapted Lurianic language and a wide variety of Lurianic conceptions in ways that were crucially important to the development of that movement's theology and spiritual outlook. As Rachel Elior puts it, "an examination of the [Hasidic] movement's literature attests clearly to the centrality of the Lurianic theosophical system in connection with its approach to God. One cannot find a [homiletic] Hasidic text which does not concern itself with [such Lurianic concepts as] *tsimtsum, shevirat ha-kelim, ʾatsilut,* . . . or with the conceptual world and theosophical tradition of Lurianic Kabbalah." In Elior's view, Lurianic teachings provided the fundamental substratum underlying Hasidic theology, despite the fact that there were other important influences upon Hasidism as well.[8]

Another way in which Lurianic mysticism exerted influence was in the realm of religious devotion and practice. Here Lurianic teaching went far beyond limited scholarly circles and appealed to a much wider audience. A great many of the rituals and customs that Isaac Luria innovated, along with earlier kabbalistic rituals that he adapted and embellished, eventually found their way into Jewish practice in communities in many parts of the Jewish world. The dissemination and adaptation of a wide variety of unusual customs and rituals, including rites at the table for the three festive Sabbath meals, the midnight vigil (*Tiqqun Ḥatsot*), the study vigils for the festivals of Shavuot (*Tiqqun leil Shavuʿot*) and Hoshanah Rabbah, the "minor Day of Atonement" (Yom Kippur Qatan), special rites at grave sites, penitential rituals, and numerous meditative instructions and liturgical variations of different types, represent the pervasive influence that Lurianic tradition had upon ritual practice. A number of important guides, instructional manuals, and Lurianic-oriented prayer books—some of which were republished over and over again in endless editions—attest to the truly extraordinary popularity of these rituals.[9]

Besides their general diffusion, Lurianic devotional practices also became the central focus for various kabbalistic fellowships. For example, an influential circle of contemplatives formed the Bet El community in Jerusalem in 1737 under the leadership of Gedaliah Hayon. When Hayon died in 1751, the mantle of leadership was passed to Israel Jacob ben Yom Tov Algazi, an important scholar of Jewish law and Kabbalah. Upon the latter's death in 1756, Shalom Mizrachi Sharabi (1720–77) became the head of Bet El. Sharabi, originally from Yemen, developed a reputation as the greatest kabbalist of Near Eastern and North African Jewry during his lifetime. Along with a small group of individuals, Sharabi established a special association of contemplative kabbalists from within Bet El, called Ahavat Shalom. Sharabi was a prolific author whose work constituted a thoroughgoing adaptation of Lurianic teachings, at both the theoretical and the practical levels.[10] He composed various esoteric commentaries to Luria's teachings, some of which were actually incorporated into certain editions of Lurianic texts themselves. These writings were distinguished by a special focus on the devotional and contemplative dimensions of Lurianic mysticism. The participants in the community of Bet El cultivated the art of contemplative prayer using meditative practices that Sharabi taught on the basis of Lurianic Kabbalah. These practices had an enormous influence on Near Eastern kabbalists and continue to be used even today by Jews with roots in the Near East and North Africa. At around the same time, in a completely different part of the Jewish world, in the Galician town of Brody, a kabbalistic conventicle, or *kloyz*, was established. Led by Hayyim ben Menahem Zanzer (d. 1783) and Moses ben Hillel Ostrer (d. 1785), the Brody *kloyz* was a highly influential community of kabbalists in which the practice and study of Lurianic Kabbalah occupied a central role.

A Brief Survey of Modern Lurianic Scholarship

These several examples provide some idea of the wide-ranging and diverse ways in which the life of Isaac Luria and his teachings influenced the religious culture of Jewry. Given all this, it is more than a little surprising that the scholarship on Luria is so sparse. If we confine ourselves to what may be properly called the modern period of scholarly research in the field of Jewish mysticism, that is, beginning with the work of Gershom Scholem (1897–1982), we find that Lurianic Kabbalah has enjoyed relatively little attention.[11] Scholem himself should be credited with having brought Luria and his teachings into sharp focus with the "Seventh Lecture," entitled "Isaac Luria and His School," in his seminal book *Major Trends in Jewish Mysticism*.[12] But aside from this highly influential chapter, and several important articles published in the early 1940s, Scholem did not return in any significant way to fresh study of Lurianic Kabbalah.[13]

A significant contribution to the scholarship on Lurianic mysticism that appeared around the same time as *Major Trends* was a slim Hebrew volume by Scholem's first doctoral student and colleague, Isaiah Tishby. In 1942, Tishby published *Torat ha-Raᶜ ve-ha-Qelippah be-Kabbalat ha-Ari* (The Doctrine of Evil and the "Shell" in Lurianic Kabbalah). Amazingly, Tishby's Hebrew work would remain the only serious and sustained study of Luria's teachings for the following forty-five years, dominating the scholarly landscape alongside Scholem's own relatively limited Lurianic oeuvre.[14] While Scholem may have argued that Lurianic Kabbalah was the decisive influence upon the development of Sabbateanism, and while he and others frequently asserted the centrality of Lurianic Kabbalah in the historical evolution of Jewish mysticism, its rigorous and systematic study has nevertheless for the most part remained neglected. Fortunately, however, this regrettable state of affairs has begun to change somewhat over the past few years, as I shall show below.

In recent years, a number of scholars of Jewish mysticism have observed with increasing frequency the extent to which the history of kabbalistic research has tended to reflect a preoccupation with the mythic and theoretical ideas of Kabbalah at the expense of its social, devotional, and experiential dimensions. As Moshe Idel has pointed out, the tendency to conceive of Kabbalah in primarily philosophical or doctrinal ways goes back at least as far as some of the earliest nineteenth-century European scholars, including Salomon Munk, Nachman Krochmal, and Adolph Frank.[15] Modern authors as well, including Scholem and Tishby, along with Alexander Altmann and Georges Vajda, all groundbreaking scholars, devoted the vast preponderance of their energies to the study of mythical and theological ideas rather than to the actual rituals and practices of Kabbalah, including the great range of mystical experiences to which kabbalistic sources attest.[16] Nor did they pay much attention to either the social communities in which Kabbalah came to life or the important personalities at the center of those communities.[17]

These general observations are certainly true with respect to the study of Lurianic mysticism. Consider, for example, Scholem's aforementioned chapter on this subject in *Major Trends*, the largest portion of which is given over to an account of Luria's theosophical or metaphysical system, in contrast to brief discussions of Luria as a charismatic personality and the ritual aspects of his teachings. Similarly, in a lengthy essay devoted to the evolution and history of the notion of transmigration of souls (*gilgul*) in Jewish mystical tradition, including Lurianic Kabbalah, Scholem does not breath a word about the practical application of these ideas and beliefs. It is possible to read what Scholem has to say about Luria's conceptions of transmigration without learning anything whatsoever about the central role it played in the religious practices and experiential life of his fellowship. So, too, with Tishby's monograph mentioned above, the very title of which discloses its virtually exclusive interest in the doctrinal aspects of Lurianic Kabbalah.[18] It hardly diminishes the contributions of these great pioneers—upon whose work all subsequent research has been built— to suggest that they depicted the phenomenon of Lurianic mysticism in ways that were far too limited by conceptualizing it almost exclusively in terms of its theogonic and cosmological ideas.

Some recent research, however, has taken a more panoramic view of Lurianic Kabbalah. Ronit Meroz's important doctoral dissertation,

"Torat ha-Ge'eulah be-Kabbalat ha-Ari" (The Teachings of Redemption in Lurianic Kabbalah), adopts a significantly more expansive approach than earlier work.[19] To begin with, Meroz's field of vision encompasses virtually the entirety of the Lurianic corpus. Meroz seeks to enumerate all of the various versions and editions of Luria's teachings, in which she identifies what she considers to be five stages in the development of Luria's thought. In the course of her elaborate account of these developmental stages, Meroz addresses a wide range of questions, all organized around the notion of redemption in Lurianic teaching. Among other things, Meroz takes a strong interest in Luria's relationship to his disciples in the context of his aspirations to bring about cosmic redemption. In addition to Meroz's research, the work that is closest in spirit to the present book is that of Yehuda Liebes. In a lengthy, pathbreaking essay devoted to a study of Luria's understanding of certain passages from the *Zohar*, Liebes places Luria the individual, and his existential relationship to his circle of disciples, at the center of his concerns.[20] In my view as well, it is on these questions that Lurianic scholarship must especially focus. My own work in this area has been organized around such issues as the role Isaac Luria played as a charismatic authority, the techniques of mystical meditation he developed, and the other practical disciplines that he taught.[21]

The Embodied Nature of Lurianic Kabbalah and Embodying Its Study

This book regards Lurianic Kabbalah as an embodied phenomenon. By this I mean primarily two related things. First, *people* were at the heart of the Lurianic enterprise. Although this should perhaps be self-evident, for the most part it has not been the case in the study of Lurianic mysticism, because the protagonists of the Lurianic fellowship have been marginalized. Second, Luria and his disciples were far more interested in the life of praxis—both at the individual level and at the level of social community—than in speculative or theoretical matters. The importance of this goes beyond the need to "fill in the gaps" and add to our knowledge. Rather, it speaks to a fundamentally different way of conceiving of this subject and organizing its study. The virtually exclusive preoccupation with Isaac Luria's mythic conceptions has prevented us from seeing that what mattered to Luria and his disciples themselves were not predominately speculative systems and scholastic debates. What mattered to them was the religious life to be lived and practiced in relationship to his teachings about the origins and nature of the cosmos. While these mythic teachings were, to be sure, the object of considerable scrutiny, as attested by the abundant attention paid to them by certain of Luria's disciples, including Hayyim Vital, Joseph ibn Tabul, Moses Yonah, and others, as far as I can see, they were not in and of themselves the central fixation of Luria and his circle. Lurianic Kabbalah was no mere theoretical system or set of intellectual or theological abstractions dressed up in mythic guise. Rather, the central argument of this study is that Lurianic Kabbalah was first and foremost a lived and living phenomenon, the actual social world of a discrete, historically observable community.

If this is the case, then its study must also be embodied. One of the most basic ways in which to do so is at the historical level—that is, to focus in a serious way on the historical contexts and cultural milieus out of which it evolved. To that end, this book begins by exploring the significance of the Ottoman Empire as a haven for Jews dislocated from the Iberian Peninsula at the end of the fifteenth century, as well as from other parts of Europe. It also contextualizes Luria's life before his emigration to Safed by describing the Jerusalem of the early sixteenth century, into which he was born, and Luria's period in Egypt, where he spent most of his life. The basic biographical questions about Luria have been largely relegated to the margins by scholars of Lurianic mysticism. The documentary information that we have concerning his pre-Safed life has been either ignored altogether or insufficiently integrated into the larger questions of Lurianic Kabbalah.[22] The failure to take any meaningful interest in the actual biographical dimensions of Luria's life strikes me as entirely consistent with the tendency to focus on theoretical aspects of his teaching.

Furthermore, this book establishes in some detail the flowering of Safed in the decades immediately prior to Luria's appearance there. Much of what Luria taught was predicated on religious ideas, practices, and institutions, as well as social realities, that had developed in that community in the forty years or so before he arrived on the scene. Even more, the spiritual environment he encountered there went a long way toward making his own success as a teacher possible. I have therefore sought in this work to clarify the relationship between pre-Lurianic Safed and Luria's career there.

My most crucial biographical concern, however, is to embody Lurianic Kabbalah through a focus on Isaac Luria the person and his relationship to his circle of disciples. This focus prompts the following kinds of questions: Why did he decide to migrate to Safed from Egypt, where he had lived most of his life? Why was he so intensely attracted to the grave sites of deceased teachers and rabbis believed to be buried in the environs of Safed? Why, in particular, did Luria identify so profoundly with Shimon bar Yohai, the second-century Palestinian sage who stands at the center of the *Zohar*'s narratives?

These questions themselves, though, have a yet larger framework. Luria's life in Safed has to be seen in the context of the circle of individuals who gravitated to him, his self-understanding in relationship to that circle, the expectations he had of them, and his disciples' own understanding vis-à-vis their teacher. A series of fundamental questions present themselves in this connection: What attracted Luria's students to him in the first place? What was the nature of his authority in their eyes? What role, in particular, did Luria's charismatic behavior play in his relationship to them? With what meaning did they invest his idiosyncratic religious behavior and his pneumatic experiences? In what manner did Luria serve them as a diagnostician and physician of the soul, and to what ends? How did Luria and his disciples apply notions of the transmigration of souls so as to construct an indispensable role for themselves in the processes of messianic redemption and cosmic restitution? What was the particular relationship between Luria and his chief disciple, Hayyim Vital? What was the nature of the relationship of Luria's disciples among themselves, especially between Vital and the rest? How did Luria's disciples come to grips with their master's premature death?

These and other such questions take us, in my view, to the very center of the Lurianic world, insofar as they require us to make sense of it as a lived experience. What we sometimes refer to as Lurian*ism* was not an *ism* to Luria and his followers, but rather a highly motivated, self-conscious, intentional social community. The complex relationships among the members of this community, and the way in which they viewed those relationships, do not form a minor subtext of this study, but one of its main subjects.

This book simultaneously moves along another track, intersecting at almost every turn with the social dimensions to which I have referred. Luria and the members of his fellowship believed themselves to be the protagonists at the center of a great cosmic drama. Discipleship was not simply about imbibing the master's view of the world, but about the urgent responsibility to purify their souls and mend a ruptured divinity. In different terms, it entailed bringing an end to exiled existence at every level of being and effecting the redemption of the whole cosmos. Individual and collective action was at the heart of the Lurianic community, just as it was at the heart of Safed's kabbalistic world more generally. As such, the search for the meaning of Lurianic Kabbalah must have at its center, rather than its periphery, the highly complex ritual culture that Isaac Luria fashioned along with his disciples. Two of the most prominent features of Lurianic mysticism are its density of ritual, that is, its sheer amount of ritual, and its exceptionally wide variety of types of ritual activity.[23] While many have alluded to the various regimens and practical disciplines that Luria imparted to his disciples, these have been neither systematically spelled out and analyzed in detail nor sufficiently studied in relation to the broad issues expressed in Lurianic myth.

Luria and his disciples regarded their fellowship as a microcosm in a literal sense. They believed themselves not only to reflect the essential structures of the cosmos but also to embody those structures individually and, more crucially, collectively. The theurgical impulses so fundamental to theosophical Kabbalah—that is, the conviction that human gestures of every type exert influences upon the cosmos as a whole—reach what is perhaps their most intense and radical form in the ritual practices of Lurianic mysticism. Here Lurianic Kabbalah was embodied in the literal sense. For Luria and his disciples, their

very bodies served as the instruments for performing the work of purification and restoration that they believed had to be done.[24] While the
body was at one level construed as an obstacle on the path of spiritual
restitution, it could also help achieve that goal. The body was implicated in a vast array of ways in the practices that Luria taught. Certain
of these were clearly intended to produce changes in bodily behavior,
as well as extraordinary states of consciousness, such as in the case of
the practice of exercises known as *yiḥudim* ("unifications"), or the enactment of the prayer *nefilat ʾappayim* ("falling on the face"). Thus,
Lurianic practice became embodied in highly performative ways, in
which the body was sometimes dramatically transformed. This study
seeks to examine these rituals in the detail they deserve.

By identifying the ways in which Lurianic Kabbalah is an embodied
phenomenon, I hardly intend to go to the other extreme and suggest a
radical dichotomy between its embodiment, on the one hand, and its
intellectual or ideational aspects, on the other. In fact, there is absolutely no mind/body dichotomy whatsoever in Lurianic Kabbalah,
and its study ought not privilege one at the expense of the other. After
all, the elaborate myth that Luria taught is itself an account of (divine)
embodiment, hence a form of "embodied thinking."[25] The principal
images and motifs employed to describe the origins of all being, that
is, the history of the cosmos born out of the depths of the divine, are
drawn from experiences of the human body, especially its physiological development: conception, pregnancy, birth, nursing, maturation,
sexual intercourse, and death. Luria found it natural to speak in language of divine genitalia, seminal and vaginal fluids, lactating breasts,
divine parents, children, and lovers. Despite its characteristically arcane
complexities and apparent abstract qualities, Luria's mythic teachings
are actually grounded in the most elemental experiences of the self:
birth and growth, childhood and parenthood, eroticism and sexuality,
consciousness and memory, separation and unification, sickness and
healing, life and death.

This is consistent with Wendy Doniger's important observation
that it is in the nature of myths to exhibit abstract/universalist tendencies (a macroscopic or wide-angled view of reality), as well as more

concrete/personal ones (a microscopic or narrowly focused perspective).[26] Concomitantly, the practice of Lurianic Kabbalah—in all the variety of its expressions—should be construed in significant part as a way in which the dynamics of the myth are interpreted and brought to life by being rehearsed, recapitulated, and performed by human actors. Among many other things, one of the principal capacities of religious ritual is to establish a mythic story as "real" by existentially embodying it.[27] Hence, the ritual cultivation of the proper emotional and spiritual life, the practice of penitential exercises in the search for perfection of the soul, the contemplative performance of the mitsvot (ritual precepts) and prayer, lying prostrate on the graves of deceased sages, and the desire to create a fellowship characterized by loving-kindness were all creative strategies and techniques designed to establish the harmony of the cosmos as envisioned in Lurianic teaching.

Given the orientation so far described, this study is particularly interested in theoretical and methodological notions that derive from the closely related fields of performance theory and practice theory, especially as developed in anthropological discourse.[28] In contrast to most structuralist and functionalist approaches, "performance models suggest active rather than passive roles for ritual participants who reinterpret value-laden symbols as they communicate them. Cultural life has come to be seen as this dynamic generation and modification of symbolic systems, as something constantly being created by the community. From this perspective, change becomes a dynamic process integral to how people live and reproduce culture, not something that happens to a passive and static social entity."[29] In a rather similar way, practice theory "claims to take seriously the ways in which human activities . . . are creative strategies by which human beings continually reproduce and reshape their social and cultural environments."[30] In connection with this line of thinking, the social theoretician Pierre Bourdieu employed the term *habitus* to refer to human activity in its real and immediate context, what he called "the socially informed body."[31] The notions that ritual is a performative medium for social change, that it emphasizes human creativity and physicality, and that individuals and social communities devise practices that enable them to shape their world well match the relentlessly activist view of life so fundamental to the Lurianic aspirations to both personal transformation and cosmos-mending (*tiqqun*).

Lurianic Kabbalah and Women

Studies of Jewish culture are increasingly and appropriately being informed (to varying degrees) by questions of gender. A revolution is beginning to take place in the conceptualization of that culture now that heightened attention is being paid to the role of women. As with so much of Judaism, Lurianic Kabbalah was conceived of by men and almost exclusively for men. Luria had no female disciples. Nevertheless, women were clearly implicated in a variety of ways in Safed ritual in general and Lurianic ritual in particular. Luria's male disciples had mothers, wives, daughters, and sisters. And, living among kabbalists, these women must be presumed to have adopted both kabbalistic views of the world and kabbalistic practices, just as women in non-kabbalistic rabbinic communities shared in their weltanschauungs and ritual lives. We must thus expand our notion of what it meant to be a kabbalist. Gershom Scholem asserted that there were no female Jewish mystics, because no females had written mystical treatises.[32] If we do not limit ourselves to the question of authorship, however, but ask instead about how women living in a kabbalistic culture were affected by their environment, we are confronted by a series of new possibilities.

In the case of Lurianic Kabbalah, for example, we want to know how very particular notions of sexuality and sexual relations (not to mention anxieties about sex) may have had an impact on the lives of women. Was Isaac Luria's wife curious about why sexual relations were essentially limited to Friday nights, while non-kabbalistic wives could have sexual relations with their husbands on other nights of the week? Did she wonder why their bed was positioned in a particular way during marital relations? What did she make of the fact that her husband required twelve loaves of *challah* to be placed on the Sabbath table!? Did Luria's mother understand the meaning of his kissing her hands after he returned from welcoming the Sabbath Bride on Sabbath eve? Did the wives of Luria's disciples regard themselves as representing and embodying the female divine presence, the *Shekhinah*, or in Lurianic parlance, *Nuqba de-Ze°ir*? Could this have elevated their status in the eyes of their husbands, or in their own eyes? These and many more questions can be asked of Lurianic culture. We do not necessarily have clear answers—or even, in most cases, any answers at all—but I have tried in this study at least to raise some of these questions and put gender issues on the agenda.[33]

A General Word About Sources

Lurianic Kabbalah is notorious with respect to the complex state of the literary sources that provide the basis for its study. The huge corpus of Lurianic materials is a daunting labyrinth. It is well known that Isaac Luria himself wrote down exceedingly little of his own teachings, so it was left to certain of his immediate disciples to recall and preserve in writing what they had learned primarily in an oral fashion from their master. Hayyim Vital, Joseph ibn Tabul, Moses Yonah, and others composed versions of Luria's teachings in this way. These renditions frequently disagree with one another over matters both large and small. The problem is made even more complicated by the fact that different versions by a given disciple often conflict with one another. This is most obviously true in the case of Hayyim Vital, from whose pen the great majority of Luria's traditions flowed. Vital wrote several different recensions of his teacher's work—beginning immediately following Luria's death and continuing for at least two decades.

To this is added the still more complicating fact that a number of subsequent editors and redactors—people who had never known Luria personally—came into possession of various versions of the teachings and proceeded to subject them to still new arrangements and renditions (and thus, to some degree, to new interpretations). Most important, in Jerusalem, approximately between 1630 and 1660, Jacob Zemach and his student Meir Poppers took up the project of editing new versions of Lurianic teaching based largely on Hayyim Vital's manuscripts. It was primarily these mediated versions, especially those by Poppers, that were responsible for the dissemination of Lurianic Kabbalah in Germany, Poland, and eastern Europe in general.

One of the truly significant developments in Lurianic scholarship over the past twenty years or so has been the increasing identification of manuscript sources, a number of which have been published, along with the gradual clarification of the nature of the sources, both published and unpublished, as a whole. But although the already sprawling body of materials has thus become even larger, we now have a much clearer map of the field, thanks especially to the painstaking bibliographical analyses of Ronit Meroz and Joseph Avivi.[34] Rather than my offering a single, detailed discussion of the complex problems related to the sources at this point, however, it will be most helpful to the reader to locate such discussion throughout the study, where it can be related more particularly to the different issues with which we are concerned.

O n e   Rabbinical Scholar, Spice Dealer, Contemplative Ascetic: Luria's Life in Egypt

> The biographies of famous Jewish rabbis are rarely more than a thin cloth of hazardous combinations of guesses, wrapped round a meagre skeleton of assured fact.
>
> —R.J.Z. Werblowsky, *Joseph Karo, Lawyer and Mystic*

Ottoman Jewry

As was the case with Jews everywhere throughout the medieval period, the fortunes of the Jewish community in Palestine rose and fell in rhythm with political events largely beyond its control. In the year 1250, the Muslim Ayyubid dynasty, founded in 1170 by Saladin, gave way to the Mamluks, Turkish-speaking former slaves who had originally been brought to Egypt to serve in the Ayyubid army. The Mamluks, however, succeeded in overthrowing their oppressors and established their own sultanate, organized along the lines of a feudal military state. While they came to rule initially in Egypt, they soon expanded their conquests to include Syria and Palestine, as well as parts of North Africa and Asia Minor. In 1291, the Mamluks solidified their conquest of Palestine, which they continued to rule until they were vanquished by the Ottoman Turks in 1516.

Except for short periods of respite, living conditions for Jews under Mamluk governance were oppressive in the extreme, as was true for *dhimmi*s (non-Muslims) in general.[1] Fierce enthusiasts for Islam, the Mamluks enforced existing regulations guiding the life of non-Muslims and introduced a range of discriminatory prescriptions of their own. In general, Mamluk rule was characterized by excessive and burdensome taxation, a social climate of unrelenting hostility toward the *dhimmi*s, frequent outbreaks of violence against persons and property, and severe impoverishment and instability. It is thus small wonder that the Ottoman conquests of the Mamluks, initially in Syria and Palestine in 1516, and in Egypt in 1517, were welcomed with considerable enthusiasm by

19

the Jewish communities of these countries. By the middle of the sixteenth century, the Ottomans had extended their rule to most of the Middle East, North Africa, Asia Minor, and the Balkans.[2]

The composition of the Jewish communities under Ottoman rule by the time of these developments was highly diverse, which is not surprising in light of the far geographical reach of the empire.[3] The oldest of these communities was that of the Romaniote Jews, native Greek-speaking people whom the Turks encountered when the original provinces that formed the foundation for the Ottoman state were conquered in the second half of the fourteenth century and the first half of the fifteenth. These included Jewish residents of the Byzantine capital of Constantinople (renamed Istanbul under the Ottomans), Greece, and western Asia Minor, as well as certain cities of the Balkans.[4]

A second layer of Ottoman Jewry was added in the fifteenth century when small groups of chiefly German-speaking Jews migrated from Germany and parts of France. These Ashkenazi Jews organized separate communities of their own in such towns as Edirne (Adrianople), Nicopolis (Nikopol in Bulgaria), Salonika, Sofia, and eventually Istanbul. Many of these were inspired to migrate in response to a well-known letter sent by Isaac Zarfati of Edirne in approximately 1454. Zarfati wrote in praise of the Ottomans and their benevolent treatment of the Jews, urging his brethren in Ashkenaz to settle in the empire. His impassioned plea graphically portrays the dismal realities of Jewish life in Ashkenaz during this period, and anticipates Ottoman generosity toward the Jews:

> I have heard of the afflictions, more bitter than death, that have befallen our brethren in Germany—of the tyrannical laws, the compulsory baptisms and the banishments, which are of daily occurrence. I am told that when they flee from one place a yet harder fate befalls them in another. . . . on all sides I learn of anguish of soul and torment of body. . . . Brothers and teachers, friends and acquaintances! I, Isaac Zarfati, though I sprang from a French stock, yet I was born in Germany, and sat there at the feet of my esteemed teachers. I proclaim to you that Turkey is a land wherein nothing is lacking, and where, if you will, all shall yet be well with you. The way to the Holy Land lies open to you through Turkey. Is it not better for you to live under

Muslims than under Christians? Here every man may dwell at peace under his own vine and fig tree. Here you are allowed to wear the most precious garments. In Christendom, on the contrary, you dare not even venture to clothe your children in red or blue, according to our taste, without exposing them to the insult of being beaten black and blue, or kicked green and red, and therefore, are you condemned to go about meanly clad in sad colored raiment. . . . and now, seeing all these things, O Israel, wherefore sleepest thou? Arise! And leave this accursed land forever![5]

The reign of Sultan Bayezid II, between 1481 and 1512, coincided with the most significant Jewish migration in the late medieval, early modern period. While Iberian Jews had already begun to travel to the Ottoman Empire in the late fourteenth century, massive migrations were set off with the expulsion of the Jews from Spain in 1492 and the subsequent forced mass conversion of Portugal's Jewish community in 1497. Although many sought refuge in Italy and North Africa, the vast majority ultimately made their way to the Ottoman Empire. Of these desperate exiles, Bayezid is alleged to have made the following oft-quoted remark: "You call Ferdinand [of Spain] a wise king; him, who by expelling the Jews has impoverished his country and enriched mine!"[6]

Tens of thousands of weary, despondent Jews seeking refuge settled in Istanbul, the Ottoman capital, as well as Edirne, Salonika, Izmir (Smyrna), and various cities and towns in Anatolia and the Balkan peninsula. Out of a desire to preserve local identities, the Iberian immigrants established numerous congregations of their own according to the communities from which they had come. Thus an exceedingly wide range of synagogues were established, calling themselves the congregation of *Gerush Sepharad* ("Exile from Spain"), Catalonia, Calabria, Andalusia, Cordoba, Saragossa, Aragon, Toledo, Lisbon, and so on. Due to their large numbers and unrivaled cultural stature, the Jews of the Iberian peninsula quickly became the dominant factor in Ottoman Jewish life.

Still other exiles from Provence and other French areas arrived in the late fifteenth century, along with émigrés from the kingdom of Naples in 1510–11. Moreover, *conversos* (Spanish Jews who had converted under duress), fleeing the perils of the Inquisition also sought the refuge of the Ottoman Empire in the hope of reestablishing normal Jewish life. Finally, we may add to these groups the Arabic-speaking Jews of the Near East who came under the rule of the Ottomans in the conquests of 1516–17. These were known to the Ottomans as *Mustariba*, or *Mustarabim*, a word meaning "Arabized" used to distinguish these individuals from Greek, Turkish, and Spanish-speaking Jews.

While the benevolence of the Ottomans toward the Jews has sometimes been exaggerated by historians, it is true that, by and large, Jewry prospered and thrived under their rule.[7] The rise and expansion of the empire could not have been more propitious for the Jews of Europe. Given the nearly universal intolerance of European Jewry by Christian governments, and the resulting wave of deportations and exiles from the thirteenth through the fifteenth centuries, the openness of the Ottomans toward the Jews served as a perfect opportunity for vast numbers of refugees to settle under favorable circumstances.[8]

The fundamental reason for this openness was that the Ottomans regarded the Jews as a highly useful and productive people, capable of benefiting the empire in important ways. This was especially true with respect to those who had migrated from the Iberian peninsula. Iberian Jews were in a position to make valuable contributions to the cultural life of the Ottomans in a variety of fields.[9] For example, Jewish physicians brought with them the much higher level of medical knowledge that characterized Europe in contrast to the Near East. In a way strongly reminiscent of Jewish life in Muslim Spain, many assumed positions as courtier-physicians in Istanbul. Among the most influential of these was Joseph Hamon, scion of a distinguished family of Spanish physicians and a native of Granada. Entering the service of the Ottoman court during the final years of the reign of Bayezid II, Joseph became the personal physician to Selim I. Joseph launched a virtual dynasty of courtier-physicians, which lasted for more than a century. The most prominent of these was Joseph's son, Moshe Hamon (c. 1490–c. 1554), who served as the personal physician to Suleiman the Magnificent, a position he used, as had his father before him, to intercede on behalf of the welfare of the Jewish community.[10]

Jews had also brought with them the art of the theater, something that had been virtually unknown in the empire. Iberian Jews were responsible for introducing printing to the Ottoman Turks, establishing Hebrew presses in Istanbul (1493), Salonika (1510), and many other places throughout the empire. The Ottomans were cautious about the printing press, however, allowing Jews to print in Hebrew or Latin only, but not in Turkish or Arabic. In fact, it was not until the eighteenth century that Turkish Muslims established their own presses; when they did, they sought out Jewish printers for help.[11]

Even more important than these cultural contributions was the role Jewry played economically. The Ottomans welcomed the economic capital that Jews brought with them, helping to alleviate an always financially stressed government. They immediately began to assume a significant place in the commercial life of the empire. With their knowledge of languages and of European society, their cosmopolitan disposition, and their experience in international commerce, Jews quickly became prominent in an enormous textile trade. Besides serving as middlemen between European, local, and Eastern merchants, they were the impetus behind an indigenous Ottoman textile industry. In Salonika, Istanbul, Bursa, Rhodes, Safed, Izmir, and Cairo, Jews engaged in every aspect of textile production, as investors, contractors, merchants, weavers, dyers, and pressers. While some worked in special workshops, many labored at home, where the head of the household worked alongside his wife and children.[12] Women did not, however, limit themselves to such activity. Unusual numbers of Jewish women were independently engaged in various kinds of commercial enterprises, from employment as prestigious as purveyors of goods for the women of the imperial palace, such as clothing and jewelry, to something as ordinary as common peddling. We know of at least one woman, the wife of a Romaniote Jew from Istanbul, whose success in commercial and real estate businesses drove her husband to seek tax relief from the rabbinic authorities.[13]

Additionally, Jews were extremely active in the whole arena of taxation, as collectors, inspectors, and tax farmers.[14] As was the case with the Romaniotes, large numbers of Iberian Jews were able to draw upon their considerable experience in these areas and as managers of ports and customhouses before the Expulsion. As a result of these various activities, many in the Jewish community acquired influence and wealth, although we also know that certain Jewish communities were far better off than others.[15]

Still another contribution that Jews made, and for which the Ottomans were especially grateful, was, curiously enough, in the arts of warfare. They had expertise in the manufacture of weapons and associated technology. Visiting Turkey in the year 1551, the Christian traveler Nicolas de Nicolay wrote of the *conversos* that they "have taught the Turk several inventions, artifices and machines of war, such as how to make artillery, arquebuses, gunpowder, cannonballs and other weapons."[16]

In addition to these wide-ranging cultural and economic contributions that newly arrived Jews made in the late fifteenth and sixteenth centuries, there was yet another significant reason why the Ottomans looked so favorably upon their Jewish subjects. Generally speaking, the Ottoman Muslims were considerably more hostile to and distrusting of the Christians in their midst, given the long history of Muslim-Christian enmity. The Ottomans believed that Jews could be trusted in ways that Christians could not. Thus, Jews were called upon to play a role as diplomats and foreign policy advisors in connection with the Ottomans' relations with European Christendom.[17] Until conditions began to deteriorate toward the end of the sixteenth century, then, Jewry enjoyed economic and social acceptance that had been virtually unknown in Christian Europe. In addition, the well-organized administrative character of the Ottoman state and the political security it provided made for unusually high levels of stability and freedom of activity.

Ottoman Jewry in Jerusalem

It was into this Ottoman world of relative tranquility and well-being that Isaac Luria was born in the year 1534 in the city of Jerusalem. During the first half of the sixteenth century, the Jews were the second largest community in Jerusalem after the Muslims.[18] Population statistics available to us indicate that the number of Jews living there continued to rise from 1525 on.[19] A survey taken for taxation purposes in 1525–26 shows that there were approximately 1,300 Jewish residents.

In 1538–39, just a few years after Isaac Luria's birth, there were some 1,600, and in 1553–54 there were about 2,350 Jews. Other evidence suggests, however, that these official figures may understate the actual number of Jews then living in the city.[20] Between about 1525 and 1575, Jerusalem underwent important changes. The rulers in Istanbul initiated a variety of projects that served to enhance life in the city. The walls surrounding Jerusalem were rebuilt and the gates were locked each evening, finally putting an end to the insecurity that had plagued it, especially in the last decades of Mamluk rule, when the city was perpetually vulnerable to Bedouin raids. Markets and shops that had been neglected were renovated. The water system, which had fallen into disrepair under declining Mamluk authority, was rebuilt and improved. Financial endowments (*waqf*) were set up for the support of Muslim institutions and scholarly activities.

The Jews of Jerusalem were autonomous in relationship to other Jewish communities. They maintained their own internal organization and were led by the community representative, known under the title *shaykh al-yahud* (elder of the Jewish community).[21] The community administered its own courts and educational and religious institutions, and appointed rabbis to oversee religious affairs. These were known by the Hebrew titles *dayyan* (religious judge) or *ḥakham* ("wise man" or rabbi). Nonetheless, the community was beholden to the Muslim authorities, with whom it had complex and ongoing involvement. This included first and foremost the collection of appropriate taxes, along with the general administration of the Jewish community in its relations with the local Muslim authorities. For example, legal and social disputes were adjudicated under the auspices of the Muslim courts. If the Jewish community felt mistreated by the local authorities, as it often did, it could appeal to regional governors and to the central authorities in Istanbul itself.

While there was no official Jewish quarter in Jerusalem during this period, there were three areas in which the Jews tended to live. These were the al-Risha and al-Sharaf quarters, in which both Muslims and Jews resided, and a primarily Jewish area known as Maslakh. All three of these neighborhoods were close to one another in the southeast section of the walled city. The main synagogue of Jerusalem—the

Ramban synagogue—was at the center of these neighborhoods and in close proximity to the al-Umari mosque, an unfortunate situation that was the cause of continual conflict between Muslim and Jewish worshippers.[22] The detailed testimony of an Italian Jewish traveler to Jerusalem, Rabbi Moses Basola (1480–1560), allows us an unusual glimpse into the Ramban synagogue. Basola, who visited Jerusalem during 1521–1522, wrote:

> There is but a single synagogue in Jerusalem; it is beautiful, with four supporting columns. It is sixty-three feet long and twenty-eight wide, and behind the Torah ark there is a room where more than sixty Torah scrolls are housed. They pray facing east, that is, facing the Temple. The synagogue has no natural light except from the western doorway, which has a small window above it. By day as well they make use of the illumination from the lamps that they light all around.[23]

Basola goes on to describe the constituency of the congregation and the sources of its financial support:

> The congregation has all types of Jews: there are fifteen Ashkenazi householders, and many Sephardim, and Mustarabs, they are Moriscos, the ancient inhabitants of the land, and Maarabim [Maghrebis] who come from Barbary, all together some three hundred households, in addition to more than five hundred widows who earn a good living in Jerusalem, for they pay no taxes and bear no other financial burden. They support the congregation for when they die intestate the congregation takes everything; most of the congregation's needs are provided for thereby. Those who receive charity number more than two hundred persons, and much charity is sent from Egypt and Turkey and elsewhere, but the Ashkenazi poor are not included—their support comes from Venice.[24]

The Jews of Jerusalem in the sixteenth century made their living in a broad range of activities and were fully integrated into the economic life of the city.[25] There is evidence, especially from the first half of the century, that Jews held positions in the bureaucracy of the government. They also worked as moneylenders, ritual slaughterers and butchers, shoemakers and processors of hides, jewelers, spice merchants, physicians, locksmiths, cloth merchants, grape and wine dealers, cheese makers, millers and bakers, as well as dealers in olive oil, soap, and other products. According to the research of Amnon Cohen, the conventional portrait of the Jewish community in Ottoman-ruled Jerusalem—as well as in other towns in Palestine—as pitiful and impoverished is inaccurate on the basis of new evidence to the contrary. Though there was certainly poverty during the sixteenth century, and the community continued to require substantial financial support from the diaspora, many Jews were well off, and a few were quite wealthy. The picture we now have is of a Jewish community that enjoyed relative well-being and whose citizens engaged in a wide range of economic activities.[26]

Luria's Life in Egypt

Would that our knowledge about the family into which Isaac Luria was born resembled our knowledge about the Jerusalem community as a whole. Unfortunately, this is hardly the case. Documentary evidence about Luria's life is woefully meager. In his study of another important sixteenth-century figure, Joseph Karo (1488–1575), R.J.Z. Werblowsky aptly describes the situation confronting the biographers of premodern rabbis in general:

> The biographies of famous Jewish rabbis are rarely more than a thin cloth of hazardous combinations of guesses, wrapped round a meagre skeleton of assured fact. The "literary" attitude in religious and spiritual matters that made for the prevalence of the book over its author leads to the result that the historian who wants to reconstruct a medieval rabbi's *vita* is engaged on a jig-saw puzzle made up of occasional letters, stray indications, and incidental personal references in the writings and *responsa* of his hero and his contemporaries. In the circumstances great gaps are the rule rather than the exception, and contradictions abound.[27]

If Werblowsky was driven to this lament in his attempt to reconstruct Karo's life, the problem is even greater in the case of Isaac Luria. Karo, after all, lived a very long life and was a leading rabbinic legal authority. As a consequence, his name is associated with a wide array of legal decisions and documents, letters and responsa. In addition there is the extraordinary mystical diary that Karo left behind, the *Maggid Mesharim* (Preacher of Righteousness).[28] Karo's diary is a great treasure trove of information about his activities, as well as his psychological and emotional life. Luria, on the other hand, lived a mere thirty-eight years, most of which were spent in relative obscurity. Except for approximately two and a half years during which he served as a teacher in Safed, Luria had virtually no public role. Thus, there is only the scantiest documentary evidence attesting to his activities. What is more, to pursue the contrast with Karo, Luria wrote very little, and nothing about himself.

The situation is further complicated by the existence of a considerable body of hagiographical literature about Luria, which rushes in to fill the gaps. Even modern scholars have sometimes had trouble restraining themselves from admitting the paucity of the evidence and then hastening to tell us what "legend says."[29] The unwitting effect of filling in the gaps with legend, even while acknowledging it to be such, is to provide the reader with a certain degree of false assurance that we know more about Luria than is actually the case. My intention is to set aside the hagiographical traditions altogether for the purposes of this chapter and instead to present a picture of Luria's actual activities prior to his emigration to Safed, at least to the extent allowed us by the fragmentary historical sources at our disposal.[30]

We have precious little information about Luria's parents. His father's name was Solomon, and he appears to have migrated from Germany or Poland, that is Ashkenaz, on account of which he was called Solomon Luria Ashkenazi. Thus, his son Isaac was frequently referred to as Rabbi Isaac Ashkenazi or as Isaac Ashkenazi Luria. The acronym ARI (referring to ha-ʾelohi Rabbi Yitshak, the saintly rabbi Isaac), by which Luria came to be called, was not used during his lifetime. None of the early sources refer to him in this way. Gershom Scholem wrote that Solomon was "a member of the Ashkenazi family of Luria,"[31] apparently implying that he was from the renowned family by this name whose roots can be traced back to the fourteenth century; but an alternative view contends that "there is certainly no connection between this family and the Luria family (who were Levites) to which Isaac

Luria belonged."[32] While we do not have his mother's name, we do know that she was of Sephardic ancestry.

The famous scholar and historical chronicler Hayyim Joseph David Azulai (1724–1806) preserved a series of brief traditions concerning Luria's activities in his well-known biographical collection *Shem ha-Gedolim*, which remains one of the few (presumably) reliable sources for Luria's early biography. There Azulai informs us that he had personally heard "from the elders of the city [i.e., Jerusalem] about the house in which he [Luria] was born, and we have been privileged to see it."[33] It is also from Azulai that we learn that Luria's father died when Luria was a young child (*qatan*), as a result of which his mother took the family to Cairo.[34] We do not know precisely how old Luria was when the family moved to Egypt, although the Hebrew term *qatan* certainly denotes a boy less than thirteen years old. If the tradition that Azulai possessed is accurate, Luria was thus living in Egypt at least by the year 1547, and probably somewhat earlier. In Cairo, again according to Azulai, they lived in the home of Luria's uncle, Mordechai Franses, his mother's brother. Franses (meaning French in Ladino) was a common Sephardic name in the Middle East, suggesting that the family may at some point have resided in France. In any event, Franses was a well-to-do tax farmer. In Ottoman Egypt, much of the government's financial administration, including the collection of taxes and customs duties, was in the hands of Jews. These individuals (*multezim*) not only collected taxes from farmers but also often levied and collected customs duties in the ports of Alexandria and Damietta.[35] The people involved in this activity, "often wealthy merchants who thereby sought to increase their income, belonged to the affluent upper echelon of Jewish society."[36] According to Azulai, Luria "grew up in his uncle's home" and was given his cousin—Franses's daughter—in marriage.

In Egypt, Luria became a student of David ben Solomon ibn abi Zimra (c. 1480–1573). Ibn Zimra had been born in Spain into a wealthy family. Along with thousands of other Spanish Jews, he and his family were victims of the exile of 1492. By the age of thirteen, ibn Zimra was in Safed, after which he moved to Jerusalem. Shortly before 1513, he traveled to Egypt, initially to Alexandria and then to Cairo. Ibn Zimra remained in Egypt for approximately forty years, until sometime in the mid-1550s.[37] An accomplished scholar by the time he arrived in Egypt, ibn Zimra became a member of the rabbinic court of the Nagid, the religious leader of Egyptian Jewry, Isaac Sholal. Following the Ottoman conquest of Egypt from the Mamluks in 1517, the office of the Nagid was abolished, and ibn Zimra was eventually appointed chief rabbi of the prestigious Jewish community in Cairo, thus also becoming the leader of all of Egyptian Jewry. In this capacity, he served not only as chief rabbinic judge, or *dayyan*, but also as the head of a yeshiva and administrator of charity collection. Ibn Zimra's rabbinical academy was among the most important and well known in his day, attracting scholars from considerable distances. He was a master of rabbinic law whose influence in halakhic matters was unsurpassed and extended far and wide. He authored over 2,500 rabbinic legal opinions, as well as a variety of other rabbinic works. What is more, as we shall see below, ibn Zimra also composed several important kabbalistic treatises.

Azulai preserves a story that he summarized on the basis of the testimony of Elijah ha-Cohen ha-Ittamari of Smyrna (Izmir) (d. 1729), author of a popular moralistic treatise known as *Shevet Musar*.[38] According to this tradition, one day Luria went to his teacher David ibn Zimra and remarked that there were three pupils in ibn Zimra's academy whose names were Isaac: he himself, Isaac Apomado, and Isaac Fasi. Ibn Zimra responded that everyone knew this and asked Luria what his purpose was in bringing him this information, whereupon Luria told him that each of these three individuals would go on to achieve fame in different areas of scholarly endeavor. The legendary nature of this story is apparent; nevertheless, it presupposes as established fact that Luria was a student of ibn Zimra's, as we know to have been the case with the other two Isaacs mentioned.

Luria's tie to ibn Zimra is also attested through a document of unusual interest. This is a formal agreement (*haskamah*), apparently from 1557, signed by nine rabbis from David ibn Zimra's circle in Cairo.[39] The fifth signature is that of Isaac Luria.[40] The document addresses three matters. First, it obligates the signatories to refrain from making appointments—presumably of rabbis to the *bet din* (rabbinic court of law)—without the consent of the majority. More generally, they agree to make all decisions on the basis of collective deliberation and majority approval. Second, they agree to accept as binding all decisions passed by a *bet din* of three individuals appointed by their teacher, without questioning it either in private or in public. Finally, and most intriguing, they pledge to treat one another with love, kindness, and honor. If one of them were to see another act disrespectfully toward one of the group, by word or by deed, he had to bring it to the attention of the offending party within twenty-four hours. If the latter extended his apology to the wronged colleague, it had to be accepted. Failure to apologize called for public reproach, so that he did not behave that way again.

This text is illuminating from several points of view. It places Luria in the midst of the most important rabbinic circle of Egypt, disciples of David ibn Zimra, at the age of twenty-three. From the contents of the text, it appears that this circle constituted something along the lines of a fellowship. The interpersonal concerns that it expresses are reminiscent of the sort of guidance that Luria himself would provide for his own disciples years later in Safed, as well as the rules guiding other Safed brotherhoods.[41]

One of the other signatories to this pledge was Betsalel Ashkenazi (c. 1520–1591/4). Ashkenazi was among ibn Zimra's foremost students and became a talmudist and halakhist of great renown in his own right. He was born in either Jerusalem or Safed and studied under Israel di Curiel. Ashkenazi went to Egypt to live in about 1540, where he became ibn Zimra's student. When the latter left Egypt, Ashkenazi succeeded him as head of the Egyptian rabbinate, a position he held until he left for Jerusalem in 1578.

It is thus clear that Luria and Ashkenazi were both members of David ibn Zimra's circle for a time together, although Ashkenazi was Luria's senior by fourteen years. Following ibn Zimra's departure, Luria continued his association with Ashkenazi, but the latter, as head of the Egyptian rabbinate, would at this point have become Luria's teacher, or at least a senior colleague. We know, in fact, that they were scholarly collaborators. One of Betsalel Ashkenazi's halakhic projects was the collecting and copying of the novellae (rabbinic interpretations) of earlier medieval scholars, the *geonim* and *rishonim* on the Babylonian Talmud. This material served as the basis for his important work *Asefat Zeqenim*, better known under the title *Shitah Mequbbetset*. Isaac Luria collaborated with Ashkenazi in the writing of the *Shitah Mequbbetset* on the talmudic tractate *Zevaḥim*. This is attested to by Azulai, who says that it was done in Luria's youth (*baḥuroto*) and that it was lost in a fire in Izmir along with all the books of a certain Aaron Alfandari.[42] Ashkenazi and Luria also joined one another in the writing of annotations to some of the works by the famous North African halakhist Isaac Alfasi. In his introduction to Rabbi Tam ibn Yahya's book *Sefer Tummat Yesharim*, Benjamin Motal indicates that he possessed Abraham Monzon's "copy of Alfasi's code, which he brought from Egypt, [which had been] proofread by the two great luminaries, the eminent rabbi Betsalel Ashkenazi, of blessed memory, and the 'divine' rabbi Isaac Ashkenazi, of blessed memory."[43] Still another collaboration took place when the two endorsed a halakhic decision along with another rabbi, Simeon Castellazzo, in 1558, when Luria was twenty-four years old.[44] Luria's halakhic interests are further evidenced in a legal inquiry made to Joseph Karo, which Azulai tells us he saw in manuscript.

From all of this we learn two important things. Luria was well trained in halakhic and rabbinic studies. He was sufficiently interested in and adept at such studies—apparently at a rather young age—to permit collaboration on a number of significant projects with Betsalel Ashkenazi, a great legal scholar. Luria engaged in this type of halakhic scholarship until at least as late as 1558.

Luria as Commercial Trader

History has been kind enough to preserve a good deal of information about a completely different aspect of Isaac Luria's life in Egypt, that is, his business activities from the same general time period, the 1550s.[45] Over the past few years, a variety of documents from the Cairo Geniza have come to light attesting to Luria's commercial dealings in several types of goods, including pepper, wine, cucumbers, wheat, and leather.

Luria lived in Cairo, but it seems that business took him to the ports of Alexandria and Rashid (Rosetta), located not far from Alexandria at the western mouth of the Nile Delta. He engaged in business with various local agents and partners, trading goods between Egypt, Turkey, and Italy. It is worth describing some of the details found in these documents.

1. The earliest testimony we have concerning Luria's commercial activity is found in a bill of sale in the Geniza that dates from the beginning of the Hebrew month of Elul (August), in the year 1554, at the age of twenty.[46] According to this document, Luria sold a certain amount of pepper belonging to him in the port of Alexandria to Nathan Chefetz for the sum of 150 Venetian gold pieces. Luria had to travel to Alexandria and was required to make sure that the pepper was delivered to Cairo within a few days. Pepper was presumably imported either from India or the Far East.[47]

2. Several months later, in 1555, another bill of sale indicates that a certain Isaac Ashkenazi paid a sum of money to individuals in the land of Israel and in Syria for the purchase of pepper.[48] In support of the likelihood that Isaac Ashkenazi and Isaac Luria are one and the same person is the fact that we know that Luria had been involved in pepper dealing just several months earlier, and that the document mentions a certain Jacob Elyakim, a name expressly associated with Luria's business activities elsewhere.[49]

3. According to a document dated 1559, Luria borrowed a sum of money from Raphael Kalonymous for the purpose of business investment.[50]

4–5. A certain Moshe Benjamin sent two letters from Rashid to Luria in Egypt, probably in either 1555 or 1562.[51] According to the contents of these letters, Benjamin owed Luria a certain amount of money for goods with which Luria had provided him, and he requested that Luria collect the debt from a Moses Krispin, with whom Benjamin was associated in business. The letters appear to suggest that Luria had sold Benjamin leather.

6. We also possess two letters by Luria in his own handwriting and signed by him. Simcha Assaf, who originally published the first of these letters,[52] believed that it was written by Luria late in his life, af-

ter he had settled in Safed, but it appears to date from close to the time of the letters sent by Moshe Benjamin, while Luria was still in Egypt.[53] Although it is not clear to whom the letter was addressed, it was sent to Rashid. In it, Luria makes an inquiry concerning the whereabouts of wheat that was to be sent to him.

7. The second letter written by Luria was sent to Rashid to a relative of his, a certain Shimon.[54] It appears that Shimon would buy cucumbers in Rashid and send them to Luria in Cairo. In this letter, Luria asks him to try to obtain fresh produce. It seems that Luria owed the sum of 68 gold coins, a debt he would pay with the profits from his sale of cucumbers. It also appears from this letter that Luria traded in silk cloth.

8. We also have a lengthy letter sent by a certain Yehudah Ash[kenazi?] to a wealthy businessman and scholar by the name of Solomon.[55] This appears to be none other than Solomon Alaskhar, a well-known figure in Egypt during this period. (Alaskhar provided the funds for the first printing of Joseph Karo's *Shulḥan Arukh* in Venice in 1565.) Yehudah was Solomon's agent in connection with the purchase of a large amount of cucumbers being delivered from Damietta to the port of Alexandria. It appears that Luria—whose name is mentioned in an incidental way near the end of the letter—owed money to one of the parties to this transaction.

We should not be too surprised that an Egyptian rabbi and scholar such as Isaac Luria was also a businessman. It was altogether common for scholars in the Middle East during this period to engage in commercial activities, and we know of many others who did exactly the same. Still, we cannot help but be somewhat amazed at evidence that even after he migrated to Safed, Luria continued his involvement in business. This is attested by the report of a certain Yedidiah Galante.[56] We learn that three days before he died, Isaac Luria—the originator of what is arguably the most profound form of contemplative mysticism in all of Jewish tradition—settled his business accounts. It seems that the same mind capable of mapping the spiritual cosmos in the most imaginative and visionary way had some room left over for accounts of pepper and cucumbers.

Solitude on the Nile

What do we know about Isaac Luria's study and embrace of Kabbalah during the period of his life spent in Egypt? Egypt was the home of a number of kabbalistic authors during the time that Luria lived there. Perhaps the most important representative of Kabbalah in Egypt was none other than Luria's own teacher in rabbinic studies, David ibn Zimra. Ibn Zimra wrote several kabbalistic works. The first of these was *Magen David*, a mystical explanation of the letters of the Hebrew alphabet, written "in the days of my youth," according to its author. In addition, he composed *Metsudat David* in 1556 on the meaning of the shape of the letters, and *Migdal David* in 1560 on the Song of Songs.[57] Thus Luria's primary teacher in halakhic studies was also intensely active as a kabbalistic writer. While there is no unambiguous evidence that Luria formally studied Kabbalah with ibn Zimra, there is good reason to believe that ibn Zimra's work influenced Luria in important ways, especially in connection with the doctrine of transmigration of souls.[58]

It is worth noting that some of the signatories to the rabbinic agreement discussed earlier already were, or were to become, active kabbalistic authors. Thus, Judah Masud translated portions of the *Zohar* into Hebrew and commented on sections of it.[59] It is possible that the name Samuel Tatalah actually refers to Samuel ibn Fodeila, one of Luria's earliest acquaintances in Egypt and a person with kabbalistic interests, as evidenced in a letter by Luria to him.[60]

According to Azulai, Luria engaged in nearly total solitude for a period of time while still in Egypt. Azulai reports that he personally saw the place where Luria had secluded himself every day except Sabbaths for six years.[61] It appears that Luria spent this time on a small island on the Nile known as Jazirat al-Rawda, owned by his uncle and father-in-law, Mordecai Franses. Although it is impossible to establish precisely when this took place, or for that matter to verify Azulai's contention that it lasted for six years, it stands to reason that it occurred primarily in the 1560s. Luria's activities as a legal scholar and businessman appear to have taken place in the 1550s and possibly early

1560s according to all of the evidence presented thus far. It seems highly unlikely that he could have pursued any of these activities while practicing a life of virtual solitude. Moreover, the *absence* of any clearly documentable activity from the 1560s suggests that it was during this period that his seclusion took place.[62] It was presumably during this period of his life that he studied *Zohar* intensively, those writings of Moses Cordovero that were available in Egypt in manuscript by this time, and other kabbalistic works.

Similarly, it is likely to have been during this time that Luria began to engage in the composition of kabbalistic writings of his own. These comprised miscellaneous commentaries on passages from the *Zohar*, including a portion of the *Zohar* known as *Sifra di-Tseniuta* (Book of Concealment).[63] In a letter on kabbalistic matters sent by Luria—apparently from Safed to Egypt—to the aforementioned Samuel ibn Fodeila, he refers to his own work and suggests that ibn Fodeila study it in the home of Luria's brother in Egypt.[64] These commentaries, which reflect Cordovero's influence upon Luria, were eventually incorporated into certain of Hayyim Vital's versions of Luria's teachings following Luria's death.[65] The existence of these commentaries is important for more than one reason. In the first place, Luria wrote little besides these texts, although he continued to compose a certain amount of similar material during the time he lived in Safed. In addition, it unmistakably attests to the fact that he had the most profound interest in the *Zohar*, a work that stood at the center of his kabbalistic thinking.

We cannot know with any certainty what inspired Isaac Luria to enter such a period of withdrawal from his family and others. It seems likely, though, that Luria used this time to experiment contemplatively. It stands to reason that the profound teachings that he eventually developed in Safed emerged, in part, as a result of his own contemplative experiences. This makes sense given the nature of Lurianic Kabbalah. But it is also compatible with one of the most significant arguments about the nature of authentic kabbalistic tradition put forward by Luria's circle of disciples. As we shall see, Luria's students claimed that their teacher was inspired by heaven, and that only works written under such inspiration constituted authentic Kabbalah. It may be that this belief was partly based on mystical practices that he began to develop while still in Egypt.

Did Luria travel outside of Egypt at any time prior to his permanent settlement in Safed? We have two attestations that appear to place Luria in Jerusalem as a mature man. Luria's principle disciple in Safed, Hayyim Vital, once reported that Luria informed him that he had heard a particular teaching from a great sage by the name of Kalonymous.[66] This would seem to be a certain, somewhat obscure Rabbi Kalonymous, an Ashkenazi sage living in Jerusalem during the first half of the sixteenth century.[67] In addition to this, research by Ronit Meroz has brought to light a brief sermon apparently given by Luria in Jerusalem.[68] The contents of this sermon indicate that it represented a rather incipient stage in Luria's thinking, rather than the teachings that characterized his Safed period. Two possibilities present themselves to explain Luria's presence in Jerusalem at a mature age. Either he lived in Jerusalem for a much longer time than previously thought, leaving for Egypt with his mother as a young adult rather than as a young child, or he returned to Jerusalem at some point (or points) in his life. The latter explanation is almost certainly the correct one, particularly if we accept Azulai's testimony that Luria left Jerusalem as a *child*, and that he was brought up in Mordechai Franses's home in Egypt. We know without any doubt that he was active in business in Egypt by the age of twenty. Luria must have returned to Jerusalem as an adult. It is altogether possible that this took place on a visit that he apparently made to the Safed area prior to settling there permanently. A single report by Hayyim Vital indicates that before his permanent settlement in Safed, Luria had visited the nearby village of Meron with his household to celebrate the holiday of Lag ba-Omer at the grave of Rabbi Shimon bar Yohai.[69] Another possibility is that he spent time in Jerusalem on his way to live in Safed permanently, in late 1569 or early 1570.

*

According to the above chronology of events, then, we can identify three basic periods of Isaac Luria's life in Egypt. Sometime in the late

1540s and early 1550s, before the departure of David ibn Zimra, he was the latter's student in rabbinic studies. Through the 1550s, he was active in halakhic affairs and in the circle of Betsalel Ashkenazi in Cairo, collaborating with Ashkenazi in the writing of a number of halakhic works. During this period, he made the transition from being a student to being a member of the most important rabbinic circle of Egypt. Also during the 1550s, he engaged in a wide range of commercial activities. Sometime during the 1560s, he immersed himself in a sustained manner in the study of Jewish mystical texts, went into virtually complete seclusion, and engaged in his own first attempts at kabbalistic creativity. While he clearly came into contact with individuals who were themselves kabbalistically inclined, David ibn Zimra included, there is no hard evidence that he ever actually studied esoteric lore in a formal way with ibn Zimra or anyone else in Egypt.

While we do not know enough about Isaac Luria's early life to say what impelled him toward Kabbalah, there is no doubt that by the middle of the sixteenth century, Kabbalah was very much in the air in many parts of the Mediterranean and Ottoman worlds. Considerable interest had been aroused by the mystical community in Safed, which had become the major center of kabbalistic practice and scholarship. The increasing dissemination of kabbalistic books—made possible by their printing in Italy in the middle of the sixteenth century—exerted a powerful impact upon the growing importance of Kabbalah. These developments presumably made strong impressions upon Isaac Luria.

On the basis of what we know, Luria's life in Egypt was pleasant and free of any unusual travail. As we have seen, the rule of the Ottomans provided a reasonably secure and prosperous environment for Jewish life in mid-sixteenth-century Egypt. There were no major social, economic, or political dislocations. On the contrary, life went on in a pretty much undisturbed way.[70] On the personal level, Luria married into a well-to-do family when he wed Mordechai Franses's daughter, and was apparently secure enough to support himself as a student and scholar, evidence of his having been engaged in business activities notwithstanding. He was privileged to study and collaborate with the leading rabbinic personalities of his day in David ibn Zimra and Betsalel

Ashkenazi. And he was clearly an accepted and productive member of the Cairo rabbinical community. Finally, circumstances permitted him the luxury of leaving the demands of family and communal life behind in order to seclude himself for the purpose of kabbalistic study and practice. Nevertheless, for reasons that will become clear, Isaac Luria chose to leave Egypt. He arrived in Safed in late 1569 or early 1570.

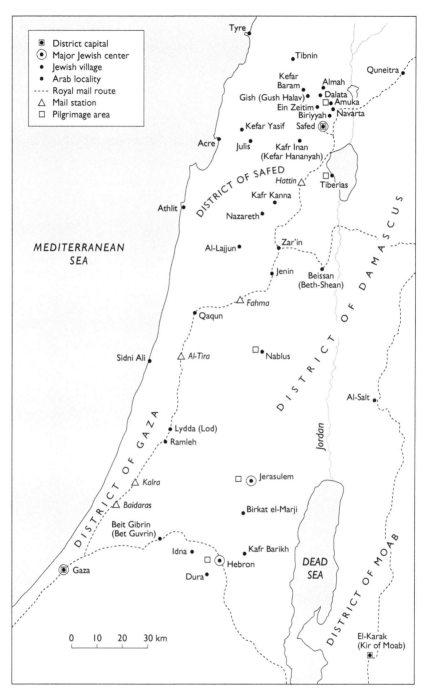

Map 1. Northern Israel, with detail of Safed and its environs.

Two   Lamenting Exile, Striving for Redemption: Pre-Lurianic Safed

> After nearly fifteen hundred years of living in exile and persecution, God recalled unto his people his covenant with their fathers and brought them back from their captivity, one of a city and two of a family, from the corners of the earth to the land of Israel.
>
> —Joseph Karo

Safed's Early History

The village of Safed lies nestled high in the eastern mountains of the Upper Galilee, twenty-five miles northwest of Tiberias, thirty miles east of the Mediterranean Sea. It commands the high ground just west of the great African-Syrian rift, which, in Israel, stretches from the Hula Valley in the north, to the Sea of Galilee, down to the Dead Sea. The old Jewish quarter of the city, with its labyrinth of narrow, winding streets, and reconstructed sixteenth-century synagogues, sits upon the eastern slope of a mountain. In the valley below lies an ancient cemetery where, even today, Jews make pilgrimage to the graves of Safed's leading kabbalists.

There is no mention of Safed in the Hebrew Bible and scant reference to it in the literature of the rabbinic period. Safed is cited in the Jerusalem Talmud as one of the mountaintop points from which fire signals were given to announce the arrival of the New Moon and festivals during the period of the Second Temple.[1] Two synagogue poems for the commemoration of the holiday of the 9th of Av by Eleazar Kallir, who lived in the Galilee sometime in the early Middle Ages, refer to Safed as a place where priestly families settled in the wake of the destruction of the Temple. There is little known about Safed, however, between the talmudic period and the Crusades.

The name of the town resurfaces in 1140 as a "fortress of very great strength between Acre and the Sea of Galilee" constructed by Fulk of Anjou, the third Crusader king of Jerusalem. It was handed over by Fulk's son, Amalric I, to the Knights Templar in 1168. In 1188, it was conquered by the great Muslim general Saladin, but it was later re-captured by the Crusaders. Eventually, in 1266, it was taken by the Mamluks, who made it the capital of a *mamlakhah*, or province, that included the Galilee and Lebanon.

While documents from the Cairo Genizah indicate that there was some Jewish settlement in Safed from the first half of the eleventh century, the celebrated traveler Benjamin of Tudela, who passed through the city in 1170–71, testifies that no Jews resided there.[2] It appears on the basis of Geniza documents, however, that a Jewish community did exist in Safed in the thirteenth century, and Jewish settlement in Safed from this period on is corroborated by the testimony of a number of travelers, including Samuel ben Shimson, who visited Palestine in 1210. Samuel traveled as part of a group from Europe, including several important scholars, among them Rabbi Jonathan ha-Kohen of Lunel. According to him, there were then more than fifty Jews living in the city.[3] We also have evidence that kabbalistic activity took place in Safed as early as the fourteenth century. Shem Tov ben Abraham ben Gaon, a well-known talmudist and kabbalist, migrated from Spain to Safed in 1313 and authored various kabbalistic treatises over the next few decades.[4] Among other things, Shem Tov studied the works of Moses Maimonides in an attempt to demonstrate the supposed influence of Kabbalah upon the great Spanish master, reflecting what was apparently a strong interest in Maimonides' halakhic legacy during this time in Safed.

According to the report of a certain Joseph de Montagna, an Italian rabbi who visited Safed in 1481, there was "a fine community, with three hundred householders including those of the surrounding villages which are within its limits. Numerous graves of prophets, saints, *tanna ͗im* [i.e., sages from the Mishnaic period], and *amora ͗im* [sages from the period of the Gemara], as well as that of Queen Esther, are to be found there."[5] Obadiah of Bertinoro, a distinguished Italian rabbi of the fifteenth century, reported in 1488: "It is said that the Jews live quietly and peaceably with the Arabs in Safed, in the village of Cana, and in all Galilee, yet most of them are poor and support themselves by peddling, and many go about the villages seeking scanty means of subsistence."[6]

An anonymous disciple of Obadiah's gives us an especially detailed and colorful description of Safed, which he visited a few years later, in the year 1495. It has wonderful value as a rich picture of the town and its environs, especially the account of the graves of various important sages, a subject of considerable interest to this study:

Safed is built on the slopes of a mountain and is a great city. The houses are small and modest, and when the rain falls it is impossible to walk about town on account of the dirt, and also because it is on the hillside. It is also difficult to go out in the markets and the streets even during the summer, for you must always be climbing up or down. However, the land is good and health giving and the waters are quite good. And this is the absolute truth: I saw men in Safed who are far older than sixty or seventy years. Among them was an old man aged a hundred and thirty, who was still flourishing, strong and healthy indeed. The holy congregation numbers about three hundred householders, and most of the Jews have shops of spices, cheese, oil, and sundry pulses and fruits. I have heard that a man can make twenty-five ducats out of one of those shops, on which five people can live. The foodstuffs are also cheap in Safed. . . . Around Safed there are many caves in which great and pious men have been buried. Most of these are about six miles from the town, and I saw some of them. Therefore I shall now inform you of what I have heard and what I have seen with my own eyes. First of all, near the Jewish quarter in Safed is the burial place of the prophet Hosea ben Beeri of blessed memory. There is no tombstone or inscription above it, and only a large stone at the cave mouth; and as soon as I reached Safed I said prayers at this grave. About as far from Safed as one may walk on a Sabbath is the grave of the talmudic master Rabbi Judah bar Ilai; and there is a little village there called Ein Zetim. On the grave is a handsome tomb at which candles are lit, and there I went and prostrated myself and lit candles to his memory. About six miles from Safed is a certain village called Meron, where very great and pious saints whose names I shall mention are buried. Before I came to the place I saw three graves by the wayside, one being that of Rabbi Judah the Punished of saintly and blessed memory, over whose grave there is only a small heap of stones. A little farther away is the burial place of Rabbi Tarfon of saintly and blessed memory, with a lovely monument above it. A little farther yet is the grave of Rabbi Jose ben Kisma of saintly and blessed memory, over which there is also a heap of stones without any monument. After this we reached the village [of Meron] itself and saw the cave of Hillel and his disciples of saintly and blessed memory, who were buried with him there; and they number twenty-four. We entered a certain cave nearby in which twenty-two scholars lie, and they said that these were the disciples of Rabbi Shimon bar Yohai of saintly and blessed memory; and near the spot on the hillside there is an extremely fine monument, which can be seen as far as Safed. But together with the disciples were buried their wives, and there is nothing over their graves. The local residents said that monuments had frequently been set over their graves, but they were all destroyed at night; however, I do not know whether it is true.[7]

By the turn of the sixteenth century, Safed was already the home of a number of important rabbis. A letter sent by the scholars of Safed to the heads of the Jerusalem yeshiva (rabbinical academy) in the year 1504 indicates that the Safed rabbinate conceded the primacy of Jerusalem and acknowledged that "the law goes forth from Zion, [and the word of the Lord from Jerusalem]."[8] The scholars of Jerusalem had rendered a decision having to do with the Sabbatical year without consulting their colleagues in Safed. Although the Safed rabbis recognized the superiority of the Jerusalem rabbinate, they protested that weight be given to "the fledgling sheep of the holy community of Safed that is in Upper Galilee," for "we are not men of no account." The signatories to the Safed letter included Joseph ben Abraham of Saragossa (David ibn Zimra's teacher), a number of *Mustarabim* and North African rabbis, but primarily sages from among the exiles from the Iberian Peninsula. We thus see that even by this early period, Safed had already begun to attract exiled Jews.

In contrast to the Jews of Jerusalem, who were not adversely affected by the conflict between the Mamluks and the Ottoman Turks in 1516, Safed appears to have suffered considerably. Retreating Mamluks attacked the community, while Arabs in nearby villages exploited the opportunity to do likewise. The Egyptian Jewish community came to the aid of their fellow Jews. Rabbi Nissan Biba of Egypt organized a project of assistance and traveled to Safed to help rehabilitate the Jewish community there. The recovery was quick, because the city at-

Figure 2. Path leading to the ancient cemetery, with the Galilean mountains in the distance. Courtesy Aaron Fine, photographer.

tracted considerable numbers of newcomers from around the Ottoman Empire in the wake of the Turkish conquest. By 1522, the traveling Moses Basola could report that he found three hundred Jewish families in Safed, made up of both Sephardim and *Mustarabim*, as well as Jews from North Africa:

> Safed is the northernmost district of the land of Naphtali, with a strong walled enclosure at the mountaintop. The walled enclosure on the peak is surrounded by four mountains, [of which] two [are] inhabited entirely by Muslims, and the slopes of the other two are completely covered with Jewish homes. They number more than three hundred households. The city has three [main] synagogues; a Sephardic one, a Morisco one, and a Maghrebi one known as "Elijah of blessed memory's synagogue," for it is ancient, and they have a tradition that Elijah, may his memory be blessed, prayed there.[9]

The fact that Basola placed Sephardim first in this list is probably no accident. As they did in just about every other place to which they

migrated, Sephardic Jews—arriving from every corner of the Ottoman diaspora—quickly became the dominant political, social, and cultural force in Safed.[10] The other Jewish communities of Safed, *Mustarabim*, Ashkenazim, North Africans, Romaniotes, and Provençal and
Italian Jews, as well as smaller numbers from such places as Hungary,
Kurdistan, and Bosnia, all had to struggle to maintain their identities and independence in the face of the powerful influence of the
Sephardim. At its peak, there were perhaps as many as several dozen
different Sephardic communities alone in Safed, many with their own
"quarter," such as those from Portugal, Cordova, Castile, Aragon, Catalonia, and Seville.[11]

Basola also paints a picture of an economy beginning to flourish in
Safed in the early 1520s, involving substantial commercial trade with
Beirut and Damascus. Nevertheless, he cautions his countrymen in
Italy to whom he is writing that there are many poor, and that those
with neither a craft nor capital should not consider immigrating there:

> The city is filled with an abundance of good things and excellent
> foodstuffs: grain, wine, and oil in great abundance and cheap for the
> person who purchases everything in its season. If it were not for the
> large amount of oil and grain that they export from there to Damas-
> cus and to other places, it [this produce] would have no value. All
> manner of succulent fruits are available there, and whatever is not
> available locally is imported from Damascus. Trade is widespread in
> this region, with shops for woolen garments, haberdashery, and
> spices. Many Jewish shops specialize in these three ventures; they im-
> port the haberdashery and the spices from Damascus and sell them in
> the city, and at the time of the galleys, they go to Beirut to purchase
> garments and other items. Many Jews make fixed rounds of the vil-
> lages in order to sell notions and other peddleable wares, thus they
> are able to fill their houses with all manner of good things. In addi-
> tion, there is profit to be made in buying cotton, thread, wax, and
> [the] scammony [plant] when they are cheap and selling them later at
> an opportune moment. Jews also sell fruits and vegetables, oil,
> cheeses, and other items in the bazaar. He who so desires can deal in
> grain, wine, and oil, each in its proper season. Generally speaking,
> there is much more trade in this land than in Italy, for the Muslims

purchase more willingly from Jews than from others. But he who has no capital to invest in trade must be a craftsman. There are four types of craftsmen in demand in the land of Israel as a whole: weavers, silversmiths, leatherworkers, and tanners, also builders. He who has the strength to be a *per diem* worker in this last field is well paid. A tailor also earns his living. On the other hand, one cannot expect to hire oneself out as a teacher or as a house servant or as a shop assistant. Nor can one live at public expense, for the poor are many. Therefore, he who possesses neither craft nor funds should not leave Italy, lest he regret his actions and [be obliged to] return, and a word to the wise is sufficient.[12]

Following the Ottoman victory, Safed quickly established itself as far and away the largest and most vibrant community in Palestine for a variety of reasons. The Jewish population of Safed—the majority of its inhabitants—increased steadily until the last quarter of the sixteenth century. At the time of the Ottoman conquest, there were somewhere between 200 and 300 households; in 1538, there were approximately 850, and in 1544–45, there were 1175. Safed's Jewish population appears to have peaked around the years 1567–68, when there may have been as many as 1,800 households, a remarkably high number for a small city.[13] As political and economic conditions deteriorated during the last quarter of the century, Safed's Jewish community began to dwindle. In a letter written in 1591 describing these conditions, Moses Alsheikh reported that it had declined "to the extent that of the five thousand people who formerly resided in the city, some four hundred alone remained."[14]

Several reasons help to account for Safed's immense popularity throughout most of the sixteenth century. In the first place, even though Jerusalem had revived under the auspices of the Ottomans, taxation was higher there and economic conditions were far less favorable than those in Safed. In fact, economic opportunities in Safed played a much greater role in the emergence of that city as a center of Jewish life than is usually appreciated. Along with Salonika and various other Ottoman cities, as mentioned earlier, Safed became a leading textile manufacturer for the empire and beyond.[15] At an earlier period in Spain, Jews had been known for their involvement in various aspects of the textile industry, as weavers, dyers, tailors, and traders. As we have already seen, these skills accompanied Jews to the Ottoman Empire, where they were able to apply them successfully. In the sixteenth century, especially between 1500 and 1580, thousands of Jews were engaged in all stages of the production of cloth.

Conditions in Safed were exceptional for the development of the textile industry. High-quality raw, short-fibered wool was sent from the Balkans to Safed by way of the port of Sidon. In order to facilitate dying on a large scale, as well as mechanical fulling (a process in which woolen cloth is beaten, scoured, and cleansed with a detergent), which was done by water power, clear soft running water was critical. Along with the springs in the city itself, and in the village of Ein Zetim, the streams of Ein Poem, Meron, and Yakhin in the upper part of Naḥal Ammud were able to accommodate this process.[16] The manufacturing was controlled by merchants who imported the wool in special ships and provided it to the workers, who were paid fees agreed upon in advance. Spinning was done by women at home, while weaving was performed in workshops. Fulling was carried out in special mills, which were known by their Spanish name, *batan*. The building in which the biggest fulling mill was housed is still standing in Safed today. The cloth industry brought in large sums of money to the treasury of the country and provided a good living for a vast number of Safed's Jews during the peak years, 1530–60. David dei Rossi, an Italian Jewish merchant who visited Safed in 1535, describes how the textile industry dominated the commercial life of the city even then: "He who saw Safed ten years ago, and observes it now, has the impression of a miracle. For more Jews are arriving here continually, and the tailoring trade grows daily. I have been told that more than 15,000 suits have been manufactured in Safed during this year, besides fancy suits. Every man and every woman who works woolen fabric earns an abundant living."[17]

Textiles, however, were not the only commercial activity. "All articles of commerce are available in these regions," dei Rossi says. "Fibers, spun and unspun, are exported from Safed in great quantities, also gall nuts, scammony, oil, honey, and silk in smaller quantities. From the adjoining regions [to Safed] come crimson silk, Cordovan carpets, and all kinds of spices, including pepper, cloves, ginger, and cane-spices. Many people, including Jews, buy these goods as merchandise."[18]

Because of its strategic importance to the Ottoman Empire, the authorities sought to keep Safed well protected. In 1549, during the reign of Suleiman the Magnificent, a wall was constructed, and the city was henceforth guarded by Turkish soldiers against the perpetual threat of marauders from neighboring villages. It appears to have provided insufficient protection, however, as evidenced by the request of the Jewish community to build a fortified section for Jewish homes that could be locked at nightfall. Sometime in the middle of the century, the Ottoman district ruler erected such a fortress, or khan, near the Jewish quarter, within which some of Safed's Jews presumably lived.[19] These relatively secure conditions continued to exist until the last quarter of the sixteenth century, when the disciplined control of the authorities in Istanbul began to fail. In the meantime, however, the Jewish community in Safed enjoyed a significant degree of prosperity and peace.[20]

Besides these material and political factors, Jews were attracted to Safed for a variety of religious reasons. In the travel accounts of 1481 and 1495 quoted earlier, we saw the importance attached to the presence of graves of various prophets and sages. The grave in Meron, just a few miles west of Safed, of the second-century rabbi Shimon bar Yohai, to whom kabbalistic tradition attributes the *Zohar*, was by far the most important of these. Pilgrimages to this site, as well as to others, go back at least as far as the fourteenth century.[21] In the sixteenth century, when Kabbalah had become increasingly popular, the opportunity to live in the area where Shimon bar Yohai and his disciples were supposed to have lived, studied, and died must have been an irresistible attraction to kabbalistic enthusiasts. We shall see later on the crucial importance that these grave sites held for the Safed kabbalists, especially Isaac Luria and his disciples.

More generally, the Ottoman conquest was construed as bearing religious significance, especially for Spanish and Portuguese exiles. Insofar as it enabled Jews to travel and settle freely in Palestine, it could not help but be regarded by many as a divinely ordained opportunity to fulfill the dreams of medieval Jews to live in the land of Israel. These dreams were frequently accompanied by new confidence in the possibility of messianic redemption.

Thus, in the 1520s and 1530s, Safed began to be populated in significant numbers by rabbis and scholars from various parts of the empire. In either 1535 or 1536, for example, Solomon Alkabets (1505–76) arrived in Safed after sojourns in Salonika, Nicopolis, and Edirne (Adrianople).[22] Alkabets had been a student of Joseph Taitasak, the leader of an important circle of kabbalists in Salonika, where Alkabets delivered a sermon in the spring of 1534 that provides unusual and valuable testimony with respect to the thinking behind his decision to emigrate to the land of Israel. From the contents of this sermon it is possible to infer that Alkabets was motivated by dreams of the rebuilding of the ancient Sanctuary in Jerusalem, something imaginable only in the context of Israel's messianic redemption.[23] That Alkabets was also interested in encouraging others to go to the land of Israel is apparent from a well-known letter that he sent from Safed to the kabbalistic brotherhood in Salonika describing in detail a case in which Joseph Karo's *maggid*, or mentor angel, had spoken to Karo in the presence of Alkabets. Alkabets depicts the *maggid* as urging Karo and those with whom the latter associated to go to the land of Israel:

> Go up to the land of Israel, for not all times are opportune. There is no hindrance to salvation, be it much or little. Let not your eyes have pity on your worldly goods, for you eat of the goodness of the higher land. If you will but hearken, of the goodness of that land you shall eat. Make haste, therefore, to go up to the land, for I sustain you here and shall sustain you there. . . . Awake, O drunken ones, for the day comes when a man must cast away his gods of silver, worldly desires, and his gods of gold, and lust for wealth. Go up to the land of Israel, which you would be able to do were you not trapped in the mud of worldly desires and vanities.[24]

It seems clear from these remarks that Alkabets sent this letter to his compatriots in Salonika to persuade them to follow in his footsteps. Alkabets played an exceedingly important role in Safed as Moses

Cordovero's (1522–70) teacher in esoteric studies. Cordovero—Alkabets's brother-in-law—would go on to become Safed's leading kabbalist, at least until the appearance of Isaac Luria. Joseph Karo (1488–1575), a prominent rabbinic figure in Turkey, where he had lived for forty years after emigrating there, perhaps from Portugal, came to Safed in 1536 or 1537. As we shall see, Karo was a central figure in Safed during his many years there, not only as its most important halakhic authority, but also as a kabbalist. Other scholars who were better known as talmudists than as kabbalists and who made Safed their home during this early period of settlement included Jacob Berab (c. 1474–c. 1541) and his students, such as Moses di Trani (1500–80), Abraham Shalom (d.c. 1557), and Israel di Curiel (c. 1502–after 1571).

The Renewal of Rabbinic Ordination

The religious significance that these individuals and others attached to the revitalization of the *yishuv*, the Jewish community in Palestine, can be vividly illustrated by a description of the attempts to renew rabbinic ordination along traditional lines in 1538.[25] This effort was initiated by the aforementioned Jacob Berab, a scholar who settled permanently in Safed in 1535 and who served as its leading rabbinic authority until his death in 1541.[26] According to Jewish law, the authority of sages was believed to have originated with Moses, who, after being empowered by God, had passed on his divine investiture to Joshua, and so on. This chain of succession was believed to have been transmitted to the biblical judges and prophets, the "men of the Great Assembly," and eventually to the sages of the talmudic period. The process of formal succession was considered to have been broken sometime in the early Middle Ages, although individuals continued to be trained and appointed as rabbis. Their authority and powers were believed, however, to be limited in comparison to earlier times. Thus, there were always hopes that full, formal ordination (*semikhah*) might someday be reestablished.

It is precisely this that Jacob Berab sought to accomplish. Berab based his opinion that it was now possible to do so on his interpretation of the views of Moses Maimonides, the preeminent Spanish-born rabbi, philosopher, and physician. Centuries earlier, Maimonides had contended that "if all the Palestinian sages would unanimously agree to appoint and ordain judges, then these new ordinants would possess the full authority of the original ordained judges."[27] Based on this ruling, Berab convened twenty-five Safed rabbis in 1538 and asked them to reintroduce *semikhah* by ordaining him. He, in turn, would then possess the authority with which to ordain others. Although there were misgivings about the whole project, those assembled acceded to Berab's request. Unfortunately, when a messenger was sent to Levi ibn Habib, the chief rabbi of Jerusalem, in order to gain his acceptance and approval of what had taken place, ibn Habib vigorously refused to give it, on various grounds, including a different understanding of Maimonides' ruling. Ibn Habib argued that Maimonides' ruling was not a legal decision per se, but merely an opinion. What is more, he claimed that Maimonides had retracted this opinion at a later time. The objections of the Jerusalem rabbinate clearly threw a damper on Berab's hopes, not only to gain acceptance for his own ordination, but also to reinstitute the Sanhedrin, the supreme court of Jewish law, in the land of Israel.

A full-blown, well-documented controversy ensued, which lasted for years. Despite the fact that the ordination never achieved the intended results, Berab conferred *semikhah* upon four other individuals. These were Joseph Karo, Moses di Trani, Abraham Shalom, and Israel di Curiel. In 1541, when Karo succeeded Berab as Safed's leading rabbinic figure, he perpetuated the tradition by ordaining Moses Alsheikh, Elisha Gallico, and Jacob Berab II. In the 1590s, Alsheikh ordained Hayyim Vital, and between the years 1594 and 1599, Jacob Berab II ordained seven more scholars: Moses Galante, Eleazar Azikri, Moses Berab (Jacob's brother), Abraham Gavriel, Yomtov Tsahalon, Hiyya Rofe, and Jacob Abulafia. Thus, despite the acrimonious controversy that swirled around the original events, Safed halakhic authorities remained convinced of the validity of the *semikhah*, although there was reluctance to invoking it as the basis for authority.

While this controversy is fascinating on its own terms, what is especially interesting is the possibility that Berab's aspirations were motivated in part by a belief in the redemptive possibilities inherent in the dramatic events taking place around them. Surely the opening up of the land of Israel under the benevolence of the Ottomans, its continuing resettlement, and the economic prosperity it was enjoying were all signs that conditions were increasingly ripe for Israel's redemption. The attempt to regain the full, formal authority of old, with all of the attendant suggestions of sovereignty and independence under rabbinic jurisdiction, may have been symptomatic of the hopeful mood that characterized the renascent community in Safed.

Rabbinic Study

While sixteenth-century Safed has over time become virtually synonymous with Kabbalah, it is clear from what we have already said that rabbinic study and talmudic life also had an exceedingly firm foundation there. In fact, the truly remarkable concentration of rabbinic scholars in one rather small place is perhaps as impressive as Safed's concentration of kabbalists. During the period in which Jacob Berab resided in Safed, the renowned yeshiva that he headed was the center of this rabbinic activity.[28] Berab was the chief rabbinical judge (*dayyan*) and appears to have enjoyed unchallenged authority in all matters of a halakhic nature. Berab's yeshiva, like others of its type elsewhere, served a range of purposes. Besides its most obvious function as an academy of rabbinic training, it also constituted an assembly of scholars that debated all manner of practical religious law, passing judgment on the basis of majority opinion. The curriculum and methods of study were largely modeled on those that had been employed in the talmudic academies of Spain.[29] Berab had studied under one of Spain's most outstanding rabbis, Isaac Aboab (1433–93), "the last *gaon* of Castile," head of a great and influential yeshiva in Toledo and later Guadalajara. Aboab himself had been a disciple of one of the preeminent Spanish masters, Isaac Canpanton. Among Berab's fundamental accomplishments, then, was to establish in the Galilee a link with the great traditions of talmudic scholarship as they had been practiced in Spain, and to create a training ground for young rabbinical scholars. The method of study "incorporated close intellectual-didactic scrutiny of the talmudic text (*sugya*) with an eye to derivation of practical *halakha* in matters of current relevance," and relied significantly on the legal writings of Rashi, the Tosafists, Maimonides, and Moses ben Nahman.[30]

Joseph Karo eventually assumed the mantle of rabbinic leadership in Safed. Karo was born in either Portugal or Spain in 1488, but at a young age he found himself journeying with his family to Egypt and eventually to various Balkan cities, such as Edirne, Salonika, and Nicopolis. As noted earlier, he arrived in Safed in 1536 or 1537. Karo is one of the greatest luminaries in the history of Jewish religious law. He authored the monumental halakhic compendium known as the *Bet Yosef* (House of Joseph), itself a commentary on Jacob ben Asher's seminal code *Arbaʿah Turim*, but is most famous on account of his condensation of the *Bet Yosef*, the *Shulḥan Arukh* (Set Table). The latter was intended to be a mere digest of his voluminous original work, but it turned out to be a far more useful and practical handbook to Jewish legal practice than its source. To this day, the *Shulḥan Arukh* is regarded as a foundational code for traditional Jewish law. In addition to leading a yeshiva, Karo also served as head of Safed's *bet din*, or religious court of law. This court also included the aforementioned Moses di Trani, another eminent halakhist, with whom Karo had fierce and ongoing disagreements,[31] and Israel di Curiel. Luria's teacher in Egypt, David ibn Zimra, joined the ranks of Safed's illustrious legal scholars between the years 1564 and 1573 and also became a member of its *bet din*.

In addition to the numerous rabbinical academies that flourished in Safed, study also appears to have taken place on a wide scale among laymen. For those who were not full-time students or scholars, the numerous synagogues provided plentiful opportunities for study. Although written in the early 1600s, the following (somewhat exaggerated) description by Solomon Shlomiel of Dresnitz of lay study in Safed no doubt reflects the general nature of such study at an earlier time as well:

> Following prayers, the entire congregation studies regularly. They sit before the rabbis and are divided into about six classes in each synagogue. Each class studies before leaving the synagogue. One class studies *Ein Yaʿaqov*, another the laws of blessings, another studies

Maimonides, another studies Mishnah, another studies the Talmud with Rashi and *Tosafot*, another studies the *Zohar*, and another studies the Bible. Consequently, no individual leaves for work or business in the morning without regularly devoting time to the Torah, and in the evenings after prayers, they study at greater length.[32]

We thus see that despite the fact that Safed's fame in the sixteenth century rests primarily upon the kabbalistic renaissance that occurred there, it was also a place where traditional rabbinic scholarship and study more than held its own. Indeed, during this period, Safed was the greatest center of such activity throughout the Near Eastern, Mediterranean, and North African regions.

Kabbalistic Life in Pre-Lurianic Safed

The teachings and practices of Lurianic Kabbalah must be understood against the background of the kabbalistic life that preceded Luria in Safed. When he arrived in Safed, Isaac Luria found a well-developed mystical community with a clearly identifiable kabbalistic culture. Thus, it is important to describe—at least in fairly broad strokes—the nature of this community. Here it is worth saying a few words about certain motifs deriving from Spanish Kabbalah of the thirteenth century.[33]

According to kabbalistic theology, divine life has two aspects, the first of which is known as *Ein-Sof* (literally, "Infinite" or "Without End"). *Ein-Sof* is the ultimate source of all reality, the divine Mystery from which all else derives. It is regarded by the kabbalists as a dimension of God that is utterly unknowable, concealed beyond all human comprehension. As the hidden and perfect root of all reality, it can be neither positively named nor imagined by the human intellect. At best, it can be described by such expressions as "that which thought cannot attain," or "perfect unity." It thus constitutes the absolutely transcendent aspect of divinity, God as known only to God, so to speak.

This conviction, with its insistence on the inability of human beings to apprehend God's essence, closely resembles the *via negativa*, or "negative theology," to which many medieval philosophers subscribed. However, the kabbalists go far beyond the philosophical rationalists by means of their concept of the *sefirot*, ten aspects of the divine that *emanate* from within the inner wellsprings of *Ein-Sof*. Described as the hidden *Ein-Sof*'s "garments," "crowns," "lights," "faces," or "colors," the *sefirot* flow out of *Ein-Sof*, revealing and making manifest the life of divinity. According to this doctrine of divine emanation, the *sefirot* are not mere external attributes of God in the philosophic sense, but aspects of God's very Self, intrinsic dimensions of divine being through which God continuously manifests itself. The *sefirot* are symbols that point to spiritual realities that constitute the life of the deity. While virtually nothing can be said of God as *Ein-Sof*, the realm of the *sefirot* is accessible to human contemplation and susceptible to description. Together, *Ein-Sof* and the ten *sefirot* constitute what the kabbalists refer to as the upper world, or world of unity.

Below the sefirotic realm is the lower world, or the world of separation, our most immediate reality. What is the relationship between these two levels of existence? In the first place, the kabbalists describe the unfolding that occurs in the upper world and the creation of our world as two aspects of the very same process. Creation takes places simultaneously on two levels, the material world constituting a visible, physical manifestation of a process that occurs in a concealed manner in the realm of the *sefirot*. The essential difference between the two realms is that whereas in the world of unity there is potentially perfect harmony and integration, the world of separation is characterized by a degree of flaw and materialization. Nevertheless, insofar as the lower world was created as a result of the emanation of divine life from above, it *corresponds* to and *parallels* that world in its essential structure. The morphology or physiognomy of the two are the same, even if they are qualitatively different. Everything in our world has a counterpart, a correspondence in the world of divinity above. The earth, moon, sun, stars, rivers, oceans, mountains, trees, and all of the processes of nature of which they are a part reveal to us the processes of dynamic life that occur on the sefirotic level.

Not only does everything in the material world mirror a spiritual reality above, but everything in our created existence is invested with a degree of divine vitality from the *sefirot*. There is a continuous flow of divine nourishment from one realm of existence to the other, endowing all things in the lower world with life. In order to express this relationship, Kabbalah employs a range of images, including that of a cosmic chain of being in which everything is linked to everything else. All the elements of existence—from the most deeply concealed to the most visible—are intimately and inextricably bound to one another. All things ultimately originate from the inner recesses of the mysterious ground of all being, *Ein-Sof*.

Human beings have a central place in this mythological scheme. For the kabbalists, the human personality represents the totality of the sefirotic structure. That is, it is a microcosm of the divine world. Even more, human beings are directly imbued with divine life. This is especially true of the soul, the *neshamah*, which is regarded as deriving from God. The soul, then, establishes a direct link between the *sefirot* and each person. On the basis of this conception, the kabbalists taught a remarkable idea, namely, that human deeds have an effect upon the upper world. Every action reverberates on the level of the *sefirot*.

The early kabbalists taught that prior to Adam's sin, there was no material world at all. Adam himself was of a purely spiritual nature. Moreover, the *sefirot* stood in a relationship of complete harmony with one another. This idyllic situation ended as a result of Adam's transgression. Adam took on corporeal form and was no longer located in the upper world; the sefirotic relationship ceased to be one of perfect unity. Rather, a degree of disharmony was introduced into the life of divinity. This disharmony or flaw is most frequently conceived of as separation between two of the *sefirot*, *Tiferet* and *Malkhut* (also known as *Shekhinah*), male and female aspects of God respectively. The task of all human beings is to *restore* the original harmony that existed prior to Adam's sin. Every proper deed contributes to the well-being of divine life. In turn, the momentary reunification of God brought about by such an action enables divine light to flow downward into the material realm. That is, virtuous earthly behavior reestablishes the unity among the various aspects of divinity, most typically by restoring the love between *Tiferet* and *Malkhut*. At the same time, it reestablishes the proper relationship between an individual and the *sefirot*.

Thus, no gesture, no utterance of speech, no thought is lacking in significance with respect to its effect upon the higher realms of reality. As the *Zohar* says: "The impulse from below calls forth that from above." There is, in other words, a mutual and dynamic relationship between human beings and the transcendent realm with which they are so essentially united. As a microcosm, a perfect paradigm of the upper world, and as one link in a cosmic chain of being, a human being simultaneously reflects the life of divinity and arouses it—only to be aroused and nourished in return.

It is obvious from this that with these conceptions, Kabbalah has broken in substantial ways with conventional rabbinic theology, both in terms of the ways in which God is conceived and in terms of what human responsibility entails. In place of a relatively simple conception of God and His unity, we find a far more intricate idea in which God is perceived as a complex organism constituted of many aspects, even if the kabbalists always insist that God's oneness remains uncompromised. Moreover, the world of our reality is invested with divine abundance in a fundamentally new way. In lieu of the weak immanence of rabbinic theology, according to which God has a providential ear to the ground, so to speak, Kabbalah provides a much stronger notion of divine presence. In Kabbalah, we have a mythological conception in which the "stuff" of divinity manifests itself in this world in an ontological way.

In addition, the function of religious observance has been redefined and invigorated with altogether new status. The cosmic repercussions of religious deeds is one of the most far-reaching and radical notions of theosophical Jewish mysticism. Although the mystics themselves never quite spell out such a conclusion, the effect of kabbalistic theology is to revise thoroughly the usual conception of God's autonomy. God is no longer regarded as being in complete control of all history in the older sense; rather, God's *own* well-being is contingent upon human action. While in rabbinic theology God may be said to mourn and suffer distress upon witnessing Israel's fate, He cannot be said to experience actual injury, let alone injury that can be healed only by virtuous action on the part of human beings. Here we have the utter antithesis of the medieval philosophic point of view. Whereas the philosophers never tired of insisting that God is absolutely immutable and unchangeable, the kabbalists assert that God is ever-vulnerable to the effects of human behavior.

It was this complex configuration of mystical notions, among others, that the Safed kabbalists inherited in forging their own community. Despite the fact that they were living in the land of Israel, the kabbalists of the sixteenth century possessed a strong sense of *galut*, that is, exile. This sense of exile expressed itself most characteristically through the kabbalistic conception of *galut ha-Shekhinah*, "exile of the *Shekhinah*."[34] *Malkhut*, or *Shekhinah*, is imagined in Kabbalah as the receptive female who possesses no divine light or vitality of Her own. Instead, She is filled with the nourishment that She receives from the *sefirot* above Her, mediated most directly through the *Sefirah Yesod*, the divine "phallus." As one of the ten manifestations of the Godhead, *Shekhinah* bears a wide variety of symbolic associations, including "Daughter," "Lower Mother," "Princess," "Queen," "Bride," "Earth," "Moon," and "Sabbath," to name a few. The harmony that ideally characterizes the relationship between *Shekhinah* and Her male lover *Tiferet* is interrupted as a result of human sin. The *Shekhinah* is cut off from Her source of nourishment and remains separated or "exiled" from the rest of the *sefirot*. Even though earlier kabbalists had spoken of the exile of the *Shekhinah*, it was the Safed kabbalists, now especially gripped by a sense of individual and collective responsibility, who took up this theme with even greater passion. In the process, they exhibited a deeply and personally felt identification with the rupture within the life of God, and particularly the misery and torment of the *Shekhinah*.

One of the most vivid illustrations of this is the oft-mentioned activity of Moses Cordovero and Solomon Alkabets known as *gerushin*, that is, "wanderings" or "exiles."[35] Cordovero and Alkabets would journey in the area around Safed with special mystical intention. During the course of these "exiles," they would self-consciously imitate the exiled *Shekhinah*:

> A person should exile himself from place to place for the sake of Heaven and in this way he will become a vessel for the exiled *Shekhinah*. . . .
> he should humble his heart in exile and bind himself to the Torah
> and then the *Shekhinah* will accompany him. And he should carry out

gerushin by exiling himself from his house of rest constantly, after the fashion of Rabbi Shimon [bar Yohai] and his company, who exiled themselves in order to study the Torah. And how much better is he who bruises his feet wandering from place to place without horse and cart. Concerning him it is said: "His hope (*sivro*) is with the Lord his God" [Ps. 146:5], which they explained from the expression *shever* ("to break"), for he breaks his body in the service of the Most High.[36]

By this self-imposed act of exile and suffering, an individual is able to express as well as experience the humiliation to which the *Shekhinah* is Herself subjected. Thus, Cordovero writes that his master Alkabets "decided upon the innovation that in the summer months especially we should on occasion walk barefooted in the mystery of the *Shekhinah*."[37] Moreover, it is preferably a form of genuine self-affliction, an opportunity to "break one's body" and to bruise one's feet in the dust, just as the bruised and suffering *Shekhinah* lies in the dust.[38] Yet by such mystical peregrinations, Cordovero and Alkabets were also able to provide comfort for the *Shekhinah*, as the heart becomes a dwelling place for Her to rest. Thus, while one subjects the body to shame and humiliation in a powerful act of empathy with the *Shekhinah*, at the same time the humbled body serves as a vessel in which She finds consolation.

This identification with the *Shekhinah* goes even further when we consider that these "exiles" resulted in experiences of involuntary speech on the part of Cordovero and Alkabets, in which they would utter kabbalistic interpretations of Scripture. Thus Cordovero:

Again we wandered on the 15th day of [the Hebrew month] Shevat, my master and myself alone, and the words of Torah were shining in us and the words were spoken of themselves. We went as far as the tomb of Rabbi Joseph of Yokrat and on our return we discussed the verse "According to the days of thy coming out of the land of Egypt will I show him" [Mic. 7:15]. . . . [and] the words were shining forth of themselves. So far the proceedings of that day. Thanks be to God that we were vouchsafed all this, for these things are all supernal, infused without reflections whatsoever; they are sweeter than honey, the gift of the Queen to them that wander with Her in exile.[39]

This "prophetic" type of speech, or supernal illumination, is regarded, in kabbalistic terms, as having its origins in the *sefirah Malkhut*, or *Shekhinah*. As the culminating point of the self-revelatory process within God, the *Shekhinah* is imagined as the articulate aspect of divinity, symbolized by the "speech" of God. Thus, She is considered to be the ultimate source of virtually all vocal revelation. The *gerushin* served, then, as a ritualized technique by which an adept could transform his body into a vessel for the physical and vocalized manifestation of divine revelation.

In the revelatory experiences of another important Safed personality, Joseph Karo, we find similar themes. Mention has already been made of the fact that Karo was a leading rabbi and halakhist. At the same time, he emerged as one of its most impressive kabbalistic visionaries. Throughout his adult life, Karo had experiences of automatic speech strongly resembling those of Cordovero and Alkabets.[40] In Karo's case, these experiences followed upon the intensive repetition of passages of Mishnah. The voice that spoke through his own had a complex identity; Karo regarded it as the personification of the Mishnah and the *Shekhinah*, and it was referred to by him as his *maggid*, an angelic-type communicator.

We have already had occasion to quote from the famous letter written by Solomon Alkabets from Safed to the kabbalistic fellowship in Salonika before Karo had himself emigrated to Safed. In this letter, Alkabets described an experience of the *maggid* that Karo had had in the company of a group of individuals on the eve of the festival of Shavuot (Feast of Weeks). The following passage from this text conveys a sense of the role that the figure of the *Shekhinah* played in Karo's emotional and psychological life:[41]

> No sooner had we studied two tractates of the Mishnah than our Creator smote us so that we heard a voice speaking out of the mouth of the saint, may his light shine. It was a loud voice with letters clearly enunciated. All the companions heard the voice but were unable to understand what was said. It was an exceedingly pleasant voice, becoming increasingly strong. We all fell upon our faces and none of us had any spirit left in him because of our great dread and awe. The

voice began to address us, saying: "Friends, choicest of the choice, peace to you, beloved companions. Happy are you and happy those that bore you. Happy are you in this world and happy in the next that you resolved to adorn Me on this night. For these many years had My head fallen with none to comfort Me. I was cast down to the ground to embrace the dunghills but now you have restored the crown to its former place. Be strong, My beloved ones. Be courageous, My friends. Rejoice and exult for you belong among the chosen few. You have the merit of belonging to the king's palace. The sound of your Torah and the breath of your mouth have ascended to the Holy One, blessed be He, breaking through many firmaments and many atmospheres until it rose upwards. . . . I am the Mishnah, the mother who chastises her children and I have come to converse with you. Had you been ten in number you would have ascended even higher but you have reached a great height nevertheless. Happy are those that bore you, My friends, in that, by denying yourselves sleep you have ascended so far on high. Through you I have become elevated this night and through the companions in the great city, a mother-city in Israel. You are not like those who sleep on beds of ivory in sleep which is a sixtieth of death, who stretch themselves out upon their couches. But you cleave to your Creator and He rejoices in you. Therefore, My sons, be strong and rejoice in My love, rejoice in My Torah, rejoice in the fear of Me. If you could only imagine one millionth of the anguish which I endure no joy would ever enter your hearts and no mirth your mouths, for it is because of you that I am cast to the ground. Therefore, O My dear sons, be strong and of good courage and rejoice. Cease not from studying, for a thread of mercy is stretched out over you and your Torah study is pleasant to the Holy One, blessed be He. Therefore, stand upon your feet and raise Me up, saying in a loud voice as on the Day of Atonement: "Blessed be the name of His glorious Kingdom for ever and ever." . . . All these things did we hear with our own ears and much more of a like nature, all matters of wisdom and great promise. We all broke into tears at the great joy we had experienced and when we heard of the anguish of the *Shekhinah* because of our sins, Her voice like that of an invalid in her entreaties.[42]

We learn a variety of things pertinent to our concerns from this text. In the first place, the *Shekhinah* was hardly an abstraction for these individuals, but a reality, an active protagonist in their psychological and religious lives. Karo, and others, had a powerful desire to communicate with the *Shekhinah*, as a person might with a loved one or with a parent. In addition, the *Shekhinah* is portrayed as suffering unimaginable humiliation and as having fallen to the depths of despair. She is a bitter, chastising mother who admonishes those of her children who have deserted her. At the same time, she praises Karo and his colleagues for having lifted her up from the ground and for providing her with a degree of comfort. Thus, the *Shekhinah* is depicted as being utterly dependent upon the proper behavior of her "children." This pattern of reproach and encouragement is found over and over again in the accounts of Karo's experiences that he recorded in a diary, ultimately published under the title *Maggid Mesharim*. While we know from reading this diary that Karo suffered from an unusually intense degree of self-doubt and self-torment—a subject to which I shall return shortly—the anxiety and guilt that he clearly felt with respect to the exiled *Shekhinah* may be said to have characterized the pre-Lurianic kabbalistic community of Safed at large.

The final example of this theme that I want to adduce is from the writings of Elijah de Vidas (d. c. 1593). Although he was the author of one of the preeminent books in the whole of Jewish ethical literature, *Reshit Ḥokhmah* (Beginning of Wisdom), virtually nothing is known about his life.[43] De Vidas was probably born in Safed and was an important disciple of Moses Cordovero, to whom he refers throughout his voluminous book as "my teacher." *Reshit Ḥokhmah* is suffused with the spirit of Cordovero's approach to Kabbalah. In the course of a discussion concerning the ritual of a midnight vigil, de Vidas writes as follows:

> One who wishes to sanctify himself when he arises at midnight ought to feel the distress of the *Shekhinah*, weep and mourn over the destruction of the Sanctuary; he should weep on account of God's desecrated name, as well as on account of his sins, which prolong the exile of the *Shekhinah*. For at midnight, the Holy One, blessed be He, remembers Israel which is in exile, and the destruction of His Sanctuary.[44]

Here again we have confirmation of the depth of sorrow and sympathy felt for the *Shekhinah*'s situation and the assumption of responsibility for Her fallen state. This dependence of the *Shekhinah* upon human deeds is unequivocally spelled out by de Vidas elsewhere:

> Even during the period when the Temple still stood, following the completion of the sacrifice, there were Israelites within their divisions, and Levites in their choirs singing, such that there was continual arousal from below. How much more so now, on account of our many transgressions, during this great and bitter exile in which the *Shekhinah* is deprived of arousal from below through sacrificial activity—and is supported only slightly by means of the deeds of the righteous—must they raise Her up from Her fallen state. For She is "the tabernacle of David that is fallen" [Amos 9:11], who each day sinks even lower than the previous one. All this is because of our transgressions, as it says: "And for your transgressions was your mother put away" [Isa. 50:1]. For on account of our sins She falls lower, and by means of our righteous deeds She becomes strengthened. . . . Even though there is no [perfect] intra-divine marriage [between *Tiferet* and *Malkhut*] in our state of exile, we must still fortify Her through acts of unification which provide Her with some degree of inspiration.[45]

It is a matter of considerable paradox that the mystics of this community felt such a deep sense of exile, both human and divine. After all, this was not a community in extremis, but one that enjoyed a reasonably high degree of security and well-being. What is more, it was a community residing not in the diaspora but in the land of Israel. Why is it, then, that these individuals focused so intensely on the condition of exile? In the first place, according to conventional rabbinic theology, redemption of the Jewish people involved more than the physical residence of some Jews in the land of Israel. It entailed the ingathering of the whole Jewish people from the "four corners of the earth" and the arrival of the Messiah. The Safed community was well aware of the fact that the vast majority of Jews were still living under precarious conditions in the diaspora. Moreover, Safed was home to a significant number of *conversos*, Spanish Jews who had converted to Christianity against their will under the threat of the Inquisition, but who had continued to live as Jews clandestinely. The *conversos* served as a continuing reminder of Jewry's vulnerability; moreover, *conversos* sought to overcome their past and to embrace Jewish life openly once again.[46] There is reason to believe that one of the motivations behind the effort to reinstitute *semikhah* was the desire to be able to enjoin the appropriate rabbinic punishments so that former *conversos* could atone fully for their past behavior.

Self-Mortification

One of the most striking features of kabbalistic life in Safed was the development of a rigorously ascetic disposition. The widespread mood of exile and guilt found expression in the practice of a wide array of ascetic activities among Safed's kabbalists. Among the most common misconceptions regarding Jewish religious history is that it has known little or nothing of asceticism. This point of view is often enunciated by way of contrasting the supposed "this-worldly" character of Judaism to the "other-worldly" nature of Christianity. Such an assumption is facile even when talking about Judaism in late antiquity.[47] It is surely mistaken with respect to medieval Judaism. For example, Bahya ibn Paquda's widely influential treatise *Ḥovot ha-Levavot* (Duties of the Heart), written in the eleventh century in Spain, is permeated by a strong Sufi-influenced ascetic attitude.[48] The same may be said of another Spanish philosopher, Abraham bar Hiyya (second half of the eleventh century–d.c. 1136), whose work *The Meditation of the Sad Soul* reflects a pronounced ascetic point of view.[49] Whereas his renowned father, Moses Maimonides, insisted on the adoption of a "middle path" in the conduct of one's life, Abraham ben Moses ben Maimon follows the ascetic path of Bahya ibn Paquda. His *Comprehensive Guide for the Servants of God* exhibits high regard for the Sufis as the spiritual disciples of Israel's prophets, particularly Elijah, and prescribes a Sufi method for the attainment of human perfection.

Interest in asceticism went beyond the theoretical among medieval Jews. A movement of Egyptian Jewish pietists emerged in the twelfth and thirteenth centuries. These *ḥasidim*, as they called themselves, were inspired by a variety of factors, including Bahya's *Duties of the Heart* as well as Sufism.[50] Broadly based ascetic practice also took root among the *Ḥasidei Ashkenaz*, the German Jewish Pietists, during the same period, the twelfth and thirteenth centuries, a subject about which I shall have a good deal more to say.[51] Safed kabbalists thus had a rich legacy of ascetic conceptions and practices upon which to draw.

Ascetic rituals in which the Safed pietists engaged were of several types, chiefly in the area of food and drink. There is recurrent reference to the desirability of avoiding meat and wine, or at least to consuming these sparingly. According to Moses Cordovero, the drinking of wine was to be avoided during the day, although he allowed diluted wine at night.[52] He further cautioned against eating more than a spare amount of meat during the weekdays "as these foods endow *Samael* [Satan] with strength."[53] Abraham Berukhim (c. 1515–c. 1593) reported that "there are certain especially pious scholars of Torah who neither eat meat nor drink wine during the entire week because they mourn the destruction of the Temple and because of their own transgressions."[54] In addition to advising against eating too much meat or drinking wine, Joseph Karo's *maggid* exhorts him to "take care not to enjoy your eating and drinking and marital relations. It should be as if demons were compelling you to eat that food."[55] Karo, who was particularly obsessed with the need to avoid eating too much or enjoying it, is told by his *maggid* that "you should very much prefer it were it possible to exist without food and drink altogether."[56]

A closely related practice that was widely promoted was fasting. There are, of course, a small number of prescribed fast days according to the laws and customs of conventional rabbinic practice. The Safed mystics went beyond these by developing far more elaborate regimens of fasting. Thus, Cordovero instructed his disciples to fast for three consecutive days during each of the four seasons, adding that it is praiseworthy to increase this amount.[57] Fasting in penitence on the eve of the New Moon (*Rosh Ḥodesh*) was apparently a widespread custom, important enough to be carried out by women, according to the report of Abraham Galante, a disciple of Cordovero.[58] One anonymous authority instructed individuals to "fast on Thursdays and pray [at] the afternoon service with a quorum of ten people who are likewise fasting."[59] As we shall see, even more rigorous fasting was one of the central forms of penitence prescribed by Isaac Luria for his own disciples.

In addition to these practices, there were other kinds of self-mortification exercises performed in Safed. Abraham Galante provided the following interesting account of the observance of the New Moon festival, especially noteworthy because of its mention of women:

> On the eve of the New Moon all the people fast, including men, women, and students. And there is a place where they assemble on that day and remain the entire time, reciting penitential prayers, petitionary devotions, confession of sins and practicing flagellation. And some among them place a large stone on their stomach in order to simulate the punishment of stoning. There are some individuals who "strangle" themselves with their hands and perform other things of a like nature. There are some who place themselves into a sack while others drag them around the synagogue.[60]

We might be tempted to dismiss this report as Galante's exaggeration were it not for the fact that there is corroborating testimony about precisely this kind of activity from Abraham Berukhim, whom we shall encounter again as a disciple of Isaac Luria's. In referring to a "fellowship of penitents," Berukhim presumably alludes to a group of former *conversos*: "There is a fellowship of penitents whose members fast regularly and who pray the afternoon service each day in weeping and in tears. They practice flagellation and wear sackcloth and ashes. Among them there are some who fast two days and nights every week. Some do so for three days and nights."[61]

Berukhim himself gained a reputation for being a vigorous practitioner of the kind of mortification exercises he reports, and a few words about Berukhim and his ascetic enthusiasm are in order here. Even for a community such as Safed, with its array of striking personalities, Berukhim, who was born in Morocco and probably immigrated to Safed before 1565, stands out. Before he took up with Luria, he was associated with the Cordovero/Alkabets circle. Accounts of some of Berukhim's activities are preserved in Solomon Shlomiel's letters. He writes that Berukhim was in the habit of exhorting others to rise at midnight for purposes of study and lamentation:

There was a certain individual here in Safed, may it be rebuilt and reestablished speedily in our day, whose name was the honored Abraham ha-Levi, may the memory of the righteous be for a blessing, who composed *Tiqqunei Shabbat* [Sabbath Customs], found at the end of the *Reshit Ḥokhmah ha-Qatsar* [Abbreviated Beginning of Wisdom]. Every midnight, he would rise and make the round of all the streets, raising his voice and crying out bitterly: "Rise in order to honor God's name, for the *Shekhinah* is in exile, and our holy Sanctuary has been consumed by fire and Israel is in great distress!" Many things of this nature would he proclaim; and he would summon each of the scholars by name and would not move away from the window until he saw that he had already arisen from his bed. And by the hour of one in the morning, the entire city would be filled with the voices of those studying Mishnah, *Zohar*, and the *Midrashim* of our sages of blessed memory, as well as Psalms, the Prophets, hymns, and supplicatory prayers.[62]

The practice of rising at midnight is well-documented in our sources. Thus, for example, Moses Cordovero advocates the following to his students: "Every night one ought to sit on the ground, mourn the destruction of the Temple, and weep on account of one's transgressions which delay the redemption."[63] Berukhim himself speaks of a midnight vigil as an established practice: "Most of the scholars of Torah, when they rise in the middle of the night in order to study, sit upon the ground, wrap themselves in black, mourn and weep on account of the destruction of the Temple. Such also is the custom of the Fellowship of Penitents at the afternoon service of the eve of the New Moon."[64]

I shall have more to say about the phenomenon of midnight devotions in the context of Lurianic Kabbalah. But it is worth pointing out here that this was a practice that was clearly well established before Luria's appearance in Safed and that was motivated by a desire for mourning and lamentation. Shlomiel also provides the following tradition about Berukhim's penchant for self-mortification:

This pious one used to practice another custom. He would go out into the markets and the streets, calling for repentance. He would gather groups of penitents, lead them to the Ashkenazi synagogue and say to them: "Do as you see me do." Then he would crawl into a sack, ordering them to drag him the entire length of the synagogue in order to mortify his flesh and humiliate his spirit. After this he enjoined them to throw stones at him, each weighing a pound and a half, which they would do. Following this, he would come out of the sack. A bed, covered with nettles, which burn the flesh like fire, would be prepared for him, and he would remove his clothing, throw himself naked upon the thorns and roll around until his body was covered with blisters. In a similar way, he would simulate the four kinds of punishment meted out [in ancient times] by the rabbinic court. Then he would say to those assembled: "My brethren, whosoever desires to save his soul from Hell must do as I have done." And immediately they all rushed at once and submitted themselves to all of the same torments, crying out in bitterness of soul and confessing their sins. They would not leave there until they had accomplished complete and permanent repentance.[65]

Shlomiel's descriptions of Berukhim's self-mortification may be somewhat exaggerated; nonetheless, they are consistent with the general tenor of the ascetic practices popular among the Safed mystics, as well as with what we know about Berukhim from other sources.

Mention has already been made of Joseph Karo in connection with his ascetic attitude toward eating and drinking. Thanks to his mystical diary, we know a great deal about Karo's practices and motivations. His proclivity for abstinence was not rooted merely in some general identification with "the sins of Israel" or the bitterness of exile; Karo, as attested by his alter ego in the form of his *maggid*, was clearly possessed of a deep *personal* sense of guilt and inadequacy. The *maggid* incessantly admonishes him for his failure to restrict his eating and drinking, his having slept too much, his having failed to study as much as he ought to have, and for forsaking the *maggid* itself. Karo is forever in need of repentance in order to satisfy the high standards of ritual piety and proper behavior demanded by his *maggid*, who, it seems, was not especially easy to please.

Keep yourself from eating too much meat for this flaws the soul. As for drinking wine, you have no idea how much harm it does and how great the flaw in the soul it causes. Be far, therefore, from these and be very careful. The masses imagine that this world is all it appears to be so that there is no one to see when they eat and drink in order to satisfy their evil inclination. Woe to them. For they are fooled by the world. . . . Was it a good thing that you failed to read the Mishnah yesterday? Was it good that you have been so careless lately about thinking on the Torah? You have seen what happened to the business in which you were engaged. Note how the Holy One, blessed be He, punishes measure for measure, and take greater care in the future. How can you wish me to converse with you when you eat horse-radish? Be careful, therefore, to eat only a little. I have already hinted to you the mystery of the good smell and the bad smell. . . . If you will improve your behavior I shall reveal to you the mysteries of reincarnation. I shall show you the previous incarnations of all your friends and relatives and you will witness wondrous things and be as-tonished. Be strong, therefore, at all times in the fear of God. Mortify your flesh with all your might and burn out all the thoughts that en-ter your mind during prayer and when you study the Mishnah. Burn them out with the straw of reading the Shema, with the breath of your mouth.[66]

In Karo's case, appropriate conduct, including abstinence and mod-eration, are bound up not only with the general desire to repent for sup-posed sinful behavior, but also with the need to focus attention exclu-sively on his *maggid* and the Mishnah. The pursuit of self-gratification is egotistical diversion from the only true legitimate object of concern. Thus, the *maggid*: "Hold fast to Me, therefore, and give up bodily pleasures. . . . If you will do this, forsaking bodily pleasures so that your heart and mind become a constant nest for the Torah and if you never cease from thinking on the Torah, then the Holy One, blessed be He, will take delight in you."[67]

In fact, the very manifestation of the *maggid* depended upon Karo's having deprived himself of certain pleasures:

The eve of the Sabbath, 29th of Iyyar, portion *Ba-Midbar Sinai*. I ate but little and drank the same and I studied the Mishnah at the begin-ning of the night. I then slept until daybreak so that when I awoke the sun was shining. I was very upset, saying to myself: "Why did I not arise during the night so that the word should come to me as beforetimes?" Nevertheless, I began to rehearse the Mishnah and I studied five chapters. As I was reading the Mishnah the voice of my beloved knocked in my mouth and the lyre sang of itself. It began by saying: "The Lord is with you wherever you go, and the Lord will prosper whatever you have done and will do, but you must cleave to Me and to My Torah and to My Mishnah at all times, not as you have done this night. For, although you did sanctify yourself in your food and drink, you slept like a sluggard, for the door revolves upon its hinges but the sluggard is on his bed, and you did not follow your good habit of rising to study the Mishnah. For this you deserve that I should leave and forsake you since you gave strength to *Samael*, the serpent and the evil inclination by sleeping until daybreak. But in the merit of the Six Orders of the Mishnah that you know by heart and in the merit of the self-tortures and torments you engaged in years past, and which you still practice, it was agreed in the Heavenly Academy that I should return to converse with you as in former time and that I should neither leave you nor forsake you. . . . Therefore, My son, hearken to My voice and to that which I command you, to busy yourself with My Torah, unceasingly by day and night. Have nothing else in the world in your thoughts than words of Torah, the fear of Me and My Mishnah."[68]

Joseph Karo's ascetic tendencies found their ultimate expression in his aspiration to martyr himself "for the sanctification of [God's] Name." Karo's fervent hope was to have the opportunity to be burnt at the stake! Concerning this hope, R.Z.W. Werblowsky writes in his study of Karo's mystical life:

Karo's desire to be burned alive "for the sanctification of the Name" seems to be unique in the history of Jewish piety. To judge from the appallingly high numbers of Jewish martyrs—though Jewry never insisted on distinguishing sharply between "martyrs" and victims of persecution—there was no lack of readiness to sanctify the Name, and Jewish liturgy gratefully and proudly remembers this fact. But readiness to be killed, slaughtered, drowned, and burned if God imposes the sacrifice is one thing, the eager desire for it quite another.[69]

While some kabbalists indulged in an imaginative, contemplative exercise of martyrdom, Karo apparently believed that only actual death would satisfy his need for personal atonement and devotion to God. Through repentant acts of physical self-affliction, Karo hoped to render himself worthy of martyrdom. Yet it was only martyrdom itself that would serve to eradicate altogether the sins for which he felt himself responsible. Thus, martyrdom is conceived of as both a privilege granted for virtuous behavior and an opportunity to complete the process of atonement:

> . . . And the *Shekhinah* converses with you and you become attached in such a way never achieved by even one in a generation, nay, by one in many generations. From it you can see how great is the love the Holy One, blessed be He, bears for you. He has stretched out His right hand to receive you as you repent. These days in which you have repented now shine for you. Your glory is upon them and theirs upon you. You will be worthy of being burned for the sanctification of the Name. Then will your sins be completely erased, all the dross and rust being purged by fire. You will be clothed in a robe of light when you ascend to Heaven. There you will be among the saints of the highest degree. You will no longer be obliged to return to earth in a new incarnation, for here you will rest, as it was said to Daniel, until the resurrection of the dead, when you will rise again together with the saints.[70]

Again, while Karo was unusually obsessed with personal guilt, alternating wildly between extremes of self-aggrandizement and self-denigration, his mortification practices and his hope of giving up his life altogether in the service of God were nevertheless symptomatic of the atmosphere that had taken hold of the Safed kabbalists more broadly. The radical turn it takes in Karo's case reveals the attitude toward the body on the part of these penitential mystics. Again, Werblowsky:

> His [Karo's] martyrdom has no messianic significance or bearing whatsoever; it is a purely personal matter, the *rite de passage*, as it were, by which his sinful, material existence would be finally transmuted into a spotlessly pure and spiritual one. For that reason also martyrdom must be by fire, for "he who is killed [by the sword] or strangled for the holiness [of God's Name] is like a sin-offering or a

trespass-offering [of which part remains and is eaten by the priests], because his flesh remains in this world . . . but he who is burned for the holiness of God is like a burnt sacrifice which rises wholly upwards." The burning is a process of de-materializing and a spiritualizing transformation; as such it is actually a rite of ascension, for as the flesh is consumed by the flames "your smell will rise like frankincense" and "all your sins and trespasses will be devoured by fire and you will ascend [in radiant whiteness] like pure wool." Karo's fantasies of martyrdom and the penitential discipline of his ascetic life have a common foundation: an oppressive sense of sin and a fervent desire to rid himself of sin as well as of the material body. What mortification can achieve only imperfectly in this life is triumphantly consummated in death by the purifying flame that annihilates both body and sin. A handful of ashes remains on the altar, whilst a spotlessly pure and white soul is received into glory.[71]

That more temperate individuals shared this same general feeling about the status of materiality and the body is abundantly apparent from the testimony of many other Safed figures. Let us take, as one example, the words of Elijah de Vidas, writing in *Reshit Ḥokhmah*:

The body, which is created from a fetid drop, is a part of this world; its ultimate destiny is destruction, just as every good thing belonging to this world winds up diminished and ruined. This is so because the body derives from the serpent's skin and its evil shell. An individual who pays greater homage to his physical body than he does to his soul is like one who shows greater respect to human beings than he does the Holy One, blessed be He. Therefore, a person ought to take more care to honor his soul than he does his body; before attending to the needs of his body he is required to attend to his soul's honor.[72]

Elsewhere, de Vidas expresses this conviction in these unequivocal terms:

Scorn the needs of the body in this world, the body being governed by the six weekdays; divest yourself of love for this world which is clothed in the skin of the serpent, and clothe yourself with the love for that world where the *neshamot* (highest form of the soul) reside. There they are bound up in the bond of eternal life, cleaving to their Maker. An individual should cleave to that which will be his at the end of his life. "For who is wise? One who can foresee events" [BT *Tamid* 32a] and considers the fact that a person is like a stranger passing by in this world. Thus, he will divest his heart of love for this world and concentrate upon cleaving to the world in which the souls [*neshamot*] reside; there he will continuously cling to *YHVH*.[73]

While the sources gathered here suggest ways in which the body was the locus for intentional acts of deprivation and humiliation for Safed's kabbalists, it was at the same time the vehicle through which divinity was glorified. Thus, for example, in the case of Cordovero's and Alkabets's mystical peregrinations, as well as Karo's maggidic experiences, the body not only was used to atone for sin but also became a vessel for the *Shekhinah* when She spoke through it, enabling an individual to raise Her up from the dust. As we shall see in the case of Lurianic Kabbalah, these men did not altogether renounce the body as much as they sought to tame it, to use the body in the service of very precise spiritual goals. Left to its own devices, the body loomed as a barrier hostile to the goals of the spirit, but it could also be willfully manipulated in ways that contributed to the perfection of the true self.[74]

Joy in the Service of God

It is important to point out that the mood of these kabbalists was not an altogether dark one. The austerity depicted here was mitigated by several factors. In the first place, the requirements of Jewish law served to compel restraint or temper what might have otherwise been ascetic behavior of an even more extreme sort. Safed kabbalists, for example, may have been more interested in pleasing the *Shekhinah* than in satisfying their wives, but Jewish tradition prevented a man from renouncing marriage and sexual life altogether. Celibacy was never intentionally practiced among medieval Jews, even in the most severely ascetic settings, no matter how much some might have preferred it. In a similar way, no rabbinic Jew could, in good conscience, altogether ignore the obligation to celebrate the Sabbath and other festivals with the expected joyfulness, and to wear fine clothes and enjoy good food. Thus, Abraham Berukhim reports that "during each of the three Sabbath meals, they sing and rejoice. They do likewise on the day of the New Moon and on Festivals."[75] Such occasions—along with celebrations accompanying various life-cycle events—had to provide the opportunity for an altogether different mood. Moreover, the traditionally social character of Jewish life, with its insistence on involvement with the larger community, prevented ascetically oriented kabbalists from going off on their own to form truly private communities along the lines of a monastic sect.

Besides these factors, joyfulness in the service of God was actually a spiritual ideal among the Safed pietists. While this was to become an important tenet of the Hasidic community in the eighteenth century, it was also a feature, at least in principle, of sixteenth-century piety. Elijah de Vidas, for example, devoted an entire chapter of the "Gate of Love" from *Reshit Ḥokhmah* to examining the role joy should play in the religious life: "A person ought to derive greater pleasure from the joy of serving God and fulfilling His commandments than from all the money in the world. . . . no joy in the world may be compared with that of the commandments."[76]

Most important of all, though, was that the guilt and anxiety described here was counterbalanced by the positive kabbalistic conviction that virtuous religious action could reverse the consequences of sin and restore the well-being of God. The sense of responsibility for the bitter, fallen state of the *Shekhinah* had its parallel in the belief that righteousness could, and must, remedy the situation. Moreover, the pre-Lurianic kabbalists fashioned a wide variety of ritual techniques through which they felt they could restore their own relationship to divinity, most especially by communion of one sort or another with the *Shekhinah*. Thus, through repentance, the cultivation of a wide range of spiritual traits and behaviors, and various techniques of contemplation, the breach suffered by God, and between an individual and God, could be healed.

Intentional Fellowships

From a social point of view, much of what has been described was mediated through a number of organized circles or fellowships. While
Kabbalah permeated the air of Safed in the sixteenth century in general, and few could have been left untouched by the powerful currents
around them, some chose to devote themselves to a more disciplined
style of spiritual life than others. Most of the individuals whose names
appear with any frequency in the kabbalistic literature are likely to have
been associated with one or another of the several groups of which we
know. These fellowships served to institutionalize kabbalistic life to a
certain degree, helping to define the direction that piety ought to take
and to channel religious energy in a disciplined manner. They constituted a vehicle through which the notion of collective obligation could
find expression. From a psychological point of view, they must have
served as both a means of support and a source of peer pressure to live
the proper life. As Werblowsky observes, "The social habits and values
of the Safed kabbalists helped to integrate the individual mystic in an
ideal, normative community which gave him spiritual security and support, and which provided him with a fund of energy and discipline on
which he could constantly draw."[77] There is reason to believe that the
rules and rites that these groups practiced were intended, at least in
part, to encourage members of the wider community in Safed and even
beyond to engage in similar pietistic activities.[78]

Some of these circles were under the spiritual guidance of particular personalities, such as Moses Cordovero and Eleazar Azikri (1533–
1600). The latter, a disciple of Cordovero's in kabbalistic studies, organized two different fellowships in Safed, one under the name *Ḥaverim
Maqshivim* (The Hearkening Companions), the other *Sukkat Shalom*
(The Tent of Peace).[79] Others appear to have been more loosely structured, organized around some specialized goal. Thus, the Fellowship
of Penitents that Abraham Berukhim informs us about sought to
achieve atonement through certain especially severe ascetic practices.
Berukhim also tells us about a group whose dedicated purpose seems
to have been rejoicing at the conclusion of every Sabbath. An anony-

mous authority indicated that "there is a group which goes out on the night of the festival of *Simḥat Torah* for the purpose of singing and dancing in the presence of the Torah scroll in every synagogue."[80] Here, too, then, Isaac Luria stepped into a community that had already cultivated the art of mystical fellowship. Thus, we should not be surprised that a circle of enthusiastic devotees flocked to him not long after he arrived in Safed.

Three   Saintliness, Heavenly Communication,
and the Divinatory Arts: Luria's Charismatic
Religious Authority

> Rabbinic literature is largely indifferent to the presentation of dis-
> tinctive individuality. No document pays homage to a particular
> rabbi; none celebrates one man's virtue, reflects his thoughts, or
> recounts his deeds. . . . In all of the literature no rabbi emerges as
> central, dominant, or determinative; none appears to symbolize,
> guide, or shape rabbinic destiny. . . . the virtual anonymity of per-
> son in rabbinic literature reveals a powerful cultural disinclination,
> perhaps an incapacity, to construe rabbinic culture and religion as
> the work of powerful individuals.
> —William Scott Green, "Storytelling and Holy Man:
> The Case of Ancient Judaism"

> Charisma is not a personality attribute, but a successful claim to
> power by virtue of supernatural ordination. If a man runs down
> the street proclaiming that he alone can save others from impending
> doom, and if he immediately wins a following, then he is a charis-
> matic leader: a social relationship has come into being. If he does
> not win a following, he is simply a lunatic.
> —Bryan R. Wilson, *The Noble Savages*

In addition to the personal considerations that led Isaac Luria to leave
Egypt for Safed, his decision must be seen within the larger context of
the attitude of Egyptian Jews toward the land of Israel in the sixteenth
century.[1] Earlier we saw that Egypt possessed a lively rabbinic community, of which Luria himself was a part. In the first decades of the
century, Egypt attracted scholars from various places, including Palestine, because of the favorable circumstances there for Jewish life. The
78   presence in Egypt of leading rabbinic figures enhanced its reputation,
making it a highly desirable destination for aspiring young students.
The authority the Egyptian rabbinate exerted is evidenced in the words
of the Jerusalem sage Abraham ha-Levi, who speaks with reverence in

addressing Cairo scholars in the 1520s: "If I have erred, instruct me and I shall be silent. For you are scholars and sages well suited to teach and render judgment."[2] We see the emergence of a greater equilibrium beginning in the 1530s in the testimony of Moses di Trani:

> We know that they [the scholars of Egypt] are versed in the law . . . and know the intricacies of the calendar. In spite of that, they behave deferentially toward us and do us honor. Because we are in Palestine, they frequently consult us on legal matters on which they themselves disagree or which are problematic for them. Because they are unable to assert their authority over their community, we assist them in this and render the decision.[3]

The choice to live in Egypt was fraught with a degree of anxiety on the part of its rabbis, even before the Safed community assumed a central role in the life of Near Eastern Jewry. This anxiety was rooted in a halakhic question concerning the legitimacy of living in Egypt at all.[4] In the view of some rabbinic authorities, Jews were forbidden to live in Egypt, on the grounds that doing so violated the scriptural injunction: "Thou shalt no more return by this way" (Deut. 17:16). Obviously, many did not interpret this as meaning that it was prohibited for Jews to reside in Egypt altogether. For centuries, well-respected rabbinical figures had lived there, not least among them the foremost Jewish scholar of the Middle Ages, Moses Maimonides. Nevertheless, the question was debated with some regularity. David ibn Zimra, who, as we have seen, was the leading Egyptian scholar of his day, and Luria's teacher, felt constrained to justify his own residence there in these words:

> It is the intention of all of us to return and to dwell in the land of Israel. It is only on this basis that we permit ourselves to dwell in Egypt; for otherwise we would be violating the command in the Torah. . . . We are not in Egypt to settle permanently but only to dwell here temporarily, and as soon as we are able, we shall go to the land of Israel.[5]

Elsewhere ibn Zimra writes that "most scholars and rabbis who come to Egypt [do not settle there; rather they] are just on route to the land of Israel and that is why they do not interfere with local customs."[6] As Joseph Hacker observed, this claim is not altogether unfounded when one considers the numerous rabbinic scholars who did indeed leave Egypt for Palestine, either temporarily or permanently.[7] These included such luminaries as Isaac Sholal and members of his academy, Joseph Saragossa, Jacob Berab, Abraham Zacuto, the family of Moses and Joseph di Trani, Betsalel Ashkenazi, Jacob Castro, and ibn Zimra himself. The example of these individuals influenced many others to travel to Palestine and helped establish very strong relations between the two communities, by way of scholarly, economic, and family connections. It should be pointed out that this migratory pattern was frequently reversed, particularly in the last quarter of the sixteenth century when conditions in Palestine began to deteriorate somewhat. Indeed, we find that many scholars traveled from one place to the other—between Jerusalem, Safed, and Cairo especially—as economic and social conditions changed.

Against this background, Isaac Luria's decision to journey to Safed may be seen as part of a broader tendency. Beyond this, however, Luria must have been attracted to Safed for many of the reasons others had come in the preceding four decades, as described in Chapter 2. It is not particularly difficult to imagine why an individual who had immersed himself in the study and practice of Kabbalah would desire to live in Safed. By 1570, Safed was not only a thriving kabbalistic community; it was the very center of Jewish mystical life. For someone like Luria, the desire to join the vibrant community there must have been irresistible. It was not only living kabbalists, however, that attracted Luria to the Galilee. He was particularly drawn to Safed on account of the widespread conviction that this was the region in which Shimon bar Yohai and his disciples had engaged in the mystical activities depicted in such colorful detail in the *Zohar*, as well as being where Shimon bar Yohai was buried. As I shall show, Shimon bar Yohai and his fellowship played a central and determinative role in Luria's imagination and identity. It is fair to presume, then, that Luria came to Safed in large part because of his evolving personal identification with the protagonist of the *Zohar*.

By the time Luria arrived in Safed, Moses Cordovero (1522–70) had been the principle figure in this kabbalistic community for many years.[8] Cordovero was the teacher of what appears to have been a relatively loosely knit circle of disciples. The most important of these included Elijah de Vidas, Abraham Galante, Moses Galante, Hayyim Vital, Abraham ben Eliezer ha-Levi Berukhim, Eleazar Azikri, Samuel Gallico, and an important Italian kabbalist who studied with Cordovero for a short while in the 1560s, Mordechai Dato. Dato, who introduced Cordovero's teachings into Italy, preserved a description of his master's activities in his travel memoirs, praising him effusively.[9] Cordovero did not, however, inspire an elaborate tradition concerning his personality or his personal activities. The anecdotal traditions about his nature and habits are relatively few in number. While he was greatly revered as a teacher, and while his prolific writings exerted enormous influence in Safed, Italy, and elsewhere, Cordovero's personality does not shine through very clearly.

That his students constituted something of a circle of pietists is suggested by the list of pietistic customs, or *hanhagot,* preserved in Cordovero's name, several of which refer to the *ḥaverim,* or associates.[10] Although we know little else about this group, the *hanhagot* spell out the ritual and ethical expectations Cordovero promulgated, presumably both for his followers and for others. He enjoined, for example, that "each person commune with one of the *ḥaverim* every day for the purpose of conversing about devotional concerns," saying that "a person ought to discuss with this same *ḥaver* every Sabbath eve what he did each day of that past week. From there he should go forth to welcome the Sabbath Queen." Moreover, he instructed that "a person ought to converse in Hebrew with the *ḥaverim* at all times."

There is clear evidence that Isaac Luria regarded Moses Cordovero as his teacher. Joseph Sambari (1640–1703), an important Egyptian chronicler, testified that Cordovero was "the Ari's teacher for a very short time."[11] This is compatible with the fact that they were in Safed simultaneously for only six months or so. Luria probably arrived in early 1570, and Cordovero died on June 27 that year (the 23d day of Tammuz). Sambari's testimony that Luria studied with Cordovero is also confirmed by Luria himself. Among the fragments of authentic passages written by Luria, reference is made at least twice to Cordovero as "our teacher, whose light may be prolonged," indicating that these passages were composed while Cordovero was still living.[12]

Figure 3. The tomb of Moses Cordovero. Courtesy Aaron Fine, photographer.

Although "our teacher" might be construed as a mere honorific applied to a great man, rather than signifying an actual relationship, this is doubtful, because Luria also speaks of "*my* teacher" with reference to Cordovero in at least two other places.

We know, as well, that Luria was present at Cordovero's funeral, and that he appears to have composed a eulogy in praise of him.[13] As we shall see, Luria's affinity to Cordovero is apparent, too, from the close similarity of their teachings on certain topics. That this should be the case is not surprising. When Luria arrived in Safed he was presumably an unknown quantity (although he quickly established himself as a teacher following Cordovero's death), and it stands to reason that he would have sought out the renowned master. While one can only speculate about how differently things might have turned out had Cordovero lived longer than he did, the fact is that his death at the age of forty-eight left the kabbalists of Safed bereft of their most prominent authority and teacher. These circumstances could only enhance the opportunity for Luria to attract students of his own, thus filling the vacuum left by Cordovero's passing.

Luria as Religious Master

Vital provides us with the names of thirty-eight individuals who, according to him, made up Luria's discipleship, although we know with absolute certainty that there were other students whom Vital does not mention.[14] While the nature of the fellowship and its constituency will be a major concern later on in this study, here I simply want to indicate its composition as described by Vital. According to him, the fellowship was divided into four, hierarchically ordered groups. The first, and most important, was composed of eleven men, listed in this order: Hayyim Vital, Jonathan Sagis, Joseph Arzin, Isaac Kohen, Gedaliah ha-Levi, Samuel Uceda, Judah Mishan, Abraham Gavriel, Shabbatai Menashe, Joseph ibn Tabul, and Elijah Falko (or Falkon). The order in which these names are presented is significant. Vital regarded himself as the leading disciple and thus placed himself at the head of the list. Joseph ibn Tabul, who was actually an exceedingly important disciple, perhaps second only to Vital in influence, is placed at the end of the list. Undoubtedly, Vital regarded ibn Tabul as a rival and thus sought to relegate him to a relatively insignificant place in the hierarchy of disciples. In the second grouping, Vital includes the following ten names: Moses Alsheikh, Moses Najara, Isaac Orcha, Solomon Saban (or Avsaban), Mordechai Gallico, Jacob Masud, Joseph Altun, Moses Mintz, Moses Yonah, and Abraham Gukil.

The third group lists thirteen names, including a repetition of Moses Alsheikh: Yom Tov Tsahalon, Joseph Kohen, Jacob Altarats, David Kohen, Isaac Kerispi, Shimon Uri, Israel Uri, Abraham Arubas, Moses Alsheikh, Israel Levi, Joseph Canpilias, Judah Ashkenazi, and a certain Naphtali. Vital indicates that a possible additional member of this group was Elijah Almiridi.

The fourth and final group consists of three names only: Abraham ha-Levi, Moses Meshamesh, and Judah Romano. After setting out these four groups and their members, Vital demurs that he is *certain* only of the membership of his own group, the first. As for the others, he possesses only general knowledge of them from his teacher.

We know, however, that Luria had a number of other disciples besides these. Mention has been made elsewhere of the fact that Hayyim

Vital did not become Luria's student until a relatively late date. According to the letters of Solomon Shlomiel of Dresnitz (described below), Vital did not join the circle of Luria's disciples until six months
after Luria had arrived in Safed. According to Vital's own account, an
even longer time elapsed before the two became associated. Vital wrote
that he began to study with Luria in the month of Adar (February/
March) 1571,[15] which could have been as many as twelve or thirteen
months after Luria settled in Safed—depending on exactly when
Luria arrived there. This probably accounts for Vital's failure to mention Israel Sarug, who appears to have studied with Luria before Vital
himself became associated with the circle. There may have been others, as well, who fell into this same category, people who were no
longer students of Luria's by the time Vital took up with him, such as
Joseph Don Don.[16]

What is more, there were individuals who were associated with
Luria to one extent or another, but who were not part of the formal
structure Vital describes. Elijah de Vidas, Eleazar Azikri, Joseph ben
Moses de Segovia Benveniste, Hiyya Rofe, Joseph Ashkenazi, and
possibly Shem Tov Atiyah fall into this category.[17]

What attracted Isaac Luria's students to him? How do they describe
him? What manner of personality did he exhibit? These and related
questions about Luria are bound up with critically important issues
concerning the nature of our sources. Insofar as the scanty writings by
Luria himself do not tell us much about him as a person, we must
turn to the depictions and accounts by others of his behavior and
character. But what is the status of these characterizations? Are they
traditions that reflect a teacher long since deceased who had, with the
passage of time, become the subject of highly inventive imagining?
That is, do they create a folk hero and have little to do with Luria's actual impact on his community, and more with the perspectives of a
later time? Or do they reflect the ways in which Luria was actually perceived and experienced during the brief period of his activity in Safed,
as well as during the immediate years thereafter?

The challenge of describing Luria's activities and the way in which his
disciples regarded him is complicated by the appearance of an elaborate
hagiographical literature beginning in the early seventeenth century—

to which I have already made some reference. The first important layer of this tradition is associated with a Moravian Jew by the name of Solomon Shlomiel ben Hayyim Meinsterl of Dreznitz, who emigrated to Safed in 1602 in order to share in the kabbalistic life of that city. We have four lengthy letters that Shlomiel wrote to friends and relatives back home between 1607 and 1609, in which he describes Safed and relates stories about Luria in considerable detail.[18] These were no mere private letters. Despite the fact that Safed was in substantial decline by the time he arrived on the scene, Shlomiel was clearly motivated by a desire to impress his readers with the beauty and splendor of the land, with the atmosphere of learning and religious enthusiasm in Safed, and with stories about its kabbalists, past and present, especially Isaac Luria. One of the letters also reveals that Shlomiel sought to encourage others to emigrate to the land of Israel, inasmuch as he provides practical financial advice in this connection. The author himself requested the recipients of these letters to make copies and to circulate them, clear proof of his intention to arouse the interest of a wider audience.

Although Luria was long deceased by the time of Shlomiel's arrival in Safed, and Vital was living in Damascus, there were still several individuals there who had personally studied with Luria, and others who at least knew him. Thus, Shlomiel was in a position to hear about Luria from living disciples, as a result of which much of what he has to say has a good deal in common with biographical traditions dating from around the time of Luria's activities in Safed. Still, these letters were composed approximately thirty-five years after Luria's death, and traditions about him had, naturally enough, undergone rather significant embellishment. Add to this Shlomiel's own narrative creativity and personal motives and we can easily understand how these letters assumed the character of informal hagiography. What is more, Shlomiel's letters themselves underwent literary transformation when they were eventually printed in somewhat different versions under unambiguously hagiographic titles.[19]

If Shlomiel's *Shivḥei ha-Ari* bears a relatively strong relationship to the earliest traditions about Luria, the same cannot be said about *Toldot ha-Ari* (Biography of the Ari), an anonymous work written sometime in the second half of the seventeenth century.[20] While this collection of stories about Luria draws upon *Shivhei ha-Ari* and has much in common with it, it goes far beyond it by portraying him in ways that lack all precedent in the earlier descriptions of his behavior. Here a truly legendary version of Luria is on display. In addition to recounting Luria's wondrous knowledge of heavenly mysteries, a predominant motif in Shlomiel's *Shivhei ha-Ari*, *Toldot ha-Ari* regales the reader with numerous anecdotes about his feats of miraculous wonder-working, a theme with no genuine basis in earlier traditions. Furthermore, the author of this book depicts a heroic figure whose fame has spread far and wide, a claim consistent to some degree with the second half of the seventeenth century, but altogether incompatible with the realities during Luria's own lifetime. In general, then, *Toldot ha-Ari* bears all the earmarks of a classic hagiographical work, replete with a range of easily identifiable folk motifs.

In my view, much greater caution should be exercised than is often the case in mining Shlomiel's *Shivhei ha-Ari* to construct a picture of Luria's activities in Safed and his relationship to his disciples. As for *Toldot ha-Ari*, it is much less valuable in this respect, although it is altogether fascinating on its own terms. As noted earlier, both of these works served as inspiration for a wide variety of subsequent writers, especially Hasidim, who continually reworked Luria's image. In addition to being translated into various languages, such as Ladino and Yiddish, they provided the model for other hagiographical works, most prominently an important collection of stories about Israel ben Eliezer, the Baal Shem Tov, or Besht, *Shivhei ha-Besht* (In Praise of the Baal Shem Tov), published for the first time in 1815.

In contrast to the hagiographical literature, the accounts of Luria by his formal disciples—as well as by several others closely associated with him—constitute evidence of a fundamentally different sort.[21] These provide us with a more reliable picture of the ways in which Isaac Luria was experienced by people who studied personally with him and were close to him. I do not mean by this that they give us the "historical" Luria, that is, documentary accounts of what Luria actually said and did. We cannot produce this on the basis of the known sources. But the descriptions of him by Hayyim Vital, Joseph ibn Tabul,

Eleazar Azikri, Jonathan Sagis, Abraham Berukhim, Elijah de Vidas, Samuel de Uceda, Joseph Benveniste, and others do provide us with a richly textured portrait of how Luria was perceived by those who knew him personally. Although even these traditions were undoubtedly colored by Luria's premature passing, and on certain issues by private agendas, they have the ring of authenticity in a way that is not always true of the sacred biographies described above. There are several reasons why this is so.

The accounts I have in mind were recorded in the years immediately following Luria's death, rather than at a period significantly removed from the most personal and freshest memories. We have, for example, the eulogy written for Luria upon his death by one of his close disciples, Samuel Uceda. As for Vital, we have already seen that he began to arrange what he had learned from Luria immediately following his master's death, if not even earlier, although Vital continued to refashion his materials for a considerable period of time. It is noteworthy that Vital also included in his writings a large number of traditions concerning Luria learned from his fellow disciples, which he apparently sought to preserve faithfully. Elijah de Vidas's and Eleazar Azikri's references to Luria were likewise composed within a few years of his passing. While proximity in time does not by itself ensure authenticity, it certainly contributes to the likelihood that these descriptions reflect actual experiences their authors had of their teacher.

In addition to the fact that these accounts were written not long after Luria's death by people who had known him personally, it is also highly significant that the relatively detailed picture of Luria's personality and behavior given by Hayyim Vital is, as I show below, essentially corroborated by others. Finally, the early biographical sources by and large contrast sharply with *Toldot ha-Ari* and *Shivḥei ha-Ari* in that they are not burdened in the same way with hagiography. In Vital's case, both brief anecdotes and lengthier descriptions are embedded in a vast sea of various kinds of materials. To be sure, Vital's writings contain lavish praise of his master's virtues and talents, and such praise was clearly more than incidental in nature; but it was only a small part of a much broader literary project in which Luria's most prolific disciple presented his master's voluminous teachings. This is all the more true in connection with the occasional remarks in such works as Eleazar Azikri's *Sefer Ḥaredim* and Elijah de Vidas's *Reshit Ḥokhmah*. What they tell us about Isaac Luria, in passing, has the ring of offhand comment. The testimony of men such as Azikri and de Vidas should be considered even less likely to have been colored by hagiographic intent, insofar as they were not formal disciples of Luria's.

Luria as Moral Exemplar

How then *do* these early biographical sources, as I shall call them, portray Luria? In the first place, Vital and others depict their teacher as possessing a saintly moral character. As in the case of saintly heroes in religious literature generally, Luria is described as exhibiting various traits that constitute moral excellence and ethical virtuosity. A number of identifiable themes predominate. For example, we are told that Luria demonstrated a deep concern for proper human relations through his personal example:

> Once I was taking a walk with my teacher, may his memory be for an everlasting blessing, when a certain scholar came and deliberately walked in front of him. Upon seeing this, my teacher himself intentionally walked behind this individual, even after the latter had gone across to the other side. I said to him: "God forbid, it appears as if you are placing an obstacle in front of a blind man," inasmuch as this scholar failed to recognize my master's importance. He replied to me that seeing as how this person feels honored by behaving as he does, he [Luria] was obliged to grant him such honor and to serve him in this fashion. In this same manner, Hillel the Elder ran for three miles before a certain poor individual who was of a good family.[22]

The lengths to which Luria would go to respect the rights of others is represented in a tradition according to which the proper observance of liturgical ritual—afternoon prayer—took a back seat to moral responsibility:

> With respect to the wages owed a hired laborer, my teacher, may his memory be for an everlasting blessing, used to be exceedingly careful. He would sometimes delay in praying the afternoon service until he

had paid someone his wages. And on occasion, he would not pray the afternoon service until after sundown when he did not have the money with which to pay what he owed; he would request money from this one and that one until he could pay what he owed a hired laborer. Only afterwards would he pray the afternoon service. He would say: "How can I pray to God, may He be exalted, when I have an obligation such as this to fulfill and I have not yet done so? And how can I lift up my countenance to pray?"[23]

Luria's sensitivity extended to the humblest of animals: "My master, of blessed memory, used to be careful never to destroy any insect, even the smallest and least significant among them, such as fleas and gnats, bees and the like, even if they were annoying him."[24]

According to Vital, Luria was endowed with great generosity, but cared little about his own needs:

As regards the attribute of charitableness and generosity, I observed that my teacher, of blessed memory, was not concerned with his own vanity, as expressed [for example] in the wearing of especially fine clothes. In his eating, as well, he would consume very little. However, when it came to his wife's apparel, he was exceedingly careful to honor her and to clothe her well. He used to satisfy her every desire, even if it was not within his means.[25]

His charitableness extended, not surprisingly, to fulfillment of the religious commandments:

When it came to giving charity and fulfilling the commandments, he was in no way a miser. With respect to the ceremony of *Havdalah* that is celebrated in the synagogue, he used to give four gold florins to charity in order to provide personally for the wine to be used. Whenever he purchased something for the purpose of performing some religious obligation, such as buying phylacteries [tefillin] or an *'etrog*, he would not be concerned with finding out how much he was supposed to pay. Rather, he used to pay the amount asked of him the first time. He would say to the vendor: "Here is my money, take as much as you wish."[26]

Along the same lines, Vital reported that "it was the practice of my master to offer charity at the afternoon service, before beginning to pray. He would donate three small coins just as was his custom to do at the morning service."[27]

These concerns are rooted in what is described as Luria's most fundamental moral conviction, self-effacement:

> The most important of all worthy traits consists in an individual behaving with humility, modesty, and with the fear of sin to the greatest possible degree. He should also, to the utmost degree, keep his distance from pride, anger, fussiness, and evil gossip; and even should he have a significant reason for behaving harshly, he ought to refrain from acting in this way. He should also abstain from idle conversation, even though it is not as important as the previous admonition. And he should not lose his temper, even with the members of his household."[28]

Spiritual perfection thus entailed cultivating one's emotional life in particular ways. Luria appears to have been intensely concerned with the importance of avoiding anger:

> The quality of anger, aside from serving as an obstacle to mystical inspiration altogether, [has other injurious consequences]. My teacher, of blessed memory, used to be more exacting when it came to anger than with all other transgressions, even in a situation where a person loses his temper for the sake of some religious obligation. This is because all other transgressions injure only a single limb of the body, whereas the quality of anger injures the soul in its entirety, altering its character completely. This is the issue: when an individual loses his temper, his holy soul deserts him altogether; in its place a spirit of an evil nature enters. And this is the esoteric meaning behind the verse: "Thou that tearest thyself in thine anger" [Job 18:4]. For such a person actually tears his soul, rendering it unfit at the moment of his wrath and anger.[29]

In this connection it is interesting to note that Luria's disciple Joseph ibn Tabul apparently felt equally strongly about the detrimental consequences of anger for the spiritual life. One of Tabul's own students, Samson Bacchi, attests (some time after Luria's death) that Tabul was hesitant about teaching his own fellowship of disciples, for he felt that they were given to anger, and that "the quality of anger keeps the spirit of purity at a distance."[30] We shall see elsewhere some of the ways in which Luria encouraged his disciples to grapple with the emotion of anger.

There is other evidence as well that cultivation of the proper emotional life was crucial to Luria's conception of spiritual practice. Reminiscent of what earlier Safed kabbalists had taught, we learn the following about melancholy: "Melancholia is, by itself, an exceedingly unpleasant quality of personality, particularly in the case of an individual whose intention is to acquire esoteric knowledge and experience the Holy Spirit [*Ruaḥ ha-Qodesh*]. There is nothing that impedes mystical inspiration—even for someone who is otherwise worthy of it—as much as the quality of sadness."[31]

On the contrary, joy in the fulfillment of the commandments ought to exceed the happiness that one might experience through material wealth: "When an individual carries out any precept, be it the study of Torah or prayer, he ought to be joyful and spirited, more than if he had acquired money, or found thousands of gold pieces."[32]

According to Eleazar Azikri, Luria's own attainment of great knowledge and the Holy Spirit were a result of his having performed the precepts with unbounded joy.[33] Similarly, Elijah de Vidas reports that he too learned from Luria that "one ought to be happier in the service of the Holy One, blessed be He, His precepts and His Torah, than in possessing all the money in the world." For "no joy in the world equals the joy associated with performing the commandments."[34]

Finally, in connection with Luria's profound concern for interpersonal relations and the cultivation of certain spiritual traits, we learn that he sought to foster empathy and love, particularly among his disciples:

> My teacher, may his memory be for a blessing, cautioned me and all the brethren [*ḥaverim*] who were with him in this fellowship that before praying the morning service, we should take upon ourselves the positive commandment " . . . and thou shalt love thy neighbor as thyself" [Lev. 19:18]. He should concentrate upon loving every member of the House of Israel as he loves himself, for on account of this, his prayer will ascend, bound up with all the prayers of Israel. By this means his soul will be able to rise above and effect *tiqqun*. And especially when it comes to the love of our *ḥaverim*, each and every one of us must bind himself to the others as if he were one limb within

the body of this fellowship. My teacher, of blessed memory, went out of his way to caution me concerning this matter. And if any *ḥaver*, God forbid, was in distress, or if there was any illness in his house or among his children, all should share in his trouble and pray on his behalf; similarly, in all matters, each of the *ḥaverim* should be mindful of his fellows.[35]

In sum, Luria is portrayed as unusually sensitive to the needs and feelings of others, and as one who, possessing exemplary moral virtues, sought to cultivate in himself and others the traits of personality necessary for the spiritual life. He was especially preoccupied with being in control of one's emotions, with not allowing vanity, anger, or sadness to dominate one's behavior, traits certain to thwart mystical inspiration. All of this is consistent with the general remarks about Luria made by Samuel de Uceda in his eulogy of his teacher. Uceda wrote that Luria was "a man of great piety [*ḥasid gadol*], unlike any other."[36]

The values adduced here are typical of late medieval rabbinic piety in many ways and could be found in other Jewish cultures. What is interesting, however, is the choice made by Luria's disciples from among the large repertoire of moral virtues promoted by the Jewish ethical tradition. The attribution to Isaac Luria of these particular qualities reflects the special preoccupations of Luria and his community. Biographical attributions such as these are not simply a matter of ascribing a litany of generic moral conventions to a hero by rote. As often as not, they capture a discrete cultural milieu, a particular cluster of social concerns and tensions.

Thus, for example, the emphasis on avoiding melancholy and serving God in joy may be seen as a way of counteracting the strong tendency toward guilt and self-reproach that we know characterized the kabbalistic community of Safed. The special concern for modesty and humility—repeatedly mentioned in our sources—takes on heightened significance in the context of a culture where more than a few egos loomed large. The internecine rivalry in evidence among certain members of Luria's brotherhood helps to put into focus Luria's warning about loving one another. As such, this collection of traditions about Luria's own behavior, and his exhortations to cultivate a certain type of spiritual life, must be read as more than a set of stereotypical pietisms. They serve as one measure of some of the psychological and social conflicts that beset this community. Ethical values, as well as emotional behaviors, are social constructions, that is, they represent expectations for behavior that are learned within the context of a particular cultural setting. Emotions are *performed* in the sense that they are a function of the ways in which people are taught and expected to behave in relationship to others. As such, they are a matter of public discourse, always evolving and being acted out in dynamic, interactional ways. The values and attitudes embodied in the traditions described here thus go to the heart of some of the most significant spiritual issues with which Luria and his circle of disciples were concerned.

Charisma and Mystical Inspiration

Nevertheless, it was not Luria's moral piety or saintliness per se that had the greatest impact on his followers; other, more unusual behavior appears to have generated the most intense fascination and appeal. The most widespread reports about Luria in the early biographical literature have to do with particular kinds of "supernatural" abilities to acquire wondrous esoteric knowledge. As is usually the case, Vital provides the most elaborate descriptions of these talents, but we are fortunately not dependent on his testimony alone. Other such testimonies are found in the writings of a number of persons, including Joseph ibn Tabul, Joseph Benveniste, Samuel Uceda, Elijah de Vidas, Eleazar Azikri, Moses di Trani, and Samson Bacchi.

From Vital, we have several versions of a tradition that summarizes Luria's exceptional abilities, of which the following is a good example:

> Concerning his attainments, it is impossible for one to relate them [even] in general terms, much less in detail. However, these are the wondrous and true things that I witnessed with my own eyes: He knew how to make a future soul appear before him, as well as the soul of a living or deceased person, from among the early as well as later sages. He could inquire of them whatever he wished concerning

knowledge of the future and secret mysteries of the Torah. The prophet Elijah, may his memory be a blessing, would also appear to him and teach him. He could also recognize the letters on the forehead and [was adept at] the science of physiognomy, as well as at [recognizing] the lights that are upon the skin and body of an individual. [He was also skilled at recognizing] the lights in the hair, the chirping of birds, and the language of trees and plants. [He understood] the speech even of inanimate things, as Scripture says: "For the stone shall cry out of the wall [and the beam out of the timber shall answer it]" [Hab. 2:11]. [He knew] the language of the burning candle and the flaming coal. He was able to see the angels who announce all the proclamations [from on high], as is well known, and to converse with them. His knowledge was expert concerning all the plants and the genuine remedies [they provide]. There are many other such things that cannot even be related. Those who hear of them will not believe them when told. I have recorded that which my eyes have seen in all truth.[37]

In another version, Vital adds that Luria "knows all the deeds that people have performed or will perform in the future, [for] he can discern the thoughts of individuals even before they are carried out."[38] Moreover, he was able to determine the transmigrations (*gilgulim*) through which the souls of individuals had passed, the sins that had been committed in the past, and the current state of their souls.[39] As Hayyim Vital's dream diary makes clear, Luria was expert as well in the interpretation of dreams. He also applied himself to a careful and elaborate study of plant life. He taught in some detail about the particular characteristics of plants and the beneficial effect each had upon a person's health.[40] Remedies for problems with the skin and with eyesight seem to have been of special interest. It may be that Luria distributed natural healing remedies such as these to his disciples and others.

These reports are echoed and confirmed by others, none more important than Joseph ibn Tabul, one of Luria's principal disciples, and a person whose version of Lurianic teachings exhibits his independence from Hayyim Vital. When quoting his master's teachings, Tabul typically indicates his debt to Luria with these words: "Here end my master's words [*ᶜad kan lashon mori*], which were revealed to him from heaven by way of the Holy Spirit."[41] Following Luria's death in 1572, Tabul taught a number of disciples of his own in Safed. From the pen of one of them, the aforementioned Samson Bacchi, we have important corroborating testimony in language that is strikingly similar to that of Hayyim Vital. In one of several letters that he sent from Safed in the early 1580s, Bacchi wrote as follows about Luria:

> He used to understand the language of trees, the sounds of birds and animals, and the rushing of water. And when he would gaze upon an individual's shadow [be-tsel ha-ʾadam], that is the external aura that is outside the person's body, he could recognize the good inclination and the evil inclination that constantly accompany an individual. And he used to discern all the transgressions that that individual had committed, and he would tell him what he had done [even] in the most concealed places [be-ḥadrei ḥadarim]. He could [also] recognize in detail the transmigration of souls of every individual. And by virtue of his great holiness, he would converse with the holy souls that are found in this land. In [this] way the concealed mysteries and secrets of Kabbalah, as well as [other] wondrous things, were revealed to him.[42]

Presumably, Bacchi learned all of this from his teacher, ibn Tabul. Of particular interest here is the allusion to the external aura, or shadow, that Luria was able to discern. In the literature of the *Zohar*, and in a long tradition of other authors, Kabbalah developed the notion of a *tselem* (image, on the basis of Gen. 1:26), an astral or psychic body that serves to mediate between the body and the *nefesh*, the lowest aspect of the human soul.[43] Because the body and the soul are so dissimilar to one another, they require an entity to bridge the gap between them. This subtle, ethereal body, normally beyond physical perception by human beings, was regarded by the kabbalists as the dimension of unique individuality possessed by every individual. Moreover, the *tselem* was identified with the garment with which souls garb themselves in paradise before they descend to the lower world, and which they take on once again after death. Based on wordplay between the terms *tselem* and *tsel* (shadow), many kabbalists believed that a person's shadow was a physical projection of this ethereal inner image. Hayyim Vital indicates that "the ethereal body of [the righteous individual] is [contained] in the secret of the *tselem*, which is perceived by those who have purified vision."[44] While Vital does not mention Luria's name in this connection, Bacchi's letter provides us with the information that Luria, indeed, was believed to have been endowed with such vision.[45]

Joseph Benveniste de Segovia, who employed the blessing over living individuals in a reference to Luria, at least once in his writings, indicated that his teacher "used to acquire knowledge of halakha [i.e., Jewish law] from heavenly angels."[46] Likewise, Benveniste reported that Luria "used to learn the simple [that is, exoteric] meaning of halakha without [intellectual] inquiry, [but] by means of prophecy [nevu ʾah]."[47] Elijah de Vidas's report that Safed was the home of sages who knew the sciences of physiognomy and possessed "wonderful wisdom that is akin to possessing the Holy Spirit" undoubtedly refers to Isaac Luria.[48] Such is also the case with the report by Moses Galante, Cordovero's student in Kabbalah, who writes that he had personally seen sages who had the ability to practice metoposcopy, the art of discerning the meaning of signs on the forehead.[49] Luria's metoposcopic virtuosity is likewise explicitly described by Eleazar Azikri in his *Sefer Haredim*, as we shall see. Azikri also refers frequently to Luria's experiences of the Holy Spirit.[50] While Samuel Uceda does not mention the revelation of Elijah or the Holy Spirit in connection with Luria, he does say that secret mysteries were revealed to him, and that he was more knowledgeable than anyone else.[51] The specific nature of some of these abilities and the uses to which they were put are discussed in greater detail below. Here a more general preliminary look at the powers attributed to Luria and the significance of such attributions will suffice.

In the first place, as we have seen, Luria is said to have had the ability to converse with the souls of the dead, chiefly rabbinic sages, as well as with angels and, most impressively, the biblical prophet Elijah. As Vital reports, "Elijah would constantly reveal himself to him, speaking directly to him, and instruct him in these mysteries."[52] Elijah, active in the mid-ninth century B.C.E. in the northern kingdom of Israel, was renowned as a wonder-worker, as well as for his dramatic ascent to heaven in a "chariot of fire." This portrayal provided the basis for a wide range of subsequent traditions concerning his extraordinary capacities. Rabbinic literature represents Elijah as fulfilling a variety of roles, as precursor and herald of the Messiah, vigilant guardian of Jewish tradition, and future reconciler of competing Jewish legal opinions.[53] Of greatest significance from the point of view of kabbalistic tradition was the belief that Elijah served as a teacher from on high and as an intermediary between heaven and earth, conveying messages to and from the celestial academy. To the kabbalists, a vision and/or auditory experience of Elijah (*gillui ʾEliyahu*) was among the most exalted forms of heavenly communication that an individual could experience. The *Zohar* itself, building upon earlier rabbinic tradition, depicts the relationship between Elijah and Shimon bar Yohai as central to the latter's spiritual development: "Rabbi Shimon bar Yohai fled to the desert of Lydda and lived in a cave with his son, Rabbi Eleazar. . . . Elijah, may he be remembered for good, visited them twice a day, and instructed them, and no one [else] knew where they were."[54]

Or to take an illustration from Luria's own time, Joseph Karo's mentor angel implicitly acknowledges the relative inferiority of its own communications by promising Karo the more exalted experience of Elijah if his behavior warrants it: "Mortify yourself as I told you, so as to merit to behold Elijah while you are awake, face to face, and he will speak to you, mouth to mouth, and will give you the salutation of peace. For he will become your teacher and master, and teach you all the mysteries of the Torah."[55]

Elsewhere, Karo's diary reports: "I have told you already twice and thrice that you shall see Elijah standing before you while awake [i.e., not in a dream]. It is necessary, however, that you fast seven times for three consecutive days, and then he will reveal himself to you at the place which you know, and there you shall delight yourself with him."[56]

Thus, the claims concerning Isaac Luria's relationship to Elijah take their place in a long tradition involving other kabbalists before him, about which I say more below. What Luria learned from these different heavenly sources consisted in kabbalistic knowledge of the Torah, that is, mystical interpretations of sacred texts, in addition to other kinds of esoteric information, such as the soul-ancestries of his disciples.

In addition to these forms of direct revelatory experience, Luria is said to have engaged in various types of divinatory activities. Thus, he could discern the meaning of signs from the natural world, from both animate and inanimate objects. To Luria, for example, feeling an individual's pulse or reading the Hebrew letters that he saw on the forehead could provide him with knowledge about that person's soul. The chirping of birds, the dance of fire from a lit candle, the souls present in all types of natural objects, such as trees and rocks, contained hidden messages whose meanings he was able to fathom. While these divinatory phenomena constituted a somewhat less direct form of divine revelation than those enumerated above, they appear to have been regarded as equally authoritative.

The various kinds of revelatory experiences ascribed to Luria include both visual and auditory types.[57] Thus, he was able to see both angels and the souls of departed prophets and sages, such as Elijah, as well as people's external auras and letters on the forehead and other parts of the body, which appeared as lights. His ear could make sense of the language spoken by birds and of the speech of all sorts of animate and inanimate phenomena in nature.[58] There seems to be no clear preference for either the visual experience or the auditory one. Nor is the distinction between the visual and the auditory in Luria's case always clear; it appears that at least in certain of the phenomena described, both modes of experience came into play.[59] The manifestation of Elijah, for instance, was no doubt simultaneously visual and auditory, just as the knowledge gained from the "speech" of a burning candle or rushing water had to have been made possible in the first place by the contemplative gaze. Still, it is important to point out that the auditory occupies an unusually prominent place in Lurianic mysticism, as will be evident below in connection with the contemplative practice of *yiḥudim*. Furthermore, Luria's ability to diagnose people's spiritual condition by feeling their pulses adds the sense of touch to the modes of cognition upon which he could rely.

No matter what form of communication was involved, they were all understood to result in knowledge gained, not through intellectual means, but through a contemplative intuition nurtured by a life of intense piety. Indeed, perhaps the most remarkable claim about Luria's esoteric knowledge is precisely the explicit rejection of intellectuality as a means of arriving at religious knowledge. Such wisdom was believed by Luria and his disciples to be inaccessible through conventional methods of intellectual study: "The secrets of the Torah and her mysteries are not revealed to human beings by the power of their intellects, but by means of divine vitality that flows from on high, through God's messengers and angels, or through Elijah the prophet, may his memory be a blessing."[60]

Vital amplifies this point in unambiguous terms, saying, "there is no doubt that these matters [i.e., esoteric knowledge] cannot be apprehended by means of human intellect, but only through Kabbalah, [that is,] from one individual [directly] to another, directly from Elijah, may his memory be a blessing, or directly from those souls that reveal themselves in each and every generation to those who are qualified to receive them."[61]

The question of the authority for one's teachings in kabbalistic tradition is critically important for our purposes. Virtually all kabbalists, from the beginnings of the movement in the late twelfth and thirteenth centuries, shared with non-kabbalists the fundamental rabbinic conviction that all religious truth derives ultimately from the dual revelation at Sinai. Moses received God's revelation, part of which was written down, resulting in the Written Torah, and part of which was transmitted orally from teachers to disciples in an unbroken chain of tradition, resulting in the Oral Torah, or Oral Tradition. According to this axiomatic rabbinic perspective, there can never really be any truly new or innovative teachings; rather, all apparently new interpretations of Scripture are nothing but the results of the process of determining the meaning of God's will as it was originally intended at Sinai.

If all kabbalists agreed on these well-known principles of rabbinic theology, the history of kabbalistic literature demonstrates that there was anything but unanimous consensus on the question of *how* to discover the truths revealed at Sinai. We can identify several different hermeneutical approaches taken by the early kabbalists of Provence and Spain, which were by no means mutually exclusive. (Keeping in mind that these are claims about the way in which kabbalistic knowledge was acquired or had been transmitted and are thus not necessarily identical with the ways in which teachings were actually derived.) These hermeneutical approaches fall under the headings of (a) oral transmission from a teacher; (b) textual exegesis; and (c) direct revelation.

Among the foremost examples of a kabbalistic author who espoused the mode of oral transmission from a teacher was Moses ben
Nahman, also known as Nahmanides, or by the acronym Ramban
(1194–1270). Nahmanides was among the greatest Spanish rabbis of
his time, a scholar whose creativity embraced the diverse fields of Jewish law, ʾaggadah (nonlegal narrative rabbinic literature), scriptural
exegesis, poetry, polemics, and Kabbalah.[62] His kabbalistic writing
lent that movement the prestige of a great religious authority and imparted legitimacy to it during a crucial period of its development.
Nahmanides believed that the only legitimate way to acquire esoteric
knowledge was through personal transmission from a teacher: "Indeed, this matter contains a great secret of the secrets of the Torah,
which cannot be comprehended by the understanding of a thinker,
but [only] by a person who gains them [personally], learning [them]
from the mouth of a teacher, going back to Moses our Master, from
the mouth of the Lord, blessed be He."[63]

Nahmanides eschewed innovating kabbalistic teaching, arguing for
dependence upon those traditions that one had actually received from
one's teacher. This assures that one's knowledge is part of the unbroken
chain of tradition that goes back to Moses at Sinai. As Moshe Idel
demonstrated, Nahmanides believed that the kabbalistic knowledge
available in his time was a closed corpus of mysteries, upon which it was
not permissible to enlarge.[64] This corpus had originally been received by
Moses and had been orally transmitted until the time of Nahmanides
himself. Like others before him, he sought to preserve these teachings
as esoteric secrets. That is to say, even kabbalistic knowledge that was regarded as legitimate and authoritative tradition had to be presented in a
cryptic, fragmentary fashion. This understanding of the nature of kabbalistic authority and the rules of its transmission was handed down by
Nahmanides to his students, including Solomon ibn Adret, Yom Tov
Ashvili, Isaac ben Todros, and David ha-Kohen, who in turn also resisted the public dissemination and expansion of kabbalistic teaching,
transmitting Kabbalah primarily orally to their own students, Shem Tov
ibn Gaon, Bahya ben Asher, Joshua ibn Shuaib, and Meir ibn Sahula.

Faithfulness to Nahmanides' conservatism broke down with this
latter generation of disciples, however, all of whom eventually gave in

to the temptation to introduce the unmistakably innovative kabbalistic ideas that flourished in the second half of the thirteenth century into their writings.[65] They not only broke with Nahmanidean conservatism with respect to *what* constituted legitimate kabbalistic teachings but also gave up the pattern of presenting Kabbalah in a highly cryptic form, through hints and allusions. By the first half of the fourteenth century in Spain, Kabbalah had become more accessible in the public domain through the publication of works lacking the deliberately cryptic nature of earlier literature.

The hermeneutical approach of textual exegesis is exemplified well by the very kabbalists responsible for the innovative trends of the late thirteenth century alluded to above. The most important example of the exegetical approach, however, is the seminal work of kabbalistic theosophy in Spain, the *Zohar*, the bulk of which was written by Moses de Leon.[66] De Leon was born in about 1240 in León, near Castile. In the 1280s and 1290s, he began circulating manuscripts that he claimed were ancient midrashim, that is, commentaries on the Torah, but that were actually written by him. De Leon pretended merely to be copying from a manuscript that, he argued, had originated in the circle of the second-century Palestinian rabbi Shimon bar Yohai (also known by the acronym RaSHBI) but that had only recently made its way to Spain. Despite early skepticism and occasional challenges to the alleged antiquity of the *Zohar*, Moses de Leon's attempt to portray the *Zohar* as a text from rabbinic times succeeded. The memory of Moses de Leon himself eventually retreated into the background as the *Zohar* established itself as an authoritative work of esoteric wisdom by the great sage Shimon bar Yohai. It was this literary ploy on de Leon's part, along with the inherent fascination with which the *Zohar* was greeted, that ultimately assured the *Zohar*'s near-canonical status by the sixteenth century. Alongside the Bible and Talmud, the *Zohar* was studied with reverence, awe, and intensity by Jews in diverse communities around the world. And as with the Bible and Talmud, the *Zohar* too spawned an entire literature consisting of commentaries, guides to its study, translations, and even imitations.[67]

The point to be made about the *Zohar* for our purposes is that one of its primary approaches to the discovery of religious truth is innovative and imaginative textual interpretation.[68] Composed largely in a midrashic style consistent with its claim to be an ancient rabbinic work, the *Zohar* assumes that Scripture encodes a vast sea of esoteric and symbolic meanings. Symbolic expression is the lifeblood of the *Zohar*; the Torah, in its view, is a vast corpus of symbols alluding to one aspect or another of the divine structure. Discovery of these meanings, however, is not regarded as being dependent upon received tradition, as with Nahmanides. Rather, anyone with knowledge of the symbolic nature of Torah is potentially in a position to determine its meanings. Various figures appear in the *Zohar*, products of de Leon's imagination, who bear kabbalistic knowledge without making any claim to having been taught by others. Armed only with imagination and knowledge of "concealed mysteries," they suddenly begin teaching to the rapt attention of interested individuals. Whereas Nahmanides was a zealot for caution and conservative explanation, de Leon was extravagant in his openness to the wide-ranging, indeed, infinite possibilities of scriptural interpretation. The *Zohar* is a testament to the highly inventive, uninhibited, and imaginative interpretive resourcefulness of Moses de Leon. The compelling power of the *Zohar*, as I have suggested elsewhere,[69] has everything to do with its author's flashes of insight and intuition, and the seemingly limitless images with which God is described. It is the flights of fantasy, the ability of the author's mind to grasp and articulate in symbols the inexhaustible dimensions of divine life, which so indelibly impress themselves upon the reader. Of course, none of this is regarded as a mere product of the human imagination, but rather as the recovery and discovery of truths going back to Sinai. The most daring and original formulations are thus construed as ancient revelation.

A third type of hermeneutical claim concerning the source of kabbalistic truth is direct, personal revelation of one type or another. This kind of claim was already made about the earliest constellation of distinguished Provençal kabbalists, including Abraham ben Isaac (d.c. 1179), president of the rabbinical court at Narbonne; his son-in-law Abraham ben David of Posquieres (d. 1198), the most prominent rabbi of his time in southern France; the latter's son Isaac the Blind; and Jacob ha-Nazir. As is well known, the teachings of these Provençal kabbalists were transplanted into Spain by their disciples around the beginning of the thirteenth century. A number of slightly varying traditions reporting that these early kabbalists experienced the "appearance of the Holy Spirit" and revelations from the prophet Elijah first appear a century later, however, around the year 1300. These are preserved in the writings of disciples of Solomon ibn Adret, himself the preeminent disciple of Nahmanides. One such report by the important Italian kabbalist Menahem Recanati asserts that the first kabbalist of the Provençal circle was not Abraham ben Isaac, but Rabbi David, the father of Abraham ben David. What is interesting about Recanati's account here, however, is the information he provides concerning the way in which the earliest kabbalistic tradition was believed to have been transmitted from one generation to the next:

> For he [Elijah] revealed himself to Rabbi David, head of the rabbinical court [ʾav bet din] and taught him the mysteries of the Kabbalah. He transmitted it, for his part, to his son, the Rabad [i.e., Rabbi Abraham ben David], and he [Elijah] also revealed himself to him, and he transmitted it to his son, Isaac the Blind, blind from birth, and to him, too, he revealed himself. The latter, in turn, transmitted these teachings to two disciples of his, R. Ezra [of Gerona], author of a commentary to the Song of Songs, and R. Azriel [of Gerona], after which it was transmitted to the Ramban.[70]

Recanati's account shows how the phenomenon of transmission from master to disciple was combined with reports about heavenly inspiration, providing two different authoritative bases for kabbalistic truth. From Abraham ben David himself, we learn: "The Holy Spirit has already appeared in our school," and "it was revealed to me from the mysteries of God, which he communicates to those who fear Him."[71] It should be noted that claims of divine inspiration are made here on behalf of the Provençal kabbalists, but not those of Spain, that is, Ezra, Azriel, or Nahmanides.

In the tradition of ecstatic Kabbalah as represented in the work of the Spanish-born mystic Abraham Abulafia, it is the prophetic inspiration of the divine spirit that is understood as the ground of mystical knowledge.[72] An anonymous author of the fourteenth or fifteenth century, writing in the Abulafian tradition, articulated in a clear manner the view that knowledge of the secrets of the Torah is contingent upon "prophetic intellect" deriving from God, rather than the normal intellect: "One cannot comprehend the majority of the subjects of the Torah and its secrets, and the secrets of the commandments cannot be comprehended but by means of the prophetic holy intellect which was emanated from God onto the prophets."[73] German Pietism also claimed that Pietists had extraordinary knowledge of God's will, insofar as "God reveals His esoteric lore [*sodo*] to His servants the prophets" (Amos 3:7). Pietists regarded themselves as possessing inspiration with which to discover the concealed will of God directly from Scripture, and sometimes called themselves "prophets."[74]

Among the most important examples of this type of claim is once again the *Zohar*, especially in connection with its representation of the figure of Shimon bar Yohai. This mystical master is portrayed as a supremely charismatic personality; besides extraordinary righteousness, he possesses spiritual power that makes it possible for him to engage in discourse with angelic spirits, the souls of the departed righteous, and, as already noted, the prophet Elijah. In one exuberant passage, he describes himself as *exceeding* Moses in his power of inspiration: "I see now what no man has seen since Moses ascended Mount Sinai for the second time. I see my face shining like the powerful light of the sun. . . . And further still, I know that my face is shining, while Moses did not know, nor did he look."[75] As Isaiah Tishby writes, Shimon bar Yohai "is portrayed as the expert in mysteries, to whom all secret paths are made plain by means of revelations from heaven, and the circle of his fellow disciples, thirsting for knowledge of the hidden world, sits in the dust at his feet in order to receive instruction from his lips. Knowledge of the unknown is the magic wand whose power enables him to rule over the upper and lower worlds."[76] Even though the Shimon bar Yohai whose personality dominates the narratives of the *Zohar* was invented by its composers, we shall see that he would become the most real of all mystical teachers as far as Luria and his circle were concerned.[77]

Luria's Place in the Chain of Kabbalistic Tradition

On the basis of what we have already seen, Vital indicates Luria's acceptance of what may be called the Nahmanidean approach, namely,
personal transmission from master to disciple, as well as the revelatory
one. It is the latter, however, that is the claim made on Luria's behalf
by Vital and others. Vital provides us with an important discussion of
his own views—and presumably Luria's as well—regarding the history
of the transmission of kabbalistic knowledge.[78]

According to Vital, kabbalistic mysteries had been taught openly
and publicly until the death of Rabbi Shimon bar Yohai, to whom, as
we have seen, tradition ascribed authorship of the *Zohar*. Quoting the
Zohar's own words on this subject, Vital wrote that ever since Shimon
bar Yohai's death "wisdom has departed from this earth" (*Zohar* 1,
217a). All of those sages who had borne kabbalistic wisdom since that
time did so in great secrecy, each disclosing his knowledge to a single
disciple. What is more, even to these select disciples, kabbalistic masters taught in generalizations only, revealing but a portion of their
knowledge.[79] Kabbalistic wisdom was passed from one generation to
the next in this fragmented and fragmentary way until the time of
Moses ben Nahman. Following the well-known tradition preserved by
Recanati, quoted above, Vital informs us that during this time there
were certain sages who were privileged to merit direct, personal revelations from Elijah the prophet, and upon whom the Holy Spirit rested,
including Abraham ben David of Posquieres, and the latter's son, Isaac
the Blind. Isaac, in turn, passed his tradition on to his two important
disciples, Ezra and Azriel of Gerona, from whom it passed to the final
teacher of genuine Kabbalah, Nahmanides. In this context, Vital quotes
the passage from Nahmanides cited above, according to which kabbalistic tradition may only be learned directly from a teacher, and it cannot be acquired by intellectual means.

On the basis of these views, Vital provides us with an important
and highly illuminating report on which books represent authentic
Kabbalah and are deserving of study, according to Luria. These include first and foremost, of course, the *Zohar*. The Lurianic circle, like

virtually all other kabbalists from the end of the thirteenth century on, accepted the tradition that the *Zohar* was a work of talmudic times. Indeed, as indicated above, it was believed that with the death of Shimon bar Yohai kabbalistic wisdom went underground, for until that time, heavenly revelation and divine inspiration had been widespread. Vital declares that "most of the words of Rabbi Shimon bar Yohai, of blessed memory, in the *Zohar*, the *Tiqqunim*, and the [*Zohar's*] Midrash to the Song of Songs, were revealed to him by Elijah the Prophet, of blessed memory."[80] Rashbi also learned the mysteries of the Torah from the souls of deceased saints, as is recorded in the second introduction to the *Tiqqunei Zohar*.[81] Luria's list of approved works also included *Sefer ha-Qanah*, all the writings mentioned by Menahem Recanati in his reference to works composed under the authorship of divine inspiration, as well as the "commentary to *Sefer Yetsira* [Book of Creation] attributed to Rabbi Abraham ben David of Posquieres, of blessed memory, even though it was composed by a certain Ashkenazi sage and does not contain the Ravad's words. For despite this, its words are truthful, concealed, and wondrous."[82]

Berit Menuḥah—a work claiming to be based on revelations to its anonymous author in the fourteenth century by "a certain saint, who instructed him, and all his words are concealed and sealed"—is another book that Vital designates as divinely inspired.[83] This unusual treatise, erroneously attributed to Abraham ben Isaac of Granada, contains dramatic accounts of visions of heavenly lights achievable by meditating on vocalizations of the Tetragrammaton. Luria and Vital were not the first to regard it as special. Moses Cordovero offered the following evaluation of it:

> I observed the work *Berit Menuḥah*, a delightful work containing an exposition of the Tetragrammaton. It is certain that the contents of this book have been handed down by tradition from master to disciple [literally, "from mouth to mouth"], or else they were imparted by an angel, since these are not subjects to be grasped as a result of profound speculation and subtle reasoning but can only be the fruit of wondrous comprehension [*hasagah niflaʾah*] [made possible] by the aid of the Holy Spirit.[84]

Vital also, as we have seen, includes the work of Nahmanides himself. He alludes to the cryptic nature of Nahmanides' commentary on the Torah by suggesting that its truth will be apparent "to one who understands it."[85] Moreover, according to Recanati, Nahmanides' teachings originated in the school of Isaac the Blind, which were themselves based upon revelations from the prophet Elijah. Vital also warns against studying anything subsequent to Nahmanides—a remarkable position that both challenges the validity of a vast corpus of mystical texts and is highly ironic, because many of the works that Luria regarded as inspired Kabbalah were actually written after the time of Nahmanides:

> Now, with regard to all the books of the later kabbalists who came after the Ramban, of blessed memory, do not come near them. For from the time of the Ramban on, the path of this wisdom disappeared from before the eyes of the sages, and nothing remains [to them] but a few scant branches without their roots. Upon these, the later kabbalists, of blessed memory, constructed their words [using] human intellect [alone].[86]

What all of the sanctioned works have in common is that they were believed either to have been written under the auspices of some form of divine inspiration, be it Elijah, an angel, or the soul of a deceased individual, or, as in the case of Nahmanides, to represent tradition authentically transmitted from master to disciple.[87] Negatively put, none of them were the product of mere human intellect, for intellect alone could not penetrate the depths of esoteric truth. The argument here is not that all other writing on Kabbalah is a complete lie or devoid of any value whatsoever. Rather, in comparison to the works sanctioned, it constitutes shallow, more easily acquired human knowledge. These views also betray the profoundly negative attitude of many kabbalists of this period toward philosophic rationalism.[88] A wide range of post-Expulsion kabbalists expressed their antagonism by going so far as to contend that the roots of philosophy were associated with the *Sitra Aḥra*, the realm of evil, and that its study was responsible for the prolonging of the exile.

What was the status of Luria's teachings? Luria, according to Vital, represents nothing less than the first and only appearance of authentic kabbalistic knowledge since Nahmanides! Even more, his knowledge may be compared only to that of Shimon bar Yohai himself. For such knowledge has "been neither seen nor heard in all the land since the days of Rabbi Shimon bar Yohai, may he rest in peace, until now."[89] Despite the claim that true Kabbalah had not manifested itself since Nahmanides, Vital writes that in every generation God displays his compassion by giving Israel extraordinary individuals (*yeḥidei segullah*) "upon whom the Holy Spirit rested, and to whom Elijah, may his memory be a blessing, revealed himself, instructing them in the secrets of Kabbalah." In our generation, God has not withheld a redeemer from Israel, sending us a saintly angel, "the great rabbi, our saintly teacher, our rabbi and master, Isaac Luria Ashkenazi, may his name be an everlasting blessing, filled like a pomegranate with [knowledge of] Scripture, Mishnah, Talmud, Pilpul, Midrashim, *Maʿaseh Bereshit*, and *Maʿaseh Merkavah*."[90] All who witness Luria's knowledge and skills, and all who familiarize themselves with his teachings will recognize "that the human mind [by itself] could not attain such deep and wondrous matters without the power of the Holy Spirit, mediated through Elijah, may his memory be a blessing."[91]

We have here a vivid instance of the legitimization of charismatic religious authority. Whatever else he may have intended by *charisma,* the influential German sociologist Max Weber clearly had in mind, first and foremost, the notion of an individual believed to be endowed with "supernatural" power of some sort or another. "[T]he term 'charisma' will be applied to a certain quality of an individual personality by virtue of which he is set apart from ordinary men and treated as endowed with supernatural, superhuman, or at least specifically exceptional powers or qualities," Weber writes. "These are such as are not accessible to the ordinary person, but are regarded as of divine origin or as exemplary, and on the basis of them the individual concerned is treated as a leader."[92]

According to this definition, charisma entails both the display of certain traits or behaviors on the part of a person and the recognition on the part of others that such behavior signifies something extraordinary. While the popular tendency is to speak of charisma as having its locus in the individual, Weber stressed the social character of charismatic authority, writing that "what is alone important is how the individual is actually regarded by those subject to charismatic authority, by his 'followers' or 'disciples.'"[93] Likewise, Weber asserted that "it is recognition on the part of those subject to authority which is decisive for the validity of charisma."[94] Charisma refers, then, to a social phenomenon as much as it does to a personality type. It always denotes a relationship between followers and the person in whom they place their confidence. It involves a claim by a community that a person is authoritative by virtue of "supernatural" or some other type of exceptional competence.

It is precisely in such terms that the preceding descriptions of Isaac Luria may be understood. Luria clearly behaved in ways that made him the object of attention and fascination; but it is the interpretation of his behavior by others as being sacred, or deriving from contact with the sacred, that especially interests us. There were numerous others in Safed before Luria's appearance who were teachers of high repute or who engaged in unusual acts of piety, as we saw earlier. But their exhibition of "commerce with the sacred" failed to produce anything remotely resembling the kind of recognition accorded Isaac Luria. A combination of factors—some of which have already been identified and others that the remainder of this study will illuminate—must have set Luria apart from others who manifested charismatic behavior.

The comparative study of religious cultures has taught us that there are varied signs understood by individuals as pointing to an association between a charismatic person and the sacred. These signs are always culture-specific, even if there are similarities to be found across cultures. As Charles Keyes aptly puts it, "charisma is always construed according to particular ideas of what constitutes the sacred—according to whether one has been set apart by virtue of a trip to and from the land of the dead as in classic shamanism, or one has inherited the *baraka* of Muhammad, or has been visited by the Holy Spirit, or has realized the ultimate truth that is Brahma or Nirvana."[95]

In Isaac Luria's case, as we have seen, the decisive sign that he exhibited entailed his contact with a wide range of heavenly figures, who revealed divine mysteries to him, and his divinatory ability to discern the hidden meaning of natural phenomena. Luria, then, was regarded by his circle as having knowledge of a charismatic type, that is, extraordinary knowledge that he had been vouchsafed by means of direct, personal revelation. He was believed to possess knowledge and skills typically beyond the grasp of ordinary human beings. It was this that helped establish him as a teacher and religious mentor of unique status in Safed.

Charismatic Authority Versus Rabbinic Authority

From a historical and comparative point of view, this legitimization of charismatic authority by the Lurianic fellowship is significant, because it goes to the heart of a central issue in the history of Judaism. The effort to achieve kabbalistic knowledge (or any type of religious knowledge for that matter) through personal inspiration, and the belief that such efforts are efficacious, stands in striking contrast to traditional rabbinic notions of authority. Rabbinic authority, as it developed in late antiquity, was rooted in an intellectual process of studying sacred texts for the purpose of interpreting their meaning. For meaning is believed to reside within the written texts themselves; one need only apply the appropriate techniques of interpretation in order to ferret out the intention of the text.

This was certainly the case for the sages of the talmudic period who deliberately asserted that prophecy—direct communication from God—had ceased. The primary motivation for such a contention was the desire to assert the primacy of the Torah (and its collaborative and collective interpretation by the rabbis) as the paradigm for human behavior, rather than the example of individuals. It is certainly true that we find in rabbinic literature a strain of tradition according to which a *tsaddiq* ('righteous' person) is imagined as one who sustains the world and stands at the center of the cosmos—primarily on account of his moral virtue.[96] It is significant, though, that little effort was made to single out particular individuals and attribute such status to them. As W. S. Green writes:

> By limiting the range of issues open to question, by organizing discrete sayings of individuals to address a single point of law or to interpret a verse of scripture, and by shaping narrative accounts of rabbinical

activities to serve public goals, the authorities behind rabbinic documents created a literature dominated by consensus, by collective
opinion. It is a literature in which individual figures appear to gloss
and refine tradition, but never to invent it, a literature in which the
sense of separate existences is minimal. The structure of rabbinic documents severely limits the expression of individuality. Idiosyncrasy or
personal charisma rarely appear. No biographies are preserved; the
inner, private, psychic, imaginative and intellectual lives, as well as
the public careers of early rabbinic masters, almost totally obscured.
No individual emerges as a "whole person" in whom all wisdom and
piety are centered and who might threaten or serve as a focus of resistance against the rabbinic collective itself.[97]

By the third century, the attribution of certain kinds of supernatural
and magical powers was not an uncommon feature of rabbinic leadership, reflecting a general trend among religious holy men in the late
Roman world.[98] As Green argues, however, rabbinic Judaism claimed
that any supernatural power was a result of rabbinic piety and knowledge of Torah, and thus profoundly defused the importance of such
behavior by making intellectuality the true measure of an individual's
status. In his view, the suppression of individuality was a consequence
of the public scrutiny to which the nature of rabbinic life subjected its
protagonists. These and other factors account for the failure of rabbinic Judaism to produce any hagiography:

> Whatever personal traits, whatever magnetism or charisma a rabbi
> possessed, his standing and credibility within the rabbinic movement
> initially depended on his learning. Rabbinical status derived not from
> the exercise of mysterious and arbitrary divine favor but from the re-
> sult of intellectual labor. Whatever else being a rabbi meant, it meant
> the publicly demonstrable mastery of a considerable body of Scrip-
> ture and halachic material. Rabbis did not hide from one another in
> the desert, nor did they seclude themselves behind cloister walls. The
> evidence of the sources suggests that they lived in a world of persis-
> tent mutual scrutiny, a world of continual evaluation and judgment.
> In such a world, rabbis could not help but be aware of their mortality
> and could not possibly maintain the illusion of special power, . . .
> especially among themselves.[99]

It is important to note that in addition to a general preference for intellectuality over personal charisma, the nature and role of law in the rabbinic system itself contributed to this tendency. In a world where proper behavior counted more than intention or motive, the inner experience of an individual would, in the nature of things, have less currency than collective or institutional authority.[100] This point is well illustrated in the often-cited talmudic dispute concerning the ritual cleanness of the oven of Akhnai. The point of this story about the proper nature of rabbinic authority is not that sages do not sometimes experience heavenly communications, such as in the form of a *bat qol*, or heavenly voice. Sometimes, in fact, they do have such experiences, for this is precisely what Rabbi Eliezer enjoyed in his attempt to persuade the rabbis with whom he was disputing that his view about the law in question was correct. The point is, rather, that such divine interventions certainly have no legitimate place in a dispute over legal matters.[101]

It remains to be added that the primacy that rabbinic Judaism accorded the power of the rational intellect was, with few exceptions, true of Jewish medieval philosophers of all varieties, as well as biblical exegetes of different types. Authority was founded on an individual's knowledge and learning, his mastery of existing tradition. Whereas the talmudic sages self-consciously went out of their way to deny the possibility of further prophecy, claiming instead that the path to understanding the Torah was a more earthly one, to be pursued along legal-rational lines, Luria and his followers affirmed their belief that direct channels of communication were not only a possibility but urgently preferable. Even though the Lurianic passages adduced above were intent on privileging certain types of kabbalistic tradition, the fact is that they also served to subvert the long-standing hegemony of conventional rabbinic authority, or at least established an alternative to that authority.

It is, of course, true that Luria's kabbalistic activities, particularly in Egypt, were especially associated with *parshanut,* that is, the interpretation of texts, primarily from the *Zohar.* But even this process came to be regarded by his disciples as having its basis in Luria's inspiration, and in a contemplative approach to study. What is more, his teachings appear to have become increasingly distanced from the practice of *par-shanut* in the conventional sense of formal and systematic commentary on texts. While he continued to be intensely preoccupied with interpreting the *Zohar* until the end of his life, over the course of time, Luria related to it in a more profoundly personal way. As we shall see, Luria came to regard his circle of disciples—with himself at the center—as reenacting the mystical activities of Shimon bar Yohai and *his* circle. Thus, Luria continued to be an interpreter of the *Zohar,* but now as an existential hermeneut who brought the world of the *Zohar* to life through his personal identification with its protagonist. Just as Shimon bar Yohai's teachings were deemed a result of heavenly inspiration, so too were Luria's. A strong bond links Moses de Leon, the central author of the *Zohar,* and Isaac Luria. In each case, the imagination appears to have been too powerful to remain constrained by traditional hermeneutics. Luria seems to be saying as much about himself when he is reported to have remarked—in response to having been asked why he did not commit his teachings to writing—that it was "impossible, because all things are interrelated. I can hardly open my mouth to speak without feeling as though the sea burst its dams and overflowed. How then shall I express what my soul has received, and how can I write it down in a book?"[102]

Charismatic Authority in the Post-Expulsion Era

As we have seen, there *were* early kabbalists whom tradition regarded as having derived their knowledge from divine revelation. But in the fifteenth and sixteenth centuries, such claims proliferated dramatically. As Moshe Idel has demonstrated, *Sefer ha-Meshiv* (The Book of the Answering [Angel]), written in Spain sometime in the second half of the fifteenth century by an anonymous author, occupies an exceedingly important place in these developments.[103] According to *Sefer ha-Meshiv*, certain people employed magical means—including fasting and the recitation of divine names—for the purpose of inducing angelic visions. This was the proper, reliable way to acquire divine knowledge and be able to write under the power of divine inspiration, like the prophets of old. For example, *Sefer ha-Meshiv* describes the descent of Elijah cloaked in a garment, as all spiritual and angelic beings must be when they descend to the world. The vision of such a garment is attributed to an array of prominent rabbinic and medieval figures, including (strangely enough) the famous, decidedly nonmystical scholar Rabbi Shlomo Yitshaqi (Rashi):

> You should know that the secret causing the descent of the supernal book is the secret of the descent of the supernal chariot, and when you pronounce the secret of the great name, immediately the force of the garment will descend downward, which is the secret of [the revelation] of Elijah, who is mentioned in the works of the sages. And by this Rabbi Shimon bar Yohai and Jonathan ben Uzziel learned their wisdom, and they were deserving of the secret of the garment, to be dressed in it. And Rabbi Hanina and Rabbi Nehunya ben ha-Kaneh and Rabbi Akiva and Rabbi Ishmael ben Elisha and our holy rabbi [Rabbi Judah the Prince] and Rashi and many others [learned] likewise. And the secret of the garment is the vision of the garment, which the angel of God is dressed in, with a corporeal eye, and it he who is speaking to you. . . . And the secret of the garment was given to those who fear God and meditate upon his name; they have seen it, those men who are the men of God were worthy of this state. And they were fasting for forty days continuously, and during their fast they pronounced the Tetragrammaton forty-five times, and on the fortieth day, [the garment] descended to him and showed him whatever he wished [to know].[104]

Just as the Lurianic sources emphasize the nonintellectual nature of these processes, so, too, does *Sefer ha-Meshiv*: "Thus was it done in the days of Rashi to his master, and the latter taught him [Rashi] this secret, and by means of it he [Rashi] composed whatever he composed, by the means of his mentor and instructor. Do not believe that he [Rashi] wrote this down from his own reason, for he did it by the secret of the garment of the angel."[105]

Idel suggested that the author of *Sefer ha-Meshiv* himself may have written by means of the "application of the techniques attributed by the author to earlier Jewish authorities."[106] There is a strong likelihood that *Sefer ha-Meshiv* influenced Joseph Taitasak, Solomon Molcho, and others living in the Ottoman Empire to write in such a style. It is certain that this book was well known among a wide range of kabbalists, including many in sixteenth-century Safed, such as Ovadiah Hamon,[107] Moses Cordovero, and Hayyim Vital, with all three of whom Isaac Luria had important relationships.[108] As Idel has suggested, it is thus more than likely that Isaac Luria himself was familiar with *Sefer ha-Meshiv* and related literature.[109] While he certainly did not employ the more magical techniques described in that book, repudiating as he did this kind of "practical Kabbalah" (*kabbalah maʿasit*), he clearly shared its views about the centrality of revelations from Elijah, angels, and departed souls; the possibilities of experiencing automatic speech; and the unreliability of purely intellectual approaches to kabbalistic wisdom.

Galya Raza, an anonymous treatise on the transmigration of souls, written probably in either Greece or Turkey between 1543 and 1553, also attests to the growing phenomenon of kabbalistic composition under the auspices of pneumatic inspiration.[110] The author of this work, who himself probably came under the influence of *Sefer ha-Meshiv*, goes out of his way to emphasize that he wrote under the inspiration of visions and dreams that had the status of divine revelation: "Blessed be the Lord, God of Israel, who revealed to me exalted secrets which were never revealed to a human being in this generation, from the time the Lamp of Brightness [i.e., Shimon bar Yohai] departed from this world until this very day."[111]

Elsewhere, he informs us about the obligation he felt to reveal to others what had been disclosed to him "by heaven": "Since I saw every day that innovations were revealed to me, as well as hidden and concealed secrets, I resolved to write them down. Moreover, I have another interpretation in the manner of secrets that stir in my bowels, and I will not be quiet until I have revealed it, because it has been aroused in my heart by heaven."[112]

Belief in the centrality of divine inspiration was not limited, however, to the composition of books during the post-Expulsion era. It played a part as well in the political and religious activities of certain individuals, notably in the brief but extraordinary life of Solomon Molcho (c. 1501–32).[113] The story of Molcho's career begins with that of another person, David Reuveni (d.c. 1538). By just about any measure,

Reuveni, an Ethiopian Jew, was one of the most fantastic and intriguing personalities of the post-Expulsion period. At the beginning of the 1520s, when Iberian exiles were setting out in considerable numbers for Palestine, David Reuveni appeared in Rome, implausibly declaring himself to be a Jewish prince whose brother Joseph was king of a large and powerful Jewish realm in Arabia. Reuveni claimed that the Jews of this kingdom were descendants of the lost ancient tribes of Reuven, Gad, and Manasseh. Reuveni made a striking impression on the Jews of Rome when he appeared there in February 1524, riding upon a white horse and accompanied by a group of attendants. Reuveni announced that his brother, King Joseph, had commissioned him to initiate negotiations with Pope Clement VII and the kings of Christian Europe for the purpose of forging an alliance against the Turks. He sought to furnish the (supposed) Jewish tribes of Arabia with the weaponry with which to go to war against the Turkish sultan, expel him from the Red Sea region, and wrest Palestine from his control! In the hope that the Portuguese might accommodate Reuveni's request, the pope gave him a letter to King John of Portugal, who actually agreed to it in part before changing his mind.

It is not hard to imagine the kind of intense excitement Reuveni must have stimulated in the hearts of Jews and *conversos* when he arrived in Portugal on his richly decorated ship, flying a Jewish national flag. The Portuguese king received him with high honors as an emissary of a foreign kingdom. Among those whose imagination was fired by Reuveni's appearance was a certain Diego Pires, born in Lisbon of *converso* parents around 1501. Aroused by Reuveni's presence in 1525, Pires sought to become circumcised, perhaps partly motivated by a rumor that the Messiah had already appeared and was living quietly outside Istanbul but was visible only to circumcised Jews, a story that had long circulated among Spanish Jewish exiles and *conversos*. Although Reuveni reportedly tried to dissuade him, Pires circumcised himself, which almost cost him his life, and eventually took the Hebrew name of Solomon Molcho. At Reuveni's request, Molcho fled Portugal for safety, while Reuveni himself was also forced eventually to flee as a result of suspicion that he had taken part in Molcho's circumcision.

Arriving in Salonika, Molcho came under the influence of the vision-ary ascetic and kabbalist Joseph Taitasak and his circle. Molcho attracted disciples of his own, and with their encouragement published a collec-tion of his fiery, messianically oriented sermons in 1529.[114] Molcho's activities in Salonika, involving dreams, celestial visions, and calls for ascetic renunciation and repentance, all dressed in the garb of mes-sianic expectation, caused a considerable stir in the kabbalistic circle around Taitasak. Acknowledging his ignorance of Hebrew, and of Jewish learning in general, Molcho described the nature of his heav-enly inspiration in the following way:

> Sometimes in these days, I see the celestial academy of sages, and the books are open before them and they study the Torah . . . and from their discussions, I hear and learn something. And since I did not learn [Hebrew], nor was accustomed to the holy language, I did not comprehend all their discussions. But from what I was taught there in that Holy Academy, I answer people who ask for interpretations of verses and statements, which are seen as difficult to understand for the sages of [our] generation. And whoever wishes may ask me what-ever he wants, to comment on recondite verses and statements, [for] with the help of God, I am confident that I may answer everyone who asks me in a satisfactory manner, sublime things that are suffi-cient for any intelligent person, which are not [written] in books, [but in] which I was instructed from heaven. But I had never learned science from the mouth of a mortal master or colleague.[115]

In the end, in 1532, Molcho was condemned by the Inquisition in Italy to be burned at the stake, but his charismatic career and dramatic death inspired other sixteenth-century figures, not the least of whom was Safed's Joseph Karo, whose own longing for martyrdom was moti-vated by a desire to follow Molcho's example. Molcho's impassioned messianism helps to bring into focus the eschatological convictions that played a significant part in the lives of others who prized heavenly inspi-ration. The authors of *Sefer ha-Meshiv* and *Galya Raza*, as well as Molcho and many Safed kabbalists, understood the revelation of esoteric knowl-edge from on high as part of an unfolding messianic scenario.[116]

It is evident from all this that the formerly Byzantine cities of the Ottoman Empire were places where the kind of kabbalistic activity described here flourished, particularly during the first half of the six-teenth century. The author of *Galya Raza*, Solomon Molcho, Joseph Taitasak, Joseph Karo, and Solomon Alkabets, individuals known for having had revelatory experiences, all resided at one time or another in Salonika, Edirne, Nicopolis, or Istanbul. Salonika, in particular, served as a critically important crossroads for such activity, as a place where these men came into contact with one another. The mystical commu-nity of Safed was the direct beneficiary of the particular brand of reli-gious enthusiasm cultivated in these circles.

Charismatic Authority and Divine Inspiration in North Africa

Notions of charismatic authority and divine inspiration also played a central role in the life of another Jewish community with ties to Safed during the sixteenth century, one at a physical and cultural remove from the Byzantine-Turkish orbit. A vibrant circle of kabbalists emerged by the middle of the century in the area of the High Atlas Mountains and the Draa Valley in southern Morocco.[117] These kabbalists, indigenous Jews (*toshavim*) whose families had lived in this area for centuries, along with a smaller number of new immigrants from the Iberian Peninsula, both preserved older traditions from Spain and developed new ones.[118] A wide range of traditions attests to the fact that they cul-tivated some of the kinds of experiences under discussion: revelations of the prophet Elijah, attainment of the Holy Spirit, visionary dreams, and the composition of texts under the auspices of heavenly inspira-tion. For example, Mordechai Buzaglo contended that the revelation of kabbalistic mysteries that he experienced was a result of the inspi-ration of the Holy Spirit, which suffused his writing instrument in a form of automatic writing.[119]

The profound interest in these kinds of phenomena on the part of the kabbalists of Draa, along with a pattern of venerating those adept at such practices, is strikingly similar to the beliefs of the Muslim marabouts, among whom the Jewish community of southern Morocco lived. At the heart of marabouts' religion stands the notion of baraka, literally, blessing, that is, the strong manifestation of the holy. While baraka can infuse just about any object, natural or otherwise, its most important locus is human beings. As Clifford Geertz puts it, baraka entails "the proposition . . . that the sacred appears most directly in the world as an endowment—a talent and a capacity, a special ability—of particular individuals . . . 'baraka' is personal presence, force of character, moral vividness."[120] Those suffused with the charisma of baraka exhibit various magical and occult powers, wonder-working, foretelling the future, and moral excellence. The elaborate and pervasive veneration of such saints, living and deceased, came to characterize this type of piety throughout much of the Maghreb. Although this still requires further substantiation, there is reason to suppose that the Jews of southern Morocco, surrounded by this religious culture, appropriated various elements of it.[121]

We know, further, that in the sixteenth century, a good many North African kabbalists, including those from the region of Draa, migrated to Jerusalem and Safed by way of Egypt.[122] Two of these, whose names we have already encountered, warrant particular attention. Joseph ibn Tabul and Abraham Berukhim, both Moroccan kabbalists, settled in Safed and became prominent disciples of none other than Isaac Luria. Both may have come from Draa, although it is not certain, and each acquired a reputation for having experienced divine inspiration. Ibn Tabul's disciple Samson Bacchi attributed to his own master some of the very same mystical attainments he ascribed to Isaac Luria. In the letter quoted earlier, Bacchi describes ibn Tabul as a saint who was able to recognize the sins that people had committed and determine which of them were fit to receive his teachings, which were so luminous that only those who actually heard them could appreciate their extraordinary character.[123] It is altogether possible that these kabbalists, along with other former Moroccans living in Safed, contributed in some special way to the high regard for the charismatic authority that Isaac Luria enjoyed.

In addition to some of the major Safed figures whose activities are described in Chapter 2, we know of certain other less prominent personalities in Safed in the period prior to Luria's arrival who contributed to the atmosphere with which we are concerned.[124] The writings of Judah

Haleywa, who had emigrated from Fez, Morocco, to Safed reflect attitudes very similar to Lurianic ones. Around 1545, Haleywa wrote a lengthy work that combined kabbalistic and ethical themes, entitled *Tsafenat Paʿaneaḥ*. Haleywa evinced a strong antiphilosophical stance and asserted the superiority of knowledge of a revealed, prophetic type that is transintellectual in nature. Moreover, like the Lurianic kabbalists, he appears especially to have prized early mystical works. In *Tsafenat Paʿaneaḥ*, Haleywa refers to a certain Rabbi Lapidot as "a great sage and kabbalist, who used to foretell the future."[125] This appears to be the same person mentioned by both de Vidas and Vital as possessing occult skills. According to de Vidas's testimony, Rabbi Lapidot was expert in dreams. In an entry in his dream diary dated 1568, Vital describes Rabbi Lapidot Ashkenazi as one who could foretell the future accurately and converse with souls from both the present and the past.[126] These are, of course, virtually the same words that Vital uses to describe Luria.

Charismatic Women

Little attention has been paid to the fact that Vital's dream diary provides abundant evidence that at least a few women in sixteenth-century Safed (as well as in Damascus, where Vital subsequently lived) had revelatory experiences and possessed occult talents. In a diary entry from the year 1570, he informs us, for example, about a wise woman in Safed named Soniadora who could foretell the future, interpret dreams, and was expert in the art of divining from drops of oil on water.[127] Vital consulted her concerning his own future spiritual attainments by asking her to "cast a spell over the oil, as was customary." Vital also described the visionary experiences of a woman named Rachel, the sister of Judah Mishan, one of Luria's disciples:

> On Sabbath morning, I was preaching to the congregation in Jerusalem. Rachel, the sister of Rabbi Judah Mishan, was present. She said that during the whole of my discourse, there was a pillar of fire above my head; Elijah was at my right hand to support me. When I had finished, they both departed. She also saw a pillar of fire above

my head as I led the "additional" service on Yom Kippur in the synagogue of the Sicilian congregation in Damascus, in 5362 [1601]. This
woman was known to see visions, spirits, and angels, and she was accurate in most of her reports, from the time that she was a young girl
until now that she has grown into womanhood.[128]

It appears from what Vital says that she was not the only woman to
have experienced this type of vision. He reports that while present at
the circumcision of a child whose godfather (*sandeq*) he was, a woman
named Saadat, the wife of Jacob Nasar, saw "a pillar of fire from heaven
above my head."[129] Years later in Damascus, Simcha, the sister of a certain Zabda, saw a brilliant, blinding pillar of white light at Vital's right
side.[130] Several other women in Safed and Damascus are said to have
experienced visionary dreams, typically having to do with confirming
Vital's greatness.[131]

Even more pertinent to our interests are several reports by Vital
about women who experienced auditory revelations. One woman in
Damascus, the daughter of Raphael Anav, is said to have had visions
while awake, through the medium of souls and angels, as well as an
auditory experience of Elijah at the moment of a Sabbath eve celebration.[132] Concerning another woman in Damascus, we learn that in addition to being able to divine the meaning of drops of oil, she "also
hears a voice speaking to her."[133] Still another, Franseza Sarah, "a saintly
woman (*ʾishah ḥasida*), used to have visions while awake, and would
hear a voice speak to her. And most of her words were true."[134] This
last report is especially interesting insofar as it sheds light on the following information preserved by Joseph Sambari:

> In those days, there was a wise woman [*ʾishah ḥokhmah*] who lived in
> the upper Galilee, in Safed, may it be rebuilt and reestablished speed-
> ily in our day, whose name was Franseza and whose deeds were great.
> She had a mentor angel [*maggid*] to speak to her and to inform her
> concerning what would take place in the world. And the sages of
> Safed tested her a number of times in order to find out if there was
> substance to her words, and everything that she uttered came to pass.[135]

As far as I am aware, this is the only tradition concerning a woman
having had a *maggid*. Taken together, these stories about women are

remarkable insofar as they suggest a picture quite different from what we might have expected to find. At least some women evidently gained reputations for having visionary dreams, visions of light, auditions of angels, departed souls, the prophet Elijah, and other unidentified voices, and were expert at certain types of divination. Almost always identified by name, and as the daughter, sister, or wife of so-and-so, these women were clearly part of the community, rather than lone, marginal individuals behaving in deviant ways. In addition to its intrinsic interest—as striking evidence that some sixteenth-century women engaged in religious practices beyond the boundaries of home and family—the participation of women in the kinds of activity analyzed in this chapter serves to confirm still further the celebrated status of charismatic behavior in sixteenth-century Safed.

*

There is no question, then, that in the post-Expulsion period, the phenomenon of divine inspiration assumed a place of enormous importance in kabbalistic circles. It was more than simply a particular hermeneutical or epistemological stance, but rather, to borrow again from Geertz, "a conception of the mode in which the divine reaches into the world."[136] When Isaac Luria arrived in Safed, then, he found himself in a cultural milieu that was highly supportive of individuals with occult gifts, who sought knowledge of Torah from on high, and who were believed to be successful in those efforts. Indeed, it strikes me as likely that Luria's penchant for divine inspiration and charismatic behavior thrived precisely because of the warm receptivity he discovered in Safed. Luria was not, however, merely one more example of a general trend. Rather, in Isaac Luria we see a rich and full realization of this tendency. Luria stood out because he was perceived by his followers as a virtuoso at such activity, as one who was gifted beyond compare. Through the strength of his impressive personality, as well as through the great power of his teachings themselves, Luria was in a position to raise the status of charismatic authority to new heights.

Up until Isaac Luria, there had been no significant public figure in the entire history of postbiblical Judaism—with the obvious exception of the figure of Jesus—concerning whom a comparable cluster of such remarkable claims were made. The occasional earlier claims for charismatic behavior notwithstanding (among kabbalists or others), we find in premodern Judaism no full-fledged tradition of "sainthood" compared, for example, to those in the history of Christianity or Islam: no true literature of sacred biography, no elaborate tradition of the veneration of saints, and no highly developed history of pneumatic virtuosi. It turns out that despite an acceptance of a certain degree of miracle-working and magical behavior on the part of sages, the rabbis of late antiquity were extraordinarily successful in their efforts to deny legitimacy to charismatic authority. Over the course of centuries, Jewish communities were taught to marvel at the mastery of tradition that a teacher possessed, not at stories about this or that person having come face to face with God. People who presented themselves as pneumatics, and the communities that now and again enthusiastically embraced them, risked marginalization or repudiation by established authorities. All of this, in my view, makes Luria a unique figure. In the following century, Sabbatai Sevi's charismatic career would make Isaac Luria's behavior look rather mild by comparison. And beginning in the eighteenth century, the phenomenon of the Hasidic *tsaddiq* in eastern Europe would for the first time sanction charismatic religious leadership on a wide scale among Jewish communities.[137] But Luria and his disciples preceded both the Sabbateans and the Hasidim in laying the groundwork for the acceptance of charismatic religious authority.

ıurianic Myth

> ˌ. ˌ]e might single this out as one of the defining characteristics of a
> myth, in contrast with other sorts of narratives (such as novels): a myth
> is a much-retold narrative that is transparent to a variety of construc-
> tions of meaning; a neutral structure that allows paradoxical meanings
> to be held in a charged tension. This transparency—the quality of a
> lens—allows a myth, more than other forms of narrative, to be shared
> by a group (who, as individuals, have various points of view) and to
> survive through time (through different generations with different
> points of view).
>
> —Wendy Doniger, *The Implied Spider—Politics and Theology in Myth*

The cosmological myth Isaac Luria taught is without doubt the most elaborate such story in all of Jewish tradition. It certainly bears no re-semblance to the brevity and elegant simplicity of the biblical account of creation, and even in comparison to the far more complex cos-mogonic myth of Spanish Kabbalah, Luria's teachings are extraordi-narily intricate. While we tend to think of a creation myth in terms of a single, coherent narrative that can be told as one does a simple story, Luria's mythological teachings have not come down to us in this way. Instead, we discover a seemingly endless series of inordinately com-plex notions, presented in often fragmentary and conflicting versions by multiple authors and editors.

We already know that Luria himself taught a great deal but wrote relatively little, and that these few writings were not published as inde-pendent treatises under his own name but were incorporated into the works produced by others. Not only do we encounter conflicts and contradictions between the versions presented by different authors, es-pecially those of Moses Yonah,[1] Joseph ibn Tabul,[2] Hayyim Vital,[3] and certain anonymous writers,[4] but we sometimes also find them occur-ring even among the different versions presented by a single individ-ual. This is especially obvious in the case of Vital's voluminous writ-ings. Vital alone wrote several versions of these teachings over a period of some twenty years, which, in turn, served as the basis for numerous

124

recensions by other editors. These often disagree with one another, sometimes in minor ways, at other times in rather significant ways. Over the years, various suggestions have been put forward to explain the diverse and frequently conflicting nature of the sources, and recent scholarship has gone a significant way toward addressing these problems, most notably in the work of Ronit Meroz. The highly detailed analysis by Meroz of Luria's mythological teachings takes a developmental approach, which attributes the apparently conflicting character of the various sources largely to the fact that they represent different stages in the evolution of Luria's thinking. Luria continued to build upon his thinking from his earliest writings produced in Egypt and throughout the period that he lived and taught in Safed. Meroz, drawing upon virtually the entire Lurianic corpus, identified five different levels of Lurianic myth based on a range of conceptual and terminological criteria. The later layers of Lurianic thought according to her schema, stages four and five, are represented primarily by certain of the versions composed by Joseph ibn Tabul and Hayyim Vital. Meroz's approach does not pit one author against another so much as it seeks to show how it is possible to discern relative coherence and agreement among certain versions and authors at each of the various developmental layers.[5]

While the validity of such a methodology is certainly clear, it is also the case that certain differences among authors are to some degree a consequence of their varying subjective interpretations of what Luria taught, and of innovations that they introduced, both wittingly and unwittingly, to their teacher's words.[6] Needless to say, different students understand and appropriate their teacher's ideas in individual and creative ways, and it is perfectly reasonable to suppose that such would have been the case with mythic notions as complex as Luria's. This, no doubt, accounts for some of the differences in conception and language, for example, between the writings of Joseph ibn Tabul and Hayyim Vital. This important factor notwithstanding, one of the advantages of any developmental approach is that it takes into account the reality that Luria's thinking on just about every topic was in process. Luria clearly manifested a boundless and inventive imagination, and there is no reason to suppose that he had exhausted his creative resources when he died at the age of thirty-eight.

The purpose of the present exposition is to provide as lucid an account as possible of these teachings as represented by the more highly evolved forms in which they were expressed by Luria during the latter part of his life; as such, it is based primarily on certain representative traditions found in the writings of ibn Tabul and Vital. My goal is neither to present these conceptions in all their detail nor to trace their conceptual and literary development, a project far beyond the scope of this study, and one virtually accomplished in the work of Ronit Meroz. Rather, I wish to describe them succinctly and in a way that will make it possible to understand their relationship to the other questions with which this study is concerned.[7]

The Primordial Status of the Cosmos

In Luria's myth, theogony, the self-manifestation of divinity, and cosmogony, the manifestation of the cosmos, go hand in hand. Luria begins with a description of the state of the cosmos before the process of creation itself occurred. In its primordial condition, the cosmos was entirely filled with the presence of God, imagined as limitless divine light. Thus, in Vital's words:

> Before the emanation of any of the emanated entities, the divine light completely suffused all of existence, and there was no free space [*maqom panui*], no empty vacuum [*'avir reqani ḥalal*] whatsoever. Rather, everything was filled with the undifferentiated light of *Ein-Sof*. There was neither beginning nor end, but everything consisted of this one simple undifferentiated light, called *Ein-Sof*.[8]

In one of ibn Tabul's versions, this cosmic circumstance is described in these terms: "Know, my son, that the supernal Emanator, may He be blessed, was one and His name was one, and that all the worlds [were filled with] the light of *Ein-Sof*."[9] Or, alternatively, according to ibn Tabul, "Before the creation of the world, the Holy One, Blessed be He, and His name, were alone."[10]

According to many accounts, however, this apparently simple, undifferentiated light was actually made up of radically diverse elements, being "a mixture of good and evil, light and darkness, and [in which] the powers of strict Judgment [*ha-Dinim*] were bound up with the powers of Compassion [*Raḥamim*]."[11] The *Din*, according to some accounts, was tantamount to the "emptiness and void" (*tohu ve-vohu*) of which the second verse of the Torah speaks. The elements of *Din*, however, were subsumed under the influence of the far greater light of *Raḥamim*. The *Dinim* were akin to a mere speck of dust in a great container filled with water, or like a drop of water in a great ocean.[12] That is to say, they had no true independent life of their own, but were dominated by the powers of *Raḥamim*.

Din and *Raḥamim* are not explicitly spoken of in gendered terms in these particular accounts, but it is important to recall that kabbalistically, they are associated with feminine and masculine forces respectively. What is more, the feminine in kabbalistic symbolism is typically associated with the quality of evil, or at least with the potential for evil and severity, whereas the male is associated with the quality of compassion and righteousness. As such, it is possible to construe the above account as one in which elements of the (potentially demonic) feminine are subsumed under the influence of the goodness of the divine masculine.

Even more, according to one startling formulation of ibn Tabul's, the reason for the existence of elements of Judgment within *Ein-Sof* is that the latter—called *Adam Qadmon* ("Primal Man") in some accounts— transgressed in some fashion.[13] Here we have what appears to constitute a surprisingly anthropomorphic view of *Ein-Sof*, insofar as normally the latter is conceived of as utterly immune from such vicissitudes in kabbalistic thinking. In another passage by ibn Tabul, however, no such reason is known for the presence of severity within *Ein-Sof*: "We are unable to fathom the derivation of these 'Powers' [*Gevurot*] [in *Ein-Sof*]."[14] Whatever its origin, as we shall see below, in many accounts the elimination or *purging* of these impure elements of Judgment from within divinity comes to serve as one of the principle bases for a whole range of cosmogonic events that follow. For were it not for the creation of the world, *Ein-Sof* would have continued to consist of an admixture of good and the roots of evil, a circumstance that "necessitated the mending of the world, to separate the holy from the profane." To put this in starkly gendered terms, a masculine divinity sought to purify itself of the feminine quality of severity, or to put it more precisely, to transform these qualities so as to purify them. Over against this, there are other accounts in which the existence of *Din* within *Ein-Sof* is not apparent.

Tsimtsum: "Withdrawal" of Divinity Away from a Point

Luria imagined the very first gesture on the part of God as an act of *retreat* or *withdrawal*, known in Hebrew as *tsimtsum* (literally, "contraction" or "shrinkage"). Insofar as the entirety of the cosmos was originally filled with the light of divinity, creation required a space within which to become manifest:

> When [*Ein-Sof*] determined to create its world and to issue forth the world of emanated entities, to bring to light the fullness of His energies [literally, "activities"], names, and qualities, this being the reason for the creation of the world, . . . *Ein-Sof* then withdrew itself from its centermost point, at the center of its light, and this light retreated from the center to the sides, and thus there remained a free space, an empty vacuum.[15]

In the words of ibn Tabul, "When the Simple one decided to issue forth the four [spiritual] worlds of 'Emanation' [ʿ*Olam ha-*ʾ*Atsilut*], 'Creation' [*Beri*ʾ*ah*], 'Formation' [*Yetsirah*], and 'Actualization' [*ʿAssiyah*], He withdrew His light, leaving a free space in which He brought forth all the worlds by way of emanation."[16] This primeval space is also called *tehiru,* or "vacuum," in many accounts, a term already found in the *Zohar* (1:15a).[17] The perimeter of the empty space left by the act of *tsimtsum* was circular in shape, and equidistant from the centermost point from which the withdrawal took place: "This withdrawal [of divinity] was perfectly equal on all sides of the central point . . . a circle on all sides, perfectly equidistant . . . the reason for this being that inasmuch as *Ein-Sof* [itself] was perfectly symmetrical, it was also necessary for it to contract itself in a similar manner, rather than do so more on one side than other sides."[18]

While the notion of *tsimtsum* is usually associated with Lurianic myth, in fact, the idea and the term itself have a long history, beginning with rabbinic midrash. According to a passage in *Midrash Tanḥuma* commenting on the construction of the ark of the covenant (Exod. 25:10), God is said to have concentrated His presence in the ark (*metsamtsem sham shekhinato*).[19] As Gershom Scholem observed, the meaning here is actually the reverse of Luria's conception. In the midrash, God concentrates His presence *in* a particular place, whereas in Lurianic myth He retreats *from* a location.[20] In still other midrashic passages, God is said to have concentrated His presence in the Holy of Holies, the inner sanctum of the ancient Sanctuary, where the cherubim (*keruvim*) are located, as if His power were concentrated in a single point.[21] Despite the difference in conception, these rabbinic texts served as the basis for Lurianic passages that describe *tsimtsum* using precisely this language: "He withdrew His presence [*tsimtsum shekhinato*] in the manner described by our rabbis, of blessed memory, [when they said] 'He concentrated His presence between the two bars of the ark,' for prior to this the *Ein-Sof* filled everything."[22]

Luria was by no means the first kabbalist to employ the notion of *tsimtsum*. As Moshe Idel has demonstrated, a range of earlier kabbalists developed this idea in diverse ways.[23] Possibly the earliest attestation of the notion of *tsimtsum* derives from no less important a figure than Nahmanides. In his *Commentary on Sefer Yetsirah*, Nahmanides writes of the contraction of the *kavod* ("glory") resting between the *keruvim*, apparently employing it in a way strikingly similar to Luria, that is, as denoting withdrawal of the *kavod*, rather than its concentration in a certain place.[24] Likewise, a comparable conception may be found in a passage cited from "the writings of the kabbalists" by Shem Tov ibn Shem Tov (fourteenth to fifteenth centuries): "How did He produce and create this world? Like a person who gathers in and contracts [*metsamtsem*] his breath, so that the smaller might contain the larger, so He contracted His light into a handbreadth, according to His own measure, and the world was left in darkness, and in that darkness He carved large boulders and hewed rocks to clear wondrous paths of wisdom."[25]

Shem Tov ben Shem Tov himself developed the notion of withdrawal in connection with the emergence of evil out of the highest realms of divinity, in a manner strongly reminiscent of Luria.[26] We know that Shimon Lavi, author of an important commentary on the *Zohar*, *Ketem Paz*, also conceived of the process of divine emanation as one of withdrawal of divine light (*genizat ha-ʾor*). Lavi wrote his commentary in North Africa in 1571, precisely during the period of Luria's activity in Safed, demonstrating the simultaneous but apparently independent development of this idea in the sixteenth century.[27] Perhaps most important of all, Cordovero, with whom we have seen Luria studied personally, taught the doctrine of *tsimtsum* as well. Cordovero's conception bears a strong resemblance to Luria's, although the notion occupied a far more central role in Luria's thought.[28]

What were the reasons for the *tsimtsum* in Luria's view? Here, as usual, our sources provide more than one answer. According to one principal view, the fact that the cosmos was completely permeated by divine light made the creation of the various worlds impossible. There was simply no room in which something other than divinity could exist. God wished to benefit something other than itself and thus conceived the idea of creating "worlds" by establishing room in which this could take place. Another especially prominent view was that through the process of *tsimtsum,* divinity sought to cleanse itself of the powers of stern Judgment. *Tsimtsum* constituted a cathartic gesture in which *Ein-Sof* purified itself by gathering together and thereby expunging the elements of *Din* within it.[29] This entailed a process of disentanglement insofar as good and "the roots of Judgment" had been thoroughly intertwined. *Ein-Sof*, then, collected all the roots of *Din* in one place so as to leave them behind within the primeval space created through *tsimtsum*. This view, of course, is consistent with the conception of *Din* as female in nature, and as bearing the seeds of impurity, as already noted.

In most accounts, however, the roots of *Din* were not the only elements left behind in the empty space. These forces of Judgment were joined by a residue of the light of Compassion (*Ḥesed* or *Raḥamim*) known as *reshimu*. Just as a vessel from which oil is poured out invariably retains traces of that oil, so too the space left by *tsimtsum* retained a degree of divine light. This *reshimu*, however, is minor compared to the greater quantity of *Din*. Still, the empty space was occupied at its core by a mixture of *Raḥamim* and *Din*, Compassion and Judgment, but in reverse proportions to this admixture prior to *tsimtsum*.

The Process of Divine Emanation into the Empty Space

The powers of stern Judgment that gathered in the empty space as a result of the *tsimtsum*, according to one unusually interesting version of Lurianic myth presented by Vital, became transformed into an unformed mass, or *golem*, that is, a bundle of inchoate matter.[30] What had previously been undifferentiated—subsumed under the influence of a far greater quantity of more pure light—assumed ontological status, an independent and relatively material identity of its own. Out of this unformed mass, "four worlds" developed. These represent the multiple levels of creation, all of which were intended to be purely spiritual in nature.

Following the *tsimtsum*, *Ein-Sof* returned a ray of its light back into the empty space so as to provide this shapeless mass with a degree of divine illumination and thus to animate it. That is, this new light was intended to serve as a medium of organization so as to structure creation through the development of the ten particular lights (*sefirot*) that would suffuse the four worlds. These dynamic processes are described by Vital in the following colorful way:

> When the supernal Emanator decided to create this material cosmos, it withdrew its presence in the manner described by our rabbis, of blessed memory, [when they said] 'He concentrated His presence between the two bars of the ark,' for prior to this the *Ein-Sof* filled everything. Now, it is known that even an inanimate stone is illumined by it; otherwise the stone could not exist at all—it would disintegrate. The illumination of *Ein-Sof* clothes itself in garment upon garment. . . . At the beginning of creation, when the Blessed One withdrew its presence all around in every direction, it left an empty space in the middle, surrounded on all sides by the light of *Ein-Sof*, empty precisely at the centermost point. Had it not done so, the light would have been greater on one side than another, which was not the intention of the

Blessed One, but rather He intended that the empty space would be surrounded equally. The light withdrew like water in a pond displaced by a stone. When a stone is dropped in a pond, the water at that spot does not disappear, but it merges with the rest [of the water]. So the withdrawn light converged beyond . . . and in the middle remained a vacuum. Then all the foulness and density of Judgment within the light of *Ein-Sof*—which had [originally] been like a [mere] drop in the ocean—became measured and was separated [from *Ein-Sof*]. Descending and gathering [itself] into the empty space, it became transformed into an amorphous mass [*golem*] out of the foulness and density of the power of Judgment, as mentioned, surrounded in all directions, above and below, and on all sides, by the light of *Ein-Sof*. Out of this mass emanated the four worlds: Emanation, Creation, Formation, and Actualization. For in its simple desire to realize its intention, the Emanator returned, sending into the mass a small ray of the light withdrawn at the beginning—but not all of the light, because had it all returned, the original state [of the cosmos] would have been restored, but this was not His intention.[31]

According to this particular account, then, the ray of light that God sent back into the empty space served to give shape and dimension to the inchoate mass comprised of the collected forces of Judgment. This is similar to a potter who gives shape and measure to formless clay: "'As clay in the hands of the potter' [Jer. 18:6], so too the supernal Emanator, the Blessed One, put His hand into this inchoate mass, that is, [He issued forth] a ray of light, which returned from above, as I have said."[32]

This returning ray of light is given a number of different names in various versions of the myth, including "ten" (*yud,* the tenth letter of the Hebrew alphabet), "ten fingers," the divine "hand," "line of measure" (*qav ha-middah*), "straight line" (*qav yashar*), "first vessel" (*keli rishon*), and *Adam Qadmon,* the latter testifying most clearly to Luria's proclivity to imagine divinity in thoroughly anthropomorphic terms. All of these expressions unequivocally signify the *masculine* nature of the divine light.

The precise manner in which this light returned is described in several ways in the Lurianic literature, and in immense detail. The most important of these descriptions draws upon the aforementioned anthropomorphic image of a male deity who assumes the shape and features of a human being, a Gnostic-like *macroanthropos* called *Adam Qadmon*. According to one account by ibn Tabul, three primary types of light emanated from various anatomical features of *Adam Qadmon*.[33] Light that was unified or "bound" together (*'or 'aqudim*) emanated from his mouth, atomized light (*'or nequdim*) issued from his navel, and speckled or dappled light (*'or berudim*) flowed from his phallus. This sexualized figure of *Adam Qadmon* is represented as constituting a spiritual world of its own, existing above and beyond the four worlds. Indeed, it is the ultimate source from which the world of Emanation (*Atsilut*) derived, along with the other worlds.

According to Vital's account in which the roots of *Din* are described as assuming the form of a *golem*, in the course of the reentry of light, ten "vessels" (*kelim*) were formed out of the mixture of the residue of light (*reshimu*) and *golem*. The function of these vessels was to contain and conduct the ten different gradations of the reemergent divine light, that is, the ten *sefirot*. These vessels not only contain sefirotic light but should themselves be thought of as being composed of thicker or denser light. The sefirotic light within these vessels, in turn, proceeded to penetrate the four worlds in a continuous dialectical process of descent and reascent. It conducted light into the four worlds, then departed, only to return once again in an ongoing pattern of egression and regression (*ratso ve-shov*), an image self-evidently sexual in nature. The worlds were thus suffused with divinity, animated by the light of the *sefirot* that flowed and ebbed through these ten vessels, like ocean waves that wash upon the shore and then retreat to the source from which they came in the first place. In Lurianic thinking this pattern of ebb and flow is conceived as the paradigmatic way in which divine light functions. As such, it is not a one-time event, but an endless process of divine inhalation and exhalation, replicated at every level of existence.

It should be pointed out that in some accounts, the notion that these ten vessels were hewn out of the very roots of Judgment is more muted. In one such version, for example, the vessels were forged out of the incorporation of the lights of the divine 'Eye' within those of Primordial Man's "Ear," "Nose," and "Mouth," while in another, they were produced from the incorporation of the lights that flow from the right side of the "Mouth" within those that flow from the left side. In these accounts, the vessels are not so much derived from light that is ontologically rooted in Judgment as from light that is called this merely in order to express its relative density compared to purer light.[34] The dominant notion appears to be, though, that the vessels were fashioned out of the dark mass produced as a result of the *tsimtsum*.

Shevirat ha-Kelim: The "Shattering of the Vessels"

The account of cosmogony takes a dramatic turn in Luria's conception of a catastrophic rupture that occurs as the light of *Ein-Sof* fills ten vessels within each of the four worlds. According to one depiction of this rupture, the light that comprised the first of the ten *sefirot*, that is, *Keter*, was exceptionally pure and stable in quality, but it became decreasingly so as it descended into the lower vessels: "As this light [from *Ein-Sof*] began to enter the mass [*golem*], [ten] vessels were formed, from the purest light, [the vessel containing the light of] *Keter*, next, *Ḥokhmah*, then *Binah*, and so on through all ten *sefirot*."[35] The quality of sefirotic light that comprised *Keter* was sufficiently pure to ensure that the vessel in which it was contained remained intact. Linked to *Ein-Sof*, and consisting of the light of all ten of the qualities of divinity, it flowed into its vessel in precisely the proper manner. Not so, however, when it came to the rest of the *sefirot*. The vessels containing the light of *Ḥokhmah* and *Binah* did not shatter, but they did fall somewhat from their proper cosmic position to a lower level.

The vessels containing *Tiferet*, however, which consisted of six aspects, that is, the six *sefirot* from *Tiferet* through *Yesod*, ruptured! Whereas the light of *Keter* constituted a perfect unity, the sefirotic light within these six lower vessels (incorporated in *Tiferet*) constituted separated or atomized "points" (*nequdim*), such that their light was not as stable as that above it. This is often referred to as the "world of *Nequdim*." To put this another way, the lights that flowed through the lower vessels were in some way defective and failed to constitute a whole, perfect configuration (*partsuf*), so that the vessels containing the light of all the *sefirot* below *Binah* shattered:

> It [i.e., the vessel containing the lights within *Tiferet*] did not possess the capacity to bear the light, and [thus] these [vessels] shattered and "died," these being the "kings who ruled in the land of Edom," that is, the aforementioned mass created from the power of Judgment. These seven died, the six [dimensions] of *Ze'ir Anpin* along with [the feminine gradation] *Malkhut*. The light within them, that is, the [divine] vitality, departed [reascending] above to the womb of *Binah*, while the vessels [themselves] shattered and descended to the level of "Creation" [*Beri'ah*].[36]

These shattered vessels, now called *qelippot* ("shells" or "shards"), fell and became the basis for our world of material reality. While most of the sefirotic light that these lower vessels had contained ascended above, returning to its source, some of the light remained trapped, *clinging* to the broken shards. This had the effect of endowing the shards with a degree of continuing vitality and strength. In the archetypal language of Isaac Luria, this imprisoned light consisted of "288 sparks."

The image of the seven kings of Edom in the above passage plays an exceedingly important role in Lurianic teachings. The image derives from Genesis 36:31, "These are the kings who reigned in the land of Edom before any king ruled over the Israelites." In the Idra Rabba of the *Zohar*, the seven kings signify the forces of strict Judgment with which the divine originally sought to initiate the process of emanation. Seeing as how they consisted of Judgment, however, "they could not survive, so that after a time He concealed them. This is [the meaning of] the verse 'And these are the kings who reigned in the land of Edom.' 'In the land of Edom'—in the place where all the Judgments exist."[37] That is, God had to abandon His attempt to create the world using the forces of *Din* alone and turned instead to combining the attributes of *Ḥesed* (Compassion), *Din* (Judgment), and *Raḥamim* (Mercy). The *Zohar* further connects this theme to a well-known midrashic motif according to which the Holy One, blessed be He, "created worlds and destroyed them, before He created these."[38]

Drawing precisely upon such older mythic themes from rabbinic and Zoharic literature, Luria identified the Breaking of the Vessels with these images of stern judgment and wicked kings, that is, flawed worlds that had been created and destroyed. Here, then, we have a principal explanation for this catastrophic cosmic rupture. The effect of the Breaking of the Vessels and the death of the kings of Edom was to conceal or separate the forces of Judgment from some of the pure elements of divinity, for the vessels (though not the sefirotic light within them) were formed out of the roots of Judgment in the first place. As mentioned, their rupture resulted in the reascent of most of the pure light that the vessels had contained.

From one point of view, this may be seen as a reiteration of the process of *tsimtsum*. Just as *tsimtsum* served to purge *Ein-Sof* of the roots of *Din*, so too the *shevirah* had the effect of separating most of the light of divine Compassion from the light of divine Judgment. This catastrophe thus had a fundamentally necessary, even positive dimension to it, partaking of the character of divine mending, *tiqqun*: "*Ein-Sof* had to [accomplish] the mending of the world, to separate the holy from the profane. . . . for the purpose of mending [the world] these original kings had to be destroyed, for they were forces of harsh Judgment."[39] Here is another critical, paradigmatic motif, which we also find elsewhere in Lurianic thinking, namely, that death—in certain contexts and under certain circumstances—serves life-giving purposes.

The paradox, of course, is that the processes of *tsimtsum* and the subsequent emanation of divine light were set in motion in the first place for a reason, namely, to bring forth Creation. But it turned out that these processes were inherently flawed, that the lower vessels lacked the strength with which to conduct the light properly, or that the light itself was defective in some manner, and thus the creative process resulted in unforeseen consequences. The implication, though, is that the roots of *Din* originally had a positive role in the unfolding of the cosmos. Had the vessels been sufficiently strong, or had the light within them been sufficiently stable, the vessels would have performed a crucial role by conducting divine light properly. But the *shevirah* ended all this. What is more, even this shattering did not result in the complete separation of good and evil. On the contrary, it had the effect of endowing the shattered—and now fully materialized—forces of Judgment with the animating strength of holy sparks trapped below by their attachment to the *qelippot*. Here we have one of the quintessential images to emerge from Lurianic mysticism: particles of divine light have *fallen* into the material world, utterly alienated and estranged from their sublime and transcendent origin. These sparks of light instinctively long to be liberated and reunited with the divine source from which they originally flowed.

Notions of a gendered divinity—implied in aspects of the myth discussed thus far—are rendered explicit in certain accounts of the Breaking of the Vessels. According to one such account, the light that emanated from the "crown" (*ʿatarah*) of the *sefirah Yesod* of Primordial Man in the course of the reemergence of divine light did so without having engaged in the process of sexual union (*zivvug*). Crown, in this context, refers to the feminine gradation *Malkhut* or *Shekhinah*, in relationship to the phallic *Yesod*. A standard kabbalistic symbol for *Shekhinah*, the term *ʿatarah* simultaneously represents the corona of the penis, suggesting, as Elliot Wolfson has so elaborately contended, the degree to which the divine feminine is sometimes regarded as an extension of the masculine in theosophical Kabbalah.[40] In this case, the emission of "semen" (*qeri*) from the divine phallus without its containment in the feminine, that is, without proper sexual union, resulted in the *transformation* of these seminal fluids into feminine sexual secretions, which are in the nature of divine Judgment, *Din*. That which was ontologically masculine assumed the character of the feminine in the absence of intradivine intercourse. In this view, then, the divine light permeating the seven lower vessels that shattered, which became trapped in the fractured shards below, was female in quality, "Female Waters" (*mayyin nuqvin*) in Lurianic parlance.[41] From this perspective, *tiqqun*, cosmic healing, entails the purification and liberation of these lower Female Waters so that they can reunite with the "Male Waters" (*mayyin dukhrin*) in the proper manner.[42]

In some of the accounts employing these gendered categories, the fact that the first three vessels did not shatter—while the seven lower ones did—is accordingly explained in unabashedly sexual terms. The vessels containing the sefirotic lights *Keter*, *Ḥokhmah*, and *Binah* were created out of configurations of light within *Adam Qadmon* that were produced as a result of sexual union, enabling them to withstand the flow of light within them. By contrast the seven lower vessels were forged partly by way of light emanating from the "toenails" of *Adam Qadmon*, understood here as equivalent to the ten drops of semen that fell from the biblical Joseph as he resisted the unwanted sexual overtures of Potiphar's wife. That is to say, rather than resulting from proper sexual union, these lights derived from a wasteful emission of semen, divine seed that fell to the ground, "for they derived from the sphere of the masculine, without the feminine."[43] While this remarkably sexualized depiction appears to fly in the face of the above accounts in which it is female light that is responsible for the creation of the inferior vessels, in fact, there is no contradiction. That is because seminal emission that is not channeled properly is paradoxically construed, as we have seen, as feminine in nature and serves as the basis for the forces of strict Judgment from which the lower vessels are forged.[44] As we shall see elsewhere, this notion of male seed that is wasted occupies an absolutely critical place in Luria's thinking. While normally such an event has profoundly negative consequences, as is the case here, in other contexts it actually serves a positive purpose.

The *Partsufim*: Reorganizing the Divine Light

In the wake of the Breaking of the Vessels, divinity sought to mend itself through a complex set of processes known by the term *tiqqun* (mending, healing, restoration). The principal means by which this began to take place was through the emanation yet again of divine light in the form of *Adam Qadmon*, but now reconfigured in altogether new ways. Instead of emanating in the comparatively simple form of ten *sefirot*, divine light now reorganized itself into five major configurations or *partsufim* (literally, "faces" or "countenances"), under which the *sefirot* were subsumed. These five *partsufim* were intended to possess the stability and strength that the earlier manifestations of light lacked.

Out of the "points" of *Keter,* a complete configuration known as *Arikh Anpin* (literally, the "Long-Faced One" or "Forbearing One") was formed. This structural principle was also called by the name *Attiqa Qaddisha* (literally, the "Holy Ancient One"). The *sefirah* Ḥokhmah became transformed into the second *partsuf*, now called *Abba* ("Father"), while *Binah* evolved into the *partsuf* of *Imma* ("Mother"). Out of the six aspects of *Tiferet*, that is, the cluster of *sefirot* from *Tiferet* through *Yesod*, the *partsuf* known as *Ze^cir Anpin* (the "Short-Faced One" or "Impatient One") was constituted. That is, *Ze^cir* comprises a constellation of all of the *sefirot* below *Binah*, with the exception of *Malkhut*. As with *Tiferet* itself, *Ze^cir Anpin* (*Ze^cir*, for short) represents a male structural principle, the "son" of *Abba* and *Imma*. Its masculinity is especially reinforced by the inclusion within it of *Yesod*, an unequivocally phallic quality. The fifth *partsuf* is known as *Nuqba de-Ze^cir* (the "feminine" of *Ze^cir*), corresponding to the *sefirah Malkhut*. *Nuqba de-Ze^cir* (*Nuqba*, for short) stands in romantic and erotic relationship to *Ze^cir Anpin* and is the "daughter" of *Abba* and *Imma*. *Nuqba* Herself has two basic aspects or dimensions, Rachel and Leah. We have here, then, one *partsuf*, *Arikh Anpin*, which, at least theoretically, transcends the category of gender, and two sets of gendered *partsufim*, *Abba* and *Imma*, and *Ze^cir* and *Nuqba*.

To make things more complex, each of the five *partsufim* consists of the full structure of ten *sefirot*, the latter typically imagined as the various anatomical features of the *partsuf;* thus, for example, one can speak of Ḥokhmah of *Arikh Anpin*, or *Yesod* of *Ze^cir Anpin* . Adding to the baroque nature of this conception of the cosmos, each one of the four worlds of Emanation, Creation, Formation, and Actualization consists of an entire set of *partsufim*, along with all their subconfigurations. For instance, one can speak of *Yesod* of *Ze^cir Anpin* in the world of *Atsilut* (Emanation). This illustrates Luria's penchant for exponentially multiplying the elements that comprise the structure of divinity. Significantly, the complete pattern of the divine is recapitulated in every one of its discrete manifestations, like mirrors set up in such a way that they endlessly reflect one another. The cosmos consists of a great chain of being, in which one can discern the whole structure of reality in any particular part of it.

The process by which each of the *partsufim* emanate and establish themselves is described in extreme detail, but the greatest focus is on the development of *Ze'ir Anpin*, depicted primarily in the language of human sexuality and physiological development: loving relations, conception, pregnancy, nursing, and maturation. The birth of *Ze'ir* results from marital union between *Abba* and *Imma*; the relationship between the latter two *partsufim* is typically described as one of perpetual love and union. *Imma* becomes pregnant with her son *Ze'ir*, whom she nurses for a period of two years following birth, a process known as *yeniqah* (literally, "suckling").

Ze'ir matures through the gradual development within it of three elements it receives from *Abba* and *Imma*. These are known as *moḥin* (literally, "intellects" or aspects of "consciousness"): Ḥokhmah, Binah, and Da'at ("mind"). The *moḥin* should be thought of as aspects of divine intellect that serve to produce consciousness. They descend into *Ze'ir* in three distinct stages, corresponding to the three periods of pregnancy, nursing, and weaning. In the stage of *moḥin* of *ibbur* (pregnancy), the *moaḥ* of *Da'at* is absent altogether, while the other two are only latent. During the second stage, known as *moḥin* of *qatnut* (a lesser state of awareness), the *moḥin* exist in a weak state while the *moaḥ* of *Da'at* is still not completely developed. This occurs during the period of nursing. In the final stage, called *moḥin* of *gadlut* (an expanded state of consciousness), all three *moḥin* are present in *Ze'ir* in their mature state, something that takes place after *Ze'ir* is weaned from its mother's breasts.

It should be emphasized that *Ze'ir* receives its nourishment from both *Abba* and *Imma*. The ongoing union of these parental figures, nourished by the light they receive from *Arikh Anpin*, serves as the basis for *Ze'ir*'s development. At first, the *moḥin* descend from *Imma*, followed by those present within *Abba*. Following the complete maturation of *Ze'ir Anpin*, a similar process takes place within *Nuqba de-Ze'ir*.

The emanation from *Adam Qadmon* of all of the *partsufim* following the Breaking of the Vessels facilitated the reascent of most of the divine sparks that had remained attached to the fractured shards. The harmonious and balanced relationships among the *partsufim* made possible the recovery of much of the divine light that had been trapped.

In particular, the continuous love between *Abba* and *Imma* was paralleled by growing intimacy between *Zeᶜir* and *Nuqba de-Zeᶜir*. Both pairs of male and female related to one another "face to face," and the four worlds began to return to their original and proper positions within the cosmos. Divinity was poised to return to a state of spiritual balance and perfection.

Lurianic Anthropology: Adam and Eve

All of the events depicted thus far take place before the creation of Adam and Eve. *Tsimtsum, shevirat ha-kelim,* the reemergence of divine light in the form of the *partsufim* — all of these developments occur completely independently of humanity. In Lurianic thinking, then, the original crisis that occurred within the realm of the divine was not dependent on the misdeeds of humanity but had to do with qualities of being and dynamic processes intrinsic to divinity itself. Human beings, however, exacerbated the crisis and thus have an indispensable role to play in the completion of the work of cosmic mending.

Adam and Eve were born as a result of marital relations between *Zeᶜir* and *Nuqba de-Zeᶜir*, which took place as these two *partsufim* ascended to the chamber of *Abba* and *Imma*.[45] At the time of his creation, Adam was purely spiritual in nature, having no part in the world as we currently know it, that is, the world of *Assiyah*.[46] His spiritual "body" derived from the next to lowest world of *Yetsirah*, his lower soul (*nefesh*) from *Beriᵓah*, his middle soul (*ruaḥ*) from *Nuqba* of the world of *Atsilut*, and a still higher level of soul, *neshamah*, originated in *Zeᶜir Anpin* of the world of *Atsilut*. The *neshamah* of his *neshamah*, a yet superior dimension of soul, came from the sphere of *Abba* and *Imma* of *Atsilut*.

According to one important account, at the time of Adam's birth, on the sixth day of creation, the Holy One, Blessed be He, brought him into the Garden of Eden. When Adam was born, the various structures of divinity had already begun to reestablish themselves. The entirety of the worlds of *Atsilut* and *Beriᵓah*, as well as the first four *sefirot* belonging to *Yetsirah*, had reascended to the same level occupied presently by *Atsilut* alone. The rest of the *sefirot* had also begun to rise from the depths to which they had succumbed following the *shevirah*. This process of mending accelerated as the onset of the Sabbath neared. For example, *Ze'ir Anpin* ascended to the place in which *Arikh Anpin* is found today, whereas *Nuqba de-Ze'ir* ascended to the place where *Abba* is presently located.[47] The world of *Beri'ah* rose to where *Imma* is found today, while the world of *Yetsirah* ascended to the place where *Ze'ir Anpin* is now located. In other words, all the structures of the cosmos had begun to occupy levels of being that were higher than is presently the case.

As for Adam himself, his spiritual position also improved as the Sabbath neared. Whereas when he was born, only the upper part of his body was located in the Garden of Eden (*Gan 'Eden*), now his entire body resided there. Had Adam acted as he should have, the entirety of the divine pleroma would have reached its highest spiritual level at the moment of the afternoon prayers of Sabbath day. None of this came about, however, as a consequence of Adam's transgression: "If *Adam ha-Rishon* [literally, "the first man"] had not transgressed [by eating of] the Tree of Knowledge, he would have been able to raise up all the worlds to still higher levels by means of his contemplative devotion on that [first] Sabbath day. With each and every set of prayers, evening (*'Aravit*), morning (*Shaharit*), additional (*Musaf*), and afternoon (*Minhah*), he would have raised them up higher and higher."[48]

Adam's Sin and Its Aftermath: The Continuing Need for *Tiqqun*

In the wake of Adam's sin, the worlds fell from the positions they had attained.[49] In particular, all ten *sefirot* of the lowest world of *Assiyah*, as well as the four lowest *sefirot* of *Yetsirah* (the "feet" of *Yetsirah*), sank into the realm of the *qelippot*. The feet of *Yetsirah*, which became embedded in the *qelippot,* are alluded to in the verse "And he [Jacob] gathered his feet upon his [death]bed" (Gen. 49:33). In Luria's view, this serves as the basis for the traditional prohibition against traveling beyond a circumscribed area on the Sabbath, known as *teḥum shabbat*. That is, on the Sabbath, an individual must not place his feet—which correspond to the lower four *sefirot* of *Yetsirah*—into the sphere of the *qelippot*, the realm of the profane. As for the lowest world of *Assiyah*, which sank altogether into the sphere of the *qelippot*, it too is inherently a realm of complete holiness; the sphere of the *qelippot* is neither its original place nor one to which it belongs.

Just as the cosmos had come close to its proper condition on the original Sabbath, so every Sabbath in the present represents an opportunity to facilitate the processes of *tiqqun*. On the eve of each Sabbath, the worlds begin to ascend, "level by level, until the afternoon prayers of Sabbath."[50] In replication of the original Sabbath, this process begins to occur from the fifth hour of the day before. By the time of the additional service of Sabbath morning, the worlds achieve the same status they once occupied at the time of Adam's birth, that is, a status significantly below that at the additional service on the original Sabbath. In turn, the highest level to which the worlds can ascend currently—at the Sabbath afternoon prayers—is the level they occupied immediately before the onset of the original Sabbath.

What is more, even this level of ascent requires human action in the form of Sabbath prayer, whereas in the case of the original Sabbath, this took place even before Adam and Eve were born. What originally took place of its own accord cannot take place now without the stimulating effect of human devotional activity. In addition, whereas on the original Sabbath both the "inner" (*penimiyut*) and "external" (*ḥitsoniyut*) aspects of each of the worlds joined in their elevation on high, in the current state of the cosmos only the inner dimension ascends. In sum, while Sabbath devotion provides individuals with the opportunity to assist in *tiqqun*, there are limits to what can be achieved by this means. By contrast, Adam's original opportunity had been infinitely greater. Had he acted properly, the cosmos would have achieved a state of harmonious balance and utter perfection.

The other principal consequence of Adam's transgression was the fall into the *qelippot* of the future souls contained within Adam's own soul. While some souls departed from Adam's prior to his transgression and ascended to the realm of the divine without being implicated in his sin, all other souls eventually fell into the realm of the *qelippot*. There they remain imprisoned, awaiting liberation so as to reunite with the source on high from which they were originally hewn. Thus, two types of divine light became attached to the *qelippot*: that which fell as a result of the catastrophic Breaking of the Vessels, and those soul-sparks of light that did so as a result of Adam's transgression. As Scholem aptly puts it, Adam's sin paralleled and replicated on an anthropological level what had taken place on the theosophical level in the course of *shevirat ha-kelim*.[51] The first man, *Adam ha-Rishon*, was patterned structurally on the primal divine configuration of *Adam Qadmon*. Being a microcosmic embodiment of the divine Anthropos, Adam's devotional actions prior to the original Sabbath would have completed the restorative processes set in motion even before his birth.

In Luria's view, then, the most fundamental and ultimate goal of all human existence is *tiqqun*. The project of *tiqqun*, the liberation of divine light in all of its forms from its entrapment in the material sphere, its return to its source on high, and the ascent of all the worlds to their proper place within the structure of the cosmos, required the most elaborate and painstaking regimen of contemplative devotion. The ritual practices that Isaac Luria taught his disciples were intended to accomplish nothing less than repair of the defects engendered by the primordial processes of divine emanation and by the primal transgression of humankind. Such reparation, as we shall see, was conceived of by Luria and his circle as synonymous with messianic redemption.

Lurianic Myth as Gnostic

As far back as *Major Trends in Jewish Mysticism*, Scholem reflected upon the similarities between Lurianic Kabbalah and ancient forms of Gnostic religion, writing that "the form in which Luria presented his ideas is strongly reminiscent of the Gnostic myths of antiquity. The similarity is, of course, unintentional; the fact is simply that the structure of his thoughts closely resembles that of the Gnostics."[52] Despite the fact that

Scholem had a very strong interest in *Hekhalot* or *Merkavah* mysticism—which he (controversially) characterized as a form of ancient Jewish Gnosticism—and that he vigorously asserted the Gnostic character of much of medieval Kabbalah, he did not pursue the comparison of Lurianism and Gnosticism very far. In the observations that follow I want to suggest some of the general resemblances between certain aspects of Gnostic and Lurianic myth, as well as point to several particular motifs, for the purpose of shedding further light on the nature of Luria's thinking.[53]

A useful point of departure for any discussion of the Gnostic imagination in late antiquity is its essentially dualistic perspective. A dualistic view of existence characterizes most, though not all, Gnostic conceptions of the cosmos, although the nature of this dualism varies widely depending upon the particular brand of Gnostic thinking. In the variety of gnosticism that Hans Jonas long ago categorized as the "Iranian" type, so called insofar as it bears similarities to aspects of Zoroastrian dualism, two fundamental principles of divinity, light and darkness, good and evil, coexist *ab aeterno*, from the beginning of time, and are radically pitted against each other.[54] These two principles of divine being are irreducible opposites, having nothing in common: Light is entirely good while Darkness is entirely evil. In the course of time, however, Light and Darkness become entangled, initiating a stage of history in which the two powers clash for ultimate control of the cosmos. One of the most important representatives of this type of myth was a heretical Christian form of Gnostic belief, Manicheanism, named for Mani, a third-century figure who lived in Mesopotamia, whose eclectic doctrines had profound and widespread influence well into the Middle Ages.

In another variety of gnosticism, which Jonas labels the "Syrian-Egyptian type," there is a single primordial divine root or principle, the "Unknown God," *out of which* a second, inferior, even dark cosmic potency gradually emanates. This latter potency, at least originally, is not an absolutely independent principle as much as it is, as Jonas puts it, "a darkened level of being," or "a degraded element of divinity." While the Source of all being is transcendent, concealed and benevolent, unconnected with the creation of the world, the derivative potency occupies a central role in bringing the world into existence and is ultimately the cause of the origin of evil. The majority of Gnostic texts from late antiquity, of which Valentinian Gnosis is the finest example, conform more or less to this second pattern of a more moderate dualism. The characteristic such texts share is the notion of a downward, emanative movement in which the transcendent godhead volitionally separates itself from this "darkened level of being."

Volitional though it may be, this separation is typically conceived of as being in the nature of a breach, a fissure precipitated by a crisis that occurs within the godhead. The consequence of this crisis is the coming into being of the world as we know it, as well as of the powers that hold it in subjection. Such dualism often entails an anticosmic attitude, that is, a deprecation of the world of matter to one degree or another. Exactly what such deprecation translates into in any particular Gnostic culture, however, can vary widely and must be examined carefully.[55] Broadly speaking, though, in contrast to the general tendency of Platonic and Plotinian dualisms, certain expressions of Gnostic dualism regard the material world as tainted, having been brought into existence through the agency of an evil demiurge, or at least being the product of negative forces. One of the results of such a view is the conviction that evil and flaw are intrinsic to the world of matter, which stands in stark contrast to the transcendent deity that exists above and beyond the created world, immune from its travails.

This dualistic *mentalité* typical of much Gnostic thought extends as well to the question of humanity. As with the rest of the material world, the body is akin to a prison in which the soul is trapped. By contrast, the soul is a spark of light, a particle from on high that has fallen below and forgotten her identity, has "forgotten her original habitation, her true center, her eternal being." In the world of its body, the soul becomes enamored of sensual passions, vanity, forgetfulness, sleep, and ignorance, aware neither of itself or its supernal origin: "They [i.e., the evil forces] mixed me drink with their cunning and gave me to taste of their meat. I forgot that I was a king's son, and served their king. I forgot the Pearl for which my parents had sent me. Through the heaviness of their [i.e., the evil forces'] nourishment I sank into deep slumber."[56] It is too simple, however, to regard Gnostic attitudes toward the body in entirely negative terms, insofar as traces of divinity can be discerned even in the body.

The general similarities between these conceptions—especially as they appear in what I have called the more moderate form of Gnostic dualism—and Lurianic myth are clearly apparent. In Lurianic thinking, as well, a single godhead is composed of elements of both good and (the potential for) evil, light and darkness, although the latter principle is included in and subordinate to the former. Darkness, or *Din*, is separated from the principle of light, initially through the divine voluntary act of *tsimtsum*, but ultimately through the intradivine crisis of *shevirat ha-kelim*. And as in many forms of Gnostic myth, the material world that ultimately results from this catastrophic breach is imagined, to a certain degree at least, as dark and polluted, dominated by the realm of the *qelippot*. The latter imprison the souls and sparks of light seeking liberation from their fettered state. In Luria's case, though, the Gnostic tendency to deprecate the natural world and the human body is somewhat tempered, at least partly as a result of the traditional penchant in Judaism for regarding both world and body in fundamentally positive ways. In any event, the extent to which Lurianic Kabbalah may or may not have entailed antagonism to the world has to be determined on the basis of evidence about actual behavior, or at least, expectations for behavior.

Beyond these general resemblances, suggestive as they may be, we find certain strikingly similar details, especially in the writings of Basilides, an important second-century Gnostic figure who was the leader of a school in Alexandria. As Scholem has already pointed out, we find in Basilides a notion rather similar to that of Lurianic *tsimtsum*. In the *Book of the Great Logos,* Basilides writes of an act of divine retreat in which God "withdrew Himself into Himself," prior to emanation.[57] Moreover, in language reminiscent of Luria's notion of *tehiru*, or empty space, this divine withdrawal resulted in a "blessed space, which can neither be conceived of, nor characterized by any word, yet is not entirely deserted from the Sonship."[58] And in a way that is remarkably similar to Luria's conception of the *reshimu*, the traces of divine residue left behind in the empty space, Basilides spoke of the blessed space as a bowl that, while empty, retains the fragrance of a "sweetest smelling unguent."[59]

The conception of broken vessels may also be found in at least one highly important Gnostic text, the *Gospel of Truth*, believed to have been written around the year 150 by Valentinus, perhaps the foremost Gnostic thinker of late antiquity.[60] Yehuda Liebes has suggested that echoes of such a Gnostic idea may also be found in Augustine's *Confessions* (1.3), in which he polemicizes against Gnostic beliefs.[61] Augustine speculates upon whether the "vessels" of heaven and earth can actually contain God, following which he avers that God stabilizes these vessels by suffusing them with His presence, and that He would not pour out of them even in the event that the vessels themselves were to shatter. Liebes infers from this that Augustine was familiar with a Gnostic myth having to do with shattered vessels; indeed, we know that Augustine had himself flirted with Gnostic thinking for a number of years and had been a follower of Manicheanism at one point during his life. In addition, in a passage from *Pseudo-Clementines*, we also find an Orphic motif that parallels the conception of the *shevirat ha-kelim*.[62] Independent of the specific imagery of broken vessels, however, we find in many Gnostic texts the image of supernal "Life" and "Light" that has fallen or sunk into the world of material reality and into the body.

While I have characterized this second type of Gnostic myth as a more moderate form of dualism, insofar as light and darkness are not originally pitted against each other in unmitigated opposition, by the same token it may be said to be a more radical theological position. From the point of view of the problem of theodicy, it is far easier to comprehend how an evil world is a consequence of an evil demiurge or creator. To be sure, this is one of the considerable attractions of such a myth. It is vastly more challenging to come to grips with the notion that the origin of evil is somehow located within the very bosom of a single divinity. Speaking of Valentinian Gnosis, Hans Jonas put it this way:

> The distinguishing principle of the type is the attempt to place the origin of darkness, and thereby of the dualistic rift of being, *within* the godhead itself, and thus to develop the divine tragedy, the necessity

of salvation arising from it, and the dynamics of this salvation itself, as wholly a sequence of inner-divine events. Radically understood, this principle involves the task of deriving not only such spiritual facts as passion, ignorance, and evil but the very nature of *matter* in its contrariety to the spirit from the prime spiritual source; its very existence is to be accounted for in terms of the divine history itself.[63]

Something quite similar may be said for Lurianic myth. Its radical nature consists significantly in the potentially subversive proposition, not merely that many entities proceed from the One, but that the world as we know it is a product of flaw and error, that "the world came about through a mistake." Though eventually abetted by human transgression, the deeply flawed character of the material world is a result of developments that occur within the life of God, surely a point of view wholly incompatible with the dominant rabbinic perception of creation as harmonious and beautiful.

By drawing attention to similarities between certain ancient Gnostic and Lurianic motifs, I do not intend to suggest that Luria's myth developed as a direct result of these influences. The question of the relationship between Gnostic sources and the presence of Gnostic-type features in kabbalistic literature is among the most thorny and controversial in all of kabbalistic scholarship.[64] It is certainly plausible, however, that certain ancient Gnostic elements entered Lurianic thinking by way of various intermediate medieval sources, especially and including the *Zohar*.[65]

Aside from this, as the exposition of Luria's myth presented above makes clear, there are a number of highly significant ways in which his teachings were directly and indirectly rooted in rabbinic motifs of a mythic nature, not to mention the influence of kabbalistic sources, such as those mentioned above in connection with the conception of *tsimtsum*. It is thus clear enough that Luria drew upon an eclectic array of sources. Having said this, it is exceedingly important to emphasize the fact that Luria (and certain of his more creative disciples) fashioned from these older sources a complex set of teachings that were fresh and distinctive, marked by an original and bold imagination.

Five Physician of the Soul

> Each [Christian] has the duty to know who he is . . . to acknowledge
> faults, to recognize temptations, to locate desires, and everyone is obliged
> to disclose these things either to God or to others in the community and
> hence to bear public or private witness against oneself. The truth obliga-
> tions of faith and the self are linked together. This link permits a purifi-
> cation of the soul impossible without self-knowledge. . . . [According to]
> the medical model: One must show one's wounds in order to be cured.
>
> —Michel Foucault, "Technologies of the Self"

> Whatever we imagine when we speak of Gnostics renouncing their
> bodies, or despising the flesh, we should not ignore how intrigued
> they seemed [*sic*] to have been with their own anatomy, how often they
> seemed convinced that truths, both pleasant and unpleasant, about their
> origin and their destiny could be traced within its form and functions.
>
> —Michael A. Williams, "Divine Image—Prison of Flesh:
> Perceptions of the Body in Ancient Gnosticism," in *Fragments for a
> History of the Human Body*, ed. Michel Feher et al., vol. 1

Techniques of Diagnosis

Among the most significant roles Isaac Luria played in the lives of his
disciples was that of physician of the soul. Before they could practice
rituals intended to enable them to bind their souls to the divine realm
and to repair that realm in accordance with the teachings of Lurianic
mythology, his disciples had first to mend their own souls, to cleanse
and purify them of all imperfections. No one whose own soul had failed
to achieve a certain level of perfection could hope to engage successfully
in the intricate and elaborate contemplative rituals Luria devised. A person had to cultivate certain spiritual and moral traits and atone for whatever sins he might have committed. Luria, in fact, provided his followers with highly detailed rituals of atonement by which they were to
mend their souls. These penitential acts were known as *tiqqunei ʿavonot*

150

("amends of sin"), whose purpose, in the words of Hayyim Vital's son Shmuel, was to "mend his soul" and "cleanse him from the filth of the disease of his sins."[1]

Lurianic teaching held that each person was in a position analogous to Adam's. Just as Adam had transgressed and was in need of *tiqqun*, so too were all individuals. Indeed, every sin committed by a person constituted a reiteration of Adam's sin and further deepened the entanglement of that person in the realm of materiality. In his introduction to the *tiqqunei ʿavonot,* Hayyim Vital discusses the relationship between one's soul and sin. The following passage provides an exceptionally lucid account of the Lurianic theory of sin, and the effectiveness of genuine repentance:

> Man is created from matter and from form, [the latter] consisting of soul [*nefesh*], spirit [*ruaḥ*], and super-soul [*neshamah*], the divine portion from above, as it is said: "and [God] breathed into his nostrils the breath (*nishmat*) of life" [Gen. 2:7]. And his body is dark matter from the side of the shell (*qelippah*), luring and preventing man from [achieving] perfection of his soul [in order] to cut it off from the Tree of Life. . . . and so "there is not a righteous man upon the earth that doeth good and sinneth not" [Eccles. 7:20]. It is known that sin is a blemish, stain, and rust in the soul, and that it is the sickness of the pure soul. When it [is immersed] in filth and stain, it is unable to perceive and achieve the true perfection, which is [attainment of] the mysteries of the Torah. . . . And the transgression becomes a barrier separating the soul from her Creator, preventing her from perceiving and comprehending holy and pure supernal matters, as it is said: "The law of the Lord is perfect, restoring the soul" [Ps. 19:8]. When the soul is pure and unblemished, then the supernal holy matters take shape in her, and when she dwells in rust and stain, everything becomes bittersweet, [i.e., evil appears as good]. [This is] similar to the sick person who, when he is ill, abhors the good things and loves things that aggravate his illness. The doctor, in order to restore his health, gives him spices, including gall, by which his nature will return to what it originally was, and his health as before. So, too, the sick soul, to remove the sickness from her, must receive the bitterness of medicine and "return" from filth and the stains of sin [by way of]

mortification and fasts, sackcloth, ashes and stripes, ritual immersions, and purifications. [This is] in order to be able to attain and comprehend supernal matters, which are the [hidden] mysteries of the world.[2]

The conceptions expressed in this passage may appear surprising. The notion that the "body is dark matter from the side of the shell" has the ring of a theology of original sin, something that the rabbis of the talmudic period did not actually teach. Rabbinic Judaism does teach that every individual is susceptible to the temptations of an "evil inclination," or *yetser ha-ra*ᶜ. This inclination is sometimes seen as an inherent force within an individual, and sometimes personified as an external power, along the lines of a demonic spirit whose business it is to lure people into sin. In either case, the *yetser ha-ra*ᶜ is an impulse that can be controlled, not an ontological taint inescapably inscribed on every individual at birth. The passage quoted above, though, comes much closer in tone to a theory of original sin. It is couched not simply in moral terms but in the language of pollution and purification, of defilement and cleansing. The polluted nature of the human body follows from the mythic notions discussed in the previous chapter concerning the tainted nature of the material world at large. Such pollution frustrates the human ambition to gain access to the sacred, in this case defined in general terms as contact with the soul's creator and comprehension of the concealed mysteries of the world. We also learn here the means by which the consequences of sinfulness and pollution can be reversed, that is, by rites of atonement and purification. Only the weapons of ascetic piety are potent enough to cleanse the soul of the stain that clings to it. Luria himself, proclaims Vital, is the diagnostician and healer of diseased souls! This healing and purification was critically important insofar as Luria only revealed his esoteric knowledge to those disciples who were completely pure and worthy. To this end he prescribed penances for various sins:

> He would not reveal any of the mysteries of this holy knowledge to one in whose soul he perceived, with the aid of the Holy Spirit, a blemish—until he gave him penitential acts to straighten out all he did crookedly. And like the expert doctor who prescribes for each sick

person the proper medicine to cure this illness, so too [Isaac Luria], may he rest in peace, used to recognize the sin, tell him where he had incurred a blemish, and prescribe for him the penitential act needed for this transgression in order to cleanse his soul, so that he could receive the divine light, as it is written, "O Jerusalem, wash thy heart from wickedness, that thou mayest be saved" [Jer. 4:14].[3]

Luria's role as a physician of the soul was explicitly corroborated several years after his death by Eleazar Azikri, who tells us that "when the Holy Spirit descended upon him, he helped many to repent, for he informed them about the extent to which each transgression causes injury . . . and he instructed the enlightened [*maskilim*, i.e., kabbalists] in the remedies [*tiqqunim*] that they must perform for the sake of their souls."[4]

Isaac Luria did what any good physician would do; he carefully diagnosed the specific sickness that his "patient" had and prescribed the appropriate cure. Before turning to these purification rites themselves, I want first to consider in some detail the diagnostic role that Luria played. Among the several diagnostic techniques that he had at his disposal, the one about which we have the greatest amount of information, and presumably the most important, was his capacity to discern and interpret the meaning of Hebrew letters visible upon an individual's forehead. This technique constituted a variation on the medieval practice known as metoposcopy.

Metoposcopy was one of the wide array of divinatory or mantic arts aimed at discovering the personal significance of events, past, present, or future, by "reading" or interpreting signs from nature or from phenomena devised by human beings. The Latin noun *divinatio* derives from the verb *divinare*, meaning "to predict," although divination is not restricted to foretelling the future. It encompasses a broader category of discovering hidden truth or grasping the meaning of things by some sort of unusual or extrasensory perception. Thus, as with certain other forms of divination, such as chiromancy (palmistry), oneiromancy (the interpretation of dreams), necromancy (consulting the dead), geomancy (divination from stones or geographic features), and physiognomy (reading the form and shape of facial and other features), metoposcopy was employed for purposes of judging an individual's character and personality and not merely for predicting one's future. As Jewish sources themselves attest, a variation of this art was already known in late antiquity, although it flourished especially in the late Middle Ages and the Renaissance. In the sixteenth and seventeenth centuries, the publication of metoposcopic works proliferated.

Like chiromancy, or palm reading, metoposcopy was primarily concerned with the significance of lines, in this case, on the forehead, and was typically associated with astrological notions.[5] In Isaac Luria's case, however, metoposcopy was practiced by discerning the meaning, not of the *lines* on the forehead but of Hebrew letters. Earlier we learned that Luria "could also recognize the letters on the forehead and [was adept] at the science of physiognomy, as well as at [recognizing] the lights that are upon the skin and body of an individual." Here we have a particularly fascinating example of how a general occult technique was practiced within a kabbalistic framework.

The theoretical basis for the recognition of letters upon the forehead has to do with a set of kabbalistic beliefs concerning the relationship between language and creation as a whole. These beliefs go back, in part, to the first systematic attempt at speculative thought in Hebrew, *Sefer Yetsirah* (Book of Creation), written perhaps sometime between the third and sixth centuries.[6] According to the opening chapter of this brief and highly enigmatic book, God brought all of creation into existence "by means of thirty-two wondrous paths of wisdom." These thirty-two paths comprise "ten *sefirot belimah*," the ten fundamental numbers, and the twenty-two letters of the Hebrew alphabet. The bulk of the book's speculative efforts concern the function and role of these letters in the cosmogonic process. Everything that exists came into being through combinations of the alphabet's letters, particularly by means of two hundred and thirty-one "gates," combinations of the letters into sets of two, in which every letter of the alphabet is joined to every other. All existence is invested with these different combinations of letters and nourished by their power.

When, centuries later, medieval kabbalists appropriated the ideas of *Sefer Yetsira,* this linguistically founded world was understood as an expression of divine self-disclosure or emanation. Whereas on its own terms *Sefer Yetsirah* regards the Hebrew letters and their combinations as *instruments* by which the Creator wrought creation, the kabbalists conceived of them as not only instruments but also forms assumed by the divine itself. Thus, not only can the revelation of God be described in terms of the ten *sefirot,* the most familiar and typical symbolic system of the kabbalists, but it can be imagined as well as the ever-unfolding word of God, which expresses itself in a virtually infinite variety of combinations and gradations. In this symbolism, the Torah is understood to comprise a vast network of "names," each of which signifies a particular concentration of divine power or energy. As such, these names possess a plenitude of meaning, not exhausted by conventional human language.

Nowhere is the divine/linguistic constitution of all creation more evident than in the case of human beings themselves. According to Hayyim Vital, the twenty-two letters of the alphabet are present in *each* of the three primary aspects of the human soul, in ascending hierarchical order, *nefesh, ruah,* and *neshamah.*[7] Each grade of soul is constructed, so to speak, on the basis of the letters of the Hebrew alphabet. The quality of each set of letters is somewhat different in accordance with the different levels of the soul's tripartite division. The letters present in the *nefesh* are small, those of the *ruah* are medium in size, and those of the *neshamah* are largest of all. These three dimensions of the soul clothe one another, as it were, with the body's skin constituting the outer covering of all. The skin is tantamount to the husk or shell of materiality, the *qelippah,* which surrounds all the lights of holiness in the world. The lights, or letters of the various parts of the soul, on the other hand, are manifestations of divinity itself, inasmuch as the constituent elements of the soul are identical with God.

Now, in the case of a sinful individual, the lights/letters of the soul remain covered and concealed by the skin. But when one perfects oneself by practicing the commandments and studying the Torah, that person gradually purifies the various parts of the soul, thus enabling the power and light of the letters within each part to come to the surface. The letters are unveiled and manifest themselves in a way visible to the skilled eye. The appearance of the letters on the skin allows one who can recognize them and determine their meaning virtually to see the divine part of the human personality, the soul itself. One "sees" the soul in the sense that the letters are a faintly material expression of something that is essentially immaterial. In the case of one who has sufficiently mended all three grades of soul, the entire alphabet belonging to *each* grade of soul at one time or another appears on the skin, most especially upon the forehead.[8] According to Vital, the forehead discloses the soul's letters best of all, in part because the letters of the alphabet as a whole correspond to the *sefirah Binah*, which, in turn, is symbolized by the forehead.[9]

The particular letters that appear on a person's forehead depend upon the commandments that individual performs properly, for there is a letter to correspond to each and every precept (although we are informed about only a few of the details of this correspondence). One who performs all the commandments on a regular basis, and in whom there is no sin, will thus bear all the letters upon the forehead. Certain letters, however, will appear more brightly at some times than at others, under various conditions. When one performs particular mitsvot, the corresponding letters shine especially brightly on that same day. Sometimes a certain word—such as the word *ḥayyim* (signaling that a person can expect to continue in life)—will appear briefly and then disappear. One skilled in this art, then, must be careful to gaze at the right time upon an individual's forehead. An exception is the deed of charity (*tsedaqah*), whose letters remain shining brightly upon a person's forehead for an entire week. This is supported by the scriptural text "And his righteousness [*tsidqato*] endureth forever" (Ps. 111:3).

The *level* of soul-purification that one has achieved is also discernible on the basis of the letters that appear. For example, if a person has only perfected the level of *nefesh,* the letters will be small, and so on. If an individual manifests only one set of letters, having attained only the level of *nefesh,* and more than one letter of a particular letter is required to spell out a word on his forehead, it will initially appear brightly in one place in the word, and reappear a second or third time as needed. The letters of the alphabet also possess a sefirotic correspondence. That is, it is possible to identify different letters with each of the ten *sefirot*. By virtue of this, one can figure out the sefirotic root of a person's soul, for the appropriate letters will appear more frequently than the others.[10]

The recitation of the 100 *berakhot* (blessings) required daily of everyone also induces the appearance of letters.[11] For just as the 613 mitsvot as a whole have their corresponding letters, so too do the *berakhot* that one recites, such as in the course of daily prayer. The lights of the letters that appear on the skin as a result of reciting *berakhot* are special insofar as there is light *surrounding* each letter; this surrounding light is more luminescent than that of the letter itself. If one sees that the opposite is the case, that the light of the letter is more intense than the surrounding light, it signals that the blessing was not performed properly. Moreover, if one fails to perform certain *berakhot* altogether, their corresponding letters do not appear at all. If a *berakhah* is recited with a mistake, then the letter will appear, but will be incomplete or imperfectly formed. And if it is performed correctly, but without appropriate contemplative intention, the letter will be present, but will be dark and unillumined.

If the appearance of letters signifies virtuous behavior, then their *absence* indicates sinfulness, whether of commission or omission. A person who is responsible for some transgression will be lacking in the corresponding letters, which will thereby fail to display themselves on his forehead. In the worst case, someone upon whose forehead *no* letters are detected can expect to meet with death within thirty days, unless he performs acts of exceptional restitution and repentance.[12]

There are other indications of the presence of sinfulness, or that something tragic has befallen the individual involved. Sometimes a particular letter will appear broken in the middle. In the case of the letter *bet*, for example, this indicates that one's son has died. At other times, letters may appear upside down or lying on their side. There is one letter, for example, that, if it appears abnormally, indicates that a man has had intercourse with his wife in an improper manner. In this connection, Vital relates the following anecdote. The wife of a certain individual had demanded of her husband that he engage in intercourse, which he did not want to do, since it happened to be a weekday rather

Figure 4. The mikvah, or ritual bath, known today as the
mikvah of Isaac Luria. Courtesy Aaron Fine, photographer.

than a Sabbath, the preferred time for marital love. Luria informed
Vital that he had recognized the letter *gimel* on the man's forehead
but it appeared upside down. The *gimel*, Luria said, symbolizes the
sefirah Yesod, associated with male procreative vitality, human and divine. Insofar as the man involved did not intend to stimulate *Yesod* by
having sexual relations at what he considered to be an improper time,
the *gimel* appeared in this unusual manner. Luria indicated that such
an act should not be considered a transgression, despite the fact that
it occurred on a weekday. Were it a sin, the letter would still have been

turned upside down but would not have shone brightly as it did. In general, when a letter manifests itself upside down, it signifies that the realm of the feminine is somehow involved. For this reason, the letters on the forehead of a male whose soul-ancestry (*gilgul*) derives from the feminine side of the divine structure will consistently appear upside down.[13]

If a person experiences an involuntary nocturnal seminal emission (*tumat qeri*), the evidence of his defilement will appear on his forehead the following day. If he seeks to cleanse himself of this impurity through ritual immersion in water (*tevilah*), then the evidence will remain during the day but will be only faintly visible. However, if he does not undergo ritual immersion, the sin will be discernible until he does so.[14]

The transgressions of a person who—by virtue of other positive deeds—merits the "extra" soul (*neshamah yeterah*) that people can acquire on the Sabbath will not be visible upon the forehead during the course of the Sabbath itself. The very presence of the additional Sabbath soul can be determined by gazing upon the forehead. For as soon as one performs the ritual immersion required as preparation for the Sabbath, the extra soul manifests itself, the evidence for which is found upon one's forehead. Scholars were the beneficiaries of an unusual prerogative in this connection. If one were a great scholar, particularly a student of Kabbalah (*ḥokhmat ha-ʾemet*), study had the effect of covering over any minor sins, which would not be visible upon the forehead. Significant sins would, however, be visible, scholarly merit notwithstanding.[15]

Vital reports that there were limitations to his master's abilities to diagnose the status of the soul on the basis of metoposcopy. At times, he had to resort to more direct communication with an individual's soul:

He possessed another kind of skill; he could call forth the *nefesh, ruaḥ,* or *neshamah* of an individual, and speak with it [directly]. He would inquire of it and ask it questions, and it would answer whatever it was he desired to know, even including matters of detail. He told me that there are some things that he was unable to discern when he gazed upon the letters of the forehead, their being too subtle and concealed. However, when he inquired and searched out a person's soul [directly], then he was able to learn things with great accuracy and clarity.[16]

While the forehead was the most common place for the materialization of the soul's letters, they could appear on any part of the body. "Know that in each and every organ of a person's body there are letters engraved, informing us about that individual's actions. But the primary place is the forehead, as indicated earlier."[17] In addition, other parts of the body have special features that are instructive with respect to an individual's conduct and character, especially the eyes, fingernails, and all types of bodily hair. In the case of hair, for example, its color, length, and type, and the way it lies, are all clues to a person's status, although we are provided no details about this more general physiognomic approach.

In addition to that cited above, there are a substantial number of anecdotal reports concerning Luria's practice of the art of metoposcopy.[18] Such evidence leads one to the conclusion that Luria actually engaged in this activity, and that it was not merely a matter of theoretical discussion. Reports by Moses Galante, Elijah de Vidas, and Eleazar Azikri were mentioned earlier in connection with this. Galante writes that he had personally seen sages who had the ability to practice the art of "determining [the letters on] the countenance." Similarly, according to de Vidas,

> [O]ur sages taught: "On seeing the sages of Israel one should say, 'Blessed be He who hath imparted of His wisdom to them that fear Him'" [BT *Berakhot* 58a]. In Safed, located in the upper Galilee, there have already appeared sages for whom it was appropriate to recite this blessing. They were capable of practicing the art of physiognomy [*ḥokhmat ha-partsuf*] and were able to inform a man concerning all that he had done—whether it was good or evil. To be sure, these individuals did not merit this wonderful wisdom (which is akin to possessing the Holy Spirit) except on account of their virtuous deeds and saintly behavior.[19]

There can be little doubt that both Galante and de Vidas had Luria in mind, although it is interesting to note that each of them implies that there were others with this skill. Indeed, we noted earlier that Joseph ibn Tabul was described by his disciple Samson Bacchi as a person with the power to discern the sins that individuals had committed and to determine who was worthy of receiving his teaching. Azikri preserved a story bearing upon Luria's practice of metoposcopy, according to which Luria once gazed upon the face of a certain sage and told him that "the transgression of cruelty toward animals is inscribed upon your countenance." The distressed man returned home to discover that his wife had failed to feed their chickens and had left them to wander in the street. After making sure that his wife had taken steps to care properly for the birds, he went back to Luria. Without knowing what had taken place, Luria informed him, upon looking into his face, that the transgression had been expiated. The sage then proceeded to tell Luria what had transpired. Vital reports an incident in which Luria gazed upon the forehead of a certain sage and informed him that in the course of his entire life this man had never recited a certain prayer correctly.[20]

Elsewhere, we learn in more general terms that Luria

> used to recognize upon the forehead of a person the virtuous deeds and the sins that he had committed or had contemplated committing. He knew the gravity of the injury brought about by each transgression, where [on high] the harm had its impact, and the nature of the harm. He [also] knew the restitution that was required [for its repair], in terms of fasts, contemplation, and the recitation of scriptural verses. He would provide each and every individual with the means of atonement in accordance with the sin he had committed.[21]

Vital also preserved several anecdotes in which he himself was involved. On one occasion, he writes, Luria identified the letters *alef*, *bet*, and *gimel* on his forehead. This demonstrated, according to Luria, that Vital needed to show compassion toward his father.[22] In a different version of this tradition, we learn that the letters *alef* and *bet*, spelling out the word *ʾav* (father), were written in normal fashion, while the *gimel* was upside down.[23]

In *Sefer ha-Ḥezyonot*, Vital describes an incident according to which Luria is reported, on a Sabbath eve, to have seen on Vital's forehead the words, "Prepare a throne for Hezekiah, king of Judah."[24] This revealed that he was invested with the soul of King Hezekiah as his "extra" Sabbath soul, says Vital. Sometime during that Sabbath day, Vital became angry while in his house, by reason of which Hezekiah's soul departed. The following week Vital repented for having been angry, whereupon, on the next Sabbath eve, Luria recognized the spirits of both Hezekiah and Rabbi Akiva upon Vital's forehead. Again, however, Vital had a bout of anger, causing these spirits to leave him. After Vital had wept and repented once again for the sin of anger, Luria informed him that the spirit of Ben Azzai had invested itself in him, despite the fact that Ben Azzai and Vital did not share the same soul-ancestry. Ben Azzai was, however, Akiva's son-in-law. In this story, then, Luria was able to determine the coming and going of Vital's visiting souls by gazing on his forehead. In this series of incidents, Luria is said to have determined not the deeds for which Vital was responsible but the effect those deeds had upon his spiritual state.

In another diary entry, Vital relates a story with a similar theme.[25] Luria was able to explain the meaning of a dream that Vital had by reference to the name of Rami bar Hami, which he had seen on Vital's forehead the evening before. The conclusion Luria reached was that Vital was invested with the soul of this Babylonian sage. Elsewhere, Vital preserves yet another story according to which he spoke the name of *Samael* (i.e., Satan) while conversing with someone at night. The following morning Luria looked upon his face and told him that he had violated the prohibition against uttering the names of other gods. "He strictly warned me that under no circumstances, neither during the day nor the night, should I utter *Samael*'s name," Vital writes. To do otherwise could have injurious consequences, causing one to fall prey to sin or to be punished.[26]

The common feature in these anecdotes is Isaac Luria's role in bringing to Vital's attention a sin he had committed, either by explicitly informing him of what he had done wrong or, as in the case of the Hezekiah story, by determining whether the souls with whom he had been invested had deserted him. These reports, along with those described earlier, suggest that Luria did not use this technique for purposes of predicting the future. Rather, he practiced the art of metoposcopy in order to determine the status of a person's spiritual condition on the basis of his actions.

While it is quite obvious that we cannot know whether the incidents reported here occurred as described, what these stories do tell us is that Luria's practice of this art was sufficiently commonplace for it to be mentioned as a matter of fact. In Vital's case, the motivation in narrating these incidents does not appear to have been to impress the reader with Luria's skill as much as to inform him about Vital himself. Generations later, various legendary traditions would preserve the memory of Luria's divinatory skill. We learn, for example, that Abraham Galante, best known as a disciple of Moses Cordovero, beseeched Isaac Luria to repair Galante's soul and asked him to "tell me all that you perceive upon my forehead."[27]

Before turning from this subject, it is interesting to note that Luria is reported to have utilized this skill for a purpose other than determining a person's moral status, although even here the soul's perfection was at issue. Vital wrote that every single evening his master would gaze upon the faces of his disciples. He would see a scriptural verse shining upon the forehead. The visualized verse was one that pertained to that particular student's soul, in accordance with the Lurianic notion that every soul possesses interpretations of Scripture that are unique to it. Luria would then partially explain the esoteric meaning of the verse in terms of the significance that it held for that individual's spiritual condition. The disciple was then instructed to concentrate upon the explanation he had been given and to recite the verse before going to sleep. He did this so that when his soul ascended to the upper realm during sleep, he might gain full knowledge of the verse's meaning. In this way, the individual's soul would increase in purity and ascend to still higher levels in the divine realm, where it would enjoy the revelation of additional mysteries of the Torah.[28]

Elsewhere, Vital described this activity in a somewhat different way. Luria would gaze upon the forehead of each student after sunset and determine what *kind* of text his soul would study that night when it ascended on high, be it some rabbinic work, such as the Mishnah, or an esoteric one, such as the *Zohar*. Here, too, he instructed the disciple to recite this text before falling asleep.[29]

Aside from the formal theories associated with this divinatory skill on Luria's part, as well as the formal (facial) signs he relied upon for interpretive purposes, we presume this practice attests to his intimate, personal relationship with his circle of disciples and his finely honed intuitive capacities. Patrizia Magli puts it aptly in speaking of the art of physiognomy more generally:

> Physiognomic perception is a form of daily knowledge, a treasure belonging to all of us. It is based on subtleties which are hard to formalize, at times even untranslatable into words. The face of those near us presents itself as the space upon which it is possible to perceive infinitesimal traces which, in turn, sometimes allow us to glean a deeper reality, one hidden to most eyes. It is part of the local knowledge of which Carlo Ginsburg spoke. . . . The form of knowledge involved in understanding physiognomics is the result of concrete needs.[30]

A rather different type of diagnostic technique that Luria is reported to have practiced was feeling the pulse. Just as a physician who treats the body utilizes the pulse of his patient for diagnostic purposes, says Vital, Luria was able to diagnose specific illnesses of the soul (*ḥolei ha-nefesh*) by doing likewise: "Be aware that just as physical illnesses are detected by means of the pulse by physicians of the body, so too my teacher, may his memory be for an everlasting blessing, used to discern in the same way an individual's illnesses of the soul."[31]

We are given a fascinating explanation concerning how this worked. The light of *Ein-Sof,* which suffuses the world of *Atsilut*, clothes itself, first and foremost, within the *partsuf Abba*, equivalent to the *sefirah Ḥokhmah*. It is through the agency of *Abba* that *Ein-Sof* permeates and enlivens the entirety of the world of *Atsilut*. This is the esoteric meaning of the verse, "With wisdom (*Ḥokhmah*) hast Thou made everything" (Ps. 104:24). Now, this *Ḥokhmah* flows through an individual's blood vessels; and thus the divine vitality of *Ein-Sof* within *Ḥokhmah* is concealed within the pulse beat. It is precisely this vitality that sustains the life of a human being. *Ḥokhmah*, in turn, serves as a medium by which all things are physically cleansed and purified. Thus, in the case of blood, the "impure" blood is supposed to exit the body as a waste product, leaving the "pure" blood to sustain it. Sometimes, however, as a result of a person's sins, this process of clarification does not take place as it ought to, and a person becomes ill as a result. That is, the unclean blood builds up in the body and causes disease. When this happens, it is necessary for a physician to perform bloodletting so as to relieve the body of the illness-causing blood. It is through the accumulation of impure elements within the bloodstream, discernible by feeling the pulse, that the physician of the *soul*, as well, can determine that a person has sinned, and even more, the nature of the spiritual illness.

There are, according to this diagnostic theory, no fewer than ten different types of pulse beat, corresponding to all the possible vocalizations available in the Hebrew language—*qamats, patah, tsere, shva, segol*, and so on. Each of these vocalizations can be felt through the pulse. By sensing the various points and lines, much the way a blind person reads by feeling Braille, the skilled diagnostician can determine the condition of someone's soul. Thus, if two pulse beats in a row feel like dots or points, it represents the vowel *tsere*. The feel of one point on top of another indicates the vowel *shva*, and so on. Insofar as each vowel derives from a different source within *Hokhmah*, it is possible to determine the nature or precise quality of a person's (divine) vitality at any moment.

For instance, if the vowel *qamats* is felt, this demonstrates the dominance of the aspect of *Keter* within *Hokhmah*. If a *patah* is felt, it indicates that *Hokhmah* within *Hokhmah* prevails over the other elements comprising this *sefirah*. When two different vowels can be felt at the same time, in a *single* beat of the pulse, such as *shva patah*, it signifies an anomaly, which reveals the presence of sin, as well as its source. Much as the body rallies to fight off infection, transgression seems to cause a weakness in the appropriate vowels, which compensate by increasing in size, "for anything that is weakened gathers its strength in order to survive."[32] A *balance* of the various vital elements within the blood, in which none dominate, signals a state of spiritual well-being, the absence of sin. Dominance of the vowel *tsere*, associated with *Binah* within *Hokhmah*, indicates a transgression having to do with the domain of *Imma*, such as the failure to honor one's mother, or that one did not exert sufficient effort at seeking to understand the Torah (*te-vunat divrei ha-Torah*). Discernment of the vowel *pataḥ* reveals that one has transgressed in connection with the wisdom of the Torah (*ḥokhmat ha-Torah*), by failing to properly acquire Torah. The vowel *segol*, associated with *Ḥesed* within *Ḥokhmah*, signifies that a person has transgressed the obligation to perform deeds of loving-kindness. Taking the pulse was widely used as one form of medical diagnosis in the Middle Ages.[33] Luria's belief that *spiritual* life-giving forces were to be found in the blood reflects a general premodern notion that the arteries were the channels through which life-bearing vital spirits flowed throughout the body.

Unfortunately, we are not given more in the way of detail about this technique, although we do have some anecdotal evidence about the way in which it could be applied in the case of demonic possession and the practice of exorcism. Safed kabbalists believed that the soul of a sinful individual who had died could enter into a living person, cleave to that person's soul, cause emotional illness, and speak through him or her. The recipient of such an evil spirit (*ruaḥ raʿah*) was normally a person considered to be responsible for some sin.[34] *Eleh Toldot Yitshaq* preserves a tradition in which Hayyim Vital describes a woman in extreme distress who was brought before Luria. Luria was asked to determine whether the woman was physically ill or possessed by an evil spirit. He was able to determine that she was indeed suffering from demonic possession by feeling her pulse.[35] Elsewhere, we learn from Vital that Luria instructed him how to perform an exorcism, entailing the technique of taking the individual's arm and placing one's hand on the pulse, "for the evil soul is enclothed in the pulse."[36]

The common assumption underlying each of these diagnostic techniques, metoposcopy and feeling the pulse, is that the human soul manifests itself in signs that appear within and upon the body. There is, in other words, a solidarity between the body and the soul, between that which is internal and that which is external, reminding us of Aristotle's observation that "the soul's passions all seem to be linked with a body, as the body undergoes modifications in their presence."[37] However else they may be opposed to one another, there is a necessary link between body and soul. Moreover, in both cases, these signs are linguistic in nature and appear as lights. While they may be extremely subtle, they can be interpreted by those sensitive and skilled enough to do so. The divine portion that enlivens every human being is present within the body. Although it is highly vulnerable to injury or disease when a person transgresses the mitsvot, at the same time, proper diagnosis of the soul's condition allows for the possibility of restoring it to health. It is through acts of penitence that cure can be effected and defilement overcome. Isaac Luria was regarded as having not only diagnostic skills but also knowledge with which to bring about the soul's cure.

Penitential Rites of Purification

Hayyim Vital provides a detailed account of the "medicine" that one must take to bring about purification of the soul and reverse the consequences of sinful acts, as related to him by his teacher.[38] He preserves, he says, all of the *tiqqunim* that he was taught, although he indicates that certain prescriptions were actually devised by Abraham ben Eliezer ha-Levi Berukhim, whom we already know to have taken a strong interest in the question of repentance. Some of the *tiqqunim* cited by Vital were also transmitted by another of Luria's students, Moses Yonah.[39] For many of the identified sins, multiple versions of the penance are given. As we shall see, these *tiqqunei ʿavonot* served two purposes simultaneously. They helped to cleanse the soul of the "stain" caused by a sinful or polluting act and constituted a means by which the injury incurred by divinity could also be repaired. From Vital, we have instructions concerning the following sinful acts:

1. The transgression of positive commandments in general, such as neglect of prayer, neglect of *tefillin* and *tsitsit* (wearing phylacteries and a prayer shawl), and neglecting to recite the Shema prayer
2. Thinking about committing a transgression
3. Engaging in the practice of *kabbalah maʿasit* ("practical" Kabbalah)
4. Writing an amulet on behalf of a woman having trouble giving birth

5. Drinking non-kosher wine (*yayin nesekh*)
6. Swearing a false oath
7. Haughtiness
8. Dishonoring one's father and mother
9. Cursing one's father and mother
10. Humiliating another person
11. Speaking ill of the dead
12. Anger
13. For sins deserving one of the four forms of capital punishment (as taught in the Talmud): stoning, burning, strangulation, and hanging
14. Sexual relations with a menstruant
15. Sexual relations with an animal
16. Sexual relations with a gentile woman
17. Adultery
18. Homosexual relations
19. Masturbation

This is a rather interesting collection of sins, and it is likely that there were other transgressions whose *tiqqun* Luria specified besides those spelled out here. Indeed, with respect to the entire category of positive commandments, Vital suggests that each precept requires its own particular *tiqqun*, the severity of which depends on the particular mitsvah involved, although here he provides general instructions for them as a whole. The *tiqqunim* described by Moses Yonah include most of those treated by Vital, and Yonah adds one for the sin of consuming *nevelah*, referring to the flesh of an animal that has died as a result of any process other than ritual slaughter. For the most part, the details of Yonah's *tiqqunim* are the same as Vital's. Virtually all of the kinds of behavior found here are discussed in various other Lurianic contexts. For example, we have already mentioned Luria's particular concern about the sin of anger. Some of the items listed here are not mitsvot in the technical sense, insofar as they do not represent one of the 613 precepts as determined by rabbinic tradition. Thus, thinking about committing a transgression and speaking ill of a deceased person are considered sinful even though they are not among the formal established corpus of mitsvot.

Leaving aside the first item on this list, the general category of positive precepts, two other categories of deeds stand out. The first of these is proper ethical conduct. Thus, six of the items are concerned with matters of interpersonal relations, such as haughty behavior or humiliating another person. Personal vanity and disregard for the dignity of others was believed to constitute a particularly powerful source of defilement. The second category is the whole arena of sexual behavior. The exceptional concern with sexual misconduct is evidenced by the enumeration of six different examples of sexual impropriety, including adultery, homosexual intercourse, and masturbation. A person who had injured or incapacitated his soul by transgressing any of these prohibitions had to perform elaborate penitences in order to restore the soul to purity.

Let us have a look at a few examples of these penitential instructions in order to illustrate their character. In the case of a person who transgressed a positive commandment, particularly the obligations to pray, don phylacteries and prayer shawl, and recite the Shema prayer, Luria enjoined a fast of sixty-one days. Such implausibly lengthy fasting was mitigated in two ways. Vital explains that a day of fasting does not include the night, and that two such successive fast days are equivalent to twenty-seven days, whereas three consecutive days *and* nights are the equivalent of forty days of fasting.[40]

The figure of sixty-one was arrived at by an interesting but convoluted method, employed in all of the penitences. According to Luria, all of the positive commandments (*mitsvot ʿaseh*) derive from the divine realm of Ḥesed (Compassion), whereas all of the negative commandments (*mitsvot lo taʿaseh*) derive from the realm of Gevurot (Stern Judgment). Now, the term Ḥesed is associated with the divine name ʾEl, by virtue of the fact that these two words are found together in Psalm 53:3, "The mercy [ḥesed] of God [ʾEl] endures continually." If we take the two letters in the word ʾEl, *alef* and *lamed*, and spell out these letters as complete words, a process known as *millui* ("filled out"), their numerical equivalent, or *gematria*, equals 185. When we double this figure, to arrive at 370, and add five more, we have the number 375.[41] This figure is the same as the numerical equivalent of the word ⁽*ASeH*, referring to the positive commandments. Having demonstrated the "intrinsic" connection between the words *°El* and ⁽*ASeH* in this mathematically acrobatic manner, we can isolate the word *°El*, which in simple *gematria* equals 31. By doubling this number and subtracting 1 (since the first *°El* is included in the second) we arrive at the figure of 61, the number of fasts required for transgressing an ⁽*ASeH*, a positive precept.[42]

In the case of merely thinking about committing a transgression, a fast of 87 days is required for atonement.[43] A person must concentrate on the Tetragrammaton, *YHVH*, as it is written "filled out," or *plene*, in such a way that it equals 45 in *gematria* (*shem mem heh*). By adding up the number of letters utilized in this spelling, that is, 10, plus the number of letters involved in spelling out the *millui* of the *millui*, that is, 28, and the 4 letters of the simple *YHVH*, we arrive at 42. Adding 45 and 42, the figure of 87 is achieved, accounting for the fast of 87 days.

The prescription for the transgression of the mitsvah of honoring one's father and mother more clearly indicates a relationship between the exegetical manipulation of *gematria* and correspondences with aspects of divinity. According to Luria, the *partsufim* of *Abba* (Father) and *Imma* (Mother) are associated with the divine name *YaH*. The *millui* of *YaH* equals 26, which is the number of fasts required to expiate this sin. In addition, 26 lashings are prescribed. Performance of this penance atones for the sin, not merely by raising the sinner's consciousness with regard to his act, but also by mending the damage done to the corresponding aspects of the divine structure through such transgression. Thus, the number 26 is hardly arbitrary or contrived, all appearances to the contrary, but represents the intrinsic connection between a specific action and its effect upon God. By concentrating on the precise number of fasts and lashings, their relationship to *YaH* and the *partsufim* of *Abba* and *Imma*, the individual repairs the injury suffered by the divine Anthropos.

The remedy required for one who has publicly humiliated another person is unique. He must roll upon thorns called *ortigas*, the Spanish word for stinging nettles.[44] Luria is said to have derived this practice from Proverbs 24:31, "The face thereof was covered with nettles." The word *face* is taken to mean the red face of one who has been put to shame in public. Just as the humiliated person is covered with "net-tles," so too the guilty party must suffer affliction with actual thorns.

Corroborating earlier testimony that Isaac Luria was especially con-cerned with the problem of anger, Vital reports that his teacher had intended to provide each member of their fellowship with a *tiqqun* for this transgression.[45] Luria's premature death, however, prevented him from doing so. Vital recalls that the essential basis for the *tiqqun* was a fast of 151 days, corresponding to the *gematria* of the Hebrew word *Ca'AS*, plus 1 for the word as a whole. Additionally, one should con-centrate on the divine name *'EHeYeH* as it is spelled in *plene* form us-ing the letter *heh*, since this spelling equals the *gematria* of *Ca'AS*. The special importance attached to the sin of anger is evidenced by the fact that Vital discusses quite a number of *tiqqunim* for its expiation.[46]

It should come as no surprise that the *tiqqunei 'avonot* exhibit spe-cial interest in various forms of illicit sexuality. As we have already be-gun to see from our consideration of Lurianic myth, a pervasive and intense preoccupation with the body and with sexuality—human and divine—is central to Lurianic Kabbalah on multiple levels. Improper sexual behavior was, of course, a prominent concern of Jewish law from its very inception in ancient Israel. Proscriptions against adul-tery, incestuous relationships, homosexual intercourse, and a variety of other forms of sexual conduct occupy an important place in the Torah, as they do, of course, in rabbinic literature and law.[47]

While this is a highly complex problem, where generalizations can be dangerous, on the whole, rabbinic Judaism taught that sexuality within the bounds of marriage was not simply to be begrudgingly tolerated as a "concession to the flesh," but was a positive and divinely favored condition of human existence. Such a stance is ultimately grounded in the attitude toward the body among Jewish thinkers of late antiquity. Whereas Hellenistic culture, including its most prominent Jewish rep-resentative in the Greek-speaking figure of Philo, conceived darkly of the body as "wicked and a plotter against the soul," as "a cadaver and always dead," the general view of evolving rabbinic Judaism resisted such dualistic tendencies. It did so by displaying an acceptance of flesh-liness insofar as both body and soul "form a whole, rather than a po-larity."[48] In this view, human sexual desire is a legitimate and natural quality of being, rather than the result of a "fall" from a prior, more spiritually sublime metaphysical condition. As a consequence, rabbinic culture tended to look upon marriage and marital sexuality warmly, as the most natural means by which women and men could express physical desire and love and experience joyful companionship.

These views contrast strikingly with the perspective of the Roman Catholic Church. One of the most basic principles of traditional Christian morality in its classical form was a radical disapproval of enjoying fleshly pleasures even within marriage, a point of view taught at least as early as Paul and reinforced by centuries of Church teaching. As Daniel Boyarin has argued, Paul's views were founded not so much on an absolute rejection and devaluation of the body in favor of the soul as on a hierarchical view in which the body is vastly inferior to the soul by virtue of its physical desire and is thus in need of constant vigilance and cleansing.[49] One of the practical consequences of these conceptions was an acceptance of marriage and married sexuality as legitimate, but as profoundly inferior to the single, celibate state. This is implied in Paul's famous (or perhaps infamous) pronouncement on these questions to the people of Corinth in what would become a foundational message of Christian thinking: "It is a good thing for a man to have nothing to do with women; but because there is so much immorality, let each man have his own wife and each woman her own husband. The husband must give the wife what is due to her, and the wife equally must give her husband his due. . . . I say this by way of *concession*, not of *command*. . . . for it is better to marry than to burn" (1 Cor. 7:1–9; emphasis added).

For most Christian thinkers of the Middle Ages, marital sex was for two purposes only: to avoid all other (and even worse) sexual temptations and to procreate (while giving one's partner what is "due" to her or him). Vastly superior to marriage and the sexual life, however, was complete abstinence. Typical was Gregory of Nyssa's praise of virginity at the expense of marriage: "The more exactly we understand the riches of virginity, the more we must bewail the other life, . . . how poor it is."[50] The implications of these views were considerable for medieval Christians, including exhortations to virginal chastity, the development of a rich monastic vocation for both men and women, the discouragement of remarriage for widows, and the introduction of celibacy for priests.

Thus, whereas in medieval Christianity celibacy and virginity were not only permitted but celebrated as the ideal state, the reverse was true of Judaism. Not only was sexual abstinence not an ideal, but it entailed a failure to fulfill one's obligation to produce children.[51] Marriage in Judaism was thus more than merely the preferred state, but an absolutely necessary and beneficial one. Indeed, say the talmudic rabbis in a classic formulation: "There are three partners in [the creation of] man, the Holy One, blessed be He, the father, and the mother."[52] Even more, beyond the obligation merely to procreate, the pleasures of joyful companionship in marriage—including *sexual* pleasure—were considered to be important and positive in their own right. Such were the partial motives, for instance, behind rabbinic rules requiring a husband to ensure his wife's sexual satisfaction on a regular basis by meeting his conjugal obligations.[53]

Traditional Jewish attitudes toward sexuality, though, can hardly be called unequivocal. Sexuality—even within the bounds of marriage—was fraught with considerable ambivalence and anxiety, and in some quarters a pronounced ascetic tendency can be found. This paradox is captured by the fact that from the point of view of the talmudic rabbis, one of the primary motives for marriage in the first place (consistent with Christian views) was to give a man a legitimate way to channel an otherwise unruly and troublesome libido. What is more, sexual relations in marriage were supposed to be carried out with the utmost modesty, along with meticulous observance of the laws of *niddah*, the rules that prohibit intercourse between a husband and wife during menstruation and for a period of seven "clean" days following it. As for nonmarital forms of sexual behavior, rabbinic and medieval literatures are replete with exhortations to resist the temptations of transgressive types of conduct. At the furthest end of the ascetic spectrum, an occasional sage in late antiquity sought to avoid marriage altogether, although he did so at the cost of severe disapproval.[54]

This same double-edged attitude toward sexuality may be seen in the traditions of the kabbalists, but taken to a new level of intensity. As is well-known, and as Chapter 6 explores in more detail, for the kabbalists, sexual relations between a wife and her husband represent corresponding dynamic processes within the divine realm. In addition to mirroring the life of God, sexual love is a theurgic rite that stimulates and facilitates love between the *sefirot Tiferet* and *Malkhut*. Thus, married sexual life takes on the quality of a mystical rite with the most profound cosmic repercussions.[55]

These ideas are expressed colorfully in one of the most intriguing texts of the early kabbalistic period, the anonymous *ʾIggeret ha-Qodesh* (Letter on Holiness) from the late thirteenth century, which resembles a marriage manual and addresses issues of sexuality on both exoteric and esoteric levels.[56] It is the most important example of the way in which kabbalistic thinking decisively influenced the theory and practice of sex. Among other things, the *ʾIggeret ha-Qodesh* affirms the centrality of proper mindfulness for both women and men in the course of sexual relations and presents an elaborate treatment of its theurgic consequences.

Over and against this positive regard for human sexuality, however, Spanish Kabbalah exhibited an equally intense fear and loathing of illicit sexual temptation and misconduct. Unconstrained sexual lust, evil, and the demonic are all knit together in an intricate pattern of symbolism and mythology. In its simplest terms, sexual misconduct arouses the dark cosmic forces, upsets the equilibrium necessary for the proper functioning of divine life, and cuts off individuals from the source of their nourishment and blessing. Thus, whereas proper sexual behavior serves to reestablish harmonious relationships among the various elements of divinity, as well as between God and humanity, illicit sexual conduct violates the laws of the cosmos, interfering with the natural order of things.

Against the background of this set of mythic notions in which the realm of the divine (and, by extension, the cosmos as a whole) is thoroughly sexualized, we can better appreciate the Lurianic interest in sexual misconduct and its consequences. The atonement for these deeds, as with the others we have already seen, was based upon the *gematria* of the word denoting the sin itself. Thus, for example, a man who was guilty of having had intercourse with his wife while she was a menstruant (*niddah*) was to fast for a total of 59 days, insofar as the three letters which make up the word *NiDaH* equal this number.[57] Moreover, he had to be lashed and to ritually immerse himself in water as a form of purification on each of these days. He was further required to abstain from sexual relations during this period, except for the eves of Sabbaths, Festivals, and the New Moon. The penitent also had to sleep on the ground (*ʿafar*, literally, "dust") during these 59 days. The explanation for this is found in the letters that make up the word *NiDaH*, *nun*, *dalet*, *heh*. The *heh* represents the *Shekhinah,* who is Herself "lying in the dust" as a consequence of Her exiled condition. She is a roving wanderer (*NaH ve-NaD*) in exile who is in need of restoration. This is symbolized by the *NaD*, or *nun dalet*, in the word *NiDaH*. The implication, then, is that violation of the law of *niddah* further entrenches the *Shekhinah* in the dust of exile. The penitent must imitate the *Shekhinah,* whose prolonged suffering he has helped cause.

But at the same time these activities contribute to the process of extricating the *Shekhinah* from exile. These penitential gestures are encoded in the very word for repentance, *TeShUVaH*: *tav* stands for *taʿanit* (fasting), *shin* for *saq* (wearing of a sackcloth), *vav* for *va-ʿefer* (dust), *vet* for *bekhi* (weeping), and *heh* represents *hesed* (lament) over having sinned.

The *tiqqun* for a person who has had intercourse with the wife of another man is to fast for 325 days, which corresponds to five times the *gematria* of the name *ʾADoNaY*.[58] This divine name is associated with the *Shekhinah,* who, as in the violation of the laws of *niddah*, is injured on account of this sin. For every one of the fasts, he must don sackcloth and rub dust on his forehead, traditional signs of mourning. Moreover, the final portion of each meal that breaks a day of fasting must be dipped in dust before eating, unless the new day to be ushered in is a Sabbath. In this case, the number 325 is equated with 320 "judgments" (*dinim*) on God's part, whose severity is "sweetened" by adding five times the letter *ʾalef* (1) from the five times *ʾADoNaY*. Thus, concentration on this word by means of the 325 days of fasting serves to atone for this transgression. The wearing of sackcloth and the application of ashes signify the reunification of *Zeʿir Anpin* and *Nuqba de-Ze͑ir*. This is possible because these two *partsufim* are symbolized by heaven (*ShaMaYiM*) and earth (*ʾAReTS*), the combined *gematria* of which equals that of the Hebrew words for sackcloth and dust, 681.

Vital reports that he learned the penance that Luria prescribed for the sin of having practiced homosexual intercourse (*ha-ba͑al ha-za-khor*) from three individuals who carried out this *tiqqun*. In fact, he goes out of his way to mention that *he* did not receive this teaching personally. This report, along with the fact that Vital recorded an unusually large number of lengthy *tiqqunim* for this transgression, suggests the fact that it was considered an especially egregious act, and that it was certainly known to have been practiced. While there is no reason to assume that homosexuality was unusually widespread in Safed, it would be naive to assume that it was unknown. In his dream diary, Vital alleges that Israel Najara engaged in homosexual behavior in his drunkenness, and contends, in connection with Damascus, that "there is much homosexuality . . . in this land."[59]

Vital introduces this subject by saying that it is important to understand the nature of this transgression and the harm precipitated by it.[60] In the normal course of events, the sefirotic qualities of *Netsaḥ*, *Hod*, and *Yesod* within the *partsufim* of *Abba* and *Imma* descend below to the upper part of *Ze͑ir Anpin*. In particular, *Yesod* comes to rest within the "chest" of *Ze͑ir Anpin*. The act of anal intercourse disrupts this normal process, however, by causing *Yesod* to descend further than it should, to the lower portion or "feet" (*RaGLayim*) of *Ze͑ir Anpin*, a place in which it should not be found. As a result, the normal development of the *partsuf* of *Ze͑ir* is impeded. In addition, *Abba* and *Imma* find themselves dislocated from their proper, elevated place, one in which they are prevented from engaging in proper *zivvug*.

The remedy for all this is a fast of 233 days, which corresponds to the *gematria* of the word *ReGeL*, or foot, denoting the place within *Ze͑ir* to which *Yesod* has improperly traveled.[61] These fast days are to be accompanied by meditative concentration on certain divine names associated with *Abba* and *Imma*, in accordance with a specific daily schedule.[62] The purpose in doing so is to raise up *Abba* and *Imma* to their proper place. The first 72 days of the fast repair the injury incurred by *Abba*, whereas the remaining 161 days bring about the repair of *Imma*.

The 161 fast days are supposed to include the winter season in order to enable the penitent to roll in the snow on at least one of these days.[63] This immersion in snow is done while the penitent is completely naked, hardly compatible with the concern for modesty that characterized Safed culture. He rolls on his front and back up to nine times. The *gematria* of the Hebrew word for snow, *SheLeG*, is manipulated in such a way that it is shown to denote the *partsuf* of *Ze'ir*, the place into which aspects of *Abba* and *Imma* have improperly descended. Thus, rolling in the snow symbolizes the intradivine processes that have gone awry.

Moses Yonah warns those who fabricate all sorts of excuses for failing to perform the *tiqqun* for homosexual activity although guilty of this transgression.[64] Such a person intentionally seeks to rebel against God, since he is aware of the necessary penance but resists carrying it out. He may argue to himself that a fast of one day, no less 233 days, might kill him. Or he may neglect his obligation by putting it off until some future time. "I am old and God will forgive me," he might say to himself; or, "If I perform this fast, followed by immersion, I shall die suddenly." Actually, the contrary is true; penance strengthens one.

The sin of masturbation was also a matter of great concern to the Safed kabbalists, including the Lurianists.[65] Moses Yonah enumerates the different ways in which masturbation can occur, or to be more precise, the ways in which a man can expend his seed in a wasteful manner.[66] There are those who commit this sin merely by fantasizing about masturbating (*'al yedei maḥshavah*), without ever actually touching their penises. Their lustful imagination gets the better of them, and they suddenly find themselves having an orgasm without doing anything. Some masturbate while fantasizing about a woman (*meharher be-'ishah*), while there are those who fantasize about a man. Others use their own saliva to masturbate, while some do so in the standard fashion (*meshamesh be-yado u-motsi qeri*). Finally, and rather curiously, some "conceal the head of the penis [*rosh ha-'atarah*] with the skin of the penis [*'ever*] that extends below" as if to simulate the appearance of a foreskin.[67] It is interesting that each form this act takes inflicts a somewhat different injury upon the divine realm, and thus the penance itself varies. In each case, a fast of 84 days is required, according to Moses Yonah, but the intentions that go along with these fasts change.

The detail in which this question was considered is presumably a measure of the problem that it posed. It makes sense that in a culture where a (kabbalistic) husband and wife were supposed to have relations only a few times each month, other outlets for sexual relief would be sought, thus ironically creating a situation in which the diligent observance of certain sexual taboos may have led to an increased tendency to violate still others.[68]

The profound anxiety evidenced here concerning wasting one's seed is connected to an older set of folkloric notions having to do with the circumstances under which bodiless demons came into the world. According to rabbinic tradition, in the twilight of the first Friday evening during the week in which the world was created, God began to produce spirits. But before He had a chance to embody these spirits—as was necessary—the Sabbath entered and intervened. Obliged to cease from labor, God gave up the effort, resulting in demonic spirits without bodies.[69] This conception was combined with another motif, according to which evil spirits were produced from Adam's semen during his long separation from his wife Eve.[70] After the murder of Abel by Cain, Adam resolved to cease having sexual relations with Eve. During this prolonged period of separation of 130 years, female demons, succubi, came to him and conceived by him. Such illicit sexual relations brought forth demonic offspring known as "spirits of harm that come from Adam" (nig'ei benei Adam).

These rabbinic conceptions were taken up by various medieval writers, notably by the author of the Zohar.[71] In the Zohar, these motifs form the basis for a colorful narrative tradition concerning the figure of Lilit, a winged, long-haired queen of demons who (along with other female spirits, such as Na'amah) makes a career out of tempting men into having sexual relations with her for the purpose of conceiving still more demons.[72] Such evil female spirits also impregnate themselves with the seed derived from involuntary nocturnal emissions men have. Taken together, these conceptions led to the great fear among kabbalists (and others) that male sexual improprieties, in particular masturbation and other forms of wasteful destruction of semen, provide opportunity for the creation of demonic spirits, male and female, or at very least the entrapment of souls in the qelippot.[73]

Thus, among other things, Lurianic teaching on this matter was motivated by the fear of adding strength to the realm of the demonic. Improper emission of semen causes a man's potential sons to become demonic spirits instead.[74] A specific rite was developed in order to retrieve or redeem these "ill-bred sons" of man (*banim shovavim*). This ritual—which predates Lurianic Kabbalah—is known as *Tiqqun Shovavim Tat*, the last two words being an acrostic formed by the initial letters of the names of the eight weekly portions of the Torah (Exod. 1–30) read during the winter months.[75] According to some variations of this ritual, kabbalists fasted on Mondays and Thursdays in the period between the readings of the Torah portions *Shemot* through *Tetsave*, in order to expiate the sins of nocturnal pollution and masturbation. It was believed that by this ascetic regimen, a man's "ill-bred sons" might be rescued from the realm of the *qelippot* and returned to the sphere of the holy.

In Luria's version of this ritual, an individual was supposed to fast for this entire period (presumably using the calculations for fasting described earlier).[76] These are the most propitious days in which to atone for this transgression, inasmuch as these Torah portions describe Israel's exile in Egypt. For the future souls of the Israelites enslaved in Egypt were (mis)conceived during the 130-year period of separation between Adam and Eve! Enslavement served as a purifying process for these souls. Luria prescribed meditative concentration on particular configurations of the divine name during each day of fasting. He also extended the fast period from forty days to eighty-four days in order to make it consistent with the *tiqqunei ʿavonot* described above. As a result, the souls of those children entrapped in the *qelippot* by virtue of their father's improper spilling of seed would be restored to the realm of holiness.

In all of the *tiqqunei ʿavonot,* we discover the same essential idea at work. A particular transgression has disrupted or violated the natural course of development within the structure of divine being. The influence of human transgression causes the lights within divinity to flow in improper and unintended ways. They can be redirected, however, through the simultaneous processes of contemplative concentration and penitential action. Just as misguided behavior interrupts the normal cosmic processes, so corrective action can repair them. Fasting, receiving lashes, donning sackcloth and ashes, immersion in water or rolling in snow, sleeping on the ground, and lying upon thorns were not intended simply to punish or afflict the body. Accompanied by precise meditative intentions, they served the most consequential theurgical purposes. At the same time, these penitential activities helped to cleanse the soul by eliminating the defilement it had incurred through sin, and thus established the conditions under which an adept could attain divine inspiration.

A Comparison with the Penances of the German Pietists

The question of asceticism in Judaism was raised briefly earlier in connection with the general pattern of pre-Lurianic piety in Safed, but one ascetically inclined group merits further attention at this point, namely, the German Pietists (*Ḥasidei Ashkenaz*) of the twelfth and thirteenth centuries. The German Pietists constituted a sectarian movement with a distinctive brand of piety. They cultivated the idea of the *ḥasid* as one who constantly confronted divinely sponsored trials, whose purpose is to challenge and test faithfulness to God. Overcoming the "evil inclination," domesticating one's passions, not the least among which were vanity and sexual lust, served as opportunities to merit reward by God. In these terms, the evil inclination was regarded as a necessary and useful feature of the human personality. Asceticism was, naturally enough, a critical feature of this type of spiritual perspective. As Ivan Marcus observes: "One result of the fact that the pietist's life requires resistance to all kinds of temptations of the flesh and ego was the tendency toward asceticism. Grounded in the authors' focus on maximizing otherworldly reward by resisting temptations in this world, the pietist is told to avoid all illicit physical or psychological pleasures during his life."[77]

But beyond the simple avoidance of illicit pleasure, the *ḥasid* was actively to pursue severe rites of self-affliction, both as trial and as a form of penitence. The literary works of German Pietism include a genre of systematic catalogues of specific sins and their corresponding penances, a phenomenon that goes far beyond anything in earlier Jewish literature. The general purpose of these penances was to enable a repentant sinner to accomplish complete atonement. Such manuals of penance bear a rather strong resemblance to the vast medieval ecclesiastical literature of Christian penitentials and may have been influenced by them, or by the example of actual Christian penance. Like the treatises of the Pietists, these Christian manuals enumerate a wide array of transgressions, spell out the precise penance required for a sin's expiation, and instruct the confessor how to go about his work.[78]

The penitential instructions of the Pietists took two different forms. In his influential and important compendium *Sefer Ḥasidim* (Book of the Pietists), Judah ben Samuel the Pietist (c. 1150–1217), the leading figure of this movement, developed penances that were intended to be given at the instruction of a Sage (*ḥakham*). The latter—who was also sometimes referred to as a "guide" (*moreh*)—was to serve as a confessor for sinners. According to *Sefer Ḥasidim,* it was the sinner's responsibility to seek out a Sage. "If so-and-so comes [to a Sage] to inquire how to do penance," the aspiring repentant was to confess his sins without concealing anything.[79] The Sage was supposed to test the sinner by instructing him to enter a period in which he had to avoid any behavior that could lead to repeating the transgressions to which he had confessed. For example, in the case of a sexual transgression involving a woman, the male penitent was to avoid all contact with this particular woman for a year. Actual penitential exercises would be given to the individual only following his successful negotiation of this trial period. Judah's rules included penances for non-Pietists who sought admittance to the sectarian fellowship, who were required to practice rites of atonement for past sins. But they also included penances for sect members who had lapsed or transgressed in some way and wished to return to the proper path.

In both cases these "Sage Penitentials" served an initiatory function. As Marcus puts it, "the ritual drama of making oral confession to another Jew was one of the boldest innovations in Judah's sectarian form of pietism and he sought to legitimate it in *Sefer Ḥasidim* as being part of earlier Judaism."[80] Aware of what appeared to be the opposing views of earlier tradition, Judah felt constrained to justify this practice. In the end, Judah's more radical sectarian approach based on confession to a Sage failed to gain the acceptance he had hoped for. In its place, his most prominent disciple, Eleazar ben Judah of Worms (c. 1165– c. 1230), modified this practice by positing a form of "Private Penitentials," not for a Sage confessor to administer, but for the private use of the sinner.[81] Instead of receiving guidance from a Sage, the penitent was supposed to consult penitential manuals on his own. Eleazar argued that there were those who sinned and were contrite, but who were too ashamed to confess and "to explain the details of their sins to someone who is more important than themselves."[82]

The penitential rites themselves included many of the more extreme and unusual kinds of self-affliction that we have seen in the Lurianic texts, and often for the very same transgressions. Thus, they call for extensive regimens of fasting, immersion in icy water, periods of sexual abstinence, and flagellation. For example, according to *Sefer Ḥasidim*, one who had engaged in sexual intercourse with a gentile woman had to fast three consecutive days and nights for a period of three years, or practice three three-day fasts in the course of a single year. The "Private Penitentials" required even stricter regimens of fasting than the "Sage Penitentials" for the same transgression, insofar as expiation takes place only if the sinner fasts, undergoes flagellation, and refrains from washing for at least forty days.[83] According to Judah, if a man has sexual relations with another's wife, he is required to sit in icy water in the winter and among insects in the summer. Moreover, he has to submit to severe flagellation in private on the days during which he fasts.[84] For his part, Eleazar enumerated detailed penances for the following transgressions in his *Hilkhot Teshuvah* (Laws of Repentance): sexual intercourse with an unmarried, ritually impure woman; intercourse with a betrothed or married woman, with a Christian woman, or with an animal; kissing or fondling a woman even without sexual intercourse; intercourse with one's own ritually impure wife; stealing; harming someone monetarily, physically or verbally; publicly humiliating someone; insulting one's wife; insulting a convert to Judaism; provoking someone; murder; apostasy; taking oaths; speaking in synagogue; slandering someone; gossiping; and desecrating God's name.[85]

We thus see that the German Pietists devised an elaborate system of expiatory penitences quite reminiscent of Lurianic Kabbalah. The question, of course, is whether Luria was influenced by the Pietists. The circumstantial evidence for such influence is wide-ranging. We know that while the more radical forms of atonement promulgated by Pietism failed to transform German Jewry as its teachers had hoped, it did exert continuing influence.[86] Eleazar's own *Sefer ha-Roqeah*, incorporating his "Laws of Atonement," outlined above, was long popular. His penances, for example, appeared from time to time in collections of legal *responsa* of German rabbis between the thirteenth and fifteenth centuries and thus infiltrated the mainstream of Jewish law in Europe to a significant degree. Indeed, there is strong evidence that ascetic practices of the Pietists had an impact upon various subcultures of Jews in France, Provence, and Spain.[87]

Of even more direct pertinence, we know that pietistic asceticism left an imprint on some of the most prominent kabbalists of sixteenth-century Safed, including Moses Cordovero, Solomon Alkabets, Elijah de Vidas, and Eleazar Azikri.[88] This is evidenced by the inclusion in their writings of penitential language that derived from the German Pietists, as well as by specific reference to their penitential manuals. This is especially striking in Azikri's case, for he incorporated language from *Sefer ha-Roqeah* in the section on repentance in his *Sefer Ḥaredim*.

Azikri also provides the clearest direct evidence that Luria himself was intimately familiar with the penitential treatises of the *Ḥasidei Ashkenaz*. We noted earlier that Azikri described Luria's practice of diagnosing his disciples' transgressions and providing the proper penances for them. Elsewhere in *Sefer Ḥaredim,* he preserves the following valuable information: "I found another penitential practice [*taqqanah*] among the books of the saintly kabbalist, the holy, pious Rabbi Isaac Luria Ashkenazi, may his memory be blessed, in a certain manuscript entitled *Bet Middot*. . . . There I found recorded all of the teachings of the *rishonim* [earlier authorities] having to do with reproofs on account of transgressions, rigorous ascetic practices [including rolling in] snow, [lying upon] thorns, fasts and [other] mortifications."[89] This report confirms Luria's knowledge of the penitential teachings of German Pietism, a fact that may also be inferred from the close resemblances between the two literatures. These resemblances include both the specific transgressions that each corpus includes, especially in the realm of sexual matters, as well as the types of penitential exercises each enjoins. In addition, it is worth taking notice of the fact that Luria employed Pietists' exegetical techniques for determining the length and nature of the penances. Luria's innovation appears to have been in adopting the techniques of *notariqon* and *gematria* from German Pietism and using them in the service of the *tiqqunei ʿavonot*.[90] Finally, it is highly interesting that the analogy between medical physician and spiritual healer—crucial to Luria's role—is already found in *Sefer Ḥasidim*.[91]

It is worth asking here, as in the case of metoposcopy, whether there is reason to believe that the Lurianic penances were actually carried out. Mention has already been made of Vital's report that he learned the *tiqqun* for homosexual behavior from three individuals who had performed it, and that Luria had intended to require each of his disciples to atone for the sin of anger. He also informs us that he himself was given a *tiqqun* by Luria for one who had spoken ill of a deceased person, "for I sinned against a certain man whom I denigrated after his death, and I also had a small amount of money that belonged to him."[92] Vital indicates as well that Luria gave someone the *tiqqun* required for having drunk *yayin nesekh* (wine unfit for consumption by Jews) with an Ishmaelite, that is, an Arab.[93] Accompanying the detailed accounts of the *tiqqunei ʿavonot* to be practiced for the sin of masturbation, we have a report according to which Luria provided these *tiqqunim* to someone he counseled over a period of time.[94]

In the context of discussing his soul-ancestry, Hayyim Vital reported that he himself had committed a variety of sins for which Luria prescribed atonement. Among other things, Vital had indulged in the study of alchemy during the years 1566–68, just prior to his taking up with Luria. He also needed to purify himself for having become angry with his wife, for having drunk forbidden wine with an apostate, for having cursed his parents, and for experiencing an involuntary emission of semen.[95] For all of these sins, Isaac Luria provided Vital with the necessary penances. Taken together, these scattered testimonies leave little doubt that the *tiqqunei ʿavonot* were given to particular individuals who carried them out.

The descriptions of the nature of sin and its remedy examined here are consistent with notions commonly associated with ritual purity, as suggested earlier. Not only is the language that of purity and impurity, but the conceptions are as well. Thus, in contrast to moral misconduct, ritual defilement can be acquired through unintentional means, of which the case of involuntary seminal emission is a perfect example. Moreover, impurity is not only a situation entailing guilt and shame—essentially moral categories—but an ontological condition that radically affects the whole of one's being. The most important consequence of the defiled state in Luria's view is that it renders an individual unfit for divine inspiration. In Lurianic terms, the soul is stained or blemished, and the holy is unable to penetrate it. Insofar as it qualitatively alters the person as a whole, defilement interferes in the most fundamental way with the project of *tiqqun* on the personal level. Having taken on the quality of impurity, one becomes like the uncleanness in the material world that one seeks to eradicate. Only by first cleansing himself, by divesting himself of the *qelippot* that cling to him, can an adept ever hope to engage in the task of ridding the *world* of its impurity, as well as becoming a repository of the holy. Only one whose soul has become purified—under the guidance of Isaac Luria's diagnostic skills and regimen of penitential remedies—is qualified to receive further instruction in the contemplative task of *tiqqun*.

Earlier I argued that, taken together, the charismatic claims made about Isaac Luria were unique. The role he played in his community as a diagnostician and physician of the soul corroborates this point of view. While we may be able to find occasional examples of something similar to this type of phenomenon, we know of no figure prior to Luria who served as a spiritual guide in quite this way. The sustained, systematic approach to discovering the spiritual condition of one's disciples and helping to bring about the necessary penitence is virtually without parallel in Jewish religious history. The only precedent that comes close is the attempt by Judah the Pious to promote the Sage as personal guide and confessor.

As with the German Pietists, Luria believed that the conventional ways in which individuals identified their transgressions and alleviated themselves of guilt were inadequate to the situation at hand. The various

opportunities for self-acknowledgement of sin and repentance that rabbinic tradition made available failed to satisfy the need for the kind of
rigorous and uncompromising self-improvement that Luria's approach
called for. Luria's approach differed from those of both Judah the Pietist
and Eleazar of Worms but was closer to Judah's. Luria did not wait for
the sinner to voluntarily seek him out, but was able to determine a person's sin merely by gazing upon the person's face. While some Safed
sources flirted with the idea of regular, public confession as a way of
bringing sinfulness to the arena, Luria appears to have rejected this in
favor of what we have described here.[96] This *medical* model, in which
the "physician" is able to make a diagnosis merely by gazing upon his
"patient's" forehead, suggests a communal climate that favored a degree of public acknowledgement of transgression short of actual voluntary confession. Still, the crucial element is the exposure of one's
sin—even if it is exposed to only one other person. As Michel Foucault
has observed of penitentially oriented Christian self-disclosure:

> To prove suffering, to show shame, to make visible humility and ex-
> hibit modesty—these are the main features of punishment. Penitence
> in early Christianity is a way of life acted out at all times by accepting
> the obligation to disclose oneself. It must be visibly represented and
> accompanied by others who recognize the ritual. . . . That's the para-
> dox at the heart of *exomologesis*; it rubs out the sin and yet reveals the
> sinner.[97]

To the extent that Isaac Luria's disciples desired the penitential guidance he could provide, it also suggests a climate in which individuals
were willing to place their confidence in a spiritual mentor. In a way
reminiscent of monastic obedience to a spiritual superior—such as we
find, for example, in Roman Catholic tradition and Zen Buddhism—a
disciple's personal autonomy is compromised for the sake of a greater
good, namely, repair and perfection of the self.

Six   *Tiqqun*: Healing the Cosmos Through the
         Performance of *Mitsvot*

In the preceding discussion, we saw that one of Isaac Luria's most essential concerns was the processes through which individuals had to pass in order to cleanse their souls of sinfulness and impurity. The primary purpose in achieving a state of purified soul was to render oneself qualified to engage in higher and broader levels of *tiqqun*. Having reached a requisite stage of personal sanctification, one was considered to be in a position to accomplish more ambitious goals, variously described in Lurianic literature. These can be reduced to two basic categories: theurgical and experiential. From the theurgical point of view, one sought to liberate divine sparks imprisoned in the *qelippot*; bring about various types of *zivvug*, or "coupling," between different aspects of the divine masculine and feminine; and, more generally, theurgically realign the structure of the divine worlds. At the same time, the Lurianic adept pursued the personal goals of binding his own soul to divinity and experiencing various types of divine inspiration. Except in the most formal terms, these several processes were not strictly separable.

These processes correspond to the original events that, in the mythic categories of Lurianic thought, were responsible for having brought the world to the situation in which it finds itself. As we have already seen, the Breaking of the Vessels and Adam's failure to accomplish the final stages of *tiqqun* precipitated the crises of flaw and fracture that characterize all life. The project facing the mystical adepts of the   187 Lurianic school was not only to reverse the consequences of these primordial events, but also to bring about a new cosmos in which divine light in all of its forms would be restored to its source, divested of any vestige of impurity. To do this required systematic and sustained contemplative efforts, as we have already begun to see. This chapter and the next two analyze a variety of important types of ritual practices that served as the main vehicles for these contemplative goals, the first of these being performance of the mitsvot, the 613 ritual precepts that form the basis of religious piety in Judaism.

One of the fundamental facts of the history of Kabbalah in general, and Lurianic Kabbalah in particular, was its capacity to remain completely within the fold of "orthodox" or normative Judaism, despite radical innovations in the arenas of both religious thought and practical piety.[1] The sole exceptions to this were Sabbateanism in the seventeenth century and its subsequent incarnation in Poland in the form of Frankism. One of the decisive differences between these phenomena and all other forms of kabbalism that went before it had to do with the question of halakha, or Jewish law. For all their novel—even radical—mythic and theological notions, the kabbalists had remained committed to the meticulous observance of the mitsvot, the precepts or commandments that constitute the basic structure of Jewish law. Kabbalah was able to "get away" with its highly inventive mythic and symbolic systems of thought, largely because its practitioners never wavered in their allegiance to halakha. Kabbalah's critics could rail against what they regarded as offensive and bizarre conceptions of God, but they could not accuse the kabbalists of significant deviation from Jewish law. Sabbateanism, by contrast, became irretrievably corrupt from the perspective of the rabbinic establishment at the point at which it became identified with antinomianism. The impressive elasticity of which rabbinic Judaism had historically shown itself capable failed to extend to the overt and unabashed halakhic deviance that Sabbatai Sevi and many of his followers acted out.

Sabbateanism aside, however, the issue for kabbalists was not *whether* to practice the mitsvot but rather their purpose and function. What was the meaning behind the precepts as a whole, and each precept in particular? It is true, as we have already seen, that the kabbalists did, in fact, *add* to the structure of religious practice through ritual innovation and variation. But their primary concern when it came to ritual was to invest already existing practice with esoteric meaning, endowing the mitsvot with significance in conformity with their various mystical conceptions.

Ever since the inception of Kabbalah in the twelfth century, kabbalistic authors had developed theories about the mitsvot and a wide range of explanations for their observance.[2] There exists an extensive genre of kabbalistic literature that attests to this endeavor. As such, Kabbalah contributed in an important way to one of the popular pastimes among Jewish thinkers of the Middle Ages: discovering the reasons for the commandments (*ta'amei ha-mitsvot*).[3] The Torah itself is more often than not silent on the specific reasons for the different precepts, and the sages of the talmudic period were generally more intent on establishing principles of exegesis and tying halakha to biblical proof-texts than they were with providing reasons for the mitsvot per se. The rabbis were not, however, unaware of the problem. They drew a distinction between *ḥuqqim* ("statutes") and *mishpatim* ("judgments"). To them, *ḥuqqim* were commandments requiring no rational explanation, insofar as they were rooted simply in divine decree. *Mishpatim*, on the other hand, were obligations for which rational justification could be found: "These are the matters that are written in the Torah and that, even if they had not been written there, it would have been logical to write."[4] Even in connection with these, however, the sages of late antiquity were not especially interested in pursuing the search for rational explanations, preferring instead to encourage the observance of the mitsvot precisely because they are "the yoke of the Kingdom of Heaven." They appear to have regarded the quest for moral, theological, or rational explanations as a somewhat less pure form of devotion to God than was sheer obedience to divine will. Having said this, the talmudic rabbis certainly believed in the intrinsic merits of many of the mitsvot, especially those having to do with ethical and interpersonal matters.

Medieval religious thinkers embarked on a rather different search. Philosophers, moralists, and biblical exegetes of various types, including kabbalists, were intent on demonstrating the *meaning* behind the mitsvot. The assorted metahalakhic concerns of these authors—be they philosophical, mystical, or of some other kind—ultimately led them to explain the halakha in terms of their larger religious perspective.[5] In the medieval Jewish philosophical tradition, for example, tremendous intellectual energy was spent trying to fathom the meaning behind the commandments. Even though most religious philosophers preserved the rabbinic distinction between *ḥuqqim* and *mishpatim*, some sought to find rational or moral justification even for the former. Thus, although Maimonides acknowledged that the *ḥuqqim* are "those [commandments] whose object is not generally clear," he argued that in theory at least there are rational explanations for *all* of the 613 mitsvot.[6] In his view, all of the commandments derive from the wisdom of God; some (*mishpatim*) are easily intelligible, while others (*ḥuqqim*) are intelligible only with difficulty, or not susceptible to human understanding at all. The philosophers were absolutely certain that intellectually based devotion was a superior, even obligatory, religious path.

While theosophical kabbalists shared the philosophical conviction that the commandments had to be explained, the metaphysical ground upon which they stood was completely different. For the vast majority of kabbalistic authors, the project of establishing the meaning of the precepts was shaped by two of the most essential dimensions of kabbalism: its symbol-making and its theurgy. In Kabbalah, virtually everything was grist for the symbolizing process. Not only could symbols be drawn from the natural world and from the realm of human experience; all of the elements of Jewish tradition were fair game as well. We have already observed how the letters of the Hebrew alphabet and the Torah as a whole served as primary vehicles for kabbalistic symbolism. Not only were individual words or expressions regarded as signs or "names" for various aspects of divinity, but the Torah's precepts were also understood to refer to the various *sefirot,* and to intra-sefirotic relationships.

For example, following a tradition in *Sefer ha-Bahir*, the *Zohar* asks about the meaning of *qorban* (ritual sacrifice). According to the *Zohar,* the act of sacrifice is for the purpose of uniting all the *sefirot,* "until all turn into one, complete oneness . . . so that compassion fills all the worlds . . . and everything becomes sweetened."[7] More particularly, the *qorban* serves the purpose of uniting masculine and feminine dimensions of deity, *Tiferet* and *Malkhut*. With the ascent of the burnt offering, *Shekhinah* "ascends and joins with the Holy King [*Tiferet*] in complete union."[8] Whereas rationalist philosophers such as Maimonides had taught that the details of certain of the precepts did not always yield to explanation, the author of the *Zohar* argues altogether differently: "Rabbi Shimon said, 'If human beings knew the words of Torah, they would know that every single word and letter contains precious, supernal mysteries.' . . . Piles upon piles of mysteries of wisdom depend on each one. . . . Every word contains many mysteries, reasons, roots, and branches."[9] Moses de Leon was especially interested in bolstering certain precepts that appear to have been neglected by many in his time, including those relating to tefillin, mezuzah, sukkah, the ritual washing of hands before eating, and sexual morality.

In what may be regarded as a polemic against the philosophical preference for thought over action, such as is found in Maimonides' assertion that ultimate perfection involves true *opinions*, not actions,[10] the *Zohar* taught: "The action below is always essential in order to arouse above. Come and See: One who says that the action is not always essential, or [merely] pronouncing words or producing sounds, may his spirit deflate!"[11] Here we have a classic articulation of the theurgical notion so basic to theosophical Kabbalah. The mitsvot do not simply reflect the *sefirot*; their enactment influences them, reorganizes them into their properly balanced configuration. This theurgic realignment is more often than not understood in terms of bringing about a *hieros gamos*, a holy marriage (*zivvuga qaddisha*) between the divine masculine and feminine, *Tiferet* and *Malkhut*. Certain rituals, such as observance of the Sabbath, celebration of the holiday of Shavuot as a sacred marriage festival, and marital intercourse, were considered to be particularly effective in this regard.

General Principles of Ritual Observance in Lurianic Kabbalah

These general attitudes toward the observance of the mitsvot were adopted in various ways by almost all later kabbalists, including Isaac Luria. According to Luria, a person is absolutely obligated to fulfill all of the precepts of the Torah, except for those that are beyond an individual's control.[12] Those rituals and laws that were dependent upon the existence and operation of the ancient Temple could not, quite obviously, be carried out. Thus it was not possible for one to practice the sacrificial rites or the laws of priestly purity now that the Temple had been destroyed. Other precepts are occasioned by special circumstances that are also out of a person's hands. These include such things as the ritual of *yibbum* and *ḥalitsah*, which obligate a man to offer himself in marriage to his widowed sister-in-law in the event of his brother's death; arranging for a *get*, a certificate of divorce; and the obligation of *pidyon ha-ben*, "redemption" of one's firstborn child, should it be a male.

But all of the remaining mitsvot must be carried out, including some that present themselves only under special circumstances. As an example, Vital refers to the ethical obligation to send away a mother bird before taking eggs from her nest (Deut. 22:6). While normally one does not have to seek out such a situation, Vital says that this is the kind of mitsvah one should try to fulfill.[13] A distinction is drawn here, then, between patently undesirable situations that one would hardly wish for, such as a divorce or a brother's death, and other types of accidental situations that one *ought* to seek out.

The significance of observing all the mitsvot in one's power has to do largely with the goal of perfecting the soul. As noted earlier, Luria taught that the soul of Adam was originally made up of virtually all the future souls of humankind. The structure of this soul was complex; it possessed 613 "limbs," or parts, each corresponding to one of the 613 mitsvot in the Torah, as calculated by rabbinic tradition. Insofar as every individual soul derives from Adam's, every soul replicates Adam's and is also constituted of 613 limbs. Of these, 365 parallel the like number of negatively formulated commandments (*mitsvot lo taᶜaseh*) and 248 parallel the same number of positively formulated commandments (*mitsvot ᶜaseh*). The perfection of an individual's soul (on the part of a male, that is) requires that he properly fulfill each of the mitsvot. Otherwise, a positive commandment that has never been fulfilled, or a negative one that has been transgressed, results in injury to the corresponding aspect of that person's soul-structure. This is the root cause of the transmigration (*gilgul*) of a soul from one individual to another. A soul that has failed to perfect itself by means of the correct enactment of all of the mitsvot finds renewed opportunity in another lifetime.

The mitsvot are supposed to be performed with intense enthusiasm and joy. One of the keys to the enactment of a precept is to avoid regarding it as a burden to accomplish as quickly as possible.[14] Rather, one should carry out a precept with the joy one would feel if one thought one was gaining huge amounts of money, filled "with boundless happiness of the heart and soul and great intensity." Performance of the mitsvot merits supernal light (ʾor ʿelyon) and the inspiration of the Holy Spirit (Ruaḥ ha-Qodesh) in direct proportion to one's degree of joyfulness.[15] A person should carry out the mitsvot with the kind of fervor and enthusiasm one exhibits in serving and pleasing a king. The true service of God is utterly selfless, motivated only by the desire to carry out God's will and to provide Him with pleasure. Indeed, according to Eleazar Azikri, Luria disclosed that all the divine inspiration that he had personally attained was on account of the fact that he practiced the entirety of the mitsvot with boundless joy.[16] When a man cuts his hair, for example, it is not enough for him simply to refrain from cutting his sidecurls (peʾot), as prescribed in the Torah. Rather, he must consciously reflect on the fact that he is doing so for the sake of pleasing his Creator, who instructed him to act this way. The same holds true for the performance of each and every mitsvah; it must be accompanied by awareness of the pleasure that it provides God.

This array of sentiments—to serve God joyfully, enthusiastically, selflessly—is not radically different from what we find in medieval Jewish literature more generally. By themselves, they represent little that is especially unusual. Hayyim Vital, however, has slipped in a Lurianic twist with his allusion to the attainment of "supernal light" and the "Holy Spirit." If this is not enough to make it clear that much more is at stake here than the simple desire to please God by doing His will, Vital quickly adds that it is impossible to accomplish the latter objective without deeper mystical motivation. God's will is not served merely by the physical doing of the commandments:

> This [God's will] can only be achieved by one who knows the [kabbalistic] intentions of prayer and the mitsvot, and who [meditatively] intends to mend the upper worlds [le-taqen ʿolamot ha-ʿelyonim], and

to unite the name of the Holy One, blessed be He [i.e., *Tiferet*], with His *Shekhinah*. And his intention should have nothing to do with receiving reward in this world, nor even for his benefit in the world to come. . . . Even in connection with the study of Torah, do not think that it is for the purpose of learning its contents, but do so . . . in order to unite the Holy One, blessed be He, and His *Shekhinah*. [17]

In this connection, Vital cites a passage from the *Raᶜaya Mehemna* (*Zohar* 2, 118a), according to which the performance of the mitsvot with kabbalistic intention (*kavvanah*, pl. *kavvanot*) serves two purposes simultaneously. With the enactment of each and every mitsvah, the Holy One, Blessed be He, cleaves to the limbs of the *Shekhinah* in marital love, and the *Shekhinah*, in turn, showers blessing upon her own "limbs," namely, those who perform the mitsvot in the first place.

The point of departure for the Lurianic *kavvanot* associated with the commandments is the traditional division between the 248 positive mitsvot and the 365 negative ones. We noted earlier in the context of the *tiqqunei ᶜavonot* that the positive commandments are exegetically identified with the realm of the *Ḥasadim* (the forces of Compassion) by means of *gematria*. On the other hand, the negative precepts are identified with the realm of the *Gevurot* (the forces of Judgment). This is so by reason of the fact that the five aspects of *Gevurot* that descend to *Zeᶜir Anpin* are associated with the various types of rabbinic punishment imposed upon those who transgress the negative commandments. The *Ḥasadim* and *Gevurot* serve the purpose of assisting in the maturation process of *Zeᶜir Anpin* and *Nuqba de-Zeᶜir*.[18] The performance of positive mitsvot assists in the ongoing development and sustenance of *Zeᶜir*, while the negative mitsvot do the same in connection with *Nuqba*. The element of *Gevurot* is "sweetened" and divested of its potentially injurious aspects as a result of the performance of the negative mitsvot. Thus, the practice of *both* types of mitsvot nourishes the properly balanced development of divinity as a whole.[19]

An alternative description of the effect that the positive and negative mitsvot have upon divinity employs somewhat different categories.[20] According to these terms the performance of the mitsvot brings about two principal kinds of *zivvug*. The love between *Abba* and *Imma* is realized through the performance of the negative mitsvot, whereas coupling between *Ze'ir* and *Nuqba* is brought to fruition by means of the positive. This distinction is tied exegetically to Exodus 3:15, in which God responds to Moses' concern regarding the identity of the one who has sent him to lead the people of Israel. God tells Moses to report to the people that it is the God of their fathers that has sent him, and that "this shall be my name [*ShMY*] forever. This is my appellation [*ZiKRY*] for all eternity." Commenting on this verse, the author of the *Ra'aya Mehemna* and *Tiqqunei Zohar* teaches that the letters in the word *ShMY*, together with the letters *YH* from *YHVH*, possess the numerical equivalent of 365, and thus represent the 365 negative commandments.[21] The letters in the word *ZiKRY*, together with the letters *VH* from *YHVH*, amount numerically to 248, thus representing the 248 positive commandments.

These notions help Luria explain why women have different halakhic responsibilities than men. According to rabbinic law, women are obligated to perform all negative commandments (with one exception), as well as all those positive commandments that do not, by their very nature, have to be observed at a specific time. To put this another way, women are *exempt* from all positive time-specific precepts, such as formal prayer three times a day. Women's status reflects the status of the mythic women of Lurianic cosmology, Leah and Rachel, the two dimensions of *Nuqba de-Ze'ir*. Just as Leah and Rachel are nourished primarily and most immediately from the realm of the *Gevurot*, so too are all females. Insofar as the forces of Judgment or *Gevurot* are associated with the negative mitsvot, the latter are incumbent upon women.[22] The mythic women Leah and Rachel (and thus, by extension, all females) *are* nourished by certain elements of the *Ḥasadim*, those that descend below to *Nuqba* in a way that is contingent upon a delayed process of time. Thus, women are obligated only to comply with those positive commandments that are not bound by time. The halakhic status of women—as is their condition in general—is thus grounded in the metaphysical rules that shape all reality.

These general accounts of the purpose and effect of performing the mitsvot, however, are just the tip of the iceberg. Luria provided richly detailed explanations of the repercussions that specific mitsvot have upon the divine world. These, in turn, were to be used as the focus of mental concentration in the enactment of the precepts. These processes may be illustrated by way of a few examples.

Mystical Intentionality and Married Sexuality

The significance and manner of married sexual relations were crucially important to Lurianic mysticism, as we might infer from what we have already seen in connection with certain of the *tiqqunei ʿavonot*. Luria offers a general reason for a man to marry a woman. He cites a passage from the Babylonian Talmud (*Qiddushin* 29a), in which we learn that God, much like an impatient father or mother, waits for a man to become married. It turns out that God is prepared to wait until a person reaches the age of twenty, after which time He loses his patience and says of him, "Blasted be his bones!" Why does the Talmud refer to a man's *bones* rather than to his body or spirit? Luria's answer is that the creation of the first woman was fashioned from Adam's rib; when a man marries a woman, he restores that rib and brings wholeness once again to his bones. The bones of a man who fails to marry are thus incomplete, or scattered, as dust is scattered in every direction.[23]

In Jewish law, the obligation to procreate (and thus, by inference, to marry) is based upon Genesis 1:28, according to which God enjoins humans to "be fruitful and multiply, and replenish the earth." From the myriad of traditions found in rabbinic literature espousing the significance of marriage, the following may be considered a classic expression:

> "And God said, it is not good for the man to be alone" [Gen. 2:18]. It has been taught: one who has no wife remains without good, without help, without joy, without blessing, and without atonement. . . . R. Hiyya the son of Gumadi said, also, he is not a complete human, for it says, "And he blessed them and called their name, Adam" [Gen. 5:2]. And there are those who say that he even decreases the likeness [of God], for it says, "in the image of God, He made Adam" [Gen. 9:6], and what does it say after this? "And as for you, be fruitful and multiply" [Gen. 9:7].[24]

Marriage is thus the foundation of a range of essential human benefits, none more important than enabling individuals to augment the "likeness of God" in the world by having children. For Luria, only on Sabbath eve do "new" souls descend from on high, the most propitious occasion for marital relations whose intention is procreation. When a man sleeps (between the end of the Sabbath meal and midnight) on Sabbath eve, his soul encounters and cleaves to some particular "new" soul, one that will subsequently descend when he makes love to his wife after midnight. Should his wife become pregnant, the resulting child will be pious and holy.

Moreover, in the course of sexual relations that result in conception, the soul of the conceived person receives a garment (*levush neshamah*), to which both mother and father contribute. Insofar as immature individuals are unable to perform the mitsvot on their own, without assistance, they require such spiritual garments to help them secure the divine vitality that descends from on high. This garment cleaves to the souls of individuals throughout their lives.[25] It is in this deep sense that a woman and her husband are partners in the process of procreation, and the reason why the Torah is as strict as it is concerning the need for sanctity in the course of sexual relations. For if individuals hallow themselves while having relations, the garment bestowed upon the soul of their newly formed child will be holy, enabling the latter to serve God properly: "Even if his is a great soul [*neshamah gedolah*], he [nevertheless] needs the sanctity of his father and mother during lovemaking so as to bring forth a superior garment, lest this garment cause him to sin . . . [thus] if one's son transgresses, his father is considered responsible."[26]

Sanctity during sexual relations appears to entail a number of things. Luria, for example, vigorously cautioned against having sexual relations in the light, even at night by the light of a candle. There must be absolutely no light whatsoever in the room in which intercourse takes place. Under the inspiration of rabbinic tradition, according to which "one who cohabits by the light of a lamp will have epileptic children," Luria taught that this is true even if a woman has already conceived but has not given birth yet.[27] Most deaths from childhood epilepsy are due to such improper relations. In a similar vein, he also warned against having intercourse immediately upon waking from a dream with an erection. Should a husband and wife do so, the resulting child will be imperfect in some manner. Presumably, this has to do with a wife's willingness to have marital relations, something not necessarily to be counted on if a man awakes from a dream with an erection, for "everything requires intention on the part of both of them" (*kavvanat shnei-hem*). From a slightly different angle, this caution reflects a fear that dream-induced desire might result in the conception of demonic spirits (*ruḥin ve-shedin*), presumably because a demonic female such as Lilit has aroused the man.[28]

Are sexual relations between a husband and wife required (or permitted, for that matter) when they are not likely to result in the conception of a child? We learn that a man ought to engage in marital intercourse even while his wife is pregnant, or while she is nursing a child. He should not claim that relations during these periods constitute a "wasteful" (*le-vatalah*) act, inasmuch as it cannot result in conception. The reason for this is that there are two types of sexual relations, each with its own motive. As we have seen, there is one in which the goal is to produce children. Sexual relations for this purpose do not have to take place at all times, such as periods when conception is impossible. The second kind of lovemaking, however, can be practiced even when a woman is pregnant or nursing, insofar as its purpose is not procreation but to arouse and sustain the upper worlds.

Evidence for the Lurianic position, we are told, may be found in connection with the biblical matriarchs, Sarah, Rebecca, and Rachel; even though Abraham, Isaac, and Jacob each had wives who appeared unable to bear children during some period of their lives, they still maintained marital relations with the intention of sustaining the upper worlds. There was conflicting evidence as to whether Luria himself had relations with his wife during those periods when conception was not possible, Vital says. Luria did not do so at such times, neighbors told Vital, but the latter believed that this might not have been the case.[29] He had asked his teacher whether he himself could desist from such conjugal relations during the winter months, because the cold weather made ritual bathing following sexual relations difficult, and Luria evidently replied that Vital could refrain as long as his wife consented, but said that it was nevertheless preferable to have relations.[30]

At the heart of the processes of *tiqqun* lies the notion that there are five principal types of supernal coupling between *Ze'ir* and *Nuqba de-Ze'ir*, consisting of different combinations of various dimensions of these two *partsufim*. *Ze'ir Anpin* has two aspects, Jacob and Israel, while *Nuqba de-Ze'ir* manifests itself either as Rachel or Leah. These five, in hierarchical order, from the most perfect to the least perfect, are: Israel and Rachel, Jacob and Rachel, Jacob and Leah (after midnight), Israel and Leah, and Jacob and Leah (before midnight). A different quality of phallic vitality, *Yesod*, issues forth during each of these various forms of divine coupling. Moreover, each of these unions takes place at a different period of the day.

Given that Luria conceived of *tiqqun* in significantly sexualized terms, it follows logically that he regarded human sexual relations as among the most immediate and powerful ways in which to accomplish cosmic mending. This required, however, that sexual relations take place at times aligned with the most propitious moments for supernal relations. Which nights and hours were appropriate for marital lovemaking depended on whether one was a sage (*talmid ḥakham*) or not.[31] A man who was not a sage—that is, who was not a kabbalist—was permitted to engage in sexual relations with his wife on any night, including weeknights. He should not do so, though, during the early evening hours, but only after midnight. Relations before midnight during the week brought about the *zivvug* of Jacob and Leah, the least sublime type of intradivine love possible, because of the prevalence of forces of divine Judgment, associated especially with Leah, which were at their most potent during the evening hours, between sundown and midnight. Union during this period resulted in Jacob and Leah occupying or filling *Ze'ir Anpin* only partially, from the "chest and above." After midnight on weekdays, however, the *zivvug* of Jacob and Leah in her aspect of Rachel took place. The superiority of such a union was based on the fact that although the forces of Judgment associated with Leah were still present at this hour, they were attenuated, or "sweetened," by virtue of it being midnight. Moreover, Jacob and this particular manifestation of Leah filled the entire length of *Ze'ir Anpin*, rather than merely its top half. For all of these reasons, non-kabbalists were permitted to have sexual relations *after* midnight during the week, but not before.

Kabbalists, on the other hand, were supposed to follow a far stricter set of guidelines. For the most part, they were prohibited from engaging in sexual relations with their wives on all nights except Friday night, Sabbath eve.[32] Moreover, they too were to wait until after midnight. Sabbath eve after midnight was superior because the *zivvug* aroused on high by virtue of relations then was the most exalted type possible, that of Israel and Rachel herself. This divine union was the same as that during the *musaf* ("additional") prayers on Sabbath mornings. The unification in the world above stimulated by relations on Sabbath eve *prior* to midnight was the same as on a weekday night *following* midnight. The rules concerning the nights of a major festival (*Yom Tov*) and the New Moon were the same as for the Sabbath, although these occasions did not possess quite the same degree of sanctity as the Sabbath.[33]

The single exception to this rather austere set of regulations was the night on which a married woman performed ritual immersion in a mikvah—following menstruation and the required seven "clean" days. Even if this fell on a weeknight, relations were nevertheless permitted. Luria would remain awake until midnight on such nights studying Torah, after which time he would have relations with his wife. Following this he would rise, wash his hands, recite the Shema, and then go to sleep.[34] The acknowledged reason for this exception was to ensure that "he would not have impure thoughts whatsoever, or perhaps, God forbid, experience a [nocturnal] emission."[35] Quite obviously, this exception represented a concession to the reality of sexual desire and the need to give it appropriate expression. We are also told about the direction in which one should lie while making love.[36] One's head should be to the East, corresponding to *Da'at*, one's feet to the West, corresponding to *Yesod*, one's right hand southward, corresponding to the *sefirah Hesed*, and one's left hand northward, corresponding to *Gevurah*. This was, we are told, Adam's position when he was created.[37]

This is a fascinating set of rules for married sexual relations. Aside from the assertion that a husband and wife's intention should be the same, and the statement that a wife has the right to demur from conjugal relations, even if her husband wishes otherwise, we are told little else about the interpersonal nature of marital relations. How are men and women to approach the sexual act? In what sense are sexual relations *love*making between two people? The question of love *is* invoked to some degree, in connection with the *notariqon* of sequences of words having to do with the practice of the Sabbath found in Exodus 31:12, 17.[38] By taking the initial letters of several combinations of words in these two verses, Luria discovered encoded the words for wife, love, and marital intercourse, from which he inferred that a husband ought to "love his wife as himself" (*ʾohev ʾishto ke-gufo*).

This brief allusion to love notwithstanding, comparison with related themes in earlier kabbalistic literature is instructive in this connection. Abraham ben David of Posquieres (Rabad), the author of a set of guidelines on marital sexuality, enumerated four rationales for sexual intercourse, including the husband's legal requirement of *ʿonah*, that is, his conjugal obligation to give his wife pleasure. A man must not merely provide the minimum to his wife as required by rabbinic law, but must satisfy her desires to the extent that she wishes. While Rabad addressed his book to men rather than women, nevertheless he was concerned that a man's *kavvanah* in the course of sexual relations focus on his wife's satisfaction rather than on his own physical pleasure.[39] Along similar lines, *ʾIggeret ha-Qodesh*, to which we have already referred, addressed in elaborate detail the gentle care and consideration with which a husband must make love to his wife. The author of this marital guide has this to say, for instance, about the nature of proper sexual foreplay: "Therefore, engage her first in conversation that puts her heart and mind at ease and gladden her. . . . Speak words that arouse her to passion, union, love, desire, and longing. . . . Never force her. . . . Instead, win her over with words of graciousness and seduction. . . . Do not hasten to arouse passion until her mood is ready; enter [her] with love and willingness so that she seminates [that is, has an orgasm] first."[40] If we consider how the *Zohar* treats marital love, we see that while its primary interest is unquestionably theosophical and theurgical, unification between *Tiferet* and *Malkhut*, the *Zohar* also manifests concern that a husband properly arouse his wife's desire: "This teaches us that when a man wishes to lie with his wife he must first of all coax her and persuade her with words, and if he is unsuccessful he should not lie with her, for they must share the same desire and there must be no compulsion."[41]

The notion that "they must share the same desire" is taken a step further both in *ʾIggeret ha-Qodesh* and the *Zohar* in their elaborations upon the significance of a woman's intentionality. Thus, the author of the *ʾIggeret* avers that the purpose of arousing one's wife is so that "their thought will unite as one, and the *Shekhinah* will rest between them."[42] Elsewhere, he states that such arousal serves "to join her mind with his, and [to] unite her intention with his."[43] Similarly, in describing sexual relations between Moses' parents, Amram and Yocheved, the *Zohar* (2, 11b) tells us that "the *Shekhinah* rested upon their bed, and their will was one with the *Shekhinah*. . . . Their desire focused on uniting with the *Shekhinah*. Thus, the *Shekhinah* joined in the very act in which they were engaged."

Commenting on this passage in the sixteenth century, Moses Cordovero emphasized still further the importance of a woman's intentionality: "Their desire, both his and hers, was to unite *Shekhinah*. He focused on *Tiferet* [as his archetype] and she on *Malkhut*. His union was to join *Shekhinah*; his wife focused correspondingly on being *Shekhinah* and uniting with Her Husband, *Tiferet*."[44]

This is a striking passage. It goes beyond the general suggestion that a woman's intention be in alignment with her husband's by spelling out the requirement that a wife consciously identify with her cosmic counterpart, the *Shekhinah*, and, even more, by calling upon her to focus contemplatively on coupling with *Tiferet*. I am aware of no other kabbalistic text that goes this far in enunciating a women's active contemplative and theurgic role in the mystical practice of sexual relations. A woman's agency in the sphere of sexual matters is also attested in an unusually intriguing text of the early seventeenth century. In his manual of kabbalistic ritual practice, *Seder ha-Yom* (Order of the Day), Moses ibn Makhir, a scholar with close ties to Safed, writes as follows:

> If it is possible for a man to immerse his entire body in forty measures [of water] so that no harm will come to him, how much the better. Such was the practice of the early pietists who used to go

down to the river in order to immerse themselves, and afterwards go to greet the [Sabbath] Bride and receive an additional soul in purity and holiness. Likewise, we have found that the early pietists practiced ritual immersion with their wives [in preparation for the Sabbath] so as to bind their hearts to the same place.[45]

Exactly what ibn Makhir has in mind is far from clear. In any case, insofar as his manual is prescriptive in nature, it appears to imply some type of kabbalistic intentionality for women as part of the act of ritual immersion on Sabbath eve. And the notion that husbands and wives did so together "so as to bind their hearts to the same place" suggests preparation, not only for the onset of Sabbath in general, but also in particular for sexual relations on the Sabbath.[46]

Now, while it is fair to assume that Luria would have encouraged sensitivity and gentleness in lovemaking, and more generally concern for one's wife, these are not the concerns that leap out at us. Our sources certainly do not betray any hint that a woman ought to assume the kind of active role suggested by the passages cited above. The preoccupation articulated in our sources is not with sex as an interpersonal activity, but with procreativity per se, and even more primarily, with the theosophical and theurgical implications of sexual relations. Aside from the fact that it can produce children, sex is consequential because of the various types of intimate union it engenders in the world of divinity. That a couple should make love even when conception is not possible, with rigorous concern for the day and hour during which relations should take place, and the direction in which a couple should lie—these are what really matter. And the reason they matter is because they enable the sexual act to replicate and thus stimulate the sefirotic universe in precise and predictable ways. That is to say, they are acts of cosmic mending, or *tiqqun*. It is as if the purely personal, intimate character of sexual activity has retreated into the background as deeper concerns assume center stage. The processes of *tiqqun* seem to have become so consuming for Luria that worldly concerns paled by comparison. The conventional purposes of married sexual relations—sexual gratification, marital joy, even procreation itself to some degree—all appear to have been significantly displaced (or at least relegated to the periphery) by an intensity of focus on *tiqqun*.

In his study of Joseph Karo, Zwi Werblowsky argued that male kabbalists as a whole treated marital sexuality in purely instrumental terms:

> The kabbalists . . . made a mystical virtue of halakhic necessity. But this mystical transformation of matrimonial life was purely *formal*. The kabbalists did not seek a new type of relationship with women or a novel conception of love and spiritual intimacy. They were certainly no romantics. They were ascetic in the extreme and could justify the sexual act and praise its mystical significance only if and because it was performed without carnal pleasure. . . . The Jewish kabbalist lived with his wife but knew that he should live only in God. He performed his marital duties with mystico-theurgic intentions, but realized that he was not allowed to give himself up either to his partner or to his passion. Transformed, in theory, into a sacramental act, the "holy union" of husband and wife was in practice an ascetic exercise that admitted of no genuine relationship between the partners because the kabbalist had to identify himself with the mystical intention of the act and not with its actuality. Add to this the markedly patriarchal and masculine character of Judaism, and the one-sidedness of married life, even after the kabbalistic revolution, becomes obvious.[47]

In light of the evidence from non-Lurianic sources adduced above, Werblowsky's generalizations about this question strike me as far too extreme and sweeping in their scope. I believe that it is reasonable to argue that *some* kabbalists, *qua* kabbalists, consciously went out of their way to treat their wives as partners in a mystical rite of sexual relations, going so far as to leave room for some degree of contemplative and theurgical agency on the part of women. If this is the case, then it is certainly mistaken to assume that the intimacy between a male kabbalist and his wife invariably "admitted of no genuine relationship between the partners." Even in Luria's case, it seems to me that such a characterization goes beyond what we could possibly be able to know. At the same time, there is more than a kernel of truth in Werblowsky's analysis, especially when it comes to Lurianic Kabbalah. Aside from an occasional remark here and there, the huge corpus of Lurianic texts pays virtually no attention to women as subjects or agents in their own right. On the basis of what we are in a position to know, it does not appear as if the crucial role that women played in the kabbalistic scheme of things translated into a significant regard for women as individuals with a point of view of their own.

The Mitsvah of Charity

This same phenomenon—in which mystical concerns displace more mundane ones—can be clearly illustrated by an analysis of Luria's approach to a quintessential ethical religious precept, the mitsvah of *tsedaqah*, or charity. In Lurianic terms, the entire process of charity, its rationale, collection and distribution, turns out to be a description of particular intradivine dynamics.[48] The *sefirah Yesod* within *Ze'ir Anpin* is the "collector of charity" (*gabbai tsedaqah*). The *tsedaqah* that it "collects" is itself gathered from divine lights above. More precisely, these lights are made up of the *Ḥasadim*, which, under the right circumstances, flow into *Yesod*. In the course of this process, the *Ḥasadim* are "crushed" by *Yesod*. Far from diminishing the *Ḥasadim*, however, this process unleashes their hitherto concealed power, so that they grow in strength. (In the same way, a person who gives charity to others will actually become more wealthy.) These now crushed particles of light are ultimately scattered as "crumbs" into the realm of *Malkhut/Nuqba de-Ze'ir*, who is impoverished insofar as she is dependent on the beneficence of others. To reduce this to its most basic terms, *Yesod* (the *Tsaddiq*, or "Righteous One") "distributes" *tsedaqah* to the "poor," that is, to *Malkhut*, or *Tsedeq*, the female counterpart to *Yesod*. *Malkhut* remains impoverished until she is filled with divine light from above. The act of charity, then, is construed as a means by which sexual union between the divine masculine and feminine takes place. The human gesture of charity is itself akin to a sexual act on the part of the one who practices it, insofar as in the process of doing so he assimilates himself to *Yesod* within *Ze'ir Anpin* through his contemplative intention.

In another description, we are informed that the letter *quf* in the word *tsedaqah* symbolizes Cain, associated with the pollution of the primeval snake, whereas the letter *heh* in *tsedaqah* symbolizes Abel. When individuals give *tsedaqah* they should meditatively intend that the "foot," or long vertical line, in the letter *quf* thereby *extricates* itself from the realm of the *qelippot*. It will then ascend above and become transformed into the letter *heh*, that is, "Abel."[49] Yet another explanation: When one gives a *perutah* (a small coin) in charity, one should concentrate on the deconstruction of this word (*PRVTaH*) into two elements as *PRaT VH*, the last two letters being the second half of the Tetragrammaton. The source of the forces of Judgment are 288 (*resh*, *peh*, *het*) sparks; when we add one to this number (for the word *RPH* as a whole), we arrive at 289, which happens to be the numerical equivalent of the letters *PRT* from *perutah*. The elements of Judgment themselves are also associated with *Malkhut*, signified by the letter *heh* of *vav heh*. Thus, when one joins *vav* to *heh*, the *PRaT* of Judgment is "sweetened." In connection with these teachings, we learn, as noted earlier, that Isaac Luria used to give charity with tremendous joy and heartfelt generosity, with an open hand, sometimes not even looking to see if anything remained in his hand or not.[50]

Although there is reference here to the actual giving of charity, and we have seen that Luria himself was meticulous about this obligation, the focus of contemplative attention is devoted entirely to its theurgical consequences. As individuals who were encouraged to be ethically sensitive—in conformity with rabbinic values—the Lurianic kabbalists doubtlessly believed in the intrinsic significance of *tsedaqah*. But the unmistakable inference one draws is that such mundane concerns were only the external dimension of deeper mystical goals. And yet, of course, the latter could not be satisfied except by means of the actual physical act—accompanied by the appropriate meditative intentions.

By contrast, once again, the *Zohar* exhibits a thoroughly developed social conscience when it comes to the question of the poor and charity. In the case of the *Zohar*'s interpretation, we find much that closely resembles the Lurianic view: the giving of charity to the poor is tantamount to the bestowal of blessing by *Tiferet* upon *Shekhinah* in an act of sexual intercourse, also expressed as the completion of God's name, *YHVH*.[51] The essential dynamic is the same in both systems, although the Lurianic is theosophically more complex, as is inevitably the case. But there is a crucial difference as well. While clearly concerned about the sefirotic consequences of giving charity, the *Zohar* simultaneously demonstrates genuine interest in the actual plight of the poor. The poor individual is identified as *Tsedeq*, that is, he signifies the *Shekhinah* and is linked to Her, for like Her, he too has nothing of his own, but depends upon others for his sustenance. The poor person is likened to one who is dead, just as the *Shekhinah* is "dead" when separated from the source of Her nourishment, *Tiferet*. But when someone has compassion for him and gives him charity, the Tree of Life, *Tiferet*, hovers over him. As Scripture says, "Righteousness [*tsedaqah*] delivers from death" (Prov. 10:2).

Another example of the *Zohar*'s overt concern for the poor may be seen in a passage that describes the ritual of dwelling in the Sukkah on the festival of Sukkot.[52] On each night of the holiday, the celebrants are to welcome sefirotic/patriarchal guests—Abraham (*Ḥesed*), Isaac (*Gevurah*), Jacob (*Tiferet*), and so on. In so doing, they focus their contemplative attention on the various aspects of divinity and draw them into the community's midst. But we also learn that to welcome divine guests *without* welcoming earthly ones, namely, the poor, is to render one's celebration meaningless. In such cases, "it turns out that the table he set is his own, not divine." What is true in the case of Sukkot also obtains when it comes to the other major festivals, illustrating how the *Zohar* joined concern for the poor to more purely mystical concerns. These examples bring into relief the way in which Luria's interpretive approach to the quintessentially social act of *tsedeqah* reframes this mitsvah so as to relegate its literal meaning (the *peshat*) to the distant periphery.

The Study of Torah as a Mystical Rite

Just as Luria understood interpersonal activities such as marital love and the giving of charity in ways that shifted the interpretive center of gravity to the theosophical realm, the same can be said for another fundamental religious act, *talmud torah*, the study of Torah. In classical Judaism, the study of Torah refers, of course, not merely to engagement with the Hebrew Bible, but to the entirety of sacred teachings and texts, "Torah" in the broadest sense of the word. The choice of this mitsvah to exemplify the questions with which we are concerned is prompted by two considerations. In the first place, it enables us to see how Luria related to what is normally considered the intellectual activity par excellence in Jewish tradition. It also allows us to explore a problem that bears upon our broader inquiry in a number of important ways.

Isaac Luria and his students unquestionably engaged to some degree in the study of sacred texts in a manner that resembled conventional techniques, that is, study that entailed sustained intellectual effort, although even this was directed toward discovering esoteric meaning:

> When I [Hayyim Vital] asked my teacher how he had merited all the esoteric wisdom in his possession, however, he told me that he had invested a great amount of effort studying. But I responded that R. Moses Cordovero, of blessed memory, had also done the same. Even I, Hayyim, devoted a tremendous amount of effort in acquiring this wisdom. He then told me that while it is true that we applied ourselves extremely diligently, to an extent greater than any of our contemporaries, we did not do as he had done. For how many nights had he remained awake, poring over a single passage of the *Zohar*? Sometimes he would seclude himself, sit and study only a single passage during the course of six weekday nights. And usually, he would avoid sleeping altogether during these nights.[53]

But in addition to this sort of study, he also instructed his disciples to engage in another type, which he calls "recitation of Torah" (*qeri'at Torah*).[54] Vital informs us that such recitation of Torah refers not to study as a whole, but to the daily, fixed regimen of study that every (male) Jew is obligated to undertake. Building upon the rabbinic injunction to divide one's study along the lines of Scripture (*Miqra'*), Mishnah, and Talmud,[55] the kabbalists added to this list the study of esoteric texts. Thus, Moses Cordovero, for example, championed the cause of kabbalistic study by identifying ideal scholars as those "who follow the straight path—who in part study Scripture, in part Gemara and its teachings, which we consider to be Mishnah, and in part this wisdom [i.e., Kabbalah], for its own sake, in order to penetrate its se-

crets."[56] Cordovero retains the threefold division of the Talmud's injunction by conflating Mishnah and Gemara into one category. Luria
refined this list by enjoining the daily study of *Miqra* (here meaning
the Pentateuch), *Neviʾim* (Prophets), *Ketuvim* (Writings), Mishnah,
Talmud, and Kabbalah.[57] As we shall see, though, the kind of study
that our sources describe bears little resemblance to any conventional
form of Torah study.

Isaac Luria himself used to recite Torah as a regular part of his daily
regimen. After praying the morning service, Luria would have break-
fast, then wrap himself in prayer shawl and phylacteries again and proceed to study Scripture, Prophets, Writings, Mishnah, Talmud, and
Kabbalah, in that order.[58] This study was performed in a highly ritualized manner. The daily recitation from the Five Books of Moses was
based upon the weekly portion (*parasha*) to be chanted in the synagogue on the upcoming Sabbath morning. A specific number of verses
from the portion was to be recited each weekday morning, leading up
to the recital of the entire weekly portion on Friday morning. The
schedule that Luria prescribed was as follows:

Sunday	First six verses
Monday	Next four verses
Tuesday	Next five verses
Wednesday	Next six verses
Thursday	Next five verses
Friday	The entire *parasha*

The recitation for each day was to be carried out in the same manner. Following established rabbinic custom, each verse was to be recited twice in Hebrew and once in the Aramaic translation (*Targum*).
Vital does not specify how the texts from the Prophets and Writings
were chosen, although presumably the prophetic portion would be
the one that normally accompanies the weekly *parasha*. In any case,
this study was also to be done by reciting each verse twice in Hebrew
and once in Aramaic. The choice of specific texts from the Mishnah
and Gemara is also left undetermined. As far as the study of Kabbalah
is concerned, the primary, if not exclusive, focus was the *Zohar*.[59] Vital

preserves the following description of his teacher's own practice of reciting the pentateuchal portion in its entirety on Friday mornings:

> These were the practices of my teacher, of blessed memory: As soon as he had finished the morning service on Friday, he would walk to the synagogue or to his House of Study. If there was a proper Torah scroll there, he would remove it from the Ark and read the portion for the coming Sabbath, twice in the Hebrew and once in the *Targum*. He used to read the Hebrew [himself] from the Torah scrolls and had a certain student who would read the Aramaic translation after him out of a book. He would adopt this procedure, verse by verse, until he had completed the portion. He did not do as those who hurry by reciting the whole portion of Scripture once [in its entirety], repeat it, and then recite the *Targum* in its entirety. Rather, he recited each and every verse separately, twice in Hebrew and once in Aramaic.[60]

The fact that these texts were to be *recited* rather than studied in a conventional manner did not mean that one was to have nothing in mind as one practiced such recitation. On the contrary, the recitation was to be accompanied by detailed *kavvanot*. The basis for these particular *kavvanot* was Luria's teachings concerning the four worlds, insofar as according to him, each of the four basic levels of sacred text—Scripture, Mishnah, Talmud, and Kabbalah—correspond to one of the four worlds that constitute the cosmos:

Scripture = *Assiyah*
Mishnah = *Yetsirah*
Talmud = *Beri'ah*
Kabbalah = *Atsilut*

We have already seen that one of the results of the Breaking of the Vessels and of Adam's sin was that the ordered hierarchy of the four worlds was thrown into disarray. In particular, the world of *Assiyah* descended into the realm of the *qelippot,* so that good and evil, light and darkness, became thoroughly entangled. As such, one of the basic ways in which *tiqqun* was conceived of was in terms of the elevation of the four worlds to their proper positions within the cosmic hierarchy and the extrication of the world of *Assiyah* from the realm of materiality. Contemplative recitation of Torah was one of the most effective means by which these goals could be accomplished. At the same time, such activity also had the effect of enabling an individual to personally bind his soul to each of the worlds as he engaged in the various levels of study: "Therefore, each day a person must cleave [*yedabeq nafsho*] and bind his soul to the four worlds, reciting Scripture that corresponds to *Assiyah*, followed by Mishnah that corresponds to *Yetsirah*, Talmud corresponding to *Beri'ah*, and Kabbalah corresponding to *Atsilut*."[61]

This homologous relationship between levels of the cosmos and various texts—that is, different manifestations of the divine word—demonstrates a fundamental notion that we have encountered elsewhere, namely, that the structure of reality and divine language are actually two expressions of the same thing. The cosmos, consisting as it does of various levels of spiritual reality, all of which emerge from within the inner wellsprings of divine infinitude, also reveals itself under the guise of the different literary and linguistic expressions of God's speech. And just as the four worlds constitute a vast structured hierarchy, so, too, does divine language. The revelation of Torah is composed of layer upon layer; that which is most concealed, most difficult to penetrate and apprehend, is the deepest and truest, most sublime and perfect expression of divinity. The outermost layers, those most accessible to the casual student of Torah, comprise the more mundane—if one can use such a word in this connection—expressions of divine life. From the purest, deepest, most sublime Torah of *Atsilut*, that is, the most concealed level of Kabbalah, to the "ordinary" discourse of Scripture according to its plain, literal meaning, the Torah of *Assiyah*, divine language parallels the structure of the cosmos itself. To put it another way, the cosmos as a whole is textualized, made up of layer within layer of language, each layer serving as the garment of the one it envelops. At the same time, there is also a dimension of human soul that corresponds to each level of world and language, insofar as the soul and divinity mirror each other. The implications of these correspondences are far reaching: to raise up one's soul and cleave to the various worlds through contemplative study is to contribute simultaneously to inspiring oneself and mending the cosmos. Thus Hayyim Vital:

My teacher, of blessed memory, used to tell me that the principal purpose of a person's contemplation while studying Torah is to draw down
upon himself mystical inspiration and supernal holiness. It all depends
on this: All his mental concentration must be directed towards binding
[*le-qasher et nafsho*] and uniting his soul with its supernal source by
means of the Torah. He should do so in order that the restoration of
the supernal Adam might be accomplished [*yushlam tiqqun ʾadam ha-
ʿelyon*]. For this is God's purpose in creating human beings, and His
intention in instructing them to occupy themselves with Torah. . . .
And this will be exceedingly effective in the attainment of the Holy
Spirit, that is, by means of the study of Torah with this intention.[62]

In these terms, study ceases to be an intellectual activity, becoming
instead a meditative exercise that has as its ultimate purpose the re-
structuring of the elements of the cosmic puzzle that the kabbalists believed constituted reality. By studying Torah, Mishnah, and Talmud
with esoteric intentionality, even these "lesser" grades of textuality are
raised to higher levels and transformed in the process. But transformation, as is always the case for Luria, takes place at the personal level
as well. A person becomes inspired, drawing down divine light upon
himself, infusing himself with vitality from on high.

The *Kavvanot* of Pentateuchal Recitation

The details of these processes may be illustrated by reference to the
kavvanot Luria taught for the recitation of portions from the Pentateuch.[63] To do so, I need to say a few words about the correspondence
between the divine structure of *Adam Qadmon* and the Tetragrammaton, *YHVH*. We know that *Adam Qadmon* is described as possessing
four structural dimensions, conceived of as anatomical features of the
head: eyes, ears, nose, and mouth. Each of these, in turn, corresponds
to various configurations of *YHVH*. According to this conception,
the Tetragrammaton can assume four basic forms; these are known as
the names "seventy-two," "sixty-three," "forty-five," and "fifty-two" and
are based on the *gematria* of the different spellings (*milluim*) of the
letters that make up *YHVH*:

1. Name "seventy-two" is expressed by *millui de-yudin*, in which the letter *yud* is used to spell the last three parts of this name as follows: *YVD HY VYV HY*.

2. Name "sixty-three" is expressed by *millui de-yudin* with an *alef* in the *vav*, and is written as follows: *YVD HY VAV HY*.

3. Name "forty-five" is expressed by *millui de-ʾalfin*, in which the last three parts are written with an *alef*, as follows: *YVD HA VAV HA*.

4. Name "fifty-two" is expressed by *millui de-hein*, in which the *heh*s are written with double *heh*, as follows: *YVD HH VV HH*.

In addition to representing one of the *partsufim*, each of these names corresponds to one of the four letters of the simple Tetragrammaton. The following chart summarizes this set of associations:

Anatomy of *Adam Qadmon*

	Partsuf	Name	Letter	World
Eye	*Abba*	72	*Yud*	*Atsilut*
Ear	*Imma*	63	*Heh*	*Beriʾah*
Nose	*Zeᶜir*	45	*Vav*	*Yetsirah*
Mouth	*Nuqba*	52	*Heh*	*Assiyah*

We know that the *kavvanot* associated with the fixed recitation of the Pentateuch are tied to the cycle of the week, organized around the Sabbath. According to Lurianic teaching, the name "fifty-two," as can be seen from the chart above, corresponds to the lowest of the four worlds, *Assiyah*. Thus, the restoration of this world requires meditative concentration on this name. A single word upon which to concentrate is composed by selecting five letters from the name "fifty-two." By taking the letters *vav* and *dalet* from the word *yud*, the second *heh* from the word *heh*, the second *vav* from the word *vav*, and the second *heh* from the final *heh* in this particular spelling of *YHVH*, one derives the name *VDHVH*. These five letters represent, then, the name "fifty-two" as a whole. They are, in turn, divided into the five weekdays, Sunday through Thursday, and serve as the basis for the *number* of verses to be recited on any particular day from the approaching Torah portion of the week. Thus, for example, on Sunday, the adept concentrates on the first *six* verses from the upcoming Torah portion, corresponding to the letter *vav* (6) in the five letters *VDHVH*. Moreover, each of these five letters and their corresponding days is associated with one of the *sefirot* from *Ḥesed* through *Yesod*:

Sunday = *Ḥesed*
Monday = *Gevurah*
Tuesday = *Tiferet*
Wednesday = *Netsaḥ*
Thursday = *Hod*

On each of these days, as one recites the pertinent verses, one simultaneously concentrates on the appropriate letter from the five-letter name *VDHVH,* as well as its sefirotic equivalent. Thus, on Sunday, when one recites the first six verses from the Torah portion, one focuses contemplatively on the letter *vav* and *Ḥesed,* associated with this name. Moreover, each letter is vocalized in a special way, based on the five vowels in the scriptural phrase "ʾ*et* ʾ*asher yavi*ʾ*u*" (Exod. 16:5), which employs the vowels *shva, pataḥ, segol, qamets,* and *ḥiriq.* Inasmuch as the recitation of the Torah portion constitutes preparation for the upcoming Sabbath, these vowels, representing as they do a verse that refers to preparing for the Sabbath, are appropriate for this meditation.[64]

As we have seen, one is supposed to recite the first twenty-six verses of the Torah portion on the first five days of the week, whereas on Friday morning, one recites the whole portion, during which time one is required to concentrate on *all* of the five letters and their sefirotic equivalences from the previous five days. By doing so, one theurgically reunites the *sefirot Ḥesed* through *Hod.* At the same time, one binds these five *sefirot* to the *sefirah Yesod* insofar as the latter corresponds to Friday. Thus the Friday recitation serves the purpose of uniting *Ḥesed* through *Yesod,* which together corresponds to the *masculine* dimension of divinity. Inasmuch as the Sabbath represents the *feminine* aspect of the divine, *Malkhut,* this prepares the way for the unification of male and female that takes place on the Sabbath itself. At the same time, this unification contributes to the *tiqqun* of the realm of *Assiyah* as a whole. These associations may be summarized as follows:

Sunday/letter *vav*/first six verses of portion/*Ḥesed*
Monday/letter *dalet*/next four verses of portion/*Gevurah*
Tuesday/letter *heh*/next five verses of portion/*Tiferet*
Wednesday/letter *vav*/next six verses of portion/*Netsaḥ*
Thursday/letter *heh*/next five verses of portion/*Hod*
Friday/*VDHVH*/entire Torah portion/*Yesod*
Sabbath Day/*Malkhut*

The Contemplative Study of Jewish Law

In addition to recitation of Torah, Luria also instructed his disciples to practice the study of Jewish law in a contemplative way, which he categorized as intensive study of Halakah (*ʿiyyun halakha*).[65] This, too, had as its primary purpose the central mystical goals that suffused Lurianic mysticism and was accompanied by particular *kavvanot*. Luria provided what can only be described as an extraordinary explanation for the study of halakha. *ʿIyyun halakha* is not for the purpose of discovering the will of God, or in order to determine proper ritual behavior. Rather, it is a means by which to destroy *qelippot*, that is, the evil "shells" imprisoning all the sparks of divine light that have fallen into our world! The shell in the present case is represented by nothing less than the *qushia*, the difficult legal quandary that confronts the student of halakhic discourse:

> In connection with the intensive study of rabbinic law with our comrades, I observed that my master, may his memory be an everlasting blessing, used to gird up his strength like a lion, to such an extent that he would become exhausted and break out in a great sweat. When I asked him why he exerted such tremendous effort, he replied that the purpose of such study was to destroy the shells, namely, those difficult problems [*qushiot*] connected with particular legal questions that are not easily understood. One therefore has to expend enormous effort, exhausting one's strength. Thus, the Torah may be called wisdom that exhausts the strength of one who engages in its study.[66]

Solving the *qushia* and thus eliminating the evil shell that encompasses a halakhic problem serves to reveal the inner core at the heart of that problem:

My teacher, of blessed memory, also informed me that a source of [mystical] inspiration is the intensive study of halakha. This is so, he said, because intensive legal study consists in concentrating one's attention upon the fact that every nut possesses a shell that protects its inner core, the part constituting its holy element. This protective shell corresponds to the difficult problem in need of resolution in the particular legal question; for the shell shields the law, preventing one from comprehending it. But when one solves the problem, one must concentrate upon destroying the power of the shell, separating it thereby from the holy. Then the inner core, which is the halakha [i.e., the legal outcome itself], will be revealed. For if one does not continually strive to concentrate in this intensive way and to shatter the shells, how will the inner core be revealed to one, this constituting the secrets of the Torah and the knowledge of Kabbalah.[67]

The notion that the *qushia* in a halakhic problem is a negative thing, even evil, has its origins in the *Tiqqunei Zohar* and the *Raᶜaya Mehemna*, anonymous imitations of the *Zohar* dating from the early fourteenth century. The *Raᶜaya Mehemna,* which displays a complex, ambivalent attitude toward the halakha and the halakhic process, is devoted largely to a discussion of the reasons for the commandments. In an attempt to assert the primacy of esoteric, kabbalistic meaning over the plain (*peshat*) meaning of the Torah, the *Raᶜaya Mehemna*, in effect, calls into question the ultimate validity of halakha. This attitude is partly rooted in the idea that the Torah as we presently have it, the "Torah of the Tree of Knowledge of Good and Evil," is one that is *necessary* in a world of sin and materiality. Human sinfulness brought about the need for such a Torah, replete with its elaborate structure of limitations and restrictions. But in the messianic age, an altogether different Torah will govern humankind, the "Torah of the Tree of Life." This utopian Torah will relinquish the need for the prohibitions and boundaries that characterize the halakha as we know it now. Such an inner, primordial Torah once existed; it was the one originally intended for Israel, and would have continued to prevail had it not been for Adam's sin.[68]

These ideas led the author of the *Raᶜaya Mehemna* to regard halakhic discourse as a transitory phenomenon required in an unredeemed world. It would be incorrect to claim that the *Raᶜaya Mehemna* was genuinely antinomian in attitude, for it is entirely committed to the observance of the halakha. Yet it is impossible to avoid the conclusion that the author of this text regarded the dialectical complexities of rabbinic law as inferior relative to the Torah's concealed truths. Thus, for example, he draws a comparison between Israel's enslavement in Egypt and the strenuous nature of the efforts scholars must exert in the course of talmudic analysis![69] The hard shell (*qelippah*) of halakha is the *qushia* that must be broken and penetrated in order to arrive at the inner core, the kernel, namely, the esoteric meaning of the text. It is thus evident that the Lurianic views draw their inspiration from the language and conceptions of this work. Luria, too, believed that the *qushia* was something to be *overcome,* to be battled with as one battles with the forces of evil. Indeed, Luria taught that the messianic age would find itself governed by a utopian version of the Torah in which the halakha as we now know it would no longer be relevant, but would assume a different form.

Intensive halakhic study of this sort does not come easily to everyone. Those for whom such intellectual efforts are within their capacity were advised by Luria to engage in *ʿiyyun halakha* each and every weekday, while others were instructed to spend their time in other kinds of study:

> He told me, however, that it is improper for a person for whom intensive study does not come easily, and who has to go to great lengths until he finds what he is looking for, to ignore the study of Torah [*ʿeseq ha-Torah*] for the sake of this kind of penetrating investigation [*ʿiyyun*]. It is far better for him to concern himself with legal decisions [*dinim*] or the homilies [*midrashim*] of our sages, of blessed memory, and the like. But one for whom such intensive study is not difficult, and who does not need to exert a great deal of effort, must take an hour or two every day for purposes of this kind of study. Afterwards, he should spend the remainder of the day studying as described earlier. He should not, however, spend the whole day in intensive study.[70]

Those who pore over halakha without being able to understand it, we are told, are like "one who cracks nuts all day long, but does not eat what is inside. It is better for such a person to occupy himself with Torah itself, legal judgments, rabbinic homilies, and [kabbalistic] secrets."[71]

Luria himself was extremely adept at the rigorous study of halakha and would probe both a law's exoteric and esoteric meanings: "My master, of blessed memory, reported to me that he always used to interpret legal problems in six different ways in accordance with the exoteric meaning. The seventh interpretation would be in accordance with the esoteric meaning. This corresponds to the mystery of the six weekdays and the seventh day, the Sabbath."[72]

Vital provides us with Luria's *kavvanot* to accompany the process of ᶜ*iyyun*. They are similar in nature to those seen earlier in that they involve the combining of various forms of the Tetragrammaton. The goal in this case is "to assist you considerably in penetrating to the depths of the halakha."[73] In this connection, Vital also indicates a more general meditative intention associated with ᶜ*iyyun halakha*.[74] The focus ought to be on the correspondence, made possible by transposition of their common consonants, between the words halakha (*HaLaKaH*) and *hakalah* (*HaKaLaH*), "the Bride." Every legal quandary resolved through ᶜ*iyyun* should aim at stripping the shells away from the halakha, revealing the supernal *kalah*, or Bride, namely, *Nuqba de-Zeᶜir*.

We see here, then, that under the auspices of Lurianic teaching, the fixed regimen of daily Torah study came to serve distinctly theurgical purposes. Negatively formulated, such study is one of the ways in which the evil structures of the world, the *qelippot*, can be stripped of their potency. From a positive perspective, it is a means of making manifest the hidden, holy core of Torah, divinity itself, as well as experiencing divine inspiration.

What is the relationship between these two types of study activity? On the one hand, ᶜ*iyyun halakha* is, ideally, the preliminary step before engaging in the fixed study of Torah described above. "And just as one who wishes to eat a nut must first break its shell, so too one must begin with ᶜ*iyyun*."[75] In this instance, the nut refers not to the core of the halakha but to the activity of recitation of Torah, or ᶜ*eseq ha-Torah*. As we have already seen, however, this preliminary step can be dispensed with altogether for those who are not especially adept at halakhic inquiry. In any case, it is quite clear that it is the fixed contemplative recitation of sacred texts that is ultimately most critical. For such study is Torah ᶜ*atsmah*, Torah *itself*, in contrast to preoccupation with

Torah's garments. Thus, in justifying the exemption from ʿiyyun ha-lakha on the part of those with little talent for it, we learn as follows: "Rather than spend too much time with the outer garments of Torah [levushei Torah], one who is not particularly capable [at ʿiyyun] should engage instead in the [Torah's] inner life and vitality, which constitutes true wisdom [ḥokhmat ha-ʾemet]."[76]

Here, again, then, we encounter the undermining of halakhic discourse. As a whole, the study of halakha constitutes the mere externals of the Torah, in contrast to its inner, esoteric dimensions. While it is true that even study of halakha can yield esoteric meaning, a surer, more direct route to the inner truths of the Torah is through other kinds of study. Those not especially adept at halakhic analysis should not waste their time, but ought to go directly to the heart of the Torah by other means.

*

Taken together, the Lurianic explanations of the mitsvot exemplify the particular kabbalistic way in which Isaac Luria transformed traditional Jewish ritual. He did so in the case of the mitsvot not by abrogating any aspects of the halakha, but by endowing its fulfillment with theosophical and theurgical significance. Much the same could be said, though, for earlier theosophical Kabbalah. But Lurianic Kabbalah may be said to have taken the strategy of earlier kabbalists to a greater extreme by focusing so single-mindedly on the theurgical implications of halakhic practice, as the analysis here suggests. In addition, this approach is distinguished by the highly technical way in which Lurianic metaphysics informs the performance of the mitsvot. The dynamic processes within the organic life of the divine provide the template, or grid, to which the mitsvot are correlated. This correlation is constructed in the most thoroughgoing detail, each discrete component of any given mitsvah being interpreted in Lurianic terms. Lurianic Kabbalah also served to empower its practitioners by cultivating the theurgic art to an even greater degree than previous kabbalists had done. Each and every halakhic enactment presented one opportunity after another to transform both oneself and the cosmos.

Seven *Tiqqun*: Healing the Cosmos Through Devotional Prayer

Intentionality of Prayer in Pre-Kabbalistic Judaism

The relationship between formal liturgical devotion and intentionality (*kavvanah*) in Jewish prayer was a significant issue as early as the rabbinic period. As used in talmudic and midrashic literature, the term *kavvanah* refers to enacting a mitsvah with at least a minimal degree of awareness and conscious intention. Thus, to pray with *kavvanah* entails paying attention to one's words, in contrast, say, to one who does so merely by rote. While the talmudic rabbis were certainly concerned first and foremost with the meticulous practice of the externals of ritual, mere ritualism was insufficient: "Be careful in your reading of the Shema and the Amidah [the "Standing" prayer], and, when you pray, do not regard your prayer as a fixed mechanical task, but as an appeal to God for mercy and grace."[1] Or consider the following teaching: "Our rabbis taught: One should not stand up to say *Tefillah* [i.e., the Amidah] while immersed in sorrow, or idleness, or laughter, or chatter, or frivolity, or idle talk, but only while still rejoicing in the performance of some religious act."[2] We learn as well about a special class of individuals, "the pious ones of old," who "used to wait an hour before praying in order that they might concentrate their thoughts upon their Father in heaven."[3] Thus, rabbinic prayer in late antiquity was supposed to be performed with both mindfulness and heartfelt sincerity. Despite its ritualized, statutory nature, prayer was to be carried out as a matter of personal piety, entailing inwardness and concentration, not to mention a certain degree of spontaneity.

220

Various nonmystical medieval authors, following the lead of the ancient rabbis, elaborated upon the question of *kavvanah*. We find various conceptions of *kavvanah* among medieval moralists, exegetes, and philosophers. By far the most interesting and influential of these was Bahya ibn Paquda, whose eleventh-century *Duties of the Heart* was directed as a whole to the cultivation of inwardness, mindfulness, and heartfelt sincerity in the religious life. Composed in Arabic under the influence of Sufi asceticism, and inspired by Neoplatonic categories of thought, Bahya's views on the inner heart find classic expression in this great work of religious spirituality:

> When a man undertakes a duty that involves both the heart and the limbs, like prayer, or the glorification of God, then he must free himself of all the deeds pertaining to both this world and the next. He must discard all thoughts which may preoccupy and draw him away from the matter of his prayer. . . . Then he must recall to memory the object and purpose of his prayer, its wording and its meaning, in order to make it acceptable to his Lord. For you must know that words are a matter of the tongue, but meaning is a matter of the heart. The words are like the body of the prayer, but the meaning is like its soul. When a man prays only with his tongue, his heart preoccupied with something other than the meaning of the prayer, then his prayer is like a body without a soul, or a shell without contents, for only his body is present; his heart is absent from his prayer.[4]

Bahya thus rejected the type of religious practice that constitutes mere formal compliance (Arabic: *taqlid*) with the dictates of the law and affirmed instead the superiority of the "duties of the heart" over "the duties of the limbs," although the latter were also obligatory. Like the rabbinic sages before him, Bahya himself did not invest the notion of *kavvanah* with any type of esoteric or symbolic meaning, notwithstanding that he profoundly influenced a great range of mystical authors, who would regularly cite him as one of their most venerated authorities.[5] This development would, however, have to await the emergence of mystical speculation on prayer, beginning in the twelfth and thirteenth centuries, in the Rhineland, Provence, and Spain.

Intentionality in Early Kabbalistic Prayer

One would have to place the subject of prayer near the top of any list of important innovations introduced by the newly evolving mystical schools of this period. In twelfth-century Germany, for example, the German pietists developed dramatically new approaches to liturgical prayer. The leading figures in this movement, Judah the Pietist and his disciple Eleazar of Worms, apparently wrote the earliest systematic commentaries on Hebrew liturgy in the last decades of the twelfth century.[6] The centrality of the question of prayer to this school is evidenced by the fact that these authors placed the problem of liturgy at the center of their theological treatises.[7] The German Pietists taught that every element in Scripture, including not only the words themselves but also the physical forms of letters, punctuation, vocalization, and, most important, the *gematriot* derived from the proper numerical understanding of the text, esoterically bore witness to the mystical harmony of the world. In a comparable way, they treated the traditional prayer texts as disclosing hidden meaning of the deepest significance. Beyond its mere literal meanings, in the order of prayer, and particularly in the *gematriot* of prayer, one can fathom an otherwise concealed divine rhythm.

The importance of this was that it represented an entirely new set of concerns with regard to statutory liturgy. Exegetical and hermeneutical techniques that had never before been applied to liturgy were now employed for the purpose of deciphering the inner meaning of the prayers. In the process, the prayer book became completely transformed into an object of studious inquiry so as to discover its *esoteric* meaning.

At precisely the same time, the nascent kabbalistic movement in Provence also developed an esoteric understanding of liturgical prayer, although of an altogether different kind from that of the Rhineland. In the writings of the very earliest circle of kabbalists in Provence, that of Abraham ben David (Rabad), we encounter traditions about prayer that reveal a wholly new approach, at the heart of which lies the conception of a *symbolic* relationship between the words of liturgy and the various attributes of God, the *sefirot*. The individual words and phrases of prayer are now read as signs embodying and pointing to the hidden world of divinity. Recitation of liturgy—accompanied by consciousness of its symbolic meanings—enables the kabbalist to focus on the *sefirot*. Even more, prayer as mystical *praxis* is a theurgical act, in which the worshipper realigns and reunifies the *sefirot* in precise ways. Praying thus becomes a highly complex mental act of contemplative awareness, in which the adept directs his consciousness to a world beyond the material realm and *influences* that world.

A couple of simple examples will illustrate the process. According to a tradition attributed to Rabad himself, the first three and last three blessings of the Shemoneh Esreh, or "Eighteen Benedictions," refer to ʿ*Illat ha-ʿIllot* (literally, "Cause of Causes," i.e., *Ein-Sof*), "and the middle ones to *Yotser Bereshit* (unspecified active creative powers within deity)."[8] Rabad espouses a point of view that did not actually gain acceptance, namely, that one can direct one's contemplative attention to the most concealed dimensions of divinity, *Ein-Sof* or *Keter*. By contrast, Jacob the Nazir, an important figure in Rabad's circle, adopts a more circumspect approach to the understanding of the same prayer: "The first three and the last three [blessings of the Shemoneh Esreh refer] to *Binah,* and the middle ones—[refer] in daytime to *Tiferet* and at night all of them to *Binah*."[9] Thus, the six blessings that are viewed as praises of God are directed to *Binah,* which, while an exalted *sefirah,* nevertheless participates in the manifest processes of creation; the petitionary blessings in between are to be directed to *Tiferet,* which assists in the governance of the world. Jacob's views were more compatible than Rabad's with evolving and ultimately normative kabbalistic ideas on this issue. In this view, contemplative prayer could not be directed to the hidden root of all reality, but only to the manifest dimensions deriving from that root.[10] The common ground between Rabad and Jacob the Nazir, though, is that both approach the liturgical text in a *symbolic* fashion, to be decoded so as to reveal the mystical processes within the life of God.

In the writings of the most important figure of Kabbalah in Provence, Rabad's son Isaac the Blind, we find an especially strong interest in the mysticism of prayer, *kavvanah* and *devequt* ("cleaving" to God).[11] According to Isaac, concentration on the *sefirot* in prayer enables individuals to elevate and "expand" their thought from the lower realms of divinity to the higher, and at least indirectly, as high as *Ein-Sof* itself: "For every *middah* [i.e., *sefirah*] is filled with that which is above it, and they are given to Israel in order to meditate from the *middah* that is visible in the heart, to meditate up to the Infinite. For there is no other path to the [true] prayer than this one; by means of the limited words, man is made to enter [into their interior] and rises in thought to the Infinite."[12]

Thus, in prayer one directs one's attention in an absolutely precise way to the specific *sefirot* symbolized by the words of the liturgy. In this process, the thought of the kabbalist ascends the ladder of the *sefirot* until it reaches its highest possible point, a level identified as one of pure "Thought" by Isaac the Blind, for whom it constitutes a return to the point of origin of human thought, the place beyond which thought cannot "expand." It entails contact or communion with God, indicated by the word *devequt*, a cleaving or clinging to deity.

These notions of contemplative prayer were adapted and further developed in the thirteenth century in important and profound ways by Isaac's most important disciples, Ezra and Azriel of the Gerona circle in northern Spain. Thus, for Azriel, for example, *devequt* constitutes the cleaving of human thought and will to the "Thought" and "Will" of God.[13] Isaac, Ezra, and Azriel were especially concerned with cultivating personal attachment to divinity in the course of prayer; while they did not ignore the more purely theurgical dimensions of prayer, their theoretical contributions to mystical prayer may be said to have been more in the arena of personal communion with God than in that of theurgy per se.

Many of these ideas come together in the *Zohar* and in the Hebrew writings of Moses de Leon. The principal theosophical goal of prayer in the *Zohar* is to bring about love or union between *Tiferet* and *Malkhut*. The main sections of the morning prayer service are understood by the *Zohar* as symbolizing the processes of preparing the *Shekhinah* as one prepares a bride for marriage with her beloved, and the bringing of that marriage to fruition. Thus, the earliest part of the morning liturgy, the *Pesuqei de-Zimra* (literally, "verses of song"), made up of hymns and songs in praise of God, are interpreted as means by which the adept adorns the Bride, readying Her for the bridal canopy.[14] Just as the angels above praise God, so too, by virtue of the songs individuals below sing, the *Shekhinah* "adorns Herself and beautifies Herself with adornments as a woman does for her husband."[15] The marriage itself begins to take place as the worshipper ends the "Redemption" blessing that directly precedes the Shemoneh Esreh: "For when those praying have arrived at the words 'Who redeemed Israel' (in the last song before the Shemoneh Esreh) . . . the *Tsaddiq* [i.e., the Male, *Tiferet*] becomes aroused so as to join the proper Place [i.e., the Female, *Shekhinah*] in love and affection, in joy and desire, and all the limbs are united with each other in one longing, the higher with the lower."[16]

Our passage goes on to say that the actual consummation of this marriage takes place with the worshipper's recitation of the final blessing of the "Eighteen Benedictions": "Grant Peace." For at that moment, the "'River [*Yesod*] that goes out from Eden' [*Binah*] performs His marital duty." In other passages, we learn that the first three blessings of the Shemoneh Esreh, corresponding to the sefirot *Hesed, Gevurah,* and *Tiferet,* respectively, are the arms and torso of the divine body, which reach out and embrace *Tiferet*'s female lover in a kiss. Having brought about this preliminary state of affection, the worshipper himself is in a position of strength to make petitions. These are the three final blessings of the Shemoneh Esreh, corresponding to *Netsah, Hod,* and *Yesod,* the two legs and the phallus of divinity, which brings about the consummation of the marriage.[17] This small example should serve to provide a sense of the dual symbolic/theurgic character of the *Zohar*'s approach to prayer. Given its free-spirited literary style, the *Zohar* bears little resemblance to a systematic commentary on the liturgy, but its influence on subsequent kabbalistic thinking about mystical prayer was nonetheless considerable, not least in the case of Isaac Luria, a devoted student of the *Zohar*.

Figure 5. The title page of *Sefer Pri ʿEts Ḥayyim* (Korecz, 1786).

Intentionality of Prayer in Lurianic Kabbalah

Isaac Luria's teachings on prayer were recorded by several of his disciples, most especially by Hayyim Vital, Moses Yonah, Moses Najara, and Joseph ibn Tabul.[18] Our sources provide us with a number of general observations and precautions about prayer. Luria's concern that sadness be avoided in connection with the performance of the mitsvot generally is vigorously reiterated with respect to prayer. A person who worships in a state of sadness will be prevented from receiving the supernal light that normally descends upon an individual during prayer.[19] Still, sadness is permitted, indeed, even appropriate, during the confession of sin. While an adept must serve God in great humility, fear, and reverence, one should nevertheless be exceedingly joyous to the greatest extent possible, just as a servant serves his master joyfully. The quality and extent of a person's divine inspiration and attainment of the Holy Spirit depend upon this joyfulness, both while praying and while performing the mitsvot more generally. Moreover, it is critical to meditate upon loving one's companions in preparation for prayer and to have all of them in mind in the course of one's prayer. On the basis of this tradition, it became standard practice among those influenced by Luria, including Hasidim, to declare such love on a daily basis as a prelude to the morning service.[20]

Both Vital and Judah Mishan tell us that out of a desire to show humility, fear, and reverence for God, Luria avoided praying aloud in a raised voice, except on the Sabbath during the prayers recited while seated, such as the preliminary songs (this excludes the Shemoneh Esreh, of course, which is prayed while standing), when he raised his voice pleasantly a little more than he did during weekday prayer. Even this, however, he did only to honor the Sabbath.[21] Whenever he came to a verse from the Torah in the liturgy, he would sing it according to the notes that accompany Torah recitation.[22]

Here Luria was following a well-developed tradition of whispered or silent prayer. The Talmud taught that the Shemoneh Esreh should be recited in a whisper,[23] and the *Zohar* appropriated this tradition, endowing it with kabbalistic purpose. According to one passage, prayer as a whole corresponds to the grade of *Malkhut,* which is an unheard voice. She Herself does not speak, since She is only a reflection of the voice that is heard, *Tiferet*.[24] Elsewhere we learn that the angels who receive prayer on high refuse to pay attention to prayers that are not whispered, the reason being that the words of prayer cling to the supernal world (*ᶜolam ha-ᶜelyon*, meaning *Binah* here), which has no need for loudly spoken devotion. That is, *Binah* resides in an exalted place, transcending the level of the spoken word.[25] According to yet another passage in the *Zohar*, whispering is obligatory during the Shemoneh Esreh since this is a moment of intradivine love, in which "everything is silent above and below with the kisses of desire."[26]

The common factor behind these various explanations is the conviction that the sound of a voice—divine or human—can disturb the communion between the divine lovers, as well as that between an individual's soul and God, produced by the power of *inner*, heartfelt desire.[27] In Luria's case, softly spoken prayer would have been appealing for another, more practical reason as well. The meditative intentions accompanying prayer were doubtlessly evoked at an individual's own pace. Whispered prayer would be more conducive to this kind of devotion, since it would provide the least amount of disturbance from fellow worshippers. Luria also cautioned his disciples to be extremely vigilant about avoiding speaking with others altogether while praying in the synagogue.[28] Even while listening to words of moral reproach and exhortations to repent, he hesitated to speak so as to avoid being drawn unwittingly into profane or ordinary conversation.

There is a widespread association between devotional experience and weeping in kabbalistic literature.[29] Thus, for example, the *Zohar* (2, 20a): "He who prays and weeps and cries so much that there is no feeling left in his lips—that is perfect prayer, prayer in the heart, and it never returns empty. R. Judah said: A cry is mighty because it rules over the attribute of Judgment in the upper world." Moses Cordovero advised his followers to "weep during each of the [three] prayer services, or at least during one of them."[30] Abraham Berukhim's report that "there is a fellowship of penitents [in Safed] whose members fast regularly and who pray the afternoon service each day in weeping and in tears" was noted in Chapter 2. For Luria himself, tears were associated with those elements of Judgment (*Din*) whose locus is in the qualities of *Netsaḥ* and *Hod* within the *sefirah Ḥokhmah*. When a worshipper sheds tears during prayer, he is in a position to "sweeten" these forces of Judgment and to stimulate the powers of Compassion.[31] Elsewhere this is expressed in these terms: "Why is weeping during prayer desirable? Because tears derive from *Ḥokhmah* and *Binah*, and when these two *sefirot* are opened [through crying], the light of *Keter* penetrates them, and they draw [the quality of] Compassion to all the [other] divine qualities [*middot*]."[32] According to Abraham Berukhim, in all of your prayers, as well as when you are having difficulty comprehending some mystical secret, "stir yourself to bitter weeping until your eyes shed tears, and the more you are able to weep—do so. And increase your weeping, as the 'Gates of Tears' are not closed and the supernal gates will be opened to you."[33]

It was also Luria's custom to pray by reading from his prayer book during the early portions of the service, up through the Shema. During the Eighteen Benedictions, which are said while standing silently, however, he would close his eyes, place his right hand over his left upon his heart, and pray from memory.[34] He would keep his eyes closed throughout the reader's repetition of the Amidah as well, listening with intense concentration to the reader. During the evening service, however, he would keep his eyes closed and place his hands as indicated above throughout the entire service. The reason for covering the left hand with the right was to sweeten the strict forces of the "left side" with those of the right, precisely in the midst of the Amidah, during which time the *moḥin* from on high fill *Zeᶜir Anpin*. Luria's practice of closing his eyes during the Amidah was associated with imitating (and imagining) the aspect of *Shekhinah* or *Nuqba de-Zeᶜir* as Rachel, who is beautiful of form, but without eyes. Although unstated, doing so may have been motivated by the fear of gazing upon the *Shekhinah* or "witnessing" the sexual intimacy between the divine masculine and feminine, which, as we shall see below, takes place during this critical part of the prayer service. As Elliot Wolfson has noted, such extraordinary traditions can be found in the *Zohar* and other pre-Lurianic kabbalistic literature.[35] Consider the following striking passage:

There is another hidden secret: at the moment one prays [the prayer of the Eighteen Benedictions] in his worship he intends the true unity, and the action that a person does below causes an act above, resulting in the copulation and union above. A person must hide out of shame for his Master and close his eyes in order not to look at the moment of copulation. Even though it is impossible to see above, "for no man shall see Me and live" (Ex. 33:20), nevertheless the knowledge of the sages constitutes their vision. On account of this they said that it is forbidden to look at the fingers of the priests when they spread out their hands, for the Presence (i.e., the *Shekhinah*) rests on their hands at that moment, and it is forbidden to look at the Presence. Even though it is impossible to see, as we said, he must hide his eyes.[36]

We possess a brief account of Isaac Luria's own morning ritual routine. If he arose before dawn, he would begin his daily devotions without waiting for the sun to rise. He would recite the first several preliminary morning prayers, up until the recitation of the ʿ*Aqedah*.[37] Following this, he would pause to recite and study Torah. When the light of dawn appeared, he would first wrap himself in his prayer shawl and then don phylacteries. According to Vital, Luria claimed that those who reversed this order, putting on phylacteries before the prayer shawl, were in complete error.[38] Then he would continue with prayer.

There is somewhat diverse testimony concerning the question of *where* Luria prayed. He certainly believed in the importance of public prayer in a synagogue, within a quorum, or minyan, and even that one should seek to be among the first ten to arrive at synagogue:

> It is incumbent upon a person to be among the first ten at synagogue. Having done so, one must not leave until one has completed one's prayers there. One should not behave like those who are among the first ten in one synagogue and then leave and go to pray in a different synagogue where they are not among the first quorum. Such people are mistaken, and doing this should not be thought of as fulfilling any religious precept whatsoever.[39]

Luria himself, however, was apparently not in the habit of being among the first at synagogue:

Figure 6. The courtyard of the Sephardi Ari Synagogue, which dates from the sixteenth century and is believed to be where Isaac Luria prayed. Courtesy Neil Folberg, photographer.

I observed that it was not the custom of my teacher, of blessed memory, to be among the first ten. He informed me that this was because he was sickly and needed to remain at home for a while in order to see to his personal needs. Another reason is that after readying himself, he used to put on his prayer shawl and phylacteries in his home, and walk dressed this way to synagogue. He had to do so while it was daytime, for at night one is not permitted to don phylacteries; however, those who made up the first ten at the synagogue arrived in the dark before the break of dawn.[40]

The inference to be drawn from this is that Luria believed—at least as far as his own practice was concerned—that it was more important to walk to synagogue already having donned prayer shawl and phylacteries than it was to be among the first ten. As for his being sickly,

Figure 7. Interior of the Sephardi Ari Synagogue. Courtesy Neil Folberg, photographer.

as noted earlier, Jonathan Sagis reports that Luria refrained from practicing ritual immersion (*tevilah*) for six months one winter owing to illness. His mother refused to allow him to do so!

The significance to Luria of participating in public devotion is further suggested by a tradition according to which it is exceedingly important to pause for a moment at the synagogue door before one enters. The purpose of this is to demonstrate one's awe and reverence at entering the "palace of the King of the world," and to contribute to one's spiritual perfection and potential for mystical inspiration.[41] Upon actually entering the synagogue, one should be prepared to be suffused with divine light:

> One should bow in the direction of the Ark, after which one ought to recite the Psalm "May God be gracious to us and bless us" [Ps. 67],

which is composed of seven verses. Corresponding to the number of verses in the psalm, one should circle the reader's table, which stands in the middle of the synagogue, seven times. It is best to seek to recite one verse for each circle, until you finish the seven circles having recited all seven verses. And contemplatively intend that the [reader's] table signifies *Malkhut* and concentrate on drawing down upon Her seven encircling lights [*shevaᶜ ᵓorot maqifin*], comprised of *Ḥesed* through *Malkhut* . . . concentrate upon including yourself [in this light], so that you and *Malkhut* might receive [light] from these encircling lights together. On Sunday, concentrate [especially] on the first verse [of the psalm], and intend that it should prevail over the other verses, this verse representing the quality of *Ḥesed*. On Monday, intend that the second verse prevail over the rest, and so on until Friday. On the Sabbath, however, there is no need to circle the table more than once. . . . This is what I heard reported in my master's name. I observed, however, that he personally never actually practiced this upon entering the synagogue; perhaps this was because he was not among the first ten to arrive there.[42]

There are a number of anecdotal reports indicating that there were other venues besides the synagogue for Luria's prayer. "[I] used to pray regularly at my master's study house [*bet midrasho*]," Hayyim Vital writes.[43] Elsewhere, Vital says "that when we were praying in his study house, my teacher, of blessed memory, used to go up to the Torah on the Feast of Weeks [Shavuot] and recite the Ten Commandments in a raised voice."[44] In a passage describing Luria's practice of the public reading of the Torah, we learn from Vital that "often my master used to pray in his own home with a quorum of ten individuals, on weekdays as well as on the Sabbath, without worrying about whether there was a Torah scroll available from which to read."[45] We know from other reports that Luria sometimes taught his disciples in his own home as well.[46] In choosing to pray in his own house of study, or in his own home, Luria was presumably motivated by a desire to pray in a more private way with his own disciples. It is difficult to imagine how the highly specialized *kavvanot* of Lurianic prayer could have been comfortably practiced in a general congregation of worshippers.

For Luria, prayer was a matter of spiritually intense experience, resulting in a face aglow with supernal light. Vital gives the following account in connection with an anecdote concerning eye pain that he was having:

> I used to pray regularly at my master's study house, and I would always sit to his right, gazing at him in order to learn his habits in every detail. During his prayer, he used to employ great and wondrous meditations, on account of which celestial light would shine upon him. But I was not qualified at that time to gaze upon him. He said to me, "Seek to avoid staring at me while I am concentrating upon the prayer 'Hear, O Israel,' while I am bowing during the *modim* prayer, and while I am reciting the *Qedushah* prayer, 'Holy, Holy, Holy, is the Lord of Hosts.' For these three prayers require extraordinary contemplative concentration. If you act properly your eye pain will be relieved." The following day, I refrained from gazing at him during these three moments of prayer, and I was suddenly healed.[47]

Presumably, Vital wished to gaze upon his master's face not merely to learn his habits but also to partake of the divine light with which it was suffused. The belief that the faces of kabbalistic adepts reflect divine light—especially the light of the *Shekhinah*—is commonplace in the *Zohar*. Thus, the righteous, that is, the comrades who constitute Shimon bar Yohai's discipleship, are known as the "face of the Presence [*Shekhinah*]," since the "Presence is hidden within them."[48] Luria himself used to practice a technique of gazing within the context of prayer; he would gaze upon the divine light hidden within the letters of the scroll of the Torah in order to draw that light to him:

> It was the custom of my teacher, of blessed memory, to kiss the scroll of the Torah and to accompany it, walking behind it when it is brought from the Ark to the reader's table in order to be read. After this, he would remain there next to the table until they opened the Torah scroll and showed it to the congregation, as is known. Then he would gaze upon the letters of the Torah. He used to say that a person could draw great light upon himself by looking at the Torah so closely that he was able to read the letters clearly. Following this, he

would return to his original place and remain seated until the completion of the Torah reading, unlike those whose custom it is to remain standing.[49]

Luria believed in a degree of individuality in prayer. In the first place, he recognized the validity of the different liturgical traditions among Jews from various regions and cultures. In addition, he taught that there were different heavenly gates through which prayer passes, and that one individual's prayer was not exactly the same as another's: "My teacher, of blessed memory, used to say that there are twelve gates above, corresponding to the twelve tribes [of Israel], and the prayers of every individual ascend by way of one of these gates."[50]

The general theurgical goals of prayer are described in a number of ways, in accordance with various aspects of Lurianic myth. Among the primary purposes of prayer is to divest the *qelippot* of the divine light that clings to them as a result of the Breaking of the Vessels, also synonymous with the "death of the kings of Edom." Prayer (like the performance of the mitsvot more generally) contributes to the ongoing processes of purification (*berur*), that is, of lifting up sparks of holiness for the ultimate purpose of rendering the *qelippot* lifeless and inanimate. Such purification simultaneously helps facilitate the restoration of the feminine, *Nuqba de-Zeʿir*, to the masculine, *Zeʿir*, and the ascent of the four worlds to their proper places within the cosmos. In the course of all this, the "kings that died" are themselves gradually cleansed and purified, raised up along with the Female Waters: "The purpose of prayer and the precepts we perform in this world is none other than to purify and to cleanse these kings and to resurrect them from their death."[51]

The *Kavvanot* of Prayer

Let us now consider some of the details of the Lurianic *kavvanot* themselves. The first example I shall use for illustrative purposes is one of the central prayers in the liturgy, the well-known affirmation of God's oneness, *Shema Yisrael ʾAdonai ʾElohenu ʾAdonai ʾEḥad* ("Hear,

O Israel, the Lord our God, the Lord is One"). There are four daily occasions on which the Shema is recited: twice during the daily morning service, once during the evening service, and before one retires at night.[52] In the case of the morning service, the first recitation occurs during the preliminary prayers and includes only the primary phrase of the Shema and the line "Blessed be the name of His glorious majesty forever and ever." The main recitation of the morning service is a full one, consisting of three biblical passages (Deut. 6:4–9; Deut. 11:13–21; Num. 15:37–41), accompanied by two blessings before the Shema itself and one following it.[53]

We know that one of the general theurgical goals of prayer was the unification or *zivvug* between the *partsufim* of *Ze'ir Anpin* and *Nuqba* in their various hierarchical configurations. The maturation of the whole structure of *Ze'ir* stands at the heart of this process, for without such maturation, loving relations between *Ze'ir* and *Nuqba* cannot take place. Furthermore, this developmental process entails the unceasing need to nourish *Ze'ir* with the *mohin* from the *partsufim* above it. As we saw earlier, the *mohin* might be imagined as bundles of divine vitality originating in *Arikh Anpin,* as well as in *Abba* and *Imma,* which flow below in order to complete the structures of *Ze'ir* and *Nuqba,* filling them with strength. While there are three sets of *mohin,* for present purposes we need only concern ourselves with the final two. The first of these is *mohin de-qatnut* (small or lesser *mohin*). These relatively weak or immature *mohin* are associated with the process of suckling or *yeniqah,* whereby *Ze'ir* nourishes itself from the "breasts" of *Imma*. The second set are the *mohin de-gadlut* (large or great *mohin*), which complete the process of *Ze'ir*'s maturation following the process of suckling.

When the ancient Temple in Jerusalem still existed, the *mohin* were continuously present in *Ze'ir*. Ever since the destruction of the Temple, however, the *mohin* constantly descend and reascend. This is why there is a need now for near-continuous prayer, so as to draw down the *mohin* from on high. This was why the early pietists used to add two hours to each prayer service. The additional devotions served to sustain the descent of the *mohin*. From one point of view, all of prayer is dedicated to nourishing *Zeᶜir* by means of restoring the *moḥin* to it and thus bringing about the conditions under which *Zeᶜir* and *Nuqba* can join one another in utterly perfect and enduring marital love. This thoroughly sexualized process—some of the details of which are described below—is suppose to occur again and again, until the final and permanent *tiqqun* that will take place with the advent of the Messiah.

Of the five different kinds of *zivvugim* that can occur between *Zeᶜir* and *Nuqba*, all but the *zivvug* of Israel and Rachel are relevant to the contemplative recitation of the Shema. The qualitative difference between each of the various manifestations of these male and female principles has to do, in part, with (1) the particular *partsuf* from which *Zeᶜir Anpin* draws its nourishment, and (2) whether it draws drops of divine seed from the interior or exterior of that *partsuf*. The *zivvug* that is *prepared* for by the two recitations of the Shema of the morning service is the highest type that can occur on a weekday.

Kabbalists paid close attention to the rhythms of day and night. Different periods of the day were conceived of as dominated by the various qualities of divine vitality. According to Luria, the twenty-four-hour cycle divides into four periods of time, two during the day and two during the night: morning, afternoon, evening (prior to midnight), and from midnight on. Following earlier traditions, Luria believed the morning to be a period governed by the forces of divine Mercy (*Ḥesed*), rendering it possible for the *zivvug* that takes place during this time to be an exalted and perfect one, in contrast to those that take place during the other times of daily weekday prayer. While the forces of *Ḥesed* prevail in the morning hours, their antithesis, the forces of Judgment (*Gevurah*), dominate in the afternoon.[54] The power produced by the earlier descent of the *moḥin de-gadlut*—facilitated by the recitation of the Shema in the morning—begins to abate in the afternoon. It is powerful enough, however, for a weaker *zivvug* to take place during the afternoon service on the basis of its residual strength.[55] The resulting *zivvug,* that of Israel and Leah, is "back to back" rather than "face to face." The omission of the Shema during the afternoon service can be explained in these terms: the glow left by the morning service is sufficient to produce *zivvug* in the afternoon without the

Shema, although it is a far less potent one. The other prayers recited in the course of the afternoon service are ample enough to stir the forces necessary to sustain this more limited *zivvug*.

With the onset of evening, though, the situation changes. While during the day the *moḥin* continue to linger in the place to which they have descended, in the evening they depart altogether.[56] It is thus necessary to begin all over again and draw them down afresh, which is the purpose of the evening service, with its recitation of the Shema. If the afternoon is a period of relative judgment, evening is one during which the powers of strictness dominate completely.[57] The power inherent in the contemplative recitation of the Shema is thus again required in order to arouse the *moḥin* and bring about *zivvug*. These *moḥin* are drawn from the *exterior* of *Arikh Anpin*. The loving union that takes place during the evening prayer is that of Jacob and Leah, from the "chest" and above of *Zeʿir Anpin*.

While the afternoon benefits from the *zivvug* aroused during the morning hours, the same is not true for the *late* hours of the evening, when one retires, in relationship to the evening prayer. The *moḥin* brought forth as a result of the evening prayer do not linger, necessitating still another arousal above. The *zivvug* that results from the recitation of the Shema at bedtime, in the depth of night, when the forces of strictness grow even stronger, is inferior to the one achieved during the evening prayers. In this case, the *moḥin* are drawn from the *exterior* of *Abba* and *Imma* only, resulting in the *zivvug* of Jacob and Leah, from the "chest" and below. The chart below summarizes these different correspondences:

Time of Shema	Source of *moḥin*	Nature of *Zivvug*
First Shema, morning	Interior/*Arikh Anpin*	Jacob and Rachel
Full Shema, morning	Exterior/*Attiqa Qaddisha*	Jacob and Rachel
Afternoon, no Shema		Israel and Leah
Evening Service	Exterior/*Arikh Anpin*	Jacob and Leah
Bedtime Shema	Exterior/*Abba* and *Imma*	Jacob and Leah

Having outlined the general differences between the various daily recitations of the Shema, a few further remarks are in order concerning the two recitations of this prayer in the morning service. The theurgic goal of these has been described as helping to prepare the ground for the unification of *Ze^cir* and *Nuqba* in the particular configuration of Jacob and Rachel. But the means by which this takes place is a subtle one, involving several stages, insofar as the union of these two *partsufim* cannot take place until *Abba* and *Imma* themselves are brought into intimate relationship with each other.

There are actually two kinds of union that characterize the relationship between *Abba* and *Imma*. The first is one of permanent harmony for the purpose of sustaining the life of all the worlds. Without it, nothing whatsoever could exist. By contrast, the second serves specifically to provide strength and nourishment to *Ze^cir* and *Nuqba* through the medium of the *moḥin*.[58] It is by means of the adept's particular meditative intentions while reciting the two renditions of the Shema in the morning service that *Ze^cir* gains the strength with which to arouse relations between *Abba* and *Imma*. In turn, once the latter are united, they disseminate in a complete way the *moḥin* with which *Ze^cir* becomes fully strengthened.

This process of maturation of *Ze^cir* is construed as the *tiqqun* of the 248 "limbs" of *Ze^cir Anpin*. By virtue of this, *Ze^cir* and *Nuqba* are readied for their own subsequent union to take place during the recitation of the Shemoneh Esreh that follows the second Shema. The actual process of *zivvug* itself—described in intricate detail—depends upon the proper *kavvanot* with which all the many parts of the Shemoneh Esreh are prayed.[59] I shall, however, omit this description. Let us instead turn our attention to the events that take place immediately following the completion of the Shemoneh Esreh.

Contemplative Death and Cosmic Mending

In addition to uniting *Ze^cir Anpin* and *Nuqba de-Ze^cir*, the Lurianic adept was supposed to accomplish other critical goals simultaneously in the course of the morning prayer service. He is himself nourished and strengthened in prayer, insofar as he raises his own soul up to the highest world of *Atsilut* as a result of praying the Shemoneh Esreh. The prayer following the Shemoneh Esreh is known as *Taḥanun* and consists of a set of petitionary and supplicatory devotions.[60] It is also referred to as *nefilat ʾappayim*, "falling on the face," since it was originally recited while completely prostrated as a sign of deep humility.[61] According to the *Zohar*, an individual engages in an act of voluntary, contemplative death while reciting this prayer.[62] One "hands over one's soul" in an erotically charged ecstatic act of mystical death, the purpose of which is to atone for one's sins:

> Come and see: When a person prays in this way, with [appropriate] actions and word, and establishes the union [of above and below], by virtue of his deeds, upper and lower worlds are blessed. Then a person must regard himself, after he completes the Shemoneh Esreh, as if he has departed this world, and has separated himself from the Tree of Life and died near the Tree of Death, which returns his pledge to him, for it is said: "[H]e (Jacob) gathered up his feet into the bed [and expired, and was gathered unto his people]" [Gen. 49:33] as he confessed his sins and prayed on account of them. Now he must be gathered near the Tree of Death, and fall [upon his face] saying: "'Unto Thee, O Lord, do I lift up my soul' [Ps. 25:1]. At first glance I gave her [i.e., my soul] to Thee as a pledge; now that I have effected unification and performed act and word properly, and confessed on account of my sins, behold, I surrender my soul to Thee completely." A person ought to regard himself as if he has departed this world, that his soul has surrendered to this sphere of death. Therefore, there is no [letter] *vav* in it [i.e., in the acrostic of Ps. 25], for *vav* represents the Tree of Life, and this [psalm] signifies the Tree of Death. What does this mean to us? The mystery is that there are sins that are not expiated until a person leaves this world, as it is written: "Surely this iniquity shall not be expiated by you until you die" [Isa. 22:14]. And this person submits himself completely to death and surrenders his soul to this region, not in a pledge as at night, but as one who has truly left this world. One must perform this devotion with sincerity of heart; then the Holy One, blessed be He, will take pity on him and forgive his sins.[63]

While praying the Shemoneh Esreh, the adept sustains the unity of above and below, and between masculine (*Tiferet*) and feminine (*Malkhut*), symbolized by the Tree of Life and the Tree of Death respectively. However, when he passes to the *Taḥanun* prayer, in which he confesses his sins, he severs this holy relationship, separating himself from the Tree of Life and binding himself to the Tree of Death. Whereas one merely entrusts one's soul "as a pledge" to the *Shekhinah* while asleep at night, in the course of *nefilat ʾappayim* one gives oneself completely to Her, "falling on the face," as if one were actually departing from this world. In other words, the kabbalist, at his most vulnerable moment, the confession of sin, stands fully exposed and ready to accept the consequences of his deeds—death itself. No longer attached to life, he throws himself into the abyss of existence in the ultimate act of submission (*mesirat nefesh*) before God. Only divine mercy enables him to survive intact, his sins having been expiated through a momentary experience of voluntary death. Unsatisfied with the partial atonement possible in this world, a person chooses mystical death as a means of achieving total purification of the soul, otherwise available only through physical death.

Commenting on the Zoharic passage cited above, Moses Cordovero indicated that when a person performs this exercise, he should prostrate himself and appear as if truly dead.[64] In so doing, the male adept, whose body represents *Tiferet*, cleaves to the earth (symbolic of the *Shekhinah*), thus unifying divine male and female. Furthermore, according to Cordovero, he must regard such death as being on account of having desecrated God's name, a transgression for which death alone can atone.

Luria's *kavvanot* for *nefilat ʾappayim* are based on these mythologems. Having raised his soul up to the highest spiritual world of *Atsilut* as a result of praying the Shemoneh Esreh, and having unified the four worlds, the male adept *himself* cleaves, as in an act of sexual intimacy, to *Nuqba de-Zeʿir*, Rachel. From this extraordinary state of strength and exaltation, the worshipper—while praying *nefilat ʾappayim*—imaginatively "descends below to the farthest end of the world of *Assiyah*, as a person who throws himself from the top of a roof to the ground below."[65] That is, he hurls himself into the lowest depths of the world, the scene of material existence and the home of evil, the realm of the *qelippot*. The erotic nature of this ritual is thinly veiled. The devotee's ecstatic descent constitutes an orgasmic release that results in utter exhaustion and a depletion of energy akin to death.

Once below, he concentrates on collecting and gathering Female Waters and divine sparks concealed in each of the worlds, beginning with the world of *Assiyah* and moving progressively upward through *Beriʾah* and *Yetsirah*, until he returns to the place from which he began, *Atsilut*. He facilitates the ascent of the Female Waters and liberates these sparks by attaching them to the various elements of his own soul: in the lowest world of *Assiyah*, he joins sparks to his *nefesh*; in the next highest world of *Yetsirah*, he joins them to his *ruaḥ*; and in the world of *Beriʾah*, he binds sparks to his *neshamah*. Having done this, the male worshipper proceeds to bind these three aspects of his soul—along with the collected sparks—to *Yesod* of *Nuqba de-Zeʿir* in the world of *Atsilut*. One of the critical effects of this is to stimulate the descent of Male Waters from *Yesod*, some of whose light flows into the soul of the worshipper himself, providing him with powerful inspiration. The kabbalistic adept thus assimilates to himself both male and female seminal fluids, while at the same time becoming a conduit for their distribution. These processes are described in the following terms by Joseph ibn Tabul:

> Following this [the recitation of the Amidah], the adept performs *nefilat ʾappayim*, for after the completion of the *Tefillah* [i.e., the Amidah], which is the mystery of *Atsilut*, he throws himself down from the world of *Atsilut* to the world of *Assiyah* below, and he surrenders his *nefesh* to death. And he ought to imagine himself as if he were [truly] dead upon uttering "To You, O Lord, I lift up my soul" [Ps. 25:1]. You are already aware that in the [course of] the ascent of the soul of the righteous individual, the Female Waters become assimilated to *Tiferet* and *Malkhut* . . . which is the [esoteric] mystery of the true divine coupling [*sod zivvug ha-ʾamiti*].[66]

It is highly significant that Luria compares this process to what the rabbis of the Talmud taught regarding the fate of the righteous following death.[67] They descend to *Gehinnom* (the netherworld), the site of the soul's punishment after death, grasp the afflicted who are found there, and retrieve them. This is made possible, in the Lurianic view, by the fact that at the moment of their deaths, righteous individuals unify the divine masculine and feminine, endowing themselves with the spiritual power with which to extricate sinful individuals from the consequences of their deeds: "There is no righteous individual who is not required [upon dying] to enter *Gehinnom* . . . in order to collect from there souls found amongst the *qelippot* and raise them up along with their own souls. And [together] they enter the mystery of the Female Waters and are purified by means of the Male Waters. They then ascend to this world embodied, just as the other souls of Israel. We [thus] find that the righteous, both during their lives as well as in death, engage in this activity, extricating the souls from among the *qelippot*."[68] Luria thus likens the imagined death and ecstatic moment of *nefilat ʾappayim* to the actual death of virtuous individuals. Such a parallel makes it clear that Luria regarded the descent into the realm of the *qelippot* as akin to a genuine act of offering up one's life. This action is said to be "in the nature of true death," inasmuch as the realm of the *qelippot* is indeed a place of death. The adept aspires to such a death, since this is the only way in which to rescue certain of the divine sparks from the grip of evil. In this paradoxical construction, then, this contemplative gesture is a redemptive act of *tiqqun*, one that calls back to life those souls trapped in a place of death.

On the other hand, one needs to take care so as to avoid ensnarement by the *qelippot*, lest one become permanently mired oneself in the depths of the lower world. Given the danger that this entails, not everyone who aspires to practice this complex ritual should do so. Only one who is perfectly righteous—free of any moral or spiritual blemish—has the capacity to struggle successfully against the forces of death. If one is not wholly qualified, the only hope of succeeding rests on perfect and absolute concentration during the entire experience. Otherwise, one runs the risk not only of not accomplishing one's goal but, far worse, of sinking inexorably into the complete grasp of evil.

While a person who is less than perfectly qualified *may* actually succeed in extricating himself from the depths, even without attaining the goal, this is not the case with one who is substantially tainted, whose fate will be to remain trapped below, along with the souls of other sinners. This enables us to understand, says Vital, what the ancient sages intended when they taught that "the wicked in their lifetime are called dead."[69] These are the people who, in the practice of *nefilat ʾappayim*, succumb to the *qelippot* by virtue of their sins, thereby receiving a new soul whose nature is entirely corrupt.

If the dangers are great, the successful adept achieves a great deal at the experiential level. He elevates his soul to the highest sphere within the divine realms, is filled with supernal light, and revitalizes his soul with the abundance of divine life. According to Moses Yonah, he becomes "newly created" as one who has actually died and left this world. He receives the spiritual strength with which to struggle against the evil inclination, resist all further sin, and achieve new levels of inspiration by which to comprehend the innermost mysteries of the Torah.[70] *Nefilat ʾappayim* thus accomplishes several related goals simultaneously. As an act of cosmic *tiqqun*, it serves the purpose of raising up sparks of holiness from the *qelippot*, along with those that reside within the three lower spiritual worlds. At the same time, the adept undergoes an ecstatic experience in which he enjoys powerful spiritual rejuvenation.

I have already described some of the *kavvanot* associated with the Shema, but it is important to observe that in one teaching associated with the phenomenon of contemplative death—in a passage written by Isaac Luria himself—we find that the recitation of the Shema prayer itself can also serve as an opportunity for this type of surrender of the soul unto death.[71] The Shema is associated in Jewish tradition, as is well known, with physical martyrdom (*qiddush ha-shem*), Rabbi Akiva having recited this prayer in the act of sanctifying God's name while being tortured to death by the Romans in the second century c.e. According to Luria, imagined death performed while reciting the Shema is actually superior to *nefilat ʾappayim*. In the former, the devotee finalizes the sacred union of *Ḥokhmah* (*Abba*) and *Binah* (*Imma*), a *zivvug* that is higher than that realized through *nefilat ʾappayim*, namely, the unification of *Tiferet* and *Malkhut*:

[I]n [connection with] the *zivvug* of *Zeʿir* and *Nuqba,* we recite *nefilat ʾappayim* in the mystery of death, for we are considered as if dead and raise up our souls. This is the meaning of the verse, "To You [*ʾelekha*], O Lord, I lift up my soul" [Ps. 25:1], the word *ʾelekha* in particular signifying that we raise up our souls, unto "the Lord," which is *Tiferet*.

However, in the recitation of the Shema . . . it is not enough that we surrender our souls through the mystery of death, but rather through that of martyrdom (*qiddush ha-shem*), this being surrender of the soul to [the extent of actual] death. Therefore, one must concentrate on the name *YAHDVNHY* when uttering the word "One" [in the Shema], and imagine the four types of [punishment by] death, meted out by a *bet din* (rabbinic court of law): stoning, burning, decapitation, and strangulation. This is the meaning of the verse "For Your sake [*ᶜalekha*, literally "above you"] we are killed all day long" [Ps. 44:23]. Instead of *ᵓelekha*, Scripture says *ᶜalekha*, meaning to the One who is *above* you, namely, *Ḥokhmah*, which is above *Tiferet*. . . . and this is the mystery that our rabbis taught in connection with Rabbi Akiva, who ascended to [the grade of] *Maḥshavah* [divine "Thought"], that is, *Ḥokhmah*, in the mystery of the surrender of his soul unto death.[72]

In this passage, the emphasis is on the level within the divine hierarchy to which the adept's soul ascends, and the nature of the union that takes place, rather than the gathering of trapped souls. The divine union brought about by an act of *qiddush ha-shem*—whether actual or merely intended martyrdom—is perfect and exalted, one in which the "children" of *Ḥokhmah* and *Binah*, namely, *Tiferet* and *Malkhut*, are nourished with unlimited blessing.[73] Up until the period of Rabbi Akiva and the Ten Martyrs, *Tiferet* and *Malkhut* enjoyed sufficient illumination with which to raise up the Female Waters to the grade of *Binah*, requiring only a limited degree of help from the righteous who surrendered their souls through imagined death in the course of reciting the Shema. In the period during which Rabbi Akiva and his colleagues lived, however, the sun (divine masculine) and the moon (divine feminine) became dark on account of the sins of that generation, leaving them deprived of the strength with which to raise up the Female Waters.[74] Upon the deaths of Akiva and the other martyrs, their very souls served to illuminate *Tiferet* and *Malkhut*, and thus to elevate the Female Waters so as to draw down the influx of the Male Waters from the realm of *Ḥokhmah* once again. Thus, martyrdom—be it actual physical death or imagined death—along with the recitation of the Shema, has the enormous power to generate the dynamic processes of cosmic mending.

The messianic implications of such martyrdom are suggested by the fact that death by martyrdom is comparable to the role played by the *Mashiaḥ ben Yosef* (Messiah, the son of Joseph), whose own death, it was believed, serves to set the stage for the arrival of *Mashiaḥ ben David* (Messiah, the son of David). Presumably, these Lurianic notions were influenced not only by earlier kabbalistic literary traditions, but also by the examples of contemporary martyrs, most prominently Shlomo Molcho. We have already noted that Joseph Karo had wholeheartedly identified with Molcho's martyrdom, so much so that his greatest aspiration was to be burnt at the stake. It is thus no accident that Karo's maggidic angel exhibited great concern for the martyrological recitation of the Shema. As Werblowsky observes, "the Maggid never tires of repeating the same pun about the burning of worldly thoughts in the 'strawfire' of meditation on the unity of God during the Shema prayer."[75] These themes reverberate in the writings of other Safed kabbalists, including Eleazar Azikri, according to whom "it is a positive obligation to sanctify God's name if one is being forced to renounce one's religion . . . and one should meditate on this in one's heart when one recites the Shema . . . and fully resolve that should one be so tested one will strengthen oneself and hand over one's soul and worldly goods with joy . . . and one should consider such resolve to be tantamount to having actually performed such an act."[76]

It turns out, then, that Luria conceived of a number of different ways to accomplish quite similar goals. Two involved imagined death, in the course either of *nefilat ʾappayim* or the martyrological recitation of the Shema, and two involved actual physical death, either the natural deaths of righteous individuals or physical martyrdom in the midst of which one recited the Shema. While the language used to describe the effects of all this upon the individual clearly suggests experience of an ecstatic type, as already noted, as far as I am aware there are no anecdotal descriptions recounting such experiences by Luria or any of his disciples. (We do have a report by Vital that he once had an audition of the voice of Rabbi Yeiva Sabba—a fictitious figure of the *Zohar*—who told him to perform *nefilat ʾappayim* during the morning and afternoon prayer services so as to attain divine wisdom, that is, mystical inspiration.)[77]

Rituals of voluntary, symbolic death are a well-attested phenomenon in the history of religions. In archaic and traditional cultures, real or imagined death is typically considered a creative event, a spiritual rebirth. The ritual of imagined, ecstatic death, as we have seen, is in the nature of an initiation, a mythic passage from one mode of existence to another, in the course of which one becomes revitalized. The Lurianic ritual of *nefilat ʾappayim*, in particular, is akin to other perilous descents to a dangerous world, strikingly reminiscent of shamanic voyages to the underworld for the purpose of gathering sick souls and bringing them back to the land of the living. One of the most fundamental features of shamanic activity is to descend to the subterranean world so as to journey among the dead. Thus, among the shamans of Siberia and Inner Asia, the purpose of such a journey is to search out and retrieve the soul of a sick individual that is believed to have wandered away from his or her body or to have been carried off by demonic forces.[78]

The notion that one endangers oneself, flirts with death itself in the process of extricating the holy from the grasp of evil, became a fundamental tenet of Sabbatean theology in the seventeenth century. It is hardly surprising that Sabbateanism specifically appropriated the Lurianic ritual of *nefilat ʾappayim* as one way of explaining Sabbatai Sevi's apostasy; it served as a perfect example of how he deliberately descended into the abyss of the *qelippot* in order to complete the yet unfinished task of cosmic redemption:

> It is well known that the reason behind every prohibition is that it causes one's soul to become impure. If this is so, why are the righteous permitted to enter into the realm of impurity? Even more, [why is] one not called righteous *unless* one performs such an act? We have seen a wonderful meditative intention of Isaac Luria, may he be blessed, concerning *nefilat ʾappayim* [to the effect] that a righteous individual must hurl himself into the depths of the *qelippot*. Now, this is similar to one who transgresses all of the prohibitions of the Torah. Because he is capable of extricating himself from there, he is permitted to commit such an enormous transgression.[79]

Others who labored for redemption had remained aloof from danger, but the Messiah (i.e., Sabbatai Sevi) alone dared to assume the frightful task of struggling with evil on its own terms and on its own territory. While in Sabbateanism such struggle was believed to necessitate antinomian behavior, the violation of Jewish law, and ultimately apostasy, in Lurianic teaching we find nothing of the sort. On the contrary, exposing oneself to the dangers involved required that the worshipper be in as complete a state of holiness as possible.

Nevertheless, even this represented a radical point of view. In a tradition such as the Lurianic one, we would normally expect (and often find) exhortations to *flee* from all danger, to put as much distance between oneself and the forces of evil as one can. The rites designed to purify the soul discussed earlier make this clear. In this case, though, the adept comes face to face with the realm of evil for the purpose of *tiqqun*. We see here the paradoxical nature of the problem of *tiqqun*. On the one hand, individuals are supposed to avoid all contact with impurity so as to render themselves holy and deprive the forces of evil of their potency. Yet the sparks of light that one seeks to liberate are themselves entangled in the realm of evil, making contact with this realm a logical, even necessary strategy. For the most part, Luria resisted this more radical approach, arguing, in effect, that *tiqqun* could be accomplished largely by contemplative acts of holiness. The dramatic ritual of *nefilat ʾappayim*, however, was an important exception to this general rule. From a position of great spiritual strength, having just completed the Shemoneh Esreh, the worshipper with the proper qualifications was considered fit to assume the risk.[80]

The *Kavvanot* of Sabbath Eve: *Kabbalat Shabbat*

Traditions having to do with welcoming the Sabbath with special liturgies prior to the formal evening prayer in the synagogue had developed in Safed before Luria's arrival there. In addition to the recitation of various psalms, the centerpiece of this innovative ritual was the prayer/song "Come, my beloved, to meet the Bride" (*Lekha dodi liqrat kalah*), composed by Solomon Alkabets. As was the case with numerous other rituals, Luria adapted this in original ways. As practiced by others, the Lurianic liturgy of welcoming the Sabbath was performed outdoors, in a field identified as the "field of holy apple trees" (Aramaic: *ḥaqal tapuḥin qaddishin*), signifying the *Shekhinah*. By walking out into the field, the male kabbalistic adept, himself representing the quality of *Tiferet*, welcomed the *Shekhinah* or *Malkhut*, the Sabbath Bride, in a physical manner. Our sources also explain the purpose of going into a field in other terms. The divine worlds that ascend during the course of the Sabbath begin their ascent by means of their "exterior" aspect; hence, one ought to be outside at the onset of Sabbath eve. Afterwards, the "interior" dimension of each of the worlds ascends, facilitated by prayer that takes place inside the synagogue.[81] The ritual of going out into the field is described in the following way:

> Go out into an open field and recite: "Come and let us go into the field of holy apple trees in order to welcome the Sabbath Queen. . . . Stand in a certain place in the field; it is preferable if you are able to do so on an elevated spot, one that is clean in front of you, as well as behind you, for a distance of four cubits. Turn your face toward the west, where the sun sets, and at the very moment that it sets, close your eyes and place your left hand upon your chest and your right hand upon your left. Direct your concentration—while in a state of awe and trembling as one who stands in the presence of the King— so as to receive the extra Sabbath holiness [*tosefet qedushat shabbat*].
>
> Begin by reciting the psalm "Give to the Lord, O heavenly beings" [Ps. 29], singing it entirely in a sweet voice. Following this, recite three times: "Come, O Bride, Come O Bride, O Sabbath Queen." Next, recite "A psalm, a song for the Sabbath day" [Ps. 92] in its entirety, followed by "The Lord is King; He is robed in majesty" until "for all time" [Ps. 93]. Then open your eyes and return home.[82]

Insofar as the western direction signifies *Malkhut* in kabbalistic symbolism, facing west served as a means of orienting oneself toward the Sabbath Bride and Queen. As noted earlier, placing one's left hand within one's right was a way of "sweetening" the side of *Din* and incorporating it within the side of *Ḥesed*. The welcoming of the Sabbath as a queen and bride has its roots actually in imagery found in rabbinic tradition. Thus the Babylonian Talmud (*Shabbat* 119a): "Rabbi Hanina robed himself and stood at sunset of Sabbath eve and exclaimed,

'Come and let us go forth to welcome the queen Sabbath.' Rabbi Yannai donned his robes on Sabbath eve and exclaimed, 'Come, O bride, Come, O bride." While the talmudic rabbis themselves viewed the Sabbath in feminine terms, there is no evidence that it was hypostasized as a female dimension of divinity along the lines of kabbalistic thinking.

We know that while the kabbalists of Safed literally went out at sunset into a field to greet the Sabbath, over time this practice became attenuated. Eventually, congregations replicated the original ritual by going into the courtyard of the synagogue. A still further dilution of this ceremony took place when it became the custom simply to rise, open the door of the synagogue, and turn toward the west at the final verse of Alkabets's poem, bowing to the approaching Bride. This is the custom in most synagogues today when *Lekhah Dodi* is sung during the *Kabbalat Shabbat* service.

Bundles of Myrtle and Twelve Loaves of Bread

Luria fashioned a series of liturgical practices connected to the festive table for Sabbath eve, some of which go back to earlier rites. Vital described the rituals to be performed upon returning home as follows:

> Afterwards [i.e., after the evening service in the synagogue], return to your home, and upon entering the house sing out with great joy: "Sabbath peace!" For [at this moment] he may be compared to a bridegroom who greets his bride with tremendous happiness and warmth. If your mother is still living, go and kiss her hands. The esoteric significance of this is that in a similar way *Zeᶜir Anpin* kisses the hands of his mother each Sabbath night. . . . Then circle the table once in silence, from the right side. . . . Following this, take in your hands two bundles of myrtle . . . and encircle the table once again in silence. . . . The two bundles signify *Zeᶜir* and *Nuqba*, on account of which, after you smell them, immediately utter "remember and observe [the Sabbath, proclaimed by God] in a single command." This alludes to the mystery of *Zeᶜir* and *Nuqba,* which are united, as expressed in the words "remember" and "observe." . . . After the blessings over the meal, once again pick up the two bundles of myrtle

and hold them together while concentrating upon the intention indicated above. Recite the words "observe and remember in a single
command." Then recite the blessing: " . . . who creates fragrant trees"
and smell them.[83]

According to Luria, the Sabbath table was to be prepared with twelve
loaves of bread (*challah*) upon it, described in some detail by Vital:

I observed that my teacher, of blessed memory, used to take very great
care to eat at a table that had four legs, after the pattern of the table
used in the [ancient] Sanctuary. Further, as to the bread with which
the table was prepared, care must be taken to place twelve loaves upon
the table at every meal, corresponding to the twelve loaves of showbread [in the ancient Temple]. Place them in the following manner:
six loaves on the right side of the table and six on the left side. The six
on the right side should be arranged in three pairs; the same with the
six on the left side. The three bottom loaves on the right should be
arranged in the form of the vowel *segol*, with the upper three resting
upon them, and so too with the loaves on the left. This is their exact
placement: on the extreme right side of the table, there should be
four loaves. And in the middle, there should be four other loaves,
two pairs. But the two middle pairs are to be separated from each
other by some distance between them, for one pair is closer to the
two pairs on the right and the other pair of middle loaves is closer to
the two pairs on the left. When you are about to recite the blessing
over the bread, take the two upper loaves from the four middle
breads, bring them together in your hands, with the undersides of
the breads joined together, so that they are facing one another and
appear as a single loaf. They will thus look like the showbread in the
Sanctuary.[84]

These fascinating ritual gestures are explained in considerable detail
in the Lurianic literature. The Sabbath eve liturgies and rituals were
on the whole regarded by Luria in terms of a sacred marriage rite, at
the center of which was the adept's goal of bringing about the most
perfect and intimate form of love between *Ze῾ir Anpin* and *Nuqba de-
Ze῾ir*. We have already seen how the act of going into the "field of holy
apple trees" begins to facilitate this process. The male adept, signifying the divine masculine (as do the trees rooted in the field) welcomes

the divine feminine through the singing of certain psalms and "Come, my beloved, to meet the Bride," the Sabbath Queen. Upon returning home to his wife, he is compared to a bridegroom (*Ze͑ir*) who greets his beloved bride (*Nuqba*), filled with immense peace and joy. (This joy, as we saw elsewhere, is supposed to express itself later in the night in the final sacred act of Sabbath eve, sexual relations between wife and husband.) The other primary woman in a man's life, his mother, is also the object of loving attention, as he kisses her hands in symbolic simulation of the relationship between *Ze͑ir* and the *partsuf Imma*.

The joining together of two bundles of myrtle and the accompanying utterance of the words "remember and observe" also signify the loving marriage of *Ze͑ir* and *Nuqba*. Encircling the table while doing so suggests an act of intimacy between male and female. More specifically, it serves to suffuse *Nuqba de-Ze͑ir* with the "surrounding light" (*͗or maqif*) belonging to the sefirotic aspects of *Ḥesed*, *Gevurah*, and *Tiferet* within *Ze͑ir Anpin*. (The first encircling, without the myrtles in hand, stimulates the "surrounding light" belonging to *Netsaḥ*, *Hod*, and *Yesod* within *Ze͑ir*.) Luria's use of myrtles on Sabbath eve drew its inspiration from a passage in the Talmud: "On the eve of the Sabbath before sunset, they saw an old man holding two bundles of myrtle and running at twilight. 'What are these for' they asked him. 'They are in honor of the Sabbath,' he replied. 'But one should suffice you?' One is for 'remember' and one for 'observe'" [he said].[85] The fragrance of the myrtles presumably called to mind their aroma in the setting of a wedding ceremony, as we know that myrtle was used for preparing the bridegroom's wreaths, at least at an earlier time. The Talmud also attests to their use more generally at betrothal celebrations, indicating that some sages would juggle with myrtle branches on such occasions![86] All of this is consistent with the conception of the Sabbath eve rites as a way to bring about the betrothal of *Ze͑ir* and *Nuqba*, especially by means of the rituals at the festive table. The aromatic fragrance filling the room may also have helped husband and wife to anticipate their own "betrothal" to come, perhaps even serving as an aphrodisiac.

The use of twelve loaves of bread for the Sabbath table was rooted in Zoharic traditions. Whereas traditionally two loaves of bread are placed on the table for each of the three festive Sabbath meals, one passage in the *Zohar* says, "Whoever can, should place on the table four loaves at every Sabbath meal, making twelve loaves in all for the three meals."[87] Elsewhere in the literature of the *Zohar*, however, we discover that twelve loaves are required for *each* meal, "six loaves on this side, and six on that," signifying the joints in the body of the *Shekhinah*, "six joints of the two arms, and six joints of the two legs, so that the *Shekhinah* becomes a body for the King, properly prepared."[88] Thus, while there are various views found in the Zoharic literature, including the traditional one, Luria found the idea of twelve loaves appealing and adopted it, influencing kabbalistically inclined individuals to do the same, especially Hasidim.[89] In addition to the fact that twelve loaves were patterned after the Temple's showbread (*lehem panim*), that is, twelve breads laid out in the Temple on a display table each Sabbath, Luria naturally adduced various esoteric reasons for this practice. Through a complex calculation of *gematria*, the number twelve was associated with the thirteen strands of hair belonging to the head of *Arikh Anpin* (i.e., *Keter*), as represented in *Sifra di-Tseniuta* and the Idra Rabba of the *Zohar*, or alternatively, with the thirteen aspects of the beard of *Attiqa Qaddisha*. By means of the celebration of the Sabbath eve meal, these divine qualities shed their illumination upon *Malkhut*, or *Nuqba*.[90]

The recitation of the Friday evening *qiddush*, the sanctification over wine, serves the purpose of drawing down the "inner light" (*'or penimi*) of sefirotic aspects of *Ze'ir Anpin* upon *Nuqba*, by which the latter is nourished in the course of the meal. What is more, these lights ultimately derive from the *mohin* of *Ze'ir*, which are called "holy" (*qadosh*), hence the *qiddush* brings about this nourishment. The Sabbath eve meal, then, is literally a meal of nourishment for *Nuqba*, which clarifies the meaning of Luria's proclaiming this "the meal of the holy apple field." *Nuqba* consumes or incorporates these lights as part of the process leading up to the consummation of Her relationship to *Ze'ir*.[91]

Following the meal, wrote Vital, "my master, of blessed memory, would sing a certain poem [*pizmon*] in a sweet melody. He composed three special poems based upon esoteric knowledge [*hokhmat ha-'emet*], consisting of all the detailed contemplative intentions associated with the Sabbath, one song for the evening meal, one for the morning meal, and one for the afternoon."[92] The song for Sabbath eve begins with these words: "I sing in praises to enter the gates of the field of holy apple trees." Its erotic nature is transparent, as the poem proclaims that "Her Husband [*Ze'ir*] embraces Her [*Nuqba*] in Her foundation, giving Her pleasure, squeezing out His strength."[93]

It was also Luria's custom "to leave the table in its place on Sabbath night with the tablecloth spread out upon it, along with the *qiddush* wine cup. . . . and he would leave some drops of wine in the cup in order to preserve the blessing of the Sabbath night there."[94] He would also keep a few crumbs of bread under the tablecloth for the same reason.

These table rites on Sabbath eve are an excellent illustration of my contention that women must have been involved in certain kabbalistic rituals in significant ways. In these passages, we are provided a glimpse of what Luria's own Sabbath rituals must have looked like. We see that he would have greeted his wife with special enthusiasm and delight upon returning home from evening prayer, as a bridegroom greets a bride. We know that if the timing of her monthly cycle permitted it, he and his wife would have (kabbalistically enjoined) marital relations late that night. We see that Luria would have kissed his mother's hands, insofar as she represented to him the supernal mother, *Imma*. We infer that the women of Luria's household had to have been busy preparing unusually large amounts of *challah*, in addition to the other requisite Sabbath preparations. And we discover, more generally, that the home, the sphere of women's endeavors, became sacralized in vivid ways. The home became the locus for mystical rites in which gender relations—human and divine—were central. The thinly veiled sexualized character of these rites would presumably have heightened their dramatic nature. While women may have had no role in the study houses and only a marginal one in the synagogues, in the home of a Lurianic adept they appear to have had opportunities to experience rich and complex kabbalistic rites in the making. But in the absence of words from Luria's wife, or from any of the other women who were associated with Luria's male disciples, we are left to our imaginations to fathom what such experiences may have actually meant to them.

Luria practiced still other customs as well:

Following the song, a person ought to recite several chapters from Mishnah *Shabbat*. If you want, read the first eight on Sabbath eve, the eight middle chapters at the morning meal, and the final eight chapters in the afternoon. . . . Generally, however, my teacher, of blessed memory, used to recite the first four chapters in the evening, the second four in the morning, and the third four in the afternoon. . . . And sometimes, when he was preoccupied with conversation about Torah with other people at the table, he would recite only a single chapter at each meal.

The twenty-four chapters of Mishnah *Shabbat* were regarded as corresponding to twenty-four adornments worn by the Sabbath Bride, that is, *Nuqba*.[95] We also learn that Luria sought to speak Hebrew only on the Sabbath:

With respect to conversation on the Sabbath, my teacher, of blessed memory, was particularly careful never to speak in the vernacular, either during the day or the night. The only exception to this was when he would deliver a homily to us and was compelled to use the vernacular in order that the listening public could understand. He was also cautious about never engaging in idle conversation or weekday talk on the Sabbath, even in Hebrew. On all of the Festivals, he would behave as he did on the Sabbath in this regard.[96]

Finally, Luria also instructed his disciples how to dress properly for the Sabbath:

Know that my teacher, of blessed memory, cautioned me . . . that it is improper for a person to wear any of the clothes he wore during the week on the Sabbath. It is wrong even to wear one's Sabbath cloak during the rest of the week. Moreover, on the Sabbath, a person must wear white garments, not colored ones. My master reported to me that the color of the garment one will wear in the world to come, following death, will be the same color as the clothes we wear on the Sabbath in this world.[97]

*

Can we make any general observations about Lurianic prayer on the basis of all this? Perhaps the most obvious conclusion is one made earlier about the *kavvanot* of mitsvot as a whole. There, I pointed out that

the conventional meaning associated with performing the precepts re-
ceded into the deep background, giving way to the theurgical intentions with which they were invested. Much the same is true in the case
of prayer. Ostensibly, Jewish prayer has to do with expressing praise
and love for God, demonstrating gratitude for the blessings of life,
seeking expiation of sin, and petitioning God to intervene in human
affairs. Such are the themes embodied in the liturgy of rabbinic tradition. For Luria, however, these themes took a back seat at best in relation to the contemplative goals he pursued. Although the sense of a
personal God—one to be served with awe and reverence, joy and enthusiasm—is preserved to some extent in Lurianic prayer, the real focus
of the imagination rests elsewhere. The standard language of praise,
thanksgiving, love, and petition gives way to the Lurianic language of
myth and theurgy. Drawing down *moḥin* from the upper *partsufim* to
nourish *Zeᶜir* and *Nuqba de-Zeᶜir*, raising up the Female Waters and
stimulating the descent of the Male Waters, the marriage of *Abba* and
Imma, and *Zeᶜir* and *Nuqba*—these were what fascinated Luria and his
disciples. The mythic categories of Lurianic teaching thus transformed
the meaning of the liturgy's words into an immeasurably intricate and
dynamic account of God's inner life. As such, what normally passes for
prayer in the rabbinic sense becomes transformed into a fundamentally
different kind of experience. In addition to feelings and thoughts of love,
gratitude, humility, awe, and supplication, Lurianic prayer requires an
additional mental attitude. The adept not only is called upon to concentrate on the Lurianic tropes that correspond to the words and phrases of
liturgy but must focus on the dynamic cosmic processes his thoughts set
in motion.

Unfortunately, we know too little about the affective impact of this
kind of worship upon those who practiced it, except in the important
case of *nefilat ᵓappayim*. What we do know is that contemplative prayer
as a whole was intended to draw down divine light upon its practitioners, to enable male adepts to assimilate to themselves the energies
of the masculine divine, and to create the conditions under which they
could experience the inspiration of the Holy Spirit. Such was the experience of Luria himself, according to his disciples.

It is also clear that the *kavvanot* are not arbitrarily or atomistically strewn about. Rather, they follow coherent patterns, which correlate with the structure of the liturgy itself. Thus, in the daily morning prayer, a series of processes or events take place in a particular and necessary order. An intradivine drama takes place, as well as a human-divine one, stimulated by the worshipping kabbalist. The various elements of the liturgy—*Birkhot ha-Shaḥar*, *Pesuqei de-Zimra*, the Shema, Shemoneh Esreh, *nefilat ʾappayim*, and so on—represent a cosmic road map in which one turn leads to the next. Similarly, the various periods of prayer in the course of a full day produce varying kinds of effects and stand in meaningful relationship to one another. Different *zivvugim* take place during each of the daily services, reaching the highest point with the morning service. So, too, with the structure of the week, reaching its climactic point with the rituals and liturgies of the Sabbath. Likewise, the liturgical cycle of the year, with its various seasons and festivals, constituted a structure with a meaningful and deliberate pattern. Given this, it is clear that there is a quality of *cyclical* time to Lurianic prayer, and in many ways to Lurianic ritual altogether. The repetitive rhythms of the daily, monthly, and yearly cycle constitute a means by which the dynamics of the cosmos are recapitulated over and over again. Despite the linear, eschatological orientation that characterizes so much of Lurianic mysticism, in which time is conceived to be moving toward an ultimate redemptive *telos*, it is nevertheless the case that we also have here features of a myth of eternal return.[98] The equilibrium of the cosmos is sustained and its balance is restored on a continuous basis by means of the *kavvanot* that accompany the act of prayer. The worshipper and the divine forces of the cosmos stand in intimate, symbiotic relationship to each other, dependent upon each other for sustenance.

In such terms, the existing liturgical structure served the character of Lurianic devotion perfectly. The wide scope and immense detail of the liturgy was ideally suited to the complexities and intricacies of Lurianic teachings. Every subtlety and each nuance of intradivine activity could be read into the words of prayer. The sheer amount of liturgy was a fitting match for the seemingly endless permutations of divine interaction. Beyond this, the unwavering regularity with which liturgical devotion is celebrated, and the phenomenon of standardized prayers, provided a reliable, compulsory, institutionalized structure of ritual. Each and every day of the year presented renewed opportunity to perform rites of mystical action over and over again.

Despite the circular nature of prayer to which attention has been drawn, Luria nevertheless affirmed the *uniqueness* of each moment of devotion. Each day's prayer was somewhat different in nature and in its effect compared to that of the day before. No prayer since the world was created was believed to be exactly the same, and every individual's prayer was distinctive.

Perhaps even more than in the case of the *kavvanot* of mitsvot, the *kavvanot* of prayer were elitist in nature. Many of the mitsvot involve rather brief, discrete contemplative actions. In the context of an isolated ritual moment it is relatively easy to remember and employ the appropriate *kavvanot*. The example of giving charity described in the previous chapter is just such a mitsvah. Liturgical devotion is altogether different in that it is a long, continuous process, requiring one contemplative intention after the next in relatively rapid succession. Even if one prayed much more slowly than is normally the case, Lurianic prayer would still have been a formidable challenge to the worshipper. Indeed, it is difficult to imagine exactly how one could incorporate all of the details Luria taught. Moreover, the requirements of public or communal prayer—where one prays with a group of at least ten—would exacerbate this problem. In private prayer, one has the leisure to follow one's own pace. But in group prayer, the congregation must meet at various predetermined moments in the service for communal recitation. In short, praying with the Lurianic *kavvanot* could not have been an easy job. It would have required, at very least, a superb memory, the ability to cope successfully with the constant distractions to which worshippers are always vulnerable, and steadfast concentration to sustain prayer of such a complex and intense nature.

E i g h t Communing with the "Very Special Dead":
The Practice of *Yiḥudim*

> Like myth, which looks to the undetermined future as well as the
> sacrosanct past, spirit mediumship, especially in less standardized
> forms culminating in oracular speech, provides an essential counter-
> part to the putative closure of ritual by its continual opening toward
> unrealized potentialities of human existence. The practiced medium's
> voluntary solicitation of a condition that surpasses her ordinary
> powers and leads her toward an intrinsically unpredictable goal thus
> exhibits the form of a spiritual quest as a purposeful exploration of
> the transcendent unknown.
> —Robert Torrance, *The Spiritual Quest*

In the previous two chapters, we have seen how Lurianic practice
adapted existing normative structures of Jewish religious observance,
the mitsvot as a whole and the liturgy of the prayer book. By investing
traditional forms of ritual with altogether new intent, Luria infused
those forms with radically different meaning. But in addition to this,
Luria fashioned new rituals to serve his distinctive needs, such as we
have already seen, for example, in connection with the *tiqqunei ʿavonot*.
Safed Kabbalah as a whole was characterized by a penchant for ritual
innovation, as many of the practices described earlier clearly demonstrate. The self-imposed peregrinations of Solomon Alkabets and Moses
Cordovero, midnight vigils for purposes of prayer and study, Karo's
maggidic experiences, new rituals for ushering in the Sabbath, and original forms of celebrating the appearance of the New Moon exemplify
the inventive, experimental impulses at work in the sixteenth century.
     Isaac Luria was no exception to this tendency. On the contrary,
Luria had a peculiar genius for ritual creativity to match his originality
in the sphere of mythological thinking and should be considered one
of the preeminent innovators of ritual in the history of Judaism. In
many cases, Luria adapted earlier kabbalistic rituals—from Safed and
elsewhere—for his own purposes. But he went further by teaching his
disciples a variety of ritual practices that had little or no precedent in

259

Jewish tradition and were not tied to the performance of formal religious precepts.[1] The most important of these, for a variety of reasons, was a ritual of communion with the souls of the deceased, known as *yiḥudim* (pl.), a term that may be translated as "unifications." The *yiḥudim* introduced elements into the repertoire of Lurianic practice that are altogether lacking in the rituals discussed thus far.

Our knowledge of this rite comes from several sources. The most extensive accounts are by Hayyim Vital and are found in *Shaᶜar Ruaḥ ha-Qodesh*, as well as in a separate book entitled *Shaᶜar ha-Yiḥudim*, both of which are devoted almost entirely to this topic.[2]

In contrast to the technique of contemplative death discussed above, where we have no accounts of actual practice, descriptions of Vital's own experiences while performing these rites were preserved by him in *Shaᶜar ha-Gilgulim*, as well as in his diary, *Sefer ha-Ḥezyonot*. To our good fortune, we also have prescriptions for the performance of these exercises by Joseph ibn Tabul and Moshe Yonah, preserved primarily in manuscript.[3] In addition, there are scattered references to the *yiḥudim* in a variety of other sources, including the letters of Solomon Shlomiel of Dresnitz. There is thus an abundance of evidence from diverse sources attesting to this ritual practice.

Qualifying for the Practice of *Yiḥudim*

We have already seen the connection in Lurianic thinking between the status of one's soul and its fitness for mystical inspiration in the context of Luria's activities as a physician of the soul. Only when the soul is pure and unblemished will "the supernal holy matters take shape in her." The mortification and penitential instructions with which Isaac Luria provided his disciples were intended to purify the soul of filth and stain and ensure that it would "be able to attain and comprehend supernal matters." Thus, Luria would reveal his knowledge only to those who had perfected their souls through the practice of *tiqqunei ᶜavonot*. These exercises should be regarded, then, as prerequisites for anyone who aspired to achieve mystical inspiration. In addition to the *tiqqunei ᶜavonot*, in Shmuel Vital's arrangement of his father's version

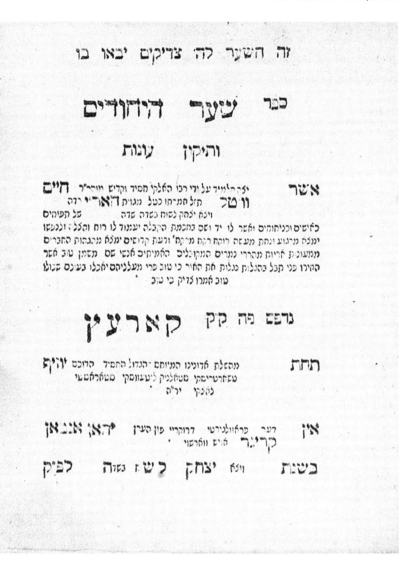

Figure 8. The title page of *Shaʿar ha-Yiḥudim* (Korecz, 1783).

of Luria's teachings, the account of the *yiḥudim* is preceded by a description of various ethical and ritual activities, some of which we have already encountered in various contexts. Shmuel tells us that he has gathered all of these items together insofar as they are necessary for achieving any kind of heavenly inspiration (*hasagah*) or enlightenment of the soul.[4] Types of moral behavior that are represented as prerequisites for success in attaining mystical illumination include the cultivation of joyfulness (and the corresponding avoidance of melancholy); the absolute avoidance of all expressions of anger; the practice of humility, meekness, and the fear of sin; as well as the avoidance of pride, jesting, gossip, and pedantry.[5] A person in pursuit of spiritual perfection should not be too strict in judging others, even if significant provocation exists. Nor should one indulge in "idle" conversation, that is, talk unrelated to Torah or spiritual matters. Success in the practice of mystical contemplation hinges on one's capacity to acquire these qualities of emotion and spirit.

Beyond this, Luria required his disciples to practice other special acts of ritual piety, the basic purpose of which was to nullify the power of the demonic and fortify the soul's purity. For example, Vital reports that Luria taught him that attainment of the Holy Spirit depends upon the care and concentration with which blessings over things one enjoys (*birkhot ha-nehenin*) are carried out. This is especially true in the case of enjoying food:

> Since through them [blessings over food recited with proper mystical intention] the strength of the shells [*qelippot*] that cling to physical foods, and thus cleave to one who eats them, is neutralized. And by virtue of the blessings over [the food] recited with contemplative intention, he removes these shells from them, purifies his physical self and becomes pure, ready to receive holiness. And he [Luria] warned me carefully in this regard.[6]

Luria also instructed his disciples to practice the custom of rising at midnight for the purpose of praying and studying through the night, an activity regarded as unusually efficacious in preparing for the performance of *yihudim*. But the midnight vigil will be effective only for an individual who has carried out certain deeds in the course of the day: enabling others to repent, giving charity anonymously, and studying the literature of the *Posekim* (rabbinic legal decisions). As we shall see, the most favorable time to perform the *yihudim* also turns out to be midnight. Other important acts of piety included meticulous observance of the Sabbath in all its details, entering the synagogue in a state of great awe and trembling, and wearing tefillin (phylacteries) the entire day. Furthermore, as we have seen, the attainment of the Holy Spirit required the regular study of Scripture, Mishnah, Talmud, and Kabbalah, as well as intensive, concentrated study of Jewish law (*ᶜiyyun halakha*).

As noted in other contexts, Vital also recorded practices that fellow disciples told him they had received directly from the mouth of their master. In the name of Jonathan Sagis, for instance, Vital reports that Luria regarded ritual immersion as essential to attainment of the Holy Spirit.[7] Immersion was believed to be a purifying exercise of such importance that it was to be practiced with the utmost diligence and regularity. As indicated elsewhere, Luria himself seems to have been prevented from engaging in ritual immersion for a period of six months because of illness, but apparently he suffered no loss of divine inspiration. Abraham ben Eliezer ha-Levi Berukhim told Vital that Luria taught him that the following were conducive to divine inspiration: avoidance of idle talk, rising at midnight and weeping on account of our lack of esoteric knowledge, and studying forty or fifty pages of the *Zohar* each day without intensive reflection.[8] Samuel Uceda reported that he was informed by his teacher that anyone who spent forty successive days speaking only words of Torah would make himself fit for mystical inspiration and knowledge.

The Context for the Practice of *Yiḥudim*

For the most part, the practice of the *yiḥudim* was intended to be an independent exercise, detached altogether from the context of traditional daily prayer. There were two places in which they were to be performed: at the grave of a *tsaddiq* (a "saintly" or righteous person) or in one's own home.[9] The purpose of performing these exercises at a grave had to do with the fact that one of the essential goals of the *yiḥudim* was to commune with the soul of a departed *tsaddiq*. They *could* be carried out in one's home, but a yet greater degree of purity on the part of the adept was necessary in order to bring about the desired communion of souls.[10]

It seems that despite Luria's instructions that the *yiḥudim* take place outside the realm of daily prayer, Hayyim Vital sought to incorporate their performance into regular prayer. In his dream diary, Vital reports that during the latter's performance of a *yiḥud* after midnight, Yeiva Sabba appeared to him and told him that by performing the *yiḥud* (s.) found in his teacher's own handwriting, he would attain all the wisdom he desired. Yeiva Sabba also informed him that he "should perform the *yiḥud* three times each day in the following fashion: in *nefilat ʾappayim* of the morning service, in *nefilat ʾappayim* during the afternoon service, and while reciting the evening Shema, and by this means I shall achieve all that I desire."[11] A couple of days later, Yeiva Sabba appeared once again to Vital, seeking to know why he failed to carry out the *yiḥud* as he had instructed him, namely, during regular prayer. Yeiva Sabba went on to instruct Vital to go to his teacher, who would teach him how to do this properly. *Shaʿar Ruaḥ ha-Qodesh* confirms this in Vital's assertion that Luria "told me that I could perform that *yiḥud* during any of the three prayer services: in the morning, afternoon, and evening, during *nefilat ʾappayim* of the morning and afternoon, and while reciting the evening Shema." Ronit Meroz suggests that this may have been an innovation of Vital's own that he presents as having been sanctioned by his teacher.[12]

Certain days were considered more propitious than others for the performance of *yiḥudim*.[13] Practice at a grave could be done on all days except for the Sabbath, New Moon (*Rosh Ḥodesh*), and Festivals. On these days, the lower souls (*nefashot*) of the righteous, which normally hover above graves, ascend to the terrestrial paradise and are thus unavailable for communion.[14] Although all other days are acceptable, the eve of the New Moon and the eve of the fifteenth day of the month are preferable, since a person is considered likely to be more spiritually prepared then. Although both types of *yiḥudim* can be properly practiced at any hour of the day, the favored time (*ʿet ratson*) is after midnight. If one performs the exercises at home, it is particularly critical to wait until the midnight hour. This dissociation of the *yiḥudim* from the context of conventional prayer—Vital's innovation notwithstanding—is significant. More often than not, mystical devotion within religious cultures tends toward private experience. Medieval Jewish mystics, however, had always to deal with the entrenched rabbinic preference for communal prayer, according to which a quorum of ten is required for public worship. As a consequence, it was more natural for earlier kabbalists of the theosophical/theurgical variety to gravitate toward the use of traditional liturgy for their meditative activities. As we have seen in relationship to the *kavvanot* of prayer, Lurianic Kabbalah also followed this path.

But there were good reasons why Luria forged ritual techniques that went beyond the boundaries of the liturgy. Although the *kavvanot* of prayer remained tied to communal worship in Lurianic devotion (in Luria's own community, that is), the nature of the contemplation involved inevitably tended to shift the emphasis from the collective dynamics of the praying community to the individual. The *kavvanot*, as we have seen, are extraordinarily complex in character, requiring intense, prolonged concentration. And besides, the primary focus of attention was no longer directed toward the text of the prayers themselves as much as toward the dynamic mythic processes to which the words of prayer correspond. It is reasonable to presume that these factors necessarily led to an increased withdrawal into oneself in the course of prayer. The step from this privatizing tendency to contemplative ritual detached altogether from regular communal worship is not a great one. Such a move allowed for the development of freer techniques to accomplish one's goals. If we add to all these considerations the fact that the *yiḥudim* involved communion with the soul of a *tsaddiq*, it is not surprising that Luria fashioned a ritual unconstrained by the requirements of public, synagogue worship.

Communion of Souls with the Dead

One of the two critical goals associated with the practice of *yiḥudim* was mystical communion between the soul of the adept and that of a departed *tsaddiq*. Hayyim Vital's account of the process of communion is contained in a series of brief introductions:

Be aware that in the case of all possible *yiḥudim*, if you perform the *yiḥud* by stretching yourself [*be-hishtatḥa*] out on the *tsaddiq*'s actual grave, you should contemplatively intend that by virtue of your stretching out on top of him, you also cause the *tsaddiq* to stretch out his lower soul [*nefesh*], which will then spread out in his bones that are in the grave: [whereupon] he comes "alive" and his bones become like a body to the soul that is stretched and spread out within them. This [particular] soul is the one that remains over the grave, as is known, which is the secret meaning of "And his soul mourneth over him" [Job 14:22]. And it is as if this *tsaddiq* lives in body and soul at this moment. And if you perform the *yiḥudim* in your house, without prostration, there is no need to practice the contemplative intention indicated above. However, you must always concentrate upon raising up your soul [*nefesh*] and that of the *tsaddiq* while they are bound to one another [*qeshurim yaḥad*], your soul included with his, regardless of whether you perform the *yiḥudim* while prostrated at the grave or while at home. You must also concentrate your attention upon that root within Adam from which both your soul and that of the *tsaddiq* derive. And concentrate upon arousing that root, for it is the "limb" within Adam from which the soul of this *tsaddiq* originates. By doing so you can raise up his soul through the mystery of the Female Waters.[15]

We have here what is certainly a highly unusual, even extraordinary ritual. There are three parts to this technique when performed at a grave. First, the adept activates the *nefesh* of the *tsaddiq* that hovers above the grave, enlivening or animating the latter's bones by completely stretching himself out on the grave. He does this face down, as a mirror image to the individual buried in the grave, so as to align himself physically with that individual. Following this, he concentrates on binding his own *nefesh* (and potentially higher levels of soul as well) to that of the *tsaddiq*. Finally, while in this state of intimate cleaving soul to soul, he concentrates on assimilating their souls to one another and thus raising them to the upper realms by concentrating on their common root within Adam's original soul. The difference between performing this at the grave as opposed to in one's home is that in the latter case the first of these three concentrative steps is omitted. Even then, however, it is still possible to cleave to the soul of the *tsaddiq*.

Here again, as in the rites associated with *nefilat 'appayim* and the martyrological recitation of the Shema, the Lurianic imagination focuses on themes of life and death. Just as in those cases, a person ritually enacts a death for the purpose of life—the renewed life of souls trapped in a place of death—similarly with the *yiḥudim*. In going to a grave and stretching out one's body upon it, one resembles one who has died; yet, by so doing, one *revitalizes* the body of the deceased *tsaddiq*. What is more, in all these cases, an adept enjoys his own personal spiritual rejuvenation through the ascent of his soul. Despite their differences, these several rites constitute a cluster of related phenomena. In the case of the *yiḥudim*, the living and the dead assist one another. By their contemplative pilgrimages to graves, the living are able to reanimate the dead, such that the lower souls of the latter ascend on high, while by cleaving "soul to soul" the mystical adept is able to journey to the world above and to enjoy communion with the celestial realms. These exercises make it possible for both the living and the dead to avoid the normal consequences of death by preserving a relationship with each other, a relationship based upon spiritual kinship, cleaving and communication. In some respects, this mutually beneficial "exchange of gifts" between the living and the dead parallels the attitudes of medieval Christians toward their saints. As Patrick Geary writes of European Christianity:

> Death marked a transition, a change in status, but not an end. The living continued to owe them [the dead] certain obligations, the most important that of *memoria*, remembrance. . . . For one category of the dead, those venerated as saints, prayers *for* changed to prayers *to*. These "very special dead" in the phrase of Peter Brown, could act as intercessors on behalf of the living before God. But this difference was one of degree, not of kind. All the dead interacted with the living, continuing to aid them, to warn or admonish them. . . . The dead were present among the living through liturgical commemoration, in dreams and visions, and in their physical remains, especially the tombs and relics of the saints. Omnipresent, they were drawn into every aspect of life.[16]

Geary's notion that the physical remains of the dead—including their tombs—constituted relics deserving of veneration for medieval

Christians is highly suggestive as well in the case of the *yiḥudim*.[17] As Peter Brown puts it in connection with the veneration of graves in late antiquity: "The graves of the saints—whether these were the solemn rock tombs of the Jewish patriarchs in the Holy Land, or, in Christian circles, tombs, fragments of bodies, or even physical objects that had made contact with those bodies—were privileged places, where the contrasted poles of Heaven and Earth met."[18] The numerous grave sites and tombstones that dotted the landscape of Safed and its environs were not merely physical reminders of the saintly dead but sites vested with sacrality, *holy* in the sense that they made access to the realm of the divine especially possible. As such, the broader landscape as a whole took on a sacral quality; to journey to a grave site, or from one grave site to another, was quite literally a matter of religious pilgrimage.

That graves became places to which Jews in the late Middle Ages and early modern period intentionally traveled in search of transformative experiences is a phenomenon that requires some explanation. This is so because Jewish tradition, beginning with religious practice in ancient Israel, regarded contact with the dead as among the most fundamental means by which to contract a state of ritual impurity, and thus something to be avoided as far as possible. Hence, the custom while the Temple in Jerusalem still existed of burying the dead beyond the physical boundaries of the living community, in caves where the impurity of the dead could not compromise the ritual status of the living.[19] *Kohanim* (priests), in particular, whose sacred work in the ancient Temple required them to maintain a state of ritual purity, had to go out of their way to avoid contact with the dead. Even in post-Temple times, Jewish tradition continued to manifest unease about unnecessary contact with the dead and with burial places.[20]

Despite these powerful strictures, however, the real and imagined grave sites of a range of important figures—biblical matriarchs and patriarchs, prophets, and rabbinic sages themselves—became sites of pilgrimage and veneration from late antiquity on, although such activity does not appear to have been especially widespread or significant in the period of the Talmud.[21] For the most part, individuals visited these sites in order to beseech the dead to intervene in the world above on behalf of the living. A few talmudic passages (*Sotah* 34b; *Taʿanit* 23b;

Baba Metsia 85b) even employ the term *hishtatḥut* in connection with supplicatory activity at grave sites. In contrast to the Lurianic meaning of this word, actual prostration upon the grave, the rabbinic accounts probably have in mind some form of bowing.[22] Thus, the enthusiasm that the author of the *Zohar* and kabbalists of sixteenth-century Safed exhibited for identifying (and multiplying) such sites builds on a limited but centuries-old tradition of grave veneration.

As for the practice of *yiḥudim* itself, its quasi-magical nature is self-evident. What distinguishes it, in part, from full-fledged magic is that the physical act by itself hardly suffices to accomplish the intended goal. No mere mechanical gesture, no simple formulaic incantation, satisfies the devotee's desire to arouse the dead. Rather, an elaborate and sustained contemplative effort is required. A similar point has been made well by Robert Torrance in connection with shamanism, with which the performance of the *yiḥudim* shares certain similarities: "[A]lthough many shamans practice magic . . . they characteristically *seek* communion with spirits instead of attempting to coerce it through mechanical formulas; the shaman's performance, unlike the magician's, is in theory a venture in the unknown. Shamanic ecstasy is no mere technique, like magic or ritual, then, but a transcendent ('ek-static') quest to restore the harmony shattered for the individual by illness or death, and for the people by loss of primordial unity with kindred spirits in the heavens and fellow creatures on earth."[23] In the case of the *yiḥudim*, not only are the methods spiritual in nature, but the ultimate goals are as well: the ascent of the soul along with that of the *tsaddiq* to the upper realms, and the unification of the divine masculine and feminine. Despite apparent similarities, then, this Lurianic rite should not be mistaken for necromancy, the divinatory art of magically conjuring up the souls of the dead.[24] Necromancy has as its main purpose communication with the dead for the purpose of obtaining information— typically concerning what the future holds in store. The broad mystical goals associated with the *yiḥudim* point to a far more subtle and complex phenomenon. Nevertheless, the theurgic, magical tendency so essential to all forms of theosophical kabbalism may be said to be taken in this case to something of an extreme, evidence that the border between magic and mysticism is often extremely difficult to discern.

The soul referred to in our passage is the *nefesh*, the lowest of the various parts of the soul as conceived of by the kabbalists. In earlier Kabbalah, the soul was generally considered to have three aspects, as we have already noted. In ascending hierarchical order, they are the *nefesh* (lower soul), the *ruaḥ* (spirit), and the *neshamah* (highest soul). The Lurianists also spoke of two additional levels of soul, *ḥayyah* and *yeḥidah*, representing still higher levels of spiritual attainment, present in only certain select individuals. According to Lurianic teaching, the various parts of the soul return to their respective places of origin following death. However, the *nefesh*, or more precisely, the *lowest* grade of *nefesh*—"*nefesh* of the lower world of *Assiyah*"—continues to hover over an individual's grave. It is this grade of *nefesh* to which our passage refers. If, however, the contemplative kabbalist has himself attained higher levels of soul, such as *ruaḥ* or *neshamah*, he can attempt to bind these as well to the *ruaḥ* or *neshamah* of the *tsaddiq* with whom he is seeking to commune.

In a previous discussion of the structure of the soul, we saw that every individual soul is part of a particular soul-root (*shoresh gadol*). That is, there exist families or constellations of souls that derive from common roots within Adam's original soul. These families have a special attraction to and affinity for one another, sharing, as they do, the same source, the metaphysical equivalent of biological ancestry. Because of this common ancestry, they are uniquely qualified to assist one another in the task of raising up soul-sparks from the now materialized realm of *Assiyah*. The knowledge of one's soul-ancestry—knowledge that Isaac Luria was able to give to his disciples—was thus of absolutely crucial importance to them. It is precisely this affinity of souls that constitutes the basis for the communion of souls at the grave. Because of their natural kinship, through intense concentration, the soul of the adept can arouse the corresponding aspect of soul of the *tsaddiq*.

It is noteworthy here that the veneration of the dead has shifted from biological to spiritual ancestors. Traditional appeals for intercession made to the souls of one's own natural family give way to an altogether different type of identity, namely, a spiritual identity with the holy dead, along the lines of a complex chain of transmigration (on

Lurianic metempsychosis, see also Chapter 9). In his classic study of the late antique cult of the saints in Latin Christianity, Peter Brown describes what he calls the "invisible companion," a dead saint who serves as a guardian angel, a patron and friend more intimate than one's own family and neighbors: "Thus, whether in times of crisis, or in the day-to-day search for protection and inspiration, the religious sensibilities of late-antique men had long been molded by an intense dialogue with invisible companions."[25] Furthermore, "the fact that the relationship can be expressed as one between two human beings means that the rich blood of late-Roman bonds of friendship and dependence now flows into the tissue of the invisible world."[26] In the case of the yiḥudim, we find something quite similar. Thus, for example, Hayyim Vital takes the advice of Yeiva Sabba, who appears to him both in dreams and in the midst of the performance of *yiḥudim*. Communication with the ancestors of one's soul is likened to the kind of conversation that takes place with neighbors and friends.

Luria's notion of soul-communion drew explicitly on themes developed in earlier kabbalistic literature, especially the *Zohar*.[27] In speaking of the fate of the soul following death, the *Zohar* teaches that the *nefashot* remain in the world, hovering over the grave, in order to protect the living in times of trouble. When the living come to them and beg for mercy, these lower souls of the departed inform their own spirits (*ruḥot*), setting off a chain reaction of celestial communication:

> We have learned that in the hour that the world requires mercy and the intervention of those righteous ones [in the world above], that [aspect of] soul that is in the world [i.e., the *nefesh*] to protect the world, ascends, goes and flits about the [upper] world to tell the *ruaḥ*, and the *ruaḥ* ascends, removes itself and tells the *neshamah*, which informs the Holy One, blessed be He. Then the Holy One, blessed be He, has pity on the world and the reverse process takes place, the *neshamah* informing the *ruaḥ* and the *ruaḥ*, the *nefesh*.[28]

Both Vital[29] and ibn Tabul[30] cite the continuation of this passage, according to which the righteous among the living weep over the graves of the departed righteous so as to inform them that the world is in distress.[31] In doing so, the living cleave "soul to soul" (*nefesh le-nefesh*) with the righteous. The *Zohar* asserts that after one has died, one actually has more spiritual power than ever:

> Even though a righteous man departs from this world, he is not removed from, or deprived of, all the worlds, because he continues to exist in all the worlds to a greater extent than during his lifetime. During his lifetime, he exists only in this world, but thereafter he exists in three worlds and is welcome there, as it is written "The maidens love you" [Song of Songs 1:3]. Do not read ʿalamot [i.e., maidens], but ʾolamot [i.e., worlds]. Happy is their portion.[32]

Although no ritual of actual prostration upon graves appears to be suggested by the *Zohar*, merely weeping, Luria's ritual was clearly inspired partly by the *Zohar*'s notion of soul-cleaving.[33] Of particular interest is Moses Cordovero's interpretation of the Zoharic passage under consideration: "This is the secret of 'soul bound up with soul'—this is when he pours [*shofekh*] his soul upon the grave of the *tsaddiq*, cleaving soul to soul [*u-mitdabeq nefesh ʾim nefesh*], and speaks with the soul of the *tsaddiq*. He informs him of the world's distress, and the soul of the *tsaddiq* arouses other souls."[34]

Cordovero also tells us that there were pietists (*ʾanshei maʿaseh*) in Spain who knew how to do this! Elsewhere, he indicates that such a graveside ritual is only necessary when the generation suffers from too much sinfulness. At other times, the deeds of the righteous are themselves sufficient to protect the world. In the event that there are no living righteous able to intercede successfully on behalf of the world, a Torah scroll should be brought to a cemetery to arouse the intercession of the souls of the departed.[35] While it is not clear whether Cordovero intends to describe prostration in using the word *pours* in the above text, many other passages from Cordovero's writings suggest that his practice of *gerushin* involved actual prostration upon the graves that he visited, including the tomb of Shimon bar Yohai. In his commentary on the *Zohar*, he writes, "[N]ow I will explain how the Creator bestowed graciousness upon me [i.e., granted me esoteric knowledge] . . . when I prostrated myself upon the tombs of Rabbi Shimon bar Yohai and his son Rabbi Eleazar, in Meron. There the way of grace and compassion was transmitted to me."[36] Cordovero goes beyond the *Zohar* by intimating a physical act of prostration through which a person actively comes close to the *nefesh* hovering above a grave. His occasional but explicit use of the term *hishtatḥut*, prostration, in *Sefer Gerushin* and *Shiᶜur Qomah* further suggests that Cordovero and his circle did indeed practice this technique, although it does not seem to me that it was a necessary element in their practice of *gerushin*.[37] It is highly probable that the example of Cordovero's practice contributed to the development of Luria's own ritual.

As noted in Chapter 2, we know also of the widespread practice of visiting the grave sites of important prophets, rabbis, and teachers in the Safed area from a variety of pre-Lurianic and post-Lurianic sources.[38] There are reports as early as the thirteenth century of visits to the cave of Hillel and Shammai in Meron—a small village near Safed—in order to pray for rain. Even before the Spanish expulsion, visits were made to the grave in Meron of Shimon bar Yohai, whose mystical teachings the *Zohar* purports to contain, as we know. Moses Basola's travelogue on the land of Israel, covering the years 1521–23, contains a rich description of his visits to "venerated tombs in the Galilee," including this account of his journey to Meron:

> On Thursday, the 23d of the month, I rode to Meron, a village half a day's journey from Safed. Midway, there is a village named Qayama. Nearby, on the road, the son of Rabbi Yose of Yokeret is buried. . . . Meron is a fruitful place, with a good spring, but no Jews live there. There I saw the burial cave of Rabbi Shimon bar Yohai and his son [Eleazar], may their memory be blessed, but it is sealed, [and] there is insufficient room to gain entry. On the cave, there are two lovely drawings opposite each other. Rabbi Shimon bar Yohai's is slightly closer to the outside.[39]

Testimony by various Safed kabbalists, including Joseph Karo, Moses Cordovero, Abraham Galante, and Eleazar Azikri, indicates how popular the custom of visits to Shimon bar Yohai's grave for study, prayer, and contemplation had become by the middle of the century.[40] Karo's *maggid*, for example, informs him that Shimon bar Yohai and his son Eleazar reveal heavenly mysteries to those who study the *Zohar* at their graves.[41] Even more important, as we have already noted, Luria himself made a pilgrimage to Meron along with members of his family prior to settling permanently in Safed. It is clear, then, that by the time Luria arrived in Safed, the custom of visiting the graves of sages for a range of devotional purposes was already quite common and well established.

The veneration of saints among the marabouts of North Africa has already been mentioned, and it is also of considerable interest in the present context that communion with saints at their grave sites had an exceedingly important place in medieval Sufi practice. Many Sufis, especially among the widely spread Qadiriyah and Naqshbandiyah sects,[42] performed what was known as "spiritual communion with a shaykh" by means of contemplatively concentrating on the image of a shaykh, living or dead. This was done in a state of solitude as preparation for the practice of *dikhr*, consciousness of God.[43] According to the Egyptian Sufi master Ibn Ata Allah (c. 1252–1309), it was incumbent upon a disciple "to imagine his shaykh between his eyes, to draw him into his heart, and believe that by doing so he draws upon the spiritual essence of the Prophet [Muhammad] represented by the shaykh."[44] Such a practice is said to result in cleaving to one's master, and through it, one attains a state of mystical inspiration. Najm al-Din Kubra (1145–1221), an influential Iranian Sufi who studied in Egypt, describes how in the course of such practice he was able to ask his master questions concerning devotion to God, and to hear his answers.[45] Especially pertinent to us, among some Sufis, following the death of one's master, this technique was practiced at his grave for the purpose of uniting with his soul and communing with him. Just as kabbalists believed that the lower soul, the *nefesh* of the deceased, continued to hover above the grave following death, so the Sufis believed that a portion of the soul known as *ruhaniyyah* (Arabic for *ruah*) did likewise.[46] According to Abd Allah Alharad (d. 1490):

> The purpose of revelation at grave sites is to imaginatively depict the spirit of the deceased in a form that resembles his ethereal image. One who experiences such a revelation will envision the deceased with his inner eye. Since there are demons that have the power to appear in different forms, the masters among the Naqshbandiyah used

to concentrate in this way. When they visited grave sites . . . their technique was to lie down [upon the grave] when they arrived at the tomb of an important individual. . . . They sat down and awaited the appearance of a spirit, whereupon they knew from the nature of this appearance that it belonged to the individual buried in the grave.[47]

The similarities between these Sufi accounts and the Lurianic practice are striking. It is altogether likely that such Sufi practices were known to Safed kabbalists, and that both Cordovero and Luria were influenced by them. Not only was sixteenth-century Safed part of an Islamic milieu, but as noted earlier, a number of its kabbalists had emigrated from southern Morocco, where they had undoubtedly been familiar with the widespread veneration of Muslim saints at their grave sites.[48] Various influences notwithstanding, Luria's rather intricate ritual incorporated features that make it a distinctive practice. In what amounts to a kabbalistic cult of saints, Luria's exercise of devotion at the graves of *tsaddiqim* speaks to the exuberant confidence he had in the spiritual power of the righteous, among both the living and the dead, to join together the otherwise estranged regions of heaven and earth. Despite evidence of some degree of early grave veneration in Judaism in late antiquity, on the whole rabbis "did not choose to lean upon tombs, as Christian bishops did, with the result that these [i.e., tombs] maintained a low profile."[49] By contrast, Safed's tombs assumed a decidedly high profile. Set against the background of other strategies employed by the kabbalists of Safed to traffic with the dead, we might say that Peter Brown's description of what took place on a broad scale in the context of the late antique Christian world of the Mediterranean applies in some measure to sixteenth-century Safed: "The breaking down and the occasional inversion of ancient barriers in the late-antique cult of saints seems to mark the end of a way of seeing the relation between the human dead and the universe, and, as an immediate consequence, a shifting of the barriers by which Mediterranean men had sought to circumscribe the role of the dead, and especially of those dead to whom one had strong links of kinship or place."[50]

Contemplating Divine Names

In addition to communion with the soul of a departed *tsaddiq*, the *yiḥudim* involved concentrating on an intricate array of divine names. Many of the names used in the performance of the *yiḥudim* correspond to the *partsufim* and their multiple subconfigurations, the unification of which is effected through formalized and sustained contemplation. As we saw in Chapter 5, some of these names constitute different spellings of the Tetragrammaton and are known by their *gematria*. Thus, they are called by the names 72, 63, 45, and 52, and correspond to the *partsufim* of *Abba*, *Imma*, *Zeᶜir*, and *Nuqba* respectively. As with the *partsufim*, the names of God to which they correspond constitute a vast and complex map of the divine structure. That is, the names are linguistic symbols, denoting various discrete concentrations of divine power. As such, they are not really names in the conventional sense. In a way highly reminiscent of the seemingly arbitrary deconstruction and reconstruction of Hebrew words so strikingly characteristic of Abulafian mysticism, Luria's use of divine names is, to a significant extent, beyond rational understanding altogether. This is more evident in some cases than in others, when Vital himself admits that, in some instances, he does not understand their meaning well. For many of the *yiḥudim* consist of long sequences of names in deconstructed and reconstructed forms that do not bear any clear meaning.[51] These are typically vocalized in ways that only add to the difficulty of making sense of them. Some of the meditations consist of combinations of such names, along with unusually constructed names of angels, such as those often found in certain Hebrew magical texts.[52]

While most of the *yiḥudim* were for the purposes we have described, quite a few of them are similar to the *tiqqunei ᶜavonot*, in the sense that they were intended to rectify specific transgressions on the part of the individual performing them, or sometimes on behalf of someone else. For example, Moses Alsheikh was given a *yiḥud* by Luria for the purpose of his son's repentance, his son having become an apostate. Vital reported that it was successful, as Alsheikh's son returned to the community.[53] Others were for the *tiqqun* of various transgressions, including adultery, homosexual relations, and anger, while still others were for the purpose of exorcising an evil spirit, or for enhancing one's memory.[54]

As an example of this type of contemplative ritual, let us turn to one of the *yiḥudim* that exhibits some of the essential elements of these exercises.[55] This is the only *yiḥud* said to have been recorded on the basis of a manuscript written by Luria himself. It is concerned with the unification of *Ḥokhmah* and *Binah* (the *partsufim Abba* and *Imma*), as well as that of *Tiferet* and *Malkhut* (the *partsufim Zeᶜir Anpin* and *Nuqba de-Zeᶜir*), the total unity of which represents the complete and perfect name of God, *YHVH*.

This meditation begins with the attempt to unite the upper parents, *Ḥokhmah* and *Binah* (*Abba* and *Imma*). The adept concentrates on the aspect of *YHVH* within *Ḥokhmah* and on the name *ᵓEHYH* within *Binah*. One mentally combines these two names by interspersing their letters—a technique known as *ḥibbur*—thus forming the single divine appellation: *YAHHVYHH*. After concentrating on this name, the adept is instructed to turn his attention to the name 72, itself corresponding to *Ḥokhmah/Abba*. Contemplation of the name 72 serves to stimulate the initial unification of *Ḥokhmah/Abba* and *Binah/Imma*. The name 72 also corresponds to the quality of divine compassion, *ḤeSeD*, the *gematria* of which is 72. *ḤeSeD* helps to facilitate the love between *Abba* and *Imma*. This meditative action represents *yud*, the first letter of the simple *YHVH*.

In the next stage, the adept focuses on the completion of this unification by bringing about the ascent of the Female Waters. This is done by concentrating on the name 63, whose source is *Binah/Imma*. The ascent of the Female Waters aroused by an individual's contemplation of the name 63 acts as the catalyst that finalizes the unification of *Abba* and *Imma*. This action represents *heh*, the second letter of the simple *YHVH*.

Following this, the adept is instructed to turn his attention to the unification of the lower two *partsufim*, *Tiferet* and *Malkhut* (*Zeᶜir* and *Nuqba*). He concentrates upon the name *YHVH* within *Tiferet* and the name *ADNY* within *Malkhut*. In his imagination, he combines the two names by interspersing their letters, thus forming *YAHDVNHY*. He then turns his attention to the name 45, which itself corresponds to *Zeᶜir*, the contemplation of which serves to stimulate the initial unification of *Zeᶜir* and *Nuqba*. This action represents the third letter of the Tetragrammaton, *vav*. In the second stage, an individual finalizes the unification of these two *partsufim* by raising up the Female Waters from *Malkhut*. This is achieved by contemplation on the name 52, itself rooted in *Nuqba*. This corresponds to the fourth letter of the Tetragrammaton, *heh*.

Through this exercise, then, both sets of male and female within *Adam Qadmon* are united with one another, *Abba* and *Imma*, and *Zeᶜir* and *Nuqba*. The net result on the theurgical plane is the total reunification of *YHVH*. Inasmuch as each *partsuf* corresponds to one of the four letters of the simple *YHVH*, when the *partsufim* are brought into proper relationship to one another through contemplation, divinity is restored to a state of complete harmony. The following chart outlines this exercise:

Ia.   Unification of *Ḥokhmah* and *Binah*: YAHHVYHH
      YVD HY VYV HY (72)
Ib.   Arousal of Female Waters to complete unification:
      YVD HY VAV HY (63)
IIa. Unification of *Tiferet* and *Malkhut*: YAHDVNHY
      YVD HA VAV HA (45)
IIb. Arousal of Female Waters to complete unification:
      YVD HA VAV HH (52)

I want also to describe a second *yiḥud* that exhibits an unusual degree of complexity. Vital reports that this *yiḥud* is one that Luria instructed him to perform following the New Moon during the Hebrew month of Elul.[56] As it precedes the "Ten Days of Penitence" that usher in the Rosh Hashanah festival, the entire month of Elul became a period of repentance characterized by special ascetic and devotional exercises: "On the day of the New Moon, Elul, the year 5331 (1571), my teacher, may his name be blessed, said to me that I should fast successively the two days directly following the day of the New Moon. And that by virtue of this I shall attain some degree of inspiration."[57]

The focus of this *yiḥud* is the names *YHVH* (*yud, heh, vav, heh*) and *ᵓEHYH* (*alef, heh, yud, heh*), representing the *partsufim Abba and Imma*. The *gematria* of these names when combined, including one for the total name as a whole, is forty-eight. This corresponds to the number of hours in the two days during which the meditation is to be performed. Forty-eight names are derived from these two names in the following way: each name possesses four letters and, by means of their total number of combinations, they can each assume twelve different forms:

Twelve Forms of *YHVH*		Twelve Forms of *ᵓEHYH*	
YHVH	VHHY	AHYH	YHHA
HVHY	HYVH	HYHA	HAYH
VHYH	YVHH	YHAH	AYHH
HYHV	HHVY	HAHY	HHYA
YHHV	VYHH	AHHY	YAHH
HVYH	HHYV	HYAH	HHAY

From these twenty-four names, an additional twenty-four can be derived by interspersing the different variations of *AHYH* and *YHVH* to create a single name, and then reversing each combined name, for example, *AYHHYVHH* and its reverse *HHVYHHYA*. The chart on the following page shows the totality of these names, including their various vocalizations. Every line of this chart represents four meditative hours.

During the first hour, the adept is to contemplate the simple name *ᵓEHYH*. During the second hour, he should contemplate this same name interspersed (*ḥibbur*) with the name *YHVH*, as above. In this manner, he proceeds from one of the forty-eight names to the next. Vital indicates that it is ideal if the adept can contemplate each name during its properly assigned hour. But if one lacks the strength for this (it would require two full days of no sleep!), one may condense the exercise by contemplating all four names of the first four hours during the initial hour, then wait until the beginning of the next four-hour cycle and contemplate the second four names during that hour. Whether or not one chooses this abbreviated method, Vital was instructed how to condense the meditation to be performed during the nighttime hours. One may include in one hour of meditation the twelve hours that would normally include the night hours. The best way to do it,

שער רוח הקדש

(ד) יֵאֲהֲוִיֵהֲהָ הְ	(ג) יהוה פֶּ	(ב) אֵיהָהֲיֵהֲהָ ל	(א) אֶהְיֶה א
(ח) יֵאֲהֲהֲהֲוִיְ דְ	(ז) יההו וְ	(ו) אִיְהֲהֲהֵיֵוְ יְ	(ה) אֲהֲיֵ יֵ
(יב) יֵאֲוְיֵהֲרָה וְ	(יא) יֵוֹהה יְ	(י) אֵיֲוְהֲהָהֶ יֵ	(ט) אִיְהֶה הְ
(טז) הֵהֲוֹיֵהֲהָיֵא וְ	(טו) הֵוֹהִיְ יְ	(יד) הֵהֲיֵוָהֲהֲאֵי הְ	(יג) הֵיֵהֲא דְ
(כ) הֵהֲוִיֵיאֵהֲהֶ יְ	(יט) הֲוִיֵה הְ	(יח) הֵהֲיֵוֲאֵיהֲהֶ וְ	(יז) הֵיאֵהֶ יְ
(כד) הֵהֲהֲוִיֵיֵא הְ	(כג) הֲהֲוִיְ יְ	(כב) הֵהֲהֲהֲוֲאֵי הְ	(כא) הֲהֲיֵא א
(כח) וַיֵהֲיֵאֵהֶה הְ	(כז) וֲהֲיֶה דְ	(כו) יֵוֲהֲהֲאֵיהֶה ו	(כה) יֵהֲאֵהֶ יְ
(לב) וַיֵהֲהֲהֲיֵא וְ	(לא) וֲהֲיְ יְ	(ל) יֵוֲהֲהֲהֲאֵי וְ	(כט) יֵהֲהֲא יְ
(לו) וְיֵיֵאֲהֲהֲהֲהֶ ל	(לה) וֲהֲיֶה א	(לד) יֵוֲאֵיֲהֲהֲהֶ יְ	(לג) יֵאֲהֶה הְ
(מ) הֵהֲיֵאֲהֲהֲוִיְ יֵ	(לט) הֵיְהוּ יֵ	(לח) הֵהֲאֵיהֲהֲיֵוְ הְ	(לז) הֲאֲהֵיֵ פֶּ
(מד) הֵהֲיֵאֲוֲיֵהֲהֶ יְ	(מג) הֵיֲוֲהֲ הְ	(מב) הֵהֲאֵיֲוֲהֲהֶ דְ	(מא) הֲאֵיהָ וְ
(מח) הֵהֲהֲהֲיֵאֲוִיְ הְ	(מז) הֲהֲיְהוּ וְ	(מו) הֵהֲהֲהֲאֵיֲהֲוְ הְ	(מה) הֲהֲאֵי יְ

however, would be to contemplate the six hours that precede midnight in condensed fashion, prior to going to sleep. That is, at 6:00 P.M. one concentrates on the names for the first six hours during that one hour and then retires. At midnight, one then arises and stays up through the night. This enables one to meditate upon each of the next six names for the full hour allotted to each of them.

Achieving Prophetic Inspiration

What kind of experience did an individual have in the course of practicing the *yiḥudim?* What were the effects upon the psyche and the body of the adept, and what were the ultimate consequences of this practice? What partial answers we are able to provide to these questions derive from two kinds of sources. First, we rely upon fragmentary and incidental statements in the theoretical accounts describing the *yiḥudim* in Hayyim Vital's *Shaᶜar Ruaḥ ha-Qodesh* and *Shaᶜar ha-Yiḥudim*. Second, as noted earlier, Vital recorded some of his own experiences in *Shaᶜar ha-Gilgulim* and *Sefer ha-Ḥezyonot*, in addition to some evidence of Luria's own experiences.

We learn that the flow of divine power stimulated by the uniting of *Zeᶜir* and *Nuqba* in the course of contemplation constitutes the source of the inspiration that the successful adept attains—either in the form of prophecy (*nevuᵓah*) or the Holy Spirit. Vital does not distinguish clearly between these two terms; they appear to be used virtually interchangeably, each being a form of inspiration or illumination (*hasagah*). Nevertheless, given their historical usages, there is no question that prophecy was held to be a more exalted form of experience, although more rarely attained than that of *Ruaḥ ha-Qodesh*: "All of the prophecy that prophets experience derives only from [the *sefirot* of] *Netsaḥ, Hod* and *Yesod* within *Zeᶜir Anpin*—because from there an illumination shines upon *Malkhut*, the feminine [aspect of *Zeᶜir*]. From this illumination, prophets draw their prophecy. . . . There is no comprehension for any prophet except by means of *Nuqba de-Zeᶜir*."[58]

That prophetic inspiration derives from *Nuqba de-Zeᶜir* is in complete accord with the traditional kabbalistic notion that virtually all prophecy is mediated through the feminine, or *Malkhut*. Based upon a tradition in the Babylonian Talmud (*Yevamot* 49b), according to which "all the prophets looked through a glass [or mirror] that did not shine [*ʾaspaqlariyah she-ʾeinah meʾirah*], but Moses looked through a glass that shined [*ʾaspaqlariayah she-meʾirah*]," the kabbalists associated Moses' prophecy with the divine masculine, and that of all others with the feminine. Thus, while Moses prophesied directly, through the higher grade of *Tiferet*, other prophets gained their illumination indirectly, through the medium of *Malkhut* or *Shekhinah*, whose own light is nothing but a reflection of the light She receives from above.[59] Uniting the *partsufim* of *Zeʿir* and *Nuqba* contemplatively infuses an individual with divine inspiration and enables him to speak words of prophecy. The spirit of prophecy begins to rest upon him and manifests itself through spontaneous unreflected speech, a form of motor automatism in which a person suddenly and involuntarily begins to articulate. Prophetic utterance such as this requires great power of concentration and is not achieved easily:

> There is one who begins to achieve some inspiration [*hasagah*] and the Spirit [*ha-Ruaḥ*] rests upon him. But it [i.e., the Spirit] does not possess perfection with which to cause the voice of prophecy and the Holy Spirit to dwell upon his lips and tongue. Without speaking, he only feels at the moment of *yiḥud* that his hair stands up, his body and limbs shake, his lips tremble—but the power of speaking is not in his mouth.[60]

This condition may afflict an adept only after he has already achieved a certain degree of inspiration. The Spirit speaks within him but does not manifest itself vocally in an external way. Luria thus prescribes several particular *yiḥudim* whose specific function is to invest the adept in need of special assistance with the power to bring forth prophetic speech: "If the person who performs *yiḥudim* has already obtained some arousal on the part of his *neshamah*, which speaks to him by means of some *yiḥud* that he has performed, but he does not yet have the strength to bring forth [actual] speech upon his lips from the potential to the actual—he should perform this *yiḥud* before he does the other one."[61]

Although Vital writes in one place that "God will reveal to him wondrous things from His Torah," the speech itself, which the contemplative either hears from without or utters with his own mouth, derives from the *tsaddiq* with whom he is communing: "On account of these *yiḥudim*, they [i.e., the *tsaddiqim*] reveal to them secrets of the Torah and matters having to do with the future."[62] Elsewhere, this process is described in the following way:

> And how is this mystery of cleaving [*devequt*] performed? Let a righteous person stretch out on the grave of one of the *tanna'im* [rabbis from the period of the Mishnah], or one of the prophets, and cleave with his lower soul [*nafsho*] to that of the *tsaddiq*, and with his spirit [*ruḥo*] to his spirit. Then the *tanna'* begins to speak with him as a person talks to a friend—and answers all that he asks, revealing to him all the mysteries of the Torah.[63]

The successful practitioner is compared to an angel on high in a position to gain access to heavenly mysteries:

> There is no doubt that if the individual always practices these *kavvanot*, he will be as one of the angels on high who minister in heaven. And he will attain knowledge of all that he wishes, especially if he does not cease, [but] concentrates continuously, not separating his thought [from this meditation]. And everything depends upon the power of his concentration and his cleaving [*hitdabquto*] above.[64]

What do we know about Luria's own performance of *yiḥudim*? According to one account by Vital, on a certain occasion Luria communed with the soul of the talmudic sage Rabbi Yannai:

> On the first of the intermediate days of Passover, I traveled with him [i.e., Luria] to a certain village known as Akbarah. We entered the cave of Rabbi Yannai [by walking] through an orchard. A spring flowed from the entrance of the cave itself, the entrance being exceedingly narrow. He told me that Rabbi Yannai is not buried there alone, but so are Rabbi Dustai and Rabbi Nehorai . . . and there his [i.e., Luria's] soul cleaved to that of Rabbi Yannai. In the course of his words, Rabbi Yannai said to him, "I, Rabbi Yannai, am the inhabitant of this grave site. Know that God, may He be blessed, has said to you, 'Go and tell this person, Hayyim Vital, who has accompanied

you, that he should guard against slander, evil gossip, and idle conversation, and that he ought to behave in an exceedingly humble way, and that I shall be with him wherever he is.'"[65]

Another description of Luria's practice of *yiḥudim* is found in Shlomiel's letters. The details in the following account are consistent with what we have already learned about this ritual:

> Once the rabbi went to prostrate himself upon the grave of Shemaya and Avtalyon in Gush Ḥalav,[66] at a distance of one *parsa*, for the purpose of inquiring of them the true secrets of the Torah. For such was his custom. Whenever he desired to speak with a prophet or a certain *tanna'*, he would travel to his grave and lay himself down upon it with outstretched arms and feet, "putting his mouth upon his mouth . . . " [2 Kings 4:34], as did Elisha with Habakkuk.[67] He would concentrate upon a *yiḥud*, and elevate the *nefesh, ruaḥ* and *neshamah* of this *tsaddiq* through the mystery of the Female Waters. . . . He would bind his [own] *nefesh, ruaḥ,* and *neshamah* to those of the *tsaddiq*, and bring about supernal unification. By means of the *yiḥud,* the soul of this *tsaddiq* would be invested with a new light, greater than that which he had previously [during his life]. In this way, the dry bones that lie in the grave revived: the *nefesh, ruaḥ,* and *neshamah* of that *tsaddiq* descended to his bones, bringing him to actual life, [and] speaking with him [i.e., Luria] as a man speaks to his neighbor, revealing to him all the secrets of the Torah concerning which he asks of him. All of these *yiḥudim* are in my possession, written down, praised be God. For the rabbi transmitted them to his disciples, all ten of whom successfully practiced them. As a consequence, the *tsaddiqim* [with whom they commune] spoke to them, answering all their questions. However, they possessed the strength to do this only during the rabbi's lifetime. After his death, their efforts were without success, with the exception of [those of] our teacher, Rabbi Hayyim Calabrese, may God protect and preserve him, who successfully practices them to this day.[68]

Chapter 9 explores the nature of Luria's personal identification with Shimon bar Yohai in some depth; here, it is important to note a tradition having to do with their communion of souls by means of *yiḥudim*. On visits to Shimon bar Yohai's tomb in Meron:

He [Luria] used to stretch himself out on the tomb of the *tanna* ⁼ [Shimon bar Yohai], and he knew how to cleave *ruaḥ* to *ruaḥ* [*le-ᵓidabqa ruḥa be-ruḥa*], and to concentrate on binding and raising up his soul [*nishmato*] with that of the *tanna* ⁼ in the mystery of Female Waters until he brought about unity above. Afterwards, the soul of the *tanna* ⁼ descended into his body, and he [Shimon bar Yohai] would speak with him, revealing to him all that he had learned in the academy on high, as a man speaks with his neighbor.⁶⁹

As we shall see below, the spiritual affinity between Luria and Shimon bar Yohai played a crucial role in Luria's self-understanding and in the redemptive project in which he believed he and his disciples were engaged.

Finally, we should note one further mention of Luria's personal practice of the *yiḥudim*.⁷⁰ Vital reports that Luria used to perform one particular *yiḥud* for the purpose of raising up certain soul-sparks that still remained in the netherworld, among the *qelippot*. These sparks derived from the soul of Cain and included the following biblical figures: Korach, Jethro, Yuval, Datan, Abiram, Jubal, and Lamekh. Because they were living in the "final generation," it was thought possible to raise up all these remaining souls.

The Experiences of Hayyim Vital

Turning to Hayyim Vital's account of his own experiences, it will be recalled that Luria had prescribed particular *tiqqunei ᶜavonot* for sins Vital had committed.⁷¹ Among other things, Vital had indulged in the study of alchemy during the years 1566–68, a couple of years prior to his taking up with Luria—a practice that he later regretted. He also needed to purify himself for having become angry with his wife, for having drunk forbidden wine with an apostate, having cursed his parents, and having committed a minor sexual transgression on his wedding night. Luria instructed him to undergo a two-and-a-half-year period of absolution in order to qualify himself fully for mystical inspiration. Vital also reports that Luria reproached him for failing to practice *yiḥudim* regularly, a matter to which Luria attached great importance:

One day I visited him [i.e., Luria], a whole month having passed
during which I had performed none of the *yiḥudim* he had prescribed
for me. Recognizing this by looking upon my face, he said to me:
"'If you leave me for a day, I shall leave you for two' [JT *Berakhot* 9:5;
14d]. You cause great harm by failing to perform the *yiḥudim*, for it
causes the souls who wish to become attached to you to remain separated from you." I excused myself in that I desired only to study the
Torah at that time, especially since those souls did not come to me as
openly as they should have done. He replied that in spite of this, I
must not fail to perform the *yiḥudim* daily. It is more important than
the study of the Torah, since it unifies the upper worlds, and so serves
the dual purpose of Torah and study and unification. He cautioned
me that when I perform the *yiḥudim*, my intention should not only
be to attract the souls but to put things right on high.

He also said to me, when I went with him to the sepulcher of
Rabbi Akiva,[72] that Rabbi Akiva had told him I was to mention
Akiva's name ten times consecutively before each of the three daily
prayers, evening, morning, and noon. As a result, he will become impregnated in me and will greatly assist me.[73] He told me that there
was no need for me to say "Rabbi Akiva," only "Akiva."

He further said to me that until the festival of Tabernacles [Sukkot]
in the year 5334 [1573], I shall require much assistance, and that he
will assist me whenever I perform *yiḥudim*. But from then on, I shall
require no assistance whatsoever, for then atonement will have been
made for the two and a half years I sinned by failing to study the Torah.
Furthermore, until that time, even if he did assist me, it would only
be occasionally.[74]

We learn from this intriguing text that Vital suspended his practice
of *yiḥudim* out of frustration at failing to experience the communion of
souls, "since those souls did not come to me as openly as they should
have done." Luria repudiated this excuse, arguing that one can still
unify the upper worlds through the *yiḥudim*. What is remarkable in
this passage is what it reveals about the status assigned to the practice
of *yiḥudim*. This type of devotional practice is more important than
the study of Torah! Insofar as the ultimate goal of the study of Torah
is the unification of the upper worlds, a ritual that accomplishes this
more directly takes priority. Luria thus challenged a well-established

rabbinic priority according to which the study of Torah was considered of paramount importance.

Although Vital refers in quite a number of places to his own practice of *yiḥudim*,[75] I want to quote in full the most detailed account that he gives of his experiences. I believe it provides the richest account we have of the nature of the experience involved:

On the eve of the New Moon of the month of Elul in the year 5331 [1571], my master, of blessed memory, sent me to the sepulcher of Abbaye and Rava.[76] There I prostrated myself at the grave of Abbaye, of blessed memory, and first performed the *yiḥud* of the Mouth and Nose of the Holy Ancient One [*Attiqa Qaddisha* or *Arikh Anpin*]. Sleep fell upon me, and then I awoke, but I saw nothing. Then I again prostrated myself on Abbaye's actual grave and performed the *yiḥud* recorded in my master's own handwriting. But as I was engaged in combining, as is well known, the letters of the Tetragrammaton with those of ADoNaY, my thoughts became confused and I was unable to combine them, so I ceased from reflecting on that combination of letters. It then seemed to me as if a voice was saying to me: "Retract! Retract!" many times, and I thought to myself that these were the words Akavyah ben Mahalalel addressed to his son, as is well known.[77] So I tried again to combine the letters, and this time I was successful. It then seemed to me in my thoughts that they were saying to me: "God will provide Himself the lamb for a burnt-offering, my son" (*ᵓelohim yireh lo ha-seh le-ᶜolah beni* [Gen. 22:8]), and it seemed as if they were explaining the meaning of the verse to me, namely, I was apprehensive that I had not performed the first *yiḥud* adequately, but it was not so. It had, in fact, been effective before God, hence: "God will provide Himself the lamb." And it seemed in my thoughts as if they were explaining to me that the whole of the first *yiḥud* I had performed was hinted at in the verse. For the initial letters of *ᵓelohim yireh lo ha-seh* have the numerical value of forty-six, the same as that of the Tetragrammaton and *AHYH*. And the initial letters of *ha-seh le-ᶜolah beni* form the word *hevel* ("breath") of the Supernal Mouth, which I had in mind while performing the *yiḥud*. And it seemed to me as if they were saying that Hillel the Elder is hinted at in the initial letters of *lo ha-seh le-ᶜolah*, but I failed to grasp the meaning of this. Behold, all this passed through my mind.

Then a great dread and trembling seized hold of all my limbs and my hands trembled. My lips, too, were trembling in a highly exaggerated manner, moving quickly and concurrently, and with great speed, as if a voice was perched on my tongue between my lips. It said with great speed more than a hundred times: "What can I say? What can I say?" I tried to steady myself and prevent my lips from moving but was unable to still them at all. Then I had in mind to ask for wisdom, upon which the voice broke out in my mouth and on my tongue, saying, more than twenty times, "Wisdom, Wisdom." Then it repeated many times: "Wisdom and Knowledge." Then it repeated: "Wisdom and knowledge will be given to you from heaven like the knowledge attained by Rabbi Akiva." Then it repeated: "And more than that of Rabbi Akiva." Then it repeated: "Like that attained by Rabbi Yeiva Sabba." And then it repeated: "And more than that of Rabbi Yeiva Sabba." And then it said: "Greetings to you." And then it said: "They send you greetings from heaven." All this was said at a great speed, repeatedly, many times, utterly wondrous, while I was in a waking state and while prostrated in the sepulcher of Abbaye.

Then I went to my master, of blessed memory, who said to me that I was most effective in performing these two *yiḥudim* one after the other, and this was, indeed, the right way to perform them. And my master, of blessed memory, said to me that when I returned from that place and entered my house, he saw the soul of Benayahu ben Yehoyada accompanying me. He told [me] that Benayahu did not belong to my soul-root, but the reason he accompanied me was that he is always revealed together with anyone who performs the supernal *yiḥud*. For this was his habit during his lifetime on earth, as we have stated elsewhere. My teacher, of blessed memory, said to me at the time of the afternoon prayer that if I am worthy on the coming Sabbath, the soul of Rabbi Yeiva Sabba will remain with me for ever, never to depart, as do the other reincarnations. Through him I shall be worthy of receiving powerful illuminations, especially during the Amidah prayer while reciting the benedictions "the years," "the shoot," and "hearkening to prayer."[78] The reason for it is that Rabbi Yeiva Sabba also reveals himself to the righteous, just as Benayahu does, as we have explained. Furthermore, he belongs to my soul-root. Therefore, if I shall be worthy of having him reveal himself to me, he will disclose to me, God willing, marvelous things.[79]

Hayyim Vital's experience consisted of two distinct stages. The first stage involved the contemplation of the *yiḥudim* themselves. His initial efforts at unification appeared to him to be unsuccessful. His mind became confused after attempting a second *yiḥud*, following which he heard a voice uttering the request of the dying Akavyah ben Mahalalel to his son. We learn from Vital's diary that this sage was one of the various *tsaddiqim* who comprised his soul-ancestry. Having heard this voice, he returned to contemplation of the second *yiḥud*, which he successfully completed. Again he heard a voice, which this time uttered a scriptural verse (Gen. 22:8), the *notariqon* and *gematria* of which elucidated the meaning of the initial *yiḥud*. The initial letters of several words in this verse, forming as they do the word *hevel* ("breath"), indicated to Vital the mystery of the supernal Mouth intended by the first meditation. This demonstrated to him that it had been successful after all.

Having achieved a level of inspiration in which he heard the external voices of others speaking *to* him, Vital entered a more intense stage of experience. He was overcome with physical trembling and began to utter short phrases repeatedly and quickly in the manner of automatic speech. The identity of the voice is left undetermined, though there is no doubt that he was invested with the voice of another, insofar as it was "as if a voice was perched on my tongue between my lips." The substance of the disclosure elicited after his having asked "for wisdom" consisted in this case not in esoteric kabbalistic knowledge but in a confirmation of the exalted status of his soul. He was promised the attainment of knowledge exceeding that of the distinguished Rabbi Akiva, and that of Yeiva Sabba, a figure known from the *Zohar*, whom we have encountered above. According to Vital's diary, both of these men were part of his *gilgul* ancestry. That such matters should be part of Vital's experiences comes as no surprise. The exceptionally elevated status of his soul, the transmigrations through which it had gone, and the unlimited possibilities for mystical illumination of which he regarded himself capable were themes with which Vital was obsessed, as we shall see in Chapter 9.

Interpreting the *Yiḥudim*

This technique and the nature of the experience that resulted from its practice can be illumined by setting it within the context of other pneumatic techniques known to us from Safed, some of which have already been mentioned. These include Cordovero's and Alkabets's peregrinations, Karo's maggidic experiences, Vital's technique of reciting Mishnah, and Luria's own technique of acquiring a *maggid*. By identifying the structural features of these techniques, we can better understand the experience of practicing *yiḥudim*.

1. Preparation and Transition

From a structural point of view, mystical techniques almost invariably require a stage in which an individual deliberately negotiates a transition from a normal mode of activity to a contemplative one. Thus, Joseph Karo's accounts repeatedly emphasize the need for Karo to prepare himself by depriving his body of all pleasures, especially food and drink. Moreover, the recitation of Mishnah texts should take place at night, and he must deprive himself of sleep in order to induce the *maggid* to manifest itself. In the case of Vital's technique of reciting Mishnah, detachment or separation from ordinary life is achieved through solitude and cutting oneself off from all material sensation:

> You already know that all types of inspiration require a person to be alone in a house so that his mind will not be distracted. The individual must seclude himself mentally to the farthest limits and divest his body from his soul as if he does not feel that he is clothed in matter at all—as though he is only soul. The more he separates himself from matter, the more his inspiration will be increased. If he senses any voice or movement that disturbs his concentration, or if any material thought comes to him of its own accord, this will stop his soul's concentration on cleaving to the upper realms. And he will not gain any inspiration whatsoever, insofar as the supernal holiness does not rest upon a man while he is [still] clinging to matter, be it even a hairsbreadth [of attachment to matter]. . . . The second condition is that a man should annul all those things that cause solitude to be inter-

rupted. For in the first condition, we mentioned only the material things of a natural character [i.e., things external to him] that cause the interruption of solitude. And these [i.e., with regard to the second condition] are the powers of impurity derived from the evil inclination with which a man invests himself. They are strengthened by virtue of man's sin. Therefore, he who intends to seclude himself must first repent of all transgressions. . . . Seclude yourself in a lonely house, as mentioned above; wrap yourself in a prayer shawl, and sit and close your eyes, divesting yourself of the material world as if your soul had left your body, and was ascending to heaven.[80]

Such rituals of physical and mental preparation serve as means by which a person leaves this world for the sake of entering another one. The anthropologist Victor Turner argued, as is well-known, that rituals such as rites of passage, pilgrimages, festivals, and certain types of mystical experience involve a transition between two fixed states. Following the work of the French anthropologist Arnold van Gennep, Turner labeled this transitional state as liminal, meaning a condition of "in-betweenness" or limbo as one deliberately passes from one state to another or from one world, whether cosmic or social, to another. In the case of mystical experience, such transition often entails leaving behind normal social life, dissolving existing ties to community and everyday reality, and entering into a new life, even if on a temporary basis.[81] Techniques or rituals that intend such a transition have little in common with experiences purported to come about in a spontaneous, unsolicited way. In the case of the *yiḥudim*, as with the other techniques mentioned here, one sets out to call forth a certain experience. The process of journeying to a grave site and physically isolating oneself there, cut off from social community, preferably in the dead of night, serves such a transitional function.

2. Loss of Bodily Control

In every one of the techniques under consideration, successful practice was understood as involving a physiological condition in which one is not in complete control of one's body. Thus, we saw in the case of an individual struggling to achieve full-fledged inspiration in the course of the *yiḥudim* that "he feels at the moment of *yiḥud* that his hair stands up, his body and limbs shake, his lips tremble." Vital himself describes how he experienced dread and trembling in all his limbs.

Descriptions such as these are remarkably reminiscent of accounts of ecstatic experience in Abulafian literature. For example, in *Sitrei Torah,* Abulafia writes: "Know that so long as you combine letters rapidly, and the hairs of your head do not all stand up in trembling, you have not yet attained one of the levels of the spirit in which all of the limbs [of the body] are moved, and you have not known even His existence, let alone His essence."[82] Similarly, in Abulafia's *ʾOtsar ʿEden Ganuz*: "The hairs of your head will begin to stand up . . . and all your body will begin to tremble, and your limbs will begin to shake, and you will fear a tremendous fear, and the fear of God shall cover you. . . . And the body will tremble, like the rider who races the horse, who is glad and joyful, while the horse trembles beneath him."[83]

The most obvious expression of loss of bodily control, however, is speech automatism, a universal element in all of the techniques. The adept is filled or seized by a voice that takes control of his vocalization. Here, too, Abulafian accounts of ecstatic experience bear strong parallels. Speech automatism was a critical ingredient in Abulafia's experiences:

> and they [i.e. practitioners] ascend from light to light . . . to the union, until their inner speech returns, cleaving to the primordial speech that is the source of all speech, and they further ascend from speech to speech until the inner human speech [is a] power in itself, and he prepares himself to receive the divine speech, whether in the aspect of the image of speech, whether in the aspect of speech itself; and these are the prophets in truth, in justice and righteousness.[84]

In the Abulafian treatise *Shaʿarei Tsedeq*, speech is described as emanating from an individual's inner heart: "Behold, like the speech that emerges from my heart and comes to my lips, forcing them to move; and I said that perchance, God forbid, it is a spirit of folly that has entered me, and I perceive it speaking wisdom. I said that this is certainly the spirit of wisdom."[85]

Automatic speech was also a feature of the experiences of Isaac of Acre, who was influenced by Abulafian Kabbalah: "For the one who speaks with the Holy Spirit does not hear that voice, but that spirit comes within him and speaks by itself, as it comes from a high place, that from which the prophets draw [which is] in *Netsaḥ* and *Hod*. . . . And there is no bringing together of lips there nor any other thing."[86]

We already know that experiences of this type were common in Safed. Thus, for Cordovero and Alkabets in the course of their practice of *gerushin*, "the words of Torah were shining in us and the words were spoken of themselves . . . all supernal, infused without reflections whatsoever." Karo characteristically describes his maggidic experience by saying that "the voice of my beloved knocked in my mouth and the lyre sang of itself."[87] In Vital's technique of Mishnah recitation, the goal is to become invested with the voice/soul of the *tanna*ʾ whose Mishnah one is repeating:

> When you become exhausted from reciting the text of the Mishnah—if you are worthy of it—it is possible that the soul of this *tanna*ʾ will abide in your mouth, and he will become invested within your mouth while you are reciting the Mishnah. And then while you are still reading the Mishnah, he will speak with your mouth and offer you a salutation of peace. Everything that you then think of asking him will he answer you. He will speak with your mouth and your ears will hear his words. It is not you yourself speaking, but he is the one who speaks. This is the meaning of: "The spirit of the Lord speaks by me and His word is upon my tongue" [2 Sam. 23:2].[88]

Luria's own theory of maggidic revelation, in which prayer and study of Torah induces an angelic revelation, also results in such vocalization:

> And here is the secret of prophecy and the Holy Spirit. It is assuredly a voice sent from above to speak with the prophet, or with this man endowed with the Holy Spirit. But this same supernal spiritual voice cannot by itself materialize and enter the ears of this prophet unless it first clothes itself in his physical voice, which emerges from this man's mouth when, at a give moment, he studies Torah or prays and the like. And then it [i.e., the supernal voice] clothes itself in it [i.e., the physical voice], joining it and comes to the ear of this prophet who [then] hears it. And without the individual's own present physical voice, it cannot achieve existence.[89]

In the case of the *yiḥudim*, two variations appear to have been possible. The adept could hear a voice speaking *to* him, a lesser degree of inspiration, or his own vocal organs could serve as the medium for the soul/voice of another. In the first example, "the *tanna*ʾ begins to speak with him as a man talks to his friend," as we saw in one passage, or in Luria's own case, "speaking with him as a man speaks to his neighbor." In the second example, as we saw from Vital's account, it was "as if a voice was perched on my tongue," and "the voice broke out in my mouth and on my tongue." That this was a matter of overt concern is attested by a report in Vital's diary. He indicates that he asked Luria whether the voice of the *tsaddiq* that he has experienced is actually that of the *tsaddiq* himself or merely his own voice. Luria assures Vital that the voice he has experienced is indeed that of the *tsaddiq*, inasmuch as the soul of the *tsaddiq* invests itself in Vital's heart through proper concentration. As Vital reports it: "From there [i.e., his heart] the sound of the *tsaddiq*'s speech ascends to my mouth [*maᶜaleh dibburo be-fi*] and speaks with my mouth, whereupon I hear his voice."⁹⁰ Elsewhere in his diary, he confesses that sometimes the voice of the *tsaddiq* speaks to him rather than through his own voice. He explains this by attributing the inferior degree of inspiration to his laxness in fulfilling his religious responsibilities.⁹¹ Vital also draws precisely such a distinction in his account of soul-communion using Mishnah recitation. Here, too, the experience of hearing a voice speaking to you rather than through your own voice is attributed to an individual's insufficient preparation for the higher level of inspiration.⁹²

We are struck by the fact that these particular mystical experiences are decidedly oral, as well as aural in nature, rather than visual or visionary. It is the speaking of words that engenders the experience in almost each of the techniques under consideration. In the case of Cordovero and Alkabets, their experiences of involuntary speech appear to have occurred while they were already discoursing on Scripture. With Joseph Karo, the indispensable and essential feature of his technique was to recite as many *mishnayot* as possible in order to arouse his *maggid*'s voice. As we have seen, Luria's theory of maggidism likewise asserts as an absolute requirement that the physical speech of the adept in the course of study or prayer serve as the vehicle through which the voice from afar, be it that of an angel or a deceased *tsaddiq*, manifests itself. In Vital's technique of Mishnah recitation, as we have already noted, it is the continuous vocal repetition of a single Mishnah that arouses the voice of the soul from afar. Only in the case of the *yiḥudim* themselves is it unclear whether such vocalization is a necessary condition for stimulating the voice with which one communes, whether the practitioner merely visualizes the names he contemplates, or whether he also pronounces them. In every one of the techniques, however, including the *yiḥudim*, involuntary vocal automatism is the way in which the experience successfully culminates.

It is worth recalling, however, that there are plenty of examples of visionary experiences on the part of Safed kabbalists, especially in connection with Abraham Berukhim and Hayyim Vital. Such visions more often than not involve an appearance of the *Shekhinah* or some vision of light. Still, the techniques in question here betray the degree to which the *linguistic* dominated this particular culture. Virtually everywhere we turn, language is the most potent force; in various guises, divinity is no further than one's throat, "knocking" in the mouth, gathered upon the lips.[93]

3. The Voice's Identity

The identity of the voices that speak through the individual varies in these techniques. In the case of Cordovero's and Alkabets's peregrinations, the voice is left undetermined, whereas Karo identifies his *maggid* as the Mishnah personified, and as the voice of the *Shekhinah*. The goal of Vital's technique of Mishnah recitation was to become invested with the soul or voice of the *tanna*ʾwhose Mishnah was being recited. Luria's technique of maggidic revelation allowed for two possibilities: the *maggid* could manifest itself in an angelic voice or that of the Holy Spirit, on the one hand, or as that of a deceased *tsaddiq*, on the other. The latter would occur providing either that the contemplative adept was from the same soul-root as the *tsaddiq* or that the religious precept performed by the adept was "in accordance with this *tsaddiq*'s character."[94] The practice of *yiḥudim*, of course, resulted in speaking with the voice of the prophet or teacher upon whose grave one was performing the ritual, a person with whom one shared a common soul-root.

Among the things we learn from all this is that the agents of communion and communication available to Safed's kabbalists were diverse, and that there was a considerable degree of fluidity in establishing the identity of a particular communicant. In an instructive passage in his treatise *Sha'arei Qedushah* (Gates of Holiness), Hayyim Vital delineates this range of cultural options, a sort of celestial smorgasbord: "We have already explained in part three, gate seven, that there are five means of achieving inspiration: The Holy Spirit, the souls of departed *tsaddiqim*, angels called *maggidim*, Elijah, and dreams."[95] Of these, the revelation of Elijah was indisputably the most desirable. We know, of course, that Vital repeatedly praised his teacher by proclaiming that Luria had attained the revelation of the prophet Elijah, making it clear that this was an exceptional accomplishment. Vital himself aspired to auditions of Elijah, judging by his own testimony.[96] As we saw earlier, the superiority of receiving Elijah's revelation is also attested by Joseph Karo, who reported that his own *maggid* held out the promise of this exalted experience.

Isaac Luria was distinguished by the fact that he was believed to be able to achieve *all* of these various types of revelation, as well as still others. Beyond this or that particular technique, Luria was regarded, as we have seen, as capable of perceiving the souls of all things, animate or inanimate, and able to call upon the souls of departed individuals at will. In other words, his was a deep and broad intuitiveness that permitted him knowledge of the inner voice at the heart of all reality.

4. Revelatory Gnosis

The final feature that the practice of *yiḥudim* has in common with the other techniques surveyed here concerns the content of the communication that these exercises yielded. The first thing to note is that in each and every case, the communication was intelligible and lucid. Others who were present were able to hear and understand the communications, as we learn explicitly in connection with Karo's *maggid*. In the case of Vital's account of his experience with performing *yiḥudim*, even though the voice became independent, speaking at will beyond Vital's control, the message itself was a coherent one. As noted earlier, in several passages describing the practice of *yiḥudim*, we are told that the *tsaddiq* and the adept converse with one another as would friends. Thus, these experiences should not be taken for nonsensical glosso-lalia that requires decoding, although Luria is asked to interpret the meaning of the message by Vital.

Moreover, the content of the speech produced in the course of these various experiences consisted of either personal information or kabbalistic knowledge. In the case of Karo's *maggid*, both types of communication occurred. The *maggid* served as an alter ego, reprimanding him for his imperfections and praising him for his virtues. But the *maggid* also communicated kabbalistic knowledge, usually in a midrashic style, that is, as scriptural interpretation. In Vital's description of his experiences, the voice that spoke through him promised him future greatness. In other descriptions of the *yiḥudim*, the adept is supposed to be able to receive whatever esoteric or heavenly knowledge he seeks. In Luria's case, as we know, his esoteric knowledge was claimed to have been gained primarily as a result of heavenly communication. In the context of Safed's eschatological climate, both types of communication, personal or impersonal, were in the nature of salvational gnosis. All knowledge from on high was deemed consequential, as bearing upon one's personal perfection and as contributing to larger redemptive goals, a subject to be explored in depth in Chapter 9.

The Practice of Yiḥudim as Spirit Possession

With what kind of phenomena in the history of religions and ethnographical anthropology can this practice be meaningfully compared? The purpose in posing this question is to shed further light by situating this ritual within a broader context of cross-cultural behavior. Of the great variety of mystical practices known to us, the *yiḥudim* bear strong similarities to the cluster of related phenomena that includes spirit possession, spirit mediumship, and shamanism. The precise meaning of these several terms is by no means self-evident, and much of the scholarly literature on these subjects is concerned with their clarification.

Spirit possession or spirit mediumship, of one type of another, is encountered in both literate and nonliterate traditions. Following the anthropologist and psychologist Victor Crapanzano, spirit possession may be defined in a fairly broad way as "any altered or unusual state of consciousness and allied behavior that is indigenously interpreted in terms of the influence of an alien spirit, demon, or deity."[97] Among the considerable range of altered states of consciousness to which the history of mysticism attests, the one most frequently associated with spirit possession or mediumship is trance. For our purposes, trance can be described as "a condition of dissociation, characterized by the lack of voluntary movement and frequently by automatisms in act and thought, illustrated by hypnotic and mediumistic conditions."[98] In such an experience, individuals feel detached from the frames of reference that form the basis for their normal understanding of their world. As the Balinese say, such a person is "away," literally separated from his own usual behavior, as well as from companionship and community.

The possessed behaves as if another personality—some spirit or soul—has entered his or her body and assumed some degree of control. Typically, there are dramatic changes in voice, body movement, and general physiognomy. While possession can be somnambulistic, where the possessed remembers nothing of what occurred, it is just as likely for possession to involve lucidity, where everything is remembered, as we have seen in connection with the *yiḥudim*. Finally, spirit possession can be undesirable, as in cases where an individual is believed to be seized or attacked against his or her will by an evil spirit, or afflicted with a physical or emotional illness. As noted elsewhere, Safed sources attest to such experiences, with demonic possession requiring professional, ritualized exorcism. In many cultures, however, possession may also be a desirable state, one to be cultivated and practiced out of a variety of motivations, as was the case with Lurianic kabbalists. Here the spirits are *sympathetic*, and communication with them or through them is socially, morally, and religiously acceptable. In contrast, demonic possession intolerably violates the social, moral, and religious order of things. Desirable spirit possession is typically voluntary, whereas malignant possession is usually involuntary, although this can vary, even in the same person.[99]

Ritual trance, or possession trance, can be induced by means of a variety of physiological, psychological, and pharmacological means. Certain techniques employ sensory bombardment, while others use sensory deprivation, or even some combination of the two. The former includes such things as singing, chanting, drumming, repetitive dancing, the inhalation of incense, or the experience of repetitive play of light and darkness, while sensory deprivation might entail seclusion, darkness, silence, abstention from eating and drinking, and sustained concentration on an object. In the case of the *yiḥudim,* we have an example of the latter, the concentration and restriction of perception, insofar as they were generally performed in private, at night, at a grave site. Communing with the soul of the *tsaddiq* did not entail any physical commotion or stimulation, but rather a quiet concentration. Nor did the contemplation of divine names involve external stimulation. Thus, while the resulting possession experience itself may have entailed physical trembling, uncontrolled body movement, and involuntary speaking, these were induced more by way of quiet inner concentration than by stimulation from without.

The practice of *yiḥudim* was considered to be part of a more general yearning to communicate and commune with diverse heavenly agents for the purpose of meriting concealed knowledge, and in pursuit of the broad redemptive task of cosmic mending. Moreover, such experiences were clearly regarded as desirable inasmuch as they enabled one to reach beyond the limitations of the material world to a world construed as constituting a deeper reality. Finally, they were unquestionably socially desirable, insofar as one's status appears to have depended, to some degree at least, on one's success at achieving such experiences. Beyond all this, as we shall see below, this ritual practice should also be understood in terms of the very personal messianic ambition that stood at the heart of Luria's vision for himself and his disciples.

Nine　Metempsychosis, Mystical Fellowship, and
Messianic Redemption

One of the most intriguing traditions in the entire Lurianic corpus
gives an account of an experience that Isaac Luria and his disciples had
not far from Meron. Vital writes:

> I once traveled with my master, may his memory be blessed, to the
> place where Rabbi Shimon bar Yohai's disciples assembled when they
> held the Idra Rabba [described in portion] *Naso* [in the *Zohar*]. There,
> on the eastern side of the road, there is a cave (lit. "great rock") in
> which there are two large openings. In the opening on the northern
> end was the place where Rabbi Shimon bar Yohai, peace be upon him,
> sat on the occasion of the Idra. And Rabbi Abba sat in the opening on
> the southern side. And next to the tree opposite these two openings, to
> their west, sat Rabbi Eleazar. And [on the present occasion] my master,
> may the memory of the righteous be for a blessing, sat in the opening
> to the north, in the [same] place where Rabbi Shimon bar Yohai, peace
> be upon him, had sat. And I sat, unwittingly, in the opening to the
> south, in the place of Rabbi Abba. Afterwards, my master, blessed be
> his memory, explained something to me of which I had been unaware,
> namely, that one of the companions who took part in the Idra was part
> of my soul-ancestry (*gilgul*), that is, Rabbi Abba. I had therefore sat in
> his place without realizing it. With respect to our positions in these two
> openings, I am uncertain whether it was not the reverse.[1]

A somewhat different, and more elaborate, version of this episode
is preserved in the letters of Solomon Shlomiel of Dresnitz, according
to whom this event took place in Meron itself:

> Occasionally, [Isaac Luria] traveled with his disciples to Meron, where
> he would have them sit in the place where Rabbi Shimon bar Yohai,

peace be upon him, revealed the Idra Rabba. And he would say: "Here sat Rabbi Eleazar, here sat Rabbi Abba, in this spot sat Rabbi Judah, and so on with the rest. And then he would place each one [of his own disciples] in the proper place in accordance with his soul. He himself sat in the place of Rabbi Shimon, and Rabbi Hayyim [Vital] sat in Rabbi Eleazar's place, and Rabbi Jonathan [Sagis] in Rabbi Abba's place, Rabbi Gedaliah [ha-Levi] in the place of Rabbi Judah, Rabbi Joseph [ibn Tabul] sat in Rabbi Yose's place, Rabbi Isaac Kohen Ashkenazi in the place of Rabbi Isaac, and so on with the rest. He would tell them that today the soul of the *tanna* [rabbinic teacher from the period of the Mishnah] so and so is invested in your soul. He would say that he saw a fire burning around the companions, but that they did not have permission to see it with their own eyes, only he could see it.[2]

There are significant inconsistencies between these two versions. First of all, Shlomiel says that this happened in Meron itself, whereas Vital's account implies a different location. It is clear here that Vital's version is accurate. In Vital's detailed description of the precise locations of the grave sites of numerous sages in the vicinity of Safed that Luria identified for his disciples, we learn about a certain place in the vicinity of Gush Ḥalav, which is four kilometers *north* of Meron, where Rabbi Yose bar Jacob, one of the three companions who died during the Idra, was buried: "This is the field where they [Rashbi and his companions] assembled to carry out the Idra, and Rabbi Shimon bar Yohai, peace be upon him, sat in the spot to the north, where Rabbi Yose is buried, and to the south sat Rabbi Abba, and Rabbi Eleazar sat where the tree is located."[3] As far as Luria was concerned, then, the Idra had not taken place in Meron itself, where Rabbi Shimon bar Yohai is buried, but rather near Gush Ḥalav.

Second, in Vital's account, Vital himself occupied Rabbi Abba's place, whereas according to Shlomiel, he sat in Rabbi Eleazar's position. Shlomiel's account of this episode is unquestionably accurate when it indicates that Luria brought with him a number of his disciples and not Vital alone. As we shall see, the visit to the site of the Idra makes sense only if we assume it involved a group of Luria's closest disciples, as indicated in Shlomiel's account.

What was the purpose of such pilgrimage? Why did Isaac Luria bring his closest disciples to the place where he believed the Idra to have taken place? And why did he arrange each of them "in the proper place in accordance with his soul," that is, in the precise position that each of Rashbi's disciples had occupied during the Idra? Finally, how are we to understand the fact that Isaac Luria himself occupied the place of Shimon bar Yohai? These questions will help provide a framework within which to make sense of both Luria's self-understanding and that of his mystical fellowship.

The Idra Rabba

The Zoharic corpus, as is well known, consists of a rather wide variety of discrete literary sections, written in a number of different styles. The Idra Rabba (Great Assembly) is found in volume 3, folios 127b–145a, of the printed editions of the *Zohar* that follow the pagination of the original Mantua edition. The Idra discusses passages from another important section of the *Zohar*, the Sifra di-Tseniuta, or Book of Concealment (*Zohar* 2, 176b–179a). The Idra constitutes—even from the point of view of the *Zohar* itself—the book's most profound and esoteric teachings, consisting largely of enigmatic anthropomorphic explanations of features of the body of God, or more precisely, the divine head. The Idra Rabba, along with a closely related section known as the Idra Zuta (Lesser Assembly), may be considered the central events in the *Zohar*. For present purposes, we are especially interested in the narrative structure of the Idra. In the Idra Rabba, Shimon bar Yohai calls together his nine primary disciples, whose names are enumerated in the text: Shimon's own son, Rabbi Eleazar; Rabbi Abba; Rabbi Judah; Rabbi Yose bar Jacob; Rabbi Isaac; Rabbi Hizkiyah bar Rav; Rabbi Hiyya; Rabbi Yose; and Rabbi Yesa. This special assembly began with teachings by Rashbi, following which he invited every one of the companions to reveal his own teachings, each of which was developed further by their teacher. Besides Shimon bar Yohai himself, Eleazar and Abba assumed a place of special prominence in the Idra, as they tend to in much of the *Zohar*: "He called Rabbi Eleazar, his son, and sat him in front, and called Rabbi Abba on the other side. He said, 'We are the sum of the whole! Now the pillars stand firm!'"

The Idra comes to an end with the unexpected deaths of three of the companions: Yose bar Jacob, Hizkiyah, and Yesa. From one point of view, their deaths appear to be a punishment, "because through us has been revealed something not revealed since the day Moses stood on Mount Sinai." That is, they engaged in the disclosure of the Torah's most profound and recondite mysteries, by the nature of things something fraught with enormous danger. On the other hand, the surviving companions are consoled when they learn about the ecstatic nature of the experience that led to the deaths of their three comrades: "For by intense desire, their souls joined the divine the moment that they were taken. Happy is their portion. They rose in perfection."[4] As evidence of their perfection, we learn that these three disciples of Shimon bar Yohai merited the most sublime form of dying, that is, from a kiss by God, precisely the type of death that rabbinic tradition attributed to Moses, Aaron, Miriam, and the three patriarchs, Abraham, Isaac, and Jacob.[5] As a whole, the Idra describes circumstances that result in an experience of ecstasy on the part of all of its participants, a transformative moment in which they have cleaved to God. The world is now blessed through them, and all their faces shine with a luster such that other human beings could not look upon them. The spiritual dependence of the six surviving companions upon their teacher is proclaimed by Rabbi Abba: "We are six lights shining from the seventh. You are the seventh of all. The six exist only because of the seventh. All depends on the seventh."[6]

Isaac Luria brought his disciples to the place where he believed the Idra to have taken place, on account of his personal identification with Shimon bar Yohai, and, even further, by virtue of his conviction that his closest disciples were to be identified with those of Shimon bar Yohai. To put this more precisely, Luria believed his soul to be a transmigration of that of Rashbi, and the souls of his inner circle of students to be the transmigrated souls of those of Rashbi's disciples! Luria's elaborate teachings bearing upon the subject of *gilgul*, metempsychosis or the transmigration of souls, are thus far more than a set of theoretical doctrines.[7] They had to do with his most intimate and personal concerns, especially during the latter months of his life, when his interest in the soul-ancestries of his students assumed increasing significance to him. Luria's quest for *tiqqun* in its many forms—personal, communal, cosmic, and historical—was inexorably tied to his beliefs concerning his own soul-ancestry and those of his disciples.

Transmigration of Souls in Early Kabbalah

Before turning to a discussion of these questions, it will be worth our while to place Isaac Luria's teachings on this subject in some perspective. Earlier, I reflected on the fact that despite a rich history of ascetic practice in Judaism, it is commonly assumed that Jewish tradition is one that eschewed asceticism in all of its forms. Precisely the same observation can be made in connection with the question of the transmigration of souls. Transmigration is a conception associated especially with Asian religious traditions, particularly Buddhism and Hinduism. Yet the fact is that we find in Judaism an extensive and significant history of teachings about this subject, although it must be acknowledged that belief in transmigration—outside of certain kabbalistic communities—never achieved the kind of normative status it occupies in Buddhist and Hindu traditions.[8]

The earliest ideas about transmigration of souls in Judaism predate Kabbalah and appear to have emerged among Jews living in the Near East, especially Iraq, in the eighth through tenth centuries, perhaps under the influence of Mutazilite Muslims and Gnostics of an Ismailian orientation. Proclivities of this type among some Jews inspired polemical rejection of the doctrine of transmigration on the part of the great tenth-century Baghdad Jewish authority Saadia Gaon, who bitterly denounced it as "madness and confusion."[9] Anan ben David, to whom the Karaite tradition attributed the beginnings of the Karaite schism with rabbinic authority in the eighth century, appropriated the idea of transmigration.

It was in the earliest circles of Kabbalah in Provence and Spain, however, that metempsychosis took root in a truly significant way, ultimately providing legitimacy for teachings that had hitherto existed exclusively at the margins of Jewish life. We find in kabbalistic sources widely varying notions about transmigration with respect to just about every aspect of the idea. The *Sefer ha-Bahir*, the earliest extant work of Kabbalah, which appeared anonymously in southern France in the last third of the twelfth century, taught the doctrine of transmigration as a mystery upon which only initiates ought to reflect. On the other hand, the author of the *Bahir* apparently felt no need to defend or justify these teachings, unlike the Cathars, who developed such ideas at precisely the same time and place, and who were condemned for doing so by the Catholic Church, which had formally rejected the doctrine of transmigration. In the thirteenth century, Spanish kabbalists continued to teach metempsychosis, including Nahmanides, according to whom Job had been required to suffer in this life so as to atone for sins he had committed in an earlier one. Another, more positive explanation for transmigration in the thirteenth century had to do with the biblical notion of Levirate marriage, according to which the brother of a man who dies without having had a child must offer to marry his brother's widow; a son created through such a marriage contains within him the soul of the deceased husband, thus providing an opportunity for the latter to fulfill his obligation to procreate through his brother's (and former wife's) son! This was the primary interest of the Gerona circle of kabbalists in the notion of metempsychosis. As far as the *Zohar* is concerned, Moshe de Leon taught the doctrine of *gilgul*, but he also tended to be especially interested in transmigration in connection with a man who had died childless.[10]

Transmigration and Luria's Fellowship

In the sixteenth century, following the Spanish Expulsion, the interest in metempsychosis became more widespread and developed in dramatic and significant new ways. The most important work devoted to this subject prior to Luria was a voluminous treatise entitled *Galya Raza*, written in either Greece or Turkey in the middle of the sixteenth century, to which we have already referred. In Safed, kabbalists of virtually every type subscribed to belief in this doctrine, none with more enthusiasm than Isaac Luria himself. While Luria's teachings on this subject include a great deal of theoretical discussion, as already noted, his primary motivation was neither speculative nor abstract, but personal and practical.

Luria regarded his own soul and that of his disciples as participating in long chains of soul transmigrations, reaching back, in fact, to the very beginnings of humanity. As we have seen, Adam's soul originally contained within it all of the future souls of humankind, although these were divided hierarchically into several groups: "My teacher, of blessed memory, informed me . . . how all the souls were originally included in *Adam Rishon*, but afterwards, on account of his sin, his [613] limbs dropped away and his stature became diminished."[11]

The first category is "genuinely new souls" (*neshamot ḥadashot ʾamitiyut*), consisting of souls that were not part of Adam when he was born but only joined him at a later time. These souls departed from Adam's at the time of his transgression, ascended to the realm of the divine, and thus avoided participating in his sin. Insofar as they were never tainted by sin, when these souls descend to the world and become incarnated in an individual's body, they are capable of perfecting themselves completely in a single lifetime, from the lowest grade, *nefesh* of the realm of *Assiyah*, to the highest grade, the level of *neshamah* in the world of *Atsilut*. Even more, they are able to do so without much effort. In the event that such a soul should fall prey to sin, however, and die before managing to perfect itself, it transmigrates into the body of another individual as an "old soul."[12]

A second category of "new souls" remained with Adam's soul while he sinned. A third group—in effect, a subcategory of the previous one, became the souls of Cain and Abel (and their lineage), which enjoyed the special merit of being considered as if they were still included in Adam. Their ability to perfect their souls within a single lifetime is more limited than the first category. Normally, these souls can only ascend in perfection to the level of *nefesh* of *Atsilut*. Even these individuals, however, can potentially perfect their *ruaḥ* and *neshamah*, if after having achieved perfection of their *nefesh*, they engage in special meditative practices at night.[13] If they fail to accomplish this, though, their souls return to the world following the death of their original body, at least once, possibly twice, so as to perfect their *ruaḥ* and *neshamah*. The fourth group from Adam's soul are those that fell directly into the realm of the *qelippot* at the time of Adam's transgression and separated into numerous sparks within the physical world. These inferior souls are the lowest type of all and are called by Luria "old souls" (*neshamot yeshanot*). The inferior quality of this category of souls normally necessitates a *series* of transmigrations before they are able to achieve complete perfection. Just as with the previous category, however, these too can speed up the process of soul perfection, through the ritual of *nefilat ʾappayim*. They can, under these circumstances, manage to perfect their *ruaḥ* even before having completed the perfection of their *nefesh*. They must, however, definitely undergo at least one additional *gilgul* in order to perfect their *neshamah*. The fifth and final division of souls are those that enter into the bodies of proselytes.

Of these five groups, all but the first eventually fell into the realm of the *qelippot*, although they do not all share the same status. Those of category two exhibit a single flaw (by virtue of their "participation" in Adam's sin), while those of category three possess a twofold flaw, one as a result of Adam's sin and one as a result of the sins of Cain and Abel.[14] When souls are liberated from the *qelippot* in order to enter the world and become incarnate in an individual, they require a period of incubation for purposes of purification, a process that takes place within the Female Waters of *Malkhut*. Paradoxically, those categories of soul that are superior merit a more prolonged period of purification, which they are able to withstand by virtue of their greater spiritual strength. Thus, souls of level two incubate for a period of nine months, level three for seven months, level four for forty days, and those of the fifth level for a mere three days. The longer the time spent in this process of healing, the greater will be their illumination and purification.

The primary importance of all this from the Lurianic point of view has to do with its existential significance for Luria's own contemporaries, and most particularly for Luria's own personal soul-history and those of his disciples. For the souls of righteous individuals correspond in precise ways to the various dimensions of divinity of which the cosmos is composed: "The souls of the righteous [*neshamot ha-tsadiqqim*] constitute the inner essence [*penimiyut*] of the divine worlds."[15] That is to say, the different gradations and configurations of the divine find earthly expression in the lives of individuals in every generation, linking them to the past in a complex chain of transmigration. Mythic history and personal history combine in such a way as to shape both the identities of individuals and the collective identities of certain groups of people.

The manner in which this applies to Luria and his closest disciples is especially clear in connection with his highly developed conception of the *garments* with which all souls are garbed, a topic intimately related to the vicissitudes of souls themselves. In accordance with the kabbalistic notion that everything—including spiritual phenomena—requires protection, or "clothing," Luria taught that souls that emerge from their imprisoned state within the realm of the *qelippot* cannot go naked in the world but are in need of a protective garment: "Know that there is no soul [*neshamah*] in the world, God forbid, that can exist naked, without a garment [*levush*] in which it is clothed in this world."[16] Remarkably enough, these soul-garments (*levushei neshamot*) are produced as a result of seminal emissions on the part of certain extraordinary individuals (*tsaddiqim*) in various generations.

The biblical figure of Joseph occupies an absolutely critical position in Luria's conception of soul-garments. As noted in Chapter 4, ten drops of semen seeped through Joseph's fingers while he was resisting the illicit sexual overtures of his master Potiphar's wife.[17] This motif originated in rabbinic literature, where we learn that as Joseph was defending himself against her unwanted seduction of him, "he stuck his hands in the ground so that his lust came out from between his finger nails," or alternatively, "his semen was scattered and dripped through his finger nails."[18] That is to say, rather than give in to the sexual passion that Potiphar's wife had aroused in him, he spilled his semen on the ground. According to Lurianic teaching, Joseph sought to avoid looking at her face, but did so when Potiphar's wife physically forced him to lift up his head. Upon looking at her, "these drops came."[19] Joseph's earthly actions reflected and stimulated a parallel process in the divine realm. Everything that happened to Joseph on earth also "occurred [simultaneously] on high within *Yosef ha-Tsaddiq* [i.e., the sefirotic Joseph], which is the *sefirah Yesod.*"[20] When these ten drops of "semen" flowed from *Yesod* on high and were not received by *Nuqba de-Ze͑ir*, the supernal womb of the divine female (*be-reḥem ha-neqevah ha-͑elyonah*), they became trapped within the *qelippot*, where they served as garments for the purpose of protecting souls. By virtue of this, the human Joseph does not so much symbolize cosmic processes within the realm of the divine as much as he participates in them. He does so by embodying phallic energy from on high and by arousing corresponding phallic dynamics above by his own sexual activity. While the involuntary emission of male seed in this fashion would normally be considered a great transgression, in this case it served an important positive purpose. Joseph's act is regarded as paradigmatic in connection with the formation of certain kinds of souls, as well as soul-garments. It is important to point out that in the case of some of the individuals described below, this wasted seed appears to signify drops of semen "left over" in the wake of coitus.

These mythic traditions served as the basis for Luria's conviction that central figures in *other* generations had also expended their seed in a similar manner, a belief that he correlated with the five primary types of divine *hieros gamos*, or *zivvugim.*[21] In each instance, seminal emission "wasted" in this manner generated soul-garments for a particular *group* of souls trapped in the realm of the *qelippot* and in need of *tiqqun*:

> It has already been explained to you how many *partsufim* there are on high that are dependent upon [the union] of *Ze͑ir* and *Nuqba*. And each of these *partsufim* possesses a dimension of *Yesod*. We find that from every *Yesod* on high there come holy soul-sparks [i.e., soul-gar- ments] in a wasteful manner, which become trapped by the *qelippot*. For all of the *Yesodot* are signified by *Yosef ha-Tsaddiq*. There are five types of *zivvug* on high, from each of which came sparks in this way.[22]

In other generations, too, we find a group of individuals, usually with a clearly identifiable figure at its center, who correspond to and embody particular aspects of the divine. Moreover, in each case the central figure assumes the earthly role of *Yesod* within *Zeᶜir Anpin*, whose seminal emission results in the creation of soul-garments for protecting souls in the realm of *qelippot*. The details of Vital's account of this set of notions are not only fascinating but central to our analysis.

1. The most superior form of supernal *hieros gamos*, that of the divine qualities called Israel and Rachel, is unique insofar as it has two aspects to it. *Yesod* of *Zeᶜir Anpin* in its particular configuration known as Israel, which engages in relations with *Nuqba de-Zeᶜir* in her aspect of Rachel, possesses both ten *Gevurot* and ten *Ḥasadim*. The ten *Gevurot*— five that originate in *Abba* and five in *Imma*—correspond to the Ten Martyrs whose souls became garbed in ten drops of semen from this particular grade of *Yesod*. The five *Gevurot* that derive from *Abba* correspond to the soul-garments of the following rabbis (five of the Ten Martyrs) of late antiquity: Akiva, Shimon ben Gamaliel, Yeshevav the Scribe, Ishmael ben Elisha, and Yehuda ben Baba. The remaining five Martyrs correspond to the *Gevurot* that derive from *Imma*.

Insofar as these ten individuals derived their soul-garments from the realm of *Gevurot*, that is, the sphere of divine strictness, it was necessary for them to experience premature death as martyrs. What is more, their deaths parallel and reiterate the primordial "death of the Kings [of Edom]," which occurred at the beginning of creation.[23] As we have seen elsewhere, however, their martyrdom was ultimately a positive, even necessary event, insofar as it provided the opportunity for the *tiqqun* of their own souls, as well as the gathering and restoration of other sparks trapped below.[24] For as we already know, the death of the Ten Martyrs, as with certain other forms of (righteous) death, paradoxically stimulates the processes of *tiqqun* through the arousal and ascent of the Female Waters, ultimately to the level of *Abba* and *Imma*.

The ten *Ḥasadim* of *Abba* and *Imma* correspond to the soul-garments of the disciples of Rabbi Shimon bar Yohai. Unlike the Ten Martyrs, these did *not* have to be killed, since by virtue of their association with the *Ḥasadim*, that is, the divine quality of Compassion, they did not fall into the grasp of the *qelippot*. As for those three disciples of Shimon bar Yohai who did actually die prematurely in the course of the Idra Rabba—Rabbis Yose bar Jacob, Hezekiyah, and Yesa—their soul-garments derived from three *Ḥasadim* of *Imma* that had ascended to a sublime level of divinity. Thus, these three individuals shared a common destiny—an ecstatic ascent to the deepest realms of the divine. Shimon bar Yohai stood at the heart of this latter group of individuals, constituting "the *Yesod* himself from whom these drops flowed." Thus, Rashbi's activity generated the soul-garments for his own disciples, on account of which he bore a unique and urgent responsibility to teach them and to see to their complete spiritual maturation and redemption.

Because the soul-garments of Rashbi's companions derived from the realm of *Hasadim* and shared in the highest possible form of *hieros gamos*, Israel and Rachel, these individuals were eligible to enjoy the revelation of all of the Torah's mysteries through the mediation of their teacher. This is something that will not happen again until the generation of the King Messiah (*dara de-malka meshiha*). In contrast to Shimon bar Yohai and his circle of disciples, no single figure stood at the center of the Ten Martyrs, by virtue of the particular manner in which the seminal fluids to which the Martyrs correspond flowed on high.

2. The *hieros gamos* of the supernal figures Jacob and Rachel involves the *Hasadim* and *Gevurot* only of *Abba*. This is the case insofar as there exist no judgmental forces (*dinin*) within Rachel, and because Jacob receives its illumination only from the *mohin* of *Abba*. Rabbi Judah ha-Nasi, compiler of the Mishnah, embodies *Yesod* in this instance and thus his disciples are garbed in the soul-garments produced by his seminal emission: Rabbis Hiyya, Oshaya, Bar Kappara, Levi bar Sissi, Hananyah bar Hama, Rav, and others.[25] Judah ha-Nasi's obligation to teach his students and help perfect their souls derived from this special relationship.

3. The third *zivvug*, between Jacob and Leah, occurs following midnight so as to "sweeten" the elements of judgment within Leah. This *zivvug* entails five *Hasadim* from the realm of *Abba* and five *Gevurot* from *Abba*. As in the case of the previous type of marital union, this one as well involves no need for the premature death of its protagonists, insofar as it involves Jacob, who derives from the realm of the masculine, that is, from the side of *Abba*. It is significant that Jacob and Leah indulge in relations *twice*, once after midnight and once again immediately before dawn, a period of even greater divine compassion

than the moment of midnight itself.[26] Whereas the initial sexual act between Jacob and Leah at midnight produces the customary ten drops of semen, the second one produces only two drops, the first of these drops consisting of five *Ḥasadim*, the second consisting of five *Gevurot*. The ten additional soul-garments that result from these two drops are superior in nature to the first ten. The individual who embodies *Yesod* of *Zeᶜir Anpin* in these two *zivvugim* is none other than Isaac Luria himself. In the words of Hayyim Vital: "These twelve drops [of semen] constitute [the soul-garments of] my companions who used to study with my master, of blessed memory. And he himself is the *Yesod* from whom these twelve drops came."[27]

4. The fourth type of *hieros gamos* is that of Israel and Leah, occurring at *minḥah* (afternoon prayers), resulting in only two drops of semen. The two individuals whose soul-garments resulted from this *zivvug* are Pappus and Lulianus, two brothers from the second century who according to rabbinic tradition were condemned to death by the Roman emperor Trajan. The medieval rabbinic commentator Rashi identified these two brothers with the "Martyrs of Lydda" mentioned in the Talmud.[28] There is no identifiable aspect of *Yesod* above involved in this *zivvug*, and thus they have no special teacher serving as their earthly *Yesod*.

5. The final *zivvug*, of Jacob and Leah, occurring prior to midnight, entails elements of complete Judgment. This marital union resulted in the soul-garments of the "Martyrs of Betar," at whose center stood Rabbi Eleazar ha-Modai, killed at Betar.[29]

Even though it is third in the hierarchical order presented above, the group to which the most intimate disciples of Luria belong is the most significant in a chronological and historical sense.[30] In a view brimming with messianic hopefulness, Luria and his disciples believed themselves to be living "in this final exile" (*be-galut zeh ha-ʾaḥaron*), hinted at in Isaiah's prophecy by the verses: "The 'Dumah' Pronouncement: A Call comes to me from Seir: 'Watchman, what of the night [*laylah*]?' The watchman replied, 'Morning came, and so did night [*leil*]'" (Isa. 21:11–12). The two different forms of the word *night* in these verses are associated by Luria with sexual relations after midnight, one following closely upon midnight and the second close to the rising of the sun, as we saw above.[31] Luria's closest disciples bear unique, urgent responsibility to set things right in light of the fact that they find themselves at the culmination of history, at the very edge of the messianic age, "in the final generation of the Messiah" (*be-dara batra'ah shel ha-Mashiah*). The exigency of the historical moment demands of them that they engage more vigorously than ever before in acts of repentance, in petitioning God, and in prayer, "so that they may be extricated from exile and be redeemed." Luria made a great effort to caution the disciples belonging to this group that they were absolutely required to rise at midnight, surely so as to engage in the devotional rites necessary to facilitate the processes of redemption.

A number of decisive elements of Isaac Luria's thinking come together here. The entire regimen of ritual practices with which Luria provided his disciples was clearly intended to enable this particular community to bring about the redemption of the divine realm, and thus of the cosmos as a whole. The *tiqqun* for which this group is collectively responsible constitutes nothing less than the restitution appropriate "in the final generation of the Messiah," "in this final exile." What is more, Luria himself embodies the male generative forces at the epicenter of these processes. It is his most vital energies that animate the community of individuals who look to him for spiritual sustenance. Together, Luria and his closest disciples personify and incarnate the totality of the divine organism. Thus, the stakes could hardly have been higher with respect to their relationship to one another, about which more will be said shortly.

Earlier we noted the names of those disciples enumerated by Vital who composed Luria's inner circle, the first of the four groups that made up the larger fellowship: Hayyim Vital, Jonathan Sagis, Joseph Arzin, Isaac Kohen, Gedaliah ha-Levi, Samuel Uceda, Judah Mishan, Abraham Gavriel, Shabbatai Menashe, Joseph ibn Tabul, and Elijah Falkon. These corresponded to the *zivvug* between Jacob and Leah, and their soul-garments derived from the interior of the *mohin* of *Da'at*. The fact that there should be twelve individuals on this list—corresponding to twelve drops of semen rather than the eleven we find here—may be explained by the fact that Vital confesses to some uncertainty about the exact composition of this group and indicates as well that some may be replaced by others.[32] In particular, he is unsure about the identities of the two people whose soul-garments correspond to the "two drops" produced by the *zivvug* just prior to the dawn.

Moses and Shimon bar Yohai

The various circles of disciples and their leaders across the generations are not linked merely by virtue of the fact that they perform similar functions. They are bound together across time in an organic way insofar as they constitute a series of crucial sets of *gilgulim*. As such, the activities of each circle reiterate and build upon those prior to it, all leading to progressive purification, restoration, and redemption. The central figures who constitute the *Yesod* of each circle stand in intimate spiritual kinship with one another, going back as far as Adam.

In a reiteration of Adam's transgression, the sins of Cain and Abel resulted in the further fall of soul-sparks (now *actual* souls, not soul-garments) into the realm of the *qelippot*, as a consequence of which good and evil once again became thoroughly mixed.[33] Abel's soul, which derived from the realm of *Daᶜat* in *Zeᶜir*, the same as his father Adam's, eventually transmigrated into that of Moses,[34] the latter occupying an especially critical role in the cosmic and historical processes of *tiqqun*. As with Abel, Moses' soul partakes of the sphere of *Ḥesed*. Thus, as an infant, Moses was drawn from the waters, that is, from the waters of Compassion. Also, like Adam and Abel, Moses' soul ascended to the level of *Daᶜat* within *Zeᶜir* when he received the Torah at Mount Sinai. But Moses' soul is also directly comparable to Adam's insofar as Moses contained within himself all of the souls of Israel, as "he is patterned after *Adam Rishon* [i.e., Adam] who incorporates all souls. . . . all of Israel were his sons."[35]

The souls of the individuals who left Egypt, including the "mixed multitude" (*ᶜerev rav*), all derived from this same aspect of *Zeᶜir*, through the mediation of Moses himself. Moses' sin, in replication of Adam's, had been in the nature of wasteful seminal emission, causing souls to be entrenched in the *qelippot*. Thus, Moses bore the responsibility for ensuring their restoration and redemption: "Since they are branches of [the soul of] Moses, he is required to be their redeemer [*go°el*]." All of the children of Israel who went out from Egypt are considered Moses' sons and are thus literally called "the *generation* of Moses," all of whose nourishment derives directly from him. Even more, Moses' soul is reincarnated anew in every generation and will continue to be until the messianic generation: "For Moses himself will return by way of *gilgul* in the final generation. . . . For there is no generation in which [the soul of] Moses, peace be upon him, is not present in order to mend that generation, in the mystery of [the verses from Eccles. 1:4–5]: 'One generation goes, another comes, but the earth remains the same forever. The sun rises, and the sun sets [and glides back to where it rises].'"[36]

In the generation of Shimon bar Yohai, Moses' soul became incarnate in the person of that preeminent mystical figure, for "Rabbi Shimon bar Yohai was a spark of Moses our teacher, peace be upon him,"[37] a tradition already present in the *Zohar*.[38] At first, Rashbi's soul occupied the lower rung of *Yesod* within *Ze°ir*, but in the course of the Idra Rabba, his soul ascended to the same level occupied by Moses at the time of his having received the second tablets of the Ten Commandments, that is, to the higher level of *Da°at* of *Ze°ir*.[39] Vital sums up some of these associations in these words: "With respect to Moses, peace be upon him, *Rabbenu ha-Qadosh* [literally, "our holy teacher," i.e., Judah ha-Nasi], Rashbi, peace be upon him, and the Ten Martyrs, all of them partake of the aspect of *Yesod* within *Ze°ir Anpin* . . . although Moses ascended [even higher] . . . to the sphere of *Da°at* of *Ze°ir*."

The "Seventh Day of Passover"

Where does Isaac Luria fit into this transmigratory progression of distinguished archetypal souls? We have already seen from his inclusion in the above account of the various figures associated with the five types of *hieros gamos* that Luria occupied the same position as these other great righteous individuals, namely, as *Yesod* within *Ze°ir*. From this alone we may be permitted to infer that Luria stood in the same relationship to the other *tsaddiqim* as they do to one another. But, in addition to this, we have other diverse and wide-ranging evidence attesting to the ways in which Isaac Luria personally identified with these figures, most significantly with Moses and Shimon bar Yohai. We want to pursue these questions further through an analysis of one especially important passage in which Luria taught his disciples—just a few months before he died—the kabbalistic significance of the "seventh day of Passover," that is, the final day of this festival.[40] According to Hayyim Vital, the transmission of these particular teachings was fraught with the gravest danger:

> And on the day that my master, of blessed memory, explained to us this passage, we were sitting in a field, under the trees, when a raven passed above him, crying out in its characteristic fashion, following which my master, of blessed memory, announced: "Blessed be the true Judge."[41] I asked him the meaning of this, and he told me that this raven informed him that because he [i.e., Luria] revealed this secret to everybody in public, he would be punished by the Heavenly Tribunal [bet din shel maʿalah]. They had decreed that his young son would die. And as soon as he returned home, he found his son in the courtyard, and on that very night [his son] became sick, and [he] died three days later, may God save us. Thus, it is necessary for every person who heard these teachings to conceal them completely, except from those who are worthy of this wisdom, for God's honor is bound up with this secret, and it is unseemly [for me] to elaborate upon this. For with respect to these matters, one who conceals these secrets from one who is not fit to receive them will be praised and honored among the celestial retinue. A person who does otherwise places himself in a position of great danger in this world, [risking] his own death, God forbid, as well as the lives of his young children, in addition to rendering himself vulnerable to punishment in the netherworld [gehinnom], a punishment to which there is no end, just as Rashbi, peace be upon him, indicated at the end of the Idra Zuta.[42]

Luria's mistake was to disclose highly recondite teachings that should not have been revealed except to those who were absolutely worthy. From this arose the urgent concern about not conveying these teachings to yet others who were unfit. The expression "everybody in public" probably refers to disciples of Luria about whose worthiness he was uncertain, or to individuals who were not among his closest students. Vital goes on to say that the reason for such harsh punishment has to do with the state of divinity on the seventh day of Passover, presumably the day on which Luria actually conveyed these teachings. If a person engages in the most esoteric mysteries of the Torah during a time of spiritual "maturity" or ascendancy (*gadlut*) on high, he faces far less danger compared to doing so at a time of relative impoverishment (*qatnut*) within the divine realm. For the exterior elements of the *moḥin*—which are characterized by severe judgment—are strengthened during periods of *qatnut*. What is more, an individual's transgressions are brought to the surface when he indulges in the revelation of such secrets at a cosmically unpropitious time.

What exactly were these mysteries that posed this kind of danger? Despite the fact that Vital indicated that "it is unseemly for me to elaborate," he committed to writing the contents of this teaching. It is based upon a number of highly curious passages in the *Zohar* concerning a pregnant hind (*ʾayala*)—symbolic of the *Shekhinah*—who has difficulty giving birth until she is "bitten" by a serpent. Thus, the *Zohar*:

> When her [i.e., the "hind" or *Shekhinah*] time comes [to give birth],
> the Holy One, blessed be He [i.e., the "husband" of the *Shekhinah*],
> summons a great, supernal snake, and he "bites" her in that place
> [i.e., her womb], and she gives birth. And this is the esoteric meaning
> of "I will greatly increase your pain and your travail, [with pain shall
> you bear children] . . . [Gen. 3:16]" because she is in anguish every
> day and immersed in pain because of the sins of the world. "With
> pain shall you bear children." "With pain"—this is the mystery of the
> snake who brings pain upon the world. . . . You might ask what need
> is there for the snake in a matter like this. The answer is that he opens
> the way for the descent of souls into the world; for if he were not to
> open the way for the descent below [the soul] would not dwell in an
> individual. It is written "Sin lies at the door" [Gen. 4:7]. What does
> "at the door" mean? It means the door that is prepared for birth, for
> the discharge of souls into the world, and at this door [the snake] lies.
> But with regard to the souls that are to descend [immediately] into
> holy bodies [i.e., bodies formed as a result of intercourse conducted

in a holy way], he does not lie by that door, and he has no power over that particular soul. Otherwise, the snake bites and that place is defiled, resulting in an impure soul.[43]

In this passage, concerned with the birth or release of souls from within the womb of the *Shekhinah*, the latter has difficulty giving birth insofar as "her existence depends upon Judgment," that is, she is connected to the realm of divine strictness. As a result, when the power of evil, the "Other Side," makes accusations on account of the sins of the world and seeks to do harm, the womb of the *Shekhinah* is shut up. In a strangely paradoxical fashion, however, by "biting" her womb—a thinly disguised expression denoting a sexual act—at the request of the hind's "husband," the snake itself makes birth possible.[44] This is the case because while the snake strengthens itself by doing so (in order to continue to perpetrate evil), at the same time its "appetite" is assuaged.[45] As a result, the snake leaves the *Shekhinah* free to give birth to holy souls unharmed by the nefarious powers of the "Other Side."

Now, in Luria's transformation of this motif, the pregnant hind signifies *Nuqba de-Ze'ir*, beloved by her husband *Ze'ir 'Anpin*. On the first night of Passover, they engage in marital relations, a union that is of the highest order insofar as *Ze'ir* is in a state of complete maturity, or *gadlut,* at this time. Such *zivvug* takes place of its own accord, without the stimulation of human activity, making sexual relations between a man and a woman unnecessary on the first night of Passover. (Indeed, Luria goes so far as to prohibit marital relations on this night.) As a result, *Nuqba* becomes pregnant and gives "birth" on the seventh day of the festival. But this birth does not take place without great struggle and danger. The problem is that as soon as the first day of the festival comes to an end, *Ze'ir* returns to a state of immaturity or *qatnut*, requiring it to undergo a renewed process of maturation, *tiqqun*. The same holds true for *Nuqba*, insofar as Her womb is lacking *Hasadim*, filled only with the qualities of *Gevurot*, causing it to become constricted (*'ayala she-raḥma tsar*). This renders her unable to give birth to the souls within her (conceived on the first night of Passover) without placing them in danger of the "sin that crouches at the door."

The remedy for this predicament is for *Ze^cir* to have relations with *Nuqba* once again on the seventh night of Passover, thereby opening up the latter's womb and enabling her to give birth. These relations are clearly not for the purpose of impregnation—which has already occurred—but to facilitate birth. In the course of this second *zivvug*, assisted by arousal of *Ze^cir* from the sphere of *Attiqa Qaddisha* on high, the powers of evil nurse, as it were, on the dross and refuse associated with the birth process.[46] In the course of this, *Nuqba* Herself is cleansed and purified of the harsh forces within Her, as a result of which the external powers do not attach themselves to the newly born souls.

The "Other Side" is strengthened by such nursing and its attention is diverted long enough to permit the birth of holy souls without harm. But there is a dramatic and crucial difference between the *Zohar*'s view and Luria's. Whereas in the *Zohar* the "biting" is done by the snake, from the Lurianic perspective the "biting" of the womb is enacted by *Ze^cir* itself, in its aspect of *Yesod*! In fact, in a startling association, we learn explicitly that *Ze^cir* and the snake are one and the same. That is to say, from Luria's point of view the serpent's "bite" constitutes a sexual act on the part of *Ze^cir ʿAnpin* while in a state of relative spiritual weakness: "And since this *zivvug* derives from the aspect of *Yesod* of *qatnut*—which is called *naḥash* [snake], entailing as it does harsh judgment—it is a *zivvug* known as 'biting.'"[47]

In the case of the *Zohar*, the snake may be regarded as "benevolent" in the limited, relative sense that its bite is necessary for the successful birthing of unharmed souls, but it is not ontologically good. With Luria, the situation is far more complicated. The boundary between good and evil is blurred much further by *identifying Ze^cir* with the snake. Hence *Ze^cir* performs two contrasting but essential functions at once. From a negative point of view, *Ze^cir* incorporates or serves as the embodiment of demonic forces that need to be appeased so as to contain them and divest *Nuqba* of harmful elements. But more positively, *Ze^cir* is a creative force whose sexual activity opens the way for the birthing of souls.

These teachings also constitute the esoteric meaning of the splitting of the sea that took place when Moses led the people of Israel out of slavery in Egypt, this also being the narrative portion from the Torah read on the seventh day of Passover. The splitting of the sea corresponds at the cosmic level to the "splitting" or opening of the hind's womb, accomplished "by means of the *zivvug* of the supernal serpent's bite in its aspect of *qatnut*."[48] What is more, Moses himself may be identified with *Ze^cir Anpin*, that is, with the snake whose bite opens up the womb of *Nuqba de-Ze^cir*! That there is an aspect of Moses that is characterized by the grade of *qatnut* is confirmed by a complex process of *gematria* in which Luria explicitly identified the name of Moses with the word *NaḥaSh* (snake). This explains the meaning of Exodus 4:2–3 in which God asks Moses, "What is in your hand? He said: A staff. He said: Throw it to the ground! He threw it to the ground, and it became a snake, and Moses recoiled from it." The transformation of Moses' "staff" into a "snake" by his casting it to the ground represents the act of biting, or opening, on the snake's part, which is itself an expression of Moses' own being:

> And this is the esoteric [significance] of Moses our teacher, peace be upon him, greatest of all the prophets, of whom it is said: "and Moses recoiled from it," on account of the staff that turned into a snake, this being *Ze^cir ^cAnpin* in its aspect of *qatnut*. . . . And when he (Moses) engaged in this teaching, he became fearful, and recoiled from it. Thus, this mystery needs to be concealed, for his [Moses'] own sake, and because we cannot fathom the true meaning of this mystery, even as much as a single grain of mustard seed.[49]

Moses, then, was both expositor of this sublime mystery as well as its subject. The danger he faced was inherent, not merely in his revelation of this teaching, but in *being* the snake whose bite was required for the safe birthing of souls into the world. Moses took on the guise of evil and performed an act that placed him in the gravest danger, on account of which he became afraid and "recoiled." The requirement to guard this secret, then, has to do in significant part with the peril posed by the performance of the act. The profoundly esoteric and dangerous nature of these activities is rooted in the teachings of the *Zohar* itself. In another Zoharic version of the pregnant hind in need of assistance, to which the Lurianic sources explicitly refer, Shimon bar Yohai warned against delving into these matters too deeply:

> When she [i.e., the pregnant hind] is about to bear a child and is in difficulty, she puts her head between her knees, and cries bitterly, and the Holy One sends a snake which bites that place, and immediately deliverance comes to her. Rabbi Shimon, however, added: "In this matter, 'thou must not ask nor tempt the Lord.'"[50]

What light, though, does all this shed on the story of Isaac Luria's role in the revelation of the secrets of the seventh day of Passover? The obvious inference is that Luria was regarded by his disciples as fulfilling the same role as Moses. Just as Moses "engaged in this teaching," that is, in the revelation of these deepest of mysteries, so did Luria. Just as this activity was fraught with the gravest danger for Moses—expressed in the fear he experienced—so too for Luria. And just as Moses' act was erotically charged, so too was Luria's, entailing the divulging of the Torah's most recondite secrets to his disciples.[51] Even from Luria's point of view, however, this *hieros gamos* was relatively inferior given the immature status of the divine at this moment.[52] Finally, it should be pointed out that the evidence for the relationship between Moses and Luria is not simply a matter of inference, as we learn explicitly that Luria's soul was a spark of Moses' soul.[53]

Similar observations may be made with respect to Luria's identification with Shimon bar Yohai. We already know that Luria (following the *Zohar* itself) believed Rashbi's soul to be a reincarnation of that of Moses, and that Luria's own soul was a spark of Moses', which manifests itself anew in every generation. The logic of this is that Luria himself was host for the transmigrated soul of Shimon bar Yohai, insofar as they both shared in Moses' soul. This logic is confirmed by the story with which this chapter began. Luria's placement of himself in exactly the same physical position of Shimon bar Yohai—as he assembled his disciples in direct imitation of Rashbi and his companions' performance of the Idra Rabba—was hardly arbitrary. He did so precisely because he regarded himself as the *gilgul* of the great master of the *Zohar*, and as performing the same role as Rashbi, and because he conceived of his disciples as the *gilgulim* of Rashbi's students.

As we have seen throughout this study, Luria was intensely focused from the beginning of his engagement with Kabbalah on (what he knew to be) the teachings of Shimon bar Yohai as found in the *Zohar*. The mysteries of the seventh day of Passover were based upon Rashbi's teachings, and our text explicitly refers to Rashbi's warning not to delve too deeply into these matters. Indeed, as with Luria, the *Zohar* itself treats these mysteries with the greatest circumspection and ambivalence. Luria was thus engaged in the revelation of precisely the same mysteries that Moses and Rashbi had revealed in their generations. And just as they had been deeply concerned about the spiritual worthiness of their generations, so was Luria. We find here, then, an intimate and direct path leading from Moses to Shimon bar Yohai to Isaac Luria, according to which the latter two figures replicated the esoteric activities of their predecessors, founded on the conviction that all three represent the same supernal grade of being and that they are all linked to one another in a series of decisively important soul migrations.

Isaac Luria as a Messianic Figure

The specifically *messianic* nature of the teaching having to do with the seventh day of Passover is suggested by Zoharic sources according to which the hind that gives birth with great difficulty will be mother to the soul of the Messiah, a motif that is rooted in well-known rabbinic traditions concerning the "birthpangs of the Messiah."[54] As far as the Lurianic narrative itself is concerned, while there is no explicit allusion to this motif, we do know that souls of the highest order are conceived as a result of these unions, and in one place we hear of a *single* birth, possibly an allusion to the singular birth of the Messiah.[55] Support for this interpretation may be found elsewhere in Lurianic literature where we learn that the erupting or opening up of the closed letter *mem* (in square Hebrew script) symbolizes the *Shekhinah*'s womb, which opens itself up for the birth of the Messiah's soul, reminiscent of the opening created by the serpent's bite in the teaching of the seventh day of Passover.[56]

In addition to this conception of Moses and Luria as begetters of the messianic soul, there is also diverse evidence suggesting that Moses, Rashbi, and Luria were all regarded as occupying messianic roles themselves. Insofar as his soul originated in *Yesod* of the *partsuf Abba* (from which *Yesod* of *Ze^cir* ultimately derived), Moses served as shepherd to the generation that left Egypt and wandered in the desert; for that generation was itself "hewn" from *Yesod* of *Abba*.[57] That is to say, the souls of the generation of the desert were branches of Moses' soul; as already intimated, their very existence was bound up with his emission of seed. Thus, while he was their "father" he was also obliged to be their redeemer (*go^el*), for he was responsible for their souls in the first place. Moses' soul was a transmigration of that of Adam, and just as Adam's emission of seed during the years in which he was separated from his wife Eve had resulted in the creation of souls in need of *tiqqun*, likewise in the case of Moses.[58] The term *go^el* in rabbinic language connotes nothing less than a messianic figure, although to be sure there are various figures representing different stages in the evolution of the messianic age. In Moses' case, he was regarded as the Messiah, son of Joseph (*Mashiah ben Yosef*), precursor of the (final) Messiah, son of David (*Mashiah ben David*). Moses' task, then, was to redeem all the soul-sparks of his generation, including those of the "mixed multitude," referring to the souls of Egyptians who sought to convert (*gerim*). Interestingly enough, in the following passage, Moses is represented as simultaneously filling the role of both father *and* mother. He carries them in his bosom as a "nursing-father" nourishes a sucking child:

> And since they [i.e., the souls of the generation of the Wilderness] are branches of [the soul of] Moses, he must be their redeemer. Therefore, the Holy One, blessed be He, pressed him [to redeem Israel from bondage] during the seven days in which he experienced the vision of the [burning] bush, as taught in the Midrash,[59] because he had to be by their side, for all of them were his actual children, and [hence] they are known as the generation of Moses. This is also the

secret meaning of "Have I conceived all this people? Have I brought them forth, that You should say to me: Carry them in thy bosom, as a nursing-father carries the sucking child, to the land which You did swear to their fathers?" [Num. 11:12].[60] Thus, they receive all their nourishment [*mezonot*] from Moses, "as a nursing-father carries the sucking child," feeding him the bread of his bosom.[61]

What is more, as we have seen, Moses' soul transmigrates in every generation anew so as to continue to carry out its mission of soul-reparation again and again. For the repercussions of Adam's sin—*his* wasteful spilling of seed[62]—manifest themselves in the generation of the Flood, the generation of the Tower of Babel, the generation of Sodom, and the generation of the Wilderness—archetypes, all of them, for *every* generation, for there is no generation without need of repair and purification, that is, *tiqqun*.

As for Shimon bar Yohai, "a spark of Moses," he, too, played the same redemptive role from the Lurianic perspective. Here Luria clearly drew on the *Zohar*'s own portrayal of Rashbi in such terms, es-pecially in connection with the Idra Rabba and the Idra Zuta. Yehuda Liebes's penetrating analysis of these *Zohar* texts demonstrates the unique redemptive function Rashbi fulfilled in the lives of his disci-ples.[63] Influenced by notions emanating from the thirteenth-century "Gnostic" circle of Spanish kabbalists, according to which the Mes-siah—who is known as *Tsaddiq* (the "Righteous" one)—manifests the grade of the *sefirah Yesod*, the Idra Rabba depicts Shimon bar Yohai as occupying "the place of the pillar" (*qaima de-ḥad samkha*). That is, he is the "foundation" of the world, the phallic center of the cosmos, through whom all existence is sustained and through whom it will be redeemed, in significant part by the guarding and disclosing of the depths of the Torah's mysteries.

As inheritor of this spiritual legacy by way of soul transmigration, Isaac Luria was likewise believed to be fulfilling a messianic role. He, too, is the "Righteous" one, the *Yesod* whose very being stands in inti-mate and harmonious relationship with *Yesod* on high, and whose ac-tions as diagnostician and physician of souls, as master of the mysteries of the Torah, were capable of facilitating the redemption of the cosmos.

Luria was the reincarnation of Adam, Abel, Moses, and Rashbi, literally occupying the exact physical place in which Shimon bar Yohai sat during the revelations of the Idra Rabba to his disciples. His disciples, like Rashbi's, were his "children," for whose spiritual nourishment and *tiqqun* he was responsible. In light of this, the notion that Luria's teachings had not been revealed since the days of Shimon bar Yohai takes on an even richer resonance, as Isaac Luria's redemptive and messianic role is explicitly articulated. Luria was a redeemer insofar as his activity had begun to usher in the messianic age. Such a role is consistent with the traditional image of the Messiah, son of Joseph:

> [T]his wisdom has been concealed from the days of Rashbi, peace be upon him, until now, as he said, "there is no permission to reveal them until the final generation." That time is now, for through our teacher, the holy, the saintly, our master, Rabbi Isaac Luria, of blessed memory, on account of the spirit of prophecy that appeared in him, our eyes have begun to become enlightened in the light of this supernal wisdom, hidden from the eyes of all living beings. This is so as to provide assistance from below, as it is said, the upper spheres need the lower, and as Rabbi Shimon bar Yohai, peace be upon him, taught, there is a need for arousal on high from below, so as to assist the arrival of the redeemer [*go'el*], so that it may take place quickly in our days. For we witness the troubles that abound, and all the signs that Rabbi Ishmael, peace be upon him, mentioned would manifest themselves on the heels of the messianic age, we have seen right now, for not one of them is missing. And [redemption will occur] by means of the revelation of the light of this wisdom, mediated through the true saintly one [i.e., Luria], peace be upon him.[64]

Explicit evidence that Luria was regarded as fulfilling the role of *Mashiah ben Yosef* may be found in an important report about a visit he made with his disciples to the graves of Shemayah and Avtalyon:

> When one recites [the blessing from the *Amidah* prayer]: "Establish in it [i.e., Jerusalem] soon the Throne of David your servant," one must accompany it with this meditative intention, which Shemayah and Avtalyon revealed to my master, of blessed memory, one day when we traveled to Gush Ḥalav in order to prostrate ourselves on

their tombs. There they themselves told him that one must concentrate upon praying on behalf of *Mashiaḥ ben Yosef*, so that one may live and not die at the hands of Armilus the wicked, during each of the three daily prayer services.[65]

The versions of this episode in the letters of Solomon Shlomiel of Dresnitz and *Pri ʿEts Ḥayyim* provide additional information pertaining to Luria's personal role in these matters. Shlomiel says that this event took place not long before Luria died and adds the following postscript by Vital: "And my teacher, of blessed memory, warned us that we should concentrate on this, and his end validated [the significance of] this warning, for my teacher, of blessed memory, died on account of our numerous and grievous sins." Both Shlomiel and the account in *Pri ʿEts Ḥayyim* indicate that at the time of the original event, the disciples had not understood what Luria meant. That is to say, after Luria's death, Vital and his disciples belatedly came to fathom the significance of Luria's warning, that he had in mind the threat to his own life as *Mashiaḥ ben Yosef*.[66]

In sum, Luria's circle of disciples believed that God, in His compassion, sends a redeemer to every generation. In their generation, too, God had not withheld a redeemer but had sent "the great rabbi, our saintly teacher, our rabbi and master, Isaac Luria . . . filled like a pomegranate with [knowledge]."[67] Moreover, the penitential remedies that Luria provided for his disciples to mend their souls had an unmistakable messianic motive: "He gave him [i.e., each of his disciples] the *tiqqun* he required for the corresponding transgression, in order to cleanse his soul, so that he could receive the divine light, as it is written [Jer. 4:14], "[O Jerusalem,] wash your heart from wickedness, that you may be redeemed."[68]

"Two Young Roes of a Doe"

Many of the exact same themes reverberate in yet another important incident that took place in wake of the occasion concerning the seventh day of Passover. According to Vital, "following these events" he asked Luria about the esoteric interpretation of the Zoharic teaching (*tosefta*) having to do with "two young roes of a doe" (*trein ʾorzalin de-ʾayalta*).[69] Luria responded by requesting that Vital not press him to reveal this "great mystery" (*sod gadol*), for he lacked permission from on high to do so. Vital's relentless insistence wore Luria down, however, and he finally revealed the mystery of the *tosefta*, with disastrous consequences:

> And after he revealed [this teaching], he said that the edict that he [would] die in the course of that same year had already been decreed as punishment for having revealed to [Vital] this mystery. "And you yourself have brought this injury about, for if you had not insisted so strenuously, I would not have revealed it to you, and they would have not punished me from heaven. I already told you many times, but you refused to listen to me. I am not concerned about myself or about my household. Rather, I am distressed on your account [plural, *ʿaleykhem*], for how can I comfort you [plural, *ʾetkhem*] without completing your *tiqqun*."[70]

Shlomiel's account of this concludes by saying that we do not know the contents of this teaching, since Hayyim Vital has kept it hidden. Thus, in contrast to the teaching given on the seventh day of Passover, where we know exactly what Luria revealed to his disciples, the contents of this teaching appear to be a matter of speculation.

A passage in Vital's diary, however, sheds some light on our narrative. Vital describes a conversation that took place, according to Vital, in the days leading up to Luria's death.[71] According to this conversation, seven days before he died Luria reminded Vital that the very first time they had met he had warned him not to reveal to others anything about Luria's own spiritual attainments and comprehension (*ʿinyano shel hasagato u-yediʿato*), inasmuch as he had come only for the purpose of Vital's perfection, so that Vital could, in turn, perfect others. He had cautioned him at that time that were he to do otherwise, he, Vital, and the world as a whole, would incur great harm.

It transpired, says Vital, that his teacher in the study of rabbinic law, Moses Alsheikh, had eventually found out about the knowledge to which Vital was privy, and pressured him to share it with him. Vital succumbed to this pressure, as a consequence of which the numbers of people coming to Luria's house to visit him greatly increased.

While Vital thought that he had performed a great deed, helping others to achieve repentance, Luria had reproved him for having done so, "for [now] I have no free time to study with you because of all those who enter."[72] He further said that Vital was responsible for a situation in which he, Luria, was being harmed, but that he did not have the heart to send them away. As time passed, says Vital, Luria had tried to dismiss them all, but they refused to leave until he was forced to confront them: "Do you wish to cause me harm so that I return to the condition of impregnation [*ibbur*] on your account?!" Still they refused to leave him alone. Three months after Luria's initial warning to Vital, Luria took him aside and told him how much harm this was causing Vital, and that had this situation not developed, he would have elevated Vital to an exceedingly exalted spiritual plane. Luria went on to tell Vital once again how harmful the sharing of these secrets with others had been to Luria, "insofar as they [i.e., the other disciples] are not yet qualified for this." Luria asserted that he nevertheless felt obligated to teach Vital, and, as a result, the others heard teachings that they were not prepared to receive.

Luria proceeded to exhort Vital not to ask him anything further in front of the others, so that they would all depart, leaving "only you, and I shall elevate you to the level above [the firmament of] *ᶜAravot*."[73] Vital averred that he was reluctant to do as Luria wished, lest he be guilty of preventing the others from achieving repentance just so that he, Vital, could benefit. Luria again tried to convince Vital by speaking to him of the importance of his soul, but Vital refused to listen, telling Luria that "whatever happens to all [the rest] will happen to me, and if they do not study [with you] neither shall I, lest they say in heaven that I did not care about all these righteous ones who entered to study because I was concerned about myself."[74] Three days after this conversation, says Vital, Luria was afflicted by the plague, "the day before the Sabbath of the [Torah] portion *Matot Masaᶜey*, on the New Moon of [the month of] Av, 5332 (1572). And on [the following] Tuesday, the fifth day of Av, he died, [entering] the life of the next world."[75]

If we leave aside for the time being the problematic question of Luria's alleged intention to dismiss his disciples, this passage from Vital's diary provides clues as to the nature of Luria's understanding of the *tosefta*, "two young roes of a doe." The secret Luria sought to avoid revealing had to do with his spiritual stature, that is to say, it concerned the nature of Luria's own soul (*ᶜinyano*).[76] But what exactly *was* the status of his soul? On this question, too, the passage in Vital's diary provides an important clue, embedded in Luria's question: "Do you wish to cause me harm so that I return to the condition of *ᶜibbur* on your account?!" As Liebes observed in his analysis of this passage, the phrase "*ᶜibbur* on your account" resonates with language used in connection with the maturation of *Zeᶜir Anpin*, which begins its development in *ᶜibbur*, that is, in the amniotic fluids of his Mother (*Imma*).[77] Liebes suggests that in identifying himself with *Zeᶜir* in its immature state of *ᶜibbur*, Luria appears to have feared the regression of his own soul, a regression that in this instance might lead to Luria's actual death.

Aside from this, the phrase "*ᶜibbur* on your account" also parallels language used by Moses (Deut. 3: 26) in speaking to Israel of *his* punishment at the hands of God, for which Israel itself was responsible: "But *YHVH* was cross with me on your account [*Ve-yitabber ᵓadonai bi le-maᶜankhem*]."[78] According to *Tiqqunei Zohar* and the *Raᶜaya Mehemna*, Moses' sin was that he had tried to repair the souls of the "mixed multitude."[79] This, of course, is similar to the sin with which Luria himself was concerned, namely, the attempt to repair the souls of disciples who were not completely worthy by sharing secrets of the Torah with them.

The significance of this is brought into high relief insofar as Luria identified thoroughly with Moses, as we have seen. Luria believed himself to be the reincarnation of Moses, potentially the last such reincarnation in this "the final generation." Just as Moses' poor judgment had brought the punishment of death and prevented him from crossing into the land of Israel, so too Luria's actions portended ominous results. In both cases, the goal was redemption. The cosmos would have been redeemed as a result of the transformation of the souls of all Israel, as well as of the "mixed multitude," such that they would have become utterly purified. Moses' own soul would itself finally have been perfected and have ceased to transmigrate. But in both cases the redeemers fell short of their goal; neither their own souls nor those of their disciples achieved perfect *tiqqun*.[80] Finally, the many connections between the teaching having to do with the seventh day of Passover and these texts are clear.

The disclosure of the deepest mysteries of the Torah is essential for *tiqqun*, but at the same time it is dangerous in the extreme. Only the confluence of the most perfect conditions can avert the peril intrinsic to the project of cosmic redemption.

Luria's messianic role is further confirmed by an altogether different source, the homiletical eulogy given by Samuel Uceda for Luria, referred to elsewhere. Organized as an exegesis of Psalm 80, the homily as a whole paints a picture of eager messianic anticipation in Safed, consistent with the widespread belief that the year 1575 would usher in the messianic age. The suffering and troubles of Israel in its exiled state were overflowing, just as they had been at the time of the deliverance from Egypt. Such suffering, according to one traditional view, was seen as a critical condition for redemption. Uceda stresses, as well, the effect of Israel's devotion and prayer at such a time upon God, who can no longer bear to see Israel suffer.[81]

As for Luria himself, Uceda writes that his students had believed that he would live until the arrival of the Messiah, and that "his days would be prolonged on account of his great and unparalleled saintliness."[82] Luria's greatness consisted in his knowledge of the secrets of the Torah, which he revealed, and on his ability to influence many to repent. Uceda may have been hinting at something even more when he spoke at the end of his homily of Luria's replacement, by reference to Psalm 80:18: "[Grant Your help to the man at Your right hand,] the one You have taken as Your own." Earlier in his sermon, these words were interpreted as referring to the Messiah, who sits at God's right hand.[83] Furthermore, Uceda asserted that Israel's troubles had multiplied, and that this *tsaddiq* had died, on account of "our many transgressions."

Luria's Disciples and the Need for Love

Although Luria's disciples felt individual responsibility for the restitution of their souls, this personal goal was clearly part of a communal endeavor. The quality of relationships among his disciples appears to have mattered as much to Luria as the private enterprise of spiritual perfection. This concern expressed itself most strikingly in the exhortation to the disciples to care for and love one another, cited in Chapter 3. According to Luria, "especially when it comes to the love of our fellows, each and every one of us must bind himself to the others as if he were one limb within the body of this fellowship."[84]

The companions constituted an organism, a body whose limbs depended on one another to function properly, and the integrity of the fellowship was compromised by the absence of love among its members. If the companions embodied the various elements of the sefirotic universe, and the quality of their relationships influenced the cosmos as a whole, divulging the deepest mysteries to those who were not completely worthy was inherently dangerous.

In fact, Luria understood his own misjudgment in revealing certain of the Torah's secrets to unfit disciples to have its parallel in what had befallen the disciples of Rabbi Akiva precisely in the period following Passover. According to a well-known rabbinic tradition:

> Rabbi Akiva had 12,000 pairs of disciples, from Gabbatha to Antipatris. And all of them died at the same time, because they did not treat one another with respect. The world remained desolate [of Torah] until Rabbi Akiva came to our masters in the south and taught the Torah to them. These were Rabbi Meir, Rabbi Judah, Rabbi Jose, Rabbi Shimon [bar Yohai], and Rabbi Eleazar ben Shammua; and it was they who revived the Torah at that time. A *Tanna*ʾ taught: All of them [i.e., the original disciples] died between Passover and Shavuot.[85]

Luria's interpretation of this tradition sheds critical light on the nature of his own mistake in teaching what he should not have to his own disciples, and on the decisive importance of the practice of love among them. The *moḥin* that flow to *Zeʿir* between Passover and the festival of Lag ba-Omer (the thirty-third day of the counting of the ʿ*Omer*) are those of harsh Judgment (*dinim qashim*). This is due to the fact that the *zivvug* that takes place in the supernal world as a result of marital relations during the ʿ*Omer* is not a "mature" one (*zivvug gamur shel gadlut*). Rather, *Zeʿir* is still in a state of "immaturity" (*qatnut*), as on the seventh day of Passover. *Zeʿir* does not achieve a state of *gadlut* once again until the festival of Shavuot.[86] In Luria's view, Akiva's disciples who "denounced and hated one another" were thus "struck down by the attribute of Judgment" precisely during this period of time, that is, a period ruled by severity."[87]

From Lag ba-Omer until the festival of Shavuot, however, the sphere of divine Compassion begins to prevail, ushering in a period of relative maturity for *Ze'ir Anpin*. Akiva's five new disciples corresponded to these superior, mature divine forces (*ḥamesh gevurot de-gadlut*), at the heart of which stood Akiva himself. In contrast to their predecessors, these disciples related to one another with respect and love, on account of which "the Torah was revived."

These ideas have their parallel in the *Zohar*, especially in connection with the Idra Rabba, which hardly escaped Luria's attention. The locus classicus for this motif in the *Zohar* is the following passage:

> When the companions came before Rabbi Shimon, he saw a sign in their faces [that there was love among them], and he said: "Come my holy children, come beloved of the King, come my cherished ones who love one another." For as Rabbi Abba once said: "All those companions who do not love one another pass from the world before their time." All the companions in the days of Rabbi Shimon loved one another in soul and spirit. That is why [the secrets of the Torah] were disclosed in his generation. As Rabbi Shimon was wont to say: "All the companions who do not love one another divert from the straight path and cause blemish to the Torah, for the Torah is love, brotherhood, and truth. Abraham loves Isaac, and Isaac loves Abraham, and they embrace each other—and they both hold Jacob in love and brotherhood, giving their spirits to one another. The companions must follow this example and not blemish [the Torah]."[88]

The words attributed here to Abba clearly resonate with the memory of Akiva's original disciples, whose failure to love one another brought such catastrophe upon them. Rashbi could divulge the secrets of the Torah to his disciples, especially on the occasion of the Idra, precisely because he ultimately decided that they were worthy—although he surely came to this decision with the most profound anxiety and ambivalence. This ambivalence was more than justified by the deaths of three of the companions, an event understood at least partially as a punishment, as already noted. Abraham, Isaac, and Jacob in this passage represent the *sefirot Ḥesed*, *Gevurah*, and *Tiferet*. Here, too, we thus see the integral relationship between harmony in the world of humanity and the world of divinity. Suffused as his imagination was with the world of Rashbi and his discipleship, Luria clearly identified with the vicissitudes of leadership and community that play such an important role in the *Zohar*'s self-consciousness. That this was the case is apparent from his belief, or perhaps more precisely, hope, that the proper conditions for revealing the mysteries of the Torah and accomplishing *tiqqun* had not existed since the days of Shimon bar Yohai until now.

Cain, Hayyim Vital, and Isaac Luria

Much of what we know about Isaac Luria and his teachings comes from the pen of his chief disciple, Hayyim Vital. But what do we know about Vital himself and his relationship to his master? And what light does Vital shed on Luria's life in the course of describing their relationship to each other? Vital himself may be said to have been obsessed with the question of his relationship to Luria. A great portion of his vast writings on the subject of metempsychosis focuses on the subject of his own complex soul-ancestry, as well as the particular role he perceived himself to have played in relationship to Luria and his fellow disciples.[89] From a certain point of view, he tells us too much about these questions. I mean by this that Vital was so self-absorbed, so fascinated by his own accomplishments and preoccupied with his failings, so caught up in what the future had in store for him, that it is not always easy, in my view, to distinguish with precision between Vital's perception of reality and the realities themselves. If nothing else, his expansive diary of visions and dreams testifies colorfully to the richness of his fantasy life. It is thus imperative to tread very carefully in any consideration of Vital's discussions of his personal status and personal relationship to Isaac Luria.

   In addition to the line of soul-ancestry that extends from Adam to Abel to Moses to Shimon bar Yohai to Isaac Luria, there is a parallel line of soul-transmigration that begins with Adam's other son, Cain, and leads ultimately to Hayyim Vital.[90] We learn that despite the fact that the *Zohar* regards Cain as having his origin in the filth produced by the serpent in the Garden of Eden, while Abel is from the "side of Adam," we should not be misled. For the *Zohar* also speaks of Cain and Abel as united in their connection to the Tree of the Knowledge of Good and Evil. As a result of Adam's sin, good and evil became thoroughly mixed together. Thus, when Cain and Abel were born they too were each composed of elements of good and evil, the difference being that Abel was primarily good, with a minor degree of evil, while Cain was primarily evil, possessing a minor degree of good. However, the positive element in Cain was extremely high in quality, given the fact that he was the firstborn son and took for himself the most superior degree of "good." In other words, despite the fact that Cain and Abel appear to have gone in completely separate directions, they are fundamentally similar, each possessing both good and evil. Ontologically speaking, they are more alike than they are different. And in one of the most strikingly paradoxical turns in Lurianic thinking, Cain's soul is actually superior to Abel's by virtue of his having been the firstborn.

Cain's soul proceeded to go through a long series of *gilgulim*, including, among many others, Esau (whereas Jacob is a reincarnation of Abel), Jethro, Nadav and Abihu, Korah, Phineas, Samson, Elkanah, Samuel, Hever the Kenite, Yael, wife of Hever the Kenite, Elijah the prophet, Elisha, King Hezekiah, Matathias the Hasmonean, Aqabyah ben Mehalalel, Yohanan ben Zakkai, Akiva ben Yosef, Yose the Galilean, Jonathan Hyrcanus, Abba Shaul, Rabban Gamaliel, Rabbi Nehorai Sabba (from the *Zohar*), Yeiva Sabba (from the *Zohar*), Hutspit the translator, Judah bar Ilai, "and also one of Rabbi Shimon bar Yohai's companions who was present at the Idra Rabba of *Naso*, but my master, of blessed memory, did not wish to reveal [his identity] to me, and I did not know why."[91] The last person on a very long list of later rabbinic and medieval figures is none other than Joseph Karo. Vital himself was a contemporary incarnation of this impressive family of souls.

Of these individuals, Yohanan ben Zakkai and Akiva play particularly crucial roles. Both of them were unlettered (*ʿamei ha-ʾarets*) for the first forty years of their lives, the reason being that their lower souls (*nefashot*) derived from the ten drops of semen that flowed from

Joseph's ten fingers, as a result of which they were seized to a certain degree by the *qelippot*, especially in the case of Akiva. This serves to explain why both of them transgressed in their younger years, and why they had to undergo transmigration. Akiva's soul derived from that of a *ger*, a proselyte to Judaism, although unlike most such souls it was of an especially exalted quality.[92]

Vital was also associated with Akiva by way of Vital's wife Hannah, insofar as Hannah's soul was the reincarnation of Kalba Savua, Rabbi Akiva's father-in-law! The latter had undergone transmigration as a woman as a result of having committed sodomy. In addition, the *nefesh* of the wife of the evil Roman governor of Judaea, Tinneus Rufus (Turnus Rufus in rabbinic literature), who later married Akiva, was impregnated within Hannah. We find that the reparation of the souls of various central figures is bound up with their wives. In Adam's case, the soul of Eve was first "married" to the serpent, that is, to the realm of evil and sexual impropriety, and then to Adam. This same soul transmigrated into Dinah, Jacob's daughter by Leah, and had originally been married to the evil Shechem ben Hamor, and subsequently to a number of other individuals, culminating in the righteous Akiva, and so forth. In each case, the woman first marries an evil man and then a righteous one. With each evolution of this soul, it becomes increasingly purified, and thus simultaneously participates in the cleansing of the soul of her righteous husband.[93]

The souls of both Yohanan and Akiva shared an identity with Moses, being aspects of the right and left "arms" of Moses' soul. This connection explains why all three men lived to the exact same age, one hundred and twenty years. It also serves to explain why Moses asked God, as rabbinic tradition suggests, why He had not chosen Akiva rather than Moses himself to receive the Torah on behalf of the children of Israel.[94] The association of Yohanan and Akiva with Moses provides the basis for Vital's own connection to Moses. Luria informed him "that my *nefesh* is connected with that of Moses, our teacher, for all the souls were included in his, especially the souls of the righteous."[95]

As with Luria, Vital's soul-ancestry also bore messianic seeds, at the center of which stood the figure of Cain. Insofar as he was Adam's firstborn, Cain was endowed with several important spiritual gifts, these being the "crown of kingship" (*keter malkhut*), "priesthood" (*kehunah*), and the "birthright" (*bekhora*).[96] Despite the fact that Cain was a sinner, partly by virtue of his father's transgressive legacy, partly on account of his own doing, as already noted, his firstborn status makes him superior to Abel. Thus while Abel's soul-ancestry leads to the Messiah, son of Joseph, Cain's soul—and the transmigratory line that derives from it—is that of the Messiah, son of David! The fulfillment of this soul's messianic promise is contingent upon its complete purification and perfection through a succession of *gilgulim* over the course of time.

Certain other individuals who participated in this line of *gilgul* are thus also described in distinctly messianic overtones. The soul of Hezekiah, king of Judah, derived from the "head" of Cain's soul, enabling the latter to begin the process of *tiqqun*.[97] Hezekiah acquired one of the three attributes that Cain had inherited from Adam as his firstborn son, *keter malkhut*. This was the basis for God's desire "to appoint Hezekiah as the Messiah."[98] Hezekiah would have fulfilled his messianic promise had he sung song's of praise before God, as King David did, for example. The relationship between the souls of King Hezekiah and Yohanan ben Zakkai is evidenced by the fact that following the latter's death it was declared: "Prepare the throne of Hezekiah, king of Judah, who attends his funeral."[99] Yohanan likewise merited the *keter malkhut* that belonged to Cain, while Rabbi Akiva's soul was also invested with that of Cain.

The direct association between Vital's soul and these predecessors is evidenced by the various ways in which they continuously show up in his dreams and visions, and even upon his forehead! We recall, for example, that Luria saw the words "Prepare a throne for Hezekiah, king of Judah" on Vital's forehead one Sabbath eve, and that on the next Sabbath eve he was able to discern the spirits of both Hezekiah and Akiva in Vital. Thus, even if only by implication, Vital himself shared in this messianic lineage. In addition, Vital's diary is filled with numerous dreams and visions in which he occupies a redemptive or messianic role.[100]

According to Vital's testimony, Luria came to Safed from Egypt for the sole purpose of ensuring the complete restoration of Vital's soul:

On the New Moon of [the Hebrew month] Adar, in the year 5331 [1571], he told me that while he was in Egypt, he began to gain his inspiration [*le-hasig hasagato*]. He was informed there [from on high] that he should go to the city of Safed, insofar as I, Hayyim, resided there, so as teach me. And he said to me that the only reason he came to Safed, may it be rebuilt and reestablished speedily, was on my account. Not only this, but even his current incarnation was for no purpose other than to bring about my perfection. He did not return [to this current generation] for himself, as he had no need to do so. He also told me that it was unnecessary for him to teach any other individuals besides me, and when I have [properly] learned, there will no longer be any reason for him to remain in this world. He also told me that my soul was superior to [those of] many of the exalted angels, and that I could ascend above the firmament of *ᶜAravot* by means of my soul, through my deeds.[101]

Luria further informed Vital that his current need for *tiqqun* stemmed, in part, from the fact that one of his most recent previous soul-incarnations, Vidal of Tolosa, author of the book *Maggid Mishneh*, had failed to believe sufficiently in the wisdom of the *Zohar*: "Thus I need to mend myself in this current *gilgul* by engaging at all times, to the greatest degree possible, in the wisdom of the *Zohar*."[102] On the other hand, since Vidal of Tolosa had accomplished so much as a scholar of Jewish law, Vital had no need now "to expend much energy in *ḥokhmat ᶜiyyun* [intensive study of religious law]." In addition, Vital, like others, had to perform *tiqqun* for transgressions that were, in one way or another, connected to various former incarnations of his soul. He was responsible, for example, for having committed the transgression of wasting his semen during the period leading up to his wedding, which he attributed to the fact that the evolution of his lower soul could be traced back to the spilling of seed on the part of Joseph.[103] Vital regarded this sin as well as what he describes as his youthful propensity for great arrogance or conceit (*gaᵓavah*) as the two primary reasons for his current incarnation, these being "the greatest sins I have committed

during my life."[104] To counter his inclination toward vanity, he had to
try and behave with the utmost humility. On one occasion, Luria told
him to mend the related sin of mocking others by fasting and wearing
sackcloth and ashes for a full month and by refraining from ridiculing
any person. Vital displays a certain degree of self-insight here, as it
seems clear from this that he recognized that this was an ongoing
problem for him, not merely a youthful transgression.

As for making restitution for having wasted his seed, he needed to
take care to have sexual relations with his wife only after midnight,
and to make sure that during sex he was on his stomach (that is, on
top), and to ensure that no drops of semen "fell outside afterwards."
He was also supposed to avoid indulging in too much conversation
with his wife during lovemaking. Finally, he was required to fast for
eighty-four consecutive days, corresponding to the eighty-four years
during which the patriarch Jacob succeeded in not wasting his seed,
until such time as he married Leah and could channel his sexuality in
the proper manner.

We saw in an earlier context that Vital also had to perform penitential exercises for having practiced alchemy at the expense of study of
Torah for a period of two and a half years, prior to having becoming
Luria's disciple.[105] This too entailed lengthy regimens of fasting and
wearing of sackcloth. Still other transgressions for which he had to
make amends, as noted, included having cursed his mother and father
when he was very young and having drunk forbidden wine with a Jew
who had committed apostasy.

Belief in transmigration must have had appeal to the extent that
one could, in effect, hold former incarnations of one's soul responsible for one's own current transgressive behavior. Nevertheless, this
does not appear to have relieved the kabbalists of Safed of a profound
sense of personal guilt and accountability. Vital sums up many of the
obstacles in his spiritual life in these words:

> These are, in brief form, the instructions that my master, of blessed
> memory, enjoined upon me, so as to gain the [heavenly] inspiration
> consistent with my soul. First, I must always behave in the following
> ways: avoiding anger, strictness, depression, arrogance, slander,
> mockery, gossip, idle conversation, and the killing of any living thing

whatsoever, even insects.[106] Instead, I have to conduct myself with humility, joyfulness, silence, and the fear of sin. I should engage in fixed study each day of Scripture, Mishnah, Talmud, and Kabbalah, along with their proper intentions, but the main thing [for me] is the study of the *Zohar*. . . . Before prayer I must cleave [to the soul of] Rabbi Akiva, of blessed memory, recalling his name ten times in a row . . . rise every night after midnight to weep on account of the exile of the *Shekhinah* [in Her aspect of] Rachel . . . and on account of the destruction of the Holy Sanctuary, the exile of Israel, and weep over [my] sins.[107]

Vital's unique relationship to Luria is suggested by his role as his teacher's "interpreter."[108] After Vital pressed him to explain the nature of his soul-history, Luria taught him that the biblical Aaron had served as spokesman for his brother Moses, since the latter was unable to speak with facility. In Moses' return to the world by way of *gilgul* in the generation of the Messiah, he still needed an "interpreter" or "translator" to assist him in teaching Israel. This interpreter is also identified as Elijah the Prophet, who still lives on as a reincarnation of Phineas, son of Eleazar, who was Aaron's son. While he does not explicitly say so, the inference is that Luria was alluding to the role that Vital had eventually come to play on his behalf. Both Phineas and Elijah were Vital's soul-predecessors, and Moses, of course, was Luria's soul-ancestor.

Along these same lines, Luria appears to have regarded Vital as occupying the role for him that either Rabbi Abba or Rabbi Eleazar (Rashbi's son) had filled for Shimon bar Yohai. We saw at the beginning of this chapter that Luria positioned Vital in the place where Abba had sat during the companions' reenactment of the Idra Rabba, at least in Vital's own version of this event. In the version in Shlomiel's letters, Vital is seated in Eleazar's place, while Jonathan Sagis is placed in Abba's position, but Vital's own account is probably to be preferred. In the *Zohar*, Abba and Eleazar are Rashbi's closest companions, often remaining with him at times when the others are not present. At the Idra Zuta, during which Rashbi revealed mysteries immediately before his death, he gave these two special responsibilities. Abba was to write down what Rashbi taught, while Eleazar would explain the teachings.[109]

Hayyim Vital and His Fellow Disciples

Not only did Hayyim Vital believe that Luria had come to Safed for
no other purpose than to mend and elevate Vital's soul; he also contended that he played an absolutely critical role in relationship to the
small community of Luria's closest disciples. Luria regarded his most
intimate students, the members of the first group, as belonging to the
fourth category of souls described earlier, so-called "old souls" that fell
directly into the *qelippot* at the time of Adam's transgressions, requiring them to undergo a series of *gilgulim*. Such souls normally spend a
period of forty days of purification within the Female Waters after
they ascend from the *qelippot*. Vital himself, however, possessed a "new
soul" belonging to the third category, those souls deriving from Cain
and Abel; such souls undergo a superior period of purification of
seven months. Vital suggests that his soul was bound up with these
other disciples in such a way that made it possible for their souls as
well to remain within *Malkhut* for this longer (and preferable) period
of seven months.[110] A portion of Vital's *ruah* was invested in each of
these individuals, and thus "all of them are nourished [*yonqim*, literally, suckled] by me, and therefore I have to try to mend them, for
my own restitution depends upon the healing of their souls."[111] Vital
claimed, then, that because part of his own soul-structure was bound
up with these individuals, the perfection of his soul was contingent
upon the spiritual maturation of their souls.

   More generally, the origin of Vital's soul in Cain imposed unique
responsibilities upon him for bringing about *tiqqun*. One who is aware
that his soul derives from Cain's, meaning that the impurity of the
snake within him is powerful, has a special obligation to do penitence.
This is because holy souls are embedded within this very impurity.[112]
Elsewhere, Vital explained this in somewhat different terms. All of the
transgressors of the current generation are akin to the "mixed multitude" of the generation that left Egypt. The souls of most of these
people go back to Cain, such that they are primarily evil and only
somewhat good. Thus, Vital, who himself derives from Cain's soul
but has extraordinary spiritual strength by virtue of his particular soul-

ancestry, is obligated to help them achieve *tiqqun*. Vital goes on to suggest that the time is ripe for the complete mending of transgressive souls, including those from previous generations that reside in the netherworld, something he can also accomplish through his actions. He can raise them out of the netherworld so that they can enter into human bodies and find restitution in this world: "The reason that I can accomplish this is because my lower soul [*nefesh*] derives from one of the main roots of Cain's lower soul, and also because I have come now, in this final generation."[113] In fact, in the week during which Luria died, says Vital, his master taught him a particular *yiḥud* for this very purpose, to raise up the sparks that still remained in the netherworld among the *qelippot*.

According to Vital, there were some individuals even in the inner circle who were spiritually superior to the rest. The souls of some were mostly good, with a small amount of evil, while the reverse was true of others. Still others were characterized by an even balance between good and evil. Through a rather curious notion of moral transference between the two groups at either extreme, those who possessed mostly good would receive the small amount of good from those who were primarily evil. On the other hand, the latter would take the minor amount of evil possessed by those who were primarily good. This would result in a complete separating out of good and evil, such that one group would become altogether good, while the other would become altogether evil. In this connection, Vital claimed that Luria had told him the following just two days before he died:

> My teacher, of blessed memory, said to me that this was his purpose in gathering them [i.e., the disciples] together, for through the fellowship and the love among the companions, they will be drawn to one another, and the good [possessed by one who is mostly evil] will transfer to one who is mostly good, thereby perfecting him [i.e., his soul]. And the small amount of evil [possessed by one who is mostly good] will transfer and join with one who is mostly evil. And, as a result, all of those who are [now] completely evil will leave [the fellowship], and those who are perfected from the side of good will remain. And my teacher, of blessed memory, informed me that for this reason it is exceedingly important for a person to commune [*yitḥaber*] with

those evil individuals who are mostly evil, possessing a minor degree
of good, to ensure that they repent, for in this way he will appropriate the good which is in them. . . . Therefore my master, of blessed
memory, cautioned me to take very great care to love the aforementioned companions of mine, and to instruct them, for in this way, I
shall be able to purify the good portion [that belongs to me], which
is bound up with them, by appropriating it, and I shall perfect myself. However, as for one who is in between, it all depends upon his
deeds, for if he desires, he can become either completely good or the
opposite.[114]

This is, to say the least, a rather unusual theory of mystical fellowship. Can it really be that one of the reasons why Luria exhorted love
among his disciples was so that Vital (and perhaps a few others) could
perfect their souls at the expense of the others? Is it true, as Vital implies here, that Luria was seeking a way to expel certain of his disciples? Before turning to these thorny questions, however, it is important to make it clear that there was considerable tension between Vital
and others. Vital claimed, for example, that Joseph Arzin told him that
he had visited Luria one Sabbath eve at midnight "out of great jealousy."[115] Arzin asked Luria why he should have to be subservient to
Vital and study with him, given the fact that Arzin was older than Vital.
Luria allegedly answered Arzin that "he [Luria] had come into the
world only in order to teach me [Vital] alone, and that all the rest of
the companions could not study even a word with him [Luria], but
that all of them had to study with me." As if to confirm the authenticity of this conversation, Vital added that he heard this report personally from Luria.

There was jealousy and strife between Vital and other disciples as
well, especially Joseph ibn Tabul. Despite the fact that ibn Tabul was
without question one of Luria's very most important disciples, Vital
placed ibn Tabul second from last on the list of members making up
the inner circle, no doubt deliberately. While Vital mentions ibn Tabul's
name a number of times in his writings, he never once cites a teaching
of Luria's in ibn Tabul's name, in contrast to his common practice of
doing so with other disciples. Most telling, perhaps, he reported a
dream, long after Luria's death, in which his former teacher in halakhic

studies, Moses Alsheikh, inquired whether it had been verified that Israel's redemption would come about through Vital. Vital answered by singing his own praises, speaking of how everyone noticed that he had recently begun to experience heavenly inspiration and visions, and that they therefore believed this to be so.[116] In what seems a complete non sequitur, Alsheikh then proceeded to ask Vital whether he was aware that Joseph ibn Tabul had had sexual difficulties in his marriage to the daughter of Yom Tov Tsahalon, on account of which "everybody spread rumors about him." To this Vital responded: "If he is [such] a wise one, as he claims, that he [supposedly] experiences *Ruah ha-Qodesh*, why has he not cured himself [*merape ʿatsmo*] of this terrible affliction [*ha-raʿah ha-gedolah*] that has befallen him?" The inference to be drawn from this is hard to avoid: Israel is going to be redeemed on account of Hayyim Vital, whose potency is evidenced by his spiritual inspiration and visions, which everybody can see. Joseph ibn Tabul, on the other hand, who *claims* heavenly inspiration, is impotent, also something that everyone sees.

Vital's less than subtle ridicule exposes a relationship of competitiveness with ibn Tabul. It is not surprising that whatever such feelings existed between these two men during their teacher's lifetime would have continued following Luria's death. We know that despite the fact that Vital vigorously defended his exclusive right to represent Luria's teachings—going so far as to hide his writings from other people—ibn Tabul composed his own versions of those teachings in a way that was original and independent of Vital. Vital must have viewed ibn Tabul's literary activities as an arrogant attempt to usurp his own authority as the sole legitimate repository and interpreter of Lurianic Kabbalah. We do not know how ibn Tabul felt about Vital.

Competition and jealousy between them was not, however, limited to the literary sphere. Both sought to succeed Luria, in the sense that each also saw himself as a teacher of the Lurianic tradition. Three years after Luria's death, in 1575, Vital formed a group of seven individuals who agreed to study Lurianic teachings with him alone and not to share them with others.[117] Needless to say, ibn Tabul was not a member of this group. Scholem speculated, in fact, that part of Vital's motivation in creating this circle was precisely to marginalize ibn Tabul.[118] We know, of course, from the letters of ibn Tabul's student Samuel Bacchi that ibn Tabul had a group of disciples as well. Whereas Vital's fellow-ship survived for a very short time, leaving no evidence that he in-spired true allegiance, ibn Tabul gained a reputation as a charismatic teacher, at least some of whose disciples were intensely attached to him. Thus, while Vital aspired to fill the vacuum left by Luria's death as the latter's successor, he clearly lacked the personal qualities to do so—despite his insistence to the contrary. It was actually ibn Tabul, not Vital, who had genuine success in this endeavor, at least for a small group of disciples who perceived in him a direct link to Luria himself. As we saw earlier, some of the exact same claims made about Luria's charismatic qualities were made about Joseph ibn Tabul. It is not hard to see how this would have been a source of tremendous frustration for Vital.

There is evidence of ill will—or at least a deprecating attitude—on Vital's part toward some of his other fellow disciples as well. In con-nection with Abraham Berukhim, for example, Vital says that he is "a forgetful person, and is unable to learn properly, with respect to both esoteric knowledge and halakhic knowledge."[119] Concerning Moses Yonah, Vital reported that he is "an exceptional sluggard and does not conduct himself properly."[120] As for Solomon Sagis, he "was jealous of me and did not want to learn this wisdom from me, but rather [di-rectly] from him [Luria]. But my teacher, of blessed memory, did not want to instruct him [and said]: 'If you do not wish to study with Rabbi Hayyim, you will never learn this wisdom during your whole life.'"[121] Finally, Vital records an incident that took place in 1572, in which, while out in the fields with Luria, he became so angry with someone that "I did not want to listen to the instruction of my teacher, of blessed memory."[122]

While all of the evidence adduced here is from Vital's point of view, we do have one particularly intriguing tradition *about* Vital attributed to Moses Yonah. It was preserved by several individuals, including Menahem de Lonzano, who reported it in the name of Abraham Monzon. According to Monzon, Moses Yonah personally told him that at the time of his dying Luria informed his disciples that they did not possess even a single teaching of his in its entirety (*haqdamah be-shlemut*). When they asked him if this was true even with respect to Hayyim Vital, Luria is said to have responded by saying that Vital knew "somewhat more." That is to say, "the little that he knows more than you is not great."[123] The significance of this evidence is that it corroborates the existence of tension between Vital and others. It also tells us that Vital's claim to possess unsurpassed knowledge of Luria's teachings was not necessarily shared by the other disciples, a matter addressed below.

If this were not enough to suggest the tension between Vital and certain of the other disciples, upon the heels of the report concerning the importance of love among the companions for the purpose of perfecting Vital's soul Vital contends that Luria had dismissed or intended to dismiss some of his students just days before he died: "My teacher, of blessed memory, told me, on the aforementioned day, that the actions of Rabbi Elijah Falkon, of blessed memory, were those of a person in the balance [between good and evil]. . . . And this is the reason why my teacher, of blessed memory, wanted to dismiss him from our fellowship."[124] Falkon, says Vital, began to lean toward the side of evil on the Sabbath eve during which "the great anger" took place involving Joseph Arzin, following which Falkon was removed from the fellowship. Luria also wanted to expel Joseph Arzin on that same day. As for Jonathan Sagis and Gedaliah ha-Levi, both of them were largely "good" and were thus not candidates for dismissal. On the other hand, there was uncertainty about the status of Isaac Kohen, who was also primarily "good." The uncertainty had nothing to do with any lack of belief on his part in Luria, but for some other reason, which, according to Vital, Luria did not wish to share with him. Samuel Uceda's status was also uncertain, even though he was primarily "good."

Others, though, were less fortunate. Vital contended that Abraham Gavriel, Shabbetai Menashe, Judah Mishan, and Joseph ibn Tabul were expelled altogether (*nidḥu le-gamrei*), although "there is still a small amount of doubt about Judah Mishan."[125] Following this, Vital alleges, Luria told him "that his intention was to dismiss [virtually] all of the companions, and that only three or four individuals would remain with him."

What should we make of these claims, particularly the allegation that Luria dismissed, or intended to dismiss, most of his disciples in the very days immediately before he died? Among other problems, Vital's contentions appear to fly in the face of the tradition according to which Luria cautioned his disciples to love one another for their collective and *mutual* benefit, with no hint whatsoever that some special advantage would accrue to Vital himself, or only to certain individuals. It is, of course, possible that Luria viewed things differently in the period right before he died. Lurianic scholarship, however, has neither raised any question about this nor challenged the veracity of Vital's claims. In my view, there are compelling reasons to treat the latter with circumspection, including the following:

1. Hayyim Vital is the only authority for these claims. As far as I am aware, there is not a shred of other direct evidence, either in reports by Luria's other disciples or in Shlomiel's letters, to corroborate his assertions. If Luria had rejected, or intended to reject, almost all of his disciples near the very end of his life, we would almost certainly expect to find such dramatic developments alluded to by Shlomiel.

2. Joseph ibn Tabul, as we have seen, remained devoted to Luria and his teachings following his master's death. He dedicated all of his subsequent writing to Lurianic Kabbalah and always referred to his teacher in the most reverential terms. Even Tabul's disciples venerated Luria as an unparalleled kabbalistic master. Does it stand to reason that this would be the case had Tabul been rejected by Luria the way Vital suggests?

3. We know that when it came to such matters as personal status and relationship to Luria, Vital was hardly an uninterested party. His claims have to be evaluated in light of the fact that he clearly had troubled relationships with quite a few of his fellow disciples, including some of those who were supposedly dismissed, and that, in general, he exhibited an exceedingly robust sense of competition. Vital was obsessively concerned with his personal relationship to Luria, and his claims were made in a highly charged polemical and emotional frame of mind. He clearly felt the need to affirm both Luria's special regard for him and his own superiority to his fellow disciples. He frequently compared himself not only to the latter but to others as well, including Joseph Karo. One self-serving diary anecdote after another about himself is recounted at the expense of the others: Luria had come to Safed only for Vital's sake; no one else would merit what he would;

no one else's inspiration compared to his; everybody would listen only to what he had to teach. Moreover, it is noteworthy that Vital continued to have problems with interpersonal relations after he left Safed and was frequently engaged in serious controversies in Jerusalem and Damascus.[126]

4. More generally, Vital exhibited what can only be considered a narcissistic personality. Even when it was not a question of who the master's favorite disciple was, Vital was relentlessly interested in the superiority of his soul and his accomplishments. His diary is a literary monument to his own greatness, autobiography as hagiographical self-celebration. Dream after dream, incident after incident testify to the wondrous nature of his soul, the unparalleled character of his spiritual attainments, and the admiration in which he was held by all manner of individuals. As with Joseph Karo—whose own diary also attests to extraordinary self-absorption and egotism—Vital stands out as a man possessed by an impressive penchant for self-aggrandizement and self-promotion. And also like Karo, Vital was simultaneously tormented by terrific self-doubt and deep feelings of inadequacy. He constantly sought confirmation by others of the claims he made about himself. In one particularly poignant expression of this need for approval, Vital remarked that "Rabbi [Joseph] Bagilar, may God preserve him, also told me that my teacher, of blessed memory, informed him about my teacher's closeness to me."[127] Given this, it seems to me to be extremely important to avoid the temptation to take at face value the things that Vital said about his fellow disciples.

5. Perhaps the most serious problem involves the incompatibility of Vital's contentions with so much else that we know about Luria's relationship to his circle of followers. If, as I have posited, Luria identified so thoroughly with Shimon bar Yohai and his fellowship, if he truly believed that he and his followers were furthering, possibly even completing the project of *tiqqun* and redemption in which Rashbi and his companions had been engaged, then we are hard-pressed to make sense of the suggestion that he sought to rid himself of virtually his entire discipleship. To do so would have amounted to an admission of complete failure. In general, it is difficult in my view to reconcile the fact that Luria attracted, embraced, and taught a group of forty or so

disciples with Vital's contention that from the very beginning of their relationship Luria had no need for or interest in students other than Vital himself.

6. It is tempting to regard the agreement of 1575, into which a number of Luria's disciples entered with Vital to study Luria's teachings with him, as evidence that Vital had been on good terms with most of them, and that they revered him without reservation. If this were the case, it might suggest that his remarks about the dismissals were credible. In my view, this agreement actually points in the opposite direction. Had Vital been so esteemed in the eyes of his fellow disciples, presumably it would not have taken three years before certain of them agreed to study with him. In addition, the language of the agreement suggests that Vital was terribly worried about their allegiance to him. It demands that they pledge their loyalty to him, that they not share what they are learning from him now or what they have learned from him in the past, or even what they learned on their own from Luria, without first receiving Vital's permission.[128] This agreement lasted at most for two years, insofar as Vital left Safed for Jerusalem in 1577.[129] Had he established a truly devoted following as Luria's acknowledged successor, it is highly unlikely that he would have picked up and left so soon. Finally, several of the signatories to this agreement, Joseph Arzin, Judah Mishan, and Samuel Uceda, were disciples who had supposedly been dismissed or been candidates for dismissal from the circle. Such a scenario requires reconciliation with the fact that Vital wanted them as students a few years later.

7. Finally, there is diverse and plentiful evidence that Isaac Luria was frustrated and dissatisfied with Vital himself. As we have seen, even according to Vital's own testimony, Luria frequently admonished him for a wide range of misbehavior, including his penchant for anger, arrogance, and ridicule of others. Indeed, as we shall see below, Luria is said to have remarked on his deathbed that there was not one completely righteous person among his disciples.

Vital's claims about Luria's intentions concerning his fellow disciples are not disproved, of course, by any of these considerations—not even by all of them taken together. At the very least, however, they ought to raise serious suspicions.[130] Although I doubt we shall ever know the

Figure 9. The tomb of Isaac Luria, with the grave of Solomon Alkabets to the right. Courtesy Aaron Fine, photographer.

truth with any certainty, my own view is that Vital may have been engaged in a certain degree of wishful thinking and may have exaggerated. On the basis of evidence discussed in this chapter, it seems clear enough that Luria *was* dissatisfied with at least some of his students, even perhaps with his circle of disciples as a whole, feeling that they had failed to live up to his greatest expectations, and that he regarded them as too given to quarreling among themselves. It is altogether possible, as Vital contends, that Luria was thinking about replacing some of his disciples with others. Various texts certainly intimate grave uncertainty and anxiety on Luria's part about revealing his teachings to unworthy individuals. And it is also evident, aside from Vital's self-adulation, that Luria did regard him as having a special, possibly even messianic, role to play. Perhaps Luria was seeking to transfer his own responsibilities to Vital, especially if he knew himself to be dying. It may be that toward the end of his life he increasingly allowed Vital to instruct the others. Nevertheless, it is easy to imagine how tempted Vital might have been to assert his own supremacy over them in the wake of Luria's sudden and premature death, in what appears to have been an atmosphere of great despair and perhaps intense rivalry.

Death by a Kiss

According to Vital, as he was about to die Luria told Isaac Kohen that "had I found even one completely righteous [*tsaddiq gamur*] person among you, I would not be departing this world before my time."[131] He further told Kohen to convey to the others that they should from that day on desist from studying the wisdom that he had taught them, "for they have not understood it properly." Only Hayyim Vital might engage in this study, which he had to do in a concealed manner. When Kohen replied, "[W]e no longer have any hope [then]," Luria responded: "[I]f you are deserving, I shall come [back] and teach you." Isaac Kohen asked how he would teach them once he had died, whereupon Luria reproached him for inquiring into the mystery of whether he would appear to them in dreams, while they were awake, or in visions. Finally, he told Isaac to leave, "for you are a priest [*kohen*], and my time has arrived, and there is no time to elaborate further about anything, and he [Isaac Kohen] left quickly. Before he crossed the threshold, he opened his mouth, and his soul left him by a kiss, may his memory be a blessing."[132] In a different version, also attributed to Vital, Luria is said to have explained that if the disciples merited it, he would return to teach them "in dreams, or [while they are] in a waking state, by *ʿibbur* ['impregnation'], or by some other means."[133]

In one of Shlomiel's letters, the story of Luria's death follows immediately upon the account of the events having to do with the *tosefta* of the "two young roes."[134] According to Shlomiel, Luria organized communal living quarters for his closest circle of ten disciples, along with their wives. After a while the wives fell to arguing with one another, which caused hostility among the men as well. Luria cautioned them about the importance of their loving one another and maintaining peaceful relations. Nevertheless, the disciples continued to argue, and Luria perceived a sign that his fate had been sealed. He told Vital that this would not have happened had it not been for the arguing that had taken place that very day between the disciples, "for whenever there had been peace among them, the accuser [i.e., the evil one] had no point of entry." "And thus, on account of our many transgressions, the academy on high requested our teacher and rabbi, the crown of our head, may his memory be a blessing, at that very time."

Elsewhere in this same letter, Shlomiel gives an account of Luria's death that he received directly from Gedaliah ha-Levi, one of Luria's close disciples. Before his death, Luria had told his disciples that he would soon return to this world, and Shlomiel adds that Vital was even now still awaiting Luria's reincarnated self, who would reveal all the (remaining) mysteries.[135]

In Vital's account, found in *Shaʿar ha-Gilgulim* and *Sefer ha-Ḥezyonot*, he asserts his exclusive right to continue to study Luria's teachings. On the other hand, all of the versions—even Vital's—intimate the possibility that Luria would return to the disciples as a group, one way or other, should they merit it. These narratives thus suggest that although bereft by the sudden loss of their teacher, the disciples appear to have faced his death with the hope of his returning to them. It is noteworthy, in my view, that Shlomiel's accounts do not mention Vital's special status, single him out in any way, or say anything about intentions on Luria's part to dismiss members of the fellowship.

Vital's description of Luria having died by a kiss is of the utmost interest. Among other things, it links Luria yet again with Moses and with the circle of Shimon bar Yohai in the *Zohar*. According to a talmudic tradition, Moses, Aaron, and Miriam all died by a kiss from God, that is, "by the mouth of the Lord" (Num. 33:38).[136] A midrashic tradition, based upon the words "let him kiss me with the kisses of his mouth" from the Song of Songs (1:2), goes even further by teaching that, in addition to the aforementioned three, all righteous persons die by God's kiss.[137] The erotic nature of such a kiss is implicit in the use of the unabashedly sexual language of the Song of Songs and evidenced indirectly by the rabbinic explanation concerning why the Torah does not explicitly state that Miriam was kissed "by the mouth of the Lord," namely, that "it would be disrespectful to do so." Such a manner of dying is an expression of divine love, bestowed upon the especially pious who study the Torah and faithfully observe its precepts.

As noted earlier, the deaths of Rabbis Yose, Hizkiyah, and Yesa during the Idra Rabba were also perceived to be rapturous events, in which their souls "departed with a kiss."[138] At the moment of their deaths, these three enjoyed the most intimate relationship to God by "cleaving" to Him. In the words of a heavenly voice: "With how much greater delight did their souls cleave to the uppermost realms when they were taken from this world. Blessed is their portion, for they have ascended in complete perfection." Such a death is tantamount to passing over to true life, as confirmed by a second voice, which could be heard saying: "But you that cleave to the Lord, your God, are alive every one of you this day" (Deut. 4:4). Moreover, not only did their deaths accomplish personal *tiqqun*, but we may infer that they also contributed to the process of cosmic *tiqqun*, the deeper goal toward which the Idra Rabba was directed. We have seen elsewhere in the *Zohar* that the death of a righteous person constitutes a surrender of the soul, an act that stimulates the Female Waters and arouses the passion of the *Shekhinah* for Her Husband. Thus, exposition of the mysteries of the Torah, followed by the ecstatic departure of the soul, is tantamount to a sexual act that serves to restore love on high between the masculine and feminine gradations of divinity.

Shimon bar Yohai's death—described at the end of the Idra Zuta—accomplished the same thing, but to an even more profound degree than in the case of his three disciples.[139] In his discourse, Rashbi describes the supernal male and female sexual organs, followed by a description of the divine seed itself, called "life," which issues from *Yesod*, and with which Shimon bar Yohai is himself identified! In overtly sexualized language, Rashbi's death is depicted as the emergence of life from *Yesod*—which Rashbi himself embodies—into the *Shekhinah*. Indeed, he died in the very midst of uttering the word "life." His death, then, is tantamount to sexual orgasm, the effect of which is to bring about messianic *tiqqun* (at least momentarily) at every level of existence. Indeed, the death of Shimon bar Yohai was ultimately a cause for affirmation and celebration by his companions.

It is precisely these convictions that would have helped shape the understanding of Luria's death on the part of his disciples. While our sources do not go beyond describing his death as having taken place "by a kiss," the use of this expression had to have been suffused with the mythic associations of earlier rabbinic and Zoharic traditions. Luria himself, as we have seen, had conveyed to his disciples a rich and varied set of teachings, according to which both the contemplative and physical death of the righteous contributed to the healing of the cosmos. Indeed, this is one of the most central motifs in Lurianic teaching. Presumably, the death of the singular "Righteous One" of the "final messianic generation," the embodiment of divine generativity (*Yesod*), whose knowledge of the mysteries of the Torah and whose saintliness had not been seen since Shimon bar Yohai, could hardly accomplish any less. Isaac Luria's death assuredly left his disciples grieving and bereft, and uncertain as to where to turn and what to do, but perhaps they took a degree of consolation from the confidence that his departure was in some partial measure an act of cosmic restitution, and from the hope that he might yet return to them in the future to complete this task.

*

One of the primary goals of this study has been to demonstrate that the significance of Lurianic Kabbalah must be sought through a focus on Isaac Luria himself and his relationship to his fellowship. Suffused as his consciousness was with the figure of Shimon bar Yohai and *his* fellowship as portrayed in the *Zohar*, Luria appears to have been drawn to the Galilee in a quest to immerse himself in the physical and spiritual environment that they had inhabited. While he may already have possessed some sense of personal kinship with Shimon bar Yohai when he arrived in Safed, the full-fledged identification with Rashbi and his circle that I have described presumably evolved only gradually. It is impossible to know precisely what ambitions Luria harbored when he journeyed from Egypt to the land of Israel. But Moses Cordovero's death in 1570 left a vacuum of leadership among the kabbalists of Safed, which Luria was able to fill by virtue of the power of his extraordinary personality and his deeply imaginative teachings. Indeed, on both of these accounts, he made a more striking impression than did Cordovero, the latter's immense influence notwithstanding.

Luria may have been ambivalent about having students in the first place. This may partially explain why only a relatively small number of them seem to have had ongoing intimate access to him. He clearly was an elitist in the sense that he had little interest in teaching large numbers of people in public. From everything we can tell, he was not inclined toward a public role, but preferred to study with and teach a small coterie of select individuals, again, in replication of the pattern depicted in the *Zohar*. While he was unquestionably preoccupied with the circumstances and destiny of the Jewish people as a whole, he believed that the road to cosmic redemption required the commitment primarily of a small group of individuals. Thus, the community that mattered most to Luria was his own immediate circle of disciples, whose souls he sought to mend and whose spiritual maturation he cultivated, just as he hoped they would, in turn, help facilitate the mending of the cosmos. Whatever misgivings and doubts he may have had about them, our sources leave us with the impression that he cared intensely about his followers' spiritual development. For he saw in his fellowship—especially his most intimate disciples—a *microcosm* of the world of the divine, in which he stood at the center. While Hayyim Vital played a special role for Luria, the latter's vision entailed not just a *single* disciple but a group in loving and harmonious relationship to one another. It seems, alas, that even this small group did not live up to his high expectations, and that not even one of them turned out to be "completely righteous." As we have seen, there is evidence that despite Luria's exhortations, at least some of the members of the fellowship were quarrelsome with, or jealous of, one another, although most of what we know about this involved Vital's relationship with certain of his fellow disciples. Thus, social tensions played a significant role in the life of this brotherhood.

The two most prominent categories that Luria drew upon to express himself were those of the erotic, on the one hand, and life and death, on the other. These categories are thickly woven together in a complex and wide array of ways in Lurianic discourse. At the mythic level, notions of gender and sexuality surface, for example, in connection with the motif of the Breaking of the Vessels. We saw that in certain accounts the emission of divine seminal fluids that were "wasted" by not being contained in the feminine became transformed into female sexual secretions, which assumed the character of divine Judgment. The seven lower vessels, which ultimately shattered, contained flawed divine light that emanated from the "toenails" of *Adam Qadmon*. In replication of this misuse of masculine vitality, Adam and others had likewise expended their sexual energy in ways that had various negative results. These included the birth of "demonic" offspring, and the entrapment of soul-sparks in the realm of the *qelippot*, awaiting their liberation and purification. From one perspective, the flawed character of existence as a whole can be traced back to misuse of masculine sexuality.

But in characteristically paradoxical fashion, Luria also taught that while under certain circumstances such use of sexuality can have destructive consequences, under other circumstances it can bear fruitful results. Thus, the "wasted" seed of extraordinary individuals in the course of Jewish history serves as protective soul-garments within the realm of the *qelippot*, and thereby plays a critical role in the processes of *tiqqun*. Indeed, it is precisely the same persons whose transgressive behavior resulted in the entanglement of good and evil who are responsible for the *redemption* of those souls, as we have seen. They have the unique responsibility to rectify transgression whose roots go back to the very beginnings of the cosmic processes. Similarly, we see beneficial effects in connection with the ritual of *nefilat ʾappayim*, where the Lurianic adept was expected to expend his erotic energy in an act of ecstatic death for the purpose of recovering sparks of light in the netherworld. Contemplative, imagined death on the part of perfectly righteous individuals actually serves to rescue sparks of life from the realm of death. These paradoxes appear to have been absolutely central to Luria's way of understanding human existence: Death is normally associated with the demonic and the unholy, but an intentional act of death can *extricate* the holy from the demonic. Improper sexual activity in its various forms gives power to the forces of the "Other Side," while, under the right conditions, emission of seed uncontained by the female is life-giving.

Such paradoxical constructions come together, as we have seen, in the context of still another paradox, having to do with the disclosure of the esoteric secrets of the Torah. The revelation of the Torah's ultimate mysteries is fraught with danger; yet their unfolding is a requisite, intrinsic feature of the processes of *tiqqun*. Under the wrong circumstances, such revelation brings death, while under propitious circumstances, it constitutes an erotically charged act of life-giving nourishment. The vitality of Lurianic mysticism, simultaneously at the level of mythic imagination and ritual performance, is grounded in these dialectical tensions. Moreover, the relationship between Luria and his disciples was shaped in dynamic ways by precisely these same tensions.

Yet another tension—in my view related to those already identified—has to do with Luria's relationship to worldly existence and to the world of nature. On the one hand, his cosmogonic teachings exhibit an anticosmic dualism in which the material world is deprecated in favor of a divine one from which all being derives. The material world and the dark realm of the *qelippot* are bound up with each other, a consequence of the shattered vessels and of human transgression. As a result, life is to be directed toward returning divine light in all its forms to its transcendent, primordial origins. Cosmic redemption amounts to the end of material existence and the restoration of a completely spiritualized one. Nevertheless, these views did not translate into an utter devaluation of the natural world. On the contrary, the natural world for Luria was a means by which to encounter the divine. This expressed itself in a variety of ways. Luria, as we saw, was able to discern the meaning of the language of animals, particularly birds, and to discern the light that inhabits even inanimate phenomena in nature. He was sensitive about the treatment of animals, believing that even they were inhabited by souls, and he took care to avoid the killing even of insects. He was intimately familiar with the healing properties of plants and vegetation. And like others in sixteenth-century Safed, he embraced the sacred topography of the Galilee, teaching his disciples out in the fields as much as he did in the study house. This is not to romanticize Luria's relationship to the natural world, but to suggest that it was complex. As a person who believed in the sentience of natural phenomena, and as one whose intuitive capacities were finely honed, he was attuned to the divine vitality that he regarded all of nature as manifesting.

Nor did his views about the material world imply a disregard for the importance of the social order and for the significance of interpersonal relations. Even though I suggested earlier that Luria's preoccupation with the restoration of the divine worlds appears to have relegated more ordinary human concerns to the periphery, this does not mean that he did not take social responsibilities seriously. In fact, the healing of the cosmos depended in large part upon virtuous behavior in the social realm, as evidenced by his ethical concerns, adduced throughout this study. This expressed itself in Luria's advocacy of humility, generosity toward and sensitivity to the feelings of others, and most strikingly in his intense striving to encourage his disciples to treat one another well, to love one another as if they were a single body.

It is ironic in the extreme that while Luria clearly desired that his teachings remain concealed following his death, in fact, accounts of them multiplied, and they eventually came to relatively wide public attention through various teachers and a maze of writings. Hayyim Vital himself would, for a short while, continue to teach certain of Luria's disciples, although as far as we can tell, with rather limited success. Vital's great rival, Joseph ibn Tabul, appears to have accomplished more in this regard. Meanwhile, still others, including some who had personally studied with Luria and many who had not, preserved, elaborated upon, transformed, and disseminated his metaphysical teachings and ritual practices.

Even without his physical presence, and despite his own desire to have his teachings concealed, the dynamic forces that Luria unleashed during his brief but extraordinary life continued to reverberate for centuries to come in a wide range of ways, and in diverse communities throughout the Jewish world. Isaac Luria's intense personal striving to cleanse and purify the soul, to redeem sparks of light from the depths of the material domain, to comprehend the innermost mysteries of the Torah, to forge loving community, and to heal the cosmos, animated Jewish religious life well into the eighteenth century. Remarkably enough, even as the twenty-first century dawns, a good many contemporary Jews continue to drink from Luria's well, inspired by the dream that collective human effort can mend a broken world.

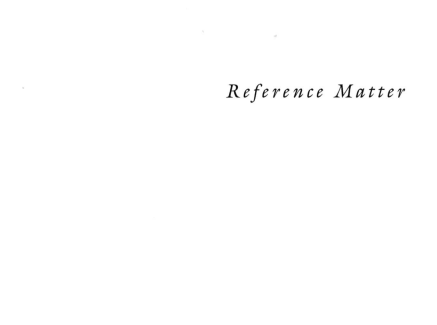

Reference Matter

Notes

Introduction

1. Israel Sarug (or Saruq) taught his version of Lurianic Kabbalah in Italy between approximately 1592 and 1599. The appearance of Lurianic manuscripts in Italy even prior to Israel Sarug's activities there was demonstrated by Joseph Avivi, "Lurianic Writings in Italy Prior to 1620" (in Hebrew), ʿAlei Sefer 11 (1984): 91–134. Sarug's version of Lurianic teachings was published for the first time as Limmudei ʾAtsilut in Lemberg (Lvov) in 1850, ironically enough, under Hayyim Vital's name, a fate that befell certain other writers as well. The question of whether Israel Sarug was actually a personal disciple of Isaac Luria's or instead learned Lurianic Kabbalah indirectly has animated kabbalistic scholarship for some time. Gershom Scholem argued, among other things, that insofar as Sarug's name is never mentioned in the sources associated with Luria's known disciples, especially in the most important lists of these individuals recorded by Hayyim Vital, Sarug's contention that he was Luria's disciple is unfounded. Ronit Meroz, on the other hand, has written a series of articles on this subject in which she argues, persuasively in my view, that Sarug had indeed known Luria personally. Meroz counters Scholem's view in various ways, including the argument that the lists contained in Vital's writing derive from a relatively late date, insofar as we know that Vital did not begin to study with Luria until some time, perhaps nine months, after the latter arrived in Safed. This leaves open the possibility that Sarug had indeed been a personal disciple during Luria's early period in Safed, in the months before Vital took up with him. On this issue, see Gershom Scholem, "Israel Sarug: Student of the Ari?" (in Hebrew), Zion 5 (1940): 214–43; David Tamar, Meḥqarim be-Toldot ha-Yehudim be-ʾErets Yisrael u-be-ʾItalyah (Jerusalem: Rubin Mass, 1973), p. 163; Ronit Meroz, "R. Israel Sarug, Student of the Ari: Reconsidered Anew" (in Hebrew), Daʿat 28 (1992): 41–50; id., "An Anonymous Commentary on ʾIdra Rabba by a Member of the Sarug School, or: 'What Is the Relationship Between Sarug and His Colleagues, and Ergas, Spinoza, and Others?'" (in Hebrew), Meḥqarei Yerushalayim 12 (hereafter MY) (1997): 207–377; Moshe Idel, "Between the Kabbalah of Jerusalem and the Kabbalah of Israel Sarug" (in Hebrew), Shalem 6 (1992): 165–73.

2. Da Fano's kabbalistic works include *ʿAsarah Maʾamarot* (Venice, 1597), *Kanfei Yonah* (Korecz, 1786), and *Gilgulei Neshamot* (Prague, 1688). Delmedigo's kabbalistic writings were published as *Matsref la-Ḥokhmah* (Basle, 1629) and *Novelot Ḥokhmah* (Basle, 1631). Herrera authored two kabbalistic treatises composed in Spanish, *Puerto del Cielo* and *Casa dela Divinidad*, in Amsterdam between 1620 and 1630. The former was translated into Hebrew in a highly abridged version and published by Isaac Aboab de Fonseca under the title *Shaʿar ha-Shamayim* (Amsterdam, 1655).

3. A considerable body of literature has focused on the kabbalistic writings of these Italian scholars, a fact that itself serves to illustrate how the repercussions of Lurianic Kabbalah have received at least as much attention as Luria's original teachings themselves. See Moshe Idel, "Major Currents in Italian Kabbalah," in D. Ruderman, ed., *Essential Papers on Jewish Culture in Renaissance and Baroque Italy* (New York: New York University Press, 1992), pp. 351–57; id., "Differing Conceptions of Kabbalah in the Early Seventeenth Century," in B. Septimus and I. Twersky, eds., *Jewish Thought in the Seventeenth Century* (Cambridge, Mass.: Harvard University Center for Jewish Studies, 1987), pp. 138–39; Isaiah Tishby, "The Tension Between Lurianic Kabbalah and the Kabbalah of Moses Cordovero in the Writings of Rabbi Aaron Berekhiah of Modena" (in Hebrew), in id., *Ḥiqrei Kabbalah u-Sheluḥoteha* (Jerusalem: Magnes Press, 1982), 1: 177–254; Alexander Altmann, "Notes on the Development of the Kabbalah of Rabbi Menachem Azariah of Fano" (in Hebrew), in J. Dan and J. Hacker, eds., *Sefer Yishayahu Tishby* (Jerusalem: Magnes Press, 1986); id., "Lurianic Kabbalah in a Platonic Key: Abraham Cohen Herrera's *Puerta del Cielo*," in B. Septimus and I. Twersky, eds., *Jewish Thought in the Seventeenth Century* (Cambridge, Mass.: Harvard University Center for Jewish Studies, 1987), pp. 1–37; Nissim Yosha, "Abraham Cohen Herrera's Philosophical Interpretation of Lurianic Kabbalah" (in Hebrew) (Ph.D. diss., Hebrew University, Jerusalem, 1991); id., "The Lurianic Concept of Prophecy in the Writings of Abraham Cohen Herrera" (in Hebrew), *MY* 10 (1992): 389–421; Gershom Scholem, *Abraham Cohen Herrera and His Book "The Gate of Heaven": His Life, Writings, and Influence* (in Hebrew) (Jerusalem: Bialik Institute, 1978); Reuven Bonfil, "Halakhah, Kabbalah and Society: Some Insights into Rabbi Menahem Azariah da Fano's Inner World," in B. Septimus and I. Twersky, eds., *Jewish Thought in the Seventeenth Century* (Cambridge, Mass.: Harvard University Center for Jewish Studies, 1987), pp. 39–61; David Ruderman, *Jewish Thought and Scientific Discovery in Early Modern Europe* (New Haven, Conn.: Yale University Press, 1995), pp. 118–52.

4. Horowitz's major kabbalistic work was *Shefaʿ Tal* (Hanau, 1612). This book was based on a combination of the writings of Moses Cordovero and (to a lesser extent) Isaac Luria. Bacharach was the author of a highly important work, *ʿEmeq ha-Melekh* (Amsterdam, 1648). Based significantly on Israel Sarug's version of Lurianic teachings, Bacharach's work exerted considerable influence on a wide range of later kabbalists. See Gershom Scholem, *Kabbalah* (Jerusalem: Keter Press, 1974),

pp. 394–95; Yehuda Liebes, "Toward a Study of the Author of ʿEmeq ha-Melekh: His Personality, Writings and Kabbalah" (in Hebrew), *MY* 11 (1993): 101–37. With respect to the aforementioned Italian circle, as well as to these authors, I am *not* seeking to suggest that knowledge of Luria's mythic teachings became widespread in the seventeenth century, but rather to indicate that they took root in certain important new ways. I am in substantial agreement on this question with Moshe Idel, who has persuasively contested Scholem's view that Lurianic Kabbalah was widely diffused in the first half of the seventeenth century. Idel has shown that knowledge of Luria's complex mythic and theosophic system was limited in the seventeenth century to relatively small numbers of sophisticated authors and teachers. His most elaborate account of this question is found in his "'One from a Town, Two from a Clan': The Diffusion of Lurianic Kabbalah and Sabbateanism: A Re-Examination," *Jewish History* 7, 2 (Fall 1993): 79–104.

5. Moshe Idel, *Kabbalah: New Perspectives* (New Haven, Conn.: Yale University Press, 1988), p. 259. However, Idel vigorously rejects Gershom Scholem's longstanding argument that Sabbateanism as a whole, and especially its messianic ideology, was intimately connected with the dissemination and popularity of Lurianic Kabbalah. Whereas Scholem contended that the messianic elements of Lurianic Kabbalah played a decisive role in the success of the Sabbatean movement, Idel has argued, among other things, that insofar as knowledge of Lurianism was limited in the first half of the seventeenth century to members of the elite, it had nothing to do with the appeal of Sabbateanism among the masses (see n. 4 above). More generally, Idel has contested Scholem's view that Lurianic Kabbalah served as the central basis not only for Sabbateanism but for Hasidism as well (see n. 7 below). See Idel, *Kabbalah*, pp. 257–60; id., "'One from a Town, Two from a Clan.'" Sabbatai Sevi himself was uninterested in the complex theosophical system that Luria had taught. On this, see Yehuda Liebes's discussion of Sabbatai Sevi's disavowal of Lurianic theology in favor of a more personal conception of God, in his "Sabbatai Zevi's Religious Faith," in id., *Studies in Jewish Myth and Jewish Messianism* (Albany: State University of New York Press, 1993), pp. 109–10. For Scholem's own views on this question, see his *Sabbatai Sevi: The Mystical Messiah* (Princeton, N.J.: Princeton University Press, 1973), pp. 66–93 and passim. For evidence of the pervasive use of the language of Lurianic myth by Nathan of Gaza, see also Abraham Elqayam, "The Mystery of Faith in the Writings of Nathan of Gaza" (in Hebrew) (Ph.D. thesis, Hebrew University, Jerusalem, 1993).

6. See Scholem, *Sabbatai Sevi*, pp. 290–97; Elqayam, "Mystery of Faith," pt. 2.

7. See Moshe Idel, *Hasidism: Between Ecstasy and Magic* (Albany: State University of New York Press, 1995), esp. introduction, pp. 1–30, and passim.

8. Rachel Elior, "Lurianic Kabbalah, Sabbateanism, and Hasidism: Historical Sequence, Spiritual Affinity, and Differences of Identity" (in Hebrew), *MY* 12 (1997): 379–97, esp. 389–91; id., *The Paradoxical Ascent to God* (Albany: State University of New York Press, 1993), pp. 79–91. See, in addition, Arthur Green, *Menahem Nahum*

of Chernobyl (New York: Paulist Press, 1982), pp. 14–16; id., "Hasidism: Discovery and Retreat," in P. Berger, ed., *The Other Side of God: A Polarity in World Religions* (Garden City, N.Y.: Anchor Press/Doubleday, 1981), pp. 114–16; Rivka Schatz Uffenheimer, *Hasidism as Mysticism* (Princeton, N.J.: Princeton University Press; Jerusalem: Magnes Press, Hebrew University, 1993), pp. 204–14, 361–62, and passim; Miles Krassen, *Uniter of Heaven and Earth: Rabbi Meshullam Feibush Heller and the Rise of Hasidism in Eastern Galicia* (Albany: State University of New York Press, 1998), pp. 81–93, and passim.

9. As was the case with the dissemination of Luria's theoretical and mythological teachings, the rituals, customs, and liturgical innovations emanating from the Lurianic school also took quite a while before they spread to various parts of the Jewish world. Although collections of Lurianic customs circulated in manuscripts not long after Luria's death, the first printing of such rituals did not occur until the beginning of the second half of the seventeenth century with the anonymous publication in Prague of *Shulḥan Arukh ha-Ari* (The "Set Table" of the Ari), in 1660. This book was based upon the work of Jacob Zemach who collected such materials in Damascus in the 1630s, drawing on the Lurianic writings of Hayyim Vital. Attesting to its popularity, *Shulḥan Arukh ha-Ari* was reprinted numerous times: in Frankfurt in 1691; in Amsterdam in 1709; in Lemberg (Lvov) in 1788, 1850, 1859, and 1861; in Slavuta in 1793; in Kapust in 1810; in Sudylkov in 1811; in Amsterdam in 1848; in Jerusalem in 1867; and in Kraków in an undated edition. Zemach, who pursued Kabbalah in Safed, Damascus, and Jerusalem during the first half of the seventeenth century, was the central figure in the editing and disseminating of such materials. Even more popular than *Shulḥan Arukh ha-Ari* was his book *Nagid u-Metsaveh*, published for the first time in Amsterdam in 1712 and no fewer than seventeen times altogether by 1907. It was published four times in Zolkiew (Ukraine) alone between 1756 and 1800. On Zemach, see Gershom Scholem, "On the Life of the Kabbalist Jacob Zemach and His Literary Activities" (in Hebrew), *QS* 26 (1950): 185–94; id., "Remarks on the Article by Dr. Zanah on Rabbi Jacob Zemach," *QS* 27 (1951): 107–10; Zev Gries, *Sifrut ha-Hanhagot* (Jerusalem: Bialik Institute, 1989), pp. 16, 80–91.

Lurianic liturgical rites and prayers were collected by Nathan Nata Hannover (d. 1683) in his widely popular treatise *Shaʿarei Tsiyon*, published originally in Prague in 1662 and reprinted 119 more times throughout Europe by 1863! It was especially popular among printers in Amsterdam and Venice, where it was published approximately 13 and 6 times, respectively. Lurianic penitential rites, *Tiqqunei Teshuvah*, appeared as early as 1595 in Venice, under the title *Marpe le-Nefesh*. On the role of these penitential rites, see Jacob Elbaum, *Teshuvat ha-Lev u-Kabbalat Yesurim* (Jerusalem: Magnes Press, 1993), pp. 137–51.

An important vehicle for the dissemination of Lurianic prayers and meditative intentions (*kavvanot*) to accompany prayers (and those in the Lurianic style) were prayer books designed specifically for this purpose or that to some degree incorporated Lurianic ritual. These included, among others, Isaiah Horowitz's *Shaʿar ha-Shamayim* (Amsterdam, 1717), *Shaʿarei Raḥamim* (Salonika, 1741), *Ḥesed le-ʾAvraham* (Smyrna [Izmir], 1764), *Mishnat Gur ʾAryeh* (Königsburg [Kaliningrad], 1756), *Siddur ha-Ari* of the kabbalists of the Brody *kloyz* (Zolkiew, 1781), and the Lurianic prayer book of Shalom Sharabi, *Nehar Shalom* (Salonika, 1806), which achieved widespread popularity in much of the Near East and in North Africa. See Ismar Elbogen, *Jewish Liturgy: A Comprehensive History*, trans. Raymond P. Scheindlin (Philadelphia: Jewish Publication Society, 1993), pp. 291–95; Stefan C. Reif, *Judaism and Hebrew Prayer* (Cambridge: Cambridge University Press, 1993), pp. 240–55; Moshe Hallamish, "The Confrontation with the Obligation of the *Kavvanot*" (in Hebrew), *MY* 12 (1997): 217–57, esp. 227–50. On the (relatively limited) role of Lurianic teachings in the work of Isaiah Horowitz, see Elliot R. Wolfson, "The Influence of Luria on the Shelah," *MY* 10 (1992): 423–48; and Miles Krassen, *Isaiah Horowitz* (New York: Paulist Press, 1996), pp. 5–10.

The *tiqqunim* were enormously popular. *Tiqqun Ḥatsot* was published for the first time in Kraków in 1638, and around 42 more editions had appeared by 1863. *Tiqqun Leil Shavuʿot,* originally published separately in Frankfurt am Main in 1728, had appeared in 43 more printings by 1863, in addition to being bound together with *Tiqqun Leil Hoshanah Rabbah* in 89 editions. On the Lurianic ritual of the midnight vigil, see Gershom Scholem, *On the Kabbalah and Its Symbolism* (New York: Schocken Books, 1965), pp. 146–50; Shaul Maggid, "Conjugal Union, Mourning, and Talmud Torah in R. Isaac Luria's *Tikkun Ḥazot,*" *Daʿat* 36 (1996): xvii–xlv; Moshe Idel, *Messianic Mystics* (New Haven, Conn.: Yale University Press, 1998), pp. 308–20. For the bibliographical data concerning the printing of the Lurianic books mentioned here, and for much of the other bibliographical information found in this study, I have relied primarily upon Y. Vinograd, ed., *ʾOtsar ha-Sefer ha-ʿIvri* (Thesaurus of the Hebrew Book) (Jerusalem: Institute for Computerized Bibliography, 1995).

10. In addition to the prayer book mentioned in n. 9, Lurianic-based works by Sharabi include *Reḥovot ha-Nahar* (Salonika, 1806) and *ʾEmet ve-Shalom* (Salonika, 1806), composed of glosses to Hayyim Vital's *ʿEts Ḥayyim*, published subsequently as part of Vital's *ʿEts Ḥayyim* (Salonika, 1842; Jerusalem, 1866–67). On the Bet El community, *ʾAhavat Shalom*, and Sharabi, see Louis Jacobs, *Jewish Mystical Testimonies* (New York: Schocken Books, 1977), pp. 192–207; Shraga Weiss, *Ḥokhmei ha-Sefardim be-ʾErets Yisrael* (Jerusalem: Rubin Mass, 1981), pp. 117–63.

11. This observation has also been made by Yoram Jacobson, "The Aspect of the 'Feminine' in the Lurianic Kabbalah," in P. Schäfer and J. Dan, eds., *Gershom Scholem's "Major Trends in Jewish Mysticism" Fifty Years After* (Tübingen: Mohr, 1993), p. 239: "In spite of its profound influence on both Jewish thought and history, the Lurianic Kabbalah has not had much success on the stage of modern scholarly research: In comparison with all other important fields of Kabbalah . . . the negligence of the Lurianic teachings can easily be seen."

12. Gershom Scholem, *Major Trends in Jewish Mysticism* (Jerusalem: Schocken Publishing House, 1941; rev. ed., 1946; 3d rev. ed., New York: Schocken Books, 1954), pp. 244–86. *Major Trends,* perhaps the single most influential title in all of twentieth-century Jewish scholarship, was based on lectures given in New York at the Jewish Institute of Religion in 1938.

13. Gershom Scholem, "The Document on Solidarity of Luria's Disciples" (in Hebrew), *Zion* 5 (1940): 133–60; id., "Israel Sarug: Student of the Ari?"; id., "The Authentic Kabbalistic Writings of Isaac Luria" (in Hebrew), *QS* 19 (1943): 184–99.

14. Isaiah Tishby, *Torat ha-Ra^c ve-ha-Qelippah be-Kabbalat ha-Ari* (Jerusalem: Akademon, 1942; rev. ed., Jerusalem: Magnes Press, 1984). In a special preface to the 1984 edition of this book, Tishby himself remarked on this circumstance: "Since 1942, many studies concerned with Lurianic Kabbalah have appeared. Most of them have to do with its dissemination and influence, while only a few treat the teachings themselves. No new monograph, however, has been produced so as to depict and to clarify Lurianic Kabbalah in a systematic fashion." In addition to the new preface, the 1984 edition includes indices. Joseph Dan also remarked at some length on this phenomenon in an essay devoted to Tishby's scholarly achievements. Dan concedes that he remains mystified by the remarkable fact that not only did Tishby and Scholem not return to the subject of Lurianic Kabbalah in a fresh way, but neither did any of their many students:

> In the course of forty [more] years of research by Scholem, and fifty by Tishby, not a single new thing was produced on this subject. The two of them had many students, but not one doctoral dissertation was written under their supervision on the subject of Isaac Luria and his circle, and these students did not turn on their own to the investigation of this central subject . . . all this at the same time as Luria and his teachings occupied a central place in their prospective. . . . I am unable to explain this phenomenon; there are other areas of Kabbalah concerning which there has not been new scholarship during a certain period of time, but it appears that it is impossible to find such a blatant example as this with respect to a topic as central as this one. (Joseph Dan, "Dimensions of the Scholarship of Isaiah Tishby" [in Hebrew], *Mada^{c}ei ha-Yahadut* 32 [1992]: 50–51)

15. Idel, *Kabbalah*, pp. 7–10.

16. In Scholem's case the issue is complex. Scholem did recognize that "nothing could be farther from the truth than the assumption that the religious experience of the kabbalists is barren of that which . . . forms the essence of mystical experience, everywhere and at all times. The ecstatic experience, the encounter with the absolute Being in the depths of one's own soul, . . . has been shared by the heirs of rabbinical Judaism." At the same time, however, Scholem tended to dismiss the possibility of studying such phenomena by his contention that kabbalists lacked the willingness to describe their personal experiences. See *Major Trends*, pp. 15–16.

This claim notwithstanding, Scholem himself *did* pay some attention to these matters, as attested, for example, in his groundbreaking chapter on Abraham Abulafia in *Major Trends*, his publication of portions of the Abulafian-inspired *Sullam ha-ʿAliyah*, in "Chapters from *Sullam ha-ʿAliyah* by R. Yehudah Albotini" (in Hebrew), *QS* 22 (1945): 161–71, and "Tradition und Neuschöpfung im Ritus der Kabbalisten," *Eranos Jahrbuch* 19 (1950): 121–80, trans. as "Tradition and New Creation in the Ritual of the Kabbalists," in Scholem, *On the Kabbalah and Its Symbolism*, pp. 118–57. In contrast to Scholem's assertion that kabbalists assuredly did have mystical experiences, R.J.Z. Werblowsky argues in *Joseph Karo, Lawyer and Mystic* (Oxford: Oxford University Press, 1962), p. 40, that "the *discursive* and even dialectical elements are so prominent in kabbalistic literature that we may almost speak of an intellectualistic hypertrophy. . . . more often than not kabbalistic literature is less the record of the *cognitio experimentalis dei* than the substitution of a theosophical *pilpul* for the halakhic one of the rabbinic lawyers." Ironically, Werblowsky enunciates this view in a full-length study of the mystical experiences of Joseph Karo. On the privileging of mystical ideas over the practical and experiential in Altmann's study of Jewish mysticism, see Lawrence Fine, "Alexander Altmann's Contribution to the Study of Jewish Mysticism," *Leo Baeck Institute Year Book* 34 (1989): 421–31. Altmann was particularly interested in establishing lines of connection between Jewish esotericism and the *philosophical* traditions of Judaism. This is one of the primary reasons why his research on Kabbalah was oriented toward mystical ideas and motifs.

17. This historiographical problem has been widely discussed. See, e.g., Lawrence Fine, "Approaching the Study of Jewish Mystical Experience," *Association for Jewish Studies Newsletter* 19 (1977): 10–11; id., "Popularizing the Esoteric: Recent Studies in Jewish Mysticism," *Judaism* 28 (1979): 494–96; id., "The Contemplative Practice of *Yihudim* in Lurianic Kabbalah," in A. Green, ed., *Jewish Spirituality*, vol. 2 (New York: Crossroad, 1987), pp. 64–98; Idel, *Kabbalah*, pp. 27–29; Yehuda Liebes, "New Directions in the Study of Kabbalah" (in Hebrew), *Peʿamim* 50 (1992): 150–54; Elliot R. Wolfson, *Through a Speculum That Shines: Vision and Imagination in Medieval Jewish Mysticism* (Princeton, N.J.: Princeton University Press, 1994), pp. 1–11, 284–88. Arthur Green observes that even the study of eastern European Hasidism has traditionally been concerned more with historical questions of the origins and causes of the movement than with Hasidism as mysticism: "We students of hasidism sometimes forget that we are dealing with *mystics*, people who see the inner life as primary and who come to 'know God' through inner experience." See Arthur Green, "Early Hasidism: Some Old/New Questions," in A. Rapoport-Albert, ed., *Hasidism Reappraised* (Portland, Or.: Vallentine Mitchell, 1996), pp. 442–43.

18. A noteworthy, frequently cited exception to this tendency is Solomon Schechter, "Safed in the Sixteenth Century: A City of Legists and Mystics," in id.,

Studies in Judaism, Second Series (Philadelphia: Jewish Publication Society, 1908), pp. 202–85; see esp. pp. 251–80. This essay, written in a charming, popular style, takes a keen interest in questions having to do with Luria's *persona* and charisma.

19. Ronit Meroz, "Torat ha-Geʾeulah be-Kabbalat ha-Ari" (Ph.D. diss., Hebrew University, Jerusalem, 1988).

20. Yehuda Liebes, "'Two Young Roes of a Doe': The Secret Sermon of Isaac Luria Before His Death" (in Hebrew), *MY* 10 (1992): 113–69. Liebes also takes up related issues in portions of two other essays, "The Messiah of the *Zohar*: Concerning the Messianic Image of R. Shimon bar Yohai," in *Ha-raʿayon ha-Meshiḥi be-Yisrael* (Jerusalem: Israel Academy of Sciences and Humanities, 1982) (in Hebrew), abbreviated English trans., "The Messiah of the *Zohar*," in id., *Studies in the Zohar* (Albany: State University of New York Press, 1993) (all references are to the Hebrew version); and "Myth vs. Symbol in the Zohar and in Lurianic Kabbalah," in L. Fine, ed., *Essential Papers on Kabbalah* (New York: New York University Press, 1995), see esp. pp. 223–33.

21. See, e.g., Lawrence Fine, trans. and ed., *Safed Spirituality: Rules of Mystical Piety, the Beginning of Wisdom* (New York: Paulist Press, 1984), pp. 61–80; id., "Maggidic Revelation in the Teachings of Isaac Luria," in J. Reinharz and D. Swetschinski, eds., *Mystics, Philosophers, and Politicians: Essays in Jewish Intellectual History in Honor of Alexander Altmann* (Durham, N.C.: Duke University Press, 1982), pp. 141–157; id., "Recitation of Mishnah as a Vehicle for Mystical Inspiration: A Contemplative Technique Taught by Hayyim Vital," *Revue des études juives* 141 (1982): 183–99; id., "The Art of Metoposcopy: A Study in Isaac Luria's Charismatic Knowledge," *Association for Jewish Studies Review* 11, 1 (1986): 79–101; id., "The Contemplative Practice of *Yiḥudim* in Lurianic Kabbalah," pp. 64–98; id., "The Study of Torah as a Theurgic Rite in Lurianic Kabbalah," in D. R. Blumenthal, ed., *Approaches to Judaism in Medieval Times*, vol. 3 (Atlanta: Scholars Press, 1988), pp. 29–40; id., "Purifying the Body in the Name of the Soul: The Problem of the Body in Sixteenth-Century Kabbalah," in H. Eilberg-Schwartz, ed., *People of the Body: Jews and Judaism from an Embodied Perspective* (Albany: State University of New York Press, 1992), pp. 117–42.

22. Neither Tishby's *Torat ha-Raʿ* nor Joseph Avivi's *Binyan ʾAriel* (Jerusalem: Misgav Yerushalayim, 1987), for example, includes a word about Luria's biography.

23. For discussion of the question of ritual density, see Catherine Bell, *Ritual: Perspectives and Dimensions* (New York: Oxford University Press, 1997), pp. 173–209.

24. See Fine, "Purifying the Body," pp. 127–36. It is true, of course, that traditional Judaism as a whole is bound up with the exercise of the body in the course of ritual and praxis. My point here, however, is that Lurianic Kabbalah went even further both in its ritual innovation and in its accentuation of ritual practice.

25. This important point has also been made by Rachel Elior, "The Metaphorical Relation Between God and Man, and the Significance of the Visionary Reality in Lurianic Kabbalah" (in Hebrew), *MY* 10 (1992): 47–57.

26. Wendy Doniger, *The Implied Spider: Politics and Theology in Myth* (New York: Columbia University Press, 1998), pp. 8–25.

27. See N. J. Girardot, *Myth and Meaning in Early Taoism* (Berkeley: University of California Press, 1983), p. 7. For a recent pioneering study of Jewish ritual that, like the present work, places the question of ritual at the forefront of its concerns, see Ivan G. Marcus, *Rituals of Childhood: Jewish Acculturation in Medieval Europe* (New Haven, Conn.: Yale University Press, 1996). As I have here, Marcus also invokes the notion of embodiment in his approach to ritual: "As the symbolic language of the body, ritual mediates between the unexpressed inner world of the self and 'gestures forth the world as meaningful and ordered.' It is a visible expression of the individual's unseen values, beliefs, and attitudes, and is 'a way of conceptualizing the world'" (pp. 4–5). He further points out that in Jewish historiography, ritual "has been relatively neglected both as a subject in its own right and as a key to understanding the culture of medieval European Jewry as a whole" (p. 5).

28. For an excellent discussion of these two models, see Bell, *Ritual*, pp. 72–83. For an example of various approaches to the question of religion and the body, see J. Law, ed., *Religious Reflections on the Human Body* (Bloomington: Indiana University Press, 1995).

29. Bell, *Ritual*, p. 73.

30. Ibid., p. 76.

31. Pierre Bourdieu, *Outline of a Theory of Practice* (Cambridge: Cambridge University Press, 1977), pp. 72–95, 124.

32. Scholem, *Major Trends*, pp. 37–38. Scholem put it this way: "Both historically and metaphysically, it [i.e., Kabbalah] is a masculine doctrine, made for men and by men. The long history of Jewish mysticism shows no trace of feminine influence. There have been no women kabbalists." Scholem attributed this to the fact that in Jewish mysticism women were associated with the quality of strict (divine) judgment and the realm of the demonic. One problem with this explanation, in my view, is that Muslim and Christian women were generally regarded similarly, without preventing them from participating in mystical life.

33. There are few studies of the role of women in the history of Kabbalah. See, for now, Talya Fishman, "A Kabbalistic Perspective on Gender-Specific Commandments: On the Interplay of Symbols and Society," *Association for Jewish Studies Review* 7 (1992): 199–245; Chava Weissler, *Voices of the Matriarchs: Listening to the Prayers of Early Modern Jewish Women* (Boston: Beacon Press, 1998), pp. 89–102; David Biale, *Eros and the Jews* (New York: Basic Books, 1992), pp. 101–20; Judith R. Baskin, "From Separation to Displacement: The Problem of Women in *Sefer Ḥasidim*," *Association for Jewish Studies Review* 9 (1994): 1–18; Elliot R. Wolfson, *Circle in the Square: Studies in the Use of Gender in Kabbalistic Symbolism* (Albany: State University of New York Press, 1995); Sharon Koren, "Mystical Rationales for the Laws of Niddah," in R. S. Wasserfall, ed., *Women and Water: Menstruation in Jewish Life and Law* (Hanover, N.H.: Brandeis University Press, 1999), pp. 101–21.

On the more general subject of Jewish women in the sixteenth century, see Ruth Lamdan, *A Separate People: Jewish Women in Palestine, Syria and Egypt in the Sixteenth Century* (Brill: Leiden, 2000).

34. See Avivi, "Lurianic Writings in Italy Prior to 1620"; id., *Binyan ʾAriel*.

Chapter 1

1. Though it provided little consolation for Jewry under Mamluk rule, the Mamluks in fact reserved their greatest animosity for their Christian subjects, particularly the Egyptian Copts. On the Jews under Mamluk rule, see Norman A. Stillman, *The Jews of Arab Lands: A History and Source Book* (Philadelphia: Jewish Publication Society, 1979), pp. 67–75; Salo Wittmayer Baron, *A Social and Religious History of the Jews*, rev. ed. (New York: Columbia University Press, 1980), 17: 154–228; Joseph Drory, "Jerusalem During the Mamluk Period," in L. Levine, ed., *The Jerusalem Cathedra* (Jerusalem: Ben Zvi Institute, 1981), 1: 190–213; Donald P. Little, "Relations Between Jerusalem and Egypt During the Mamuluk Period According to Literary and Documentary Sources," in A. Cohen and G. Baer, eds., *Egypt and Palestine: A Millennium of Association (868–1948)* (Jerusalem: Ben-Zvi Institute for the Study of Jewish Communities in the East; New York: St. Martin's Press, 1984), pp. 73–93. For studies of the relationship between Muslim society and *dhimmis*, see A. S. Tritton, *The Caliphs and Their Non-Muslim Subjects: A Critical Study of the Covenant of Umar* (London: H. Milford, Oxford University Press, 1930); Antoine Fattal, *Le Statut légal des non-musulmans en pays d'Islam* (Beirut: Imprimerie catholique, 1958); Bernard Lewis, *The Jews of Islam* (Princeton, N.J.: Princeton University Press, 1984), pp. 3–66; Bat Yeʾor, *The Dhimmi: Jews and Christians Under Islam* (Rutherford, N.J.: Fairleigh Dickinson University Press; London: Associated University Presses, 1985).

2. For a general history of the Ottoman empire, see Stanford Shaw and Ezel Shaw, *History of the Ottoman Empire and Modern Turkey* (New York: Cambridge University Press, 1976–77).

3. In the recent past the study of Jewish life under Ottoman rule has received a considerable amount of well-deserved scholarly attention, including Lewis, *Jews of Islam*, ch. 3; Stillman, *Jews of Arab Lands*, pp. 87–94; Itzhak Ben-Zvi, "Eretz Yisrael Under Ottoman Rule," in L. Finkelstein, ed., *The Jews: Their History, Culture, and Religion* (3d ed., New York: Harper, 1960), pp. 602–89; Baron, *Social and Religious History*, 18: 3–295; Benjamin Braude and Bernard Lewis, eds., *Christians and Jews in the Ottoman Empire: The Functioning of a Plural Society*, 2 vols. (New York: Holmes & Meier, 1982); Aryeh Shmuelevitz, *The Jews of the Ottoman Empire in the Late Fifteenth and the Sixteenth Centuries* (Leiden: E.J. Brill, 1984); Jacob Landau, ed., *Toldot Yehudei Mitsrayim be-Tequfat ha-Otomanit* (Jerusalem: Misgav Yerushalayin, 1988); Cohen and Baer, *Egypt and Palestine*; Joseph Hacker, "The Jewish Community of Salonika from the Fifteenth to the Sixteenth Century" (in

Hebrew) (Ph.D. diss., Hebrew University, Jerusalem, 1978); Mark Alan Epstein, *The Ottoman Jewish Communities and Their Role in the Fifteenth and Sixteenth Centuries* (Freiburg: K. Schwarz, 1980); Stanford J. Shaw, *The Jews of the Ottoman Empire and the Turkish Republic* (New York: New York University Press, 1991); Esther Juhasz, ed., *Sephardi Jews in the Ottoman Empire: Aspects of Material Culture* (Jerusalem: Israel Museum, 1990); Jane Gerber, *The Jews of Spain: A History of the Sephardic Experience* (New York: Free Press, 1992), pp. 145–75; Aron Rodrigue, "The Sephardim in the Ottoman Empire," in E. Kedourie, ed., *Spain and the Jews* (London: Thames & Hudson, 1992), pp. 162–88; Esther Benbassa and Aron Rodrigue, *Sephardi Jewry: A History of the Judeo-Spanish Community, Fourteenth–Twentieth Centuries* (Berkeley: University of California Press, 2000), pp. 1–10, 36–49; Avigdor Levy, ed., *The Jews of the Ottoman Empire* (Princeton, N.J.: Darwin Press; Washington, D.C.: Institute of Turkish Studies, 1994).

4. On the history of Byzantine Jewry, see Steven B. Bowman, *The Jews of Byzantium, 1204–1453* (Tuscaloosa: University of Alabama Press, 1985). On the struggle between Romaniote Jews and newly arrived Iberian Jews, see Rodrigue, "Sephardim in the Ottoman Empire," pp. 165–66.

5. The complete text of this letter is found in F. Kobler, ed., *A Treasury of Jewish Letters: Letters from the Famous and the Humble* (New York: Farrar, Straus & Young, 1952), 1: 283–85. A portion of the letter is also given in Lewis, *Jews of Islam*, pp. 135–36. Cf. Schechter, "Safed in the Sixteenth Century," pp. 251–52.

6. This famous report is attributed to Bayazid's courtiers by Eliyahu Capsali, *Seder ʾEliyahu Zuta*, ed. A. Shmuelevitz (Jerusalem, 1975). Immanuel Aboab ascribes it to Bayazid himself in his *Nomologia, o Discursos legales compuestos* (Amsterdam, 1629), p. 195.

7. Lewis, *Jews of Islam*, pp. 137–38; Joseph Hacker, "Ottoman Policy Toward the Jews During the Fifteenth Century," in Braude and Lewis, *Christians and Jews in the Ottoman Empire*, vol. 1, pp. 117–26.

8. By the beginning of the sixteenth century, Jews had been driven out of most of western Europe, except for certain portions of Italy and Germany. Jewish life shifted to two great centers in the East: Ashkenazi Jews settled in Poland and Lithuania, while, as we have seen, Sephardic Jews (along with others) made a home for themselves in the vast reaches of the Ottoman Empire.

9. Lewis, *Jews of Islam*, pp. 129–35.

10. A. Levy, ed., *The Sephardim in the Ottoman Empire* (Princeton, N.J.: Darwin Press, 1992), p. 31.

11. Gerber, *Jews of Spain*, p. 159.

12. See Benjamin Braude, "The Rise and Fall of Salonica Woolens, 1500–1650: Technology, Transfer and Western Competition," in A. M. Ginio, ed., *Jews, Christians, and Muslims in the Mediterranean World After 1492* (Portland, Or.: Cass, 1992), pp. 216–36; id., "The Cloth Industry of Salonika in the Mediterranean Economy," *Peʿamim* 15 (1983): 82–95; Shmuel Avitsur, "Contribution to the History

of the Woolen Textile Industry in Salonika" (in Hebrew), *Sefunot* 12 (1971–78): 147–68; id., "Safed — Center of the Manufacture of Woven Woolens in the Fifteenth Century [should read sixteenth century]" (in Hebrew), *Sefunot* 6 (1962): 41–69; Levy, *Sephardim in the Ottoman Empire*, p. 35; Benbassa and Rodrigue, *Sephardi Jewry*, pp. 39–42. One of the chief contributions of the Spanish Jews appears to have been the introduction of the water-driven, mechanical fulling process.

13. Benbassa and Rodrigue, *Sephardi Jewry*, p. 38; Levy, *Sephardim in the Ottoman Empire*, pp. 36–37.

14. See, e.g., Robert Mantran, "Foreign Merchants and the Minorities in Istanbul During the Sixteenth and Seventeenth Centuries," in Braude and Lewis, *Christians and Jews in the Ottoman Empire,* vol. 1, pp. 127–37; Eliezer Bashan, "The Rise and Decline of the Sephardi Communities in the Levant: The Economic Aspects," in R. D. Barnett and W. M. Schwab, eds., *The Western Sephardim* (Grendon, Northants: Gibraltar Books, 1989), pp. 349–88; Simon Schwarzfuchs, "Quand commença le déclin de l'industrie textile des Juifs de Salonique," in A. Toaff and S. Schwarzfuchs, eds., *The Mediterranean and the Jews: Banking, Finance and International Trade (XVI–XVIII Centuries)* (Ramat Gan: Bar-Ilan University Press, 1989), pp. 215–36; Benbassa and Rodrigue, *Sephardi Jewry*, pp. 36–49.

15. Levy, *Sephardim in the Ottoman Empire*, pp. 34–35.

16. See Lewis, *Jews of Islam*, pp. 134–35.

17. Lewis, *Jews of Islam*, p. 139.

18. For much of the information that follows, I draw upon the important study of this subject by Amnon Cohen, *Yehudim be-Shilton ha-Islam* (Jerusalem, 1982), trans. as *Jewish Life Under Islam: Jerusalem in the Sixteenth Century* (Cambridge, Mass.: Harvard University Press, 1984). Cohen drew on hitherto unexamined Muslim court archives in East Jerusalem, which enabled him to paint a rich and detailed portrait of Jewish life in Jerusalem during the period in which we are interested. Other studies of sixteenth-century Jerusalem include Amnon Cohen and Bernard Lewis, *Population and Revenue in the Towns of Palestine in the Sixteenth Century* (Princeton, N.J.: Princeton University Press, 1978); A. Cohen, ed., *Jerusalem in the Early Ottoman Period* (in Hebrew) (Jerusalem: Ben Zvi Institute, 1979) ; id., *Ottoman Documents on the Jewish Community of Jerusalem in the Sixteenth Century* (in Hebrew and Turkish) (Jerusalem: Ben Zvi Institute, 1976); Bernard Lewis, *Notes and Documents from the Turkish Archives: A Contribution to the History of the Jews in the Ottoman Empire* (Jerusalem: Oriental Notes and Studies, 1952); W. Hutteroth, "The Pattern of Settlement in Palestine in the Sixteenth Century," in M. Ma'oz, ed., *Studies on Palestine During the Ottoman Period* (Jerusalem: Magnes Press, 1975), pp. 3–9; Abraham David, *To Come to the Land: Immigration and Settlement in Sixteenth-Century Eretz Yisrael* (Tuscaloosa: University of Alabama Press, 1999), pp. 57–92.

19. Cohen, *Jewish Life*, pp. 12–35.

20. See David, *To Come to the Land*, pp. 59–61.

21. See Cohen, *Jewish Life*, pp. 36–58; David, *To Come to the Land*, pp. 73–78.

22. Cohen, *Jewish Life*, pp. 76–86. Cf. also David, *To Come to the Land*, pp. 57–59.

23. Abraham David, *In Zion and Jerusalem: The Itinerary of Rabbi Moses Basola (1521–1523)* (Jerusalem: C.G. Foundation, Jerusalem Project Publications of the Martin (Szusz) Department of Land of Israel Studies, Bar Ilan University, 1999), p. 81.

24. Ibid., p. 82.

25. See Cohen, *Jewish Life*, pp. 140–219.

26. Abraham David's view is somewhat less positive about the economic circumstances of the Jews of Jerusalem in the sixteenth century: "The new prosperity and economic opportunities in Eretz-Yisrael notwithstanding, Jews still bore the burden of heavy taxation and owed their survival, in Jerusalem especially, to massive support by Diaspora Jews" (David, *To Come to the Land*, p. 47).

27. Werblowsky, *Joseph Karo*, p. 84.

28. Joseph Karo, *Maggid Mesharim* (Preacher of Righteousness), published for the first time in Lublin in 1646.

29. A good example of this tendency to blur the distinction between critical analysis and traditional sacred biography is the treatment of Luria in Schechter, "Safed in the Sixteenth Century."

30. Studies treating the biographical details of Luria's life in Egypt, especially his commercial activities, include David Tamar, "Isaac Luria's Beginnings in Egypt" (in Hebrew), in id., *Meḥqarim be-Toldot ha-Yehudim be-ʾErets Yisrael u-be-ʾArtsot ha-Mizrach* (Jerusalem: Mossad Harav Kook, 1981), pp. 70–85; E. Shochetman, "New Sources from the Geniza Concerning the Business Activities of the Ari in Egypt" (in Hebrew), *Peʿamim* 16 (1983): 56–64; Abraham David, "Halakhah and Commerce in the Biography of Isaac Luria" (in Hebrew), *MY* 10 (1992): 287–97; id., "More Concerning the Life of the Ari in Egypt" (in Hebrew), *ʿAlei Sefer* 14 (1987): 135–37; Meir Benayahu, "Documents from the Geniza Concerning the Business Activities of the Ari" (in Hebrew), in id., ed., *Sefer Zikkaron le-ha-Rav Yitshak Nissim*, 4: 225–53 (Jerusalem: Yad Harav Nissim, 1985).

31. Gershom Scholem in *EJ*, 10: 572. Scholem's view was voiced earlier by Schechter, *Studies in Judaism, Second Series*, p. 251.

32. J. Rothschild, *EJ*, 11: 569.

33. Hayyim Joseph David Azulai, *Shem ha-Gedolim* (Jerusalem: Otsar ha-Sefarim, 1994), entry *"Rabbenu ha-Ari."*

34. Ibid.

35. Ibid. On the economic activities of the Jews of Ottoman Egypt, including the phenomenon of tax farming, see Eliezer Bashan, "Economic Life Between the Sixteenth and Eighteenth Centuries," in Landau, *Toldot Yehudei Mitsrayim*, esp. pp. 98–102; and Shaw, *Jews of the Ottoman Empire*, pp. 86–97.

36. David, *To Come to the Land*, p. 41.

37. Concerning ibn Zimra, see Israel Goldman, *The Life and Times of Rabbi David Ibn Abi Zimra* (New York: Jewish Theological Seminary of America, 1970); Melila Helner, "Transmigration of Souls in the Kabbalistic Writings of Rabbi David ibn Zimra" (in Hebrew), *Pe'amim* 43 (1980): 16–50; David, *To Come to the Land*, pp. 142–44. For general observations concerning the life of Spanish Jewry in sixteenth-century Egypt, see Jacob Barnai, "The Jews of Spain in Egypt," in H. Beinart, ed., *Moreshet Sepharad: The Sephardi Legacy* (Jerusalem: Magnes Press, 1992), 1: 72–76.

38. The story is reported in full form by Elijah ha-Cohen (ha-Ittamari) in his *Midrash ʾEliyahu* (Izmir, 1759), 12, 4. While this story has a legendary quality to it, I draw upon it despite my earlier insistence on avoiding the hagiographical traditions about Luria to learn about his life in Egypt. It is possible, in my view, to draw an inference of historical value from Azulai's anecdote.

39. The agreement signed by the rabbis of David ibn Zimra's circle in Cairo is published in *Levushei Sered* (Kraków, 1882), p. 15, as well as *Birkat ha-ʾArets* (Jerusalem, 1904), p. 61. In *Shem ha-Gedolim,* Azulai refers to this document, which he reports having seen in a copy written by Hayyim Vital. If the date 1557—indicated at the end of the text—is accurate, then it places ibn Zimra in Egypt at this time, insofar as the agreement was made at ibn Zimra's decree. If this is the case, then the conventional scholarly view that ibn Zimra left Egypt for Jerusalem in 1553 is incorrect. See Tamar, "Isaac Luria's Beginnings," p. 75, n. 20.

40. The other signatories included Isaac Modena, Betsalel Ashkenazi, Elijah Mizrachi, Abraham ha-Levi, Judah Masud, Samuel Tatlah (possibly Samuel Fodeila), Isaac Berab, and Isaac bar Abraham Berab. On the identity of these individuals, see Tamar, "Isaac Luria's Beginnings," pp. 76–77.

41. See ibid., p. 77.

42. Azulai, *Shem ha-Gedolim*, p. 73.

43. Published in the introduction by Benjamin Motal to Tam ibn Yahya, *Tummat Yesharim* (Venice, 1622).

44. David Conforte, *Qore ha-Dorot* (Berlin, 1846), 40b. Conforte (c. 1617–c. 1690) was a Sefardi rabbi, literary historian, and kabbalist. *Qore ha-Dorot,* a chronicle of authors from post-talmudic times until the author's own, was published from manuscript for the first time in Venice in 1746, and in an enhanced edition in 1846.

45. For studies treating Luria's commercial activities, see above, n. 30. The article by Benayahu is the most comprehensive of these and the basis for much of what follows here, although see the reservations about some of Benayahu's assertions expressed in David, "Halakhah and Commerce."

46. Published originally by E. J. Worman, "Un Document concernant Isaac Luria," *REJ* 57 (1909): 281–82, based on Cambridge University Library MS T.S. 112, 589. Worman believed that the date was 1559, but it is actually 1554, as Tamar

and Benayahu have shown. See Tamar, "Isaac Luria's Beginnings," p. 72; Shochetman, "New Sources," p. 60, n. 23; Benayahu, "Documents," p. 227.

47. Benayahu, "Documents," p. 227.

48. Jewish Theological Seminary of America MS Adler 3726. See Benayahu,
"Documents," p. 227.

49. See Shochetman, "New Sources," p. 60, n. 25.

50. Benayahu, "Documents," p. 228.

51. Cambridge University Library MS T.S. 6J4. See Shochetman, "New
Sources," p. 61; Benayahu, "Documents," p. 228. While these letters indicate the
day of the week and month of their composition, the year is missing. In Shochetman's view, however, 1562, 1565, 1567, or 1569 are the possible years, while Benayahu narrows the choices down to 1555 and 1562.

52. Simcha Assaf, *Meqorot u-Meḥqarim be-Toldot Yisrael* (Jerusalem: Mossad
ha-Rav Kook, 1946), p. 204.

53. See Scholem, *Kabbalah*, p. 421; Tamar, "Isaac Luria's Beginnings," pp. 72–73;
Shochetman, "New Sources," p. 60; Benayahu, "Documents," pp. 229–30.

54. Benayahu discovered this letter, unnumbered, in the Adler collection of
the Jewish Theological Seminary of America. See Benayahu, "Documents," p. 230.

55. Jewish Theological Seminary of America, n.s., 47, MS Adler. See Benayahu,
"Documents," pp. 231–32. The date of this document is uncertain.

56. Galante's report is found in Leon Modena's *Sefer Ari Nohem*, ed. S. Rosenthal
(Leipzig, 1840).

57. David ibn Zimra, *Magen David*, Amsterdam, 1713; id., *Metsudat David*,
Zolkiew, 1862; id., *Migdal David*, Lemberg (Lvov), 1883. On the nature of these
writings, see Helner, "Transmigration of Souls."

58. Helner, "Transmigration of Souls."

59. Reported by the Egyptian chronicler Joseph ben Isaac Sambari, *Seder ha-
Ḥachamim ve-Qorot ha-Yamim*, vol. 1, ed. A. Neubauer (Berlin, 1888), p. 160.

60. See Tamar, "Isaac Luria's Beginnings," p. 77, n. 25. Tamar speculates concerning the possibility that Abraham ha-Levi, whose name is also found on this rabbinic agreement, may be none other than Abraham ben Eliezer ha-Levi Berukhim,
who became a well-known kabbalist in Safed and a student of Luria's.

61. Azulai, *Shem ha-Gedolim*, p. 73.

62. Tamar ("Isaac Luria's Beginnings," p. 78) speculates that this seclusion began between the years 1558 and 1560, and that it lasted for six or seven years. Cf.
Scholem, *Kabbalah*, p. 421.

63. Scholem's attempt to determine what Isaac Luria personally wrote is
found in his "Authentic Kabbalistic Writings of Isaac Luria." In connection with
the question of Luria's authorship, see also Joseph Avivi, "The Lurianic Writings
of Rabbi Hayyim Vital" (in Hebrew), *Moriah* (1981): 77–91; id., "Lurianic Writings in Italy Prior to 1620"; id., *Binyan ʾAriel*, p. 19; Meroz, "Torat ha-Geʾeulah,"
pp. 70–80.

64. See Scholem, "Authentic Kabbalistic Writings," pp. 187–90; Tamar, "Isaac Luria's Beginnings," pp. 80–82.

65. Luria's commentaries to *Sifra di-Tseniuta*, for example, were published as part of Vital's *Shaʿar Maʿamarei Rashbi* (in the 1898 Jerusalem edition, hereafter *ShMR*), fols. 22a–30c.

66. Vital, *Shaʿar ha-Pesuqim* (hereafter *ShP*), *Parashat Be-Haʿalotekha*, p. 171.

67. In 1565, Joseph Karo noted that "the elder, R. Kalonymous, of blessed memory, used to be there [in the *yeshivah*] with the other Ashkenazi sages." According to Abraham David, he is "to be identified with "Kalonymus ben R. Jacob," who, in conjunction with other Jerusalem sages, signed an agreement to a tax exemption for scholars in late 1547. There is a strong likelihood that he was none other than the "R. Kalman" who headed one of the mid-sixteenth-century Jerusalem Ashkenazi yeshivot. See David, *To Come to the Land*, p. 160.

68. Ronit Meroz, "Selections from Ephraim Penzieri: Luria's Sermon in Jerusalem and the *Kavvanah* on Eating Food" (in Hebrew), *MY* 10 (1992): 211–57.

69. Vital, *Shaʿar ha-Kavvanot* (hereafter *ShK*), vol. 2, *Sefirat ha-ʿOmer*, *Derush* 12, p. 189. Luria speaks of the "first time he came from Egypt."

70. While the general circumstances of Egyptian Jewry in the sixteenth century were positive, it should be pointed out that the status of this community was somewhat less stable than that of Jewish communities in the larger Ottoman centers. It is the case, for example, that the Ottomans transferred some Egyptian Jews to Istanbul under the *sürgün* (exile) system that applied throughout the empire. In addition, Islamic laws against *dhimmis* were apparently applied more strictly in Egypt than in other Ottoman communities. See Barnai, "Jews of Spain in Egypt," p. 74.

Chapter 2

1. JT *Rosh Hashanah* 2:1, 58a.

2. Benjamin of Tudela's famous travelogue, *Sefer ha-Massaʿot* (Book of Travels), was published for the first time in Istanbul in 1543. A critical Hebrew edition and English translation was published by E. N. Adler (London, 1907). A portion of the English translation is reproduced in E. N. Adler, ed., *Jewish Travellers in the Middle Ages: Nineteen Firsthand Accounts* (New York: Dover, 1987), pp. 38–63.

3. Adler, *Jewish Travellers*, p. 107. Cf. Joshua Prawer, *The History of the Jews in the Latin Kingdom of Jerusalem* (Oxford: Oxford University Press, 1988), pp. 76–77; 215–21.

4. See David Levinger, "Rabbi Shem Tov ben Abraham ben Gaon"(in Hebrew), *Sefunot* 6 (1963): 9–39.

5. Joseph de Montagna's letter is to be found in A. Yaari, ed., *ʾIggrot ʾErets Yisrael* (Ramat Gan: Masada, 1971), pp. 89–93.

6. Adler, *Jewish Travellers*, p. 245.

7. Yaari, ʾIggrot, pp. 144–160. I have drawn on the English translation found in K. Wilhelm, ed., Roads to Zion (New York: Schocken Books, 1948), pp. 15–27.

8. See Itzhak Ben-Zvi, ʾErets Yisrael ve-Yishuvah be-Yemei ha-Shilton ha-Otamani (Jerusalem: Ben Zvi Institute, 1967), p. 145.

9. Translation based on David, In Zion and Jerusalem, pp. 61–62. As David points out (p. 62, n. 33), there were "additional smaller congregations: Ashkenazim, Italians, Hungarians, among others." See the delineation of the numbers of individuals in each of the different Jewish communities in Safed, in Cohen and Lewis, Population and Revenue, pp. 34–41, 155–61.

10. Abraham David, "The Spanish Exiles in the Holy Land," in H. Beinart, ed., The Sephardi Legacy (Jerusalem: Magnes Press, 1992), 2: 77–108.

11. Joseph Hacker, "The Sephardim in the Ottoman Empire in the Sixteenth Century," in Beinart, The Sephardi Legacy, 2: 113. See also Cohen and Lewis, Population and Revenue, pp. 155–61. On Jews in Safed from other communities, see David, To Come to the Land, pp. 100–114.

12. David, In Zion and Jerusalem, pp. 62–64. Slightly adapted translation.

13. It is never easy to establish reliable population statistics for the premodern period, and our case is no different. For a number of years, population statistics for Safed were based on censuses studied by Cohen and Lewis in their Population and Revenue. The figures I have cited are based on calculations by Joseph Hacker, whose study of a controversy in Safed concerning whether or not scholars should be exempt from taxation suggests that Cohen and Lewis's numbers were too low. In contrast to Hacker's figures, the numbers upon which Cohen and Lewis's research is based indicate 719 households and 63 bachelors in 1555–56, and 945 households and 12 bachelors in 1567–68. See Joseph Hacker, "The Payment of Djizya by Scholars in Palestine in the Sixteenth Century" (in Hebrew), Shalem 4 (1984): 92–94; Abraham David, "Demographic Changes in the Safed Jewish Community of the Sixteenth Century," in R. Dan, ed., Occident and Orient: A Tribute to the Memory of A. Scheiber (Leiden: E.J. Brill, 1988), pp. 85–86; id., To Come to the Land, pp. 97–99.

14. See David, To Come to the Land, p. 98.

15. The definitive study of Safed's textile industry is Avitsur, "Contribution to the History of the Woolen Textile Industry in Salonika." See as well Y. Canaani, "Economic Life in Safed and its Environs in the Sixteenth Century and the First Half of the Seventeenth Century" (in Hebrew), Zion, o.s., 6 (1933–34): 195–201.

16. Shmuel Avitsur, "The Batan, a Water-Powered Fulling Mill in Nahal Ammud— Relic of the Wool-Textile Industry in Safed," Israel, Land and Nature 7 (1981): 18–21.

17. Stillman, Jews of Arab Lands, p. 290.

18. Ibid., p. 292.

19. This structure was still standing in the middle of the seventeenth century, according to the testimony of a Turkish tourist who described it in 1649. He referred to it as "a large caravanserai, with an iron gate like that of a castle, and square

in plan. Right round it measures six hundred paces. It stands four stories high." See David, *To Come to the Land*, pp. 95–97.

20. For the testimony of Christian travelers to Safed in the second half of the sixteenth century, see M. Ish-Shalom, ed., *Masᶜe notsrim le-Erets Yisrael* (Tel Aviv: Am Oved, 1965), pp. 109–13, 284–85, 299–300, 304–5.

21. Traditions concerning pilgrimage to Meron are collected and studied in Meir Benayahu, "Customs of the Kabbalists of Safed at Meron" (in Hebrew), *Sefunot* 6 (1962): 9–40; Abraham Yaari, "History of the Pilgrimage to Meron." For a discussion of Moses Basola's visit to grave sites in the environs of Safed, including that of Shimon bar Yohai in Meron, see David, *In Zion and Jerusalem*, pp. 32–36, 64–69.

22. See Mordechai Pachter, "The Emigration of Rabbi Solomon Alkabets to the Land of Israel and His Departure Sermon in Salonika" (in Hebrew), *Shalem* 5 (1987): 251–63 .

23. Ibid., pp. 252–53.

24. Alkabets's letter appears in the introduction to Karo's diary *Maggid Mesharim*, as well as in the section on *Shavuᶜot* in Isaiah Horowitz's *Shnei Luḥot ha-Brit* (Amsterdam, 1648). An English translation of the entire letter is to be found in Louis Jacobs, *Jewish Mystical Testimonies*, pp. 99–104, from which I have adapted the present translation.

25. The attempt to renew rabbinic ordination in Safed and the ensuing controversy have been well studied. See Jacob Katz, "The Controversy Concerning Ordination Between Rabbi Jacob Berab and Rabbi Levi ibn Habib" (in Hebrew), in id., *Halakha ve-Qabbalah* (Jerusalem: Magnes Press, 1986), pp. 213–36; Meir Benayahu, "The Revival of Ordination in Safed" (in Hebrew), in S. W. Baron et al., eds., *Sefer Yovel le-Yitshaq Baer* (Jerusalem: Ben Zvi Institute, 1960), pp. 248–69; H. Z. Dimitrovsky, "Two New Documents Concerning the Ordination Controversy in Safed" (in Hebrew), *Sefunot* 10 (1966): 112–92. An English version of Katz's study may be found in J. Dan, ed., *Studies in Jewish History*, Binah, 1 (New York: Praeger, 1989), pp. 119–41.

26. Concerning Berab's activities, see David, *To Come to the Land*, pp. 124–26.

27. Mishneh Torah, *Yad*, Sanhedrin 4:11.

28. See H. Z. Dimitrovsky, "The Study House of Rabbi Jacob Berab in Safed" (in Hebrew), *Sefunot* 7 (1963): 41–102.

29. See Avraham Gross, "Centers of Study and Yeshivot in Spain," in Beinart, *The Sephardi Legacy*, 1: 407–10.

30. See David, *To Come to the Land*, p. 124.

31. See H. Z. Dimitrovsky, "The Controversy Between Rabbi Joseph Karo and Rabbi Moses di Trani" (in Hebrew), *Sefunot* 6 (1962): 73–123.

32. Based upon translation in David, *To Come to the Land*, p. 132. ᶜ*Ein Yaᶜaqov* refers to a collection of aggadic texts from the Talmud collected by Jacob ibn Habib, arranged according to the order of talmudic tractates. Laws of blessings

may refer to the talmudic tractate *Berakhot*, while the reference to Maimonides alludes no doubt to his great legal code, the Mishneh Torah.

33. For selected studies of early Kabbalah, see Gershom Scholem, *Origins of the Kabbalah* (Philadelphia: Jewish Publication Society, 1987); id., *Major Trends*, lectures 5 and 6; I. Tishby and F. Lachower, eds., *The Wisdom of the Zohar: An Anthology of Texts* (Oxford: Oxford University Press, 1989), 3 vols., trans. D. Goldstein (hereafter *WZ*). For more succinct presentations, see Lawrence Fine, "Kabbalistic Texts," in B. Holtz, ed., *Back to the Sources* (New York: Simon & Schuster, 1984), pp. 305–59; Arthur Green, "The Zohar: Jewish Mysticism in Medieval Spain," in Fine, *Essential Papers on Kabbalah*, pp. 27–66; Daniel Matt, *Zohar: The Book of Enlightenment* (New York: Paulist Press, 1983).

34. On the concept of the *Shekhinah* in kabbalistic literature, see Gershom Scholem, "*Shekhinah*: The Feminine Element in Divinity," in id., *On the Mystical Shape of the Godhead: Basic Concepts in the Kabbalah* (New York: Schocken Books, 1991), pp. 140–96; *WZ*, 1: 371–422; Wolfson, *Through a Speculum*, ch. 7.

35. These experiences are recorded in Cordovero's *Sefer Gerushin* (Venice, c. 1602; Jerusalem: Makor Hayyim, 1962).

36. Cordovero, *Tomer Devorah* (Venice, 1589), ch. 9. Translated by Louis Jacobs as *The Palm Tree of Deborah* (1960; 3d ed., New York: Sepher-Hermon Press, 1981).

37. Cordovero, *Sefer Gerushin*, ch. 9.

38. The image of the downtrodden *Shekhinah* lying in the dust is found, e.g., in *Zohar* 1,4a, and *Zohar Ḥadash*, 47d.

39. Cordovero, *Sefer Gerushin*, as quoted in Werblowsky, *Joseph Karo*, p. 53.

40. A full-length study of Karo's mystical life and experiences is Werblowsky's *Joseph Karo*.

41. Even though this letter describes an experience that took place sometime prior to Karo's migration to Safed, it is perfectly consistent with what we know about Karo and his mystical life in Safed.

42. *Maggid Mesharim*, in which this letter appears as the introduction. The present translation is from Jacobs, *Jewish Mystical Testimonies*, pp. 100–101.

43. Concerning Elijah de Vidas and *Reshit Ḥokhmah*, see Fine, *Safed Spirituality*, pp. 81–156.

44. Ibid., p. 107.

45. Ibid, p. 149.

46. Concerning the presence of *conversos* in Safed, see Abraham David, "Safed, foyer de retour au judaïsme de *conversos* au XVIe siècle," *REJ* 146 (1987): 63–83; id., "Spanish Exiles in the Holy Land," pp. 105–7; id., *To Come to the Land*, pp. 103–6. As David has pointed out, "Signs of the longing of Spanish *conversos* to settle in Eretz-Israel and throw off the mask of Christianity are discernible as early as the mid-fifteenth century, sparked by messianic expectations that intensified following the Ottoman conquest of Constantinople" (*To Come to the Land*, p. 103).

47. See, e.g., Steven Fraade, "Ascetical Aspects of Ancient Judaism," in A. Green, ed., *Jewish Spirituality* (New York: Crossroad, 1980), 1: 253–88.

48. Concerning asceticism in Bahya, see Alan Lazaroff, "Bahya's Asceticism Against Its Rabbinic and Islamic Background," *Journal of Jewish Studies* 21 (1970): 11–38. For a translation of Bahya's work into English, see *The Book of Direction to the Duties of the Heart*, trans. and ed. M. Mansoor et al. (London: Routledge & K. Paul, 1973).

49. For an English translation, see Abraham bar Hiyya, *The Meditation of the Sad Soul*, trans. and ed. Geoffrey Wigoder, Littman Library of Jewish Civilization (New York: Schocken Books, 1969).

50. See Obadiah ben Abraham Maimonides (1228–65), *The Treatise of the Pool = al-Maqala al-hawdiyya*, trans. and ed. Paul Fenton (London: Octagon Press, 1981).

51. For a study of the theology of the German pietists, see Joseph Dan, *Torat ha-Sod shel Ḥasidut ᵓAshkenaz* (Jerusalem: Mossad Bialik, 1968). The practical piety and asceticism of the pietists is studied in Ivan Marcus, *Piety and Society: The Jewish Pietists of Medieval Germany* (Leiden: E.J. Brill, 1981).

52. This tradition, as well as others described here, are found in texts of *hanhagot*, descriptive and prescriptive rules of piety written by several Safed kabbalists. The *hanhagot* are in the form of lists, which, in a terse, systematic format, enumerate practical behavioral standards and customs. These materials provide us with an invaluable source of information about the pietistic activities of this community. We possess *hanhagot* by Moses Cordovero, Abraham Galante, Abraham ben Eliezer ha-Levi Berukhim, Moses of Liera, and an anonymous Safed kabbalist. These were published for the first time from manuscripts by Schechter as an appendix to his essay "Safed in the Sixteenth Century," pp. 202–306. All but Moses of Liera's text are translated in Fine, *Safed Spirituality*, where the *hanhagot* literature is discussed, pp. 27–80. Cordovero's tradition, cited here, is found on p. 35. In connection with this literature, see also Mordechai Pachter, "Kabbalistic Ethical Literature in Sixteenth-Century Safed," in J. Dan, ed., *Studies in Jewish History, Thought, and Culture*, Binah 3, (Westport, Conn.: Praeger, 1994), pp. 159–78.

53. Fine, *Safed Spirituality*, p. 35.

54. Ibid., p. 59.

55. Jacobs, *Jewish Mystical Testimonies*, p. 105.

56. Fine, *Safed Spirituality*, p. 56.

57. Ibid., p. 38. See also Berukhim's report that "some pietists fast for three days and nights, four times each year, during each of the four seasons" (ibid., p. 53).

58. Ibid., p. 42.   59. Ibid., p. 58.

60. Ibid., p. 42.   61. Ibid., p. 51.

62. Hayyim Vital, *Sefer ha-Ari ve-Gurav*, ed. Yaᶜakov Moshe Hillel (Jerusalem: Ahavat Shalom, 1992), p. 86. For a more detailed description of Solomon Shlomeil's letters, see Chapter 3, n. 18.

63. Fine, *Safed Spirituality*, p. 36.

64. Ibid., p. 51.

65. Dresnitz, letter 4, p. 88.

66. Jacobs, *Jewish Mystical Testimonies*, pp. 106–7.

67. Ibid., p. 112.

68. Ibid., p. 111.

69. Werblowsky, *Joseph Karo*, p. 152.

70. Jacobs, *Jewish Mystical Testimonies*, p. 115. On this subject, see Werblowsky, *Joseph Karo*, pp. 148–55; Mordechai Pachter, "The Concept of Devekut in the Homiletical Ethical Writings of 16th Century Safed," in I. Twersky, ed., *Studies in Medieval Jewish History and Literature* (Cambridge, Mass.: Harvard University Press, 1984), pp. 193–202.

71. Werblowsky, *Joseph Karo*, pp. 153–54.

72. Fine, *Safed Spirituality*, p. 130.

73. Ibid., p. 141.

74. For a study of this question, see Fine, "Purifying the Body."

75. Fine, *Safed Spirituality*, pp. 51–52.

76. Ibid., p. 151.

77. Werblowsky, *Joseph Karo*, p. 62. On these brotherhoods, see also Pachter, "Kabbalistic Ethical Literature," pp. 160–64; and David Tamar, "On the Fellowships of Safed," in id., *Meḥqarim be-Toldot ha-Yehudim be-ʾErets Yisrael u-be-ʾItalyah*, pp. 95–100. See, as well, Moshe Idel, "On Mobility, Individuals and Groups: Prolegomenon for a Sociological Approach to Sixteenth-Century Safed," *Kabbalah: Journal for the Study of Jewish Mystical Texts,* ed. D. Abrams and A. Elqayam, 3 (1998): 145–73.

78. Pachter, "Kabbalistic Ethical Literature," pp. 161–63.

79. Concerning Cordovero's circle, see Fine, *Safed Spirituality*, pp. 30–38. Azikri's mystical life is studied in Mordecai Pachter, "The Life and Personality of Rabbi Eleazar Azikri According to His Mystical Diary and *Sefer Ḥaredim*" (in Hebrew), *Shalem* 3 (1981): 127–47; id., *Millei de-Shemaya le-Rabi Eleazar Azikri* (Tel Aviv: Mifalim Univeristaim, 1991); Werblowsky, *Joseph Karo*, pp. 57–65; and Moshe Idel, *Studies in Ecstatic Kabbalah* (Albany: State University of New York Press, 1988), pp. 132–34.

80. Fine, *Safed Spirituality*, p. 11.

Chapter 3

1. The relations between the Jews of Egypt and Palestine are treated in Joseph Hacker, "Spiritual and Material Links Between Egyptian and Palestinian Jewry in the Sixteenth Century," in A. Cohen and G. Baer, eds., *Egypt and Palestine* (New York: St. Martin's Press, 1984), pp. 241–50.

2. *Kerem Ḥemed*, vol. 9 (1856), p. 141, cited in Hacker, "Spiritual and Material Links," p. 244.

3. Moses di Trani, *Responsa* (Venice, 1630), vol. 2, no. 206.

4. See Hacker, "Spiritual and Material Links," p. 242, esp. n. 4, where references to the literature concerning this issue are provided.

5. David ibn Zimra, *Responsa*, vol. 4, no. 73. See also Goldman, *Life and Times of Rabbi David Ibn Abi Zimra*, p. 13.

6. Ibn Zimra, *Responsa*, vol. 3, no. 94.

7. Hacker, "Spiritual and Material Links, p. 242.

8. Cordovero, known by his acronym RaMaK, was born c. 1522, perhaps in Salonika, although his family apparently came from Portugal. He arrived in Safed at the age of twenty, studied Jewish law under Joseph Karo, and Kabbalah under his brother-in-law, Solomon Alkabets. By the beginning of the 1560s, Cordovero was the head of a yeshivah established by the Portuguese community in Safed, as well as a *dayyan* (judge) and *ʾav bet din* (head of a rabbinic court). He was a prolific writer who sought to systematize previous kabbalistic thought comprehensively. On Cordovero's life and career, see Meir Benayahu, *Yosef Beḥiri* (Jerusalem: Yad Harav Nissim, 1991), pp. 189–229; Bracha Zack, *Be-Shaʿarei ha-Kabbalah shel R. Moshe Cordovero* (Jerusalem: Ben Gurion University Press, 1995), pp. 1–32; Joseph ben Shlomo, *Torat ha-ʾElohut shel R. Moshe Cordovero* (Jerusalem: Mossad Bialik, 1965); Ira Robinson, *Moshe Cordovero's Introduction to Kabbalah* (New York: Ktav, 1994), pp. xxiv–xxxiv; Lawrence Fine, "Moshe Cordovero," in M. Eliade et al., eds., *The Encyclopedia of Religion* (New York: Macmillan, 1987), 4: 87–88; David, *To Come to the Land*, pp. 163–64.

9. On Dato's relationship to Cordovero, see Isaiah Tishby, "The Image of R. Moses Cordovero in the Writing of R. Mordechai Dato" (in Hebrew), *Sefunot* 7 (1963): 119–66.

10. For an English translation of Cordovero's *hanhagot*, see Fine, *Safed Spirituality*, pp. 34–38.

11. Joseph ben Isaac Sambari, *Sefer Divrei Yosef*, ed. S. Shtober (Jerusalem: Ben Zvi Institute, 1994), p. 64.

12. Concerning this question, see Benayahu, *Yosef Beḥiri*, pp. 196–98.

13. Benayahu, *Yosef Beḥiri*, p. 212, see esp. n. 100.

14. These lists are found in two sources: pt. 4 of Vital's dream diary, *Sefer ha-Ḥezyonot* (hereafter *SeH*), ed. A. Z. Aeshcoly (Jerusalem: Mossad ha-Rav Kook, 1954), pp. 217–20; and id., *Shaʿar ha-Gilgulim* (hereafter *ShG*), ed. Yehudah Ashlag (Tel Aviv: Eshel, 1961), *Haqdamah* 39, p. 171. For an English translation of Vital's diary, see Morris Faierstein, *Jewish Mystical Autobiographies* (New York: Paulist Press, 1999).

15. Vital, *SeH*, p. 134.

16. Concerning Joseph Don Don's relationship to Luria, see Ronit Meroz, "Selections from Ephraim Penzieri," pp. 214–22. With respect to the question of identifying Luria's disciples, in general, see ibid., pp. 214–15; and id., "R. Israel Sarug, Student of the Ari," pp. 41–44.

17. Concerning the question of whether Shem Tov Atiyah was a student of Luria's, see Tamar, *Meḥqarim be-Toldot ha-Yehudim be-ʾErets Yisrael u-be-ʾItalyah*, pp. 147–49. With respect to Benveniste, see below, n. 46.

18. Three of these letters were originally published in Joseph Delmedigo's *Taʿalumot Ḥokhmah* (Basle, 1629–31) under the title *Kitvei Shevaḥ Yaqar u-Gedulat ha-Ari*, and subsequently in a different version in Naphtali Bacharach's *ʿEmeq ha-Melekh*. They were republished numerous times as *Shivhei ha-Ari*. A fourth letter was published by Simcha Assaf in *Qovets ʿal Yad* (1940): 120–33. Unless otherwise noted, all references are to Yaʿakov Moshe Hillel's edition of these letters, *Sefer ha-Ari ve-Gurav* (Jerusalem: Ahavat Shalom, 1992) (hereafter *SeA*).

19. Concerning Shlomiel's letters, see Joseph Dan, *Ha-Sippur ha-ʿIvri be-Yemei ha-Beinayim* (Jerusalem: Keter, 1975), pp. 238–51; id., "On the History of the Literature of Hagiography" (in Hebrew), *MY* 1 (1981): 82–100; id., "Hagiographic Literature: East and West" (in Hebrew), *Peʿamim* 26 (1986): 77–86; Tamar, "Concerning the Book *Toldot ha-Ari*" (in Hebrew), in id., *Meḥqarim be-Toldot ha-Yehudim be-ʾErets Yisrael u-be-ʾItalyah*, pp. 166–93.

20. After circulating in numerous manuscripts, a portion of the cycle of stories that make up the anonymous *Toldot ha-Ari* was printed under the title *Sefer Kavvanot u-Maʿaseh Nissim* for the first time in Istanbul in 1720, and many times thereafter. It was edited in a modern edition by Meir Benayahu, who contends that this work served as the basis for *Shivhei ha-Ari*, not the reverse, as is the prevailing scholarly view. See his *Sefer Toldot ha-Ari* (Jerusalem: Ben Zvi Institute, 1967), and the studies by Dan and Tamar cited in n. 19 above. Tamar's "Concerning the Book *Toldot ha-Ari*" offers a detailed and convincing refutation of Benayahu's views regarding the chronological relationship between these two works.

21. The view taken here differs markedly from the one espoused by Mordechai Pachter. In his discussion of Samuel Uceda's eulogy of Luria, Pachter distinguished between the "realistic" evidence of the eulogy and the "legendary" evidence, which, in his view, includes not only *Shivhei ha-Ari* and *Toldot ha-Ari*, but also the anecdotal traditions scattered throughout Vital's writing. Insofar as Vital depicts Luria's "supernatural" abilities, Pachter regards such descriptions as legendary. In my view, such an approach fails to appreciate the significant differences between the earliest biographical traditions given to us by Luria's actual disciples and the subsequent hagiographies. What is more, the "realistic" portrayal evident in the eulogy is entirely compatible with what we learn from Luria's other disciples, including Vital. See Mordechai Pachter, "The Homiletic Eulogy by R. Samuel Uceda upon the Death of the Ari" (in Hebrew), in id., *Matsfunot Tsfat* (Jerusalem: Merkaz Zalman Shazar, 1994), pp. 39–68.

22. Hayyim Vital, *Shaʿar ha-Mitsvot* (hereafter *ShM*), *Parashat Qedoshim*, p. 55. This anecdote appears in the context of a discussion of the obligation to honor sages and elderly persons.

23. *ShM*, *Parashat Ki Tetse*, p. 143.

24. *ShM, Parashat Noaḥ*, p. 9.

25. *ShM, Parashat ʿEqev*, p. 89.

26. Ibid.

27. *ShK, Tefilat Minḥah, Derush* 2, p. 335.

28. HayyimVital, *Shaʿar Ruaḥ ha-Qodesh* (hereafter *SRH*), p. 34.

29. *SRH*, p. 33.

30. We know of three letters by Samson Bacchi, which were published by A. M. Luncz in *Yerushalayim* (Jerusalem, 1889), ed. D. Kaufman, 2: 140–47. These comments are found in the second letter, p. 145. Bacchi, whose exact dates are unknown, was active in the second half of the sixteenth century. Probably originally from Italy, he emigrated to Safed around 1582 and became a disciple of ibn Tabul. Soon thereafter, in 1583 or 1584, he moved to Jerusalem, where he came into contact with ibn Tabul's former rival, Hayyim Vital. In 1585, Bacchi sent a brief Lurianic treatise written by Vital entitled *Seder ha-ʾAtsilut be-Qitsur Muflag*, to Italy. It appears that Bacchi may have been the head of a yeshiva in Jerusalem. See David, *To Come to the Land*, p. 168.

31. *SRH*, p. 33.

32. Ibid.

33. Eleazar Azikri, *Sefer Ḥaredim* (Jerusalem, 1958), "Introduction."

34. Elijah de Vidas, *Reshit Ḥokhmah* (Venice, 1579), "The Gate of Love," ch. 10.

35. *SeH*, p. 156. Cf. *ShK*, p. 2, where the passage concludes with these words: "My teacher, of blessed memory, took great care to caution me about the love we ought to bear toward our associates, the members of our brotherhood."

36. Pachter, "Image of the Ari," p. 67.

37. *SRH*, p. 19. Cf. Vital's introduction to *Shaʿar ha-Haqdamot*, found at the beginning of id., *ʿEts Ḥayyim* (hereafter *EH*) (Warsaw, 1891). Cf., as well, Meroz, "An Anonymous Commentary on ʾIdra Rabba by a Member of the Sarug School," p. 312.

38. Vital's introduction to *EH*, p. 8.

39. See, e.g., *SeA*, letter 1, pp. 11–12.

40. *ShG, Haqdamah* 36, pp. 124–125.

41. See, e.g., Joseph ibn Tabul, Columbia University MS X893 M6862, fols. 144a, 152a. Cf. Zvia Rubin, "The Zoharic Commentaries of Joseph ibn Tabul" (in Hebrew), *MY* 10 (1992): 370.

42. Bacchi, letter 3, in D. Kaufman, ed., *Yerushalayim*, p. 146.

43. See Gershom Scholem, "*Tselem*: The Concept of the Astral Body," in id., *On the Mystical Shape of the Godhead*, pp. 251–73.

44. Hayyim Vital, *Sefer ha-Gilgulim* (Przemysl, 1875), ch. 69 (hereafter *SeG*).

45. According to some authorities, under the proper circumstances individuals can envision their own *tselem*, a type of encounter with one's "self" in the manner of a doppelgänger phenomenon. Thus, Moses Cordovero taught in his *Pardes*

Notes to pages 96–99   385

Rimmonim (gate 31, ch. 4) that "some of the pious achieve the observation of their image even in this world." See Scholem, *"Tselem,"* pp. 266, 316, n. 33.

46. Joseph Benveniste, *Dovev Siftei Yeshenim* (Izmir, 1671), p. 23a. Benveniste, as noted above, was not listed among Luria's disciples by Vital, or by anyone else, as far as I am aware. We know that he lived in Safed, beginning around the middle of the sixteenth century, and that he studied halakha with Elisha Gallico, and eventually studied as well with Samuel de Uceda. On Benveniste, see M. Benayahu, ed., *Sefer Toldot ha-Ari* (Jerusalem: Ben Zvi Institute, 1967) (hereafter *STA*), pp. 362–64; Tamar, *Meḥqarim be-Toldot ha-Yehudim be-ʾErets Yisrael u-be-ʾItalyah*, pp. 144–147; David, *To Come to the Land*, pp. 146, 168.

47. Benveniste, *Dovev Siftei Yeshenim*, p. 36a.

48. De Vidas, *Reshit Ḥokhmah*, "The Gate of Love," ch. 6.

49. Moses Galante, *Kohelet Yaʿaqov* (Safed, 1578), p. 57a.

50. See Benayahu, *STA*, pp. 361–62.

51. Samuel Uceda, *Midrash Shmuel* (Venice, 1578), p. 236a.

52. *ShG*, p. 27. The Lurianic literature is replete with stories about Luria's experience of the revelation of Elijah. See, e.g., the references to "Elijah" in Benayahu, *STA*, index to the names of individuals, p. 379.

53. Concerning the role of Elijah in Jewish literature, see Aharon Wiener, *The Prophet Elijah in the Development of Judaism: A Depth-Psychological Study* (Boston: Routledge & K. Paul, 1978). On his place among the kabbalists, see Werblowsky, *Joseph Karo*, pp. 40–41, 269–70; Scholem, *On the Kabbalah*, pp. 19–21.

54. *Zohar Ḥadash*, 59c.

55. *Maggid Mesharim*, 2b, adapted from Werblowsky's translation in *Joseph Karo*, p. 269.

56. *Maggid Mesharim*, 19b, adapted from Werblowsky, *Joseph Karo*, pp. 269–70.

57. Elliot Wolfson persuasively demonstrated the prominent role of the visual in the history of Jewish mystical literature. See his *Through a Speculum*, esp. chs. 6 and 7, where he explores this question in the context of theosophic Kabbalah.

58. Concerning the notion of the sentience of all creation in Jewish tradition, see Everett Gendler, "A Sentient Universe," in E. Bernstein, ed., *Ecology and the Jewish Spirit: Where Nature and the Sacred Meet* (Woodstock, Vt.: Jewish Lights, 1998), pp. 58–68.

59. This point is addressed in Wolfson's observation that "[m]ystical knowledge, in contrast to normal modes of perception, entails synesthesia, wherein the two epistemic modes [i.e., the visual and the auditory] converge and interpenetrate." Wolfson goes on to suggest that "even in those contexts that indicate the supremacy of hearing over seeing, the two systems, light and sound, are so conflated that it is impossible to speak of hearing the divine voices without seeing them." See Wolfson, *Through a Speculum*, pp. 287–88.

60. Vital's introduction to *EH*, p. 7.

61. Ibid.

62. For studies on the varied nature of Nahmanides' literary activities, see I. Twersky, ed., *Rabbi Moses Nahmanides (Ramban): Explorations in His Religious and Literary Virtuosity* (Cambridge, Mass.: Harvard University Press, 1983).

63. *The Commentary on Job, Kitvei ha-Ramban*, I: 23. This topic is the focus of a study by Moshe Idel, "We Have No Kabbalistic Tradition on This," in Twersky, *Rabbi Moses Nahmanides*, pp. 51–73; id., "Nahmanides: Kabbalah, Halakhah, and Spiritual Leadership," in M. Idel and M. Ostow, eds., *Jewish Mystical Leaders and Leadership in the Thirteenth Century* (Northvale, N.J.: Jason Aronson, 1998), pp. 15–96. For a somewhat different view of Nahmanides' hermeneutical stance, see Elliot R. Wolfson, "By Way of Truth: Aspects of Nahmanides' Kabbalistic Hermeneutic," *Association for Jewish Studies Review* 14, 2 (1989): 103–78.

64. Idel, "We Have No Kabbalistic Tradition," pp. 63–64.

65. Ibid., pp. 64–65.

66. A revised view of the authorship of the *Zohar* was espoused by Yehuda Liebes, according to which a *group* had a part in its development, although de Leon still emerges as the central figure in this process. See Liebes, "How the Zohar Was Written," in id., *Studies in the Zohar*, pp. 85–138.

67. Concerning the influence of the *Zohar*, see *WZ*, I: 13–30.

68. A considerable amount of attention has been devoted to questions bearing on the midrashic nature of the Zoharic literature. See, e.g., Matt, *Zohar*, pp. 25–32; id., "*Matnita Dilan*: A Technique of Innovation in the Zohar" (in Hebrew), in *MY* 8 (1989): 123–45; Moshe Idel, "Midrashic Versus Other Forms of Jewish Hermeneutics: Some Comparative Reflections," Michael Fishbane, "'The Holy One Sits and Roars': Mythopoesis and the Midrashic Imagination," and Elliot R. Wolfson, "Beautiful Maiden Without Eyes: *Peshat* and *Sod* in Zoharic Hermeneutics," all in Fishbane, *The Midrashic Imagination: Jewish Exegesis, Thought, and History* (Albany: State University of New York Press, 1993). For studies that describe the relationship between revelatory experience and textual interpretation in the Zohar, see Elliot Wolfson, "Circumcision, Vision of God, and Textual Interpretation: From Midrashic Trope to Mystical Symbol," in Fine, *Essential Papers on Kabbalah*, pp. 495–524; id., "The Hermeneutics of Visionary Experience: Revelation and Interpretation in the Zohar," *Religion* 18 (1988): 311–45.

69. Fine, "Kabbalistic Texts," pp. 313–14.

70. Menahem Recanati, *Perush ʿal ha-Torah* (Jerusalem, 1961), *Parashat Naso*. Cf. Scholem, *Origins*, p. 37, n. 61.

71. As cited in Scholem, *Origins*, p. 206; see also on this ibid. pp. 35–39, 238–43; id., *On the Kabbalah*, pp. 5–31. Scholem (*Origins*, p. 206) cautions that "expressions of the kind mentioned here do not necessarily indicate a mystical inspiration. They also occur in the Talmud in purely halakhic contexts in order to designate the source of statements that do not emanate from oral tradition but

that nevertheless claim authority. . . . The evaluation of the significance of such expressions in the case of the Rabad is a matter of subjective judgment." See as well Isadore Twersky, *Rabad of Posquieres: A Twelfth-Century Talmudist* (Cambridge, Mass.: Harvard University Press, 1962), pp. 286–300; A. J. Heschel, *Prophetic Inspiration After the Prophets* (Hoboken, N.J.: Ktav, 1996).

72. Idel, *Kabbalah*, pp. 234–37. In Abulafia, prophetic experience itself is contingent upon a complex and distinctive hermeneutical system in which the letters that make up the Torah and God's names are "deconstructed" and recombined into new patterns. For a discussion of Abulafia's hermeneutics, see Moshe Idel, *Language, Torah, and Hermeneutics in Abraham Abulafia* (Albany: State University of New York Press, 1989). On the nature of mystical experience in Abulafian mysticism, see Idel, *Mystical Experience in Abraham Abulafia*, esp. ch. 3.

73. Idel, *Kabbalah*, pp. 236, 387, n. 163.

74. Ivan Marcus, "Religious Virtuosi and the Religious Community: The Pietistic Mode in Judaism," in J. Neusner, ed., *Take Judaism, for Example* (Chicago: University of Chicago Press, 1983), p. 100. For a thorough analysis of visionary experience as a form of prophecy among the German Pietists, see Wolfson, *Through a Speculum*, ch. 5.

75. *Zohar* 3, 132b (Idra Rabba). Translation from *WZ*, 1: 10.

76. Ibid.

77. For a set of remarks about the importance of this fictional Shimon bar Yohai in the life of the great Hasidic master Nahman of Bratslav, see Arthur Green, *Tormented Master: A Life of Rabbi Nahman of Bratslav* (Tuscaloosa: University of Alabama Press, 1979), pp. 10–15.

78. See Vital's introduction to *EH*, pp. 8–9. See on this Moshe Idel, "Inquiries into the Doctrine of *Sefer ha-Meshiv*" (in Hebrew), *Sefunot* 17 (1983): 239–43.

79. Vital's introduction to *EH*, p. 8.

80. Ibid., p. 7.   81. Ibid.

82. Ibid., p. 9.   83. Ibid.

84. These words were incorporated in the title page of the printed editions of *Berit Menuḥah* by its publishers, who drew it from Cordovero's *Pardes Rimmonim*, *Shaᶜar ha-Nequdot*, ch. 1. I have adapted the English translation of this passage from Jacobs, *Jewish Mystical Testimonies*, p. 87.

85. Vital's introduction to *EH*, p. 9.

86. Ibid.

87. For more on this subject, see Idel, "Inquiries," pp. 241–42.

88. Ibid., pp. 232–43.   89. Vital's introduction to *EH*, p. 8.

90. Ibid.   91. Ibid.

92. Max Weber, *The Theory of Social and Economic Organization*, trans. A. M. Henderson and T. Parsons (Glencoe, Ill.: Free Press, 1947), p. 329.

93. Ibid.

94. Ibid, p. 330.

95. Charles Keyes, "Charisma: From Social Life to Sacred Biography," in *Charisma and Sacred Biography*, ed. M. Williams, *Journal of the American Academy of Religion, Thematic Studies* 48, 3–4 (1982): 2.

96. See, e.g., Arthur Green, "The *Zaddiq* as *Axis Mundi* in Later Judaism," *Journal of the American Academy of Religion* 45, 3 (1977): 327–47, reprinted in Fine, *Essential Papers on Kabbalah*, pp. 291–314.

97. W. S. Green, "What's in a Name? The Problematic of Rabbinic 'Biography,'" in J. Neusner, ed., *Approaches to Ancient Judaism: Theory and Practice* (Missoula, Mont.: Scholars Press, 1978), pp. 89–90.

98. Jacob Neusner, *A History of the Jews in Babylonia* (Leiden: E.J. Brill, 1969), 4: 334–69; W. S. Green, "Palestinian Holy Men: Charismatic Leadership and Rabbinic Tradition," in W. Haase and H. Temporini, eds., *Aufstieg und Niedergang der römischen Welt: Geschichte und Kultur Roms im Spiegel der neueren Forschung* (Berlin: W. de Gruyter, 1979), 19.2, pp. 619–47. On the question of the relative absence of charismatic attribution in Judaism more generally, see Robert Cohn, "Sainthood on the Periphery: The Case of Judaism," in J. S. Hawley, ed., *Saints and Virtues* (Berkeley: University of California Press, 1987), pp. 87–108.

99. W. S. Green, "Storytelling and Holy Man: The Case of Ancient Judaism," in Neusner, *Take Judaism, for Example*, p. 41.

100. My thanks to Professor Robert Goldenberg for this observation, in a personal communication.

101. Concerning this point, see Bruce Chilton and Jacob Neusner, *Types of Authority in Formative Christianity and Judaism* (New York: Routledge, 1999), p. 78. Neusner remarks that "the sages are represented as holy men, able to do miracles, but the law is set forth by sages in their capacity as masters of tradition and reasoning concerning tradition."

102. Joseph Solomon Delmedigo, *Taʿalumot Ḥokhmah*, 37b; Hayyim Vital, *Liqqutei Shas* (Leghorn, 1790), 33c.

103. See Idel, *Kabbalah*, pp. 237–40; id., "Inquiries"; Gershom Scholem, "The *Maggid* of Rabbi Joseph Taitasak and the Revelations Attributed to Him" (in Hebrew), *Sefunot* 11 (1978): 47–112.

104. The translation of this passage is based on Idel, *Kabbalah*, p. 237. On the traditions according to which Rashi was the recipient of divinely inspired knowledge, see ibid., pp. 238–39.

105. Ibid., p. 237.

106. Ibid., p. 238.

107. Concerning the activities of Ovadiah Hamon, see Moshe Idel, "Rabbi Judah Haleywa and His Book *Sefer Tsefanat Paʿaneaḥ*" (in Hebrew), *Shalem* 4 (1984): 139–45.

108. Idel, "Inquiries," pp. 193–94, 220–26, and passim.

109. Ibid., pp. 240–43.

110. See Rachel Elior, "The Doctrine of Transmigration in *Galya Raza*," in Fine, *Essential Papers on Kabbalah*, pp. 243–69, an abbreviated English translation based upon the original article in Hebrew in *Meḥqarim be-Kabbalah be-Pilosophia Yehudit u-Besifrut ha-Musar ve-Hehagut*, pp. 207–39.

111. Elior, "Doctrine," p. 244.

112. Ibid.

113. On Molcho, see R.J.Z. Werblowsky, "R. Joseph Karo, Solomon Molcho, Don Joseph Nasi," in Beinart, *The Sephardi Legacy*, 2: 187–91; Moshe Idel, "Solomon Molcho as Magician" (in Hebrew), *Sefunot* 18 (1985): 193–219.

114. Molcho's collection of homilies was printed under the title *Sefer ha-Mefoʾar* (Salonika, 1529), and composed in response to a request "by the beloved brethren in Salonika." Accounts of his visionary experiences were preserved in his epistle addressed to Joseph Taitasak, *Ḥayyat Qaneh* (Amsterdam, 1648), written in Monastir in Macedonia.

115. Based upon Idel's translation in *Kabbalah*, p. 240.

116. Cf. Idel, *Kabbalah*, p. 234. For a discussion of the connections between visionary experience, mystical inspiration, and messianic impulses among a range of sixteenth-century figures, see Rachel Elior, "Messianic Expectations and Spiritualization of Religious Life in the Sixteenth Century," in D. Ruderman, ed., *Essential Papers on Jewish Culture in Renaissance and Baroque Italy* (New York: New York University Press, 1992), pp. 283–98.

117. Concerning the history of the kabbalists of Morocco, see Rachel Elior, "The Kabbalists of Draa" (in Hebrew), *Peʿamim* 24 (1985): 36–73; Moshe Hallamish, "The Origins of Kabbalah in Morocco" (in Hebrew), *Peʿamim* 15 (1983): 29–46; id., "The Kabbalists of Morocco" (in Hebrew), *Mi-Mizrach u-be-Maʿarav* 2 (1980): 205–35; id., "Concerning the Kabbalists of Morocco" (Corrections and Additions) (in Hebrew), *Daʿat* 16 (1986): 87–131; and Moshe Idel, "The Beginnings of Kabbalah in North Africa" (in Hebrew), *Peʿamim* 43 (1990): 4–15. For general information about North African Jewry, especially in the sixteenth century, see H. Z. Hirschberg, *A History of the Jews in North Africa* (Leiden: E. J. Brill, 1974–81); Jane S. Gerber, *Jewish Society in Fez, 1450–1700: Studies in Communal and Economic Life* (Leiden: E.J. Brill, 1980); D. Corcos, *Studies in the History of the Jews of Morocco* (Jerusalem: Rubin Mass, 1976); M. Avitbul, "North African Jewry after the Spanish Expulsion" (in Hebrew), in I. Cohen, ed., *Ha-Pezurah ha-Yehudit ha-Sefardit ʾAḥarei ha-Gerush* (Jerusalem, 1992), pp. 9–26; Abraham David, "Relations Between North African Jewry and the Land of Israel in the Fifteenth and Sixteenth Centuries" (in Hebrew), *Peʿamim* 24 (1985): 74–86.

118. According to scholarly estimates, some 30,000 Jews from the Iberian Peninsula settled in North Africa following the Expulsion, most of them in northern Morocco. The influence of Sephardim in the south was far more limited. In

contrast to our extensive knowledge about the Sephardic Jewish communities that relocated in the Ottoman Empire, there is much less documentation concerning North African Jewry. See J. Barnai, "The Jews of Spain in North Africa," in Beinart, *The Sephardi Legacy*, 2: 68–71; David, *To Come to the Land*, pp. 70–71, 106–8.

119. Elior, "Kabbalists of Draa," pp. 61–65.

120. Clifford Geertz, *Islam Observed: Religious Development in Morocco and Indonesia* (New Haven, Conn.: Yale University Press, 1969), pp. 43–55. See also Ernest Gellner, *Saints of the Atlas* (Chicago: University of Chicago Press, 1969); Edward Westermarck, *Ritual and Belief in Morocco*, 2 vols. (1926; new ed., New Hyde Park, N.Y.: University Books, 1968).

121. Elior, "Kabbalists of Draa," pp. 66–68.

122. See David, "Relations Between North African Jewry and the Land of Israel in the Fifteenth and Sixteenth Centuries" (in Hebrew), *Peʿamim* 24 (1985): 74–81.

123. Bacchi's letters, in D. Kaufman, *Yerushalayim*, pp. 146–47.

124. See Idel, "Rabbi Judah Haleywa," pp. 119–30.

125. Ibid., pp. 146–48.

126. *SeH*, pp. 2–3. On Rabbi Lapidot, see as well p. 60; Idel, "Rabbi Judah Haleywa," p. 147.

127. *SeH*, pp. 3–4. Cf. pp. 120, 122.   128. Ibid., pp. 6–7.

129. Ibid., p. 36.   130. Ibid., pp. 36–37.

131. Ibid., pp. 28–29, 87–88, 113–14.   132. Ibid., pp. 27–28.

133. Ibid., p. 122.   134. Ibid., pp. 10–11.

135. Joseph ben Isaac Sambari, *Sefer Divrei Yosef*, p. 364. This remark is followed by a couple of stories that serve to confirm the reliability of her knowledge.

136. Geertz, *Islam Observed*, p. 44.

137. On the subject of Sabbatai Sevi, see Scholem, *Sabbatai Sevi*. For a study of the controversies between rabbinic authorities and Sabbateans in the eighteenth century, see Elisheva Carlebach, *The Pursuit of Heresy: Rabbi Moses Hagiz and the Sabbatian Controversies* (New York: Columbia University Press, 1990). On the role of the *tsaddiq* as a charismatic figure in the development of eastern European Hasidism, see Arthur Green, *Tormented Master*, ch. 4; id., "*Zaddiq* as *Axis Mundi* in Later Judaism;" id., "Typologies of Leadership and the Hasidic Zaddiq," in id., *Jewish Spirituality*, 2: 127–56. The phenomenon of charisma in both Sabbateanism and Hasidism is also studied in Stephen Sharot, *Messianism, Mysticism, and Magic: A Sociological Analysis of Jewish Religious Movements* (Chapel Hill: University of North Carolina Press, 1982).

Chapter 4

1. Moses Yonah's version represents Luria's teachings at an early stage in Safed. It was published as *Kanfei Yonah* in Lemberg (Lvov), 1884 (reprint, Jerusalem,

1975). An important version of Yonah's rendition is found in Sassoon MS 993, written in 1584, and is accompanied by the signature of the author, who made corrections to the scribe's work. While this manuscript is missing a number of the initial folios, a complete manuscript is Ben Zvi Institute MS 2218. *Sha'ar ha-Kelalim*, printed at the beginning of Meir Popper's version of *'Ets Hayyim*, is also associated with Moses Yonah. This material, which parallels *Kanfei Yonah*, is variously attributed in a number of manuscripts to Moses Yonah, Moses Najara, and Joseph Arzin, and probably predates the period in which Vital became Luria's student. The identification of Moses Yonah's writing has been complicated by the existence of a great number of other manuscripts entitled *Kanfei Yonah*, attributed to other authors, most prominently the Italian kabbalist Azariah da Fano. For detailed accounts of Moses Yonah's compositions, see Meroz, "Torat ha-Ge'eulah," pp. 90–91, who regards *Kanfei Yonah* as the most significant representative of level three in her schema; Avivi, "Lurianic Writings in Italy Prior to 1620"; Meir Benayahu, "Rabbi Moses Yonah, the Ari's Disciple, and the First to Record His Teachings" (in Hebrew), in id., ed., *Sefer Zikkaron le-ha-Rav Yitshak Nissim* (Jerusalem: Yad Harav Nissim, 1985), pp. 7–74.

2. Joseph ibn Tabul, as we have already noted, was among Luria's most prominent disciples, second in importance after Vital. The main rendition by Tabul of Luria's mythological teachings was published as *Derush Heftsi Bah*, found at the beginning of a book entitled *Simhat Kohen* (Jerusalem, 1921) by Masud ha-Kohen al Haddad. Ironically, it was attributed to Hayyim Vital, who considered himself Tabul's rival. Important manuscript versions of this material include Jewish Theological Seminary of America MS 1759 and Columbia University MS X893 M6862. Among the many other manuscripts containing Tabul's version of Lurianic myth, mention should be made of *Sod Gavhei Shamayim*, recorded by one of Tabul's disciples, found in British Museum MS Or. 10627, fols. 77–81b. Ibn Tabul also composed numerous commentaries to the *Zohar*, influenced in part by Luria's teachings. His commentary to the Idra Rabba was published from manuscript by Israel Weinstock, "Rabbi Yosef ibn Tabul's Commentary on the Idra" (in Hebrew), in *Temirin*, vol. 2 (Jerusalem, 1982), pp. 123–67. Ibn Tabul's writings are described in Meroz, *Ge'eulah*, pp. 81–89; Avivi, "Lurianic Writings in Italy Prior to 1620"; Rubin, "Zoharic Commentaries of Joseph ibn Tabul."

3. Vital's compositions account for the vast majority of Luria's teachings, although it is also true that many writings by other students of Luria's were falsely or mistakenly attributed to Vital. The questions having to do with the many renditions of Vital's writings are exceedingly complex, and the present remarks are limited to a very brief account of Vital's first version. Vital began to record Luria's teachings probably even before the latter died, and continued to engage in this work for approximately twenty years, in Safed, Damascus, and Jerusalem. In his "first version" (*mahadura qamma*), entitled *'Ets Hayyim* (*Tree of Life*), Vital organized

Luria's teachings into eight book-length divisions or "gates." The first gate
brought together teachings that Luria himself had committed to writing, while
the remaining gates included what Vital had learned orally from Luria. At the end
of each of these final seven gates, Vital added traditions, which he had not personally heard but had learned from Luria's other disciples. Vital says that these
people heard these teachings, at least in part, "during the period that I was not
present," referring to Luria's earliest months in Safed, when Vital was not yet his
disciple. The eight original gates were organized as follows: (1) Teachings that
Vital copied from Luria's own manuscripts; (2) Teachings (*haqdamot*) concerning
mythological themes that Vital had heard from Luria; (3) Luria's commentaries
on selected passages from the *Zohar*; (4) Luria's commentaries on verses from the
TaNaKh; (5) contemplative intentions (*kavvanot*) to accompany liturgical prayer;
(6) contemplative intentions to accompany the performance of the mitsvot, organized according to the portions into which the Torah is divided; (7) teachings
having to do with achieving the "Holy Spirit" (*Ruaḥ ha-Qodesh*) by means of the
practice of *yiḥudim*; and (8) teachings having to do with reincarnation (*gilgul*).
This original version exists in manuscript form only. On the basis of this version,
Vital's son Shmuel produced a revised edition in Damascus following his father's
death, employing the following titles: (1) *Shaʿar ha-Haqdamot*; (2) *Shaʿar Maʾamarei Rashbi*; (3) *Shaʿar Maʾmarei Razal*; (4) *Shaʿar ha-Pesuqim*; (5) *Shaʿar ha-
Mitsvot*; (6) *Shaʿar ha-Kavvanot*; (7) *Shaʿar Ruaḥ ha-Qodesh*; and (8) *Shaʿar ha-
Gilgulim*. Shmuel eliminated the first gate from the original version, distributed
its material into other sections, and divided the original third section into two different gates, thus retaining his father's original structure of eight parts. In addition, instead of leaving the traditions that other disciples had conveyed to Hayyim
Vital at the end of each gate, Shmuel integrated these materials according to topic
into the edition as a whole. In other words, whereas Hayyim Vital had sought to
keep separate what Luria had written, what he had heard directly from his teacher,
and what he had learned from others, Shmuel's goal was to reorganize the materials in a more thoroughgoing thematic way. It is this version that is generally
known as the *Shemonah Sheʿarim* (Eight Gates). Remarkably, it was not brought
to the printing press until the middle of the nineteenth century, when it was published in Jerusalem for the first time between the years 1850–98.

Two further strata of Vital's writings became the basis for a complex maze of
editions and recensions of Lurianic teachings by a variety of individuals, including Jacob Zemach, Meir Poppers, Abraham Azulai, and Nathan Shapira. For detailed and considerably different accounts of Vital's versions and the numerous
editions by other editors based upon Vital's work, see Meroz, "Torat ha-Geʾeulah,"
pp. 39–69; and Avivi, *Binyan ʾAriel*, pp. 20–108. For an overview, in English, of
the Lurianic writings, see P. Giller, *Reading the Zohar: The Sacred Text of the Kabbalah* (New York: Oxford University Press, 2001), pp. 21–26.

4. See Meroz, "Torat ha-Geʾeulah," pp. 92–94.

5. This is one of the main differences between Tishby's approach in his *Torat ha-Raʿ* and more recent research. Tishby based his study almost entirely on certain of the writings of Hayyim Vital, with one notable exception. In his discussion of Luria's conceptions of *tsimtsum* and *reshimu*, Tishby contrasted Vital's views with those of Joseph ibn Tabul and argued that Tabul's description of these ideas is the authentic Lurianic perspective. But newly available evidence demonstrates that Vital actually articulated views similar to Tabul's. This kind of evidence strengthens the argument that there is much greater similarity among the versions than was once believed, and that Luria's thinking evolved over time. For Tishby's own comments on this, see the new introduction to the 1984 edition of *Torat ha-Raʿ*, pp. 10–11, and pp. 21–27. In his book *Binyan ʾAriel*, Joseph Avivi also describes various layers of Lurianic teaching. Avivi's approach differs greatly from Meroz's, however. In the first place, Avivi draws distinctions between *nine* layers of Luria's thought, in contrast to Meroz's five. Second, Meroz differentiates between levels based upon bibliographical considerations as well as clearly articulated "internal" terminological and conceptual criteria, whereas Avivi depends primarily upon bibliographical factors. Third, Avivi draws only upon Luria's own writings, along with the renditions by Vital, leaving out the versions by Moses Yonah and Joseph ibn Tabul. Nor does he take into account traditions that Vital himself heard from fellow disciples and preserved in his writings. One of the results of this, as Meroz herself points out, is that levels one and three in her schema are missing altogether from Avivi's. For Meroz's remarks on Avivi's work, see "Torat ha-Geʾeulah," pp. 371–82.

6. Meroz has also made this point. See her "Faithful Transmission Versus Innovation: Luria and His Disciples," in P. Schäfer and J. Dan, eds., *Gershom Scholem's "Major Trends in Jewish Mysticism" Fifty Years After* (Tübingen: Mohr, 1993), pp. 257–74, where she offers examples of ways in which Vital contributed his own originality to the teachings he had received.

7. My exposition of Lurianic myth draws in significant respects on Meroz, "Torat ha-Geʾeulah," pp. 181–254, incorporating the closely related stages four and five in her schema.

8. Hayyim Vital, *ShH, Haqdamah* 4, p. 14.

9. Joseph ibn Tabul, *Perush ha-ʾIdra Rabba le-Rabbi Yosef ibn Tabul*, ed. I. Weinstock, in *Temirin*, vol. 2 (Jerusalem, 1982), p. 137, edited on the basis of Jewish National and University Library MS 452 8 and Musayof MS 160, Jerusalem.

10. Joseph ibn Tabul, *Kerem Hayah le-Shlomo*, Columbia University MS X893 M6862. This language has its origins in rabbinic midrash, *Pirquei de-Rabbi ʾEliezer*, ch. 3, and served as the basis for a passage in *Zohar Ḥadash* 2d, according to which "Before the world was created the Holy One, blessed be He, was one and his name was one."

11. Ibn Tabul, *Kerem Hayah*. Cf. id., *Gavhei Shamayim*, British Museum MS Or. 10627, fols. 78b–79a.

12. See, e.g., Hayyim Vital, *Derush she-Masar Hayyim Vital le-Rabbi Shlomo Sagis*, in Toyetto, *Liqqutim Hadashim* (Jerusalem: Mevaqqshei ha-Shem, 1985), p. 17. This text is found in Livorno (Leghorn) MS 74, fols. 12b–13a, in the handwriting of Nathan Shapiro, and Jewish National and University Library MS 1161. While it is found in neither Vital's original *ʿEts Hayyim* or the subsequent *Shemonah Sheʿarim*, it appears to belong to the original stage of Vital's writings and to stage four in Meroz's schema.

13. Ibn Tabul, *Kerem Hayah*.

14. Ibn Tabul, *Derush Heftsi Bah, Derush* 1, 1.

15. *ShH, Haqdamah* 4, p. 14.

16. Ibn Tabul, *Perush*, p. 137.

17. There, however, it has an altogether different meaning, referring to a luminous splendor, the *sefirah Keter*, that was co-eternal with and surrounded *Ein Sof*: "In the beginning [Gen. 1:1] when the will of the King began to take effect, He engraved signs into the supernal luster *(tehiru)* [that surrounded Him]."

18. Ibn Tabul, *Perush*, p. 137.

19. *Midrash Tanhuma, Vayakhel* 7. Cf. Exodus Rabbah, 24:1, where God says he "will descend and even concentrate My presence within one square cubit [of the ark]."

20. Scholem, *Major Trends*, p. 260.

21. See the sources cited by Scholem, *Major Trends*, p. 410, n. 43.

22. Vital, *Derush she-Masar*, p. 17. See Meroz, "Torat ha-Geʾeulah," pp. 187–88.

23. Moshe Idel, "Concerning the Concept of *Tsimtsum* in Kabbalah and in Scholarship" (in Hebrew), *MY* 10(1992): 59–112.

24. Ibid., pp. 60–68. Idel (p. 60) asserts that it is reasonable to assume "that the fact that Ramban takes this approach made an impression upon the Ari, who elaborated upon the idea of *tsimtsum*."

25. Ibid., p. 69. Cf. Scholem, *Major Trends*, pp. 260, 410, n. 42.

26. Ibid., pp. 69–85, and passim.

27. Boaz Huss, "*Genizat ha-ʾOr* in Simeon Lavi's *Ketem Paz* and the Lurianic Doctrine of *Tsimtsum*" (in Hebrew), *MY* 10(1992): 341–61.

28. See Zack, *Be-Shaʿarei ha-Kabbalah*, pp. 57–82.

29. See, e.g., Vital, *Derush she-Masar*. As noted earlier, the discovery of this source serves to disprove Isaiah Tishby's contention that ibn Tabul knew of this explanation for *tsimtsum* but Vital did not. See Meroz, "Torat ha-Geʾeulah," pp. 190–91. As is well known, Scholem drew an interpretive connection between Luria's notion of *tsimtsum* and that of exile. In *Major Trends* (p. 261), he writes:

One is tempted to interpret this withdrawal of God into his own Being in terms of Exile, of banishing Himself from His totality into profound seclusion. Regarded this way, the idea of *Tsimtsum* is the deepest symbol of Exile that could be thought of, even deeper than the "Breaking of the Vessels." In the "Breaking of the Vessels," . . . something of the Divine Being is exiled out of Himself, whereas the *Tsimtsum* could come to be considered as an exile into Himself.

Elsewhere (*Sabbatai Sevi*, p. 31), Scholem conceded that the "Kabbalists did not explicitly say that the act of *simsum* was a divine type and prefiguration of the exile, although the analogy seems obvious." This view was part of a larger tendency on Scholem's part, not only to interpret Lurianic myth in terms of the categories of exile and redemption, but also to strongly imply that these concerns were a (logical) consequence and thus mystical interpretation of the recent Spanish Expulsion. Moshe Idel, in particular, has vigorously challenged the validity of this historically oriented interpretation, arguing, among other things, that what Scholem asserted in rather hypothetical terms became reified in subsequent scholarship, where it has been largely accepted as hard fact. See Idel, *Kabbalah*, pp. 264–66; id., "Concerning the Concept of *Tsimtsum*," pp. 91–101; id., "Particularism and Universalism in Kabbalah: 1480–1650," in Ruderman, *Essential Papers on Jewish Culture in Renaissance and Baroque Italy*, pp. 334–37; id., *Messianic Mystics*, pp. 179–80. While I myself long ago echoed certain of Scholem's views on this question, I am in complete agreement with Idel that there is no explicit evidence in Lurianic literature that the historical experience of the Spanish Expulsion played a part in Luria's mythic conceptions. Neither this historical event nor any others are mentioned in this literature. On the other hand, I remain convinced that the notion of exile and the striving for redemption occupied a critical place in Lurianic Kabbalah, as attested by diverse evidence in the present study. As seen in Chapter 9, for example, the members of Luria's fellowship believed that they were living "in this final exile" (*be-galut zeh ha-ʾaḥaron*), "in the final generation of the Messiah." One of the ways in which they expressed the purpose of their religious task was that they performed it in order to be "extricated from exile and be redeemed." While exile and redemption was by no means the only set of categories through which Luria and his disciples understood the meaning of their lives, it was certainly a fundamental one.

30. Concerning the history of the various conceptions of the *golem* in Jewish literature, see Moshe Idel, *Golem: Jewish Magical and Mystical Traditions on the Artificial Anthropoid* (Albany: State University of New York Press, 1990).

31. Vital, *Derush she-Masar*, p. 17. This translation draws on Daniel Matt, *The Essential Kabbalah* (San Francisco: Harper San Francisco, 1995), p. 94.

32. Vital, *Derush she-Masar*, p. 18.

33. Joseph ibn Tabul, *Sod Gavhei Shamayim*, British Museum MS Or. 10627, fols. 79b–81a.

34. Cf. Meroz, "Torat ha-Geʾeulah," pp. 237–38.

35. Vital, *Derush she-Masar*, p. 18.

36. Ibid., p. 20.

37. *Zohar* 3, 135a–135b, Idra Rabba. See *WZ*, 1: 332–33; Liebes, *Ha-Mashiah*, pp. 195–99.

38. Genesis Rabbah 3:9.

39. Ibn Tabul, *Kerem Hayah*.

40. One of the central arguments in Wolfson's *Through a Speculum* is that the kabbalistic Godhead is ultimately conceived of as an androgynous male. The divine female originates as an extension of the male and is ultimately reincorporated back into the male such that the female is subsumed, divested of its independent identity: "The underlying theosophic assumption is that the phallus is the ontic source of both masculinity and femininity. . . . the contextualization of the female in the male organ allows the kabbalists to envision the penis as the locus of the union of both genders." See Wolfson, *Through a Speculum*, pp. 357–58; id., "Crossing Gender Boundaries in Kabbalistic Ritual and Myth," in id., *Circle in the Square*, pp. 79–121. On the development of the conception of crown in kabbalistic tradition more generally, and its sexual associations in particular, see Arthur Green, *Keter: The Crown of God in Early Jewish Mysticism* (Princeton, N.J.: Princeton University Press, 1997), esp. chs. 13–14.

41. The conception of "Male Waters" and "Female Waters" has its origins in rabbinic literature. According to a passage in Genesis Rabbah (13:13), there are two kinds of waters: rain, which flows from above, and water, or moisture, which wells up from the earth. Of these, says R. Levi, "the upper waters are male while the lower are female." Cf. JT *Berakhot* 9:3, 14a.

42. See Ibn Tabul, *Perush*, pp. 139–40. Cf. Meroz, "Torat ha-Geʾeulah," pp. 230–31. This gendered understanding of the Breaking of the Vessels is consistent with and intimately related to another important set of symbols: "circles and a straight path" (*ʿiggulim ve-yosher*). Many accounts of Luria's myth emphasize that the light of *Adam Qadmon* that was reintroduced into the empty space following the *tsimtsum* did so, at first, in the form of a series of concentric circles, conceived as female configurations. Having done so, they proceeded to assume male anthropomorphic form, as a straight line, akin to the shape of the masculine body. Some explanations of the *shevirah* stress the fact that the four worlds were created only in the pattern of feminine circles, without the participation of the male configuration of a straight line. As a result, these circles failed to constitute a whole or perfect configuration. In such terms, *tiqqun* requires the uniting of these *ʿiggulim ve-yosher*, that is, the "marriage" of feminine and masculine qualities. The weakness of the light that reentered the empty space—whether it was conceived as the "crown" of *Yesod* or "circles"—was thus a function of its isolation, the separation of female light from male light. On this motif, see Meroz, "Torat ha-Geʾeulah," pp. 232–34, 239–41.

43. *Mavo Sheʿarim,* ed. Yehudah Ashlag (Tel Aviv: Eshel, 1961), *Shaʿar* 2, pt. 1, ch. 5, pp. 18–19.

44. Cf. Meroz, "Torat ha-Ge'eulah," pp. 241–44.

45. *ShMR, Qedoshim*, p. 175.   46. Ibid., p. 174.

47. Ibid., 178.   48. Ibid., p. 179.

49. Ibid., p. 179.   50. Ibid., 180.

51. Scholem, *Major Trends*, p. 279.

52. Ibid., p. 260. See also Isaiah Tishby, "Gnostic Doctrines in Sixteenth-Century Jewish Mysticism," *Journal of Jewish Studies* 6 (1955): 146–52.

53. Definitions and characterizations of *Gnostic, Gnosis*, and *Gnosticism* have been the subject of endless debate among scholars. What *is* clear is that these terms refer to a wide and variegated collection of religious movements concerning which there is evidence in the Roman empire beginning in the second century C.E., rather than to a monolithic phenomenon susceptible to easy universal characterization. An international conference held in Messina, Italy, in 1966, arrived at a working definition of *Gnosticism* that included the following language:

a coherent series of characteristics that can be summarized in the idea of a divine spark in man, deriving from the divine realm, fallen into this world of fate, birth and death, and needing to be awakened by the divine counterpart of the self in order to be finally re-integrated. . . . this idea is based ontologically on the conception of a downward movement of the divine whose periphery . . . had to submit to the fate of entering into a crisis and producing—even if only indirectly—this world.

The Messina conference, however, hardly solved the problems inherent in seeking to understand what these various religious movements have in common. In his *Rethinking "Gnosticism": An Argument for Dismantling a Dubious Category* (Princeton: Princeton University Press, 1996), Michael Williams argues that the very use of the terms *Gnostic* and *Gnosticism* to describe these movements should be abandoned insofar as they serve to obscure the truly differentiated nature of the ideas found in this literature. Still, in my view, there is heuristic value in the characterization of Gnostic myth presented here.

54. See Hans Jonas, *The Gnostic Religion: The Message of the Alien God and the Beginnings of Christianity*, 2d ed. (Boston: Beacon Press, 1970). Even though Jonas's binary categorization is dated, as more nuanced typologies and phenomenologies of Gnostic sects have been developed, it is still frequently invoked, and still useful. Jonas himself regarded the terms "Iranian" and "Syrian-Egyptian" as shorthand for two basic orientations that characterize much Gnostic speculation: "Our division is typological and therefore not much affected by what is made of the geographic and ethnic intimations of the names chosen for it" (ibid., p. 237). See also ibid., pp. 112–46; and Kurt Rudolph, *Gnosis: The Nature and History of Gnosticism* (San Francisco: Harper & Row, 1983), pp. 59–67.

55. For a discussion of the wide variety of "anticosmic" positions, see Williams, *Rethinking "Gnosticism,"* pp. 96–115.

56. "Hymn of the Pearl" in the *Acta Thomae*, as quoted by Jonas, *Gnostic Religion*, p. 69.

57. Scholem, *Major Trends*, p. 264.

58. As cited in ibid., p. 264. Scholem writes there that *sonship* "is Basilides's term for the most sublime consummation of the universal potentialities."

59. Ibid.

60. Although born in Greece around the year 100, Valentinus, like Basilides, was active in Alexandria, Egypt. The attractiveness of his teachings resulted in a Valentinian school of Gnostic thought.

61. Yehuda Liebes, "The Kabbalistic Myth as Told by Orpheus," in id., *Studies in Jewish Myth and Messianism*, p. 85.

62. Liebes, "Kabbalistic Myth," p. 86.

63. Jonas, *Gnostic Religion*, p. 174.

64. Among the extensive literature on this question, see esp. Scholem, *Origins*, esp. pp. 67–97, 316–20, 363–64, 389–90; Idel, *Kabbalah*, esp. chs. 1 and 6; Joseph Dan, "Kabbalistic and Gnostic Dualism," in id., ed., *Studies in Jewish History, Thought, and Culture*, pp. 19–33; Kalman Bland, "Neoplatonic and Gnostic Themes in R. Moses Cordovero's Doctrine of Evil," *Bulletin of the Institute of Jewish Studies* 3 (1975): 103–29; Elliot R. Wolfson, "The Tree That Is All: Jewish-Christian Roots of a Kabbalistic Symbol in *Sefer Ha-Bahir*," in id., *Along the Path: Studies in Kabbalistic Myth, Symbolism, and Hermeneutics* (Albany: State University Press of New York, 1995), pp. 63–88.

65. See, e.g., Liebes, "Kabbalistic Myth," p. 85; Idel, *Kabbalah*, pp. 119–120.

Chapter 5

1. *SRH*, p. 39.

2. Ibid.

3. Ibid., p. 40.

4. Azikri, *Sefer Ḥaredim*, *Mitsvot ha-Teshuvah*, ch. 2. Azikri himself was preoccupied with questions of sin and penance. This section of his book comprises a sustained treatment of penitential practices that is strikingly similar in certain ways to Luria's. Even though Azikri was not a formal disciple of Luria's, he clearly was influenced by him and drew upon his teachings.

5. For treatments of non-Jewish approaches to metoposcopy, see the monumental classic by Lynn Thorndike, *A History of Magic and Experimental Science* (New York: Macmillan, 1923–58), esp. vols. 6–8; Kurt Seligman, *Magic, Supernaturalism, and Religion* (1948; New York: Pantheon Books, 1973), pp. 256–61; and Sarane Alexandrian, *Histoire de la philosophie occulte* (Paris: Éditions Seghers, 1983), pp. 201–3. On the general subject of divination, see the entry "Divination" in M. Eliade et al., eds., *Encyclopedia of Religion*, 4: 375–82. The subject of divination in its earliest stages in the Western world is discussed in Georg Luck, *Arcana*

Mundi: Magic and the Occult in the Greek and Roman Worlds (Baltimore: Johns Hopkins University Press, 1985), pp. 229–305; and E.R. Dodds, *The Ancient Concept of Progress and Other Essays on Greek Literature and Belief* (Oxford: Clarendon Press, 1985), pp. 156–210.

6. For discussion of *Sefer Yetsirah*, see Scholem, *Origins*, pp. 24–35; id., "The Name of God and the Linguistic Theory of the Kabbalah," *Diogenes* 79 (1972): 59–80; id., *Kabbalah*, pp. 23–30. See as well the studies by Israel Weinstock and Nehemya Aloni in *Temirin*, vol. 1 (Jerusalem, 1972), pp. 9–99. Luria's use of *Sefer Yetsirah* in connection with metoposcopy is explicitly acknowledged in *SRH*, pp. 15–16. For broader discussions of the relationship between language and Kabbalah, see Scholem, *On the Kabbalah*, pp. 32–86; id., the *Diogenes* article mentioned above, as well as its continuation in *Diogenes* 80 (1972): 164–94.

7. *SRH*, p. 6. This idea is already found in the *Zohar*, in the context of its discussion of physiognomic matters. See, e.g., *Zohar* 2, 73a, where we learn that the mystery of the twenty-two letters is engraved within the *ruaḥ* of an individual, and that these letters can appear on the face.

8. *SRH*, pp. 15–16. The primary Lurianic account of metoposcopy is found in *SRH*, pp. 15–22. The earliest Jewish interest in physiognomy in general appears to go back to the Qumran document published as 4Q186. According to this text, certain physiognomic criteria, such as the size and shape of the thighs, toes, fingers, hair, eyes, beard, teeth, height, and quality of voice, can be examined to ascertain an individual's moral and spiritual status. Such criteria, along with a person's zodiacal sign, were used to determine a person's fitness for membership in the "House of Light," that is, the righteous among Israel. See John M. Allegro and Arnold A. Anderson, eds., *Qumrân Cave 4: 4Q158–4Q186* (Oxford: Clarendon Press, 1968), pp. 89–91.

Physiognomic considerations play little role in conventional rabbinic materials, but they were of great interest to the Merkavah mystics. As in the Qumran text, the Merkavah literature indicates that physiognomic criteria were employed to determine eligibility for admission into the circle of mystics. These criteria have to do with the character of the nose, lips, eyes, eyebrows, eyelashes, and sexual organs, although greatest significance was attached to the lines and letters upon the palm and forehead. These texts already speak, albeit in an unsystematic and exceedingly obscure way, of certain letters that appear on the hand and forehead. The primary text in this connection is *Hakkarat Panim le-Rabbi Yishmael*, which speaks of twelve letters that are visible on the forehead, although it does not specify which letters these are. This text and related materials are analyzed in two articles by Gershom Scholem, "Physiognomy of the Face" (in Hebrew), in U. Cassuto, ed., *Sefer Assaf* (Jerusalem: Mossad ha-Rav Kook, 1952–53), pp. 459–95; and id., "Ein Fragment zur Physiognomik und Chiromantik aus der Tradition der spätantiken jüdische Esoterik," in *Liber amicorum: Studies in Honor of Professor Dr. C. J. Bleeker* (Leiden: E.J. Brill, 1969), pp. 175–93. See also id., "Chiromancy," in Scholem's *Kabbalah*, pp. 317–19; Ithamar Gruenwald, "New Texts from the Literature of Hakkarat Panim ve-Sidrei Sirtutin" (in Hebrew), *Tarbiz* 40 (1970–71): 301–19; id., *Apocalyptic and Merkavah Mysticism* (Leiden: E.J. Brill, 1980), pp. 218–24; Peter Schäfer, "Ein neues Fragment zur Metoposkopie und Chiromantik," in id., *Hekhalot-Studien* (Tübingen: Mohr, 1988), pp. 84–95; and id., *The Hidden and Manifest God: Some Major Themes in Early Jewish Mysticism* (Albany: State University of New York, 1992), pp. 137–38.

In Abraham Abulafia's *Sefer ha-ʾOt*, we find a description of prophetic experience in which an individual imagines a human form upon whose forehead a letter is inscribed: "On his forehead was a letter inscribed in blood and ink on two sides, and the shape of the letter was like the shape of a staff separating them, and it was a very hidden letter." According to Moshe Idel, who cites this passage, this description can be understood as a battle within the soul (between "blood" and "ink"), which is projected externally upon the forehead. Elsewhere in *Sefer ha-ʾOt*, Abulafia speaks of seventy tongues that flow from between the signs on his forehead. While this is clearly different compared to the Lurianic material, there are two important similarities. In both cases, letters appear on the forehead, and in each case they appear to be manifestations of the soul. See Idel, *Mystical Experience in Abraham Abulafia*, pp. 95–100. More generally, visions of letters, as is well known, are an intrinsic aspect of Abulafian ecstatic experience.

The most extensive treatment of physiognomy, chiromancy, and metoposcopy in theosophical kabbalistic literature prior to the Lurianic texts is found in the zoharic corpus, concerning which see the following note. For a discussion of physiognomy and metoposcopy in connection with Abraham Yagel, a physician, kabbalist, and naturalist who lived in northern Italy in the sixteenth and early seventeenth centuries, see David Ruderman, *Kabbalah, Magic, and Science: The Cultural Universe of a Sixteenth-Century Jewish Physician* (Cambridge, Mass.: Harvard University Press, 1988), pp. 132–35. It is worth noting that Yagel mentions Luria's prominence as a practitioner of the art of metoposcopy.

9. *SRH*, pp. 15–16. While the Lurianic notions of metoposcopy described here do not appear to have any direct link to the material found in the Merkavah literature, they are unmistakably indebted, at least to a degree, to the extensive discussions in the zoharic corpus. The literature of the *Zohar* treats physiognomic, chiromantic, and metoposcopic issues in several places, including: (1) *Zohar* 2, 71a–78a (along with the parallel version in *Raza de-Razin*); (2) *Zohar* 2, 272b–276a; (3) *Zohar Ḥadash* 35b–37c; and (4) *Tiqqunei Zohar, tiqqun* 70. Cf. as well *Zohar* 3, 75b–76a. These speculations are based, in part, on exegesis of Exod. 18:21. There are certain substantial differences between the *Zohar*'s discussions and the Lurianic one: (1) Whereas the *Zohar* treats in some detail the several subjects of physiognomy, chiromancy, and metoposcopy—discussing the significance of the hair, forehead, eyes, face, lips, lines on the hands, and the ears—Luria was almost ex-

clusively concerned with metoposcopy, that is, the forehead. He takes up other matters in the most passing way. (2) The *Zohar's* analysis of metoposcopy is mostly concerned with the shape of the forehead and with the lines or creases appearing on it, and less with letters. In Luria's case, there is no discussion of anything but the letters and words that manifest themselves. (3) Whereas the *Zohar* incorporates elements of astrological speculation, the Lurianic account has only the briefest passing reference to this (see *SRH*, p. 16) and is clearly not genuinely concerned with astrology. (4) The *Zohar* tends to indicate how physical characteristics, such as the shape of the forehead or eyes, signify certain moral and spiritual traits in general ways. Thus, for example, a person is said to be inclined toward anger, impulsiveness, or joyfulness. In our texts, Luria is able to determine the specific sins or righteous acts that a person has performed.

10. *SRH*, p. 17.

11. Ibid., p. 18. According to BT *Menaḥot* 43b, R. Yose declares it to be the duty of everyone to recite one hundred blessings daily, whereas *Numbers Rabbah* 18 indicates that King David instituted this tradition.

12. *SRH*, p. 16.

13. Ibid., p. 17.

14. The relationship between seminal emission and ritual impurity has a long history in Jewish tradition, beginning with the Torah. According to Lev. 15:16, a man who experiences an apparently involuntary seminal emission is required to bathe himself and remains in a state of impurity until evening. According to Lev. 15:17, sexual intercourse requires immersion by both a man and a woman for purposes of purification. Cf. Lev. 15:13 for the laws concerning the impurity contracted by a man who has had a continuing genital discharge. In rabbinic tradition, these laws became the basis for a range of restrictions, including the requirement for a *baʿal qeri* (one who has experienced a seminal emission) to immerse himself before saying the Shema out loud, or to abbreviate the recitation of the Amidah prayer. The Talmud also takes up the question of whether a *baʿal qeri* is permitted to study Torah. While R. Joshua b. Levi prohibits study, subsequent halakhic opinion avers that "words of Torah are not susceptible of impurity" (BT *Berakhot* 22a). In the *Hekhalot* literature of late antiquity—where this subject is exceedingly important—seminal emission requires ritual purification so as to render an adept's adjuration of angels successful. Five of these texts instruct the practitioner to avoid seminal emission before as well as during his performance of the adjuration. Thus, for example, the Sar ha-Torah text in *Hekhalot Rabbati* indicates that "the one who binds himself by the Sar ha-Torah should wash his garments and cloaks and perform a stringent immersion rendering him free from any doubt of nocturnal pollution." On these rabbinic and *Hekhalot* traditions, see Rebecca Lesses, *Ritual Practices to Gain Power: Angels, Incantations, and Revelations in Early Jewish Mysticism* (Harrisburg, Pa.: Trinity Press International, 1998), pp. 117–34; Michael

D. Swartz, *Scholastic Magic: Ritual and Revelation in Early Jewish Mysticism* (Princeton, N.J.: Princeton University Press, 1996), pp. 157–66. The medieval renewal of the practice of ritual immersion as an exercise in purification for men following a nocturnal emission is associated with the eleventh-century Babylonian authority Hai Gaon. On this, and the question of male ritual ablution among medieval kabbalists, see Elliot K. Ginsburg, *The Sabbath in the Classical Kabbalah* (Albany: State University of New York Press, 1989), pp. 227–31, 248–51, nn. 34–42.

15. *SRH*, p. 22.

16. Ibid., p. 17.

17. Ibid., p. 20.

18. Although, as noted earlier, the *Zohar* contains a considerable amount of theoretical material having to do with chiromancy, physiognomy, and metoposcopy, it is worth pointing out that one passage (3, 75b–76a) provides an account of a practice similar to Luria's. Given its relevance to our subject, I quote it at length on the basis of the translation in *WZ*, 3: 1478–79:

> Rabbi Abba was once traveling to Cappadocia with Rabbi Yose. During their journey they met a man who had a scar on his face. Rabbi Abba said: Let us pause here, for this man's face testifies that he has transgressed the sexual prohibitions in the Torah. That is why he has a mark on his face. Rabbi Yose said to him: If he has had this mark from birth, what sexual offenses could he have committed? He said: I can see that his face bears witness to sexual acts prohibited by the Torah. Rabbi Abba called to him, and said: Tell me. What is that scar on your face? He said to them: Do not, I pray you, give a man more punishment than his sins have already brought upon him. Rabbi Abba said: What do you mean? He replied: One day I was on a journey with my sister. We stopped at an inn, and I became drunk, and all that night I lay with my sister. We arose in the morning and found the innkeeper struggling with another man. I came between them, but they got hold of me, one on either side, and I received this blow on the head. My life was saved by a doctor who happened to be there. He said to him: Who was this doctor? He replied: It was Rabbi Simlai. He said: What kind of cure did he give you? He replied: A cure for the soul. From that day onward I have repented. Every day I look at my face in the mirror and weep for that sin before the Holy One, blessed be He, who is Master of all worlds. And I wash my face with those tears. Rabbi Abba said: If [total] repentance were possible in your case, I would remove that mark from your face. But I shall pronounce over you "Your iniquity is taken away, and your sin expiated" [Isa. 6:7]. He said to him: Say it three times. He said it three times, and the mark disappeared. Rabbi Abba said: Since your Master wished to remove [that mark] you must be in a state of true repentance. He said to him: I vow that from this day forth I shall study Torah day and night.

19. De Vidas, *Reshit Ḥokhmah*, "The Gate of Love," ch. 6.

20. *PEH* (Jerusalem, 1980), *Shaᶜar ha-ᶜAmidah*, ch. 19.

21. *ʾEleh Toldot Yitshaq*, in Benayahu, *STA*, p. 251.

22. *SRH*, p. 17.   23. Benayahu, *STA*, p. 190.

24. *SeH*, p. 165.   25. Ibid., p. 173.

26. *ShM, Parashat Mishpatim*, p. 36.

27. *Ḥemdat Yamim* (Leghorn, 1763), 53a–b. See the English translation of this story in Aryeh Wineman, *Beyond Appearances: Stories from the Kabbalistic Ethical Writings* (Philadelphia: Jewish Publication Society, 1988), pp. 107–8. *Ḥemdat Yamim* is a vast compendium of kabbalistic customs and traditions written under the influence of moderate Sabbateanism, published for the first time in Smyrna in 1731. It incorporates a rich repository of Lurianic narratives and legends. It is also interesting to note a story told by Naphtali Hertz Treves, an Ashkenazi kabbalist of the middle of the sixteenth century: "Once a rabbi died and appeared before his disciple in a dream. He had a stain on his forehead. The disciple asked why this happened. He replied: Because I was not careful to refrain from talking during the benediction of *meᶜein shevaᶜ* [on Friday evening] or while the Cantor recited the blessing over wine, nor was I careful to trim my nails on Sabbath eve." See Ginsburg, *Sabbath in the Classical Kabbalah*, p. 246, n. 21.

28. *ShG, Haqdamah* 17, pp. 48–49.

29. *ShM, Parashat Ve-ʾethanan*, p. 87.

30. Patrizia Magli, "The Face and the Soul," in M. Feher et al., eds., *Fragments for a History of the Human Body* (New York: Zone, 1989), 2: 89.

31. *SRH*, pp. 14–15; cf. Vital, *ShMR, Perush ᶜal Sefer ha-Tiqqunim*, p. 7. This practice was inspired, in part, by *Tiqqunei Zohar, tiqqun* 69.

32. *SRH*, p. 15.

33. See Nancy G. Siraisi, *Medieval and Early Renaissance Medicine* (Chicago: University of Chicago Press, 1990), pp. 125–27.

34. Concerning the phenomenon of possession by an evil spirit and exorcism, see Benayahu, *STA*, pp. 290–306; Raphael Patai, "Exorcism and Xenoglossia among the Safed Kabbalists," in id., *On Jewish Folklore* (Detroit: Wayne State University Press, 1983), pp. 314–25; Scholem, *Kabbalah*, pp. 349–50; and J. H. Chajes, "Judgements Sweetened: Possession and Exorcism in Early Modern Jewish Culture," *Journal of Early Modern History* 1, 2 (1997); id., "Jewish Exorcism: Early Modern Traditions and Transformations," in L. Fine, ed., *Judaism in Practice: From the Middle Ages Through the Early Modern Period* (Princeton, N.J.: Princeton University Press, 2001); M. Goldish, ed., *Spirit Possession in Judaism: Cases and Contexts from the Middle Ages to the Present* (Detroit: Wayne State University Press, 2003). Beginning in the seventeenth century, among German and Polish Jews, such evil spirits were known by the term *dibbuq*, an abbreviation of the words *dibbuq me-ruaḥ raᶜah* ("cleaving of an evil spirit"), or *dibbuq me-ruaḥ ḥitsonim* ("cleaving from the demonic side").

35. Benayahu, *STA*, p. 253.

36. *SRH* (Jerusalem, 1863), p. 31a. Cf. Benayahu, *STA*, p. 190.

37. Aristotle, *De anima* 1A.1.403a.15.

38. Vital's versions of the *tiqqunei ʿavonot* are found primarily in *SRH*, pp. 40–74; and *Tiqqunei ʿAvonot* (Korecz, 1783), pp. 30–40.

39. See *Kanfei Yonah* (Lemberg [Lvov], 1884), 54c–58d; and the various manuscript sources of *Kanfei Yonah* described in detail by Benayahu, "Rabbi Moses Yonah," pp. 45–74.

40. *SRH*, pp. 25–26.

41. The extra five is supposed to represent the number of letters in the full spelling of *alef* and *lamed*. The problem is that there are six letters in these two words in Hebrew, not five.

42. The connections between *ʾEl*, *Ḥesed*, and the *mitsvot ʿaseh* are made in *ShM, Haqdamah*, pp. 2–3.

43. *SRH*, p. 41.

44. Ibid., p. 49. Among the various extreme self-afflictive acts Abraham ben Eliezer ha-Levi Berukhim was reported to have practiced was that of rolling upon a bed of thorns, which felt like fire to his flesh. See Benayahu, *STA*, p. 226.

45. *SRH*, p. 50.

46. Ibid., pp. 50–52.

47. A general discussion of issues having to do with sexuality in Judaism is found in D. Biale, *Eros and the Jews*; see esp. chs. 1–3. A more elaborate treatment of these issues may be found in Daniel Boyarin, *Carnal Israel: Reading Sex in Talmudic Culture* (Berkeley: University of California Press, 1993). On sexual practices in medieval Jewish culture, see, e.g., Yom Tov Assis, "Sexual Behavior in Medieval Hispano-Jewish Society," in A. Rapoport-Albert and S. Zipperstein, eds., *Jewish History: Essays in Honour of Chimen Abramsky* (London: P. Halban, 1988), pp. 25–59.

48. See Boyarin, *Carnal Israel*, pp. 31–33, who quotes Philo and cites the views of Alon Goshen-Gottstein. More generally, see ibid., pp. 44–54, and passim.

49. Daniel Boyarin, *A Radical Jew: Paul and the Politics of Identity* (Berkeley: University of California Press, 1994), pp. 57–84.

50. Gregory of Nyssa, *On Virginity* 3, in *Nicene and Post-Nicene Fathers*, 2d ser., ed. Philip Schaff and Henry Wace (Peabody, Mass.: Hendrickson Publishers, 1994). There is an enormous literature on the subject, but some of the most important recent work on the relationships among abstinence, sexuality, and marriage in Christianity includes Peter Brown, *The Body and Society: Men, Women, and Sexual Renunciation in Early Christianity* (New York: Columbia University Press, 1988); Boyarin, *Radical Jew*; James Brundage, *Law, Sex, and Christian Society in Medieval Europe* (Chicago: University of Chicago Press, 1987); Philippe Ariès and André Béjin, eds., *Western Sexuality: Practice and Precept in Past and Present Times*, trans. Anthony Forster (New York: Blackwell, 1985); David Noble, *A World Without Women: The Christian Clerical Culture of Western Science* (New York: Knopf, 1992);

Caroline Walker Bynum, *Fragmentation and Redemption: Essays on Gender and the Human Body in Medieval Religion* (New York: Zone Books, 1991); and Dyan Elliott, *Spiritual Marriage: Sexual Abstinence in Medieval Wedlock* (Princeton, N.J.: Princeton University Press, 1993).

51. On the subject of the obligation in Jewish tradition to procreate, see Jeremy Cohen, *"Be Fertile and Increase, Fill the Earth and Master It": The Ancient and Medieval Career of a Biblical Text* (Ithaca, N.Y.: Cornell University Press, 1989). With regard to marriage more generally, see Israel Gafni, "The Institution of Marriage in Rabbinic Times"; and Mordechai Friedman, "Marriage as an Institution: Jewry Under Islam," both in D. Kraemer, ed., *The Jewish Family: Metaphor and Memory* (New York: Oxford University Press, 1989), pp. 11–30, 31–45.

52. BT *Qiddushin* 30b.

53. BT *Ketubot* 61b–63a.

54. See Boyarin, *Carnal Israel*, pp. 46–47, 135–41, 159–65.

55. See Moshe Idel, "Sexual Metaphors and Praxis in the Kabbalah," in D. Kraemer, ed., *The Jewish Family* (Oxford: Oxford University Press, 1989), pp. 197–224; *WZ*, 3: 1355–79; D. Biale, *Eros and the Jews*, ch. 5.

56. On this book, see Charles Mopsik, *Lettre sur la sainteté: Le Secret de la relation entre l'homme et la femme dans la Cabale* (Lagrasse: Verdier, 1986); Karen Guberman, "The Language of Love in Spanish Kabbalah: An Examination of the *'Iggeret ha-Qodesh*," in D. R. Blumenthal, ed., *Approaches to Judaism in Medieval Times*, vol. 1 (Chico, Calif.: Scholars Press, 1984), pp. 53–105; D. Biale, *Eros and the Jews*, pp. 101–9.

57. *SRH*, p. 52. Vital indicates, as he does in several other cases, that this particular *tiqqun* was actually taught by Abraham ben Eliezer ha-Levi Berukhim rather than Luria. As with the other sexual transgressions identified here, it is impossible to know how prevalent this practice was. We have a highly interesting report from eighteenth-century eastern Europe of a man accused of beating his wife and compelling her to have relations with him during the "white days," that is, the seven days immediately following the cessation of menstruation itself. His neighbors testified that he was overheard "attacking the rabbis for instituting the restriction of the white days," and he sought to convince his wife that it was not necessary to obey this aspect of the law. Cited in D. Biale, *Eros and the Jews*, pp. 82–83. On the subject of *niddah* and sexual practice more generally, see Rachel Biale, *Women and Jewish Law: An Exploration of Women's Issues in Halakhic Sources* (New York: Schocken Books, 1984), pp. 147–74; D. Biale, *Eros and the Jews*, pp. 42–43, 50, 52, 55–56, and passim; Shaye Cohen, "Women and the Sacred: Menstrual Pollution in Judaism and Christianity," in S. B. Pomeroy, ed., *Women's History and Ancient History* (Chapel Hill: University of North Carolina Press, 1991), pp. 273–99; Judith Baskin, "Women and Ritual Immersion: The Sexual Politics of Piety," in Fine, *Judaism in Practice*. It is worth noting that marital relations during menstruation were also proscribed by the medieval Church.

58. *SRH*, pp. 54–56.

59. See *SeH*, p. 34. On the general subject of homosexuality in Judaism, see the relevant articles in the anthology edited by C. Balka and A. Rose, *Twice Blessed: On Being Lesbian, Gay and Jewish* (Boston: Beacon Press, 1989); D. Biale, *Eros and the Jews*, passim; Daniel Boyarin, *Unheroic Conduct: The Rise of Heterosexuality and the Invention of the Jewish Man* (Berkeley: University of California Press, 1997), passim. A good deal of attention has been given to the question of male homosexuality among Jews in Muslim Spain during the Golden Age, based largely upon the presence of the theme of male love in Hebrew poetry of this period. There is no scholarly consensus, though, on whether this literature reflects actual homosexual practice. See Assis, "Sexual Behavior," pp. 50–51; Norman Roth, "'Deal Gently with the Young Man': Love of Boys in Medieval Hebrew Poetry of Spain," *Speculum* 57, 1 (Jan. 1982): 20–51; id., "'Fawn of My Delights': Boy-Love in Hebrew and Arabic Verse," in J. E. Salisbury, ed., *Sex in the Middle Ages: A Book of Essays* (New York: Garland, 1991), pp. 157–72; id., "The Care and Feeding of Gazelles: Medieval Arabic and Hebrew Love Poetry," in M. Lazar and N. Lacy, eds., *Poetics of Love in the Middle Ages* (Fairfax, Va.: George Mason University Press, 1989), pp. 95–118; Raymond P. Scheindlin, *Wine, Women, and Death: Medieval Hebrew Poems on the Good Life* (Philadelphia: Jewish Publication Society, 1986), passim; Joseph Schirmann, "The Ephebe in Medieval Hebrew Poetry" (in Hebrew), *Sefarad* 23 (1963): 311–21. For views on the related question of lesbianism, see R. Biale, *Women and Jewish Law*, pp. 192–97; Rebecca Alpert, "Challenging Male/Female Complementarity: Jewish Lesbians and the Jewish Tradition," in Eilberg-Schwartz, *People of the Body*, pp. 361–77; Bernadette J. Brooten, *Love Between Women: Early Christian Responses to Female Homoeroticism* (Chicago: University of Chicago Press, 1996), pp. 61–71. A classic study of homosexuality in medieval Christian Europe is John Boswell, *Christianity, Social Tolerance and Homosexuality: Gay People in Western Europe from the Beginning of the Christian Era to the Fourteenth Century* (Chicago: University of Chicago Press, 1980). See as well Boswell's *Same-Sex Unions in Premodern Europe* (New York: Villard Books, 1994). In the latter volume, see also the author's remarks concerning Judaism and homosexuality, pp. 364–71.

60. *SRH*, p. 57. For Moses Yonah's versions of the *tiqqunim* for homosexual behavior, see *Kanfei Yonah*, sec. 103, 54c–55b; Sassoon MS 993, fols. 208–10.

61. For a study of the image of divine feet in Jewish mystical literature, see Elliot R. Wolfson, "Images of God's Feet: Some Observations on the Divine Body in Judaism," in H. Eilberg-Schwartz, ed., *People of the Body*, pp. 143–81. See esp. his remarks on Moses Yonah, p. 164.

62. *SRH*, pp. 56–57.

63. Unlike many places in Israel, Safed does experience a certain amount of snowfall, on average five days per year, owing to its high elevation. Snow usually falls in January and February, the coldest months. See Efraim Orni and Elisha Efrat, *Geography of Israel* (3d rev. ed., New York: American Heritage Press, 1971), p. 147.

64. MS in the Benayahu collection from the early seventeenth century. See Benayahu, "Rabbi Moshe Yonah," p. 5. For a set of remarks suggesting phallic and homoerotic implications in the *Zohar* in connection with the motif of the mystical fellowship of Shimon bar Yohai, and the representation of the fellowship as the "face of *Shekhinah*," see Wolfson, *Through a Speculum*, pp. 368–72, 396.

65. See, e.g., the detailed discussion of this transgression in Azikri, *Sefer Haredim, Mitsvot ha-Teshuvah*, ch. 2. On the question of masturbation in Judaism more generally, see D. Biale, *Eros and the Jews*, pp. 56–57, 79–84, and passim. On the grave concern of the Church with the sin of masturbation, esp. in the later Middle Ages, see Jeffrey Richards, *Sex, Dissidence and Damnation: Minority Groups in the Middle Ages* (New York: Routledge, 1991), pp. 30–32, 37.

66. Vital represents this as having been conveyed by Luria to Moses Yonah. It is found in *SRH*, pp. 63–64, as well as in a manuscript in the Benayahu collection. See Benayahu, "Rabbi Moshe Yonah," p. 19.

67. Simulating the appearance of a foreskin in this manner brings to mind the practice among some radically Hellenized Jews during the period of the Second Temple of having their circumcision reversed. Might the practice described in this passage have represented an unconscious male fantasy of resembling a gentile's sexual anatomy? Moses Cordovero expresses his concern about autoeroticism in his caution that one "refrain from touching his body with his hand, and from lowering his hand below his navel." See Fine, *Safed Spirituality*, p. 35. Azikri mentions still other techniques that men use to waste their seed, including rubbing the penis with one's foot (!) and having relations with one's wife "in an unnatural manner" (*ha-ba ʿal ʾishto she-lo ke-darkah*). The latter appears to refer to intercourse in which a woman is on top, or perhaps to penetration from the rear. In either case, Azikri's point is that these are unnatural forms of sex that can result in a man ejaculating in a wasteful way. Azikri provides an account of an incident in which a married woman came before a body of distinguished rabbis, including Joseph Karo, Isaac Masud, Abraham Shalom, and Joseph Sagis. She complained to them that her husband had had relations with her in an unnatural manner. According to Azikri, this rabbinic council exiled him from the land of Israel. See *Sefer Haredim*, ch. 2.

68. In the literature of German pietism, we find an interesting anecdote that speaks to this question. Judah the Pietist advises that a person who has a strong sexual impulse and is fearful that he might sin by having relations with another man's wife or with his own wife while she is a menstruant may be permitted to masturbate instead. Even so, he is obliged to atone for what he has done by carrying out the proper penance of sitting in icy water during the winter or fasting for a period of forty days in the summer. Thus, while one is permitted a certain sin in order to avoid a presumably graver one, he is still liable for the transgression. See *Sefer Hasidim* (recension Bologna, 1538), no. 509, pp. 340–41.

69. ʾAvot 5:6; Genesis Rabbah 7:5.

70. Genesis Rabbah 20:11, 24:6; Midrash Tanḥuma ha-Kadum ve-ha-Yashan (Lemberg [Lvov]), 1883), ed. S. Buber, 1: 12, 20; BT Eruvin 18b.

71. See Joshua Trachtenberg, Jewish Magic and Superstition (New York: Behrman's Jewish Book House, 1939), p. 29; Meir Benayahu, "Spirits of Harm and Their Reparation" (in Hebrew), in id., ed., Sefer Zikkaron le-ha-Rav Yitshaq Nissim (Jerusalem: Yad Harav Nissim, 1985), 6: 81–104. Cf. Rashi's commentary to 2 Sam. 7:14; Zohar 1, 54b; 2, 231b; 3, 76b, for example.

72. Concerning these motifs, see WZ, 2: 464–70, 529–32; 3: 1364–72; Joseph Dan, "Samael, Lilith, and the Concept of Evil in Early Kabbalah," Association for Jewish Studies Review 5 (1980): 17–40; Scholem, On the Kabbalah, pp. 153–57.

73. A different kind of negative consequence associated with spilling one's semen, according to the Zohar, is that the transgressor is thwarted from entering the Heavenly Palace or seeing the Shekhinah upon death. Thus, for example: "R. Judah said: 'Every sin admits of repentance except this, and every sinner may hope to see the face of the Shekhinah except this one'" (Zohar 2, 219b). See additional references to this theme in Wolfson, Through a Speculum, p. 366, n. 143, to which I am indebted for calling my attention to this motif.

74. In his diary, Joseph Karo provides an account of his experience of a nocturnal pollution, which he attributes to his having walked into a Sufi monastery (apparently while he was still living in Turkey) earlier that day. Karo's Maggid informs him that "on account of the pollution that you had they [i.e., the evil powers] have already snatched their share " (Werblowsky, Joseph Karo, pp. 138–39).

Beginning no later than the early sixteenth century, we encounter the view that all of the illegitimate children that a man has brought into the world in this way during his lifetime appear following his death and take part in his funeral! According to the early sixteenth-century Moroccan kabbalist Abraham Sabba, for example, the souls that a man has begotten in this manner cry out "while he is being carried to the grave," and "they swarm around him like bees, crying: 'You are our father,' and they complain and lament behind his bier, because they have lost their home and are now being tormented along with the other demons which hover [bodiless] in the air." Quoted by Scholem, On the Kabbalah, p. 155, from Sabba's work entitled Tseror ha-Mor (Venice, 1576), 5a. Such beliefs gave rise to magical practices intended to prevent these "children" from interfering in the funeral, harming a man's legitimate children, or claiming a portion of their father's inheritance. One exceedingly popular ritual consisted of dancing around the deceased seven times in order to form a magical circle that the illegitimate children could not penetrate. Writing in 1950, Scholem observed that even then this ritual was occasionally practiced, although the kabbalistic meaning behind it had become obscure. See On the Kabbalah, pp. 154–56.

75. These are the portions Shemot, Vaʾera, Bo, Beshallaḥ, Yitro, Mishpatim, Terumah, and Tetsaveh. For post-Lurianic accounts of this ritual, see, e.g., Isaiah

Horowitz, *Shnei Luḥot ha-Brit* (Amsterdam, 1648), 306b; Mordecai Jaffe, *Levush ha-ʾOrah* (Prague, 1604), no. 685; and, the most elaborate formulation, Moses Zakuto, *Tiqqun Shovavim* (Venice, 1716). In the seventeenth century, the emotionally (and sexually) troubled messianic pretender Sabbatai Sevi was known to have suffered egregiously from nightmarish dreams filled with sexual themes. The following anecdote is found toward the conclusion of a book entitled *The Vision of R. Abraham*:

> When he [Sabbatai Sevi] was six years old, a flame appeared in a dream and caused a burn on his penis; and dreams would frighten him, but he never told anyone. And the sons of whoredom [the demons] accosted him so as to cause him to stumble and they beat him, but he would not hearken unto them. They were the sons of Naʿamah, the scourges of the children of man, who would always pursue him so as to lead him astray.

These are clearly allusions to the demonic spirits brought about as a result of masturbation or other improper emissions of semen. What is more, among the penitential manuals composed by Nathan of Gaza in the style of Lurianic *tiqqunei ʿavonot*, we find a version of the ritual of *Tiqqun Shovavim Tat*. See Scholem, *Sabbatai Sevi*, pp. 113, 290–97, 936–39. *Tiqqun Shovavim Tat* continued to be practiced among eastern European Hasidim in the eighteenth century. See, e.g., the religious counsel proffered by Menahem Nahum of Chernobyl in Green, *Menahem Nahum of Chernobyl*, p. 42.

76. *SRH*, pp. 62–63.

77. Ivan Marcus, "Ashkenazic Hasidism," in M. Eliade et al., eds., *Encyclopedia of Religion*, 1: 458–61. See as well Marcus's full-length study of this topic, *Piety and Society: The Jewish Pietists of Medieval Germany* (Leiden: E.J. Brill, 1981), esp. chs. 3, 6, and 8.

78. On this genre of literature, see Gabriel Le Bras, "Pénitentiels," in A. Vacant, E. Mangenot, E. Amann et al., eds., *Dictionnaire de théologie catholique*, 15 vols. (Paris: Letouzey & Ané, 1903–50), 12.1 (1933): 1160–79; Ludwig Bieler, "Penitentials," *New Catholic Encyclopedia* (1967), 11: 86–87; J. T. McNeil and H. M. Gamer, eds. and trans., *Medieval Handbooks of Penance*, Columbia Records of Civilization, 29 (New York: Columbia University Press, 1938); Ludwig Bieler, ed. and trans., *The Irish Penitentials*, Scriptores Latini Hiberniae, 5 (Dublin: Dublin Institute for Advanced Studies, 1963, 1975); Pierre J. Payer, *Sex and the Penitentials: The Development of a Sexual Code, 550–1150* (Toronto: University of Toronto Press, 1984). With respect to the question of influences, it is interesting to note that one of the most important collections of Penitentials—the *Decretum*—was compiled by Bishop Burchard of Worms, who died in 1025. Worms was, of course, one of the very centers of German pietism in the following century. Marcus, however, finds no evidence for a direct literary relationship between the Latin penitential literature and German pietism. See his *Piety and Society*, p. 150, n. 54.

This, indeed, has been the prevailing scholarly opinion for many years. Various individuals have argued that penitential rites among the German pietists were rooted rather in ancient Jewish practices originating in the period of the early rabbis. Others, however, including Gershom Scholem, Yitzhak Baer, and Asher Rubin, believed that there was a link between the Christian penitentials and German pietism. This line of reasoning has been strengthened by the recent contribution of Talya Fishman to this question in "The Penitential System of Ḥasidei Ashkenaz and the Problem of Cultural Boundaries," *Journal of Jewish Thought and Philosophy* 8 (1999): 201–29. Fishman (p. 215) argues that it is "unlikely that Jews of medieval Ashkenaz would have been receptive to developments in Christian penitence at any conscious level. . . . Influence, if it occurred, was more likely to have taken place by osmosis—through conversations in the marketplace and pawn shop or upon sighting Christians fulfilling their penances in outdoor public spaces." Critical to Fishman's argument is the publication of the above-mentioned twenty-one-volume *Decretum* by Burchard of Worms, which dominated the canonical tradition of the eleventh century. The Church had formally opposed penitential literature for some four centuries, in resistance to Irish penitential treatises that had appeared beginning in the seventh century. The acceptance of Bishop Burchard's work effectively brought an end to this resistance. In Fishman's view (p. 217), "While Christians in many European lands had long engaged in acts of penance guided by confessors who consulted penitential tracts, Burchard's 'Corrector' granted these practices a new respectability and presumably catapulted them to new visibility among Jews as well as Christians." Bringing matters full circle, Fishman (pp. 227–29) provides suggestive evidence for the intriguing possibility that Irish Christian culture had itself been influenced by ancient Jewish traditions, mediated primarily through the Apocrypha literature.

79. Ivan Marcus, "*Ḥasidei ʾAshkenaz* Private Penitentials: An Introduction and Descriptive Catalogue of Their Manuscripts and Early Editions," in J. Dan and F. Talmage, eds., *Studies in Jewish Mysticism* (Cambridge, Mass.: Association for Jewish Studies, 1982), p. 59.

80. Marcus, *Piety and Society*, p. 82. The subject of penitence among the pietists is also studied in Jacob Elbaum, *Teshuvat ha-Lev ve-Kabbalat Yesurim* (Jerusalem: Magnes Press, 1993); Asher Rubin, "The Concept of Repentance among the Hasidey Ashkenaz," *Journal of Jewish Studies* 16 (1965): 161–76; and Joseph Dan, *Sifrut ha-Musar ve-ha-Derush* (Jerusalem: Keter, 1975), pp. 129–33. Although it appeared too late for me to draw upon in detail, see also Ephraim Kanarfogel, *Peering Through the Lattices: Mystical, Magical, and Pietistic Dimensions in the Tosafist Period* (Detroit: Wayne State University Press, 2000).

81. Marcus, *Piety and Society*, pp. 121–39. For an account of the literature of the "Private Penitentials," see Marcus, "*Ḥasidei ʾAshkenaz* Private Penitentials," 57–83.

82. Marcus, *Piety and Society*, p. 124.

83. Ibid., p. 125. The private penitentials tend to be more severe than the sage penitentials in the *Sefer Ḥasidim*, which Marcus attributes to the need to "compensate for the removal of penitential shame once available by confessing to a Sage."

84. Ibid.

85. Eleazar of Worms, *Sefer ha-Roqeaḥ* (Jerusalem, 1968), *Hilkhot Teshuvah*. These transgressions comprise the outline of *Hilkhot Teshuvah*. See Marcus, "*Ḥasidei ⁾Ashkenaz* Private Penitentials," pp. 75–76. As with the pietists and the Lurianists, the aforementioned Christian penitentials also devoted a disproportionate amount of attention to sexual transgressions. Sexual matters comprised the largest single category of violations in the Latin penitentials. Although the penances varied with the severity of the sin, all of them were based on restricting one's consumption to bread and water, as well as avoiding sexual relations for a number of consecutive days in multiples of ten. For the worst transgressions, penances were given in terms of *years*, but this meant penance on the three annual fasts of Christmas, Easter, and Pentecost, as well as on the Wednesday, Friday, and Saturday of every week. The penance for masturbation from the *Decretum* of Burchard of Worms serves to illustrate what they entailed. A male who masturbated by hand was liable to ten days on bread and water, while the use of a perforated piece of wood (!) warranted twenty days. Burchard was apparently relatively lenient, insofar as other penitential handbooks imposed a penalty of between forty days and a year, varying with the age and status of the individual involved, as well as with the frequency of the habit. It is evident even from these brief examples that the medieval Church cultivated the penitential art in a far more nuanced and elaborate manner than did either the German Pietists or the Lurianists. See Payer, *Sex and the Penitentials*, pp. 46–47; Richards, *Sex, Dissidence and Damnation*, pp. 22–41.

86. I draw here on the observations of Marcus, *Piety and Society*, pp. 126–29.

87. Among the many writers whose work reflects such influence are Aaron ha-Cohen of Lunel, Isaac of Corbeil, Israel al-Naqawa, and Jacob ben Judah Hazzan of London. See Fishman, "Penitential System," p. 201, n. 2; Elbaum, *Teshuvat ha-Lev*, pp. 37–38; Yedidya Dinari, *Ḥakhmei Ashkenaz Be-Shilhei Yemei ha-Beinayim* (Jerusalem: Mossad Bialik, 1984), pp. 85–93. See also Kanarfogel, *Peering Through the Lattices*, which provides rich and substantial evidence for the influence of the Pietists' penances.

88. Elbaum, *Teshuvat ha-Lev*, pp. 38–40.

89. *Sefer Ḥaredim*, *Mitsvot ha-Teshuvah*, ch. 3. While the term *rishonim* refers to prominent rabbinic authorities between the eleventh and the middle of the fifteenth centuries in Europe and North Africa in general, here it clearly refers to authorities from Ashkenaz. The manuscript to which Azikri refers, *Bet Middot*, is none other than *⁾Orḥot Tsaddiqim*, which comprises a version of Eleazar of Worm's *Hilkhot Teshuvah* ("Laws of Repentance") from his *Sefer ha-Roqeaḥ*. See Elbaum, *Teshuvat ha-Lev*, pp. 38–39, esp. n. 9; Mordechai Pachter, "Concerning Passages

from ⁾*Orḥot Tsaddiqim* in the Ethical Treatises of the Sages of Safed" (in Hebrew), *QS* 47 (1972), pp. 487–92.

90. My thanks to Ivan Marcus, who made this observation in a private communication.

91. See *Sefer Ḥasidim*, ed. J. Wistinetzki (Frankfurt am Main: Wahrmann, 1924), par. 17.

92. *SRH*, p. 49.

93. Ibid., p. 42.

94. Ibid., p. 64.

95. *ShG, Haqdamah* 36, pp. 127–28, 38, 132–37; *SeH*, pp. 146–47, 152–54, 157. In connection with the history of alchemy in Judaism, see the magnificent study by Raphael Patai, *The Jewish Alchemists* (Princeton, N.J.: Princeton University Press, 1994), esp. pp. 340–64, where he discusses the alchemical writing of Hayyim Vital.

96. On confession and its background in rabbinic Judaism, see Marcus, *Piety and Society*, pp. 82–83.

97. Michel Foucault, "Technologies of the Self," in *Technologies of the Self: A Seminar with Michel Foucault*, ed. L. Martin et al. (Amherst: University of Massachusetts Press, 1988), p. 42.

Chapter 6

1. Concerning the relationship between Jewish law and Kabbalah, see the collection of studies by Jacob Katz, *Halakha ve-Qabbalah* (Jerusalem: Magnes Press, 1984); id., *Divine Law in Human Hands* (Jerusalem: Magnes Press, 1998).

2. For studies of this topic, see, e.g., Idel, *Kabbalah*, pp. 156–99; Daniel Matt, "The Mystic and the *Mitsvot*," in *Jewish Spirituality*, 1: 367–404; Charles Mopsik, "*Les Grands Textes de la Cabale: Les Rites qui font Dieu*" (Lagrasse: Verdier, 1993); Elliot R. Wolfson, *The Book of the Pomegranate: Moses de Leon's Sefer ha-Rimmon* (Atlanta: Scholars Press, 1988); id., "Mystical Rationalization of the Commandments in Sefer ha-Rimmon," *Hebrew Union College Annual* 59 (1988): 217–51; id., "Mystical Rationalization of the Commandments in the Prophetic Kabbalah of Abraham Abulafia," in A. L. Ivry et al., eds., *Perspectives on Jewish Thought and Mysticism* (Amsterdam: Harwood Academic Publishers, 1998); *WZ* 3: 1155–1325; Katz, *Halakhah ve-Kabbalah*; Ginsburg, *Sabbath in the Classical Kabbalah*; Pinchas Giller, *The Enlightened Will Shine: Symbolization and Theurgy in the Later Strata of the Zohar* (Albany: State University of New York Press, 1993), esp. pp. 59–105; Arthur Green, *Devotion and Commandment: The Faith of Abraham in the Hasidic Imagination* (Cincinnati: Hebrew Union College Press, 1989).

3. A classic survey and study of the literature of *Taᶜamei ha-Mitsvot* may be found in Isaac Heinemann, *Taᶜamei ha-Mitsvot be-Sifrut Yisrael*, 2 vols. (Jerusalem: Jewish Agency Publications, 1956, 1966). The first volume covers the Hebrew Bible

through medieval philosophical literature, but with no attention whatsoever to kabbalistic sources. The second volume extends the discussion to the modern period, from Moses Mendelssohn to Franz Rosenzweig.

4. *Sifra* to Lev. 18:4.

5. Concerning this question, see Isadore Twersky, "Talmudists, Philosophers, Kabbalists: The Quest for Spirituality in the Sixteenth Century," in B. Cooperman, ed., *Jewish Thought in the Sixteenth Century* (Cambridge, Mass.: Harvard University Press, 1983), pp. 431–57.

6. Maimonides, *Guide of the Perplexed*, pt. 3, ch. 26.

7. *Zohar* 3, 5a.

8. *Zohar* 3, 107b.

9. *Zohar* 2, 55b.

10. Maimonides, *Guide of the Perplexed*, pt. 3, ch. 27.

11. *Zohar* 3, 105b.

12. *ShM, Haqdamah*, p. 1. The *kavvanot* of mitsvot are found in various sources; the present exposition and discussion are based primarily upon *Shaʿar ha-Mitsvot* of the *Shemonah Sheʿarim* and *Taʿamei ha-Mitsvot*. *Taʿamei ha-Mitsvot* is the "second branch" of Meir Popper's *Pri ʿEts Ḥayyim*, published in Zolkiew in 1775.

13. Ibid.

14. Ibid, p. 2.

15. Ibid.

16. *Sefer Ḥaredim, Haqdamah*, pp. 16–17.

17. *ShM, Haqdamah*, p. 2. The last words in this passage became the basis of a formulaic expression to be recited before the performance of many mitsvot. Thus, we find in *SRH* (p. 38): "Before one performs some mitzvah or gives charity, one should utter [the words]: '[This is for the sake of] the unification [of] the Holy One, blessed be He, and His *Shekhinah*, in fear and in love, in love and in fear,' in the name of all Israel. And one should contemplate joining the name *YH*, which signifies fear and love, with *VH*, which signifies the Holy One, blessed be He, and His *Shekhinah*." These are the earliest attestations of this formula in sixteenth-century sources. It appears subsequently in Elijah de Vidas's *Reshit Ḥokhmah* (The Gate of Love), ch. 9, where he teaches that in order to carry out the unification, one ought to say that one performs each deed in order to unite the Holy One, blessed be He, and His *Shekhinah*, and one should depict to oneself the Tetragrammaton and *ʾADoNaY*, representing *Tiferet* and *Shekhinah*, respectively. One ought to also have in mind the intention that by one's deed the *Shekhinah* will arise from Her exile. These formulaic expressions achieved widespread acceptance by all later kabbalists who were influenced by Lurianic traditions, including the Hasidim. In fact, it became a matter of contention between Hasidim and their rabbinic opponents, who fiercely repudiated the formula. R. Ezekial Landau (1713–93), leader of the Prague Jewish community, published a famous broadside against its recital. For a discussion of this controversy, see Louis Jacobs, *Hasidic Prayer* (New York: Schocken Books, 1973), pp. 140–53.

18. Jacobs, *Hasidic Prayer*, pp. 140–53.

19. These processes are described in considerable detail in *ShM*, *Haqdamah*, pp. 2–4.

20. See *ShM*, p. 4; Vital, *ShMR*, *Perush ᶜal-Sefer Tiqqunim*, p. 8; *Taamei ha-Mitsvot* (Vilna, 1880), p. 15a.

21. Cf. *Tiqqunei Zohar*, *tiqqun* 21, 64a; *Zohar* 3, 273b (*Raᶜaya Mehemna*).

22. *Taᶜamei ha-Mitsvot*, *Haqdamah*, p. 14b.

23. *ShM*, *Parashat Bereshit*, p. 7.

24. *Genesis Rabbah* 17:2; cf. BT *Yevamot* 62b.

25. *Taᶜamei ha-Mitsvot*, *Parashat Bereshit*, p. 15b; cf. *ShG*, *Haqdamah* 26, pp. 70–71.

26. *Taᶜamei ha-Mitsvot*, *Parashat Bereshit*, p. 15b.

27. See BT *Pesaḥim* 112a. On the insistence of having sexual relations in the dark in rabbinic literature, see Boyarin, *Carnal Israel*, pp. 125–28, who suggests (p. 126) that "there may be no doubting that these regulations were understood as promoting the rabbinic ideal of 'modesty'; however, the very extremes of privacy that were encoded in the practice also promoted the notions of intimacy and freedom in sexual behavior."

28. *Taᶜamei ha-Mitsvot*, *Parashat Bereshit*, p. 16a.

29. *ShM*, *Parashat Bereshit*, p. 7; *Taᶜamei ha-Mitsvot*, *Parashat Bereshit*, p. 16a.

30. *Taᶜamei ha-Mitsvot*, *Parashat Bereshit*, p. 16a. The question of whether or not sexual relations (and, more generally, male seminal emission) must be followed by purification through ritual immersion in water was debated by the talmudic rabbis. It seems that whereas early Palestinian sages insisted on immersion in a ritual bath before resuming the study of Torah after sexual activity, subsequent talmudic tradition made it clear that this requirement had been abrogated. According to Boyarin, "the anxiety about sexuality that was manifested by such an idea of impurity was incompatible with later rabbinic sensibilities around the body." See his observations in *Carnal Israel*, pp. 49–51. In light of this, Luria's insistence that purification take place returns to the more stringent spirit of the early Palestinian rabbinic view. See above, p. 401, n. 14.

31. *ShM*, *Parashat Bereshit*, pp. 7–8; *Taᶜamei ha-Mitsvot*, p. 16a.

32. Whereas rabbinic tradition teaches that Friday night is an ideal time for marital love, kabbalistic tradition, which Luria follows here, obviously goes much further by effectively *restricting* it to that time. See, e.g., *Zohar* 2, 89a–89b, where we learn about "the Companions who study the Torah, and who abstain from sexual intercourse during the six weekdays while they labor at the Torah, but who on Sabbath eve prepare themselves for intercourse, because they know the exalted mystery concerning the time when the Consort [i.e., *Shekhinah*] is united with the King [i.e., *Tiferet*]. . . . Blessed is the portion of the man who sanctifies himself with this holy act, and knows this mystery." On the subject of conjugal relations in the *Zohar* and other kabbalistic sources, see *WZ*, 3: 1355–1406; Ginsburg, *Sabbath in the Classical Kabbalah*, pp. 134–35; 289–93.

33. There is a conflicting Lurianic tradition, according to which the require-ment that marital relations be limited to Sabbath eve pertains only to intercourse whose goal is procreation, but not to relations intended to sustain the love be-tween *Ze^cir Anpin* and *Nuqba de-Ze^cir*. See Jacob Zemach, *^cOlat Tamid* (Jerusalem, 1907), *^cInyan Shabbat*, p. 53b; Vital, *Ta^camei ha-Mitsvot, Parashat Bereshit*, p. 16b. Such a view contradicts not only the Lurianic view presented thus far, but also the whole Zoharic tradition upon which it is based. The seventeenth-century Lithuan-ian Kabbalist Alexander Susskind quotes this tradition from a post-Lurianic source but regards it as completely mistaken. See his *Yesod ve-Shoresh ha-^cAvodah* (Jerusalem: Harry Fischel Institute, 1978), *Sha^car ha-^cElyon*, ch. 6, p. 228.

34. *ShM, Parashat Bereshit*, p. 8; Vital, *Ta^camei ha-Mitsvot, Parashat Bereshit*, p. 16a.

35. The *Zohar* also permits sexual relations following a woman's ritual purifi-cation, but for different reasons. It is a man's wife who enables her husband to cleave to the *Shekhinah*; thus, he must reward her by giving her joy, such as when he returns from a journey away from home, on Friday nights, and after her period of impurity: "When a man's wife has her menstrual period and he has proper re-spect for her, celestial intercourse is granted him during those days, so that male and female may exist together. When his wife has become purified, he must give his wife the joy of the commandment, exalted joy" (*Zohar* I, 49b–50a).

36. *ShM, Parashat Bereshit*, p. 8.

37. BT *Berakhot* 5b. *Da^cat* ("Consciousness") refers to the third of the three *mohin*, aspects of divine "consciousness" that facilitate the maturation of *Ze^cir Anpin*.

38. *PEH, Sha^car Shabbat*, ch. 18.

39. Abraham ben David, *Ba^calei ha-Nefesh, Sha^car ha-Qedushah* (Jerusalem, 1975), pp. 104–24. See also D. Biale, *Eros and the Jews*, pp. 95–97; R. Biale, *Women and Jewish Law*, pp. 132–37; J. Cohen, "*Be Fertile and Increase*," p. 218.

40. *³Iggeret ha-Qodesh*, in H. Chavel, ed., *Kitvei Ramban* (Jerusalem: Mossad ha-Rav Kook, 1973), ch. 6, pp. 335–36.

41. *Zohar* I, 42a–b, as translated in *WZ*, 3: 1389. For a discussion of the ques-tion of arousal, mutuality, pleasure, and intimacy in marital relations in rabbinic literature, see Boyarin, *Carnal Israel*, pp. 107–33. Boyarin concludes in this regard that the talmudic rabbis achieve a balance between a sexuality of "modesty" and strict boundaries, on the one hand, and the legitimization of both emotional and physical pleasure, on the other. Speaking of rabbinic men, he contends (p. 132) that "the [male] reader of the text now knows that it is possible to derive pleasure from looking at his wife's genitals, from kissing them, from 'turning the tables,' and most of all, from conversing with her, laughing and playing while making love."

42. *³Iggeret ha-Qodesh*, in H. Chavel, ed., *Kitvei Ramban*, p. 331.

43. Ibid., p. 335.

44. Abraham Azulai, *³Or ha-Hamah* (Bnei Brak: Yahadut, 1973), vol. 2, 12c. Cf. Matt, *Zohar*, pp. 236–37; Ginsburg, *Sabbath in the Classical Kabbalah*, pp. 291–92.

45. Moses ibn Makhir, *Seder ha-Yom* (Lublin, 1876), p. 21b, published originally in Venice, 1599. On this passage, cf. Ginsburg, *Sabbath in the Classical Kabbalah*, pp. 250–51. Makhir was active in the latter half of the sixteenth century and the early seventeenth. He was the founder of a yeshivah in Ein Zeitim that pursued a distinctive curriculum in rabbinic and kabbalistic studies. It was forced to close in 1599 as a result of raids by marauding Muslims, after which its students relocated in Safed. *Seder ha-Yom* became very popular and helped facilitate the dissemination of Safed kabbalistic practices to other parts of the Jewish world.

46. A passage in *Sefer Ḥasidim* also places a husband and wife in a bath together: "A certain Ḥasid was taking a bath [*hayah roḥets be-ʾambatya*], and his wife was sitting with him [*yoshevet ʾetslo*] and behold, a radiance [appeared] on the head of the *tsaddiq*, as well as in the water." This passage is cited in Moshe Idel, "Gazing at the Head in Ashkenazi Hasidism," *Journal of Jewish Thought* 6 (1997): 269–70, and is based upon the version of this work published by Ivan Marcus, *Sefer Ḥasidim*, MS Parma H3280 (Jerusalem: Dinur Center of the Hebrew University, 1985), fol. 101a. See Idel, n. 10, p. 269, where he suggests the likely erotic nature of this passage.

47. Werblowsky, *Joseph Karo*, pp. 135, 137–38.

48. *ShM, Parashat Reʾeh*, p. 111; Vital, *Taʿamei ha-Mitsvot, Parashat Reʾeh*, pp. 111a–b. Cf. *SRH*, p. 38.

49. *ShM, Parashat Reʾeh*, p. 111.

50. *SRH*, p. 38; Vital, *Taʿamei ha-Mitsvot, Parashat Reʾeh*, p. 111b.

51. *Zohar* 3, 113b, for example.

52. *Zohar* 3, 103b–104a. For an English translation and discussion of this passage, see Matt, *Zohar*, pp. 148–52, 268–71. Cf. Fine, "Kabbalistic Texts," in Holtz, ed., *Back to the Sources*, pp. 330–40. On the social concerns of the *Zohar* and early Kabbalah more generally, see Yitzhak Baer, *A History of the Jews in Christian Spain*, vol. 1 (Philadelphia: Jewish Publication Society, 1961), pp. 243–305. See esp. pp. 263–67, where Baer focuses on the *Zohar*'s critique of the moral laxity of the upper classes and its conception that God is closest to the poor and the humble.

53. *SRH*, p. 36.

54. See *ShM, Parashat ve-ʾEthanan*, pp. 76–88; Vital, *Taʿamei ha-Mitsvot, Parashat ve-ʾEthanan*.

55. According to BT *Qiddushin* 30a, "one should always divide his years into three, [devoting] a third to *Miqra*, a third to Mishnah, and a third to Talmud." The Gemara questions whether this division makes any sense since a person does not know how many years he will live, to which it responds that the division should be along days, understood by the medieval commentator Rashi to mean that two days in each week should be dedicated to *Miqra*, Mishnah, and Talmud, respectively. It is the medieval *Tosafot* that contends that the study of these three texts should be divided within *each* day. In actual practice, however, the study of the Talmud was held to incorporate all three levels of learning and was thus considered sufficient to fulfill this obligation. In the Lurianic tradition, the division

is taken more literally, such that the different kinds of texts must be attended to separately.

56. Moses Cordovero, ʾOr Neʿerav (Tel Aviv, 1965), pt. 1, ch. 6.

57. ShM, Parashat ve-ʾEthanan, p. 82.

58. Ibid. Customarily, the wearing of phylacteries (tefillin) is restricted to adult males at weekday morning services. The Lurianic practice of wearing them while studying Torah was unusual but not without precedent. From both the Babylonian and Jerusalem Talmuds we learn that Rabban Yohanan ben Zakkai and his disciple Eliezer ben Hyrcanus, in the land of Israel, as well as Ada ben Ahavah in Babylonia, "never walked four cubits without wearing phylacteries" (BT Sukkah 28a; Taʿanit 20b; JT Berakhot 2:3). Luria may, however, have been influenced more directly by traditions stemming from the Cordoverian school. Thus, according to Elijah de Vidas, it is proper to wear phylacteries throughout the day, if at all possible, and minimally one should wear them while studying Torah, a time during which one is free from the preoccupations of the world. See his Reshit Ḥokhmah, "The Gate of Fear," ch. 15, and "The Gate of Holiness," ch. 6. In this connection, it is interesting to note that the kabbalists of Safed also deviated from normative practice by calling for the donning of tefillin during the weekday afternoon (minḥah) service, in addition to the morning service. Thus, for example, Cordovero: "One should take care to recite the afternoon prayer service while wearing a prayer shawl and phylacteries; this includes the reader's repetition of the Amidah." This is echoed by Abraham ben Eliezer ha-Levi Berukhim: "It is a practice among most of the scholars of Torah, those who revere God, to pray the afternoon service while wearing a prayer shawl and phylacteries." See Fine, Safed Spirituality, pp. 36, 51. Luria, too, practiced the custom of wearing phylacteries during the afternoon prayer. He taught that one should wear two pairs of tefillin during the morning service, those prescribed by Rashi as well as those of Rabbenu Tam, reflecting the debate over proper tefillin, but "in the afternoon service he would only don the tefillin of Rabbenu Tam." See ShK, ʿInyan Tefilat Minḥah, Derush 2, p. 335. On the question of wearing two pairs of phylacteries, Luria's own practice, and its subsequent influence, see Jacob Gartner, Gilgulei Minhag ba-ʿOlam ha-Halakhah (Jerusalem: Hemed Press, 1995), pp. 134–70.

59. ShM, Parashat ve-ʾEthanan, p. 82.

60. Ibid.

61. Ibid., p. 83.

62. Ibid., p. 78. Cf. SRH, p. 34. The Lurianists were not the only ones to transform the study of Torah into a rite of mystical experience. For the German pietists, Torah study served as a means through which they could engage in the visualization of the divine glory (the Shekhinah) or the divine name. According to Sefer Ḥasidim, for example, "Whoever is occupied [with Torah study] out of love sits in the shade of the Presence and derives pleasure from the splendor of the glory." According to Elliot Wolfson's analysis of this material, such passages should be taken literally as

referring "to a technical appearance of the glory induced by the study of Torah." See Elliot R. Wolfson, "The Mystical Significance of Torah Study in German Pietism," *Jewish Quarterly Review* 84, 1 (July 1993): 43–77. In the literature of the *Zohar*, as well, study of Torah is a principal vehicle for mystical experience in the form of visions and the revelation of esoteric mysteries. See Wolfson, *Through a Speculum*, pp. 372–74, 383–84; id., "Circumcision, Vision of God, and Textual Interpretation," in Fine, *Essential Papers on Kabbalah*, pp. 495–524. Among the earliest teachers of eighteenth-century Hasidism, beginning apparently with the Baal Shem Tov himself, we find an approach that synthesizes the study of Torah with the Hasidic goal of cleaving to God, or *devequt*. Thus, according to Jacob Joseph of Polnoye: "I learned from my teacher the Besht [Baal Shem Tov] that the principal thing in [the study of] Torah and prayer is to affix oneself to the innerness and spirituality of the light of the infinite within the letters." See Joseph Weiss, "Torah Study in Early Hasidism," in id., *Studies in Eastern European Jewish Mysticism*, ed. D. Goldstein (Oxford: Oxford University Press, 1985), pp. 56–68.

63. This account is found in *ShM, Parashat ve-ʾEthanan*, pp. 84–85.

64. Exod. 16:5 refers to the injunction to Israel to gather a double portion of manna on Friday in preparation for the Sabbath: "And it shall come to pass on the sixth day that they shall prepare that which they bring in, and it shall be twice as much as they gather daily."

65. The expression *ʿiyyun halakha* appears to have originated in Spain with philosophers and talmudists, referring to a type of study characterized by inquiry and debate among students independent of their teacher. See Haim Dimitrovsky, "The Academy of Rabbi Jacob Berab" (in Hebrew), *Sefunot* 7 (1963): 41–102.

66. *ShM, Parashat ve-ʾEthanan*, p. 79.

67. *SRH*, p. 35. Cf. *ShM, Parashat ve-ʾEthanan*, p. 79.

68. Concerning these issues, see *WZ* 3: 1089–1112; Gershom Scholem, "The Meaning of the Torah in Jewish Mysticism," in id., *On the Kabbalah*, pp. 66–77; Giller, *Enlightened Will Shine*, pp. 59–79.

69. *Zohar* 3, 153a–b. Cf. *Zohar* 1, 27a–28a; 3, 124b, 229b, 254a–b.

70. *SRH*, p. 36. Cf. *ShM, Parashat ve-ʾEthanan*, p. 79.

71. *ShM, Parashat ve-ʾEthanan*, p. 79.

72. *SRH*, pp. 35–36. Cf. *ShM, Parashat ve-ʾEthanan*, p. 79.

73. *ShM, Parashat ve-ʾEthanan*, p. 81.

74. Ibid., pp. 81–82.

75. Ibid., p. 79.

76. *Taʿamei ha-Mitsvot, Parashat ve-ʾEthanan*, p. 93a.

Chapter 7

1. *Avot* 2:13. Cf. Mishnah *Berakhot* 4:4.

2. BT *Berakhot* 31a.

3. BT *Berakhot* 30b.

4. Bahya ibn Paquda, *Duties of the Heart* (Jerusalem, 1928), 8:3, par. 9. The translation is drawn from *The Book of Direction to the Duties of the Heart*, trans. and ed. by Mansoor et al., pp. 364–65. On Bahya and prayer, see Joseph Dan, "The Language of Mystical Prayer," in *Studies in Spirituality* 5 (1995): 40–60.

5. Concerning Bahya's influence upon kabbalistic authors, see Scholem, *Kabbalah*, p. 175; id., *Origins of the Kabbalah*, p. 222.

6. Concerning the question of prayer and German pietism, see Joseph Dan "The Emergence of Mystical Prayer," in *Studies in Jewish Mysticism*, pp. 85–120; id., "Prayer as Text and Prayer as Mystical Experience," in R. Link-Salinger, ed., *Torah and Wisdom: Studies in Jewish Philosophy, Kabbalah, and Halacha* (New York: Shengold, 1992), pp. 33–47; id., "Pesaq ha-Yirah veha-Emunah and the Intention of Prayer in Ashkenazi Hasidic Esotericism," *Frankfurter Judaistische Beitrage* 19 (1991–92): 185–215; id., "The Intention of Prayer from the Tradition of R. Judah the Pietist" (in Hebrew), *Daʿat* 10 (1983): 47–56.

7. Dan, "Emergence of Mystical Prayer," pp. 90–91.

8. Ibid., p. 108.

9. Ibid.

10. Concerning these traditions, see Dan, "Emergence of Mystical Prayer," pp. 107–10; Scholem, *Origins*, pp. 208–10, 243–48.

11. Concerning Isaac the Blind and his views on mystical prayer, see Scholem, *Origins*, pp. 248–309; Wolfson, *Through a Speculum*, pp. 288–93.

12. Passage quoted in Scholem, *Origins*, pp. 300–301.

13. On the subject of contemplative prayer in Ezra and Azriel of Gerona, see Scholem, *Origins*, pp. 414–21; Daniel Matt, "*Ayin*: The Concept of Nothingness in Jewish Mysticism," in Fine, *Essential Papers on Kabbalah*, pp. 77–85; Wolfson, *Through a Speculum*, pp. 289–302. A French translation of Azriel's *Commentary on the Prayers* is found in Azriel of Gerona, *Commentaire sur la liturgie quotidienne*, ed. Gabrielle Sed-Rajna (Leiden: E.J. Brill, 1974). See as well Sed-Rajna, "Sur quelques commentaires kabbalistiques sur le rituel," *REJ* 124 (1965): 307–51.

14. *WZ*, 2: 262. On the *Zohar*'s approach more generally to prayer, contemplation, and visionary experience, see Wolfson, *Through a Speculum*, pp. 326–92. For a study of the conception of devotional prayer in one of Moshe de Leon's Hebrew writings, *Sefer ha-Rimmon*, see Wolfson, "Mystical-Theurgical Dimensions of Prayer in *Sefer ha-Rimmon*," in D. R. Blumenthal, ed., *Approaches to Judaism in Medieval Times*, vol. 3 (Atlanta: Scholars Press, 1988), pp. 41–79.

15. *Zohar* 2, 200b.

16. *Zohar* 2, 128b.

17. *Zohar* 2, 200a. For still other variations on this theme, see *WZ*, 2: 273–74.

18. Vital's version, by far the most elaborate, was published in different recensions, most prominently as *Shaʿar ha-Kavvanot* of the *Shemoneh Sheʿarim*. This was printed for the first time in Salonika in 1862, and subsequently in Jerusalem in

1902. Another edition of Vital's account of the *kavvanot* of prayer was produced by Jacob Zemach as ʿ*Olat Tamid*, printed for the first time in Jerusalem in 1907. A manuscript of this work in Zemach's own handwriting is Jewish Theological Seminary of America MS Mic. 2020. For a description of ʿ*Olat Tamid*, see Avivi, *Binyan* ʾ*Ariel*, pp. 62–63. Zemach's student Meir Poppers edited a version of these *kavvanot* as part of his *Pri* ʿ*Ets Ḥayyim*, published originally in Korecz in 1785. Moses Yonah and Moses Najara preserved *kavvanot* in *Kanfei Yonah*, Sassoon MS 993, Ben Zvi Institute MS 2218, and in a printed edition of this work, Lemburg (Lvov), 1884. Brief accounts of the *kavvanot* of prayer by Joseph ibn Tabul are found in print and manuscript. Certain of his material was incorporated into printed editions of Vital's writings, including, for example, the aforementioned edition of *Pri* ʿ*Ets Ḥayyim*, p. 91, col. 3 (on the *hallel* prayer), and p. 128, col. 3–p. 130, col. 1 (on the "four species" of *Sukkot*). Miscellaneous *kavvanot* preserved by ibn Tabul have been published from manuscript by Joseph Avivi in "The *Kavvanot* of Rabbi Joseph ibn Tabul," in M. Benayahu, ed., *Sefer Zikkaron le-ha-Rav Yitshaq Nissim* (Jerusalem: Yad Harav Nissim, 1985), 4: 75–108. On ibn Tabul's *kavvanot* of prayer, see, as well, Meroz, "Torat ha-Geʾeulah," pp. 87–88.

19. *ShK, Haqdamah* ʾ*Eḥat Qetanah*, p. 2. The same is reported by Judah Mishan in his enumeration of Luria's customs and teachings. See Benayahu, *STA*, p. 336, no. 17.

20. Concerning the reverberation of this practice in Hasidism, see the remarks by A. Green, *Devotion and Commandment*, pp. 65–70, and nn. on pp. 90–91.

21. *ShK,* ʿ*Inyan Birkhot ha-Shaḥar*, p. 2; Luria's customs, in the name of Judah Mishan, preserved in manuscript, were published in Benayahu, *STA*, pp. 335–39.

22. *PEH, Shaʿar* ʿ*Olam ha-*ʿ*Assiyah*, ch. 2.

23. BT *Berakhot* 24b, 31a; *Sotah* 32b.

24. *Zohar* 1, 209b–210a.

25. *Zohar* 3, 210b (*Raʿaya Mehemna*).

26. *Zohar* 2, 128b. Cf. *Tiqqunei Zohar, tiqqun* 10.

27. *WZ*, 2: 271–72.

28. *ShK,* ʿ*Inyan Berakhot*, p. 23.

29. For extensive treatments of this theme, see Idel, *Kabbalah*, pp. 74–88, reprinted in Fine, *Essential Papers on Kabbalah*, pp. 439–53; Elliot R. Wolfson, "Weeping, Death, and Spiritual Ascent in Sixteenth-Century Jewish Mysticism," in J. Collins and M. Fishbane, eds., *Death, Ecstasy, and Other Worldly Journeys* (Albany: State University of New York Press, 1995), pp. 209–47.

30. From Cordovero's *hanhagot*, see Fine, *Safed Spirituality*, p. 38.

31. Vital, *ShMR, Ma*ʾ*amarei Sefer ha-Zohar, Parashat Bereshit*, p. 34.

32. *SRH*, p. 29; *PEH, Shaʿar* ʿ*Olam ha-*ʿ*Assiyah*, ch. 1. Vital cites this tradition in the name of Abraham Berukhim, whom Vital believes received it from Moses Cordovero.

33. See Idel, *Kabbalah*, pp. 70, 313, n. 36.

34. *PEH, Shaᶜar Qeriᶜat Shema*, ch. 29; *ShK, ᶜInyan Berakhot*, p. 23; *ShK*, vol. 2, *ᶜInyan Shinui ha-Tefillot*, p. 11. Luria also counseled his disciples to close their eyes while practicing certain of the *yiḥudim*, discussed in Chapter 8. See *SRH*, pp. 117, 130.

35. Wolfson, *Through a Speculum*, pp. 336–42. A vision of the exiled *Shekhinah* is the central theme in an often-cited dramatic story concerning Abraham Berukhim, in which the themes of weeping and visionary experience come together. In this story, Luria advises him to perform an act of personal *tiqqun* so as to prolong his life. He counsels him to travel to the Western Wall in Jerusalem, "where you should pour out your prayers and your tears; and if you are acceptable before Your Maker you will merit a vision of the *Shekhinah*." In preparation for his pilgrimage:

> he immediately secluded himself without interruption for three days and nights, which he spent in fasting, wearing sackcloth and in great weeping. After these three days, he proceeded to the Western Wall, where he began to pray and weep bitterly. While doing so, he lifted up his eyes and saw upon the Wall the likeness of a woman with her back turned toward him. I do not wish to disclose the garments that she was wearing out of respect for our Maker. As soon as he saw her, he fell upon his face, crying out and weeping: "Mother, mother, mother of Zion, woe is me that I have seen you thus!" And he continued to weep bitterly, afflicting himself, tearing hair out of his beard and head until he fainted and fell deeply asleep. Then in a dream he saw the *Shekhinah* coming toward him. And placing her hand upon his face and wiping away the tears from his eyes, She said to him: "Console yourself, Abraham my son, for 'there is hope for thy future, saith the Lord, and your children shall return to their own border' [Jer. 31:17] 'for I will cause their captivity to return, and will have compassion upon them'" [Jer. 33:26]. (*SₑA*, letter 4, pp. 87–88)

This amazing story epitomizes at once so many of the themes that animated Safed's kabbalists: penitence, ascetic mortification, divinely inspired experience, and messianic longing. Here Berukhim does actually see the *Shekhinah*, but only with Her back turned toward him, suggesting the ambivalence about such a vision. Not only this, but he falls upon his face, presumably to avoid gazing upon Her. Only in his subsequent dream, filled with clear messianic allusions, does he see Her coming toward him, that is, from the front, as She draws near to wipe away the tears from his eyes. Cf. the remarks in Idel, *Kabbalah*, pp. 80–81, and nn. on p. 314; Fine, *Safed Spirituality*, pp. 48–49; Wineman, *Beyond Appearances*, pp. 140–45; Benayahu, *STA*, pp. 228–30.

36. This passage is quoted from the translation in Wolfson, *Through a Speculum*, p. 341, based upon Medicea-Laurenziana MS 44.13, fol. 23a. See also Jewish Theological Seminary of America MS Mic. 1822, fol. 47a.

37. *ShK, ᶜInyan Birkhot ha-Shaḥar*, p. 2. The *ᶜAqedah* refers to Gen. 22:1–19, which is incorporated into the early portion of the morning liturgy, following the

prayer in which one blesses God "who removes sleep from my eyes and slumber from my eyelids."

38. Luria's order is the traditional one for putting on phylacteries and prayer shawl.

39. *ShK, ʿInyan ba-Berakhot*, pp. 19–20. The contemporary visitor to Safed's old city will find two synagogues purporting to be Isaac Luria's synagogue, one Ashkenazi and the other Sephardic. It was in the latter that Luria actually prayed.

40. *ShK, ʿInyan Bet ha-Knesset*, p. 20.

41. Ibid.

42. Ibid., p. 22. Rites of circumambulation go as far back as the Bible (see Josh. 6:13–16). The Mishnah depicts a ritual procession seven times around the altar of the ancient Temple on the festival of Sukkot (Sukkah 4:4), a practice that was eventually adapted to the synagogue, apparently during the tenth century by Saadya Gaon, as evidenced by his *Siddur*. Ritual circumambulation on Sukkot was adopted by kabbalists as well, who invested it with esoteric significance. It is interesting that in the Lurianic passage here, such practice is not limited to Sukkot but appears to have been performed on a regular basis. The devotee, an embodiment of the divine masculine, encircles the reader's table, explicitly signified as the divine feminine (*Malkhut*), seven times, the purpose being to facilitate a divine *hieros gamos* and personal illumination. For a study of such rites, see Paul Fenton, "The Symbolism of Ritual Circumambulation in Judaism and Islam: A Comparative Study," *Journal of Jewish Thought and Philosophy* 6 (1997): 345–69.

43. *ShM, Parashat ʿEqev*, p. 89. Vital's words are also found in Montifiore MS 348, fol. 26a, Safed kabbalistic traditions collected by a student of Moses Galante's.

44. *ShK, ʿInyan Shaḥarit shel Shabbat*, p. 92. Cf. Benayahu, *STA*, p. 326, n. 2.

45. *ShK, Qeriʾat Sefer Torah, Derush* 1, p. 214. Cf. *PEH, Shaʿar Qeriʾat Sefer Torah*, ch. 1.

46. *ShM, Parashat ve-ʿEthanan*, p. 78.

47. *ShM, Parashat ʿEqev*, p. 89.

48. *Zohar* 2, 163b. See Wolfson, *Through a Speculum*, pp. 368–69, where this theme is discussed at length.

49. *ShK, Qeriʾat Sefer Torah, Derush* 1, p. 314b. Cf. a passage by the thirteenth-century kabbalist Isaac of Akko, according to which you should "place in front of the eyes of your mind the letters of God's name, as if they were written in a book in Hebrew script. Visualize every letter extending to infinity. What I mean is: when you visualize the letters, focus on them with your mind's eye as you contemplate infinity. Both together: gazing and meditating." Translated by Matt, *Essential Kabbalah*, p. 120. For a study of the phenomenon of gazing in the context of kabbalistic rituals, see Idel, "Gazing at the Head in Ashkenazi Hasidism," pp. 265–300.

50. *PEH, ʿInyan Tefillah*, introduction.

51. *ShM, Parashat Behar*, p. 6. Cf. *PEH, ʿInyan Tefillah*, ch. 6, pp. 15–16.

52. The talmudic source for this nighttime recitation of the Shema is BT *Berakhot* 4b–5a.

53. For discussions of the development of the Shema as part of the fixed liturgy, see Lawrence Hoffman, *The Canonization of the Synagogue Service* (Notre Dame, Ind.: Notre Dame University Press, 1979), pp. 24–29; Ismar Elbogen, *Jewish Liturgy: A Comprehensive History*, trans. R. Schendlin (Philadelphia: Jewish Publication Society), pp. 16–24.

54. *ShK*, ʿ*Inyan Kavvanat Qeriʾat Shema*, *Derush* 4, p. 129.

55. Ibid., *Derush* 1, pp. 120–21.

56. Ibid., *Derush* 3, pp. 127–28.

57. See *Zohar, Parashat Pinḥas*, 222a (*Raʿaya Mehemna*).

58. *ShK*, ʿ*Inyan Kavvanat Qeriʾat Shema*, *Derush* 6, p. 141.

59. The *kavvanot* of the Shemoneh Esreh are described in *ShK*, ʿ*Inyan Kavvanat ha-ʿAmidah*, pp. 182–279; *PEH*, *Shaʿar ha-ʿAmidah*, pp. 44a–56b.

60. "Falling upon the face," as well as "spreading out the arms and legs," were two types of prostration customary in Babylonia at the beginning of the third century during the recitation of the *Taḥanun*. According to the Mishnah (*Tamid* 7:3), the practice of prostration before God goes back to a practice in the Temple in Jerusalem: "The Levites recited the psalm. When they reached the end of the section, they blew the *shofar*, and the people prostrated themselves. For every section, the *shofar* was blown, and for every blowing of the *shofar* there was a prostration." After the Temple's destruction in 70 C.E., this custom was transferred to the synagogues; following the Amidah, the opportunity was given to every individual to express heartfelt devotion in an entirely private and personal way. Although they began as private, unfixed prayers, eventually a collection of liturgical passages evolved, the main themes of which were confession of sin, the worshipper's unworthiness, and petitions for divine mercy. Among Jews from Spain and Portugal, this liturgy included Psalm 25, while by the eighteenth century among Ashkenazim, it included Psalm 6. On the development of *Taḥanun*, see A. Z. Idelsohn, *Jewish Liturgy and Its Development* (1932; reprint, New York: Schocken Books, 1972), pp. 110–12; Samuel Freehof, "The Origin of the Tahanun," *Hebrew Union College* 1 (1925): 339–50; Elbogen, *Jewish Liturgy*, pp. 66–72.

61. Some talmudic sages are reported to have refused to prostrate themselves on the ground, either because they considered full prostration forbidden outside the Temple or because they regarded it as unbecoming for a distinguished person. See BT *Baba Metsia* 59b; *Megillah* 22b; *Taʿanit* 14b. By the period of the Geonim, the posture had taken the form of sitting with the head inclined on the arm.

62. Concerning the phenomenon of mystical death in Judaism, see Michael Fishbane, *The Kiss of God: Spiritual and Mystical Death in Judaism* (Seattle: University of Washington Press, 1994); and L. Fine, "Contemplative Death in Jewish

Mystical Tradition," in *Sacrificing the Self: Perspectives on Martyrdom and Religion*, edited by Margaret Cormack (New York: Oxford University Press, 2002), pp. 92–106.

63. *Zohar* 3, 120b–121a. Psalm 25 is written acrostically, but the letter *vav* is lacking. For variations on this motif, see *Zohar* 2, 202b; 3: 176b, 241b. For discussions of the *Zohar*'s treatment of *nefilat ʾappayim*, see *WZ* 2: 275–76; Wolfson, *Through a Speculum*, pp. 339–40; Meroz, "Torat ha-Geʾeulah," pp. 255–56, 289; Fishbane, *Kiss of God*, pp. 107–10.

64. Moses Cordovero, *Siddur Tefillah le-Moshe* (Przemysl, 1892), 112a. Cf. Fishbane, *Kiss of God*, pp. 110–12.

65. *ShK, ʿInyan Nefilat ʾAppayim*, pp. 301–314; *ShG, Haqdamah* 19, p. 52. Cf. Tishby, *Torat ha-Raʾ*, pp. 128–30; Liebes, *Studies in the Zohar*, pp. 52–55; Fishbane, *Kiss of God*, pp. 112–16.

66. Avivi, "The *Kavvanot*," pp. 87, 89, based on Gaster MS 282, now British Museum MS Or. 10627, and Montifiore MS 348.

67. BT *Ḥagigah* 15b.

68. *ShM, Parashat Reʾeh*, p. 112.

69. *ShK, ʿInyan Nefilat ʾAppayim, Derush* 2, p. 305, where Vital cites BT *Berakhot* 18b.

70. Moses Yonah, *Kanfei Yonah*, 50c. For his general account of these *kavvanot*, see 24c–d.

71. See *ShK, ʿInyan Nefilat ʾAppayim, Derush* 5, pp. 310–14; *PEH, Shaʿar Nefilat ʾAppayim*, ch. 4. Cf. also *ShK, ʿInyan Kavvanat Qeriʾat Shema, Derush* 5, p. 137. On this passage, cf. Meroz, "Torat ha-Geʾeulah," pp. 80, 152, who ascribes it to level three of her schema.

72. *ShK, ʿInyan Kavvanat Qeriʾat Shema*, p. 137. On the messianic role that Akiva plays in Luria's view, see Chapter 9.

73. *ShK, ʿInyan Nefilat ʾAppayim, Derush* 5, p. 311.

74. Ibid. Cf. *Shaʿar ha-Kelalim*, ch. 1; Meroz, "Torat ha-Geʾeulah," pp. 256–61, 282–86.

75. Werblowsky, *Joseph Karo*, p. 152.

76. Eleazar Azikri, *Sefer Ḥaredim*, pt. 1, ch. 1, par. 16. Cf. Werblowsky, *Joseph Karo*, p. 152, n. 4.

77. *SeH*, p. 172.

78. For a brief account of the phenomenon of shamanism, see the entry "Shamanism" in M. Eliade et al., *Encyclopedia of Religion*, 13: 201–8; a classic full-length study of Shamanism may be found in Mircea Eliade, *Shamanism: Archaic Techniques of Ecstasy* (Princeton, N.J.: Princeton University Press, 1964).

79. Letter by Nathan of Gaza to Sabbatai Sevi's brother, in Jacob Sasportas, *Sefer Tsitsat Nobel Sevi*, ed. I. Tishby (Jerusalem: Mossad Bialik, 1954), pp. 201–2. See, as well, British Museum MS Margoliouth 856, fol. 75a; Gershom Scholem, ed., *ʾIggeret Natan ha-Azati ʿal Sabbatai Sevi ve-Hamarato*, in *Qovets ʿal Yad*, vol. 16

(Jerusalem, 1966), p. 454. On the question of Sabbatai Sevi's apostasy more generally, see Scholem, *Sabbatai Sevi*, pp. 687–820.

80. It is worth noting that, in addition to the Sabbateans, a wide range of other post-Lurianic authors promoted the practice of ritualized, contemplative death and martyrdom, including the famous seventeenth-century Polish rabbi and kabbalist Jacob Emden, the Hasidic masters Shneur Zalman of Lyadi and Nahman of Bratslav, and the ascetic Lithuanian kabbalist Alexander Susskind of Grodno (d. 1793). Susskind was, without any doubt, the most fervent proponent of spiritual martyrdom:

> Now it is obvious that this martyrdom, even though it is only *in potentia*, must be wholehearted and not with a remote heart. For the Creator, blessed be He and exalted, searches all hearts. For it is clear that a mere thought on one's part that one is ready to suffer martyrdom for the sanctification of God's name does not mean anything unless one really makes the firmest resolve that one will certainly survive the test, [thereby] allowing oneself to be threatened with every kind of death by torture rather than be false to one's holy religion. One should represent to oneself that at this moment they are actually carrying out these forms of killing, and one should envisage the pain and the sufferings that one will undergo and yet survive the test. The Creator, blessed be He and exalted, who searches all hearts, sees one's thoughts and the manner in which one represents to oneself the deaths and the tortures inflicted upon one and yet survives the test. This is real martyrdom, even though it is only *in potentia*. (*Yesod ve-Shoresh ha-ᶜAvodah, Shaᶜar ha-Gadol*, ch. 11, pp. 33–35, translation on the basis of Jacobs, *Jewish Mystical Testimonies*, p. 178)

81. *ShK*, 2, ᶜ*Inyan Kabbalat Shabbat, Derush* 1, p. 38.

82. Ibid., pp. 38–39.

83. *ShK*, 2, ᶜ*Inyan ᶜAravit shel leil Shabbat, Derush* 2, pp. 73–76.

84. *ShK*, 2, ᶜ*Inyan ha-Shulḥan*, p. 84.

85. BT *Shabbat* 33a. The injunction concerning the Sabbath found in Exod. 20:8 begins, "Remember the Sabbath day to keep it holy," while in Deut. 5:12, it reads, "Observe the Sabbath day. . . . " According to rabbinic tradition (*Shevuᶜot* 20b), both forms were miraculously communicated by God simultaneously. Here that linguistic miracle signifies the intimacy between divine masculine and feminine that occurs on the Sabbath.

86. Concerning the use of myrtle for preparing the bridegroom's wreath, see *Tosefta, Sotah* 15:8. On the juggling of myrtle at a wedding, see BT *Ketubot* 17a. For the use of myrtle in the celebration of the *Havdalah* ceremony at the end of the Sabbath, in the literature of the earlier Kabbalah, see Ginsburg, *Sabbath in the Classical Kabbalah*, pp. 263–67. It is worth noting that myrtle shrubs grow wild on Mount Carmel and in the Upper Galilee, making it widely available.

87. *Zohar* 3, 245a (*Raᶜaya Mehemna*). According to this passage, these represent the faces of the *ḥayyot* of the Chariot described in Ezekiel 10, that is, the lion, the ox, and the eagle, each of which had four countenances. Somewhat later in the same passage, however, the *Zohar* indicates that on the basis of the Torah, only two loaves are required for each meal, "representing the six levels of the supernal Throne," meaning the *sefirot* from *Ḥesed* through *Yesod*. Still, it is better to provide an additional six "representing the six levels of the lower Throne," that is, the angels of the *Shekhinah*.

88. *Tiqqunei Zohar, tiqqun* 47, 84a–84b. We also find in *Zohar Ḥadash, Parashat* ᵓ*Aḥarei Mot*, 48d, instructions to prepare twelve loaves, although according to Isaiah Tishby, this may be a later addition to the text. On the motif of twelve Sabbath loaves in the *Zohar*, see *WZ*, 3: 1235–36, 1269, nn. 222–23.

89. This custom was not universally practiced among the Hasidim. Some rejected the custom, partly because of the presence of different views in the *Zohar*. According to Aaron Wertheim, the custom was taken up by Hasidism in Ukraine as well as in the greater part of Poland and Galicia. A variation of this practice developed in Ukraine that involved "baking one large challah loaf made up of twelve parts, known in Yiddish as a *yudbeysnik* (i.e., "a twelvenik"). Wertheim also relates that "Karlin Hasidim who wished to invoke the high opinion that the Maggid of Miedzyrzecz held of their own rebbe, R. Aaron 'the Great,' told the story that when he sat at table with the great rabbi in Miedzyrzecz, twelve loaves were placed before him as well for all the Sabbath meals." The opponents of the Hasidim, though, repudiated the custom. According to the Vilna Gaon, for example, Luria actually intended only twelve pieces, requiring the traditional two loaves for each meal. On this question, see Aaron Wertheim, "Traditions and Customs in Hasidism," excerpted in G. D. Hundert, ed., *Essential Papers on Hasidism: Origins to Present* (New York: New York University Press, 1991), pp. 369–70.

90. *ShK*, 2, ᶜ*Inyan ha-Shulḥan*, pp. 84–85.

91. Ibid., pp. 76–82.

92. Ibid., p. 85.

93. For a translation of this poem, see Fine, *Safed Spirituality*, pp. 78–80. See also Scholem, *On the Kabbalah*, pp. 143–45; Yehuda Liebes, "Sabbath Meal Songs Established by the Holy Ari," *Molad* 4 (1972): 540–55.

94. Ibid., p. 88.

95. *ShK*, 2, p. 86.

96. Benayahu, *STA*, pp. 331–32.

97. *ShK*, 2, ᶜ*Inyan Reḥitsat Panav*, p. 30. On the question of proper dress on the part of kabbalists for the Sabbath, see Ginsburg, *Sabbath in the Classical Kabbalah*, pp. 231–42.

98. The cyclical nature of Lurianic ritual has also been remarked upon by others. Liebes ("Two Young Roes," p. 126) writes that there is "another dimension to time in Lurianic myth, that is the cyclical aspect, which is expressed in *Shaᶜar ha-Kavvanot*,

according to which the [dynamic processes of this] myth are not realized in the course of history, but once every year. . . . The acute messianic quality of Lurianic Kabbalah appeared only in its final stages." See, as well, Idel, *Messianic Mystics*, p. 314; and id., "Some Concepts of Time and History in Kabbalah," in E. Carlebach, J. Efron, and D. Myers, eds., *Jewish History and Jewish Memory: Essays in Honor of Yosef Hayim Yerushalmi* (Hanover, N.H.: University Press of New England for Brandeis University Press, 1998), pp. 153–88, where Idel aptly observes that "the basis of Luria's Kabbalah is the cyclical ritualistic microchronos, which has been combined with the more linear messianic motif. The double vision of divine guidance in the world — the grand course of history progressing toward its perfection in the eschaton, and the providence within history, concerned with the deeds of men in a microchronic period of time — became part of the development of Lurianic thought" (p. 167).

Chapter 8

1. For a survey of selected kabbalistic mystical techniques not associated with the performance of the mitsvot, see Idel, *Kabbalah*, ch. 5, reprinted in Fine, *Essential Papers on Kabbalah*, pp. 438–94. Idel applies the term *anomian* to mystical techniques essentially unrelated to halakhic practice.

2. Hayyim Vital, *Sha⁽ar ha-Yiḥudim* (hereafter *ShY*) was published for the first time in Korecz in 1783, and subsequently in Lemberg (Lvov) in 1855. This book is based upon the editing of Meir Poppers, who compiled a version of Vital's writings under three separate titles: *Derekh ⁽Ets Ḥayyim, Pri ⁽Ets Ḥayyim* (consisting of four "branches"), and *Nof ⁽Ets Ḥayyim*. The four "branches" or parts that made up the second of these, *Pri ⁽Ets Ḥayyim*, were themselves divided into three separate volumes when they were printed. The material having to do with *kavvanot* of prayer was published (making for confusion) as *Sefer Pri ⁽Ets Ḥayyim* (Korecz, 1785), the second as *Sefer Ta⁽amei ha-Mitsvot* (Zolkiew, 1775), and the third and fourth "branches" were printed in Korecz under the title *Sha⁽ar ha-Yiḥudim ve-Tiqqunei ⁽Avonot*. The contents of this volume are essentially the same as those found in *SRH*. All references are to the first edition.

3. Ibn Tabul's much briefer versions of the *yiḥudim* are extant in Jewish Theological Seminary of America MS 1995 (JTS 931), fols. 175a–180a, entitled *Mah she-Lamad Yosef ibn Tabul me-ha-Ari*, fols. 175a–180a; and Columbia MS X893 M6862, fols. 143a–152a. Ibn Tabul's material overlaps with Vital's to some degree. All but one of the *yiḥudim* that appear in the JTS 931 MS are also recorded in Vital's name in *Sha⁽ar ha-Yiḥudim*, a version edited by Meir Poppers. Of the *yiḥudim* preserved in the Columbia MS, two are not found in print, that is, in either *SRH* or *Sha⁽ar ha-Yiḥudim*. The last four *yiḥudim* in the Columbia MS are present in almost exactly the same language in *SRH*. The question of the relationship between these overlapping materials is complicated by the fact that both ibn Tabul and Vital claim to have received them personally, word for word from Luria. We find the

following in the introduction to the *yiḥudim* preserved in Jewish Theological Seminary of America MS 1995 (JTS 931), fol. 175a: "These are the words [*zeh lashon mori*] of my teacher and rabbi, Rabbi Isaac Luria Ashkenazi, may his memory be blessed, who told me personally [*peh ʾel peh*], word for word, a great esoteric teaching [*sod gadol*] . . . and this is what he said." Ibn Tabul's *yiḥudim* themselves (fol. 175b) are introduced with these words: "These are the *yiḥudim* that my teacher transmitted to me personally, word for word, letter for letter." At the very end of the relevant portion of the manuscript (fol. 180a), we find the following curious statement by ibn Tabul: "This ends the words of the perfect sage, light of the exile, who transmitted them directly to me, Joseph, at the grave of Abba Shaul. And I forgot them, but I learned them [again] in a dream following his death." The first two of these above citations are found in almost exactly the same language in *Shaʿar ha-Yiḥudim*, ch. 8, representing Vital. It thus appears that either ibn Tabul or Vital appropriated language from the other. In addition to nine separate *yiḥudim* that Vital reports Luria having given to Moshe Yonah, found in *SRH*, there are also other *yiḥudim* in Yonah's own writings found in a manuscript in the Benayahu collection. Some of the same *yiḥudim* present in *SRH*, which Vital indicates were given by Luria to Abraham Berukhim, are found as well in manuscripts of Yonah's *Kanfei Yonah*. We thus see that there is a good deal of overlapping of these texts in the writings of Vital, ibn Tabul, and Yonah, presumably because handwritten materials circulated in such a way that they were known to various individuals within Luria's circle. See Meroz, "Torat ha-Geʾeulah," pp. 86–87; Scholem, *Ketavav ha-ʾAmitiyim shel ha-Ari be-Kabbalah*, p. 185; Benayahu, "Rabbi Moshe Yonah," pp. 20–22.

4. *SRH*, p. 33.

5. Ibid., pp. 33–36.

6. Ibid., p. 34.

7. Ibid., p. 36.

8. Ibid.

9. Ibid., p. 108.

10. *ShY*, ch. 4, p. 5a.

11. *SeH*, pp. 172–73.

12. *SRH*, p. 111. Meroz cites this as an example of the way in which Luria's disciples contributed in an active and creative way to his teachings. See her "Faithful Transmission," pp. 264–65. Liebes, on the other hand, attributes the extension of the practice of *yiḥudim* to prayer itself as representing a later development in Luria's thinking. See Liebes, "New Directions," p. 166.

13. *SRH*, p. 108.

14. In an earlier version of these teachings, in a commentary on the *Zohar*, Luria held a different position on the proper days for practice of the *yiḥudim*. Here, in complete antithesis to what he taught later, he asserts that the appropriate days are precisely Sabbaths, Festivals, and the New Moon, since on these occasions the righteous in Paradise travel from world to world in order to bring about the *zivvug* of Zeʿir Anpin and Nuqba de-Zeʿir. The righteous among the living are supposed to perform prostration at the graves of the departed on these days in order

to assist them in their efforts. On the other hand, extraordinary *tsaddiqim* such as Shimon bar Yohai—who embody the principle of *Yesod*—have the ability to do this even on weekdays. See *Zohar ha-Raqia* (Korecz, 1785), pp. 41b–43a. Cf. Meroz, "Torat ha-Ge ʾeulah," pp. 287–88, who attributes this version to no earlier than level three of her schema.

15. *SRH*, p. 75.

16. Patrick Geary, *Living with the Dead in the Middle Ages* (Ithaca, N.Y.: Cornell University Press, 1994), p. 2. See, as well, pp. 77–92 where Geary frames the relationship between Christian saints and those who venerate them in terms of the model of gift exchange, such as I have suggested here in connection with the *yiḥudim*.

17. This connection has already been made by Pinchas Giller, "Recovering the Sanctity of the Galilee: The Veneration of Sacred Relics in Classical Kabbalah," *Journal of Jewish Thought* 4 (1994): 147–69.

18. Peter Brown, *The Cult of the Saints* (Chicago: University of Chicago Press, 1981), p. 3.

19. See Giller, "Recovering the Sanctity of the Galilee," p. 148: "Burial took place in two stages: an initial burial was followed by the bones of the deceased being re-buried in ossuaries. In order to contain the spread of ritual impurity generated by the corpse, the Jews of antiquity dug thousands of limestone burial tombs."

20. See, e.g., Robert Bonfil, *Jewish Life in Renaissance Italy* (Berkeley: University of California Press, 1994), pp. 280–84.

21. Giller, "Recovering the Sanctity of the Galilee," pp. 149–54.

22. Ibid., p. 154.

23. Robert M. Torrance, *The Spiritual Quest: Transcendence in Myth, Religion, and Science* (Berkeley: University of California Press, 1994), p. 155. I earlier suggested similarities between the Lurianic practice of *nefilat ʾappayim* and shamanism, and the performance of the *yiḥudim* also bears similarities to shamanic practice, primarily insofar as both activities entail elaborate attempts to visit the souls of the dead.

24. Concerning necromancy, see M. Eliade et al., *Encyclopedia of Religion*, 10: 345–46, and the bibliography listed there. Regarding necromancy as part of popular Jewish practice, see Trachtenberg, *Jewish Magic and Superstition*, pp. 222–24, who mentions such methods as (a) incantations at the grave; (b) passing the night on the grave, clothed in a distinctive garment and burning spices and incense while waving a myrtle wand "until one hears an exceedingly faint voice from the grave responding to his questions, so faint that it seems hardly to be sensed by the ear, but rather to exist in his thoughts"; (c) the stationing of a man and a woman at the head and foot of a grave, with a rattle on the earth between them, which they strike while they recite a secret invocation; and (d) invocation of the dead by

means of angelic names, while holding a mixture of oil and honey in a new glass bowl. Although rabbinic authorities might discourage or even prohibit such popular magical practices, the fact is that customs of this type could never be completely suppressed.

25. Brown, *Cult of the Saints*, p. 53. See, as well, his "The Rise and Function of the Holy Man in Late Antiquity," in id., *Society and the Holy in Late Antiquity* (Berkeley: University of California Press, 1982), pp. 103–52.

26. Brown, *Cult of the Saints*, p. 56.

27. The two primary passages that influenced Lurianic teachings are *Zohar* 1, 224b–225b; and 3, 70b–71b.

28. *Zohar* 3, 70b.

29. *SRH*, p. 109.

30. Joseph ibn Tabul, Jewish Theological Seminary of America MS 1995 (JTS 931), fols. 175a–180a; and Columbia University MS X893 M6862, fols. 143a–152a.

31. In *Ecclesiastes Rabbah* 10:10 we already find a correlation between weeping at a grave and a revelatory experience, involving none other than Shimon bar Yohai: "One of the disciples of R. Shimon bar Yohai forgot his learning; so he went weeping to the cemetery. After he had wept much [his teacher] appeared to him in his dream."

32. *Zohar* 3, 71b.

33. In a highly interesting feature of this teaching, the *Zohar* says that the presence of a scroll of the Torah in a cemetery can *also* arouse the attention of the dead:

> Rabbi Hiyya: I would be surprised if there were any who knew how to communicate with the dead apart from us. Rabbi Abba said: Sorrow communicates with them. The Torah communicates with them. For if they [i.e., the righteous among the living] cannot find someone who is knowledgeable about this, they take a scroll of the Torah to the graves, and [the dead] bestir themselves out of concern for the Torah, [wondering] why it has been exiled to such a place. Then Dumah communicates with them. Rabbi Yose said: They know that the world is in trouble, and that the living are not fit or knowledgeable enough to tell them. (*Zohar* 3, 71a)

On the basis of the entire extended passage describing this, it appears that the *Zohar* is reflecting an actual contemporary practice. Cf. also *Zohar* 1, 225a–b. Luria himself refers to this unusual technique in *Zohar ha-Raqia*, although it does not appear to have played a part in Lurianic practice. In his study of medieval Mediterranean Jewry, S.D. Goitein reported that "When a solemn excommunication was to be announced, the Torah scrolls were carried out to the cemetery and the congregation gathered there as a *memento mori* and warning to the evildoers, and probably also as an invitation to the large community of the dead to witness, and to consent to, the (sometimes) dubious action." See Goitein, *A Mediterranean Society: The Jewish Communities of the Arab World as Portrayed in the Documents of the Cairo Geniza*, vol. 5: *The Individual* (Berkeley: University of California Press, 1988), pp. 185–86.

34. Moses Cordovero's *Zohar* commentary ʾ*Or Yaqar* in Abraham Azulai's ʾ*Or ha-Ḥammah* (Bnei Brak: Yahadut, 1973), 3: 56a. Cf. the slightly different version in ʾ*Or Yaqar*, 13: 64–65.

35. ʾ*Or ha-Ḥammah*, 1, 221d. See above, n. 33.

36. ʾ*Or Yaqar*, 13: 175. Cf. Liebes, "New Directions," p. 165, n. 50.

37. See, e.g., Cordovero, *Sefer Gerushin*, par. 7; id., *Shiʿur Qomah* (Jerusalem, 1966), par. 50, p. 54b. On this subject, see also Zak, *Be-Shaʿarei ha-Kabbalah*, pp. 20–21; 218–20.

38. Traditions about the grave sites of various individuals buried in the land of Israel are collected in Michael Ish-Shalom, *Qivrei ʾAvot* (Jerusalem: Mossad Ha-Rav Kook, 1948). A voluminous, two-volume study of the same subject was done by Zev Vilnay, *Matsevot Qodesh be-ʾErets Yisrael* (3d ed., Jerusalem: Achiever, 1985–86). It should be pointed out that as far back as late antiquity, it was customary for Jews to visit cemeteries on fast days in order to offer prayers at the graves of the dead "in order that they may intercede in behalf of the living" (BT *Taʿanit*, 16a, 23b; *Sotah* 34b, Maimonides, *Yad*, *Taʿanit* 4:18). This is widely attested in the Middle Ages as well, particularly in connection with the 9th of Av and during the month of Elul, a period of repentance (Joseph Karo, *Shulḥan ʿArukh*, ʾ*Oraḥ Ḥayyim* 579:3; Moses Isserles to ʾ*Oraḥ Ḥayyim* 559:10; 581–84). In a popular practice with obviously magical appeal, it was customary in times of personal or communal crisis to measure the perimeter of the cemetery walls and to contribute an equivalent length of candles to the synagogue. A related practice involved conducting a procession around the circumference of the cemetery, accompanied by the recitation of psalms and penitential prayers in order to thwart danger. For evidence of these types of practices in Ashkenaz, see Herman Pollack, *Jewish Folkways in Germanic Lands (1648–1806): Studies in Aspects of Daily Life* (Cambridge, Mass.: MIT Press, 1971), pp. 47–49; Chava Weissler, "'For the Human Soul Is the Lamp of the Lord: The *Tkhine* for "Laying Wicks" by Sarah bas Tovim,'" in *Polin* 10 (1997): 49–65.

39. Based on the translation in David, *In Zion and Jerusalem*, p. 65. For a full account of the elaborate traditions concerning Shimon bar Yohai's grave and the various customs that developed around it, see Vilnay, *Matsevot*, 2: 118–50.

40. See the many references in Meir Benayahu, "Devotion Practices of the Kabbalists of Safed in Meron" (in Hebrew), *Sefunot* 6 (1962): 9–40.

41. Joseph Karo, *Maggid Mesharim* (Venice, 1649), *Parashat* ʾ*Emor*.

42. The Qadiriyah sect, founded by Abd al-Qadir al-Jilani (1088–1166) in Baghdad, spread as far as Yemen, Egypt, Sudan, North and West Africa, India, and Southeast Asia. The Naqshbandiyah was established by Baha al-Din Naqshband (d. 1388) in Bukhara and played an important role in India, China, Central Asia, and the Middle East.

43. Yosef Yanun (Paul Fenton), "The Influence of Sufism on Safed Kabbalah" (in Hebrew), *Maḥanayim* 6(1994): 170–79.

44. Ibid., p. 177.   45. Ibid., p. 178.

46. Ibid.   47. Ibid.

48. The influence of Moroccan Jews continues to be felt even today in Israel in connection with widespread visitations and pilgrimages to grave sites. Since the arrival of Moroccan Jews, along with other Jews from Arab countries, the veneration of saints at their tombs has proliferated and enjoyed extraordinary popularity. Yoram Bilu, for example, has reported the common phenomenon of the "translocation of a saint from Morocco through the discovery or renewal of a sacred place in the locality on the basis of folk beliefs and local traditions." In addition to this, Moroccan Jews continue to "discover" other grave sites of teachers and saints from the past and to invest contemporary figures with sainthood. Large-scale celebrations and pilgrimages by Moroccan Jews take place at various locations, including the Cave of the Patriarchs in Hebron, the tomb of Rachel the Matriarch in Bethlehem, the tomb of R. Meir Baʿal ha-Nes in Tiberias, and most significantly, that of R. Shimon bar Yohai in Meron, on the holiday of Lag ba-Omer. Among the numerous studies that document these phenomena, see Yoram Bilu and Eyal Ben-Ari, "Saints' Sanctuaries in Israeli Development Towns: On a Mechanism of Urban Transformation," *Urban Anthropology* 16, 2 (1987): 65–102; Y. Bilu and H. Abramovich, "In Search of the Sadiq: Visitational Dreams Among Moroccan Jews in Israel," *Psychiatry* 48 (1985): 83–92; Yoram Bilu, "The Role of Charismatic Dreams in the Creation of Sacred Sites in Present-Day Israel," in B. Z. Kedar and R.J.Z. Werblowsky, eds., *Sacred Space: Shrine, City, Land* (New York: New York University Press, 1998), pp. 295–315; Norman Stillman, "Saddiq and Marabout in Morocco," in S. Deshen and W. P. Zenner, eds., *Jews Among Muslims: Communities in the Precolonial Middle East* (New York: New York University Press, 1996), pp. 121–30; Alex Weingrod, *The Saint of Beersheba* (Albany: State University of New York Press, 1990); Issachar Ben-Ami, *Saint Veneration Among the Jews in Morocco* (Detroit: Wayne State University Press, 1998). See, as well, the remarks by Giller, "Recovering the Sanctity of the Galilee," pp. 167–68.

49. Brown, *Cult of the Saints*, p. 10.

50. Ibid., p. 5.

51. See, e.g., the following *yiḥudim* from SRH: *Yiḥud* 20 (pp. 141–42); *Yiḥud* 22 (pp. 146–51); *Yiḥud* 23 (pp. 151–52).

52. For examples of these in *SRH*, see *Yiḥud* 24 (pp. 152–53); *Yiḥud* 2 (p. 155); *Yiḥud* 4 (p. 155).

53. *SRH*, p. 76.

54. See, e.g., *SRH*, pp. 87, 88, 92–94, 103–4, 107.

55. *SRH*, pp. 110–11. At the end of this text, Vital indicates that he copied this from his teacher's manuscript. This exact passage is also found in ibn Tabul's brief

account of the *yiḥudim*. Descriptions and translations of a number of the *yiḥudim* are found in Aryeh Kaplan, trans. and ed., *Meditation and Kabbalah* (York Beach, Me.: S. Weiser, 1982), pp. 218–60.

56. *SRH*, pp. 121a–126a.

57. Ibid., pp. 121a–b.

58. *ShY*, ch. 1, p. 1a.

59. See the elaborate discussion of these issues in Wolfson, *Through a Speculum*, pp. 270–317, 377–80, and passim, esp. the passage quoted on pp. 343–44, n. 56. See also Abraham J. Heschel, *Prophetic Inspiration After the Prophets: Maimonides and Other Medieval Authorities* (Hoboken, N.J.: Ktav, 1996); Idel, *Kabbalah*, pp. 234, 240–42; id., *Mystical Experience*, pp. 83–95.

60. *ShY*, ch. 5, p. 6a.   61. *SRH*, pp. 115–16.

62. *ShY*, ch. 3, p. 4a.   63. Benayahu, *STA*, p. 157, n. 6.

64. *SRH*, p. 143.

65. This passage occurs in both *ShG*, p. 126, and *SeH*, pp. 135–36.

66. Shemaya and Avtalyon were sages of the late first century B.C.E. who were colleagues. They constituted the fourth of the *zugot* (pairs) of sages, and they are said to have received rabbinic tradition from Judah ben Tabbai and Shimon ben Shetah. Shemaya was *nasi* (president) and Avtalyon was *ʾav bet din* (head of the court) of the ancient Sanhedrin. The tradition according to which they were buried in the village of Gush Ḥalav, not far from Safed, is an old one, despite the fact that their activities are not associated with this place. Various testimony from the early thirteenth century on speaks of their graves in Gush Ḥalav. See Vilnay, *Matsevot*, 1: 50–54.

67. The text refers here to an incident in 2 Kings 4 in which the prophet Elisha revives the dead child of a Shunammite woman: "Then he went up and lay upon the child, putting his mouth upon his mouth, his eyes upon his eyes, and his hands upon his hands; and as he stretched himself upon him, the flesh of the child became warm." According to a legendary motif in the *Zohar* (1,7b; 2,44a–45a)— on which the text under discussion apparently draws—the revived child was the prophet Habakkuk.

68. *SeA*, letter 1, pp. 8–9. Over against the claim here that only Vital successfully practiced the *yiḥudim* following Luria's death, Joseph ibn Tabul reports that although he had forgotten the instructions given him by his teacher concerning the practice of *yiḥudim* at the grave site of the rabbinic sage Abba Shaul, "yet I relearned them after his death in a dream, and I tested them on the grave sites of the *tsaddiqim*, and they are true and his words are true." See Vilnay, *Matsevot*, 1: 21.

69. *SeA*, letter 3, p. 45. Cf. Benayahu, *STA*, p. 157.

70. *SRH*, p. 86.

71. *ShG, Haqdamah* 36, pp. 127–28; *Haqdamah* 38, pp. 132–37; *SeH*, pp. 146–47, 152–54, 157.

72. Akiva (c. 50–135 C.E.), the foremost scholar of his age and among the most influential rabbis of the talmudic period, is buried, according to folk tradition, in a cave in Tiberias. See Vilnay, *Matsevot*, 1: 87–92.

73. The belief in "impregnation" (*ʿibbur*) occupied a prominent place in Luria's thinking. Whereas *gilgul*, or metempsychosis, refers to the entrance of a past soul into an individual at the time of one's birth, *ʿibbur* denotes the entrance of a past soul at some later point during one's life. In the case of *ʿibbur*, the impregnated soul seeks to rectify itself by atoning for a past transgression or fulfilling a precept that has been left unfulfilled. At times, however, *ʿibbur* is for the benefit of the host individual, enabling him to accomplish something he is otherwise unable to do. Indeed, this was the case with Vital's impregnations. Typically, *ʿibbur* takes place by a past soul investing itself in an individual with whom it shares the same soul-root. Unlike *gilgul*, in which the soul is present throughout one's entire life, *ʿibbur* occurs for a temporary period of time, until the impregnated soul accomplishes its goal. As many as three impregnations can take place at one time. In his dream diary, Vital specifies a number of individuals whose souls became impregnated within him or who were potential candidates for impregnation, including Rabbi Akiva, as we see here; Abbaye; Eleazar ben Arakh; Eleazar ben Shamua; Yeiva Sabba; Yohanan ben Zakkai; the prophet Samuel; and King Hezekiah. Vital was intensely preoccupied with behaving in such a way as to have these souls continue to impregnate themselves into his body. For an account of the differences between *gilgul* and *ʿibbur* by Vital, see *SeH*, pp. 192–93.

74. *SeH*, pp. 149–50; cf. *ShG, Haqdamah* 38, p. 136. I have drawn on the translation by Jacobs, *Jewish Mystical Testimonies*, pp. 161–62.

75. See, e.g., *SeH*, pp. 5, 16–17, 25–26, 28–29, 36, 149–51, 172–73; *SRH*, pp. 131–32, 141–42. It is important to note that in addition to a great many generic *yihudim*, Luria provided a number of his disciples with personalized ones. In *SRH*, Vital records twenty-five *yihudim* that he says he received from Luria for himself, as well as customized ones for Joseph Arzin, Joseph Kohen, Elijah de Vidas, Gedaliah ha-Levi, Moses Alsheikh, Elijah Falkon, Abraham Berukhim, Moses Yonah, and a certain Y. Schneur. We know as well that Joseph ibn Tabul received personalized instructions for this practice from Luria, as noted above.

76. Abbaye and Rava were prominent rabbinic sages of third- and fourth-century Babylonia and are among the most important of all talmudic figures. According to kabbalistic tradition, their grave site is in the village of Avnit, northeast of Safed. Vital describes this site in *ShG, Haqdamah* 37, p. 185. See Vilnay, *Matsevot*, 2: 231–33.

77. Aqavyah ben Mahalalel was a first-century sage who was offered the position of president of the Sanhedrin on condition that he renounce four of his decisions in which he disagreed with the majority opinion. He refused to do so until on his deathbed, when he told his son to retract these four opinions on his behalf (Mishnah *Eduyot* 5:6–7).

78. These refer to three of the blessings of the Amidah or Shemoneh Esreh.

79. *SeH*, pp. 170–172. This translation is based on Jacobs, *Jewish Mystical Testimonies*, 131–33, with some changes. A slightly different version is found in *ShG*, 140–41.

80. Fine, "Recitation of Mishnah as a Vehicle for Mystical Inspiration," pp. 189–90. The practice of solitude plays a part in some of the instructions for the performance of the *yihudim*. For example (*SRH*, p. 117), "And first you must close your eyes . . . and seclude yourself for one hour." Elsewhere (*SRH*, p. 86), we learn in connection with a particular *yihud* that is performed over the course of a week's time, that "a person who practices seclusion, as described above, should meditate each day of the seven days of the week on one of the seven names of the '42 letter name of God'" (*shem mem bet*)."

81. On the concept of liminality in the work of Victor Turner, see, e.g., "Pilgrimages as Social Processes," in id., *Dramas, Fields and Metaphors: Symbolic Action in Human Society* (Ithaca, N.Y.: Cornell University Press, 1974), pp. 166–230; id., "Liminality and Communitas," in his *Ritual Process: Structure and Anti-Structure* (Chicago: University of Chicago Press, 1969), pp. 94–130; and id. and Edith Turner, *Image and Pilgrimage in Christian Culture: Anthropological Perspectives* (New York: Columbia University Press, 1978).

82. Cited in Idel, *Mystical Experience in Abraham Abulafia*, 75.

83. Ibid. The anonymous author of the Abulafian text *Sha'arei Tsedeq* also writes that "great trembling seized me, and I could not gather strength, and my hairs stood up" (Idel, *Kabbalah*, p. 76).

84. Idel, *Mystical Experience in Abraham Abulafia*, p. 83.

85. Ibid., p. 85.

86. Ibid.

87. See, e.g., the passages in Jacobs, *Jewish Mystical Testimonies*, pp. 98–122.

88. Fine, "Recitation of Mishnah as a Vehicle for Mystical Inspiration," pp. 190–91.

89. See Fine, "Maggidic Revelation in the Teachings of Isaac Luria," pp. 141–57. See this passage on p. 145.

90. *SeH*, p. 16.

91. *SeH*, p. 25.

92. Fine, "Recitation of Mishnah as a Vehicle for Mystical Inspiration," p. 191.

93. This is an excellent example of the complex connection between the phenomena of orality and revelation analyzed by William A. Graham in *Beyond the Written Word: Oral Aspects of Scripture in the History of Religion* (New York: Cambridge University Press, 1987). One of Graham's main points is that in our fixation on written Scripture, we tend to ignore or forget the extent to which orality has dominated religious cultures, a fact felicitously captured by the Muslim adage: "You can return to God nothing better than that which came from Him, namely the Recitation (*al-quran*)" (ibid., p. 96).

94. Fine, "Maggidic Revelation in the Teachings of Isaac Luria," p. 146.

95. Ibid., p. 188.

96. *ShG, Haqdamah* 38, p. 141.

97. Victor Crapanzano, "Spirit Possession," in M. Eliade et al., *Encyclopedia of Religion*, 14: 12, with an excellent, selective bibliography on this subject. For extended discussions of the issues raised here, see V. Crapanzano, and V. Garrison, eds., *Case Studies in Spirit Possession* (New York: Wiley, 1977), esp. the editors' introductory essay; Torrance, *Spiritual Quest*, chs. 8–14.

98. Arthur S. Reber, *The Penguin Dictionary of Psychology* (New York: Penguin Books, 1971), p. 38.

99. Concerning the question of desirable versus undesirable forms of spirit possession, see Erica Bourguignon, "The Self, the Behavioral Environment, and the Theory of Spirit Possession," in M. E. Spiro, ed., *Context and Meaning in Cultural Anthropology* (New York: Free Press, 1965), esp. pp. 42–43. For a study of sympathetic possession in Judaism, see L. Fine, "Benevolent Spirit Possession in Sixteenth-Century Safed," in Goldish, *Spirit Possession in Judaism*, pp. 1–23.

Chapter 9

1. *ShG, Haqdamah* 38, pp. 132–133; *SeH*, p. 153. Elsewhere in this section of *Shaʿar ha-Gilgulim*, Vital remarks that Luria had told him that one of the participants in the Idra was part of Vital's soul-ancestry, but Luria did not wish to reveal his identity at the time, nor did he explain why.

2. *SeA*, letter 3, p. 44. Still another version of this episode is found in *Toldot ha-Ari*, Benayahu, *STA*, pp. 179–80. This version clearly follows Shlomiel's account, and also indicates that Vital sat in Rabbi Eleazar's place rather than Abba's. It adds at the end that "after [they were seated in the proper places], he [Luria] taught them the Idra, and revealed to them mysteries and secrets that Rashbi had taught at the Idra."

3. *ShG, Haqdamah* 37, p. 183.

4. *Zohar* 3, 144a.

5. *Song of Songs Rabbah* 1:16; BT *Baba Batra* 17a; Rashi, ad loc.

6. *Zohar* 3, 144b. Concerning the literature of the Idrot, see Giller, *Reading the Zohar*, chs. 4–7.

7. The major accounts of metempsychosis in Lurianic Kabbalah are found in *Shaʿar ha-Gilgulim*, *Sefer ha-Gilgulim*, and *Sefer ha-Ḥezyonot*, primarily pt. 4.

8. Concerning the history of the idea of transmigration of souls in Judaism, see Gershom Scholem, "*Gilgul*: The Transmigration of Souls," in id., *On the Mystical Shape of the Godhead*, pp. 197–250; id., *Origins of the Kabbalah*, pp. 188–98, 457–60; id., *Major Trends*, pp. 278–84; Elior, "Doctrine of Transmigration in *Galya Raza*," pp. 243–69; Werblowsky, *Joseph Karo*, pp. 234–56; Alexander Altmann, "Eternality of Punishment: A Theological Controversy Within the Amsterdam Rabbinate in the Thirties of the Seventeenth Century," in Fine, *Essential Papers on*

Kabbalah, pp. 270–87; Moshe Hallamish, *An Introduction to the Kabbalah* (Albany: State University of New York Press, 1999), pp. 281–309.; Giller, *Reading the Zohar*, pp. 37–42.

9. Saadia Gaon, *Sefer ʾEmunot ve-Deᶜot* (New York: Yeshivah University, 1970), 6:7.

10. Scholem, *"Gilgul,"* p. 209.

11. *SeH*, p. 203. Cf. *ShG, Haqdamah* 39, p. 163.

12. *ShG, Haqdamah* 7, p. 28.

13. Ibid., p. 29.

14. Concerning the sins of Cain and Abel, see, e.g., *SeH*, p. 178. The tradition about their sin may be found already in *Tiqqunei Zohar, tiqqun* 69.

15. *ShK, ᶜInyan Qeriʾat Shema, Derush* 6, p. 143.

16. *ShG, Haqdamah* 26, p. 69. This notion is based, in part, on the *Zohar*, as the Lurianic passage itself makes clear. See *Zohar* 2, 96b–97b, where the word *clothing* in Exod. 21:10, "If he marries another, he must not withhold from this one her food, her clothing, or her conjugal rights," is understood to refer to the "King's [God's] garment, which is spread over the soul and always protects her."

17. See *SeH*, pp. 138, 163, 211; *SeG*, ch. 41; *ShG, Haqdamah* 26, p. 69.

18. BT *Sotah*, 36b; *Bereshit Rabbah* 98:20. Cf. R. Margoliot, ed., *Midrash ha-Gadol, Bereshit* (Jerusalem: Mossad ha-Rav Kook, 1947), p. 668.

19. *SeG*, ch. 41.

20. *ShG, Haqdamah* 26, p. 69. Cf. *ShK, ᶜInyan Qeriʾat Shema, Derush* 6, p. 147.

21. *SeH*, pp. 212–17; *ShG, Haqdamot* 26 and 39.

22. *ShG, Haqdamah* 26, p. 69.

23. Vital, *ShMR*, p. 36; Cf. Meroz, "Torat ha-Geʾeulah," p. 282.

24. *ShG*, end of *Haqdamah* 36. On the redemptive role of the Ten Martyrs, cf. Meroz, "Torat ha-Geʾeulah," pp. 282–83.

25. *SeH*, p. 214.

26. See *Zohar* 2, 10a.

27. *SeH*, p. 214.

28. BT *Taᶜanit* 18b, *Sifra ʾEmor*, 9:5; Rashi on *Taᶜanit*, 18b.

29. *SeH*, p. 215.

30. *ShG, Haqdamah* 39, p. 171; *SeH*, pp. 217–18.

31. In this connection, Vital (*SeH*, p. 218) cites *Zohar* 2, 38a–b, according to which the words *leil* and *layla* in Exod. 12:42 signify the masculine and feminine dimensions of divinity, whose sexual unification took place on the night before Israel fled from Egypt, anticipating the union that will take place in the future redemption.

32. *ShG, Haqdamah* 39, pp. 171–72; *SeH*, p. 218–20.

33. *ShG, Haqdamah* 20, p. 54.

34. *ShG, Haqdamah* 34, p. 96.

35. *ShG, Haqdamah* 34, p. 97. Cf. *SeH*, p. 136, where we learn that all souls are included in Moses', esp. those of the righteous, by virtue of which Vital is linked to Moses by way of the former's lower soul, or *nefesh*.

36. *ShG, Haqdamah* 20, p. 54.

37. *SeG*, ch. 64, p. 86b.

38. This is noted by Liebes, "Messiah of the *Zohar*," pp. 90, n. 12, 105–7, where he points out that in the Idra Rabba, Rashbi's role is similar to the messianic role attributed to Moses in certain sections of the *Zohar*, including the Idra itself. This parallel is based partly on the comparison of the event of the Idra to the giving of the Torah at Mount Sinai, an event that will not recur again until the messianic generation. On the representation of Moses in the *Zohar* more generally, see Liebes, "Myth vs. Symbol," pp. 213–17. On the link between Sabbatai Sevi and Moses, see Liebes, *Sod ha-ʾEmunah ha-Shabtaʾit* (Jerusalem: Mossad Bialik, 1995), pp. 281–82, n. 79.

39. *ShG, Haqdamah* 36, p. 123.

40. These traditions have been elaborately studied in Liebes, "Two Young Roes," to which my analysis is indebted in substantial ways.

41. This is a traditional blessing pronounced upon hearing sad tidings, most notably that a person has died.

42. *ShK*, vol. 2, *ʿInyan Sefirat ha-ʿOmer, Derush* 12, p. 187. Cf. the parallel version in *SeA*, letter 3, pp. 53–54.

43. *Zohar* 2, 219b–220a. Cf. the variations on this theme in *Zohar* 2, 52b; 3, 67b–68a; 3, 249b. This translation is based upon *WZ*, 2: 738–39.

44. The *Zohar*'s conception itself goes back to the Babylonian Talmud, *Baba Batra* 16b: "This hind has a narrow womb. When she crouches for delivery, I prepare a serpent that bites her at the opening of the womb, and she is delivered of her offspring; and were it one second too soon or too late, she would die."

45. The notion of appeasement of the *Sitra Aḥra*, the "Other Side," has deep roots in the history of Kabbalah. See, e.g., Scholem, *On the Mystical Shape*, pp. 73–87.

46. As Liebes points out ("Two Young Roes," p. 139), the dross referred to here corresponds presumably to a theme in one of the Zoharic passages describing the pregnant hind. In a lengthy description of the hind, *Zohar* 3, 249a–b speaks of the blood and water that flow in the wake of the serpent's bite. The serpent drinks of the blood, that is, the blood of childbirth, while the water nourishes the animals of the world:

> When she is pregnant, she is closed up. When the time comes for her to give birth, she lows, and utters cries, cry after cry, as many as seventy cries, which match the number of words in "May the Lord answer you in the day of trouble" [Ps. 20], which is the song sung by this pregnant one. The Holy One, blessed be He, hears her, and goes to her aid. He immediately brings forth a great snake from among the mountains of darkness, and it comes through the

hills, its mouth licking the dust. It draws near to the hind, and bites her twice at the appropriate place. The first time, blood comes out, and it licks it up. The second time, water comes out, and all the animals in the mountains drink, and she is opened and gives birth. (*WZ*, 1: 395–96)

47. *ShK*, vol. 2, ʿ*Inyan Sefirat ha-*ʿ*Omer, Derush* 12, p. 188.

48. Ibid.

49. Ibid., p. 187.

50. *Zohar* 2, 52b.

51. See Liebes, "Two Young Roes," pp. 139–40, where he speculates on whether we should regard Luria's decision to reveal these secrets to unworthy disciples, and his son's death, as forms of bribe to the "Other Side," as a parallel to the *Zohar*'s description of the appeasement of the serpent.

52. Cf. Liebes on these observations, "Two Young Roes," p. 140. Liebes suggests that this *zivvug* entailed expending semen outside of *Nuqba*, "to the sphere of the external powers to provide them with nourishment."

53. See, e.g., Vital's remarks in *SeG*, ch. 64.

54. See BT *Sanhedrin* 98b. I am indebted to Liebes's observations in this regard. See "Two Young Roes," pp. 141–44, esp. n. 261, where he identifies the relevant *Zohar* passages, and pp. 168–69, where he details the ancient sources behind these motifs.

55. See Liebes, "Two Young Roes," p. 142, n. 264.

56. While Lurianic texts do not draw this connection, precisely such a link between these two motifs is made by the Safed kabbalist Abraham Galante and in Sabbatean literature. I am indebted to Liebes for these observations ("Two Young Roes," p. 142, nn. 266–68). On this, see also Meroz, "Torat ha-Geʾeulah," p. 311–12.

57. Cf. Meroz, "Torat ha-Geʾeulah," p. 264, where she attributes this particular idea to level three of her schema.

58. Cf. ibid., p. 305, where Meroz attributes the view that Moses' messianic mission is primarily a result of his being a *gilgul* of Adam to stage four in her schema. The terms *Yesod* and *goʾel* are explicitly identified with each other. Thus, for example, in *PEH*, *Shaʿar ha-*ʿ*Amidah*, ch. 15: "*Yesod* is called *goʾel*, for through *Yesod* redemption [*geʾeulah*] occurs."

59. *Exodus Rabbah*, 3.14: "Seven whole days previously did God urge Moses to go on his mission, but he refused to go until the incident of the thornbush."

60. Here the verse is intended not as a series of questions but as assertions.

61. *ShP*, *Parashat Shemot*, on Exod. 1:8, p. 108.

62. In Meroz's schema, stage four is characterized on this issue by Luria's establishment of a connection between the notion of Adam's wasting of seed and the motif that it is the Messiah's task to rectify this transgression. See Meroz, "Torat ha-Geʾeulah," p. 335.

63. Liebes, "Messiah of the *Zohar*," esp. pp. 90–100.

64. *SRH*, pp. 39–40. Cf. Vital's introduction to *EH*.

65. *ShK, ʿInyan Kavvanat ha-ʿAmidah, Derush* 6, p. 235. According to a seminal medieval Jewish apocalyptic text, *Sefer Zerubbavel*, Armilus is a cruel tyrant who will seek to achieve dominion over the whole world. His name may be derived from that of Romulus, founder of Rome. Armilus will come to Jerusalem with nine other kings, over whom he will rule. He will wage war against Israel, driving the survivors into the desert. However, on the eve of Passover, the Messiah son of David will appear in the desert to redeem the Jewish people, proving his identity by conquering Armilus and the forces of evil. See Lawrence Fine, "Medieval Jewish Apocalyptic Literature," in M. Eliade et al., *Encyclopedia of Religion*, 1: 342–44.

66. *PEH, Shaʿar ha-ʿAmidah*, ch. 19, pp. 245–46.

67. Vital's introduction to *EH*.

68. *SRH*, p. 40.

69. *Tosefta* here does not refer to a rabbinic text, as it normally does, but to a certain section of the *Zohar*. There are numerous short passages scattered throughout the *Zohar* that are referred to by the rabbinic terms *Matnitin* and *Tosefta*. This particular passage is found in *Zohar* 3, 55b. The present anecdote is preserved in *SeA*, letter 3, pp. 54–55, and retold in a more elaborate and fanciful fashion in *Toldot ha-Ari*, Benayahu, *STA*, pp. 200–202. This anecdote does not appear in the non-hagiographic literature, as far as I am aware. Nevertheless, it may be regarded as a reliable story for a number of reasons, including the fact that Vital refers to these events in *SeH*, pp. 188–89. A detailed analysis of this narrative serves as the basis for Liebes's "Two Young Roes," to which some of my remarks here are indebted.

70. *SeA*, letter 3, pp. 54–55.   71. *SeH*, pp. 188–90.

72. Ibid., p. 189.   73. Ibid.

74. Ibid., pp. 189–90.   75. Ibid., p. 190.

76. While the account in *SeH* initially speaks of "the matter of his attainments and his knowledge" (ʿinyano hasagato u-yediʿato), as Liebes points out, the next sentence employs only the term ʿinyano, which Liebes understands as a reference to the status of Luria's soul, not merely to his attainments and knowledge. See Liebes, "Two Young Roes," p. 117.

77. Liebes, "Two Young Roes," pp. 117–18.

78. Ibid., pp. 118–20.

79. Ibid., p. 118 and n. 33 (with *Zohar* sources).

80. For still other connections of messianic import between Moses and Luria, see ibid., pp. 122–23.

81. Pachter, "Homiletic Eulogy," p. 51.

82. Ibid., p. 53.   83. Ibid.

84. *SeH*, p. 156; *ShK*, p. 2.   85. BT *Yevamot* 62b.

86. *ShK*, vol. 2, ʿInyan Sefirat ha-ʿOmer, Derush 12, pp. 188–89. There are seven weeks between the second day of Passover, that is, the 16th of Nisan, and the festival of Shavuot, a period known as the ʿOmer (literally, "sheaf"). ʿOmer refers to

an offering brought to the Temple on the 16th of Nisan; the forty-nine days between this date and Shavuot are counted on a daily basis. The thirty-third day of
the counting of the ʿOmer is known as Lag ba-Omer. At some point, the days of
the ʿOmer began to take on a character of semi-mourning. Marriage, eventually
haircutting, and later still, the playing of musical instruments were prohibited. An
eighth-century responsum by Natronai Gaon associates the mourning with the
plague said to have killed Akiva's original disciples. The origin of Lag ba-Omer is
also cloaked in some uncertainty. It is not explicitly mentioned earlier than the
thirteenth century, when Menahem Meiri, in his commentary to Yevamot, described
it as the day when, "according to the tradition of the geonim," the "plague" ceased.
Thus, in this view, the plague that befell Akiva's students ended on Lag ba-Omer,
a view to which Luria subscribed. In kabbalistic tradition, Lag ba-Omer came to
be commemorated as the anniversary of Shimon bar Yohai's death.

87. ShK, vol. 2, ʿInyan Sefirat ha-ʿOmer, pp. 189–90.

88. Zohar 2, 190b. Cf. Zohar 3, 59b: "And you companions that are here, as you
have loved before, do not part yourselves from one another from now on until
the Holy One, blessed be He, be glad with you and call peace upon you, and may
there be peace in the world on your account, as it is written [Ps. 122:8]: 'For my
brethren and companions' sake, I will now say, Peace be within you.'"

89. These are found primarily in three sources: ShG, SeG, and SeH, esp. the
fourth section. In addition, scattered references to these questions are found
throughout the rest of Vital's writings.

90. This is delineated by Vital in numerous places, but the present exposition
is based esp. on ShG, Haqdamot 34 and 36.

91. The complete list is found in ShG, Haqdamah 36, p. 106. See, as well, the
long list found in SeH, pp. 142–46. These lists are summaries of the lengthy discussions concerning Vital's soul-ancestry found in these texts.

92. See, e.g., ShG, Haqdamah 34, pp. 97–98, where we learn that even though
Akiva is called a ger, he is not actually one, but rather he became the progenitor
of converts during the twenty-four years he was separated from his wife (while
studying Torah). In general, Luria took a very strong interest in the souls of gerim,
incorporating this subject into his theory of souls and their transmigration, as we
saw above in connection with Moses and the "mixed multitude." He took an extremely positive view of the souls of converts to Judaism, rather unusual for the
premodern period. He identifies and lauds those individuals who were especially
responsible for conceiving the souls of converts while separated from their wives,
including Abraham, Moses, Shimon ben Azzai, Abbaye, and Akiva himself.

93. See, e.g., ShG, Haqdamah 38, pp. 139–140; SeG, ch. 50; SeH, pp. 168–70.
See Meroz, "Torat ha-Geʾeulah," pp. 315–21, for a fuller discussion of these themes.

94. BT Baba Metsia 58b.

95. ShG, Haqdamah 36, p. 126. Moses' soul is such that different aspects of it
transmigrate into lines originating in both Cain and Abel.

96. See, e.g., *ShG Haqdamot* 32 and 33, pp. 92–93. This is based on Targum Onkelos's (Aramaic translation of the Torah) understanding of Gen. 49:3: "Reuven, my firstborn, you, my might, first-fruit of my vigor. Surpassing in loftiness, surpassing in force." Like Cain, Reuven was a firstborn child, Jacob's first son.

97. *ShG, Haqdamah* 32, p. 92; *Haqdamah* 36, p. 109; *SeH*, p. 167. Cf. Meroz, "Torat ha-Geʾeulah," pp. 291–92.

98. BT *Sanhedrin* 94a.

99. *ShG Haqdamah* 32, p. 92.

100. See, e.g., the passages cited in Faierstein, *Jewish Mystical Autobiographies*, pp. 14–15; Tamar, "Luria and Vital as the Messiah Son of Joseph," pp. 174–77.

101. *SeH*, p. 134. Cf. *SeH*, p. 8, where Moses Alsheikh is said to have been told by Luria that "he [Luria] came into the world only to teach me [i.e., Vital], and that it was impossible to reveal this wisdom other than through me."

102. *SeH*, pp. 134–35. Vidal Yom Tov of Tolosa was a Spanish rabbi who lived in the second half of the fourteenth century. As his name indicates, he came from Tolosa in Catalonia, where he compiled his commentary to Maimonides' *Mishneh Torah*, called the *Maggid Mishneh*. The latter work was accepted as the standard commentary to the *Mishneh Torah*, and Vidal was believed by Luria to have possessed a spark of the soul of Maimonides. This is of interest since Vital, too, says that he was connected to Maimonides' soul.

103. *ShG, Haqdamah* 36, p. 128.

104. Ibid., p. 127.

105. *ShG, Haqdamah* 38, pp. 120, 122.

106. We saw earlier that Luria himself was said to avoid the killing of any insects. In Vital's case, Luria explained that since his soul derived from Cain's soul-ancestry, that is, from one who murdered his brother, as well as from the soul of Shaul of Trieste, who inadvertently killed a child upon whom he was performing circumcision, Vital himself must take care never to kill any living creature. He is even prohibited from personally performing ritual slaughter (*shehitah*) of an animal for consumption. See *ShG, Haqdamah* 38, p. 133; *SeH*, p. 154.

107. *ShG, Haqdamah* 38, pp. 158–59.

108. Ibid., p. 136.

109. *Zohar* 3, 287b.

110. *ShG, Haqdamah* 39, p. 165.

111. Ibid.

112. *SeH*, p. 229.

113. *ShG, Haqdamah* 39, p. 172.

114. Ibid.

115. *SeH*, pp. 159–60.

116. Ibid., pp. 70–71. The diary entry has the year 1608, when Vital was living in Damascus, but the dream places the incident in a synagogue in Safed.

117. The contractual document that attests to this was analyzed by Scholem in "The Document on Solidarity of Luria's Disciples." For the text of the document itself, see *SeH*, p. 254.

118. Scholem, "Document on Solidarity of Luria's Disciples," pp. 149–52.

119. *SeG*, ch. 66, p. 88.

120. Ibid., p. 89.

121. *SeH*, p. 235. Solomon Sagis (d. 1587) was the son of Moses Sagis, the latter being a rabbinic judge who sat on the court of Joseph Karo. According to one tradition, Solomon Sagis was Luria's son-in-law. See David, *To Come to the Land*, pp. 171, 252, n. 405. This same diary entry also describes Moses Alsheikh's distress over the fact that Vital, Alsheikh's own student in Jewish law, refused to take him on as a student in Kabbalah. Cf. *SeH*, pp. 52–53, where Vital describes a dream in which he inquires whether Solomon Sagis is "greater than me."

122. *SeH*, p. 237. Our text has only the initials of the individual involved, Y.M. (*yud mem*), possibly referring to Judah Mishan or Jacob Masud.

123. Menaham de Lonzano (c. 1550–before 1626) was a poet, grammarian, and kabbalist who was active in Jerusalem in the late sixteenth and early seventeenth centuries. Abraham Monzon had been a student of Betsalel Ashkenazi in Egypt, with whom we know Luria was associated as well, as student and scholarly collaborator. Monzon is reported, as noted in Chapter 1, to have had a "copy of Alfasi's code which he brought from Egypt [which had been] proofread by the two great luminaries, the eminent rabbi Betsalel Ashkenazi of blessed memory, and the saintly rabbi Isaac Ashkenazi of blessed memory." It is thus clear that Monzon and Luria had known one another. For the various places in which this tradition is preserved, see Benayahu, "Moses Yonah, the Ari's Disciple, and the First to Record his Teachings," p. 18. On de Lonzano, see David, *To Come to the Land*, p. 162.

124. *ShG*, *Haqdamah* 39, p. 172; *SeH*, p. 221.

125. *ShG*, p. 172; *SeH*, p. 222. Cf. *SeH*, p. 56.

126. See Faierstein, *Jewish Mystical Autobiographies*, pp. 8–10.

127. *SeH*, p. 160; *ShG*, *Haqdamah* 38, p. 137. This remark follows immediately upon the heels of Vital's account of how Joseph Arzin went to complain to Luria on account of his jealousy of Vital, described above. According to Joseph ben Isaac Sambari, Joseph Bagilar, a rabbi and well-to-do philanthropist from Egypt, "supported the yeshivah of the Ari, may his memory be blessed, in Safed, may it be speedily rebuilt, for ten years at his own expense, and he engaged in the study of Kabbalah" (Sambari, *Sefer Divrei Yosef*, p. 416). Luria, of course, did not live in Safed for this length of time. On Bagilar, and the question of how the *yeshivot* in sixteenth-century Safed were funded, see David, *To Come to the Land*, pp. 122–23.

128. This agreement was signed by Joseph Arzin, Jonathan Sagis, Samuel Uceda, Gedaliah ha-Levi, Jacob Masud, Judah Mishan, and Joseph Latun. There is no doubt that the name written as Joseph Latun on this document refers to the man identified elsewhere as Joseph Altun, including in the lists summarizing information about the *gilgul* ancestries of various individuals (*SeH*, p. 252, based on *SeG*). Of these, Arzin, Sagis, Uceda, ha-Levi, and Mishan were members of the inner circle of Luria's closest disciples, and Masud and Altun had been members of the second group enumerated by Vital.

129. From this point on, Vital's life was somewhat unsettled, as he traveled between Jerusalem, Safed, and Damascus. After leaving Safed in 1577, he went to Jerusalem, where he was the head of a yeshivah until no later than 1586, after which he went back to Safed. Following his ordination in Safed by Moshe Alsheikh in 1590, he appears to have returned to Jerusalem. His name appears in 1594 as a signer of an agreement from Jerusalem exempting scholars from having to pay taxes. Vital may have been called to Jerusalem to succeed Betsalel Ashkenazi, who died sometime between 1591 and 1595. It appears that Vital went to live in Damascus prior to 1597. There he served the Sicilian congregation as their rabbi until his death in 1620. See David, *To Come to the Land*, pp. 147–48; Meir Benayahu, "Rabbi Hayyim Vital in Jerusalem" (in Hebrew), *Sinai* 30 (1952): 65–75.

130. One scholar who has addressed the question of Luria's having taught near the very end of his life that some of the disciples would appropriate the good found in their largely wicked colleagues, implying the dismissal of the latter, is Menachem Kallus. He suggests "that the extreme examples of what could only . . . be characterized as vindictive and paranoid parsimoniousness . . . may have been the result of delirium, or the combination of general weakness and extreme pessimism. Luria may have suffered from these conditions as a result of high fever, after having contracted either the Black Plague or Typhoid fever. . . . R. Hayyim Vital, out of reverence for his teacher, took his words at face value, and applied them as a general principle, despite the fact that they were contradicted by other statements [by Luria]." See Menachem Kallus, "Pneumatic Mystical Possession and the Eschatology of the Soul in Lurianic Kabbalah," in M. Goldish, ed., *Spirit Possession in Judaism* (Detroit: Wayne State University Press, 2003), which addresses a number of the issues treated in this chapter. My thanks to Menachem Kallus and Professor Matt Goldish for the opportunity to read this article in manuscript.

131. *ShG, Haqdamah* 39, p. 176. This precise version is also found in *SeH*, p. 230.

132. *ShG, Haqdamah* 39, p. 176.

133. *ʾEleh Toldot Yitshaq*, Benayahu, ed., *STA*, p. 258.

134. *SeA*, letter 3, pp. 55–56.

135. Ibid., pp. 72–73. Shlomiel indicates (*SeA*, pp. 56–57) that three of Luria's most important disciples, Hayyim Vital, Joseph ibn Tabul, and Gedaliah ha-Levi, were still alive at the time of his writing.

136. BT *Baba Batra* 17a. For a penetrating analysis of these traditions, from the rabbinic period through the Middle Ages, see Fishbane, *Kiss of God*, ch. 1.

137. *Song of Songs Rabbah*, 1:2.5

138. *Zohar* 3, 144b.

139. See Liebes, "Messiah of the *Zohar*," pp. 191–207. Rashbi's death is described in *Zohar* 3, 296b. Although Rashbi's death is an ecstatic event, it is not actually depicted as having been accompanied by a kiss, as in the cases of the three companions who died during the Idra Rabba.

Select Bibliography

Primary Sources

Manuscripts

Ben Zvi Institute, Jerusalem. 2218.
British Museum, London. Margoliouth 856.
British Museum, London. Or. 10627 (formerly Gaster 282).
Cambridge University Library, Cambridge, U.K. T.S. 6J4.
Columbia University, New York. H533 X893.
Columbia University, New York. K11 X893.
Columbia University, New York. M6862 X893.
Jewish National and University Library, Jerusalem. 452 8.
Jewish National and University Library, Jerusalem. 1161.
Jewish Theological Seminary of America, New York. Adler 3726.
Jewish Theological Seminary of America, New York. Adler, n.s., 47.
Jewish Theological Seminary of America, New York. 1995 (JTS 931).
Livorno (Talmud Tora) (Leghorn) 74.
Montifiore Collection, London. 348.
Musayof, Jerusalem. 160.
Sasoon, Jerusalem. 993.

Printed Books

Aboab, Immanuel. *Nomologia, o Discursos legales compuestos.* Amsterdam, 1629.
Abraham ben David. *Ba ʿalei ha-Nefesh.* Jerusalem, 1975.
Alhadad, Masoud. *Simḥat Kohen.* Jerusalem, 1921.
Azikri, Eleazar ben Moses. *Sefer Ḥaredim.* Jerusalem, 1958.
Azriel of Gerona. *Commentaire sur la liturgie quotidienne.* Edited by Gabrielle Sed-
    Rajna. Études sur le judaisme médiéval, 5. Leiden: E.J. Brill, 1974.
Azulai, Abraham. *ʾOr ha-Ḥammah.* Bnei Brak: Yahadut, 1973.
Azulai, Hayyim Yosef David. *Shem ha-Gedolim.* Jerusalem: Otsar ha-Sefarim, 1994.
Bacharach, Naphtali. *ʿEmeq ha-Melekh.* Amsterdam, 1648.

Bahya ben Joseph ibn Paquda. *The Book of Direction to the Duties of the Heart*. Translated and edited by Menahem Mansoor, with Sara Arenson, and Shoshana Dannhauser. Littman Library of Jewish Civilization. London: Routledge and K. Paul, 1973.

——. *Ḥovot ha-Levavot*. Jerusalem, 1928.

Benveniste, Joseph. *Dovev Siftei Yeshenim*. Izmir, 1671.

Birkat ha-ʾArets. Jerusalem, 1904.

Capsali, Elijah. *Seder ʾEliyahu Zuta : Toldot ha-Otomanim u-Venitsiah ve-korot am Yisrael be-mamlekhot Turkiyah, Sefarad u-Venitsiah*. Edited by Aryeh Shmuelevitz. Jerusalem: Makhon Ben-Tsvi shel Yad Yitshak Ben-Tsvi veha-Universitah ha-Ivrit bi-Yerushalayim, 1975–83.

Conforte, David. *Qore ha-Dorot*. Berlin, 1846.

Cordovero, Moses. *ʾOr Neʿerav*. Tel Aviv, 1965.

——. *Pardes Rimmonim*. Munkacs, 1872. Reprint, Jerusalem, 1962.

——. *Sefer Gerushin*. Venice, c. 1602. Jerusalem: Makor Hayyim, 1962.

——. *Siddur Tefillah le-Moshe*. Przemysl, 1892.

——. *Tomer Devorah*. Venice, 1589. Translated and edited by Louis Jacobs as *The Palm Tree of Deborah*. 1960. 3d ed. New York: Sepher-Hermon Press, 1981.

Da Fano, Azariah. *ʿAsarah Maʾamarot*. Venice, 1597.

——. *Gilgulei Neshamot*. Prague, 1688.

——. *Kanfei Yonah*. Korecz, 1786.

De Vidas, Eliajah. *Reshit Ḥokhmah*. Venice, 1579.

Delmedigo, Joseph Solomon. *Taʿalumot Ḥokhmah*. Basle, 1629–31.

Eleazar of Worms. *Sefer ha-Roqeaḥ*. Jerusalem, 1968.

Galante, Moses. *Kohelet Yaʿaqov*. Safed, 1578.

Ha-Cohen, Elijah. *Midrash ʾEliyahu*. Izmir, 1759.

Hannover, Nathan Nata. *Shaʿarei Tsiyon*. Prague, 1662.

Ḥemdat Yamim. Leghorn, 1763.

Herrera, Abraham. *Shaʿar ha-Shamayim*. Amsterdam, 1655.

Horowitz, Isaiah. *Shaʿar ha-Shamayim*. Amsterdam, 1717.

——. *Shnei Luḥot ha-Brit*. Amsterdam, 1648.

Ibn Tabul, Joseph. *Derush Ḥeftsi Bah*. Published in Alhadad, *Simḥat Kohen* (see above).

——. *Perush ha-ʾIdra Rabba le-Rabbi Yosef ibn Tabul*. Edited by I. Weinstock. *Temirin*, vol. 2. Jerusalem, 1982.

Ibn Zimra, David. *Magen David*. Amsterdam, 1713.

——. *Metsudat David*. Zolkiew, 1862.

——. *Migdal David*. Lemberg (Lvov), 1883.

ʾIggeret ha-Qodesh. In *Kitvei Ramban*, edited by H. Chavel. Jerusalem: Mossad ha-Rav Kook, 1973.

Jaffe, Mordechai. *Levush ha-ʾOrah*. Prague, 1604.

Karo, Joseph. *Maggid Mesharim*. Lublin, 1646.

Levushei Sered. Kraków, 1882.

Marpe le-Netesh. Venice, 1595.

Modena, Leon. *Sefer Ari Nohem*, ed. S. Rosenthal. Leipzig, 1840.

Molcho, Solomon. *Ḥayyat Qaneh*. Amsterdam, 1648.

———. *Sefer ha-Mefoʾar*. Salonika, 1529.

Moses di Trani. *Responsa*. Venice, 1630.

Moses ibn Makhir. *Seder ha-Yom*. Lublin, 1876; reprint, Jerusalem, 1969.

Motal, Benjamin. *Tummat Yesharim*. Venice, 1622.

Poppers, Meir. *Taʿamei ha-Mitsvot*. Vilna, 1880.

Recanati, Menahem ben Benjamin. *Perush ʿal ha-Torah*. Jerusalem, 1961.

Sambari, Joseph ben Isaac. *Seder ha-Ḥachamim ve-Qorot ha-Yamim*. Edited by A. Neubauer. Berlin, 1888.

———. *Sefer Divrei Yosef*. Edited by S. Shtober. Jerusalem: Ben Zvi Institute, 1994.

Sarug, Israel. *Limmudei ʾAtsilut*. Lemberg (Lvov), 1850. Attributed to Hayyim Vital.

Sefer ha-ʾAri ve-Gurav. Edited by Yaʿakov Moshe Hillel. Jerusalem: Ahavat Shalom, 1992.

Sefer ha-Peliah. Korecz, 1883.

Sefer ha-Qanah. Kraków, 1894.

Sefer Ḥasidim. Edited by J. Wistinetzki. Frankfurt am Main: Wahrmann, 1924.

Sefer ha-Zohar. 3 vols. Edited by R. Margaliot. Jerusalem: Mossad ha-Rav Kook, 1964.

Sefer Kavvanot u-Maʿaseh Nissim. Istanbul, 1720.

Sefer Minhagei ha-Arizal Patora de-Abba. Edited by Uri Strelisker. Jerusalem, 1985.

Sefer Shivḥei Rabbi Hayyim Vital. Tel Aviv: Yashlian, 1988.

Sefer Torat ha-Gilgul. 2 vols. Jerusalem: Ahavat Shalom, 1982.

Sefer Tsitsat Nobel Sevi. Edited by Isaiah Tishby. Jerusalem: Mossad Bialik, 1954.

Sharabi, Shalom. *ʾEmet ve-Shalom*. Salonika, 1806.

———. *Reḥovot ha-Nahar*. Salonika, 1806.

Shlomiel ben Hayyim Meinsterl, Solomon, of Dresnitz. *Kitvei Shevaḥ Yaqar u-Gedulat ha-Ari*. Published in Delmedigo, *Ta ʿalumot Hokhmah* (see above). See also *Sefer ha-ʾAri ve-Gurav*, above

Susskind, Alexander. *Yesod ve-Shoresh ha-ʿAvodah*. Jerusalem: Harry Fischel Institute, 1978.

Tiqqun Leil Ḥatsot. Frankfurt am Main, 1728.

Tiqqunei ha-Zohar. Edited by R. Margaliot. Jerusalem: Mossad ha-Rav Kook, 1978.

Uceda, Samuel. *Midrash Shmuel*. Venice, 1578.

Vital, Hayyim. *Derush she-Masar Hayyim Vital le-Rabbi Shlomo Sagis*. In *Liqqutim Ḥadashim*, edited by D. Toyetto. Jerusalem: Mevaqqshei ha-Shem, 1985.

———. *ʿEts Ḥayyim*. Warsaw, 1891.

———. *Liqqutei Shas*. Leghorn, 1790.

———. *Mavo Sheʿarim*. Edited by Yehudah Ashlag. Tel Aviv: Eshel, 1961.

———. *Pri Ets Hayyim*. Jerusalem, 1980.

——. *Sefer ha-Gigulim.* Przemysl, 1875.

——. *Sefer ha-Ḥezyonot.* Edited by A. Z. Aeshcoly. Jerusalem: Mossad ha-Rav Kook, 1954

——. *Shaʿar ha-Gilgulim.* Edited by Yehudah Ashlag. Tel Aviv: Eshel, 1961.

——. *Shaʿar ha-Haqdamot.* Edited by Yehudah Ashlag. Tel Aviv: Eshel, 1961.

——. *Shaʿar ha-Kavvanot.* 2 vols. Edited by Yehudah Ashlag. Tel Aviv, 1961.

——. *Shaʿar ha-Mitsvot.* Edited by Yehudah Ashlag. Tel Aviv: Eshel, 1961.

——. *Shaʿar ha-Pesuqim.* Edited by Yehudah Ashlag. Tel Aviv: Eshel, 1961.

——. *Shaʿar ha-Yiḥudim.* Edited by Meir Poppers. Korecz, 1783.

——. *Shaʿar Maʾamarei Rashbi.* Edited by Yehudah Ashlag. Tel Aviv: Eshel, 1961.

——. *Shaʿar Maʾamarei Razal.* Edited by Yehudah Ashlag. Tel Aviv: Eshel, 1961.

——. *Shaʿar Ruaḥ ha-Qodesh.* Edited by Yehudah Ashlag. Tel Aviv: Eshel, 1961.

——. *Tiqqunei ʾAvonot.* Korecz, 1783.

——. *Zohar ha-Raqia.* Korecz, 1785.

Yonah, Moses. *Sefer Kanfei Yonah.* Lemberg (Lvov), 1884; reprint, Jerusalem, 1975.

Zakuto, Moses. *Tiqqun Shovavim.* Venice, 1716.

Zemach, Jacob. *Naqid u-Metsaveh.* Amsterdam, 1712.

——. *Olat Tamid.* Jerusalem, 1907.

——. *Shulḥan Arukh ha-Ari.* Prague, 1660.

Zohar Ḥadash. 2d ed. Edited by R. Margaliot. Jerusalem: Mossad ha-Rav Kook, 1978.

Secondary Sources

Adler, Elkan N., ed. *Jewish Travellers in the Middle Ages: Nineteen Firsthand Accounts.* New York: Dover, 1987.

Allegro, John M., and Arnold A. Anderson, eds. *Qumrân Cave 4: 4Q158–4Q186.* Discoveries in the Judean Desert of Jordan, 5. Oxford: Clarendon Press, 1968.

Altmann, Alexander. "Eternality of Punishment: A Theological Controversy Within the Amsterdam Rabbinate in the Thirties of the Seventeenth Century." In *Essential Papers on Kabbalah,* edited by Lawrence Fine. New York: New York University Press, 1995.

——. "Lurianic Kabbalah in a Platonic Key: Abraham Cohen Herrera's *Puerta del Cielo.*" In *Jewish Thought in the Seventeenth Century,* edited by Bernard Septimus and Isadore Twersky. Cambridge, Mass.: Harvard University Center for Jewish Studies, 1987.

——. "Notes on the Development of the Kabbalah of Rabbi Menachem Azariah of Fano" (in Hebrew). In *Sefer Yishayahu Tishby,* edited by Joseph Dan and J. Hacker. Jerusalem: Magnes Press, 1986.

Assaf, Simcha. *Meqorot u-Meḥqarim be-Toldot Yisrael.* Jerusalem: Mossad ha-Rav Kook, 1946.

Avitsur, Shmuel. "The Batan, a Water-Powered Fulling Mill in Nahal Ammud—Relic of the Wool-Textile Industry in Safed." *Israel, Land and Nature* 7 (1981): 18–21.

———. "Contribution to the History of the Woolen Textile Industry in Salonika" (in Hebrew). *Sefunot* 12 (1971–78): 147–68.

———. "Safed—Center of the Manufacture of Woven Woolens in the Fifteenth Century [should read sixteenth century]" (in Hebrew). *Sefunot* 6 (1962): 41–69.

Avivi, Joseph. *Binyan ʾAriel*. Jerusalem: Misgav Yerushalayim, 1987.

———. "The *Kavvanot* of Rabbi Joseph ibn Tabul" (in Hebrew). In *Sefer ha-Zikkaron le-ha-Rav Yitshaq Nissim*, vol. 4, edited by M. Benayahu. Jerusalem: Yad ha-Rav Nissim, 1985.

———. "Lurianic Writings in Italy Prior to 1620" (in Hebrew). *ʿAlei Sefer* 11 (1984): 91–134.

———. "The Lurianic Writings of Rabbi Hayyim Vital" (in Hebrew). *Moriah* [*Sivan*] (1981): 77–91.

Baer, Yitshak. *A History of the Jews in Christian Spain*. Vol. 1. Philadelphia: Jewish Publication Society, 1961.

Barnai, Jacob. "The Jews of Spain in Egypt." In *Moreshet Sepharad: The Sephardi Legacy*, edited by Haim Beinart, 1: 72–76. Jerusalem: Magnes Press, 1992.

———. "The Jews of Spain in North Africa." In *The Sephardi Legacy*, edited by Haim Beinart, 2: 68–71. Jerusalem: Magnes Press, 1992.

Baron, Salo Wittmayer. *A Social and Religious History of the Jews*. Rev. ed. 18 vols. New York: Columbia University Press, 1952–83.

Bashan, Eliezer. "The Rise and Decline of the Sephardi Communities in the Levant: The Economic Aspects." In *The Western Sephardim: The History of Some of the Communities Formed in Europe, the Mediterranean and the New World After the Expulsion of 1492*, edited by R. D. Barnett and W. M. Schwab, pp. 349–88. Grendon, Northants: Gibraltar Books, 1989.

Baskin, Judith R. "From Separation to Displacement: The Problem of Women in *Sefer Ḥasidim*." *Association for Jewish Studies Review* 9 (1994): 1–18.

Bat Yeʾor. *The Dhimmi: Jews and Christians Under Islam*. Translated by David Maisel, Paul Fenton, and David Littman. Rutherford, N.J.: Fairleigh Dickinson University Press; London: Associated University Presses, 1985. Originally published as *Le Dhimmi: Profil de l'opprimé en Orient et en Afrique du nord depuis la conquête arabe* (Paris: Anthropos, 1980).

Beinart, Haim, ed. *The Sephardi Legacy*. 2 vols. Jerusalem: Magnes Press, 1992.

Bell, Catherine. *Ritual: Perspectives and Dimensions*. New York: Oxford University Press, 1997.

Ben Shlomo, Joseph. *Torat ha-ʾElohut shel R. Moshe Cordovero*. Jerusalem: Mossad Bialik, 1965.

Benayahu, Meir. "Customs of the Kabbalists of Safed at Meron" (in Hebrew). *Sefunot* 6 (1962): 9–40.

——. "Documents from the Geniza Concerning the Business Activities of the Ari" (in Hebrew). In *Sefer Zikkaron le-ha-Rav Yitshak Nissim*, edited by Meir Benayahu, 4: 225–53. Jerusalem: Yad Harav Nissim, 1985.

——. "Rabbi Hayyim Vital in Jerusalem" (in Hebrew). *Sinai* 30 (1952): 65–75.

——. "Rabbi Moses Yonah, the Ari's Disciple, and the First to Record His Teachings" (in Hebrew). In *Sefer Zikkaron le-ha-Rav Yitshak Nissim*, edited by M. Benayahu. Jerusalem: Yad Harav Nissim, 1985.

——. "The Revival of Ordination in Safed" (in Hebrew). In *Sefer Yovel le-Yitshaq Baer*, edited by S.W. Baron et al. Jerusalem: Ben Zvi Institute, 1960.

——. *Sefer Toldot ha-Ari*. Jerusalem: Ben Zvi Institute, 1967.

——. "The Tax Concession Enjoyed by the Scholars of Safed" (in Hebrew). *Sefunot* 7 (1963): 103–17.

——. "Spirits of Harm and Their Reparation" (in Hebrew). In *Sefer Zikkaron le-ha-Rav Yitshak Nissim*, edited by M. Benayahu. Jerusalem: Yad Harav Nissim, 1985.

——. *Yosef Behiri*. Jerusalem: Yad Harav Nissim, 1991.

Benbassa, Esther, and Aron Rodrigue. *Sephardi Jewry: A History of the Judeo-Spanish Community, Fourteenth–Twentieth Centuries*. Berkeley: University of California Press, 2000.

Ben-Zvi, Itzhak. "Eretz Yisrael Under Ottoman Rule." In *The Jews: Their History, Culture, and Religion*, edited by Louis Finkelstein. 1949; 3d ed., New York: Harper, 1960.

——. ʾ*Erets Yisrael ve-Yishuvah be-Yemei ha-Shilton ha-Otamani*. Jerusalem: Ben Zvi Institute, 1967.

Biale, David. *Eros and the Jews*. New York: Basic Books, 1992.

Biale, Rachel. *Women and Jewish Law: An Exploration of Women's Issues in Halakhic Sources*. New York: Schocken Books, 1984.

Bland, Kalman. "Neoplatonic and Gnostic Themes in R. Moses Cordovero's Doctrine of Evil." *Bulletin of the Institute of Jewish Studies* 3 (1975): 103–29.

Bonfil, Reuven. "Halakhah, Kabbalah and Society: Some Insights into Rabbi Menahem Azariah de Fano's Inner World." In *Jewish Thought in the Seventeenth Century*, edited by Bernard Septimus and Isadore Twersky. Cambridge, Mass.: Harvard University Center for Jewish Studies, 1987.

Bonfil, Robert. *Jewish Life in Renaissance Italy*. Berkeley: University of California Press, 1994.

Bourdieu, Pierre. *Outline of a Theory of Practice*. Cambridge: Cambridge University Press, 1977.

Bowman, Steven B. *The Jews of Byzantium, 1204–1453* (Tuscaloosa: University of Alabama Press, 1985)

Boyarin, Daniel. *Carnal Israel: Reading Sex in Talmudic Culture*. Berkeley: University of California Press, 1993.

——. *A Radical Jew: Paul and the Politics of Identity*. Berkeley: University of California Press, 1994.

Braude, Benjamin. "The Cloth Industry of Salonika in the Mediterranean Economy." *Peʿamim* 15 (1983): 82–95.

———. "The Rise and Fall of Salonica Woolens, 1500–1650: Technology, Transfer and Western Competition." In *Jews, Christians, and Muslims in the Mediterranean World After 1492*, edited by Alisa Meyuhas Ginio. Portland, Or.: Cass, 1992.

Braude, Benjamin, and Bernard Lewis, eds. *Christians and Jews in the Ottoman Empire: The Functioning of a Plural Society*. 2 vols. New York: Holmes & Meier, 1982.

Brown, Peter. *The Cult of the Saints: Its Rise and Function in Latin Christianity*. Chicago: University of Chicago Press, 1981.

———. *Society and the Holy in Late Antiquity*. Berkeley: University of California Press, 1982.

Canaani, Y. "Economic Life in Safed and Its Environs in the Sixteenth Century and the First Half of the Seventeenth Century" (in Hebrew). *Zion*, o.s., 6 (1933–34): 195–201.

Chajes, J.H. "Jewish Exorcism: Early Modern Traditions and Transformations." In *Judaism in Practice: From the Middle Ages Through the Early Modern Period*, edited by Lawrence Fine. Princeton, N.J.: Princeton University Press, 2001.

———. "Judgments Sweetened: Possession and Exorcism in Early Modern Jewish Culture." *Journal of Early Modern History* 1, 2 (1997): 124–69.

Chilton, Bruce, and Jacob Neusner. *Types of Authority in Formative Christianity and Judaism*. New York: Routledge, 1999.

Cohen, Amnon. *Jewish Life Under Islam: Jerusalem in the Sixteenth Century*. Cambridge, Mass.: Harvard University Press, 1984. Originally published as *Yehudim be-Shilton ha-Islam* (Jerusalem, 1982).

———. *Ottoman Documents on the Jewish Community of Jerusalem in the Sixteenth Century* (in Hebrew and Turkish). Jerusalem: Ben Zvi Institute, 1976.

———, ed. *Jerusalem in the Early Ottoman Period* (in Hebrew). Jerusalem: Ben Zvi Institute, 1979.

Cohen, Amnon, and Bernard Lewis. *Population and Revenue in the Towns of Palestine in the Sixteenth Century*. Princeton, N.J.: Princeton University Press, 1978.

Cohen, Jeremy. *"Be Fertile and Increase, Fill the Earth and Master It": The Ancient and Medieval Career of a Biblical Text*. Ithaca, N.Y.: Cornell University Press, 1989.

Cohn, Robert. "Sainthood on the Periphery: The Case of Judaism." In *Saints and Virtues*, edited by J. S. Hawley, pp. 87–108. Berkeley: University of California Press, 1987.

Crapanzano, Victor. "Spirit Possession." In *The Encyclopedia of Religion*, edited by Mircea Eliade et al., vol. 14. New York: Macmillan, 1987.

Dan, Joseph. "Dimensions of the Scholarship of Isaiah Tishby" (in Hebrew). *Madaʿei ha-Yahadut* 32 (1992): 49–60.

———. "The Emergence of Mystical Prayer." In *Studies in Jewish Mysticism: Proceedings of Regional Conferences Held at the University of California, Los Angeles, and McGill University in April, 1978* , edited by Joseph Dan and Frank Talmage. Cambridge, Mass.: Association for Jewish Studies, 1982.

——. "Hagiographic Literature: East and West" (in Hebrew). *Pe⁰amim* 26 (1986): 77–86.

——. *Ha-Sippur ha-ᶜIvri be-Yemei ha-Beinayim.* Jerusalem: Keter, 1975.

——. "The Intention of Prayer from the Tradition of R. Judah the Pietist" (in Hebrew). *Daᶜat* 10 (1983): 47–56.

——. "Kabbalistic and Gnostic Dualism." In *Studies in Jewish History, Thought, and Culture*, Binah, 3, edited by Joseph Dan. Westport, Conn.: Praeger, 1994.

——. "The Language of Mystical Prayer." *Studies in Spirituality* 5 (1995): 40–60.

——. "On the History of the Literature of Hagiography" (in Hebrew). *Meḥqarei Yerushalayim* 1 (1981): 82–100.

——. "Pesaq ha-Yirah veha-Emunah and the Intention of Prayer in Ashkenazi Hasidic Esotericism." *Frankfurter Judaistische Beitrage* 19 (1991–92): 185–215.

——. "Prayer as Text and Prayer as Mystical Experience." In *Torah and Wisdom: Studies in Jewish Philosophy, Kabbalah, and Halacha*, edited by R. Link-Salinger. New York: Shengold, 1992.

——. "Samael, Lilith, and the Concept of Evil in Early Kabbalah." *Association for Jewish Studies Review* 5 (1980): 17–40.

——. *Sifrut ha-Musar ve-ha-Derush.* Jerusalem: Keter, 1975.

——. *Torat ha-Sod shel Ḥasidut ᵓAshkenaz.* Jerusalem: Mossad Bialik, 1968.

——, ed. Binah Series. 1: *Studies in Jewish History*; 2: *Studies in Jewish Thought*; 3: *Studies in Jewish History, Thought, and Culture.* New York: Praeger, 1989–94.

David, Abraham. "Demographic Changes in the Safed Jewish Community in the Sixteenth Century." In *Occident and Orient: A Tribute to the Memory of A. Scheiber*, edited by R. Dan. Leiden: E.J. Brill, 1988.

——. "Halakhah and Commerce in the Biography of Isaac Luria" (in Hebrew). *Meḥqarei Yerushalayim* 10 (1992): 287–97.

——. *In Zion and Jerusalem: The Itinerary of Rabbi Moses Basola (1521–1523).* Translated by Dena Ordan. Jerusalem: C.G. Foundation, Jerusalem Project Publications of the Martin (Szusz) Department of Land of Israel Studies, Bar Ilan University, 1999. In English followed by the Hebrew text of the manuscript.

——. "More Concerning the Life of the Ari in Egypt" (in Hebrew). *ᶜAlei Sefer* 14 (1987): 135–37.

——. "Relations Between North African Jewry and the Land of Israel in the Fifteenth and Sixteenth Centuries" (in Hebrew). *Pe⁰amim* 24 (1985): 74–86.

——. "Safed, foyer de retour au judaïsme de *conversos* au XVI siècle." *Revue des études juives* 146 (1987): 63–83.

——. "The Spanish Exiles in the Holy Land." In *The Sephardi Legacy*, edited by Haim Beinart, 2: 77–108. Jerusalem: Magnes Press, 1992.

——. *To Come to the Land: Immigration and Settlement in Sixteenth-Century Eretz Yisrael.* Translated by Dena Ordan. Tuscaloosa: University of Alabama Press, 1999.

Deshen, Shlomo, and Walter P. Zenner, eds. *Jews Among Muslims: Communities in the Precolonial Middle East.* New York: New York University Press, 1996.

Dimitrovsky, H. Z. "The Controversy Between Rabbi Joseph Karo and Rabbi Moses di Trani" (in Hebrew). *Sefunot* 6 (1962): 72–123.

——. "The Study House of Rabbi Jacob Berab in Safed" (in Hebrew). *Sefunot* 7 (1963): 41–102.

——. "Two New Documents Concerning the Ordination Controversy in Safed" (in Hebrew). *Sefunot* 10 (1966): 112–92.

Doniger, Wendy. *The Implied Spider: Politics and Theology in Myth.* New York: Columbia University Press, 1998.

Drory, Joseph. "Jerusalem During the Mamluk Period." In *The Jerusalem Cathedra*, ed. L. Levine, 1: 190–213. Jerusalem: Ben Zvi Institute, 1981.

Eilberg-Schwartz, Howard, ed. *People of the Body: Jews and Judaism from an Embodied Perspective.* Albany: State University of New York Press, 1992.

Elbaum, Jacob. *Teshuvat ha-Lev ve-Kabbalat Yesurin.* Jerusalem: Magnes Press, 1993.

Elbogen, Ismar. *Jewish Liturgy: A Comprehensive History.* Translated by Raymond P. Scheindlin. Philadelphia: Jewish Publication Society, 1993.

Eliade, Mircea. *Shamanism: Archaic Techniques of Ecstasy.* Translated by Willard R. Trask. Bollingen ser., 76. Princeton, N.J.: Princeton University Press, 1964. Originally published as *Chamanisme et les techniques archaïques de l'extase* (Paris: Payot, 1950).

Eliade, Mircea, Charles J. Adams, et al., eds. *The Encylopedia of Religion.* 16 vols. New York: Macmillan, 1987.

Elior, Rachel. "The Doctrine of Transmigration in *Galya Raza.*" In *Essential Papers on Kabbalah*, edited by Lawrence Fine. New York: New York University Press, 1995.

——. "The Kabbalists of Draa" (in Hebrew). *Pe'amim* 24 (1985): 36–73.

——. "Lurianic Kabbalah, Sabbateanism, and Hasidism: Historical Sequence, Spiritual Affinity, and Differences of Identity" (in Hebrew). *Mehqarei Yerushalayim* 12 (1997): 379–97.

——. "Messianic Expectations and Spiritualization of Religious Life in the Sixteenth Century." In *Essential Papers on Jewish Culture in Renaissance and Baroque Italy*, edited by D. Ruderman. New York: New York University Press, 1992.

——. "The Metaphorical Relation Between God and Man, and the Significance of the Visionary Reality in Lurianic Kabbalah" (in Hebrew). *Mehqarei Yerushalayim* 10 (1992): 47–57.

——. *The Paradoxical Ascent to God.* Albany: State University of New York Press, 1993.

Elqayam, Abraham. "The Mystery of Faith in the Writings of Nathan of Gaza" (in Hebrew). Ph.D. diss., Hebrew University, Jerusalem, 1993.

Epstein, Mark Alan. *The Ottoman Jewish Communities and Their Role in the Fifteenth and Sixteenth Centuries.* Freiburg: K. Schwarz, 1980.

Faierstein, Morris. *Jewish Mystical Autobiographies.* New York: Paulist Press, 1999.

Fattal, Antoine. *Le Statut légal des non-musulmans en pays d'Islam.* Recherches publiées sous la direction de l'Institut de lettres orientales de Beyrouth, 10. Beirut: Imprimerie catholique, 1958.

Feher, Michel, Ramona Naddaff, and Nadia Tazi, eds. *Fragments for a History of the Human Body.* 3 vols. New York: Zone, 1989.

Fenton, Paul B. "The Influence of Sufism on Safed Kabbalah" (in Hebrew). *Maḥanayim* 6 (1994): 170–79.

——. "Solitary Meditation in Jewish and Islamic Mysticism in the Light of a Recent Archeological Discovery." *Medieval Encounters* 1, 2 (1995): 271–96.

——. "The Symbolism of Ritual Circumambulation in Judaism and Islam: A Comparative Study." *Journal of Jewish Thought and Philosophy* 6 (1997): 345–69.

Fine, Lawrence. "Alexander Altmann's Contribution to the Study of Jewish Mysticism." *Leo Baeck Institute Year Book* 34 (1989): 421–31.

——. "Approaching the Study of Jewish Mystical Experience." *Association for Jewish Studies Newsletter* 19 (1977): 10–11.

——. "The Art of Metoposcopy: A Study in Isaac Luria's Charismatic Knowledge." *Association for Jewish Studies Review* 11, 1(1986): 79–101.

——. "Benevolent Spirit Possession in Sixteenth-Century Safed." In *Spirit Possession in Judaism,* edited by M. Goldish. Detroit: Wayne State University Press, 2003.

——. "Contemplative Death in Jewish Mystical Tradition." In *Sacrificing the Self: Perspectives on Martyrdom and Religion,* edited by M. Cormack. New York: Oxford University Press, 2002.

——. "The Contemplative Practice of *Yiḥudim* in Lurianic Kabbalah." In *Jewish Spirituality,* edited by Arthur Green, vol. 2. New York: Crossroad, 1987.

——. "Kabbalistic Texts." In *Back to the Sources: Reading the Classic Jewish Texts,* edited by B. Holtz. New York: Simon & Schuster, 1984.

——. "Maggidic Revelation in the Teachings of Isaac Luria." In *Mystics, Philosophers, and Politicians: Essays in Jewish Intellectual History in Honor of Alexander Altmann,* edited by Jehuda Reinharz and Daniel Swetschinski with the collaboration of Kalman P. Bland. Durham, N.C.: Duke University Press, 1982.

——. "Medieval Jewish Apocalyptic Literature." In *The Encyclopedia of Religion,* edited by Mircea Eliade et al., vol. 1. New York: Macmillan, 1987.

——. "Popularizing the Esoteric: Recent Studies in Jewish Mysticism." *Judaism* 28 (1979): 494–96.

——. "Purifying the Body in the Name of the Soul: The Problem of the Body in Sixteenth-Century Kabbalah." In *People of the Body: Jews and Judaism from an*

Embodied Perspective, edited by Howard Eilberg-Schwartz. Albany: State University of New York Press, 1992.

——. "Recitation of Mishnah as a Vehicle for Mystical Inspiration: A Contemplative Technique Taught by Hayyim Vital." *Revue des études juives* 141, 1–2 (1982): 183–99.

——. "The Study of Torah as a Theurgic Rite in Lurianic Kabbalah." In *Approaches to Judaism in Medieval Times*, vol. 3, edited by David R. Blumenthal. Atlanta: Scholars Press, 1988.

——, ed. *Essential Papers on Kabbalah*. New York: New York University Press, 1995.

——, ed. *Judaism in Practice: From the Middle Ages Through the Early Modern Period*. Princeton, N.J.: Princeton University Press, 2001.

——, trans. and ed. *Safed Spirituality: Rules of Mystical Piety, the Beginning of Wisdom*. New York: Paulist Press, 1984.

Fishbane, Michael. "'The Holy One Sits and Roars': Mythopoesis and the Midrashic Imagination." In id., ed. *The Midrashic Imagination: Jewish Exegesis, Thought, and History*. Albany: State University of New York Press, 1993.

——. *The Kiss of God: Spiritual and Mystical Death in Judaism*. Seattle: University of Washington Press, 1994.

——, ed. *The Midrashic Imagination: Jewish Exegesis, Thought, and History*. Albany: State University of New York Press, 1993.

Fishman, Talya. "A Kabbalistic Perspective on Gender-Specific Commandments: On the Interplay of Symbols and Society." *Association for Jewish Studies Review* 7 (1992): 199–245.

——. "The Penitential System of Hasidei Ashkenaz and the Problem of Cultural Boundaries." *Journal of Jewish Thought and Philosophy* 8 (1999): 201–29.

Foucault, Michel. "Technologies of the Self." In *Technologies of the Self: A Seminar with Michel Foucault*, edited by L. Martin, H. Gutman, and P. Hutton. Amherst: University of Massachusetts Press, 1988.

Fraade, Steven. "Ascetical Aspects of Ancient Judaism." In *Jewish Spirituality*, vol. 1, edited by Arthur Green. New York: Crossroad, 1986.

Gartner, Jacob. *Gilgulei Minhag ba-ʿOlam ha-Halakhah*. Jerusalem: Hemed Press, 1995.

Geary, Patrick J. *Living with the Dead in the Middle Ages*. Ithaca, N.Y.: Cornell University Press, 1994.

Geertz, Clifford. *Islam Observed: Religious Development in Morocco and Indonesia*. New Haven, Conn.: Yale University Press, 1969.

Gellner, Ernest. *Saints of the Atlas*. Chicago: University of Chicago Press, 1969.

Gendler, Everett. "A Sentient Universe." In *Ecology and the Jewish Spirit: Where Nature and the Sacred Meet*, edited by Ellen Bernstein. Woodstock, Vt.: Jewish Lights Publishing, 1998.

Gerber, Jane S. *The Jews of Spain: A History of the Sephardic Experience.* New York: Free Press, 1992.

Giller, Pinchas. *The Enlightened Will Shine: Symbolization and Theurgy in the Later Strata of the Zohar.* Albany: State University of New York Press, 1993.

——. *Reading the Zohar: The Sacred Text of the Kabbalah.* New York: Oxford University Press, 2001.

——. "Recovering the Sanctity of the Galilee: The Veneration of Sacred Relics in Classical Kabbalah." *Journal of Jewish Thought* 4 (1994): 147–69.

Ginsburg, Elliot K. *The Sabbath in the Classical Kabbalah.* Albany: State University of New York Press, 1989.

Girardot, Norman J. *Myth and Meaning in Early Taoism.* Berkeley: University of California Press, 1983.

Goitein, S.D. *A Mediterranean Society: The Jewish Communities of the Arab World as Portrayed in the Documents of the Cairo Geniza.* Vol. 5: *The Individual.* Berkeley: University of California Press, 1988.

Goldish, Matt, ed. *Spirit Possession in Judaism: Cases and Contexts from the Middle Ages to the Present.* Detroit: Wayne State University Press, 2003.

Goldman, Israel M. *The Life and Times of David Ibn Abi Zimra.* New York: Jewish Theological Seminary of America, 1970.

Graham, William A. *Beyond the Written Word: Oral Aspects of Scripture in the History of Religion.* New York: Cambridge University Press, 1987.

Green, Arthur. *Devotion and Commandment: The Faith of Abraham in the Hasidic Imagination.* Cincinnati: Hebrew Union College Press, 1989.

——. "Early Hasidism: Some Old/New Questions." In *Hasidism Reappraised*, edited by A. Rapoport-Albert. Portland, Or.: Vallentine Mitchell, 1996.

——. "Hasidism: Discovery and Retreat." In *The Other Side of God: A Polarity in World Religions*, edited by Peter L. Berger. Garden City, N.Y.: Anchor Press/ Doubleday, 1981.

——. *Keter: The Crown of God in Early Jewish Mysticism.* Princeton, N.J.: Princeton University Press, 1997.

——. *Menahem Nahum of Chernobyl.* New York: Paulist Press, 1982.

——. *Tormented Master: A Life of Rabbi Nahman of Bratslav.* Tuscaloosa: University of Alabama Press, 1979.

——. "The *Zaddiq* as *Axis Mundi* in Later Judaism." *Journal of the American Academy of Religion* 45, 3 (1977): 327–47. Reprinted in *Essential Papers on Kabbalah*, edited by Lawrence Fine. New York: New York University Press, 1995.

——. "The Zohar: Jewish Mysticism in Medieval Spain." In *Essential Papers on Kabbalah*, edited by Lawrence Fine, pp. 27–66. New York: New York University Press, 1995.

——, ed. *Jewish Spirituality.* 2 vols. New York: Crossroad, 1986–87.

Green, William Scott. "Palestinian Holy Men: Charismatic Leadership and Rabbinic Tradition." In *Aufstieg und Niedergang der römischen Welt: Geschichte und Kultur Roms im Spiegel der neueren Forschung*, edited by W. Haase and Hildegard Temporini, 19.2, pp. 619–47. Berlin: W. de Gruyter, 1979.

——. "Storytelling and Holy Man: The Case of Ancient Judaism." In *Take Judaism, for Example*, edited by J. Neusner. Chicago: University of Chicago Press, 1983.

——. "What's in a Name? The Problematic of Rabbinic 'Biography.'" In *Approaches to Ancient Judaism: Theory and Practice*, edited by J. Neusner. Missoula, Mont.: Scholars Press, 1978.

Gries, Zev. *Sifrut ha-Hanhagot*. Jerusalem: Bialik Institute, 1989.

Hacker, Joseph. "The Jewish Community of Salonika from the Fifteenth to the Sixteenth Century" (in Hebrew). Ph.D. diss., Hebrew University, Jerusalem, 1978.

——. "Ottoman Policy Toward the Jews During the Fifteenth Century." In *Christians and Jews in the Ottoman Empire: The Functioning of a Plural Society*, ed. Benjamin Braude and Bernard Lewis, vol. 1. New York: Holmes & Meier, 1982.

——. "The Payment of *Djizya* by Scholars in Palestine in the Sixteenth Century" (in Hebrew). *Shalem* 4 (1984): 63–117.

——. "The Sephardim in the Ottoman Empire in the Sixteenth Century." In *The Sephardi Legacy*, edited by Haim Beinart, 2: 109–33. Jerusalem: Magnes Press, 1992.

——. "Spiritual and Material Links Between Egyptian and Palestinian Jewry in the Sixteenth Century." In *Egypt and Palestine*, edited by Amnon Cohen and Gabriel Baer. New York: St. Martin's Press, 1984.

Hallamish, Moshe. "The Confrontation with the Obligation of the *Kavvanot*" (in Hebrew). *Mehqarei Yerushalayim* 12 (1997): 217–57.

——. *Ha-Kabbalah be-Tefillah be-Halakha u-be-Minhag*. Ramat Gan: Bar Ilan, 2000.

——. *An Introduction to the Kabbalah*. Translated by Ruth Bar-Ilan and Ora Wiskind-Elper. Albany: State University of New York Press, 1999.

——. "The Kabbalists of Morocco" (in Hebrew). *Mi-Mizrach u-be-Maʿarav* 2 (1980): 205–35.

——. "The Origins of Kabbalah in Morocco" (in Hebrew). *Peʿamim* 15 (1983): 29–46.

Helner, Melila. "Transmigration of Souls in the Kabbalistic Writings of Rabbi David ibn Zimra" (in Hebrew). *Peʿamim* 43 (1980): 16–50.

Heschel, A.J. *Prophetic Inspiration After the Prophets*. Hoboken, N.J.: Ktav, 1996.

Heyd, Uriel. *Ottoman Documents on Palestine, 1552–1615*. London: Oxford University Press, 1960.

Hirschberg, H. Z. *A History of the Jews in North Africa*. Translated from the Hebrew. 2d rev. ed. 2 vols. Leiden: E.J. Brill, 1974–81.

Hoffman, Lawrence. *The Canonization of the Synagogue Service*. Notre Dame, Ind.: Notre Dame University Press, 1979.

Hundert, Gershon D., ed. *Essential Papers on Hasidism: Origins to Present*. New York: New York University Press, 1991.

Huss, Boaz. *ʿAl ʾAdnei Paz: Ha-Kabbalah shel Rabbi Shimon Ibn Lavi*. Jerusalem: Magnes Press, 2000.

——. "*Genizat ha-ʾOr* in Shimon Lavi's *Ketem Paz* and the Lurianic Doctrine of *Tsimtsum*" (in Hebrew). *Meḥqarei Yerushalayim* 10 (1992): 341–61.

Hutteroth, W. "The Pattern of Settlement in Palestine in the Sixteenth Century." In *Studies on Palestine During the Ottoman Period*, edited by Moshe Ma'oz, pp. 3–9. Jerusalem: Magnes Press, 1975.

Idel, Moshe. "The Beginnings of Kabbalah in North Africa" (in Hebrew). *Peʿamim* 43 (1990): 4–15.

——. "Between the Kabbalah of Jerusalem and the Kabbalah of Israel Sarug" (in Hebrew). *Shalem* 6 (1992): 165–73.

——. "Concerning the Concept of *Tsimtsum* in Kabbalah and in Scholarship" (in Hebrew). *Meḥqarei Yerushalayim* 10 (1992): 59–112.

——. "Differing Conceptions of Kabbalah in the Early Seventeenth Century." In *Jewish Thought in the Seventeenth Century*, edited by Bernard Septimus and Isadore Twersky. Cambridge, Mass.: Harvard University Center for Jewish Studies, 1987.

——. "Gazing at the Head in Ashkenazi Hasidism." *Journal of Jewish Thought* 6 (1997): 265–300.

——. *Golem: Jewish Magical and Mystical Traditions on the Artificial Anthropoid*. Albany: State University of New York Press, 1990.

——. *Hasidism: Between Ecstasy and Magic*. Albany: State University of New York Press, 1995.

——. "Inquiries into the Doctrine of *Sefer ha-Meshiv*" (in Hebrew). *Sefunot* 17 (1983): 185–266.

——. *Kabbalah: New Perspectives*. New Haven, Conn.: Yale University Press, 1988.

——. *Language, Torah, and Hermeneutics in Abraham Abulafia*. Albany: State University of New York Press, 1989.

——. "Major Currents in Italian Kabbalah." In *Essential Papers on Jewish Culture in Renaissance and Baroque Italy*, edited by D. Ruderman. New York: New York University Press, 1992.

——. *Messianic Mystics*. New Haven, Conn.: Yale University Press, 1998.

——. "Midrashic Versus Other Forms of Jewish Hermeneutics: Some Comparative Reflections." In Michael Fishbane, ed. *The Midrashic Imagination: Jewish Exegesis, Thought, and History*. Albany: State University of New York Press, 1993.

——. *The Mystical Experience in Abraham Abulafia*. Translated by Jonathan Chipman. Albany: State University of New York Press, 1988.

——. "'One from a Town, Two From a Clan': The Diffusion of Lurianic Kabbala and Sabbateanism: A Re-Examination." *Jewish History* 7, 2 (Fall 1993): 79–104.

——. "On Mobility, Individuals and Groups: Prolegomenon for a Sociological Approach to Sixteenth-Century Safed." *Kabbalah: Journal for the Study of Jewish Mystical Texts,* edited by D. Abrams and A. Elqayam, 3 (1998): 145-73.

——. "Particularism and Universalism in Kabbalah: 1480–1650." In *Essential Papers on Jewish Culture in Renaissance and Baroque Italy,* edited by D. Ruderman. New York: New York University Press, 1992.

——. "Rabbi Judah Haleywa and His Book *Sefer Tsefanat Paʿaneaḥ*" (in Hebrew). *Shalem* 4 (1984): 119–48.

——. "Sexual Metaphors and Praxis in the Kabbalah." In *The Jewish Family,* edited by D. Kraemer. Oxford: Oxford University Press, 1989.

——. "Solomon Molcho as Magician" (in Hebrew). *Sefunot* 18: (1985): 193–219.

——. "Some Concepts of Time and History in Kabbalah." In *Jewish History and Jewish Memory: Essays in Honor of Yosef Hayim Yerushalmi,* edited by Elisheva Carlebach, John M. Efron, and David N. Myers. Hanover, N.H.: University Press of New England for Brandeis University Press, 1998.

——. *Studies in Ecstatic Kabbalah.* Albany: State University of New York Press, 1988.

——. "We Have No Kabbalistic Tradition on This." In *Rabbi Moses Nahmanides (Ramban): Explorations in His Religious and Literary Virtuosity,* edited by Isadore Twersky. Cambridge, Mass.: Harvard University Press, 1983.

Idel, Moshe, and Mortimer Ostow, eds. *Jewish Mystical Leaders and Leadership in the Thirteenth Century.* Northvale, N.J.: Jason Aronson, 1998.

Idelsohn, A. Z. *Jewish Liturgy and Its Development.* 1932. Reprint. New York: Schocken Books, 1972.

Ish-Shalom, Michael. *Qivrei ʾAvot.* Jerusalem: Mossad Ha-Rav Kook, 1948.

——, ed. *Masʿe notsrim le-Erets Yisrael.* Tel-Aviv: Am Oved, 1965.

Ivry, Alfred L., Elliot R. Wolfson, and Allan Arkush, eds. *Perspectives on Jewish Thought and Mysticism,* Amsterdam: Harwood Academic Publishers, 1998.

Jacobs, Louis. *Hasidic Prayer.* New York: Schocken Books, 1973.

——. *Jewish Mystical Testimonies.* New York: Schocken Books, 1977.

Jacobson, Yoram. "The Aspect of the 'Feminine' in the Lurianic Kabbalah." In *Gershom Scholem's "Major Trends in Jewish Mysticism" Fifty Years After: Proceedings of the Sixth International Conference on the History of Jewish Mysticism,* edited by Peter Schäfer and Joseph Dan. Tübingen: Mohr, 1993.

Jonas, Hans. *The Gnostic Religion: The Message of the Alien God and the Beginnings of Christianity.* 1958. 2d ed. Boston: Beacon Press, 1963, 1970.

Juhasz, Esther, ed. *Sephardi Jews in the Ottoman Empire: Aspects of Material Culture.* Jerusalem: Israel Museum, 1990.

Kallus, Menachem. "Pneumatic Mystical Possession and the Eschatology of the Soul in Lurianic Kabbalah." In *Spirit Possession in Judaism*, edited by M. Goldish. Detroit: Wayne State University Press, 2003.

——. "The Relationship of the Baal Shem Tov to the Practice of Lurianic Kavvanot in Light of His Comments on the *Siddur Rashkov*." In *Kabbalah: Journal for the Study of Jewish Mystical Texts*, edited by D. Abrams and A. Elqayam, vol. 2. Los Angeles: Cherub Press, 1997.

Kanarfogel, Ephraim. *"Peering through the Lattices:" Mystical, Magical, and Pietistic Dimensions in the Tosafist Period*. Detroit: Wayne State University Press, 2000.

Kaplan, Aryeh, trans. and ed. *Meditation and Kabbalah*. York Beach, Me.: S. Weiser, 1982.

Katz, Jacob. *Divine Law in Human Hands*. Jerusalem: Magnes Press, 1998.

——. "The Controversy Concerning Ordination between Rabbi Jacob Berab and Rabbi Levi ibn Habib" (in Hebrew). In id., *Halakha ve-Qabbalah*, pp. 213–36. Jerusalem: Magnes Press, 1986.

Kedourie, Elie, ed. *Spain and the Jews: The Sephardi Experience, 1492 and After*. London: Thames & Hudson, 1992.

Keyes, Charles. "Charisma: From Social Life to Sacred Biography." In *Charisma and Sacred Biography,* edited by M. Williams. *Journal of the American Academy of Religion, Thematic Studies* 48, 3–4 (1982).

Kobler, Franz, ed. *A Treasury of Jewish Letters: Letters from the Famous and the Humble*. 2 vols. New York: Farrar, Straus & Young, 1952.

Koren, Sharon. "Mystical Rationales for the Laws of Niddah." In *Women and Water: Menstruation in Jewish Life and Law*, edited by Rahel S. Wasserfall, pp. 101–21. Hanover, N.H.: Brandeis University Press, 1999.

Krassen, Miles. *Isaiah Horowitz*. New York: Paulist Press, 1996.

——. *Uniter of Heaven and Earth: Rabbi Meshullam Feibush Heller and the Rise of Hasidism in Eastern Galicia*. Albany: State University of New York Press, 1998.

Lamdan, Ruth. *A Separate People: Jewish Women in Palestine, Syria and Egypt in the Sixteenth Century*. Brill: Leiden, 2000.

Landau, Jacob, ed. *Toldot Yehudei Mitsrayim be-Tequfat ha-Otomanit*. Jerusalem: Misgav Yerushalayin, 1988.

Lazaroff, Alan. "Bahya's Asceticism Against Its Rabbinic and Islamic Background." *Journal of Jewish Studies* 21 (1970): 11–38.

Law, Jane Marie, ed. *Religious Reflections on the Human Body*. Bloomington: Indiana University Press, 1995.

Lesses, Rebecca. *Ritual Practices to Gain Power: Angels, Incantations, and Revelations in Early Jewish Mysticism*. Harrisburg, Pa.: Trinity Press International, 1998.

Levy, Avigdor, ed. *The Jews of the Ottoman Empire*. Princeton, N.J.: Darwin Press; Washington, D.C.: Institute of Turkish Studies, 1994.

——, ed. *The Sephardim in the Ottoman Empire*. Princeton, N.J.: Darwin Press, 1992.

Lewis, Bernard. *The Jews of Islam*. Princeton, N.J.: Princeton University Press, 1984.

——. *Notes and Documents from the Turkish Archives: A Contribution to the History of the Jews in the Ottoman Empire*. Jerusalem: Oriental Notes and Studies, 1952.

Liebes, Yehuda. "The Messiah of the *Zohar*: Concerning the Messianic Image of R. Shimon bar Yohai." In *Ha-raᶜayon ha-Meshiḥi be-Yisrael* [The Messianic Idea in Jewish Thought: A Study Conference in Honour of the Eightieth Birthday of Gershom Scholem (in Hebrew)]. Jerusalem: Israel Academy of Sciences and Humanities, 1982. English translation in id., *Studies in the Zohar* (see below).

——. "Myth vs. Symbol in the Zohar and in Lurianic Kabbalah." In *Essential Papers on Kabbalah*, edited by Lawrence Fine. New York: New York University Press, 1995.

——. "New Directions in the Study of Kabbalah" (in Hebrew). *Peᶜamim* 50 (1992): 150–70.

——. "Sabbath Meal Songs Established by the Holy Ari" (in Hebrew). *Molad* 4 (1972): 540–55.

——. *Sod ha-ʾEmunah ha-Shabtaʾit: Kovets Maʾamarim*. Jerusalem: Mossad Bialik, 1995.

——. *Studies in Jewish Myth and Jewish Messianism*. Translated by Batya Stein. Albany: State University of New York Press, 1993.

——. *Studies in the Zohar*. Translated by Arnold Schwartz, Stephanie Nakache, and Penina Peli. Albany: State University of New York Press, 1993.

——. "Toward a Study of the Author of ᶜ*Emeq ha-Melech*: His Personality, Writings and Kabbalah" (in Hebrew). *Meḥqarei Yerushalayim* 11 (1993): 101–37.

——. "'Two Young Roes of a Doe': The Secret Sermon of Isaac Luria Before His Death" (in Hebrew). *Meḥqarei Yerushalayim* 10 (1992): 113–69.

——. "*Zohar* and Eros" (in Hebrew). ᶜ*Alpayyim* 9 (1994): 67–119.

Liebes, Yehudah, and Rachel Elior, eds. *Lurianic Kabbalah: Proceedings of the Fourth International Conference on the History of Jewish Mysticism = Jerusalem Studies in Jewish Thought*, vol. 10 (in Hebrew). Jerusalem: Magnes Press, 1992.

Little, Donald P. "Relations Between Jerusalem and Egypt During the Mamuluk Period According to Literary and Documentary Sources." In *Egypt and Palestine: A Millennium of Association (868–1948)*, edited by Amnon Cohen and Gabriel Baer, pp. 73–93. Jerusalem: Ben-Zvi Institute for the Study of Jewish Communities in the East; New York: St. Martin's Press, 1984.

Maggid, Shaul. "Conjugal Union, Mourning, and Talmud Torah in R. Isaac Luria's *Tikkun Hazot*." *Daᶜat* 36 (1996): xvii–xlv.

——. "From Theosophy to Midrash: Lurianic Exegesis and the Garden of Eden." *Association for Jewish Studies Review* 22 (1997): 37–75.

Magli, Patrizia. "The Face and The Soul." In *Fragments for a History of the Human Body*, edited by Michel Feher with Ramona Naddaff and Nadia Tazi. 3 vols. New York: Zone, 1989.

Mantran, Robert. "Foreign Merchants and the Minorities in Istanbul During the Sixteenth and Seventeenth Centuries." In *Christians and Jews in the Ottoman Empire: The Functioning of a Plural Society*, edited by Benjamin Braude and Bernard Lewis, 1: 127–37. New York: Holmes & Meier, 1982.

Marcus, Ivan G. "Ashkenazic Hasidism." In *The Encyclopedia of Religion*, edited by Mircea Eliade et al., vol. 1. New York: Macmillan, 1987.

——. "*Hasidei Ashkenaz* Private Penitentials: An Introduction and Descriptive Catalogue of Their Manuscripts and Early Editions." In *Studies in Jewish Mysticism: Proceedings of Regional Conferences Held at the University of California, Los Angeles, and McGill University in April, 1978* , edited by Joseph Dan and Frank Talmage. Cambridge, Mass.: Association for Jewish Studies, 1982.

——. *Piety and Society: The Jewish Pietists of Medieval Germany*. Leiden: E.J. Brill, 1981.

——. "Religious Virtuosi and the Religious Community: The Pietistic Mode in Judaism." In *Take Judaism, For Example*, edited by J. Neusner. Chicago: University of Chicago Press, 1983.

——. *Rituals of Childhood: Jewish Acculturation in Medieval Europe*. New Haven, Conn.: Yale University Press, 1996.

Matt, Daniel C. "*Ayin*: The Concept of Nothingness in Jewish Mysticism." In *Essential Papers on Kabbalah*, edited by Lawrence Fine. New York: New York University Press, 1995.

——. "*Matnita Dilan*: A Technique of Innovation in the Zohar" (in Hebrew). *Mehqarei Yerushalayim* 8 (1989): 123–45.

——. "'New Ancient Words': The Aura of Secrecy in the Zohar." In *Gershom Scholem's "Major Trends in Jewish Mysticism" Fifty Years After: Proceedings of the Sixth International Conference on the History of Jewish Mysticism*, edited by Peter Schäfer and Joseph Dan. Tübingen: Mohr, 1993.

——. *The Essential Kabbalah*. San Francisco: Harper San Francisco, 1995.

——. *Zohar: The Book of Enlightenment*. New York: Paulist Press, 1983.

Meroz, Ronit. "An Anonymous Commentary on *Idra Rabba* by a Member of the Sarug School, or: What Is the Relationship Between Sarug and His Colleagues, and Ergas, Spinoza, and Others?" (in Hebrew). *Mehqarei Yerushalayim* 12 (1997): 207–377.

——. "Contrasting Opinions Among the Founders of R. Israel Sarug's School." In *Expérience et écriture mystiques dans les religions du livre: Actes d'un colloque international tenu par le Centre d'études juives, Université de Paris IV–Sorbonne,*

1994, edited by Paul B. Fenton and Roland Goetschel. Leiden: E.J. Brill, 2000.

——. "Early Lurianic Compositions" (in Hebrew). In *Massuot*, edited by A. Goldreich and M. Oron. Jerusalem: Mossad Bialik, 1994.

——. "Faithful Transmission Versus Innovation: Luria and His Disciples." In *Gershom Scholem's "Major Trends in Jewish Mysticism" Fifty Years After: Proceedings of the Sixth International Conference on the History of Jewish Mysticism*, edited by Peter Schäfer and Joseph Dan. Tübingen: Mohr, 1993.

——. "R. Israel Sarug, Student of the Ari: Reconsidered Anew" (in Hebrew). *Daᶜat* 28 (1992): 41–56.

——. "Selections from Ephraim Penzieri: Luria's Sermon in Jerusalem and the *Kavvanah* on Eating Food" (in Hebrew). *Meḥqarei Yerushalayim* 10 (1992): 211–57.

——. "Torat ha-Geᵓeulah be-Kabbalat ha-Ari" (The Teachings of Redemption in Lurianic Kabbalah). Ph.D. diss., Hebrew University, Jerusalem, 1988.

Mopsik, Charles. *Les Grands Textes de la Cabale: Les Rites qui font Dieu: Pratiques religieuses et efficacité théurgique dans la Cabale, des origines au milieu du XVIIIe siècle*. Lagrasse: Verdier, 1993.

——. *Lettre sur la sainteté: Le Secret de la relation entre l'homme et la femme dans la Cabale*. Lagrasse: Verdier, 1986.

Neusner, Jacob. *A History of the Jews in Babylonia*. Volume 4. Leiden: E.J. Brill, 1969.

Orni, Efraim, and Elisha Efrat. *Geography of Israel*. 3d rev. ed. New York: American Heritage Press, 1971.

Pachter, Mordechai. "The Concept of Devekut in the Homiletical Ethical Writings of 16th Century Safed." In *Studies in Medieval Jewish History and Literature*, vol. 2, edited by Isadore Twersky. Cambridge, Mass.: Harvard University Press, 1984.

——. "Concerning Passages from ᵓOrḥot Tsaddiqim in the Ethical Treatises of the Sages of Safed" (in Hebrew). *Qiryat Sefer* 47 (1972): 487–92.

——. "The Emigration of Rabbi Solomon Alkabets to the Land of Israel and His Departure Sermon in Salonika" (in Hebrew). *Shalem* 5 (1987): 251–63.

——. "The Homiletic Eulogy by R. Samuel Uceda upon the Death of the Ari" (in Hebrew). In id., *Matsfunot Tsfat*, pp. 39–68. Jerusalem: Merkaz Zalman Shazar, 1994.

——. "Kabbalistic Ethical Literature in Sixteenth-Century Safed." In *Studies in Jewish History, Thought, and Culture*, Binah, 3, edited by Joseph Dan. Westport, Conn.: Praeger, 1994.

——. "The Life and Personality of Rabbi Eleazar Azikri According to His Mystical Diary and *Sefer Ḥaredim*" (in Hebrew). *Shalem* 3 (1981): 127–47.

——. *Matsfunot Tsfat*. Jerusalem: Merkaz Zalman Shazar, 1994.

———. *Millei de-Shemaya le-Rabi Eleazar Azikri*. Tel Aviv: Mifalim Univeristaim, 1991.

Patai, Raphael. *The Jewish Alchemists*. Princeton, N.J.: Princeton University Press, 1994.

———. *On Jewish Folklore*. Detroit: Wayne State University Press, 1983.

Payer, Pierre J. *Sex and the Penitentials: The Development of a Sexual Code, 550–1150*. Toronto: University of Toronto Press, 1984.

Prawer, Joshua. *The History of the Jews in the Latin Kingdom of Jerusalem*. Oxford: Oxford University Press, 1988.

Rapoport-Albert, Ada, ed. *Hasidism Reappraised*. Littman Library of Jewish Civilization. Portland, Or.: Vallentine Mitchell, 1996.

Reber, Arthur S. *The Penguin Dictionary of Psychology*. New York: Penguin Books, 1971.

Reif, Stefan C. *Judaism and Hebrew Prayer*. Cambridge: Cambridge University Press, 1993.

Richards, Jeffrey. *Sex, Dissidence and Damnation: Minority Groups in the Middle Ages*. New York: Routledge, 1991.

Robinson, Ira. *Moshe Cordovero's Introduction to Kabbalah*. New York: Ktav, 1994.

Rodrigue, Aron. "The Sephardim in the Ottoman Empire." In *Spain and the Jews: The Sephardi Experience, 1492 and After*, edited by Elie Kedourie, pp. 162–188. London: Thames & Hudson, 1992.

Rubin, Asher. "The Concept of Repentance among the Hasidey Ashkenaz." *Journal of Jewish Studies* 16 (1965):161–76.

Rubin, Zvia. "The Zoharic Commentaries of Joseph ibn Tabul" (in Hebrew). *Meḥqarei Yerushalayim* 10 (1992): 363–87.

Ruderman, David, ed. *Essential Papers on Jewish Culture in Renaissance and Baroque Italy*. New York: New York University Press, 1992.

———. *Jewish Thought and Scientific Discovery in Early Modern Europe*. New Haven, Conn.: Yale University Press, 1995.

———. *Kabbalah, Magic, and Science: The Cultural Universe of a Sixteenth-Century Jewish Physician*. Cambridge, Mass.: Harvard University Press, 1988.

Rudolph, Kurt. *Gnosis: The Nature and History of Gnosticism*. 2d ed. Translated and edited by R. McLachlan Wilson. San Francisco: Harper & Row, 1983.

Schäfer, Peter. "Ein neues Fragment zur Metoposkopie und Chiromantik." In *Hekhalot-Studien*, edited by Peter Schäfer. Tübingen: Mohr, 1988.

———. *The Hidden and Manifest God: Some Major Themes in Early Jewish Mysticism*. Translated by Aubrey Pomerance. Albany: State University of New York, 1992. Originally published as *Der verborgene und offenbare Gott: Hauptthemen der frühen jüdischen Mystik* (Tübingen: Mohr, 1991).

Schatz Uffenheimer, Rivka. *Hasidism as Mysticism: Quietistic Elements in Eighteenth-Century Hasidic Thought*. Translated by Jonathan Chipman. Princeton, N.J.: Princeton University Press; Jerusalem: Magnes Press, Hebrew University, 1993.

Schechter, Solomon. *Studies in Judaism, Second Series*. Philadelphia: Jewish Publication Society, 1908.

Scholem, Gershom. *Abraham Cohen Herrera and His Book "The Gate of Heaven": His Life, Writings, and Influence* (in Hebrew). Jerusalem: Bialik Institute, 1978.

———. "The Authentic Kabbalistic Writings of Isaac Luria" (in Hebrew). *Qiryat Sefer* 19 (1943): 184–99.

———. "The Document on Solidarity of Luria's Disciples" (in Hebrew). *Zion* 5 (1940): 133–60.

———. "Ein Fragment zur Physiognomik und Chiromantik aus der Tradition der spätantiken jüdische Esoterik." In *Liber amicorum: Studies in Honor of Professor Dr. C. J. Bleeker*. Leiden: E. J. Brill, 1969.

———. "Israel Sarug: Student of the Ari?" (in Hebrew). *Zion* 5 (1940): 214–43.

———. *Kabbalah*. Jerusalem: Keter Press, 1974.

———. "The Maggid of Rabbi Joseph Taitasak and the Revelations Attributed to Him" (in Hebrew). *Sefunot* 11 (1978): 47–112.

———. *Major Trends in Jewish Mysticism*. Jerusalem: Schocken Publishing House, 1941. 3d rev. ed. New York: Schocken Books, 1954.

———. *On the Kabbalah and Its Symbolism*. Translated by Ralph Manheim. New York: Schocken Books, 1965.

———. "On the Life of the Kabbalist Jacob Zemach and His Literary Activities" (in Hebrew). *Qiryat Sefer* 26 (1950): 185–94.

———. *On the Mystical Shape of the Godhead: Basic Concepts in the Kabbalah*. Translated by Joachim Neugroschel. Edited by Jonathan Chipman. New York: Schocken Books, 1991.

———. *Origins of the Kabbalah*. Philadelphia: Jewish Publication Society, 1987.

———. "Physigonomy of the Face" (in Hebrew). In *Sefer Assaf*, edited by U. Cassuto. Jerusalem: Mossad ha-Rav Kook, 1952–53.

———. "Remarks on the Article by Dr. Zanah on Rabbi Jacob Zemach (in Hebrew)." *Qiryat Sefer* 27 (1951): 107–10.

———. *Sabbatai Sevi: The Mystical Messiah*. Princeton, N.J.: Princeton University Press, 1973.

———. "Tradition und Neuschöpfung im Ritus der Kabbalisten." *Eranos Jahrbuch* 19 (1950): 121–80. Translated by Ralph Manheim as "Tradition and New Creation in the Ritual of the Kabbalists," in Scholem, *On the Kabbalah and its Symbolism*, pp. 118–57.

Schwarzfuchs, Simon. "Quand commença le déclin de l'industrie textile des Juifs de Salonique." In *The Mediterranean and the Jews: Banking, Finance and International Trade (XVI–XVIII Centuries)*, edited by Ariel Toaff and Simon Schwarzfuchs, pp. 215–36. Ramat-Gan: Bar-Ilan University Press, 1989.

Sharot, Stephen. *Messianism, Mysticism, and Magic: A Sociological Analysis of Jewish Religious Movements*. Chapel Hill: University of North Carolina Press, 1982.

Shaw, Stanford J. *The Jews of the Ottoman Empire and the Turkish Republic*. New York: New York University Press, 1991.

Shaw, Stanford, and Ezel Shaw. *History of the Ottoman Empire and Modern Turkey*. 2 vols. New York: Cambridge University Press, 1976–77.

Shmuelevitz, Aryeh. *The Jews of the Ottoman Empire in the late Fifteenth and Sixteenth Centuries*. Leiden: E.J. Brill, 1984.

Shochetman, E. "New Sources from the Geniza Concerning the Business Activities of the Ari in Egypt" (in Hebrew). *Peʿamim* 16 (1983): 56–64.

Siraisi, Nancy G. *Medieval and Early Renaissance Medicine*. Chicago: University of Chicago Press, 1990.

Stillman, Norman A. *The Jews of Arab Lands: A History and Source Book*. Philadelphia: Jewish Publication Society, 1979.

Swartz, Michael. *Scholastic Magic: Ritual and Revelation in Early Jewish Mysticism*. Princeton, N.J.: Princeton University Press, 1996.

Tamar, David. *Meḥqarim be-Toldot ha-Yehudim be-ʾErets Yisrael u-be-ʾArtsot ha-Mizrach*. Jerusalem: Mossad Harav Kook, 1981.

——. *Meḥqarim be-Toldot ha-Yehudim be-ʾErets Yisrael u-be-ʾItalyah*. Jerusalem: Rubin Mass, 1973.

Thorndike, Lynn. *A History of Magic and Experimental Science*. 8 vols. New York: Macmillan, 1923–58.

Tishby, Isaiah. "Gnostic Doctrines in Sixteenth-Century Jewish Mysticism." *Journal of Jewish Studies* 6 (1955): 146–52.

——. "The Image of R. Moses Cordovero in the Writing of R. Mordechai Dato" (in Hebrew). *Sefunot* 7 (1963): 119–66.

——. "The Tension Between Lurianic Kabbalah and the Kabbalah of Moses Cordovero in the Writings of Rabbi Aaron Berekhiah of Modena" (in Hebrew). In *Ḥiqrei Kabbalah u-Sheluḥoteha*, vol. 1, edited by Isaiah Tishby. Jerusalem: Magnes Press, 1982.

——. *Torat ha-Raʿ ve-ha-Qelippah be-Kabbalat ha-Ari*. Jerusalem: Akademon, 1942. Rev. ed. Jerusalem: Magnes Press, 1984.

Tishby, Isaiah, and Fischel Lachower, eds. *The Wisdom of the Zohar: An Anthology of Texts*. 3 vols. Translated by David Goldstein. Oxford: Oxford University Press, 1989.

Torrance, Robert M. *The Spiritual Quest: Transcendence in Myth, Religion, and Science*. Berkeley: University of California Press, 1994.

Trachtenberg, Joshua. *Jewish Magic and Superstition*. New York: Behrman's Jewish Book House, 1939.

Tritton, A. S. *The Caliphs and Their Non-Muslim Subjects: A Critical Study of the Covenant of ʿUmar*. London: H. Milford, Oxford University Press, 1930.

Turner, Victor. *Dramas, Fields and Metaphors: Symbolic Action in Human Society*. Ithaca, N.Y.: Cornell University Press, 1974.

——. *Ritual Process: Structure and Anti-Structure*. Chicago: University of Chicago Press, 1969.

Twersky, Isadore. "Talmudists, Philosophers, Kabbalists: The Quest for Spirituality in the Sixteenth Century." In *Jewish Thought in the Sixteenth Century*, edited by B. Cooperman. Cambridge, Mass.: Harvard University Press, 1983.

——. *Rabad of Posquieres: A Twelfth-Century Talmudist*. Cambridge, Mass.: Harvard University Press, 1962.

——, ed. *Rabbi Moses Nahmanides (Ramban): Explorations in His Religious and Literary Virtuosity*. Cambridge, Mass.: Harvard University Press, 1983.

Vilnay, Zev. *Matsevot Qodesh be-ʾErets Yisrael*. 2 vols. 3d ed. Jerusalem: Achiever, 1985–86.

Vinograd, Yeshayahu, ed. *ʾOtsar ha-Sefer ha-ʿIvri* [Thesaurus of the Hebrew Book]. 2 vols. Jerusalem: Institute for Computerized Bibliography, 1995.

Weber, Max. *The Theory of Social and Economic Organization*. Translated by A.M. Henderson and Talcott Parsons. Edited by Talcott Parsons. Glencoe, Ill.: Free Press, 1947. Originally published as part 1 of Weber's *Wirtschaft und Gesellschaft* (Tübingen: Mohr, 1922).

Weinstock, Israel. "Rabbi Yosef ibn Tabul's Commentary on the Idra" (in Hebrew). In *Temirin*, vol. 2 (Jerusalem, 1982), pp. 123–67.

Weiss, Joseph. *Studies in Eastern European Jewish Mysticism*. Edited by David Goldstein. Littman Library of Jewish Civilization. Oxford: Oxford University Press, 1985.

Weiss, Shraga. *Ḥokhmei ha-Sefardim be-ʾErets Yisrael*. Jerusalem: Rubin Mass, 1981.

Weissler, Chava. *Voices of the Matriarchs: Listening to the Prayers of Early Modern Jewish Women* . Boston: Beacon Press, 1998.

Werblowsky, R.J.Z. *Joseph Karo, Lawyer and Mystic*. Oxford: Oxford University Press, 1962.

——. "R. Joseph Karo, Solomon Molcho, Don Joseph Nasi." In *The Sephardi Legacy*, edited by H. Beinart, 2: 187–91. Jerusalem: Magnes Press, 1992.

Wertheim, Aaron. "Traditions and Customs in Hasidism." In *Essential Papers on Hasidism*, edited by G. D. Hundert. New York: New York University Press, 1991.

Wiener, Aharon. *The Prophet Elijah in the Development of Judaism: A Depth-Psychological Study*. Littman Library of Jewish Civilization. Boston: Routledge & K. Paul, 1978.

Wilhelm, Kurt, ed. *Roads to Zion*. New York: Schocken Books, 1948.

Williams, Michael A. *Rethinking "Gnosticism": An Argument for Dismantling a Dubious Category*. Princeton, N.J.: Princeton University Press, 1996.

Wilson, Bryan R. *The Noble Savages: The Primitive Origins of Charisma and Its Contemporary Survival*. Berkeley: University of California Press, 1975.

Wineman, Aryeh. *Beyond Appearances: Stories from the Kabbalistic Ethical Writings*. Philadelphia: Jewish Publication Society, 1988.

Wolfson, Elliot R. *Along the Path: Studies in Kabbalistic Myth, Symbolism, and Hermeneutics*. Albany: State University Press of New York, 1995.

——. "Beautiful Maiden Without Eyes: *Peshat* and *Sod* in Zoharic Hermeneutics." In Michael Fishbane, ed. *The Midrashic Imagination: Jewish Exegesis, Thought, and History*. Albany: State University of New York Press, 1993.

——. *The Book of the Pomegranate: Moses de Leon's Sefer ha-Rimmon*. Brown Judaic studies, 144. Atlanta: Scholars Press, 1988.

——. "By Way of Truth: Aspects of Nahmanides' Kabbalistic Hermeneutic." *Association for Jewish Studies Review* 14, 2 (1989): 103–78.

——. *Circle in the Square: Studies in the Use of Gender in Kabbalistic Symbolism*. Albany: State University of New York Press, 1995.

——. "Circumcision, Vision of God, and Textual Interpretation: From Midrashic Trope to Mystical Symbol." In *Essential Papers on Kabbalah*, edited by Lawrence Fine. New York: New York University Press, 1995.

——. "The Hermeneutics of Visionary Experience: Revelation and Interpretation in the Zohar." *Religion* 18 (1988): 311–45.

——. "Images of God's Feet: Some Observations on the Divine Body in Judaism." In *People of the Body: Jews and Judaism from an Embodied Perspective*, edited by H. Eilberg-Schwartz. Albany: State University of New York Press, 1992.

——. "The Influence of Luria on the Shelah" (in Hebrew). *Meḥqarei Yerushalayim* 10 (1992): 423–48.

——. "The Mystical Significance of Torah Study in German Pietism." *Jewish Quarterly Review* 84, 1 (July 1993): 43–77.

——. "Mystical-Theurgical Dimensions of Prayer in *Sefer ha-Rimmon*." In *Approaches to Judaism in Medieval Times*, edited by D. R. Blumenthal, 3: 41–79. Atlanta: Scholars Press, 1988.

——. *Through a Speculum That Shines: Vision and Imagination in Medieval Jewish Mysticism*. Princeton, N.J.: Princeton University Press, 1994.

——. "Weeping, Death, and Spiritual Ascent in Sixteenth-Century Jewish Mysticism." In *Death, Ecstasy, and Other Worldly Journeys*, edited by J. Collins and M. Fishbane. Albany: State University of New York Press, 1995.

Worman, E. J. "Un Document concernant Isaac Luria." *Revue des études juives* 57 (1909): 281–82.

Yaari, Abraham. "History of the Pilgrimage to Meron" (in Hebrew). *Tarbiz* 31 (1961): 72–101.

——, ed. *ʾIggrot ʾErets Yisrael*. Ramat Gan: Masada, 1971.

Yosha, Nissim. "Abraham Cohen Herrera's Philosophical Interpretation of Lurianic Kabbalah" (in Hebrew). Ph.D. diss., Hebrew University, Jerusalem, 1991.

——. "The Lurianic Concept of Prophecy in the Writings of Abraham Cohen Herrera" (in Hebrew). *Meḥqarei Yerushalayim* 10 (1992): 389–421.

Zack, Bracha. *Be-Shaʿarei ha-Kabbalah shel R. Moshe Cordovero*. Jerusalem: Ben Gurion University Press, 1995.

Index

Lightning Source UK Ltd.
Milton Keynes UK
UKHW010156010221
377821UK00011BA/103